Microsoft Official Academic Course
MICROSOFT OUTLOOK 2013

WILEY

Editor	Bryan Gambrel
Publisher	Don Fowley
Director of Sales	Mitchell Beaton
Technical Editor	Joyce Nielsen
Executive Marketing Manager	Chris Ruel
Assistant Marketing Manager	Debbie Martin
Editorial Program Assistant	Allison Winkle
Senior Content Manager	Kevin Holm
Senior Production Editor	Jill Spikereit
Creative Director	Harry Nolan
Cover Designer	Tom Nery
Product Designer	Jennifer Welter
Content Editor	Wendy Ashenberg

This book was set in Garamond by Aptara®, Inc. and printed and bound by Courier/Kendallville. The covers were printed by Courier/Kendallville.

ISBN 978-0-470-13311-8

Printed in the United States of America

10 9 8 7 6 5 4 3 2 1

Foreword from the Publisher

Wiley's publishing vision for the Microsoft Official Academic Course series is to provide students and instructors with the skills and knowledge they need to use Microsoft technology effectively in all aspects of their personal and professional lives. Quality instruction is required to help both educators and students get the most from Microsoft's software tools and to become more productive. Thus our mission is to make our instructional programs trusted educational companions for life.

To accomplish this mission, Wiley and Microsoft have partnered to develop the highest quality educational programs for Information Workers, IT Professionals, and Developers. Materials created by this partnership carry the brand name "Microsoft Official Academic Course," assuring instructors and students alike that the content of these textbooks is fully endorsed by Microsoft, and that they provide the highest quality information and instruction on Microsoft products. The Microsoft Official Academic Course textbooks are "Official" in still one more way—they are the officially sanctioned courseware for Microsoft IT Academy members.

The Microsoft Official Academic Course series focuses on workforce development. These programs are aimed at those students seeking to enter the workforce, change jobs, or embark on new careers as information workers, IT professionals, and developers. Microsoft Official Academic Course programs address their needs by emphasizing authentic workplace scenarios with an abundance of projects, exercises, cases, and assessments.

The Microsoft Official Academic Courses are mapped to Microsoft's extensive research and job-task analysis, the same research and analysis used to create the Microsoft Office Specialist (MOS) exams. The textbooks focus on real skills for real jobs. As students work through the projects and exercises in the textbooks they enhance their level of knowledge and their ability to apply the latest Microsoft technology to everyday tasks. These students also gain resume-building credentials that can assist them in finding a job, keeping their current job, or in furthering their education.

The concept of life-long learning is today an utmost necessity. Job roles, and even whole job categories, are changing so quickly that none of us can stay competitive and productive without continuously updating our skills and capabilities. The Microsoft Official Academic Course offerings, and their focus on Microsoft certification exam preparation, provide a means for people to acquire and effectively update their skills and knowledge. Wiley supports students in this endeavor through the development and distribution of these courses as Microsoft's official academic publisher.

Joe Heider
Senior Vice President, Wiley Global Education

Illustrated Book Tour

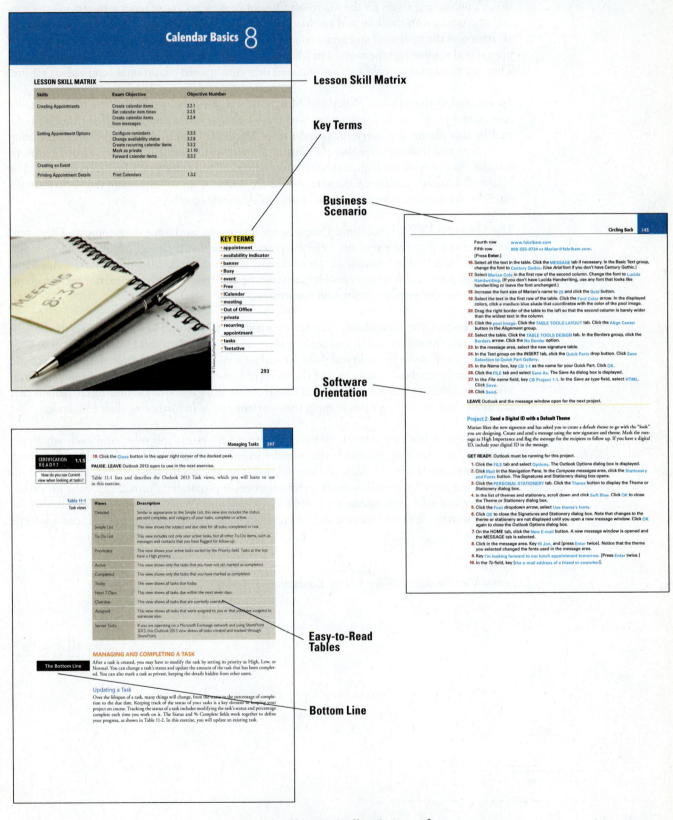

Lesson Skill Matrix

Calendar Basics 8

LESSON SKILL MATRIX

Skills	Exam Objective	Objective Number
Creating Appointments	Create calendar items	3.2.1
	Set calendar item times	3.2.5
	Create calendar items from messages	3.2.4
Setting Appointment Options	Configure reminders	3.3.3
	Change availability status	3.2.8
	Create recurring calendar items	3.2.2
	Mark as private	2.1.10
	Forward calendar items	3.3.2
Creating an Event		
Printing Appointment Details	Print Calendars	1.3.2

Key Terms

KEY TERMS
- appointment
- availability indicator
- banner
- Busy
- event
- Free
- iCalendar
- meeting
- Out of Office
- private
- recurring appointment
- tasks
- Tentative

293

Business Scenario

Software Orientation

Circling Back 145

Fourth row	www.fabrikam.com
Fifth row	800-555-8734 or Marian@fabrikam.com.
	[Press Enter.]

16. Select all the text in the table. Click the MESSAGE tab if necessary. In the Basic Text group, change the font to Century Gothic. (Use Arial font if you don't have Century Gothic.)
17. Select Marian Cole in the first row of the second column. Change the font to Lucida Handwriting. (If you don't have Lucida Handwriting, use any font that looks like handwriting or leave the font unchanged.)
18. Increase the font size of Marian's name to 20 and click the Bold button.
19. Select the text in the first row of the table. Click the Font Color arrow. In the displayed colors, click a medium blue shade that coordinates with the color of the pool image.
20. Drag the right border of the table to the left so that the second column is barely wider than the widest text in the column.
21. Click the pool image. Click the TABLE TOOLS LAYOUT tab. Click the Align Center button in the Alignment group.
22. Select the table. Click the TABLE TOOLS DESIGN tab. In the Borders group, click the Borders arrow. Click the No Border option.
23. In the message area, select the new signature table.
24. In the Text group on the INSERT tab, click the Quick Parts drop button. Click Save Selection to Quick Part Gallery.
25. In the Name box, key CB 1-1 as the name for your Quick Part. Click OK.
26. Click the FILE tab and select Save As. The Save As dialog box is displayed.
27. In the File name field, key CB Project 1-1. In the Save as type field, select HTML. Click Save.
28. Click Send.

LEAVE Outlook and the message window open for the next project.

Project 2: Send a Digital ID with a Default Theme

Marian likes the new signature and has asked you to create a default theme to go with the "look" you are designing. Create and send a message using the new signature and theme. Mark the message as High Importance and flag the message for the recipient to follow up. If you have a digital ID, include your digital ID in the message.

GET READY. Outlook must be running for this project.

1. Click the FILE tab and select Options. The Outlook Options dialog box is displayed.
2. Click Mail in the Navigation Pane. In the Compose messages area, click the Stationery and Fonts button. The Signatures and Stationery dialog box opens.
3. Click the PERSONAL STATIONERY tab. Click the Theme button to display the Theme or Stationery dialog box.
4. In the list of themes and stationery, scroll down and click Soft Blue. Click OK to close the Theme or Stationery dialog box.
5. Click the Font dropdown arrow, select Use theme's fonts.
6. Click OK to close the Signatures and Stationery dialog box. Note that changes to the theme or stationery are not displayed until you open a new message window. Click OK again to close the Outlook Options dialog box.
7. On the HOME tab, click the New E-mail button. A new message window is opened and the MESSAGE tab is selected.
8. Click in the message area. Key Hi Jon, and [press Enter twice]. Notice that the theme you selected changed the fonts used in the message area.
9. Key I'm looking forward to our lunch appointment tomorrow. [Press Enter twice.]
10. In the To field, key [the e-mail address of a friend or coworker].

Managing Tasks 397

CERTIFICATION READY? 1.1.5
How do you use Current view when looking at tasks?

19. Click the Close button in the upper right corner of the docked peek.

PAUSE. LEAVE Outlook 2013 open to use in the next exercise.

Table 11-1 lists and describes the Outlook 2013 Task views, which you will learn to use in this exercise.

Table 11-1
Task views

Views	Description
Detailed	Similar in appearance to the Simple List, this view also includes the status, percent complete, and category of your tasks, complete or active.
Simple List	This view shows the subject and due date for all tasks, completed or not.
To-Do List	This view includes not only your active tasks, but all other To-Do items, such as messages and contacts that you have flagged for follow-up.
Prioritized	This view shows your active tasks sorted by the Priority field. Tasks at the top have a High priority.
Active	This view shows only the tasks that you have not yet marked as completed.
Completed	This view shows only the tasks that you have marked as completed.
Today	This view shows all tasks due today.
Next 7 Days	This view shows all tasks due within the next seven days.
Overdue	This view shows all tasks that are currently overdue.
Assigned	This view shows all tasks that were assigned to you or that you have assigned to someone else.
Server Tasks	If you are operating on a Microsoft Exchange network and using SharePoint 2013, this Outlook 2013 view shows all tasks created and tracked through SharePoint.

Easy-to-Read Tables

MANAGING AND COMPLETING A TASK

The Bottom Line

After a task is created, you may have to modify the task by setting its priority as High, Low, or Normal. You can also change a task's status and update the amount of the task that has been completed. You can also mark a task as private, keeping the details hidden from other users.

Updating a Task

Over the lifespan of a task, many things will change, from the status to the percentage of completion to the due date. Keeping track of the status of your tasks is a key element to keeping your project on course. Tracking the status of a task includes modifying the task's status and percentage complete each time you work on it. The Status and % Complete fields work together to define your progress, as shown in Table 11-2. In this exercise, you will update an existing task.

Bottom Line

Illustrated Book Tour

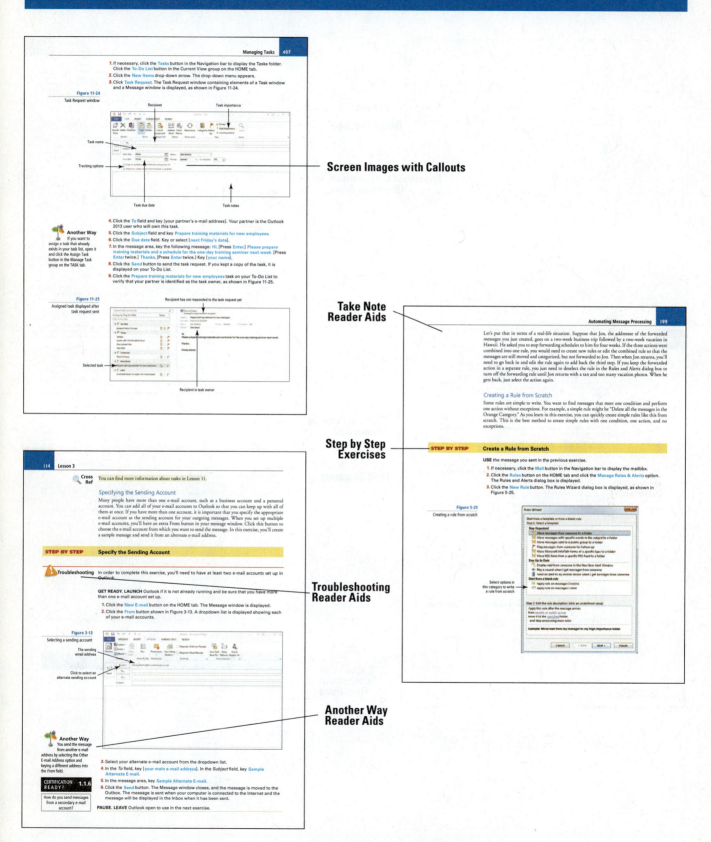

Screen Images with Callouts

Take Note Reader Aids

Step by Step Exercises

Troubleshooting Reader Aids

Another Way Reader Aids

Illustrated Book Tour

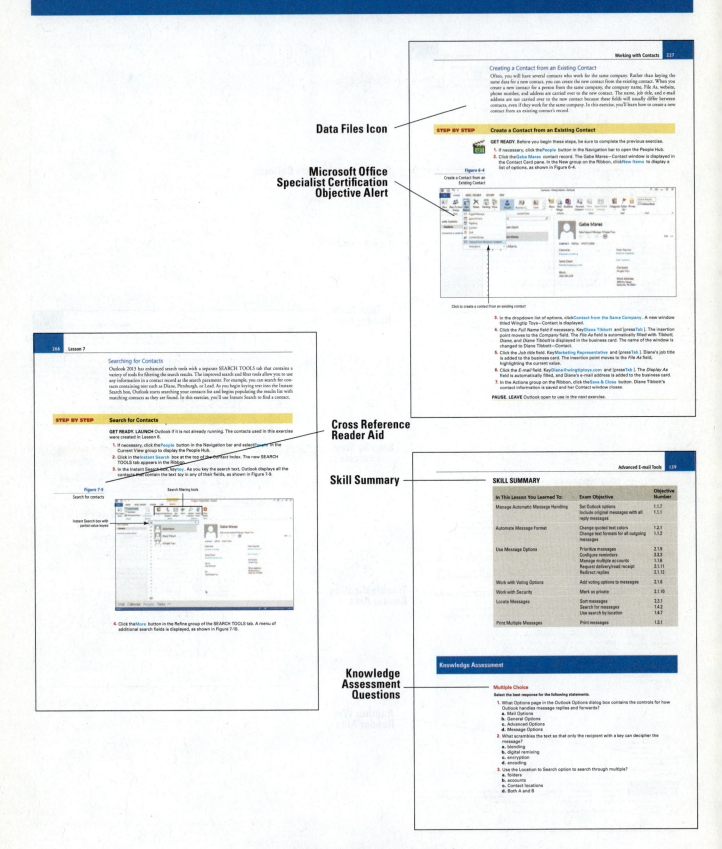

Data Files Icon

Microsoft Office Specialist Certification Objective Alert

Cross Reference Reader Aid

Skill Summary

Knowledge Assessment Questions

Illustrated Book Tour

Competency Assessment

Proficiency Assessment Project

Mastery Assessment Projects

Circling Back Exercises

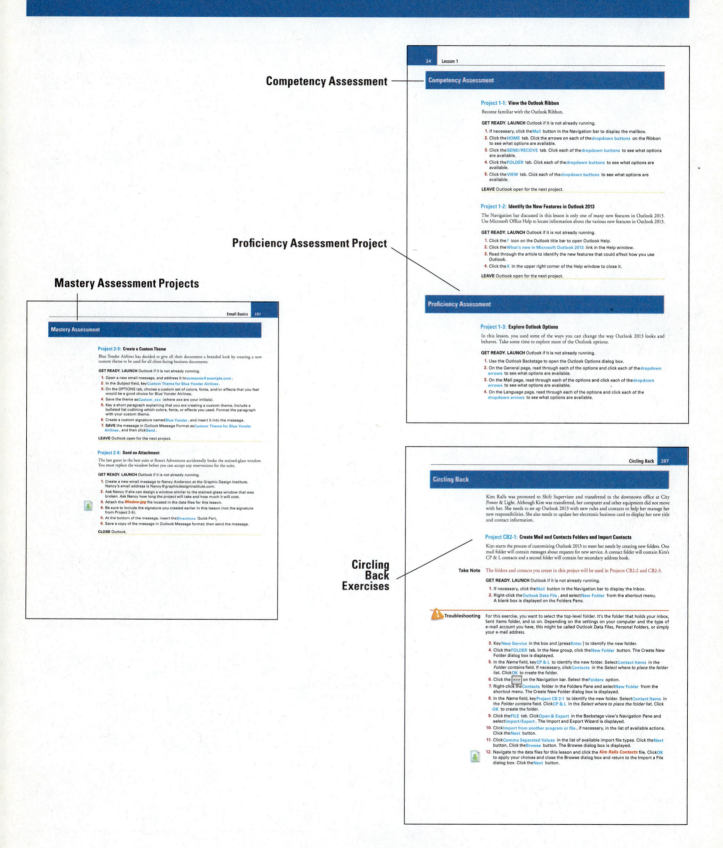

Preface

Welcome to the Microsoft Official Academic Course (MOAC) program for Microsoft Office 2013. MOAC represents the collaboration between Microsoft Learning and John Wiley & Sons, Inc. publishing company. Microsoft and Wiley teamed up to produce a series of textbooks that deliver compelling and innovative teaching solutions to instructors and superior learning experiences for students. Infused and informed by in-depth knowledge from the creators of Microsoft Office and Windows, and crafted by a publisher known worldwide for the pedagogical quality of its products, these textbooks maximize skills transfer in minimum time. Students are challenged to reach their potential by using their new technical skills as highly productive members of the workforce.

Because this knowledgebase comes directly from Microsoft, architect of the Office 2013 system and creator of the Microsoft Office Specialist (MOS) exams (www.microsoft.com/learning/mcp/mcts), you are sure to receive the topical coverage that is most relevant to students' personal and professional success. Microsoft's direct participation not only assures you that MOAC textbook content is accurate and current; it also means that students will receive the best instruction possible to enable their success on certification exams and in the workplace.

THE MICROSOFT OFFICIAL ACADEMIC COURSE PROGRAM

The Microsoft Official Academic Course series is a complete program for instructors and institutions to prepare and deliver great courses on Microsoft software technologies. With MOAC, we recognize that, because of the rapid pace of change in the technology and curriculum developed by Microsoft, there is an ongoing set of needs beyond classroom instruction tools for an instructor to be ready to teach the course. The MOAC program endeavors to provide solutions for all these needs in a systematic manner in order to ensure a successful and rewarding course experience for both instructor and student—technical and curriculum training for instructor readiness with new software releases; the software itself for student use at home for building hands-on skills, assessment, and validation of skill development; and a great set of tools for delivering instruction in the classroom and lab. All are important to the smooth delivery of an interesting course on Microsoft software, and all are provided with the MOAC program. We think about the model below as a gauge for ensuring that we completely support you in your goal of teaching a great course. As you evaluate your instructional materials options, you may wish to use the model for comparison purposes with available products.

PEDAGOGICAL FEATURES

The MOAC courseware for *Microsoft Outlook 2013* is designed to cover all the learning objectives for that MOS exam, which is referred to as its "objective domain." The Microsoft Office Specialist (MOS) exam objectives are highlighted throughout the textbooks. Many pedagogical features have been developed specifically for *Microsoft Official Academic Course* programs. Unique features of our task-based approach include a Lesson Skills Matrix that correlates skills taught in each lesson to the MOS objectives; Certification, and three levels of increasingly rigorous lesson-ending activities: Competency, Proficiency, and Mastery Assessment.

Presenting the extensive procedural information and technical concepts woven throughout the textbook raises challenges for the student and instructor alike. The Illustrated Book Tour that follows provides a guide to the rich features contributing to *Microsoft Official Academic Course* program's pedagogical plan. Following is a list of key features in each lesson designed to prepare students for success on the certification exams and in the workplace:

- Each lesson begins with a **Lesson Skill Matrix**. More than a standard list of learning objectives, the skill matrix correlates each software skill covered in the lesson to the specific MOS exam objective domain.

- Each lesson features a real-world **Business Case** scenario that places the software skills and knowledge to be acquired in a real-world setting.

- Every lesson opens with a **Software Orientation**. This feature provides an overview of the software features students will be working with in the lesson. The orientation will detail the general properties of the software or specific features, such as a ribbon or dialog box; and it includes a large, labeled screen image.

- Concise and frequent **Step-by-Step** instructions teach students new features and provide an opportunity for hands-on practice. Numbered steps give detailed, step-by-step instructions to help students learn software skills. The steps also show results and screen images to match what students should see on their computer screens.

- **Illustrations**: Screen images provide visual feedback as students work through the exercises. The images reinforce key concepts, provide visual clues about the steps, and allow students to check their progress.

- **Key Terms:** Important technical vocabulary is listed at the beginning of the lesson. When these terms are used later in the lesson, they appear in bold italic type with yellow highlighter and are defined. The Glossary contains all of the key terms and their definitions.

- Engaging point-of-use **Reader aids**, located throughout the lessons, tell students why this topic is relevant (*The Bottom Line*), provide students with helpful hints (*Take Note*), or show alternate ways to accomplish tasks (*Another Way*), or point out things to watch out for or avoid (*Troubleshooting*). Reader aids also provide additional relevant or background information that adds value to the lesson.

- **Certification Ready?** features throughout the text signal students where a specific certification objective is covered. They provide students with a chance to check their understanding of that particular MOS exam objective and, if necessary, review the section of the lesson where it is covered. MOAC provides complete preparation for MOS certification.

- Each lesson ends with a **Skill Summary** recapping the topics and MOS exam skills covered in the lesson.

- **Knowledge Assessment:** Provides a total of 20 questions from a mix of True/False, Fill-in-the-Blank, Matching or Multiple Choice testing students on concepts learned in the lesson.

- **Competency, Proficiency, and Mastery Assessment:** provide three progressively more challenging lesson-ending activities.

- **Circling Back:** These integrated projects provide students with an opportunity to renew and practice skills learned in previous lessons.

- **Online files:** The student companion website contains the data files needed for each lesson. These files are indicated by the file download icon in the margin of the textbook.

Conventions and Features Used in This Book

This book uses particular fonts, symbols, and heading conventions to highlight important information or to call your attention to special steps. For more information about the features in each lesson, refer to the Illustrated Book Tour section.

Convention	Meaning
The Bottom Line	This feature provides a brief summary of the material to be covered in the section that follows.
CLOSE	Words in all capital letters indicate instructions for opening, saving, or closing files or programs. They also point out items you should check or actions you should take.
CERTIFICATION READY?	This feature signals the point in the text where a specific certification objective is covered. It provides you with a chance to check your understanding of that particular MOS objective and, if necessary, review the section of the lesson where it is covered.
Take Note	Reader aids appear in shaded boxes found in your text. Take Note provides helpful hints related to particular tasks or topics.
Another Way	Another Way provides an alternative procedure for accomplishing a particular task.
Cross Ref	These notes provide pointers to information discussed elsewhere in the textbook or describe interesting features that are not directly addressed in the current topic or exercise.
ALT + Tab	A plus sign (+) between two key names means that you must press both keys at the same time. Keys that you are instructed to press in an exercise will appear in the font shown here.
A **shared printer** can be used by many individuals on a network.	Key terms appear in bold italic.
Key **My Name is**	Any text you are asked to key appears in color.
Click **OK**	Any button on the screen you are supposed to click on or select will also appear in color.
	The names of data files will appear in bold, italic and red for easy identification. These data files are available for download from the Student Companion Site (www.Wiley.com/college/Microsoft).
	Step-by-step tutorial videos are available for many of the activities throughout this course. For information on how to access these videos, see the Student Companion Site (www.Wiley.com/college/Microsoft).
OPEN *BudgetWorksheet1*	The names of data files will appear in bold, italic and red for easy identification.

www.wiley.com/college/microsoft
or call the MOAC Toll-Free Number: 1+(888) 764-7001 (U.S. & Canada only)

Instructor Support Program

The *Microsoft Official Academic Course* programs are accompanied by a rich array of resources that incorporate the extensive textbook visuals to form a pedagogically cohesive package. These resources provide all the materials instructors need to deploy and deliver their courses. Resources available online for download include:

- The **Instructor's Guide** contains Solutions to all the textbook exercises as well as chapter summaries and lecture notes. The Instructor's Guide and Syllabi for various term lengths are available from the Instructor's Book Companion site (www.wiley.com/college/microsoft).

- The **Solution Files** for all the projects in the book (where applicable) are available online from our Instructor's Book Companion site (www.wiley.com/college/microsoft).

- The **Test Bank** contains hundreds of questions organized by lesson in multiple-choice, true-false, short answer, and essay formats and is available to download from the Instructor's Book Companion site (www.wiley.com/college/microsoft). A complete answer key is provided.

  This title's test bank is available for use in Respondus' easy-to-use software. You can download the test bank for free using your Respondus, Respondus LE, or StudyMate Author software.

  Respondus is a powerful tool for creating and managing exams that can be printed to paper or published directly to Blackboard, WebCT, Desire2Learn, eCollege, ANGEL and other eLearning systems.

- **Test Bank Projects.** Two projects for each lesson are provided on the Instructor's Book Companion Site. These projects cover topics from within one specific lesson.

- **PowerPoint Presentations and Images**. A complete set of PowerPoint presentations is available on the Instructor's Book Companion site (www.wiley.com/college/microsoft) to enhance classroom presentations. Tailored to the text's topical coverage and Skills Matrix, these presentations are designed to convey key Microsoft .NET Framework concepts addressed in the text.

  All figures from the text are on the Instructor's Book Companion site (www.wiley.com/college/microsoft). You can incorporate them into your PowerPoint presentations, or create your own overhead transparencies and handouts.

  By using these visuals in class discussions, you can help focus students' attention on key elements of Windows Server and help them understand how to use it effectively in the workplace.

- The **Student Data Files** are available online on both the Instructor's Book Companion Site and for students on the Student Book Companion Site.

- Wiley **Faculty Network:** When it comes to improving the classroom experience, there is no better source of ideas and inspiration than your fellow colleagues. The Wiley Faculty Network connects teachers with technology, facilitates the exchange of best practices, and helps to enhance instructional efficiency and effectiveness. Faculty Network activities include technology training and tutorials, virtual seminars, peer-to-peer exchanges of experiences and ideas, personal consulting, and sharing of resources. For details visit www.WhereFacultyConnect.com.

IMPORTANT WEB ADDRESSES AND PHONE NUMBERS

To locate the Wiley Higher Education Rep in your area, go to the following Web address and click on the *"Contact Us"* link at the top of the page.

www.wiley.com/college

Or Call the MOAC Toll Free Number: 1 + (888) 764-7001 (U.S. & Canada only).

To learn more about becoming a Microsoft Certified Professional and exam availability, visit **www.microsoft.com/learning/mcp.**

DREAMSPARK PREMIUM

Free 3-Year Membership available to Qualified Adopters

DreamSpark Premium is designed to provide the easiest and most inexpensive way for schools to make the latest Microsoft developer tools, products, and technologies available in labs, classrooms, and on student PCs. Dream-Spark Premium is an annual membership program for departments teaching Science, Technology, Engineering, and Mathematics (STEM) courses. The membership provides a complete solution to keep academic labs, faculty, and students on the leading edge of technology.

Software available through the DreamSpark Premium program is provided at no charge to adopting departments through the Wiley and Microsoft publishing partnership.

Contact your Wiley rep for details.

For more information about the DreamSpark Premium program, go to Microsoft's DreamSpark website.

BOOK COMPANION WEBSITE (WWW.WILEY.COM/COLLEGE/MICROSOFT)

The students' book companion site for the MOAC series includes any resources, exercise files, and web links that will be used in conjunction with this course.

WILEY E-TEXT: POWERED BY VITALSOURCE

When you choose a Wiley E-Text you not only save money; you benefit from being able to access course materials and content anytime, anywhere through a user experience that makes learning rewarding.

With the Wiley E-Text you will be able to easily:
- Search
- Take notes
- Highlight key materials
- Have all your work in one place for more efficient studying

In addition, the Wiley E-Text is fully portable. Students can access it online and download to their computer for off line access and access read and study on their device of preference—computer, tablet, or smartphone.

WHY MOS CERTIFICATION?

Microsoft Office Specialist (MOS) 2013 is a valuable credential that recognizes the desktop computing skills needed to use the full features and functionality of the Microsoft Office 2013 suite.

In the worldwide job market, Microsoft Office Specialist is the primary tool companies use to validate the proficiency of their employees in the latest productivity tools and technology, helping them select job candidates based on globally recognized standards for verifying skills. The results of an independent research study show that businesses with certified employees are more productive compared to non-certified employees and that certified employees bring immediate value to their jobs.

In academia, as in the business world, institutions upgrading to Office 2013 may seek ways to protect and maximize their technology investment. By offering certification, they validate that decision—because powerful Office 2013 applications such as Word, Excel and PowerPoint can be effectively used to demonstrate increases in academic preparedness and workforce readiness.

Individuals seek certification to increase their own personal sense of accomplishment and to create advancement opportunities by establishing a leadership position in their school or department, thereby differentiating their skill sets in a competitive college admissions and job market.

PREPARING TO TAKE THE MICROSOFT OFFICE SPECIALIST (MOS) EXAM

The Microsoft Office Specialist credential has been upgraded to validate skills with the Microsoft Office 2013 system. The MOS certifications target information workers and cover the most popular business applications such as Word 2013, Excel 2013, PowerPoint 2013, Outlook 2013 and Access 2013.

By becoming certified, you demonstrate to employers that you have achieved a predictable level of skill in the use of a particular Office application. Employers often require certification either as a condition of employment or as a condition of advancement within the company or other organization. The certification examinations are sponsored by Microsoft but administered through exam delivery partners like Certiport.

To learn more about becoming a Microsoft Office Specialist and exam availability, visit http://www.microsoft.com/learning/en/us/mos-certification.aspx.

Preparing to Take an Exam

Unless you are a very experienced user, you will need to use a test preparation course to prepare to complete the test correctly and within the time allowed. The *Microsoft Official Academic Course* series is designed to prepare you with a strong knowledge of all exam topics, and with some additional review and practice on your own. You should feel confident in your ability to pass the appropriate exam.

After you decide which exam to take, review the list of objectives for the exam. This list can be found in the MOS Objectives Appendix at the back of this book. You can also easily identify tasks that are included in the objective list by locating the Lesson Skill Matrix at the start of each lesson and the Certification Ready sidebars in the margin of the lessons in this book.

To take the MOS test, visit http://www.microsoft.com/learning/en/us/mos-certification.aspx to locate your nearest testing center. Then call the testing center directly to schedule your test. The amount of advance notice you should provide will vary for different testing centers, and it typically depends on the number of computers available at the testing center, the number of other testers who have already been scheduled for the day on which you want to take the test, and the number of times per week that the testing center offers MOS testing. In general, you should call to schedule your test at least two weeks prior to the date on which you want to take the test.

When you arrive at the testing center, you might be asked for proof of identity. A driver's license or passport is an acceptable form of identification. If you do not have either of these items of documentation, call your testing center and ask what alternative forms of identification will be accepted. If you are retaking a test, bring your MOS identification number, which will have been given to you when you previously took the test. If you have not prepaid or if your organization has not already arranged to make payment for you, you will need to pay the test-taking fee when you arrive.

Test Format

MOS exams are Exams are primarily performance-based and conducted in a "live," or simulated, environment. Exam candidates taking exams for MOS 2007 or 2010 are asked to perform a series of tasks to clearly demonstrate their skills. For example, a Word exam might ask a user to balance newspaper column lengths or keep text together in columns. All MOS exams must be completed in 90 minutes or less.

Student Data Files

All of the practice files that you will use as you perform the exercises in the book are available for download on our student companion site. By using the practice files, you will not waste time creating the samples used in the lessons, and you can concentrate on learning how to use Microsoft Office 2013. With the files and the step-by-step instructions in the lessons, you will learn by doing, which is an easy and effective way to acquire and remember new skills.

COPYING THE PRACTICE FILES

Your instructor might already have copied the practice files before you arrive in class. However, your instructor might ask you to copy the practice files on your own at the start of class. Also, if you want to work through any of the exercises in this book on your own at home or at your place of business after class, you may want to copy the practice files.

1. **OPEN** Internet Explorer.
2. In Internet Explorer, go to the student companion site: www.wiley.com
3. Search for your book title in the upper right hand corner
4. On the Search Results page, locate your book and click on the Visit the Companion Sites link.
5. Select Student Companion Site from the pop-up box.
6. From the menu, select the arrow next to Browse By Resource and select Student Data Files from the menu.
7. A new screen will appear.
8. On the Student Data Files page, you can select to download files for just one lesson or for all lessons. Click on the file of your choice.
9. On the File Download dialog box, select Save As to save the data files to your external drive (often called a ZIP drive or a USB drive or a thumb drive) or a local drive.
10. In the Save As dialog box, select a local drive in the left-hand panel that you'd like to save your files to; again, this should be an external drive or a local drive. Remember the drive name that you saved it to.

Acknowledgments

We would like to thank the many instructors and reviewers who pored over the Microsoft Official Academic Course series design, outlines and manuscript, providing invaluable feedback in the service of quality instructional materials.

Erik Amerikaner, *Oak Park Unified*

Connie Aragon, *Seattle Central Community College*

Sue Bajt, *Harper College*

Gregory Ballinger, *Miami-Dade College*

Catherine Bradfield, *DeVry University*

DeAnnia Clements, *Wiregrass Georgia Technical College*

Mary Corcoran, *Bellevue College*

Andrea Cluff, *Freemont High School*

Caroline de Gruchy, *Conestoga College*

Janis DeHaven, *Central Community College*

Rob Durrance, *East Lee County High School*

Janet Flusche, *Frenship High School*

Greg Gardiner, *SIAST*

Debi Griggs, *Bellevue College*

Phil Hanney, *Orem Junior High School*

Portia Hatfield, *Tennessee Technology Center-Jacksboro*

Dee Hobson, *Richland College*

Terri Holly, *Indian River State College*

Kim Hopkins, *Weatherford College*

Sandra Jolley, *Tarrant County College*

Keith Hoell, *Briarcliffe College*

Joe LaMontagne, *Davenport University*

Tanya MacNeil, *American InterContinental University*

Donna Madsen, *Kirkwood Community College*

Lynn Mancini, *Delaware Technical Community College*

Edward Martin, *Kingsborough Community College-City University of New York*

Lisa Mears, *Palm Beach State College*

Denise Merrell, *Jefferson Community and Technical College*

Diane Mickey, *Northern Virginia Community College*

Robert Mike, *Alaska Career College*

Cynthia Miller, *Harper College*

Sandra Miller, *Wenatchee Valley College*

Mustafa Muflehi, *The Sheffield College*

Aditi Mukherjee, *University of Florida—Gainesville*

Linda Nutter, *Peninsula College*

Diana Pack, *Big Sandy Community & Technical College*

Bettye Parham, *Daytona State College*

Tatyana Pashnyak, *Bainbridge State College*

Kari Phillips, *Davis Applied Technical College*

Michelle Poertner, *Northwestern Michigan College*

Barbara Purvis, *Centura College*

Dave Rotherham, *Sheffield Hallam University*

Theresa Savarese, *San Diego City College*

Janet Sebesy, *Cuyahoga Community College-Western*

Lourdes Sevilla, *Southwestern College*

Elizabeth Snow, *Southwest Florida College*

Denise Spence, *Dunbar High School*

Amy Stolte, *Lincoln Land Community College*

Linda Silva, *El Paso Community College*

Dorothy Weiner, *Manchester Community College*

We would also like to thank the team at Microsoft Learning, including Alison Cunard, Tim Sneath, Zubair Murtaza, Keith Loeber, Rob Linsky, Anne Hamilton, Wendy Johnson, Julia Stasio, and Josh Barnhill for their encouragement and support in making the Microsoft Official Academic Course programs the finest academic materials for mastering the newest Microsoft technologies for both students and instructors. Finally we would like to thank Jeff Riley and his team at Box Twelve Communications, Laura Town and her team at WilliamsTown Communications, Debbie Collins, Janet Curtis, and Sandy DuBose for their editorial and technical assistance.

We would like to thank the following instructors for their contributions to particular titles in the series as well:

ACCESS 2013

Catherine Bradfield, *DeVry University*

Mary Corcoran, *Bellevue College*

Cynthia Miller, *Harper College*

Aditi Mukherjee, *University of Florida—Gainesville*

Elizabeth Snow, *Southwest Florida College*

EXCEL 2013

Catherine Bradfield, *DeVry University*

DeAnnia Clements, *Wiregrass Georgia Technical College*

Dee Hobson, *Richland College*

Sandra Jolley, *Tarrant County College*

Joe Lamontagne, *Davenport University*

Edward Martin, *Kingsborough Community College-City University of New York*

Aditi Mukherjee, *University of Florida—Gainesville*

Linda Nutter, *Peninsula College*

Dave Rotherham, *Sheffield Hallam University*

POWERPOINT 2013

Mary Corcoran, *Bellevue College*

Rob Durrance, *East Lee County High School*

Phil Hanney, *Orem Junior High School*

Terri Holly, *Indian River State College*

Kim Hopkins, *Weatherford College*

Tatyana Pashnyak, *Bainbridge State College*

Michelle Poertner, *Northwestern Michigan College*

Theresa Savarese, *San Diego City College*

WORD 2013

Erik Amerikaner, *Oak Park Unified*

Sue Bajt, *Harper College*

Gregory Ballinger, *Miami-Dade College*

Andrea Cluff, *Freemont High School*

Caroline de Gruchy, *Conestoga College*

Donna Madsen, *Kirkwood Community College*

Lynn Mancini, *Delaware Technical Community College*

Denise Merrell, *Jefferson Community and Technical College*

Diane Mickey, *Northern Virginia Community College*

Robert Mike, *Alaska Career College*

Bettye Parham, *Daytona State College*

Barbara Purvis, *Centura College*

Janet Sebesy, *Cuyahoga Community College-Western*

Dorothy Weiner, *Manchester Community College*

OUTLOOK 2013

Kari Phillips, *Davis Applied Technology College*

Erik Amerikaner, *Oak Park Unified*

Robert Mike, *Alaska Career College*

Lourdes Sevilla, *Southwestern College*

Sue VanLanen, *Gwinnett Technical College*

Janet Curtis

Author Credits

CHRISTY PARRISH

Christy Parrish has spent the last 20 years developing, designing and delivering corporate training programs. She has written to several books on Microsoft Office and other productivity software packages. As a freelance author, she has also written a magazine series and hundreds of online articles on a wide variety of topics. Christy is also a member of her community artists group and is recognized for her unique photographic skills that are on display at various galleries. She is married and has two sons that both share her love of writing and art.

Brief Contents

Contents

Lesson 1: Getting to Know Outlook

© GeorgePeters/iStockphoto

Lesson 2: Email Basics

© alohaspirit/iStockphoto

Lesson 3: Advanced E-mail Tools

© Gorfer/iStockphoto

Lesson 4: Managing E-mail Messages

© webphotographeer/iStockphoto

Lesson 5: Automating Message Processing

© GVision/iStockphoto

Lesson 6: Working with Contacts

© lisafx/iStockphoto

Lesson 7: Advanced Contact Management

© adventtr/iStockphoto

Lesson 8: Calendar Basics

© Thomas_EyeDesign/iStockphoto

Lesson 9: Managing Meetings

© Chimpinski/iStockphoto

Lesson 10: Advanced Calendar Management

© Tongshan/iStockphoto

Lesson 11: Managing Tasks

© michaeljung/iStockphoto

Lesson 12: Categories and Outlook Data Files

© GlobalStock/iStockphoto

Lesson 13: Managing Notes and Journal Entries

© rcaucino/iStockphoto

LESSON SKILL MATRIX

Skills	Exam Objective	Objective Number
Starting Outlook		
Working in the Outlook Window	Configure views	1.1.5
Personalizing Outlook	Customize the Navigation Pane	1.1.3
Using Backstage View	Set Outlook options	1.1.7

© GeorgePeters/iStockphoto

KEY TERMS

- Backstage view
- feature
- fields
- fly-out
- folders
- gallery
- groups
- item
- Navigation bar
- Peek
- Quick Access Toolbar
- Reading Pane
- Ribbon
- ScreenTip
- Status bar
- tile
- Title bar
- To-Do Bar

© GeorgePeters/iStockphoto

Resort Adventures is a luxury resort. During the summer, activities such as kayaking, canoeing, hiking, and horseback riding are available. In the winter months, visitors enjoy skiing, snowshoeing, and sleigh rides. Partners Mindy Martin and Jon Morris own and operate Resort Adventures. They work hard to ensure that guests enjoy their stay. Employees are well-trained and well-treated professionals. For one week every year, Mindy and Jon close the resort to guests and open the facilities to employees and their families.

Microsoft Outlook is an ideal tool for managing communication with their clients and their staff. Whether you need to send a message to a vendor making a late delivery, look up an old friend's phone number, or schedule a staff meeting, Outlook provides the tools that will save time and make your job easier. In this lesson, you will learn how to customize the Microsoft Outlook environment to suit your needs.

SOFTWARE ORIENTATION

The Microsoft Outlook Workspace

Before you begin working in Microsoft Outlook, you need to be familiar with the primary user workspace. When you first launch Microsoft Outlook, you will see a screen similar to that in Figure 1-1.

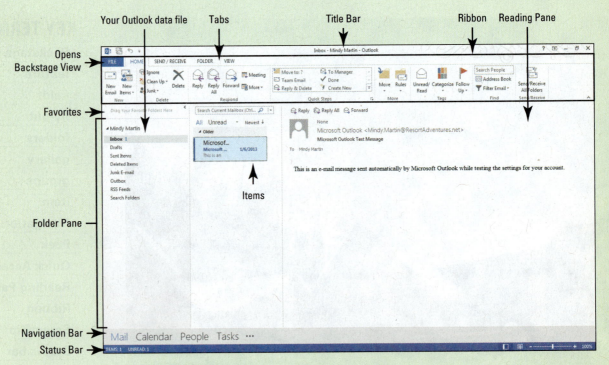

Figure 1-1

The Inbox—Outlook 2013's opening screen

The elements and features of this screen are typical for Microsoft Outlook. Your screen may vary if default settings have been changed or if other preferences have been set. Use this figure as a reference throughout this lesson as well as the rest of this book.

STARTING OUTLOOK

The Bottom Line

Microsoft Outlook 2013 can be launched in a couple of different ways. You can launch Outlook from the Windows Start screen. The Start screen displays tiles that represent the programs you use most. Using Windows 8, you can search for Outlook 2013 from the Start screen or just locate the Microsoft Office tiles and click Outlook 2013.

Launching Outlook from the Windows Start Screen

As in all Microsoft Office applications, using the Windows Start screen may be the most common method of launching Outlook. You can access Outlook 2013 by simply typing the word *Outlook* anywhere on the Windows Start screen. The Windows 8 Search feature will search through the various apps, settings, and files on the computer to find the requested application. In this exercise, you will learn how to launch Outlook from the Start screen.

STEP BY STEP   **Launch Outlook from the Windows Start Screen**

GET READY. Before you begin these steps, be sure to turn on and log on to your computer.

1. Press the Windows Key, if necessary to return to the Windows Start screen.
2. Key the word **Outlook**. As soon as you begin typing, Microsoft Windows Search will present a list of applications that match what you typed, as shown in Figure 1-2.

Figure 1-2

Windows 8 Search for Microsoft Outlook 2013

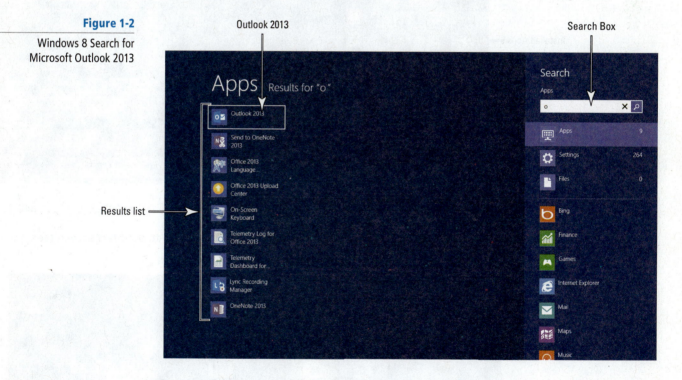

3. Click **Outlook 2013** in the results list to open the Outlook window.
4. Compare your screen to Figure 1-1, and locate each of the labeled elements.
5. Click the **Close** button in the upper-right corner.

PAUSE. You will launch Outlook again in the next exercise.

Launching Outlook from a Shortcut Tile

As you saw in the previous exercise, you can easily launch Outlook 2013 from the Start screen. However, you might find it easier to create a tile for Outlook 2013 on your Start screen. A **tile** is an icon placed on the Windows Start screen that launches an application, opens a folder, or opens a file. Simply click the tile to perform the specified action.

In the next exercise, you will create an Outlook tile and use it to launch Outlook.

STEP BY STEP   **Launch Outlook from a Shortcut Tile**

GET READY. Before you begin these steps, be sure that Microsoft Outlook is not running.

1. Click the **Start** button, or press the Windows key if necessary to return to the Windows Start screen.

2. Right-click in an area with no tiles. A bar appears at the bottom of the screen, as shown in Figure 1-3.

3. Click the **All apps** icon in the bottom right of the bar. Windows displays a list of all the apps installed on the computer.

4. Scroll to the right until you locate Outlook 2013 on the list.

5. Right-click the **Outlook 2013** tile. Options appear in the bar at the bottom of the screen.

6. Select If you "Unpin from Start" in the bottom bar instead, skip to Step 7 **Pin to Start**.

Another Way

If you frequently access Outlook 2013 from your desktop, you can also add a shortcut to the Windows taskbar. Just click the **Pin to taskbar** button as well.

Figure 1-3

Creating a Start screen tile for Microsoft Outlook 2013

Installed Apps

Pin to Start

Outlook 2013   All Apps

7. Click the **Start** button or press the Windows key to return to the Start screen (see Figure 1-4).

Figure 1-4

Start screen tile for Microsoft Outlook 2013

8. Scroll as needed to locate the Microsoft Outlook 2013 tile.

9. Click the Outlook 2013 tile. Microsoft Outlook 2013 is launched.

PAUSE. LEAVE Outlook open to use in the next exercise.

As you have just seen, Outlook can be launched in two different ways. Use the method you prefer.

• Click the Start button (or press the Windows key) and key Outlook 2013.

• Click the Outlook 2013 tile on the Windows Start screen.

In the previous exercise, you launched Microsoft Outlook. Outlook opens to your mailbox when launched, as shown in Figure 1-1. By default, the Outlook mailbox is divided into five main sections: the Ribbon, the Folder Pane, the message list, the Reading Pane, and the Navigation bar. You can use the Outlook onscreen tools to control the Outlook environment and access the various Outlook features.

WORKING IN THE OUTLOOK WINDOW

The Bottom Line

Outlook has a variety of tools that help you organize your communication and manage your time. The Outlook 2013 window was designed to help you get your work done as quickly and efficiently as possible. In this section, you'll explore different ways to navigate through the various Outlook features. You will also learn about using the Outlook onscreen tools, such as the Ribbon, which displays common commands in groups arranged by tabs, and the Quick Access Toolbar.

Navigating in Outlook

To get the most out of Outlook, you'll want to familiarize yourself with each of the onscreen tools. When you hover the mouse pointer over any command, a **ScreenTip** appears providing a brief description of the command's purpose in a small, pop-up text box.

The **Navigation bar** includes tools that help you access the Outlook features, such as Mail, Calendar, Tasks, etc. Outlook 2013 is all about accessing all of your information at a glance. To help with that, all you need to do is hover over one of the Navigation bar buttons to display a Peek. A **Peek** is a small fly-out view of your schedule, your to-do list, or what is happening with your friends without ever having to leave your inbox. In this exercise, you'll use the new Outlook Navigation bar and Folder Pane to take a quick look at some of the Outlook features and familiarize yourself with navigating in the Outlook window.

STEP BY STEP | **Navigate in Outlook**

GET READY. LAUNCH Outlook if it is not already running.

Take Note We've added some content to the screens in this section so that you can see how your content will appear. Your screen will look different if default settings have been changed or other content has been added to your PC. Use these figures as a reference.

1. Locate the Navigation bar. The Navigation bar is located in the lower left of the screen. This is the tool that helps you access each of the primary Outlook functions, such as the Calendar and the People view.

2. Hover the mouse over the Calendar button in the Navigation bar. Outlook displays the Calendar Peek showing upcoming events, as shown in Figure 1-5.

Figure 1-5

Calendar Peek in Outlook 2013

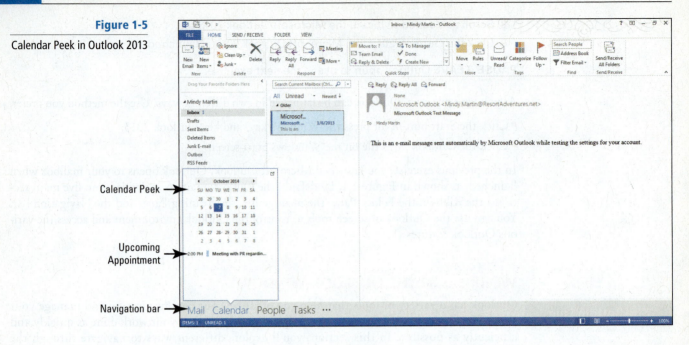

Calendar Peek ─

Upcoming
Appointment ─

Navigation bar ─

3. Click the **Calendar** button in the Navigation bar. The Calendar is displayed showing today's date, as shown in Figure 1-6.

Take Note   Notice that the contents of the Folder Pane have changed. This section updates automatically to provide you with tools for navigating within the selected Outlook component.

Figure 1-6

Outlook 2013 Calendar

Navigate within the
open component

Click a button to switch
to another component

Another Way
You can also access Outlook Calendar by using the keyboard shortcut Ctrl + 2.

4. Point to the small, left-facing arrow at the top right corner of the Folder Pane. A ScreenTip appears identifying the arrow as the Minimize the Folder Pane button (Figure 1-7). These minimize buttons are often referred to as collapse buttons.

Figure 1-7

Using ScreenTips

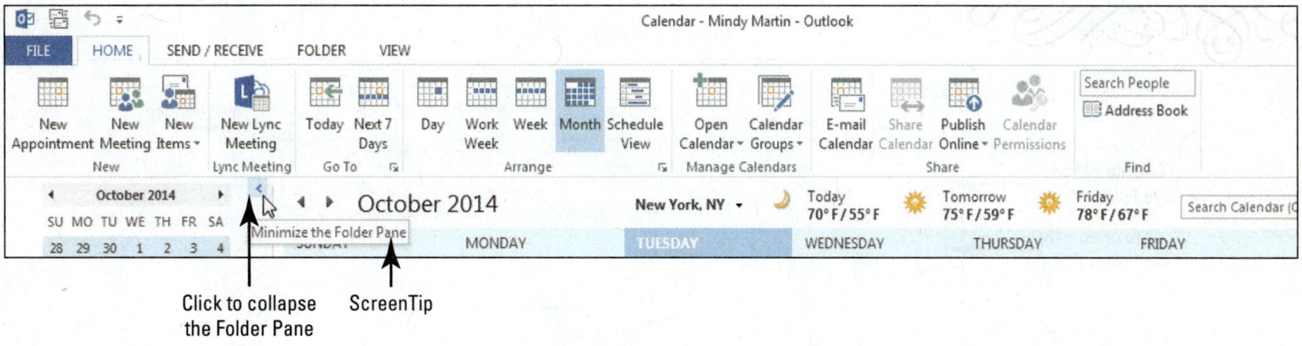

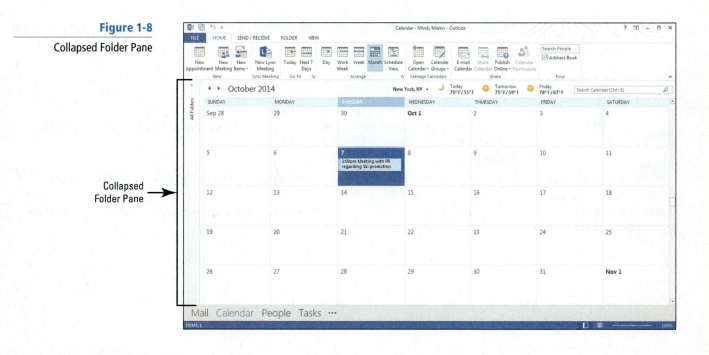

Click to collapse   ScreenTip
the Folder Pane

5. Click the **Minimize the Folder Pane** button in the Folder Pane. The Folder Pane collapses to show more of the Calendar, as shown in Figure 1-8.

Figure 1-8

Collapsed Folder Pane

Collapsed
Folder Pane

6. Click **All Folders** on the collapsed Folder Pane. A fly-out of the Folder Pane is displayed showing you all the information in the Pane, as shown in Figure 1-9.

A **fly-out** is a menu or pane that opens floating above the main window, without changing the layout of the underlying main window.

Figure 1-9

Fly-out Folder Pane

Click to expand the Folder Pane

Click to open a fly out Folder Pane

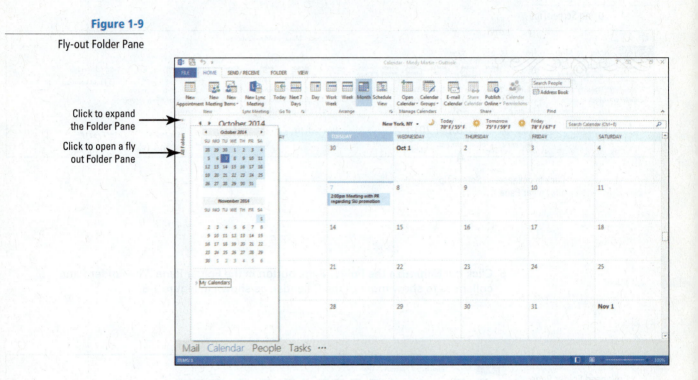

7. Click **All Folders** again to remove the fly-out.

8. Click the **Expand the Folder Pane arrow** on the Folder Pane. The full Folder Pane is restored.

9. Click the **Mail** button in the Navigation bar.

10. Click ******* on the Navigation bar. A shortcut menu listing additional Navigation bar options is displayed.

11. Click the **Folders** option. The Folder Pane changes to display the Folders List, as shown in Figure 1-10.

Another Way
You can also access Outlook Mail by using the keyboard shortcut Ctrl + 1.

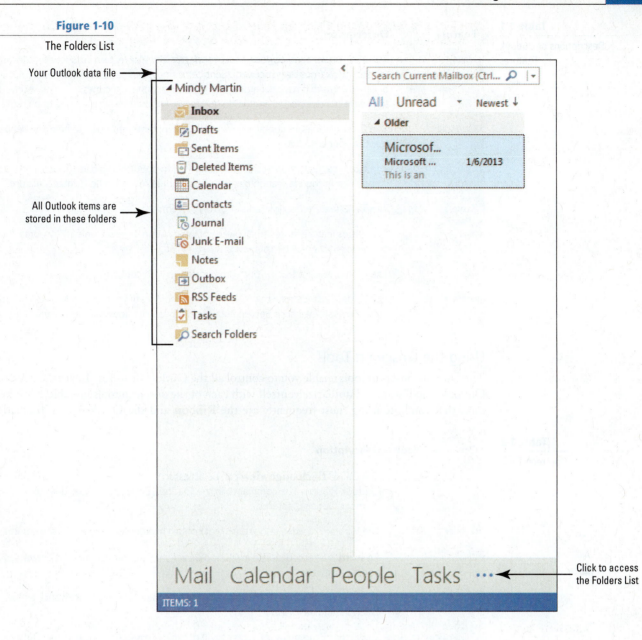

Figure 1-10

The Folders List

Your Outlook data file →

All Outlook items are stored in these folders →

Click to access the Folders List

PAUSE. LEAVE Outlook open to use in the next exercise.

When you display the Outlook Folders List, you can see that each Outlook feature has its own folder, as shown in Figure 1-10. Every Outlook item (message, meeting, task, etc.) is stored in one of the folders in the Folders List.

Take Note   Because each Outlook feature is stored in a folder, the features themselves are sometimes referred to as **folders**.

If you create folders to help organize your Outlook items, those folders will typically appear as subfolders. For example, if you create a folder to store e-mails relating to a specific project you are working on, the project folder will appear in the Folders List under the Inbox folder by default.

Table 1-1 briefly describes how these Outlook features are typically used.

Feature	Description
Mail	The Mail feature contains your e-mail messages. The Mail feature includes the following folders: Inbox (messages received), Sent Items (messages sent), Deleted Items (messages or other items that have been deleted), Junk E-mail (unwanted messages you received that were not directed to another folder), and Outbox (messages waiting to be sent).
Calendar	The Calendar feature contains a calendar and appointment book to help you keep track of your schedule.
Contacts	The Contacts feature stores contact information about individuals, groups, and companies. In the Navigation bar, the word People refers to the Contacts feature.
Tasks	The Tasks feature displays tasks and To-Do items.
Notes	The Notes feature stores small pieces of information on electronic sticky notes. Notes can be forwarded as e-mail messages.
Journal	The Journal feature tracks your communication with contacts.
Folders List	The Folders List identifies all of your Outlook folders. If your company or organization uses Microsoft Exchange Server, public folders you can access are also listed.

Using the Onscreen Tools

The Outlook onscreen tools enable you to control all the Outlook features. To get the most out of Outlook, you'll want to familiarize yourself with each of the onscreen tools in Table 1-2. The two tools that you'll be using most frequently are the **Ribbon** and the Quick Access Toolbar. The

Onscreen Tool	Description
Backstage View	The Office **Backstage view** can be accessed by clicking on the FILE tab on the Outlook Ribbon. The commands in the Outlook Backstage can be used to customize most Outlook features.
Groups	The Ribbon is divided into groups that contain buttons for frequently used commands.
Item	An **item** is a record stored in Outlook. Each message, appointment, contact, task, or note is an item.
Navigation bar	The Navigation bar provides access to each of the Outlook features, such as the Calendar and Tasks list.
Folder Pane	The Folder Pane provides access to all of the folders used in each of the Outlook features. The Folder Pane can be minimized to enlarge the Reading Pane.
Reading Pane	The **Reading Pane** displays information about the selected Outlook item. For example, in the mailbox, it displays the text of a selected e-mail message.
Ribbon	The Ribbon contains common menus and commands available in Outlook 2013. The Ribbon contains tabs that replace the menus in the old Menu bar. Each tab is divided into groups of commands.
Status bar	The **Status bar** identifies the number of items in the active feature or selected folder. For example, when the Contacts tool is active, the number of people stored is displayed in the Status bar.
Title bar	The **Title bar** identifies the application and the active feature. For example, when the Calendar is active, the Title bar says "Calendar – *Your Name* – Outlook." Depending on how your account was created, it could show either your name or your e-mail address.
To-Do Bar	The **To-Do Bar** summarizes information about appointments and tasks.
Quick Access Toolbar	The **Quick Access Toolbar** appears on the left side of the Title bar, above the Ribbon. If you want the toolbar closer to your work area, you can move it below the Ribbon. This toolbar should contain the commands you use most frequently.

Ribbon contains the most commonly used commands and buttons you need for each of the Outlook features. As you click buttons or select menu commands, the Outlook window changes to display the information you requested or to provide space to enter new information. In this exercise, you'll practice using the Outlook onscreen tools.

Table 1-2 describes the basic functions of the onscreen tools used to access the Outlook features. More detailed information about using each of the features is available in the following sections of this lesson and the remaining lessons.

STEP BY STEP **Use the Onscreen Tools**

GET READY. LAUNCH Outlook if it is not already running and ensure that the Mail feature is active.

1. Click the **Mail** button in the Navigation bar and click the **VIEW** tab. The Ribbon is divided into **groups** of related commands, as shown in Figure 1-11.

Figure 1-11

The Ribbon features a variety of tools

Click to enter
Backstage view   Tabs

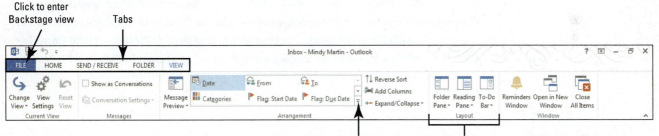

Click the More button to   The tools on each tab
open a gallery of options   are placed in groups of
                               similar functions

2. Locate the Arrangement group. When there are too many options available to store neatly as buttons in a group, Outlook places the buttons in a dropdown window called a **gallery**. The More button tells you that there are more options available in the gallery.
3. Click the **More** button to display the Arrangement gallery. A gallery of available options for arranging e-mail drops down, as shown in Figure 1-12.

Figure 1-12

The Arrangement gallery displayed

Ribbon Display Options

Inbox - Mindy Martin - Outlook

FILE   HOME   SEND / RECEIVE   FOLDER   VIEW

Change View | View Settings | Reset View   Show as Conversations   Conversation Settings   Message Preview   Date | Categories | Size | Attachments | Show in Groups | View Settings...   From | Flag: Start Date | Subject | Account   To | Flag: Due Date | Type | Importance   Reverse Sort | Add Columns | Expand/Collapse   Folder Pane | Reading Pane | To-Do Bar   Reminders Window | Open in New Window | Close All Items

Current View   Messages   Layout   Window

Drag Your Favorite Folders Here   Search Current Mailb

▲ Mindy Martin
Inbox
Drafts
Sent Items

All   Unread
▲ Older

Microsof...
Microsoft ...   1/6/2013
This is an

indy.Martin@ResortAdventures.net>
ssage

To   Mindy Martin

The Arrangement gallery   Click to collapse Ribbon

4. Click the **Ribbon Display Options** button. A list of available Ribbon options drops down, as shown in Figure 1-13.

Figure 1-13

Ribbon Display Options

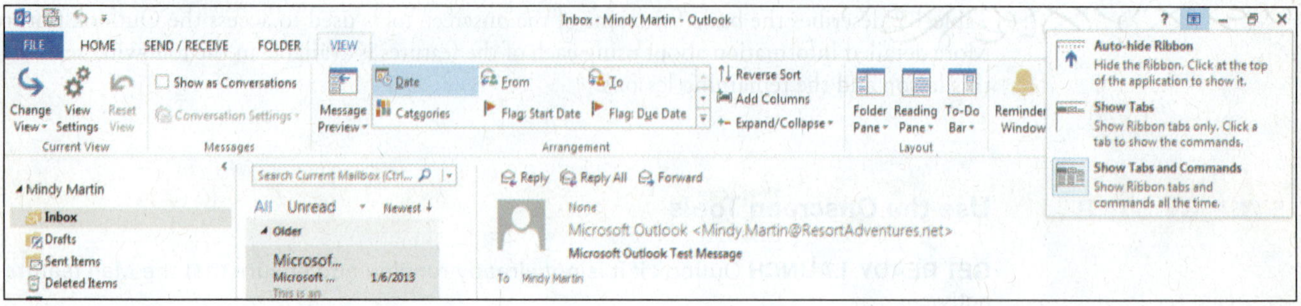

5. Click the **Auto-Hide Ribbon** option. Notice that the entire Ribbon disappears.

6. Hover at the top of the window (where the title bar used to be). Notice that a colored bar appears.

7. Click the bar at the top of the window. Notice that the entire Ribbon reappears.

8. Click anywhere else in the Outlook window and the Ribbon disappears again.

9. Click the **Ribbon Display Options** button again, and select **Show Tabs and Commands**.

10. Click the **Collapse the Ribbon** arrow on the Ribbon, as shown in Figure 1-12. The Ribbon collapses into a single bar showing only the tab names.

11. Click the **HOME** tab.

Figure 1-14

Expand the Ribbon

Click to create an
new e-mail message

Click to lock the expanded Ribbon

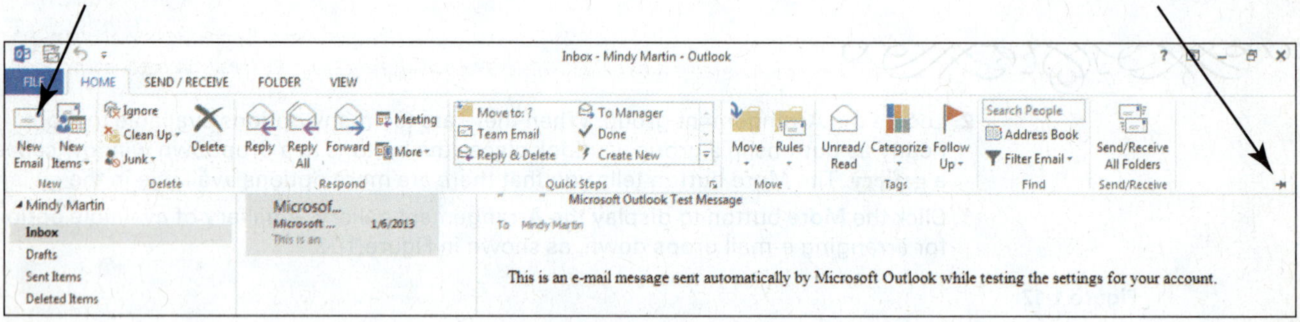

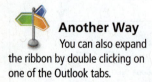
Another Way
You can also expand the ribbon by double clicking on one of the Outlook tabs.

12. Click the **Pin the Ribbon** icon to restore the Ribbon, as shown in Figure 1-14.

13. Click the **New Email** button in the New group, as shown in Figure 1-14. A message window is displayed, as shown in Figure 1-15. Notice that it has its own Ribbon. Once again, the Ribbon is divided into tabs based on the type of options available, and the options on each tab are organized into groups of similar commands.

Figure 1-15

The Untitled — Message
window

Dialog box launcher

Ribbon buttons are
gray when the option
is not available

Message area

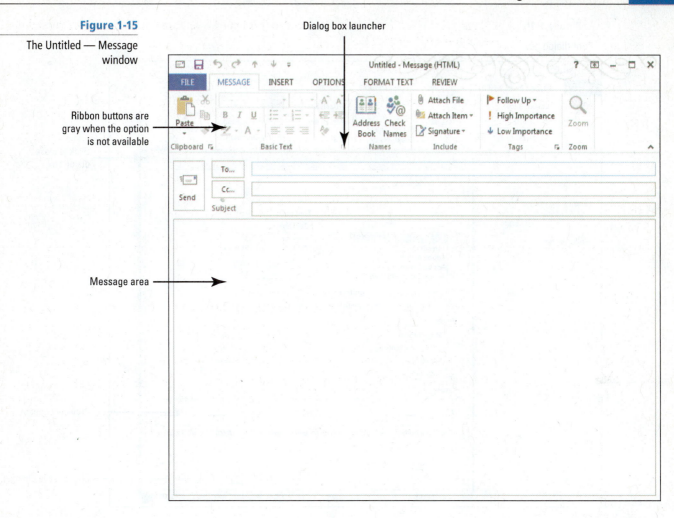

14. Locate the Title bar at the top of the window. It tells you that this window is named **Untitled — Message**. You can always identify windows and dialog boxes using the Title bar.

15. Notice that most of the buttons in the Clipboard and Basic Text groups are gray. When buttons on the Ribbon are gray, it means that the option is not available. Since this message window contains no text, the options for formatting and working with text are not yet available.

 Cross Ref You'll learn more about working with e-mail messages in Lesson 2.

16. Click in the message area. The Ribbon fills with color as options become available. Most of the buttons on the Ribbon are now available in preparation for entering text.

17. In the message area, key **Hello World**.

18. Drag the mouse over the word **Hello** in the message area to select it.

19. Click the dialog box launcher in the **Basic Text group** on the Ribbon, as shown in Figure 1-15. A traditional Microsoft dialog box is displayed containing additional options for this command group. Notice that many of the same options are available in both the dialog box and on the Ribbon.

20. In the Font Style box, click **Bold Italic**. Notice how the text *Hello* in the Preview area of the dialog box changes to reflect your choice, as shown in Figure 1-16.

Figure 1-16

Font dialog box

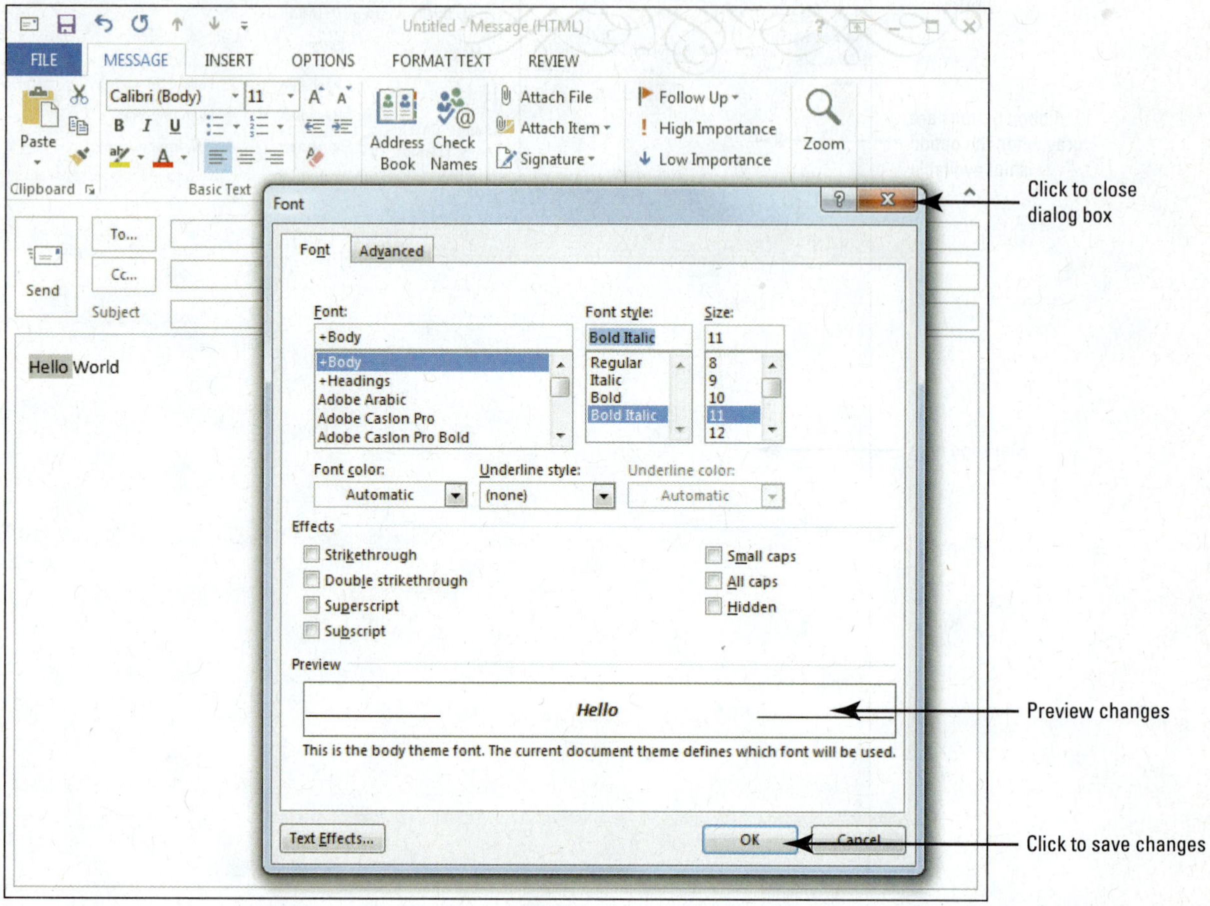

Click to close dialog box

Preview changes

Click to save changes

21. Click the **OK** button to close the dialog box and save the changes.

22. Click the **Undo** button on the Quick Access Toolbar, as shown in Figure 1-17. The bold italic formatting is removed from the word "Hello" and the Redo button appears in the Quick Access Toolbar.

Figure 1-17

Using the Quick Access Toolbar

Save Undo Redo

Customize Quick Access Toolbar

Quick Access Toolbar

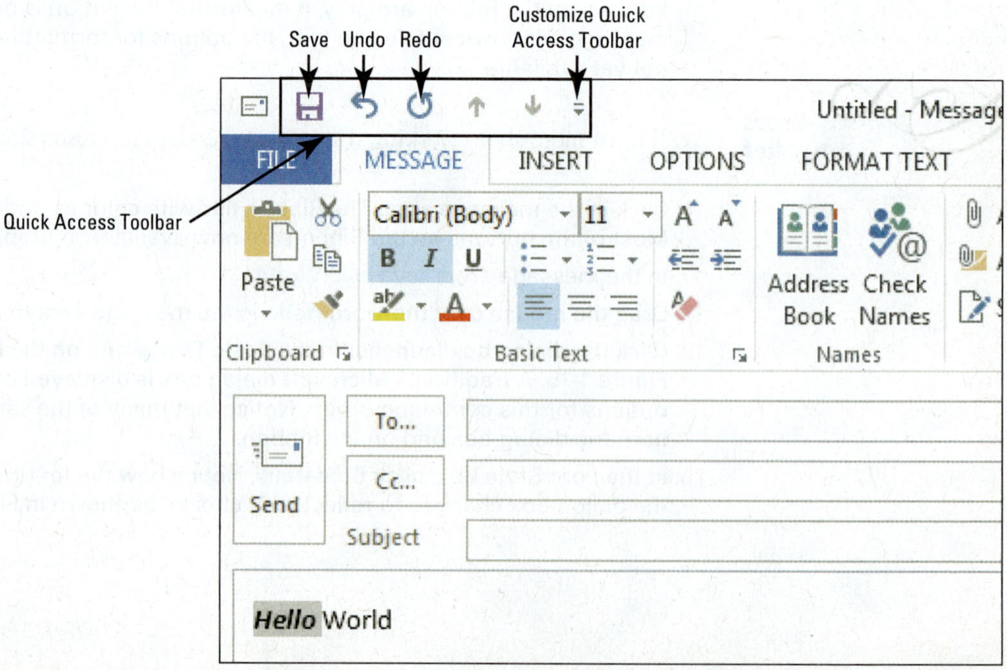

23. Click the **Redo** button on the Quick Access Toolbar to restore the text formatting. The Redo button grays out again to let you know that there are no more actions that can be redone.

24. Click the **Customize Quick Access Toolbar** button. A list of available buttons is displayed, as shown in Figure 1-18. To add or remove buttons from the Quick Access Toolbar simply select or deselect a command from the list.

Figure 1-18

Customizing the Quick Access Toolbar

Customize Quick Access Toolbar button

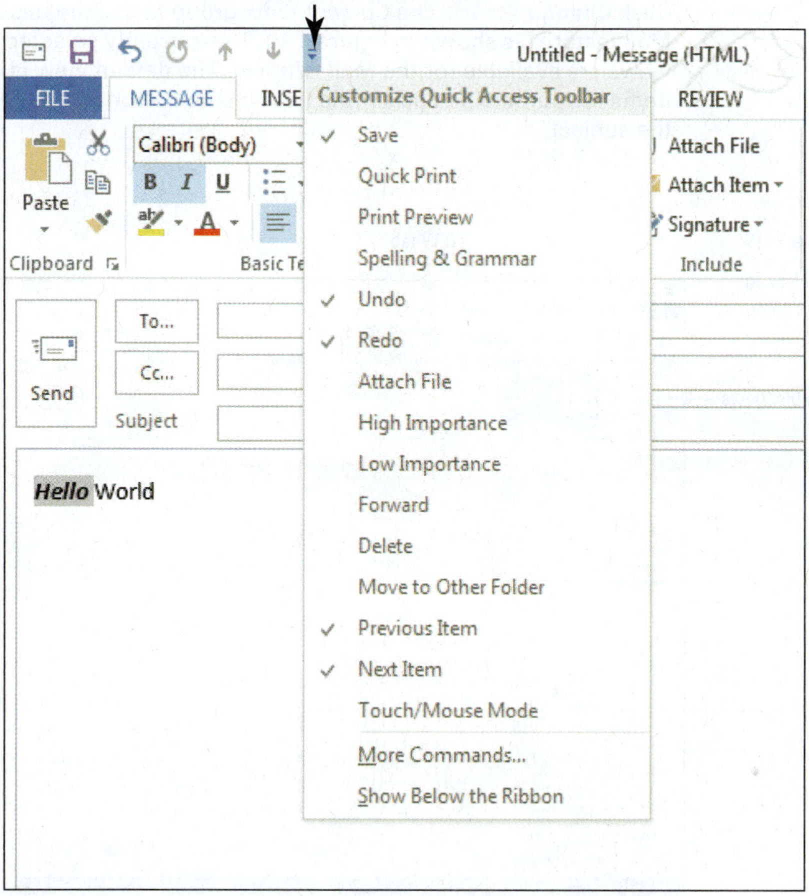

Another Way
The Customize Quick Access Toolbar menu offers a selection of commonly used buttons. If you want to add a particular command that is not in the list, you can click More Commands to open the Customize Quick Access Toolbar window, where you can choose any command in Outlook to add to your Quick Access Toolbar.

25. Click the **Close** button at the far right of the Title bar to close the message window. If Outlook prompts you to save your work, click **No**.

PAUSE. LEAVE Outlook open to use in the next exercise.

In the previous exercise, you took a quick look at the different Outlook onscreen tools. In this exercise, you will look at some of the ways you can change the viewing options available in Outlook. The features you use most frequently are covered in more detail in the following lessons.

Changing the Outlook View

Every Outlook **feature** stores specific information and offers you several options for viewing that information. For example, the Contacts feature, called People on the Navigation bar, provides the names, addresses, and phone numbers for the individuals and companies you contact. The Calendar tracks your appointments and meetings. Mail enables you to send and receive e-mail messages. You can use Ribbon commands to change the way that information is displayed to suit your needs. In this exercise, you'll use the VIEW tab and other Ribbon commands to explore some of the different Outlook views.

Change the Outlook View

GET READY. LAUNCH Outlook if it is not already running and ensure that the HOME tab is active.

1. If necessary, click the **Mail** button in the Navigation bar, and then click the **Inbox** folder to display your mailbox.

2. Click the **VIEW** tab to display more options.

3. Click **Change View** in the Current View group to see the basic viewing options for the Mail feature, as shown in Figure 1-19. The currently selected view is highlighted. Three views are available for the Mail window. The default view is Compact, which shows the items in your mailbox as simple two-line items containing the sender, the date, and the subject.

Figure 1-19

The Outlook Mailbox in Preview View

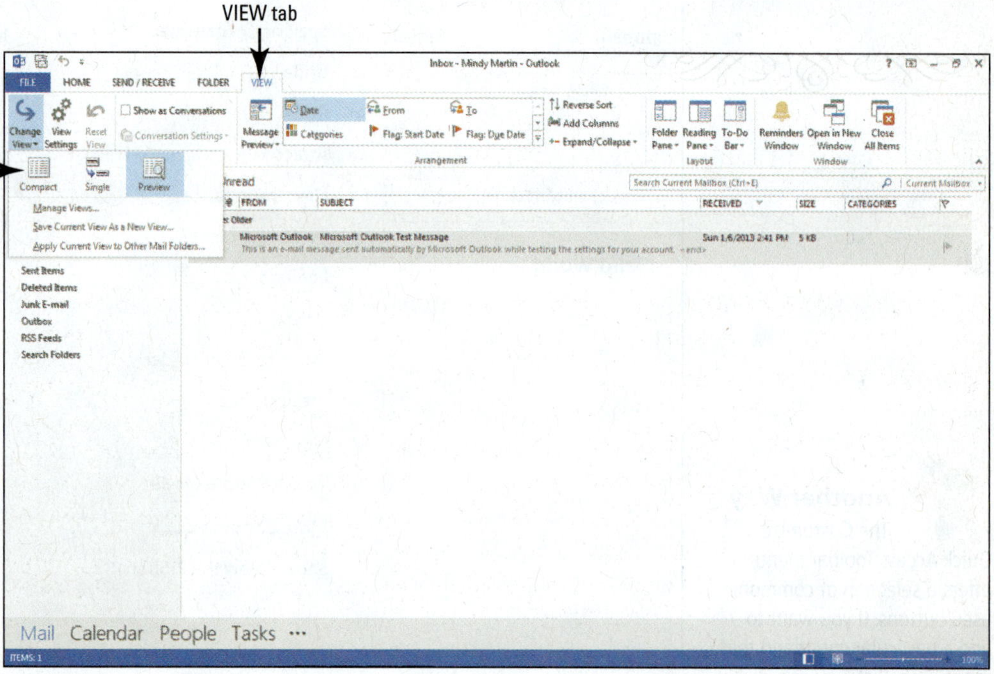

VIEW tab

Available Views →

4. Click **Single**. The Single view flattens the mailbox items into a single line with all the e-mail information spread out in columns.

5. Click **Change View** again, and click **Preview**. Notice how the screen changes to expand from a single compressed line for each item to include a short Preview of each e-mail's contents and the Reading Pane disappears.

Take Note   We've added some content to the screens in this section so that you can see how your content will appear. Your screen will look different if default settings have been changed or other content has been added to your PC. Use these figures as a reference.

6. Click **Change View** in the Current View group and select **Compact** to return to the default Mail view.

7. Click the **Calendar** button in the Navigation bar to display the Calendar feature, and click the **VIEW** tab to see the different Calendar viewing options. You can change the arrangement of the onscreen Calendar in each view. Month is the default option.

8. Click the **Day** button on the VIEW tab, to view the day's schedule.

9. Click the **Week** button to show an entire week's schedule.

10. Click the **Work Week** option. The Calendar view now displays the current work week, as shown in Figure 1-20.

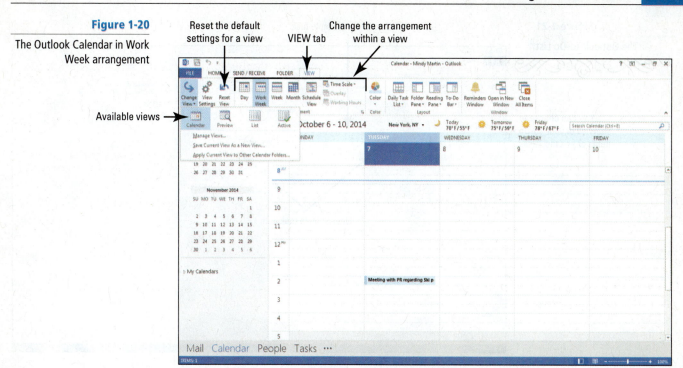

Figure 1-20

The Outlook Calendar in Work Week arrangement

Reset the default settings for a view

VIEW tab

Change the arrangement within a view

Available views

Take Note   The Work Week arrangement shows the work week as Monday through Friday, by default. However, you can change the work week to reflect your personal work schedule.

11. Click **Change View** in the Current View group to see the available views. Make sure that the default Calendar is selected.

12. Click **List**. The Calendar changes to provide a simple list of calendar items. The Active view is similar, but only shows those events that have not already occurred.

13. Click **Change View** in the Current View group, and select **Calendar**.

14. Click **Reset View** in the Current View group to change to the default Calendar view. Outlook will present you with a warning box asking you to verify that you really want to reset the view.

15. Click **Yes**.

Take Note   Throughout this chapter you will see information that appears in black text within brackets, such as [Press **Enter**], or [your e-mail address]. The information contained in the brackets is intended to be directions for you rather than something you actually type word for word. It will instruct you to perform an action or substitute text. Do **not** type the actual text that appears within brackets.

Another Way

You can also access Outlook Tasks by using the keyboard shortcut Ctrl + 4.

16. Click the **Tasks** button in the Navigation bar. Your To-Do List is displayed.

17. Click the **Type a new task** field and key **Sample**. [Press **Enter**.] The new task drops to the Task List and a flag appears indicating that the task is for today.

Cross Ref   You'll learn more about working with tasks in Lesson 11.

18. Click the **Sample** task. The Ribbon fills with color as options become available, as shown in Figure 1-21.

Figure 1-21

The Outlook To-Do List

Click to key in a simple task

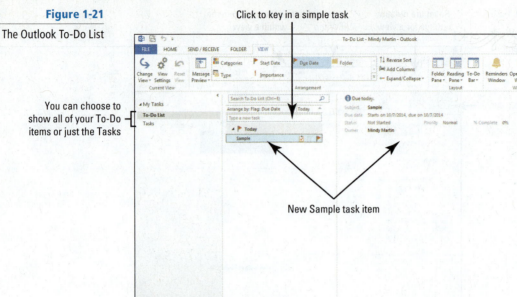

You can choose to show all of your To-Do items or just the Tasks

New Sample task item

19. Click the **VIEW** tab, and click **Change View** in the Current View group to see the viewing options.

20. Click on each option in the **Change View gallery** to see how the screen layout changes. You can choose from a number of different options—views that show all the details about a task item (Detailed) or views that let you filter your Task List to contain only items that fit the criteria you choose (Prioritized, Active, Completed, Today, Next 7 days, Overdue, Assigned).

21. Click **Change View** and select **Today**. Click the **Sample** task again, if it isn't already selected.

22. Click the **HOME** tab and select **Delete** in the Delete group to remove your sample task. Click the Undo button in the upper left corner of the screen to restore the Sample task.

23. Click **Mail** in the Navigation bar to return to the Inbox.

PAUSE. LEAVE Outlook open to use in the next exercise.

CERTIFICATION READY?   **1.1.5**

How do you configure the Outlook Calendar views?

Outlook stores and organizes many of the little pieces of information that form the core of your daily activities. In a single day, you might use the Outlook Calendar, Mail, and Contacts features to schedule meetings, look up phone numbers, send e-mail messages, and set up reminders that help you arrive on time for every meeting.

PERSONALIZING OUTLOOK

The Bottom Line

You can arrange the elements in the Outlook window to fit your needs. You have a great deal of control over the Outlook environment. In the previous exercise, you learned how to change the views for each Outlook feature, but you can go even further. You can change what appears on the Navigation bar. You can resize, rearrange, hide, or display Outlook features to create an environment that meets your requirements. In this section, you'll learn how to rearrange your Outlook window by moving the Reading Pane, displaying or hiding the To-Do Bar, adding or deleting columns in a List view, and adding and removing elements from the To-Do Bar.

Customizing the Navigation Bar

You can change which Outlook features appear on the Navigation bar or rearrange the items to suit your needs. You can also set the Navigation bar buttons to appear as either words or icons. In this exercise, you'll learn to change the appearance of the Navigation bar.

Customizing the Navigation Bar

GET READY. LAUNCH Outlook if it is not already running.

1. Click **Mail** in the Navigation bar, if necessary, to display the default Outlook opening screen.

2. Click ******* on the Navigation bar, as shown in Figure 1-22.

Figure 1-22

Customizing the
Navigation bar

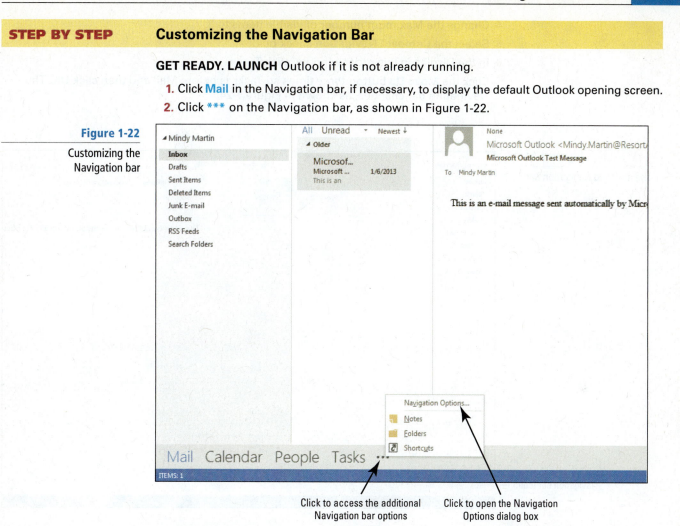

Click to access the additional   Click to open the Navigation
Navigation bar options   Options dialog box

3. Select **Navigation Options**. The Navigation Options dialog box appears, as shown in Figure 1-23.

Figure 1-23

The Navigation Options
dialog box

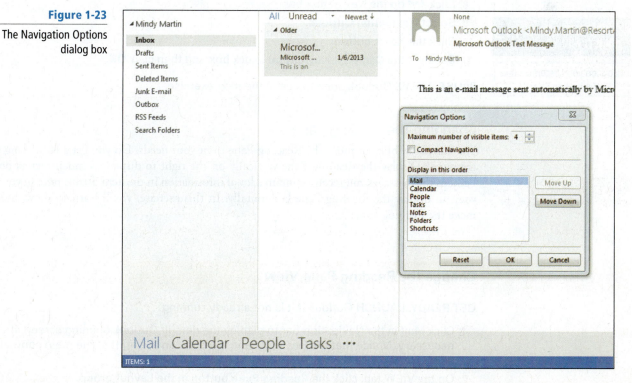

4. Change the Maximum number of visible items to **3**.

5. Select the **Compact Navigation** check box.

6. In the Display in this order window, click **Tasks**.

7. Click the **Move Up** button *three* times so Tasks is before Mail and then click **OK**. The Navigation bar changes, as shown in Figure 1-24.

Figure 1-24

The modified Navigation bar

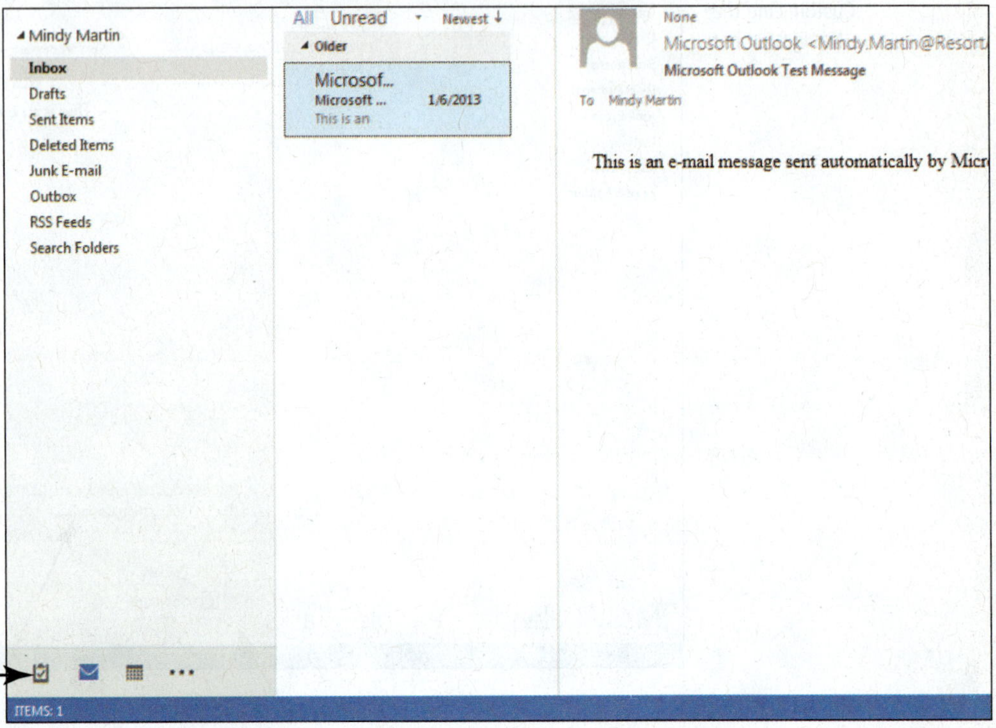

Navigation bar icons

8. Click ******* on the Navigation bar.

9. Select **Navigation Options**.

10. Click the **Reset** button.

11. Deselect the **Compact Navigation** check box and then click **OK**.

PAUSE. LEAVE Outlook open to use in the next exercise.

CERTIFICATION READY?   **1.1.3**

How do you customize the Navigation Pane?

Changing the Reading Pane View

You can show, hide, or move the Reading Pane to fit your needs. Do you get a lot of long e-mail messages? Display the Reading Pane vertically on the right to display as much text as possible. Perhaps the messages you receive contain a lot of information in the item listing area, so you might want to display the Reading Pane horizontally. In this exercise, you'll learn to show, hide, and move the Reading Pane.

STEP BY STEP   **Change the Reading Pane View**

GET READY. LAUNCH Outlook if it is not already running.

1. Click **Mail** in the Navigation bar to display the default Outlook opening screen, if necessary. Notice that the Reading Pane is visible on the right of the main content pane.

2. On the VIEW tab, click the **Reading Pane** button in the Layout group.

3. Select the **Bottom** option. The Reading Pane is displayed horizontally, across the bottom of the message viewing area. If you have any e-mails in your mailbox, you'll see a preview of the message contents in the Reading Pane, as shown in Figure 1-25.

Figure 1-25

Reading Pane displayed in the bottom position

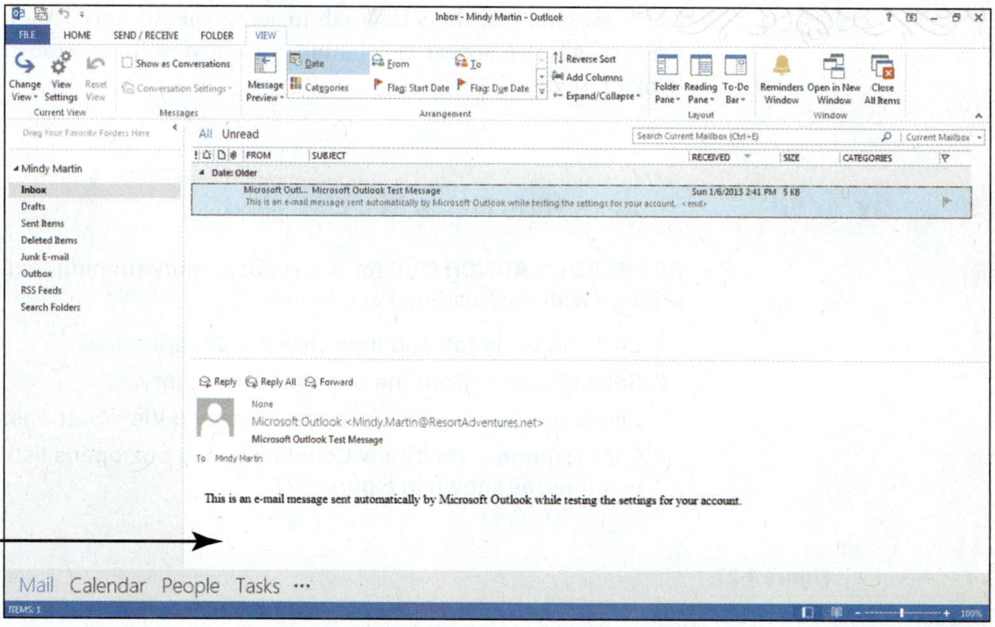

Reading Pane ───────────────▶

4. On the VIEW tab, click the **Reading Pane** button in the Layout group.
5. Select the **Off** option. The Reading Pane is hidden, as shown in Figure 1-26.

Figure 1-26

Reading Pane is hidden

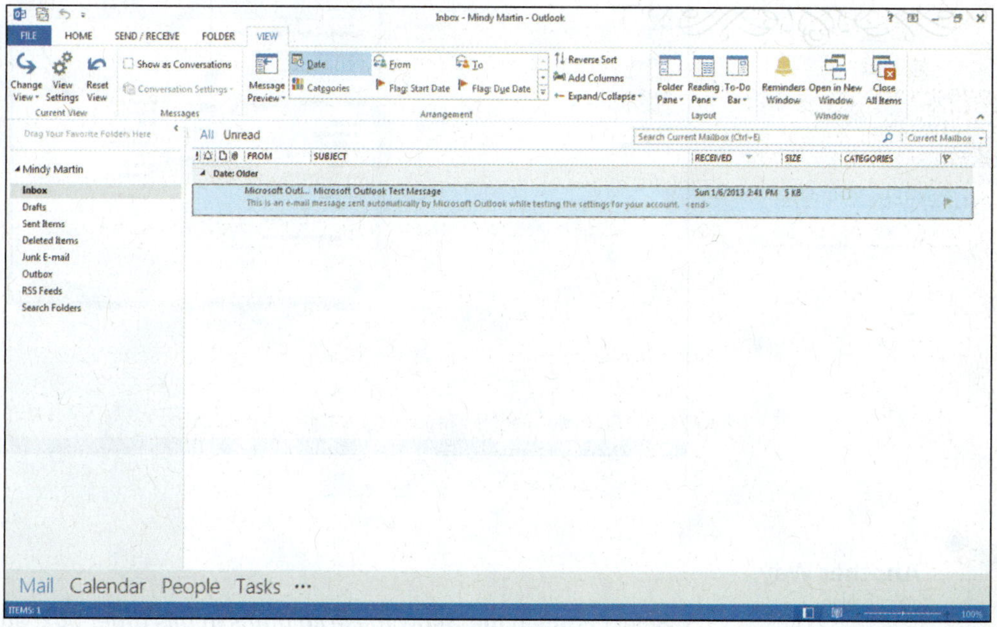

PAUSE. LEAVE Outlook open to use in the next exercise.

Showing or Hiding Fields in a List View

Another way you can personalize your Outlook window is by deciding which fields you want to see in a list view. In Outlook, **fields** are specific bits of information about an item. For example, an incoming e-mail message might contain several fields of information, such as *From, Subject, To, Received, Flag Status, Attachments*, and so on. You can click the View Settings button in the Current View group on the VIEW tab to access the Advanced View Settings dialog box to add and remove fields that appear as columns in a List view. In this exercise, you'll add and remove a field from a List view.

STEP BY STEP   ### Show or Hide Fields in a List View

GET READY. LAUNCH Outlook if it is not already running and ensure that it shows the mailbox with the Reading Pane hidden.

1. Click the **VIEW** tab and then click the **Change View**.
2. Select **Preview** from the Change View gallery.
3. Click **View Settings** to open the Advanced View Settings: Preview dialog box.
4. Click **Columns**. The Show Columns dialog box opens listing all of the available columns, as shown in Figure 1-27.

Figure 1-27

The Show Columns dialog box

Click to add selected column   Columns currently showing in List view

Click to access the Advanced View Settings dialog box

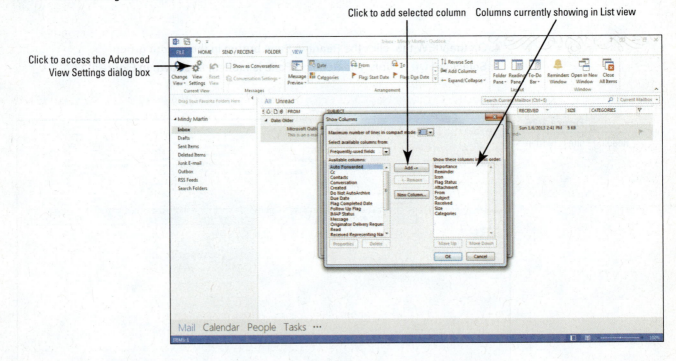

Another Way
You can also remove a field by right-clicking the field header in the List view and selecting *Remove This Column* from the shortcut menu.

5. Select **From** in the *Show these columns in this order* box, and then click the **Remove button**.
6. Click **OK** twice to apply your changes and close the dialog boxes. The column changes have been applied to the mailbox, as shown in Figure 1-28. Notice that the From column no longer appears.

Figure 1-28

The mailbox with
modified columns

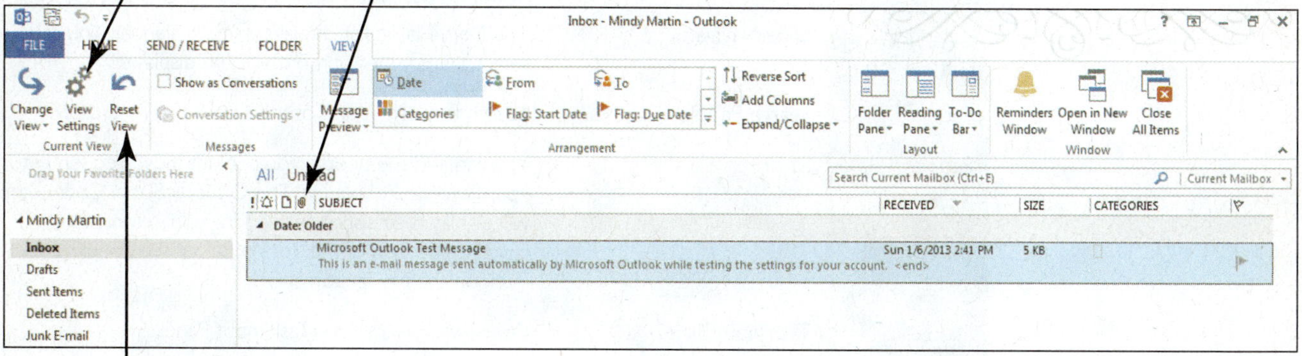

Click to access the Advanced
View Settings dialog box

From column is hidden

Click to revert back to the
defaults for the selected view

7. Click the **View Settings** button, then click **Columns** in the Advanced View Settings: Preview dialog box.

8. Select **From** in the Available Columns box on the left of the dialog box and click the **Add** button. Notice that the From column is at the bottom of the *Show these columns in this order* list, meaning that it will appear at the far right column in Preview view list.

9. Click the **Move Up** button below the list repeatedly until the From column appears at the top of the list.

10. Click **OK** twice to apply your changes and close the dialog boxes. The From column is visible again, but is located at the far left of the column headers.

11. Click **Change View** in the Current View group on the VIEW tab.

12. Click **Compact** at the prompt to restore the mailbox to the default view.

13. Click **Reset View** in the Current View group on the VIEW tab.

14. Click **Yes** at the prompt to restore the mailbox to the default view.

15. Click the Reading Pane dropdown button and select Right.

PAUSE. LEAVE Outlook open to use in the next exercise.

Another Way
You can also change the column order by selecting the field name in either the Show Columns dialog box or in the List view itself and dragging the field to the desired location.

Customizing the To-Do Bar

The *To-Do Bar* summarizes the current Outlook items that need some follow-up. With a single glance, you can see your appointments, tasks, and e-mail messages that require some action. By default, the To-Do Bar feature is turned off in Outlook 2013. You can turn it on using the VIEW tab, or it can be built by docking, or pinning, Peeks from the Navigation bar to the right of the Outlook window. You can customize the To-Do Bar by changing which elements are visible. When you use Pinned Peeks to build the To-Do Bar, you are able to customize the order in which the visible elements appear. In this exercise, you'll add and remove elements from the To-Do Bar.

Table 1-3 describes each of the To-Do Bar elements.

Table 1-3
To-Do Bar Element Descriptions

To-Do Bar Section	To-Do Bar Element	Description
Calendar	Appointments	The Appointments element displays appointments scheduled in Outlook. You can select the number of appointments to be displayed.
Calendar	Date Navigator	The Date Navigator displays a small calendar. You can select the number of months to be displayed.
People	Search People	Search through your Contacts from the To-Do Bar.
People	Favorites	You can add the people you contact most frequently to your Favorite People list. The Outlook Social Connector will display their social networking updates in the Favorites section of the To-Do Bar or the People dock Peek on the Navigation bar.
Tasks	Task Input Panel	Key new tasks into the Task Input Panel.
Tasks	Task List	The Task List displays the tasks that have been assigned to you.

STEP BY STEP Customize the To-Do Bar

GET READY. LAUNCH Outlook if it is not already running.

1. If necessary, click the **Mail** button in the Navigation bar to display the default mailbox view. By default, the To-Do Bar is not displayed.
2. Click the **VIEW** tab, and then click the **To-Do Bar** button. The To-Do Bar options are displayed, as shown in Figure 1-29.

Click to view the To-Do Bar options

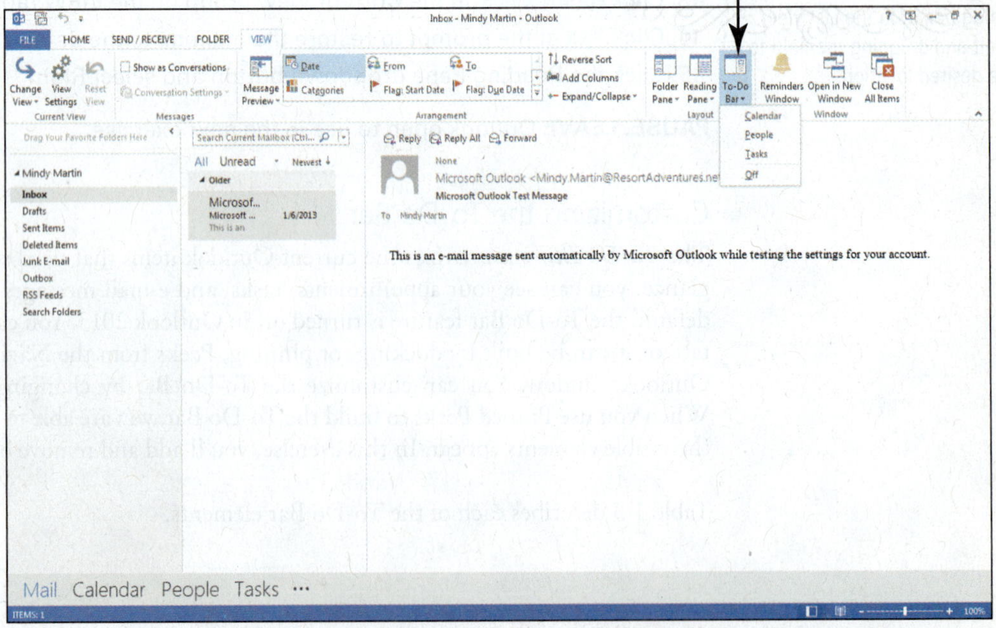

Figure 1-29
The To-Do Bar options

3. Click **Calendar**. The To-Do Bar appears on the right of the Outlook window. The Date Navigator is shown in the top half, as shown in Figure 1-30.

Figure 1-30

The Date Navigator in the To-Do Bar

Date navigator

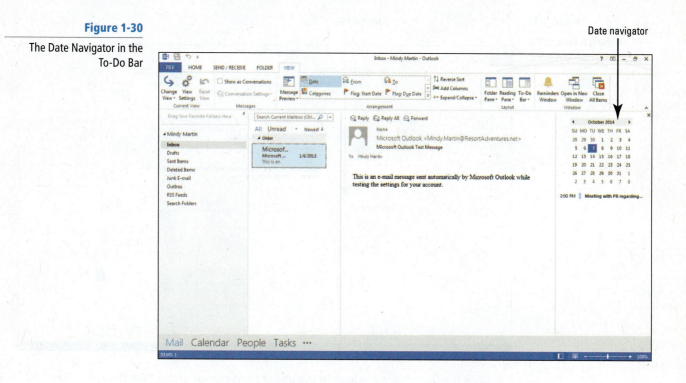

4. Click the **To-Do Bar** button and click **People**. A People section is added to the lower half of the To-Do Bar, as shown in Figure 1-31.

Figure 1-31

Adding People to the To-Do Bar

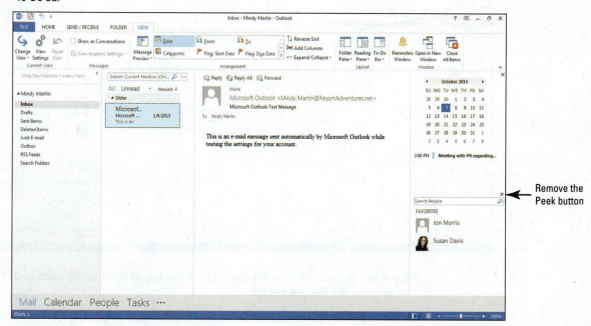

Remove the Peek button

Take Note   The To-Do Bar sections mirror the information displayed when Peeks are viewed.

5. Hover the mouse over the **Tasks** button in the Navigation bar, as shown in Figure 1-32.

Figure 1-32

Pinning a Peek to the To-Do Bar

Dock the Peek button

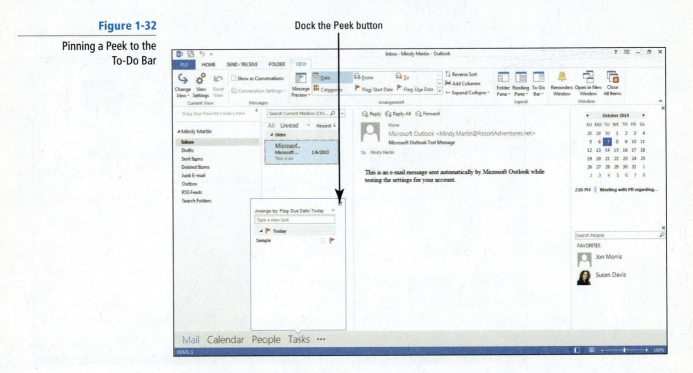

6. Click the **Dock the peek** icon in the upper right corner of the Task Peek. The Task section is added to the To-Do Bar, as shown in Figure 1-33.

Figure 1-33

The To-Do Bar

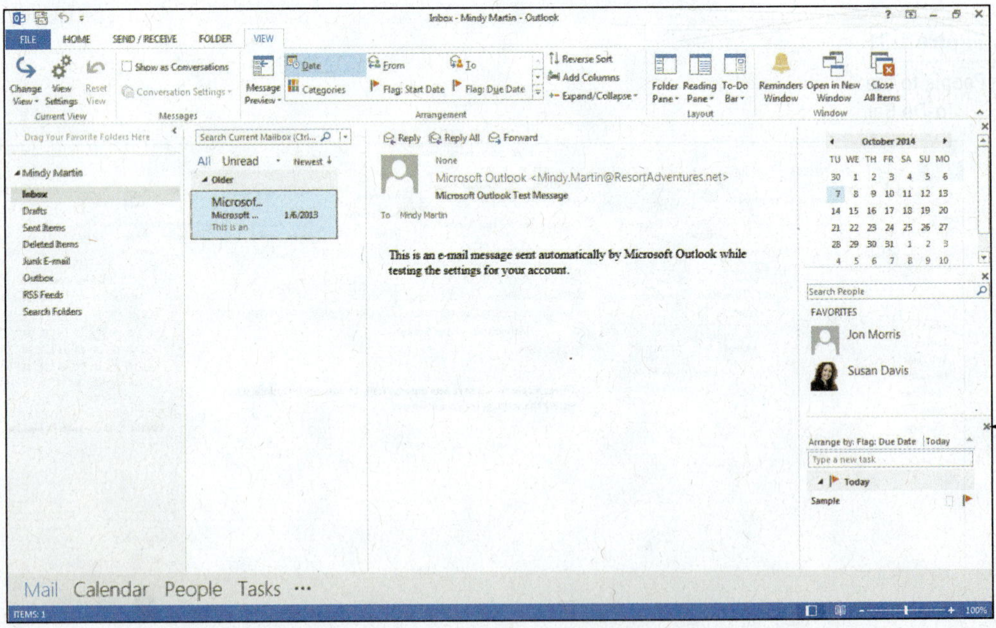

Remove the Peek button

7. Click the **Remove the Peek** button (X) at the top of the People section of the To-Do Bar to remove the People section.

8. Click the **VIEW** tab, click the **To-Do Bar** button, and select the **Off** option.

PAUSE. LEAVE Outlook open to use in the next exercise.

USING BACKSTAGE VIEW

The Bottom Line

Microsoft Outlook 2013 is designed to adapt to you. Outlook places all of the settings and controls in one easy-to-navigate place called Backstage. You can use the Backstage view options to control the way Outlook acts and looks. You can use Backstage to create and modify accounts and to clean up your Outlook file. You can also use the *Options* area of Backstage to change all the settings used for mail, calendars, tasks, journals, and people, or use the Advanced options to access settings that control the way Outlook handles your information.

Using the FILE Tab to Open Backstage View

Clicking the FILE tab opens the Microsoft Office Backstage view. You'll notice a menu-like list running down the left side of the window, called the Navigation Pane. You can click any of these commands to open a new Backstage page that contains related options. In this exercise, you learn to use the FILE tab to open Backstage view and look over the options available through some of its commands.

STEP BY STEP   **Use the FILE Tab to Open Backstage View**

GET READY. LAUNCH Outlook if it is not already running.

1. In the Outlook window, click the **Microsoft Outlook Test Message** and then click the **FILE** tab. This opens the Backstage view with the Info page active, as shown in Figure 1-34. The Info page includes information about your account and tools for maintaining your mailbox

⚠ Troubleshooting   If you no longer have the Microsoft Outlook Test Message, you can still complete the remaining steps in this exercise. However, the preview images in Backstage view will be different from those shown in Figure 1-34.

Figure 1-34

Microsoft Office Backstage view for Outlook

Backstage Navigation Pane

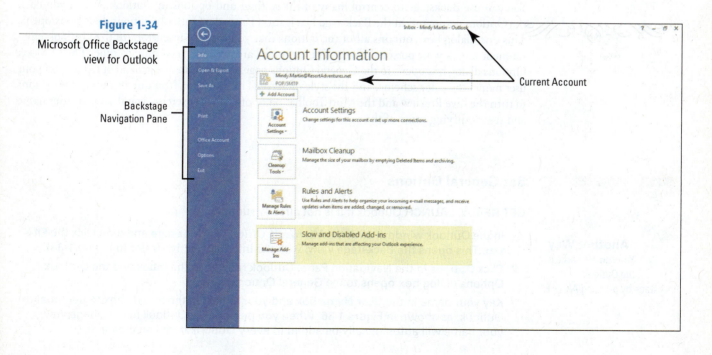

2. Click **Print** in the left Navigation Pane. The Outlook Print page opens, and a preview appears in the right Preview pane, as shown in Figure 1-35.

Figure 1-35

Microsoft Outlook Print page

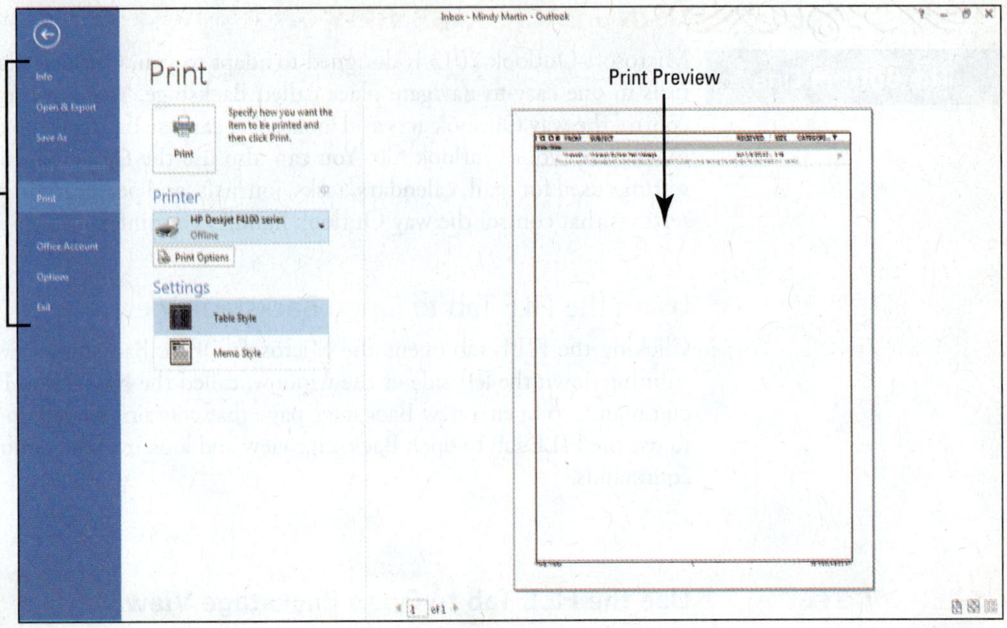

Backstage
Navigation Pane

Print Preview

3. Click the **Table Style** command in the Settings area and then the **Memo Style**. Notice how the preview changes.

4. Click the **Back arrow** icon at the top left corner of the Backstage view to return to the Inbox.

PAUSE. LEAVE Outlook open to use in the next exercise.

Setting General Options

You can use Backstage to control many of the settings and options in Outlook. When you click the Options command in the Backstage Navigation Pane, the Outlook Options dialog box opens. This one dialog box contains all of the options that you can use to customize the Outlook environment to suit your personal needs. These options are grouped according to type. The Outlook Options dialog box opens to the General Options page. You can use the general options to set your user name, the color scheme, and the style of ScreenTip you want. You can also use these options to turn the Live Preview and the Mini Toolbar on or off. In this exercise, you'll set your user name and try modifying some of the options.

STEP BY STEP	**Set General Options**

GET READY. LAUNCH Outlook if it is not already running.

Another Way
You can also access the Outlook Backstage by pressing Alt + F.

1. In the Outlook window, click the **Microsoft Office Test Message** and then click the **FILE tab**. This opens the Backstage view, with the Info page active (refer to Figure 1-34).

2. Click **Options** in the Navigation Pane. Outlook returns to the Inbox and the Outlook Options dialog box opens to the General Options page.

3. Key your name in the **User Name** box and your initials in the **Initials** box to personalize Outlook, as shown in Figure 1-36. When you personalize Outlook in Backstage view, your name will automatically be added to every Outlook item you create.

Figure 1-36

General Options page of the
Outlook Options dialog box

Hover over the information circle for more information

Each item in the Options
Navigation Pane opens an
entire page of associated
settings you can customize

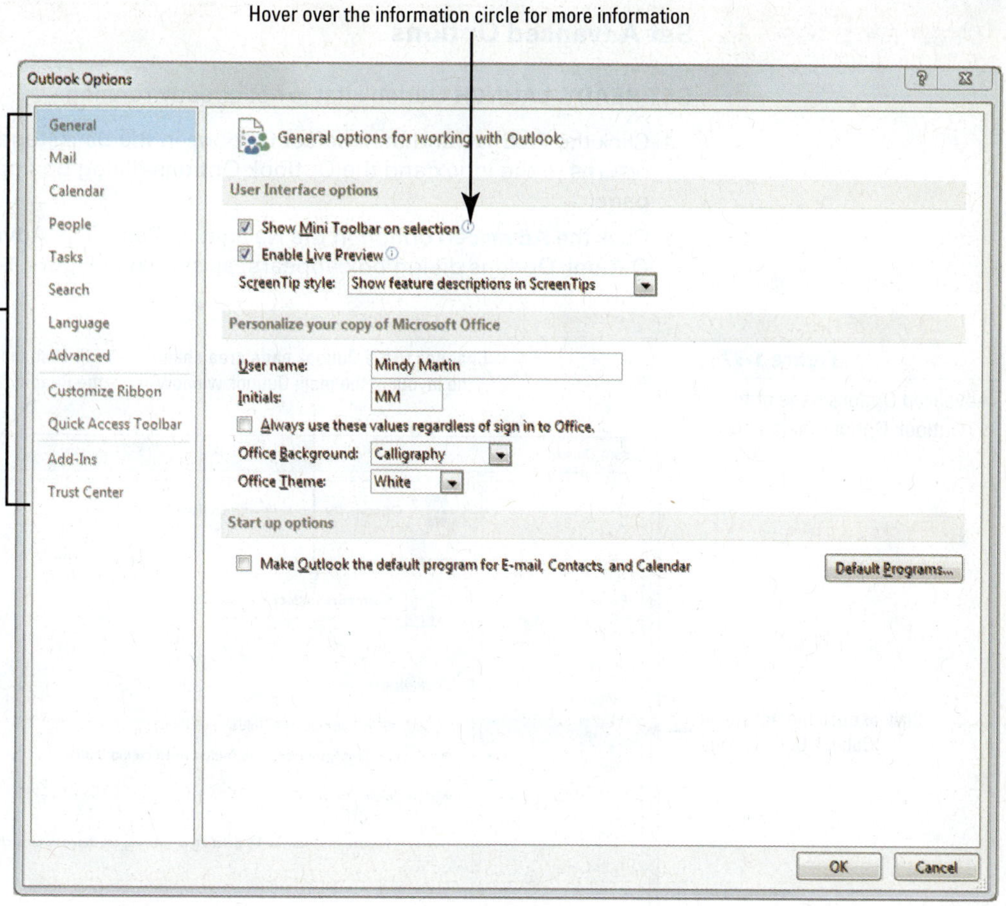

4. In the *Personalize your copy of Microsoft Office* area, click the **Office Theme** dropdown arrow and select **Dark Gray**.

5. Click **OK**. Outlook applies the color to the Outlook window.

6. Click the **FILE tab**. This opens the Microsoft Office Backstage again.

7. Click **Options** in the Navigation Pane. The Outlook Options dialog box opens to the General Options page.

8. In the *Personalize your copy of Microsoft Office* area, click the **Office Theme** dropdown arrow and select **White**.

9. Click **OK**. This will restore the default color to the Outlook window.

PAUSE. LEAVE Outlook open to use in the next exercise.

Setting Advanced Options

You can use the Advanced options page of the Outlook Options dialog box to customize how the various panes of the Outlook window appear. You can also control specific aspects of the program to suit your needs, such as determining which folder appears when Outlook opens or how often Outlook performs tasks like sending and receiving messages, AutoArchiving, and receiving RSS feeds. In this exercise, you'll change some of these settings to familiarize yourself with the process.

CERTIFICATION READY? 1.1.7

How do you set the Outlook program options?

Set Advanced Options

GET READY. LAUNCH Outlook if it is not already running.

1. Click the **FILE tab** and then select **Options** in the Backstage Navigation Pane. Outlook returns to the Inbox and the Outlook Options dialog box opens to the General Options page.

2. Click the **Advanced** option in the Navigation Pane. The Advanced options page of the Outlook Options dialog box appears, as shown in Figure 1-37.

Figure 1-37

Advanced Options page of the Outlook Options dialog box

Changes to the Outlook pane area change the layout of the main Outlook window

Click to modify the Reading Pane

Click to modify the Navigation Pane

Click to open the Advanced Outlook Options page

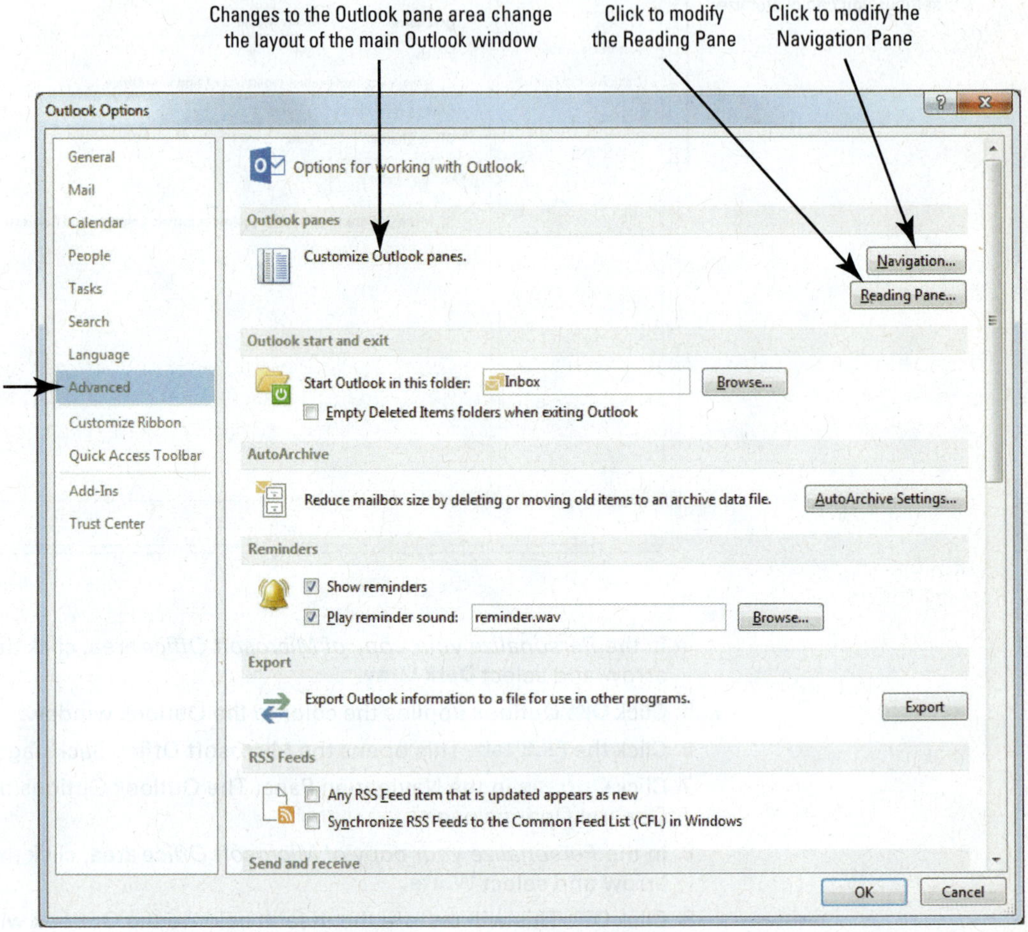

3. Find the first section on the Advanced page called the Outlook panes area. In this section, click the **Navigation** button. The Navigation Options dialog box appears. This is the same dialog box that we opened from the Navigation bar.

4. With the **Mail** option highlighted, click the **Move Down** button two times, then click **OK**. Notice that the Mail button on the Navigation bar at the bottom of the screen is now the third item in the list.

5. Click the **Navigation** button again. The Navigation Options dialog box reappears.

6. Click **Reset** and then **OK** to restore the default arrangement.

7. Click the **Reading Pane** button. The Reading Pane dialog box reappears.

8. Review the options available. Click **Cancel**.

9. Scroll down, reading each of the available options. When you get to the *Send and receive* area, deselect the **Send immediately when connected** option. This change means that you need to manually tell Outlook when you're ready to send and receive messages.

10. Click **Cancel**. This will restore the default layout and settings.

CERTIFICATION READY? 1.1.7

How do you set the advanced Outlook program options?

PAUSE. LEAVE Outlook open to use in the next exercise.

Setting Language Options

Outlook 2013 also allows you to select your default language. You can use the same language as you do for the rest of Office or choose a different language as your default. If you prefer to use English as your default language but correspond with non-English speaking friends or coworkers on a regular basis, you can also add the languages you need to the Outlook Editing Languages. When you create e-mails in another language, Outlook will look up your editing languages and offer you all the same spell-check and grammar tools that you're used to in Office. In this exercise, you'll set English as your default language and add Spanish to your Editing Languages.

STEP BY STEP	Set Language Options

GET READY. LAUNCH Outlook if it is not already running.

1. Click the **FILE tab** again and select **Options** and then **Language**. The Language options page of the Outlook Options dialog box appears.

2. Click the **[Add additional editing languages]** box in the Choose Editing Languages area of the dialog box. A long list of available languages appears.

3. Scroll down the list and select **Spanish (United States)**.

4. Click **Add**. Outlook adds the language to the Editing Language list, which turns on all of its proofing tools for that language.

5. You can use the *Choose Display and Help Languages* area to change the language that appears onscreen in ScreenTips and in the Help window. In the Display Language window, select **English**, if necessary. Your screen should look like Figure 1-38.

Figure 1-38

Language Options page of the Outlook Options dialog box

Changing the Editing Language changes the proofing tools that Outlook uses to check your writing

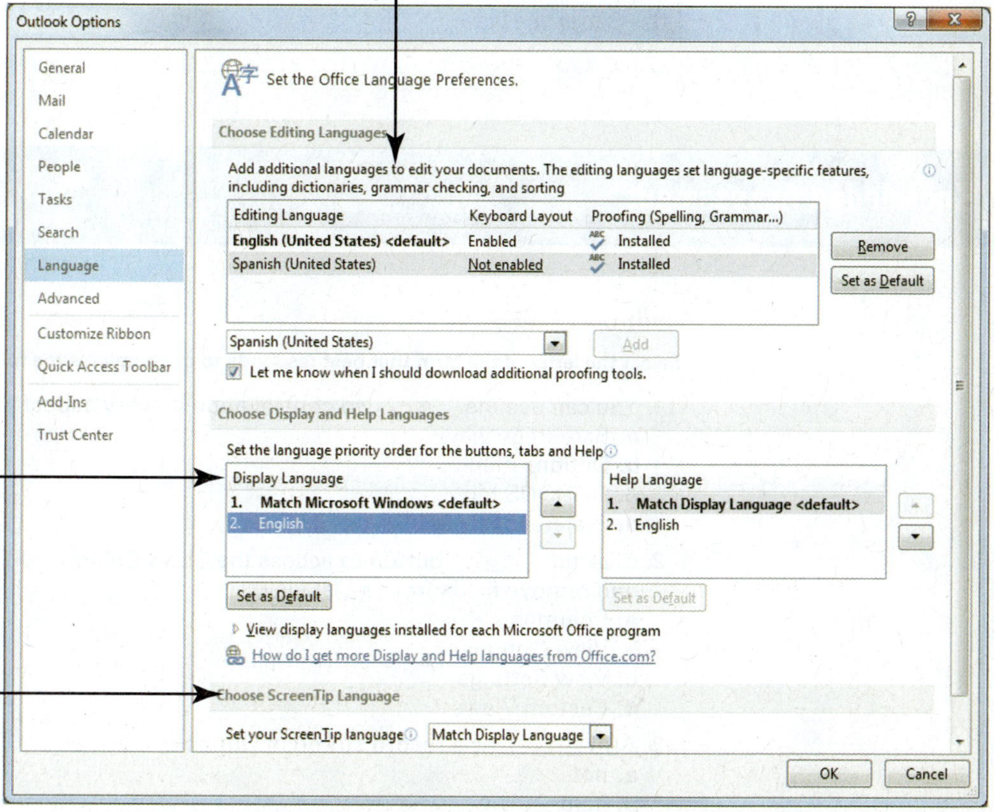

Changing the Display Language changes the language of Menus and onscreen text

Changes the ScreenTip Language

6. Click **Cancel**. Outlook will restore the default language options and return you to the main window.

PAUSE. LEAVE Outlook open to use in the next exercise.

CERTIFICATION READY?   1.1.7

How do you set the Outlook Language program options?

As you've seen, you can use the Outlook Backstage view to access a wide variety of settings to help you customize the way Outlook looks and works to suit your needs (see Table 1-4).

Table 1-4

Outlook Options

General	Personalize Outlook with your user name, turn on and off Live Preview, and change the Office Background and Themes.
Advanced	Customize the Outlook window's Navigation bar and Reading Pane. You can also AutoArchive your mailbox, set reminders, export Outlook information, synchronize RSS feeds, and set rules for international correspondence.
Language	You can add proofing tools for additional languages and set your own default language.

SKILL SUMMARY

In This Lesson You Learned How To:	Exam Objective	Objective Number
Start Outlook		
Work in the Outlook Window	Configure views	1.1.5
Personalize Outlook	Customize the Navigation Pane	1.1.3
Use Backstage View	Set Outlook options	1.1.7

Knowledge Assessment

Multiple Choice

Select the letter of the term that best responds to or completes the following statements and questions.

1. You can use the _____ to control almost every aspect of the Outlook environment.
   a. Backstage view
   b. Options menu
   c. OPTIONS tab
   d. Preferences tab

2. Click the _____ button to access the Show Columns dialog box where you can add and remove fields from a List view.
   a. Columns
   b. View Options
   c. View Settings
   d. Custom Views

3. A(n) _____ is a record stored in Outlook.
   a. note
   b. item
   c. object
   d. message

4. You can change the appearance of the Outlook workspace by changing the theme on the Outlook _____ page.
   a. Mail Options
   b. General Options
   c. Design Options
   d. Advanced Options

5. The _____ contains menus and commands available in Outlook 2013.
   a. Toolbar
   b. Ribbon
   c. Options menu
   d. Banner

6. What pane displays the text of a selected e-mail message?
   a. Preview Pane
   b. Viewing Pane
   c. Message Pane
   d. Reading Pane

7. You can customize the appearance of the Navigation bar using the Navigation Options dialog box, which can be accessed by _____.
   a. Clicking the Navigation button on the Advanced Options page
   b. Clicking Navigation Options in the View Settings dialog box
   c. Clicking *** on the Navigation bar and selecting Navigation Options
   d. both A and C

8. What is the easiest way to access the Outlook features, such as the Tasks and Calendar?
   a. Folder Pane
   b. Navigation bar
   c. FILE tab
   d. Home menu

9. The _____ button is the first feature listed in the Navigation bar.
   a. Mail
   b. People
   c. Calendar
   d. Tasks

10. You can _____ a pane to save room in the Outlook window.
    a. compress
    b. rotate
    c. minimize
    d. shrink

True/False

Circle T if the statement is true or F if the statement is false.

T F   1.   The Reading Pane can be hidden.

T F   2.   The Navigation bar can only display four items.

T F   3.   In Outlook, messages, appointments, people, tasks, and notes are called records.

T F   4.   The Calendar feature contains an appointment book.

T F   5.   By default, the To-Do Bar is displayed on the right of the Outlook workspace.

T F   6.   You can hide columns from a list by selecting the field and pressing the Delete key.

T F   7.   The Status bar identifies the application and the active feature.

T F   8.   You can use a keyboard shortcut to access the Outlook Backstage view.

T F   9.   Hovering over Contacts on the Navigation bar displays the People Pane.

T F 10.   Backstage is a help feature in Outlook.

Competency Assessment

Project 1-1: View the Outlook Ribbon

Become familiar with the Outlook Ribbon.

GET READY. LAUNCH Outlook if it is not already running.

1. If necessary, click the **Mail** button in the Navigation bar to display the mailbox.
2. Click the **HOME** tab. Click the arrows on each of the **dropdown buttons** on the Ribbon to see what options are available.
3. Click the **SEND/RECEIVE** tab. Click each of the **dropdown buttons** to see what options are available.
4. Click the **FOLDER** tab. Click each of the **dropdown buttons** to see what options are available.
5. Click the **VIEW** tab. Click each of the **dropdown buttons** to see what options are available.

LEAVE Outlook open for the next project.

Project 1-2: Identify the New Features in Outlook 2013

The Navigation bar discussed in this lesson is only one of many new features in Outlook 2013. Use Microsoft Office Help to locate information about the various new features in Outlook 2013.

GET READY. LAUNCH Outlook if it is not already running.

1. Click the **?** icon on the Outlook title bar to open Outlook Help.
2. Click the **What's new in Microsoft Outlook 2013** link in the Help window.
3. Read through the article to identify the new features that could affect how you use Outlook.
4. Click the **X** in the upper right corner of the Help window to close it.

LEAVE Outlook open for the next project.

Proficiency Assessment

Project 1-3: Explore Outlook Options

In this lesson, you used some of the ways you can change the way Outlook 2013 looks and behaves. Take some time to explore more of the Outlook options.

GET READY. LAUNCH Outlook if it is not already running.

1. Use the Outlook Backstage to open the Outlook Options dialog box.
2. On the General page, read through each of the options and click each of the **dropdown arrows** to see what options are available.
3. On the Mail page, read through each of the options and click each of the **dropdown arrows** to see what options are available.
4. On the Language page, read through each of the options and click each of the **dropdown arrows** to see what options are available.

5. On the Advanced page, read through each of the options and click each of the dropdown arrows to see what options are available.

6. Click the Cancel button to leave the Outlook Options dialog box without making any changes.

LEAVE Outlook open for the next project.

Project 1-4: Use the Folders List

Use the Folders List to display the Outlook folders.

GET READY. LAUNCH Outlook if it is not already running.

1. Click the *** button in the Navigation bar (the last item).
2. Select Folders. The Folders List is displayed in the upper area of the Folder Pane.
3. Click the Calendar folder in the Folders List. The Calendar is displayed, and the Folders list moves to the bottom of the Folder Pane.
4. Click the Contacts folder in the Folders List. The People Hub is displayed.
5. Click the Deleted Items folder in the Folders List. The Deleted Items folder is displayed. Any deleted Outlook items are stored here until this folder is emptied.
6. Right-click the Deleted Items folder in the Folders List. Note the Empty Folder option. Selecting this option permanently deletes these items.
7. Click the Inbox folder in the Folders List. By default, the Inbox folder contains any e-mail messages you have received but have not deleted or filed elsewhere.
8. Click the Tasks folder in the Folders List. The Tasks folder is displayed.
9. Click the Mail button in the Navigation bar to return to the default Outlook view.

LEAVE Outlook open for the next project.

Mastery Assessment

Project 1-5: Customize the Navigation Bar

Change the number of buttons that appear on the Navigation bar and dock some of the Peek views in your workspace.

GET READY. LAUNCH Outlook if it is not already running.

1. If necessary, click the Mail button on the Navigation Bar to display the mailbox and verify that the To-Do Bar is not displayed.
2. Click *** on the Navigation bar.
3. Select Navigation Options.
4. Change the Maximum number of visible items to display all of the available items in the *Display in this order* window.
5. Click OK to close the dialog box to view the modified Navigation bar.
6. Hover the mouse over the Tasks button in the Navigation bar.
7. Click the Dock the peek icon on the Tasks Peek.
8. Right-click on the Calendar button and select Dock the peek from the shortcut menu.
9. Take a screen capture of your customized workspace and send it to your professor following their instructions.
10. On the VIEW tab, click To-Do Bar to open the display options.
11. Select Off to close the To-Do Bar.

12. Re-open the **Navigation Options** dialog box, and click the **Reset** button.

13. Click **OK** to restore the Navigation bar defaults.

LEAVE Outlook open for the next project.

Project 1-6: Customize a List View

The columns in a list view can be added, deleted, and rearranged.

GET READY. LAUNCH Outlook if it is not already running.

1. Click the **Tasks** button in the Navigation bar to display the To-Do List.

2. Change to the Active view so that the tasks are shown as a list.

3. Remove the **Due Date** and **In Folder** columns.

4. Using the Show Columns dialog box, add the **Sensitivity** and **Company** columns to the far left of the list.

5. Add the **Reading Pane** in the bottom position.

6. Minimize the Folder Pane.

7. Add the **To-Do Bar** to Outlook populated with the Calendar and People sections.

8. **CLOSE** Outlook.

9. Restart Outlook and use the Tasks keyboard shortcut to open the Task List. The customized view should be displayed.

10. Take a screen capture of your customized workspace, and send it to your professor following their instructions.

11. Reset the Active view to the default columns and Expand the Folder Pane.

CLOSE Outlook.

LESSON SKILL MATRIX

Skills	Exam Objective	Objective Number
Creating Messages	Create messages	2.1.1
	Change text formats for all outgoing messages	1.1.2
Sending a Message	Add cc and bcc to messages	2.1.5
Reading and Responding to Messages	Reply to sender only	2.1.8
	Reply to all	2.1.7
	Forward messages	2.1.2
	Print messages	1.3.1
	Save messages in alternate formats	1.3.7
Formatting Messages	Format text	2.2.1
	Apply themes and styles	2.2.3
Personalizing Messages	Create and assign signatures	1.2.2
	Format signatures	2.2.6
	Add a signature to specific messages	2.2.5
Working with Quick Parts	Create and use Quick Parts	2.2.7
Inserting and Formatting Graphic Message Content	Insert images	2.2.4
	Insert hyperlinks	2.2.2
Working with Attachments	Add/remove message	2.1.4
	Set attachment reminder options	2.3.11
	Preview attachments	1.3.4
	Save message attachments	1.3.3

© alohaspirit/iStockphoto

<mark>KEY TERMS</mark>

- attachment
- Attachment Reminder
- AutoComplete
- AutoPreview
- Bcc
- Cc
- character
- clip art
- crop
- Draft Indicator
- font
- Format Painter
- formatting attributes
- hyperlink
- Hypertext Markup Language (HTML)
- plain text
- Quick Access Toolbar
- Quick Parts
- Quick Response
- Quick Styles
- Rich Text Format (RTF)
- signature
- SmartArt graphics
- style
- subject
- theme

Mindy Martin and Jon Morris own and operate Resort Adventures, a luxury resort. They stay busy throughout the day, and frequently work different shifts to stay on top of the activities going on at different times. They rely on email to keep each other informed. Outlook is the perfect tool for this task. Mindy and Jon also use Outlook to contact clients and create press releases. Outlook 2013's ability to format and enhance messages makes it a great way to send professional and polished messages. In this lesson, you'll learn how to create, save, format, and print messages.

© alohaspirit/iStockphoto

SOFTWARE ORIENTATION

The Microsoft Outlook Message Window

Email is the most frequently used Outlook component. The Message window, shown in Figure 2-1, should be familiar to every Outlook user.

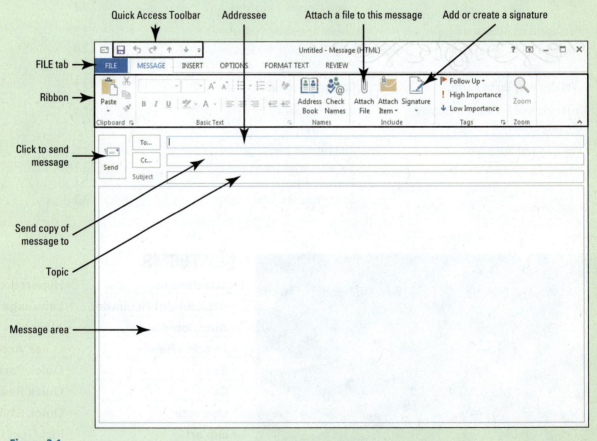

Figure 2-1

The Outlook Message window

Many of the elements in the Message window are familiar to you if you use Microsoft Word 2013. The editor used to create messages in Outlook is based on Microsoft Word 2013. Your screen may vary if default settings have been changed or if other preferences have been set. Use this figure as a reference throughout this lesson as well as the rest of this book.

CREATING MESSAGES

The Bottom Line

Creating email messages is probably the most common user activity in Outlook. Creating a simple email message is not much harder than jotting words on a sticky note. In this section, you'll create a basic email message and specify its format.

Composing a Message

The Microsoft Outlook email component is a full-featured composition tool that provides many of the same functions found in Microsoft Word. Keying, copying, cutting, and deleting text in an Outlook message are identical to the same functions in Microsoft Word 2013. The **AutoComplete** function is another Word feature available in Outlook. It helps you quickly enter the names of the months and days of the week. AutoComplete cannot be turned off in Outlook 2013. In this exercise, you create a new email message.

STEP BY STEP | **Compose a Message**

GET READY. LAUNCH Outlook if it is not already running.

1. If necessary, click the **Mail** button in the Navigation bar to display the Mail folder, as shown in Figure 2-2.

Figure 2-2

The Inbox—the Outlook opening screen

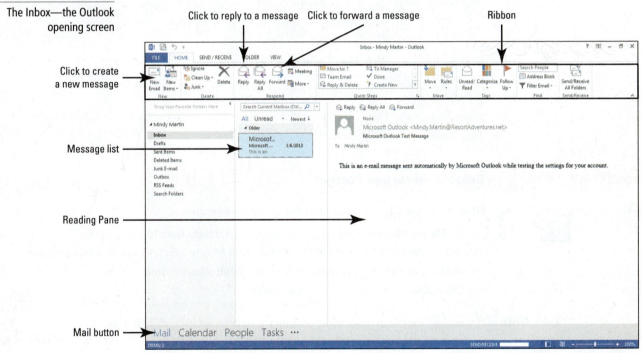

2. Click the **New Email** button on the HOME tab. The Message window is displayed, as shown in Figure 2-1.

Take Note

Throughout this chapter you will see information that appears in text within brackets, such as [Press **Enter**], or [your email address]. The information contained in the brackets is intended to be directions for you rather than something you actually type word for word. It will instruct you to perform an action or substitute text. Do **not** type the actual text that appears within brackets.

Another Way

You can also open a new Message window by using the keyboard shortcut Ctrl+N.

3. Click the message area.
4. Key **Hi Jon,** [press **Enter** twice].

5. Key **Blue Yonder Airlines is running a contest in January. The winner gets free round-trip airfare to Cincinnati. Terry Crayton, a marketing assistant at Blue Yonder, asked if we would be interested in offering a free weekend at Resort Adventures as part of the prize. What do you think?** [Press **Enter** twice.]

6. Key **Let me know.** [Press **Enter** twice.]

7. Key **Mindy Martin.** [Press **Enter**.]

PAUSE. LEAVE the Outlook Message window open to use in the next exercise.

Regardless of the tool you use, the task of writing a message is the same. In normal business correspondence, you would be more formal in addressing the correspondence. However, this example is just a quick note between the partners at Resort Adventures.

Specifying Message Content Format

The most attractive email messages contain formatted text. Formatting, including bullets, font sizes, font colors, and bold text, can help you convey just the right impression. Microsoft Outlook can send messages in Hypertext Markup Language (HTML), Rich Text Format (RTF), and Plain Text—formats described in Table 2-1. Because of its flexibility and the formatting options it provides, HTML is the default format for the message you compose and send. However, not all email applications can display these effects. In this exercise, you will change the format for a message to plain text.

Table 2-1

Message Formats

Format	Description
HTML	**Hypertext Markup Language (HTML)** is used by web browsers to display information. HTML enables you to format text and insert items such as horizontal lines, pictures, and animated graphics. Older and less robust email programs may not be able to display HTML.
RTF	**Rich Text Format (RTF)** uses tags to format text. It can be read by most word processors and newer email programs, but it can't display animated graphics and some web page formatting.
Plain Text	**Plain Text** does not use any formatting. It can be read by all email programs. Without formatting, though, the impression you can convey in your message is limited.

STEP BY STEP   **Select a Message Format**

USE the message you created in the previous exercise.

1. **OPEN** the *Picture Signature* document in the data files for this lesson.

2. Select the table containing the picture and Mindy Martin's contact information.

3. Right-click the table and click **Copy** on the shortcut menu.

4. Close the *Picture Signature* document.

Take Note   If you close the document before pasting the data in your Clipboard, Outlook will ask you if you'd like to keep the last item copied to the Clipboard. Click Yes. Otherwise, the Clipboard is empty when you return to Outlook. This message doesn't display every time—only when larger items are stored on the Clipboard (such as this one, which includes an image).

5. Select the text **Mindy Martin** in the message window that you opened in the previous exercise.

6. Click the **Paste** button in the Clipboard group. Mindy's signature, including the picture of the sunflower, is pasted into the message.

7. In the Subject field, key **Plain Text Message**.

8. Click the **FORMAT TEXT** tab, as shown in Figure 2-3.

9. In the Format group, click **Plain Text**. The Microsoft Outlook Compatibility Checker dialog box shown in Figure 2-3 is displayed. The items listed in the dialog box identify the changes that will occur in this particular message.

Figure 2-3

The Inbox—Formatted message and Microsoft Outlook Compatibility Checker dialog box

Format group | FORMAT TEXT tab | Items that will be affected by the change of format

Image and formatted text in a table

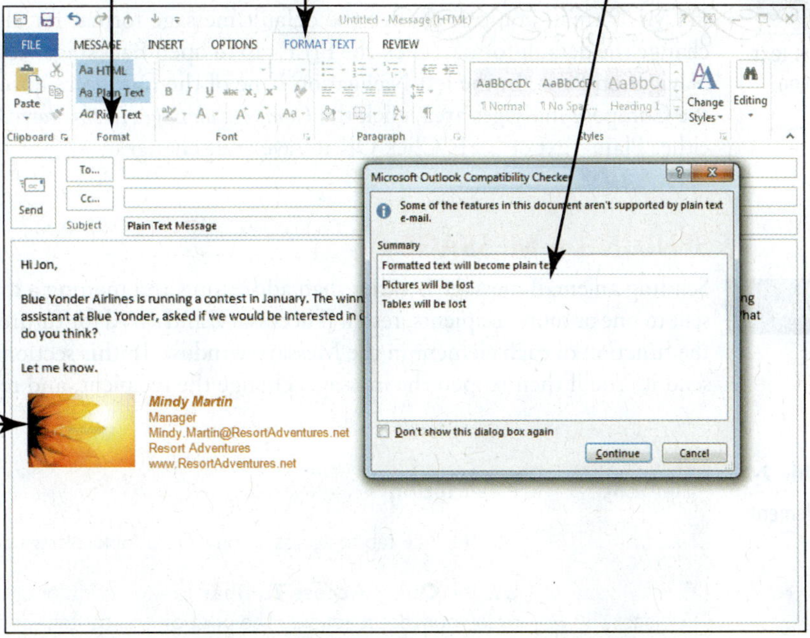

© logoboom/iStockphoto

CERTIFICATION READY? 2.1.1

How do you create a message?

10. Click the **Continue** button. The picture and formatting are removed from the message, as shown in Figure 2-4.

Figure 2-4

Message converted to Plain Text format

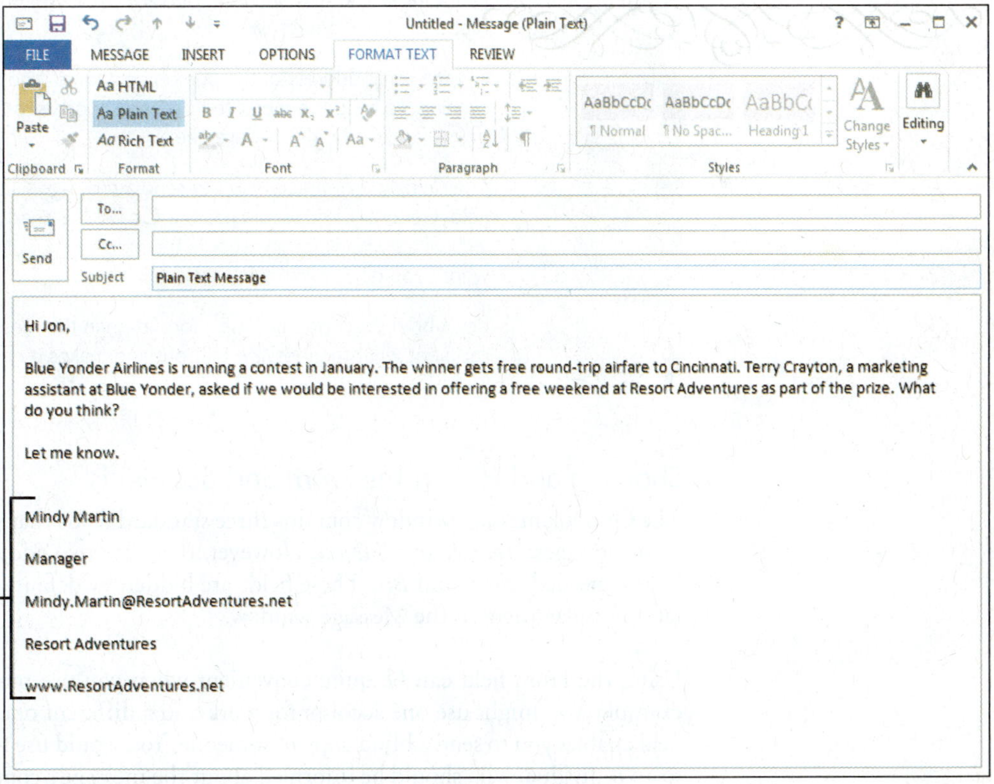

Image and formatted text is replaced with plain text

PAUSE. LEAVE the Plain Text Message—Message window open to use in the next exercise.

Take Note When you reply to a message, Outlook automatically uses the format of the received message as the format for your reply. Thus if you receive a message in plain text, your reply will automatically be sent in plain text.

CERTIFICATION
READY?   1.1.2

How do you change the text
format for all outgoing
messages?

In the previous exercise, you saw how you can choose to use RTF or plain text for an individual message. If you find that most of the people you need to send messages to can't read messages in HTML format, you can change the default message format for all your outgoing messages. To change the default format, click the FILE tab to open Backstage view and select Options from the Navigation Pane. In the left Navigation Pane of the Outlook Options dialog box, select Mail. In the Compose messages area, click the *Compose messages in this format* dropdown arrow, and select either Plain Text or RTF. Click OK to save your changes.

SENDING A MESSAGE

The Bottom Line

Sending an email message is easier than addressing and mailing a letter. An email message can be sent to one or more recipients, resent if necessary, and saved for future reference. Table 2-2 describes the function of each element in the Message window. In this section, you'll address a message and send it. You'll then reopen the message, change the recipient, and resend it.

Table 2-2

Message Window Elements

Element	Description
FILE tab	Use the FILE tab to access common Outlook settings and options.
Quick Access Toolbar	Use the **Quick Access Toolbar** to save, print, or undo your recent actions and redo your recent actions. The position and content of the Quick Access Toolbar can be customized.
Ribbon	The Ribbon organizes commands into logical groups. The groups are placed under tabs that focus on a particular activity. In the Message window, the tabs include Message, Insert, Options, Format Text, and Review. The content of the Ribbon varies by the task. The Ribbon in the Message window contains different options from the Ribbon in the Contacts window.
To	Key the email address of the person or people who will receive the message you are sending. To send the message to several addressees, key a semicolon after a name before adding the next addressee.
Cc	The *Cc* field is optional. You can send a message without entering anything in the *Cc* field. Generally, you would use the **Cc** field to send a copy of the message to individuals who you think should be informed about the message content but from whom you don't expect any action.
Subject	Key a brief description of the information in the message. The **Subject** tells the recipient what the message is about and makes it easier to find the message later.

Showing and Hiding the *From* and *Bcc* Fields

The Outlook message window contains three standard fields that you can use to create and address your messages: *To*, *Cc*, and *Subject*. However, there are two additional fields that you can use or hide as needed: *From* and *Bcc*. These fields are hidden by default, but you can use the OPTIONS tab to display them in the Message window.

Using the From field can be quite convenient when you use more than one email account. For example, you might use one account for work and a different one for personal messages. The **Bcc** field enables you to send a blind copy to someone. You would use this to send a copy of the message to an individual who should be informed about the message's content without notifying the recipient(s) listed in the *To* and *Cc* fields. The *Bcc* field is different from the *Cc* field in that no one else who receives the email message knows that someone else received a blind copy. In this exercise, you'll turn on and off the From and Bcc fields.

Show or Hide the *From* and *Bcc* Fields

USE the message you created in the previous exercise.

1. Click the **OPTIONS** tab. The OPTIONS tab displays the sending and delivery options as well as many options you can use to customize the message.

🔍 **Cross Ref**

You'll learn more about the advanced Outlook messaging options in Lesson 3.

2. In the Show Fields group, click **Bcc**. The *Bcc* field appears in the Message window, as shown in Figure 2-5.

3. In the Show Fields group, click **From**. The *From* field appears in the Message window, as shown in Figure 2-5.

Figure 2-5

Displaying the *From* and *Bcc* fields

Click to toggle on and off the From and Bcc fields

Click the From button to select an alternate email address

The Bcc field

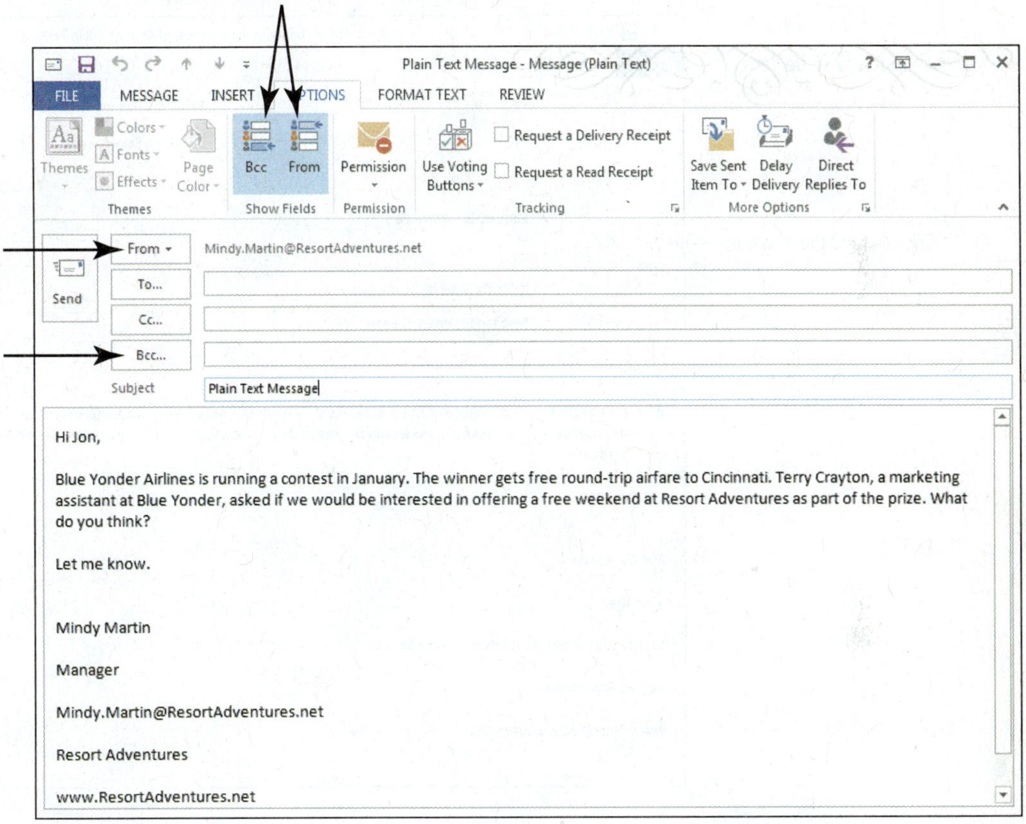

4. In the *Bcc* field, key [**your email address**].

Take Note Displaying and hiding the *From* and *Bcc* fields affects only the current Message window.

5. In the Show Fields group, click **From**. The *From* field is once again hidden from view.

PAUSE. LEAVE the Plain Text Message—Message window open to use in the next exercise.

Sending a Message

Addressing an email message is similar to addressing a letter. In seconds, you can send an email message to one or more recipients. In this exercise, you'll address an email message and send it to the recipient.

Send a Message

USE the message you worked on in the previous exercise.

1. Click the **To** field. Key **someone@example.com** or key [**the email address of a friend or coworker**]. To send the message to more than one recipient, key a semicolon (**;**), and then key another email address.

2. Select the previously keyed text in the *Subject* field and key **Blue Yonder Airlines Contest**. The message is now ready to send, as shown in Figure 2-6.

⚠ **Troubleshooting** The email addresses used in this book are owned by Microsoft Corporation. Because they are not real email addresses, you will receive either an error message or a message thanking you for using Microsoft products.

Figure 2-6

Message ready to be sent

Click to send the message →

Message →

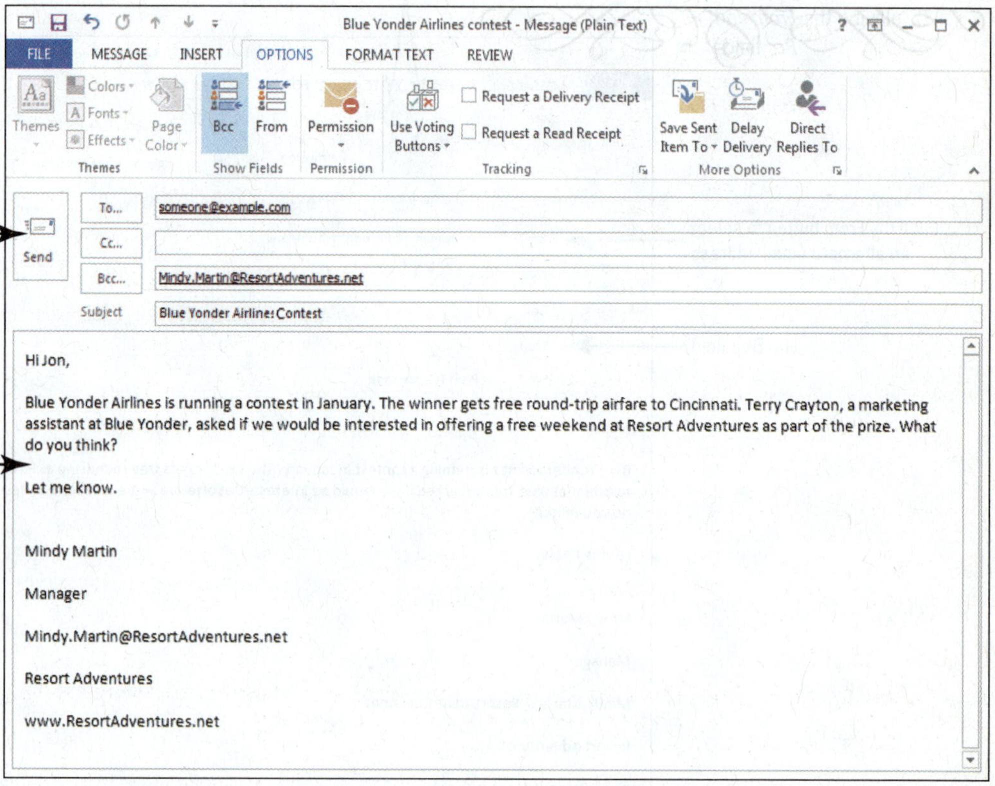

3. Click the **Send** button. The Message window closes, and the message is moved to the Outbox.

Take Note *If your computer is connected to the Internet, the message is sent to the addressee as soon as you click the Send button. If your computer is not connected to the Internet, the message will remain in the Outbox until you connect to the Internet and the message can be sent.*

PAUSE. LEAVE Outlook open to use in the next exercise.

In the previous exercises, you used the Message window to compose and send an email message. If your computer has not been connected to the Internet since you started this lesson, the message you sent will still be in the Outbox. Outgoing messages are moved to the Outbox when you click the Send button. They are moved to the Sent Items folder when you connect to the Internet and the messages are sent.

Resending a Message

Occasionally, you may want to resend a message. This commonly occurs when you want to send the same message to additional recipients or the recipient has accidentally deleted the message and needs another copy. In this exercise, you'll resend the message that you just sent.

STEP BY STEP   **Resend a Message**

USE the message you created in the previous exercise.

1. In the Folder Pane, click the **Sent Items** folder. The email messages you send will be listed as items in the Sent Items folder, as shown in Figure 2-7.

Figure 2-7

Sent Items folder

Sent message in the message list

Sent Items folder selected

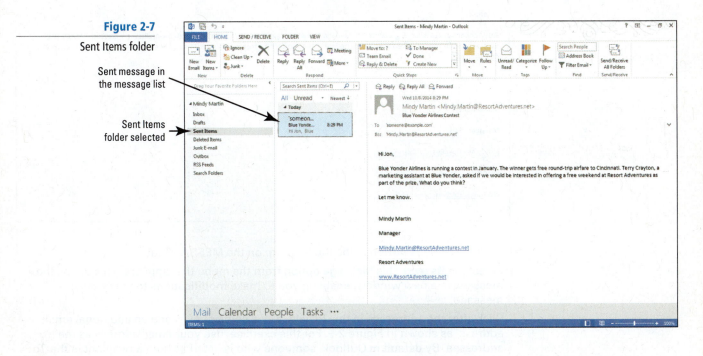

Troubleshooting   If you haven't been connected to the Internet and your message is still sitting in the Outbox, click the Outbox folder instead of the Sent Items folder. Then continue with step 2.

2. In the list of items that have been sent, double-click the message you sent in the last exercise. The message is displayed in a new window, as shown in Figure 2-8. The title bar of the new window is the subject of the message.

Figure 2-8

Sent message

Title bar matches the subject

Actions button

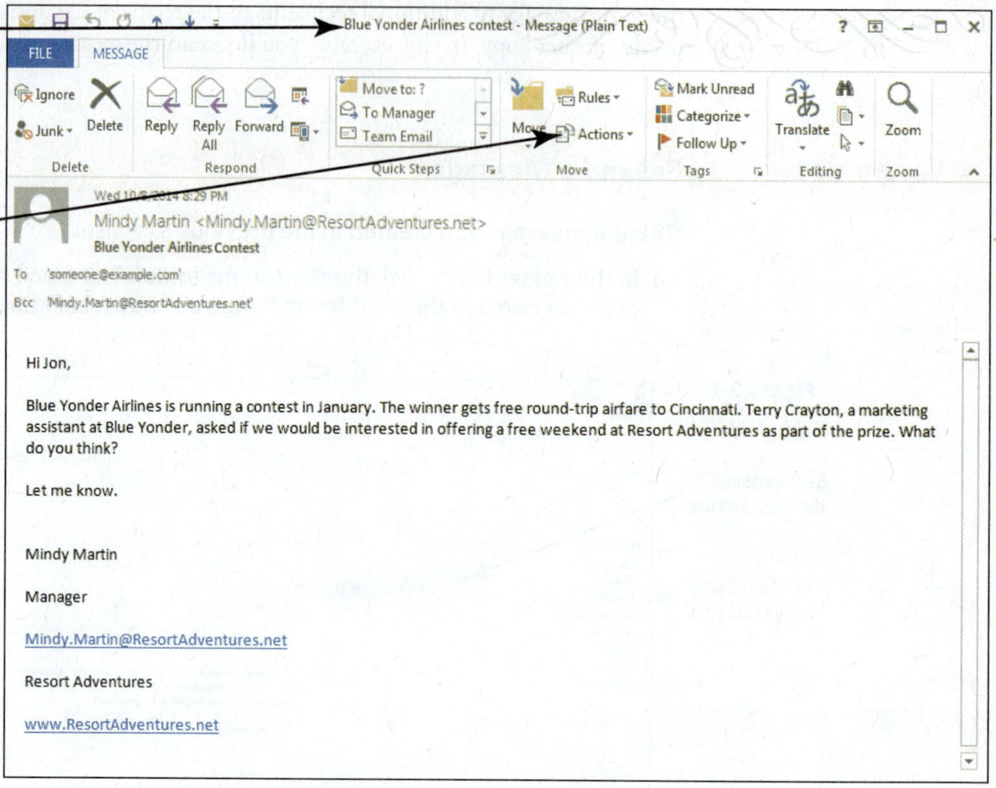

3. Click the **Actions** button in the Move group on the MESSAGE tab.
4. Select the **Resend This Message** option from the menu that appears. This opens the message in a new window, enabling you to make modifications to the original message.
5. Click after the addressee in the *To* field. Key a semicolon (;) and an additional email address, as shown in Figure 2-9. For this exercise, use your email address as the addressee. By default in Outlook, someone who is listed as both a recipient in the *To* field and the *Bcc* field will only receive the message once.

Figure 2-9

Message ready to be resent

Original message window

Addressee added before resending the message

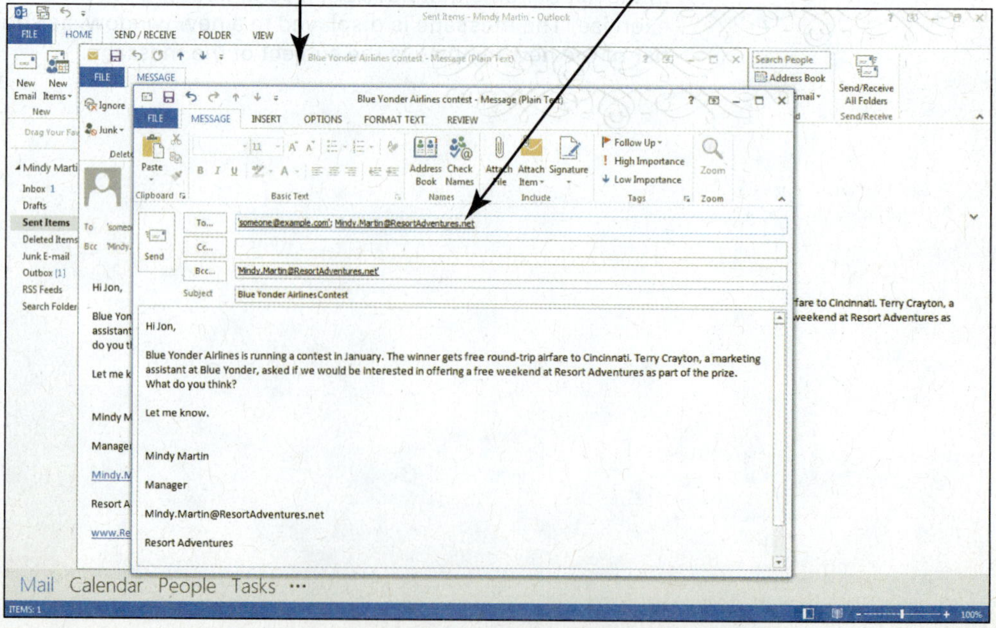

6. Click the **Send** button. The Message window closes, and the message is moved to the Outbox. The message is sent when your computer is connected to the Internet.

7. Close the original Message window.

PAUSE. LEAVE Outlook open to use in the next exercise.

In the previous exercise, you resent a message. When you resend a message, you can delete the original addressee, add new addressees, and edit the message content.

READING AND RESPONDING TO MESSAGES

The Bottom Line

When you receive an email message, you naturally want to read it and, in many cases, send a reply. Outlook enables you to preview and reply to a message with a few mouse clicks. In this section, you'll preview and read a new email message and flag it with a reminder for yourself. Finally, you'll reply to the message and then forward to a colleague.

Automatically Previewing Messages

If you return to your desk after a meeting to find 20 messages in your Inbox and have another meeting to attend in 5 minutes, it might be impossible to open all the messages and still get to the meeting on time. In this exercise, you learn how to use **AutoPreview** to view the first three lines of every message in the message list.

STEP BY STEP **Automatically Previewing Messages**

USE the message you created in the previous exercise.

1. In the Folder Pane, click the **Inbox** folder. The Inbox is displayed.

2. On the VIEW tab, click the **Change View** button. The available views for this folder appear below the Current View group.

3. Select the **Preview** option. The Inbox folder's layout changes: The Reading Pane disappears, and the messages appear in a list format. Notice that the first line of text in each unread message is displayed, as shown in Figure 2-10.

4. On the VIEW tab, click the **Message Preview** button.

Figure 2-10

Message Preview options

Message Preview options →

AutoPreview displays the first line of the message →

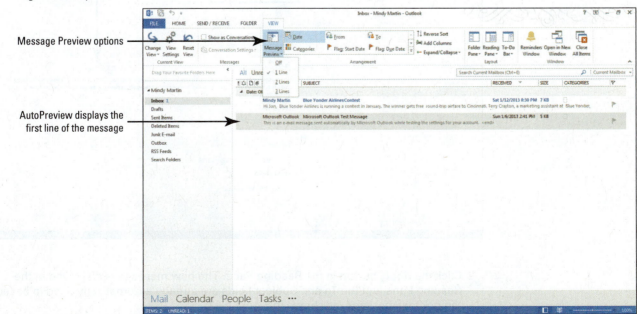

5. Select **3 Lines** from the drop list. Outlook asks you whether you want to apply the change to All Mailboxes or This Folder.

6. Click **This Folder**. The Preview view changes to display three lines per email.

7. On the VIEW tab, click the **Reset View** button and click **Yes** to return the Preview view to its default settings.

8. On the VIEW tab, click the **Change View** button.

9. Select **Compact** from the available views to return to the default view.

PAUSE. LEAVE Outlook open to use in the next exercise.

AutoPreview requires more space in the message list. Therefore, you probably want to turn off the feature most of the time.

Sending a Reply to a Message

Not every message is going to require a response of some type, but many messages do. When you use the Reply function, your response is automatically addressed to the person who sent the message to you. Outlook 2013 offers you a shortcut called Quick Response to simplify the reply process. The **Quick Response** feature allows you to reply to a message without ever leaving the Reading Pane, which eliminates the need to have multiple message windows open at the same time. In this exercise, you'll send a reply to a message.

STEP BY STEP   **Send a Reply to a Message**

USE the message you received when you sent a message to yourself in a previous exercise.

1. In the Inbox, click the message with the subject **Blue Yonder Airlines Contest**. The message is selected, and a preview appears in the Reading Pane, as shown in Figure 2-11.

Figure 2-11

Viewing a message in the Reading Pane

Quick Response buttons   Message contents appear in the Reading Pane

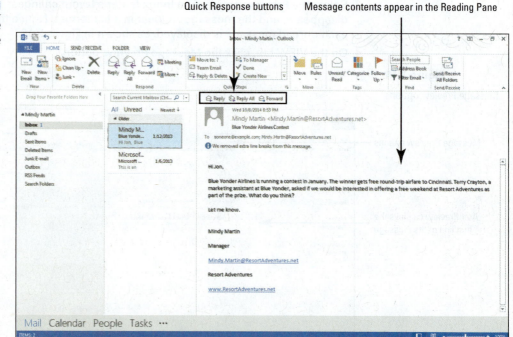

2. Click the **Reply** button in the Reading Pane. The new message is displayed in the Reading Pane and the To and Subject fields are already automatically filled in based on the original message, as shown in Figure 2-12.

Take Note Note that the Ribbon changes to the new COMPOSE TOOLS MESSAGE tab that appeared automatically and that the contents of the original message are included at the bottom of the window.

 **Another Way** You can also reply to a message by selecting a message and clicking the Reply button in the Respond group on the HOME tab.

Figure 2-12

Reply to a message
you received

Draft Indicator   A new Ribbon tab automatically appears   Click to open the message in a separate message window

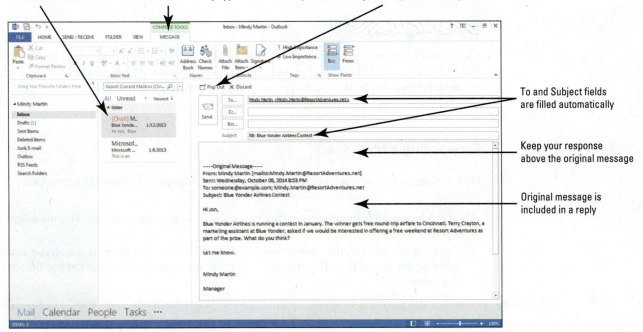

To and Subject fields
are filled automatically

Keep your response
above the original message

Original message is
included in a reply

3. Key **The contest could be a good idea. Let's set up a meeting**.

Take Note In the *Subject* field, the text "RE:" was inserted before the original subject line. "RE:", which stands for "regarding," tells the recipient that the message is a reply about the Blue Yonder Airlines Contest topic.

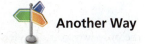 **Another Way** If you want to send a reply to everyone who received an email message, you can click the Reply All button on the HOME tab or click the Reply All (Quick Response) button in the Reading Pane.

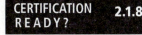

4. Click the **Send** button. The reply is moved to the Outbox. The message is sent when your computer is connected to the Internet.

PAUSE. LEAVE Outlook open to use in the next exercise.

CERTIFICATION READY?	2.1.8

How do you send a reply to a message?

How many times have you started a message and been called away before you could finish what you were doing? When you begin a response to a message in Outlook 2013, you'll notice that a **Draft Indicator** appears on the message item in the message list, as shown in Figure 2-12. The Draft Indicator will stay there until you either send the message or delete the reply that you added. This is a handy way to instantly see that you've not finished responding to a message.

When a reply has been sent, the icon next to the original message is changed. An arrow pointing left, as shown in Figure 2-13, indicates that you replied to the message. When you view the main Outlook window, this icon tells you which messages you have answered.

Figure 2-13

Icon indicates that a reply was sent

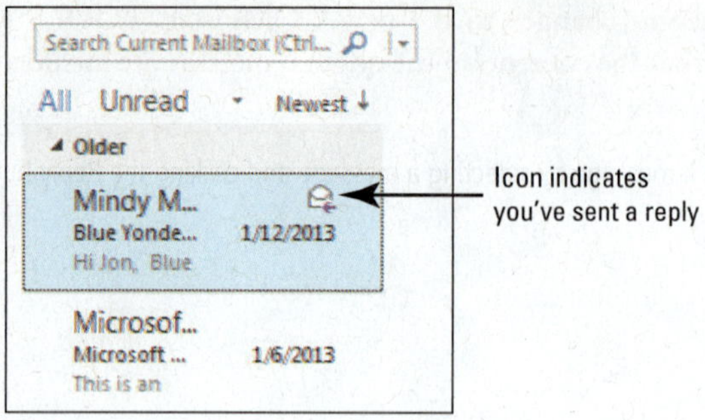

Icon indicates you've sent a reply

CERTIFICATION READY?   2.1.7

How do you send a reply to everyone addressed on a message?

Forwarding a Message

Occasionally, you receive a message that should be sent to additional people. The Outlook Forward function is a quick method of sending the message to additional people without re-creating the original message. In this exercise, you'll forward a message to a colleague.

STEP BY STEP   **Forwarding a Message**

USE the message you received when you sent a message to yourself in a previous exercise.

1. In the Inbox, click the message that you created in the last exercise. The message is selected.
2. Click the **Forward** button in the Reading Pane. The new message is displayed in the Reading Pane and the contents of the original message are included at the bottom of the message.

Take Note   Note that the *Subject* field is already filled. In the *Subject* field, the text "FW:" has been inserted before the original subject line. "FW:" tells the recipient that the message has been forwarded by the sender.

3. In the *To* field, key **someone@example.com**.
4. Click the **Pop Out** button that appears at the top of the Reading Pane, as shown in Figure 2-12. The message moves to a message window.

Another Way   You can also double click a message in the message list to open the message in a message window.

Take Note   Note that once you've popped the message out of the Reading Pane, the only way you can view your Forward/Reply message in the Reading Pane again is to save it as a draft and then select it in the message list in the Drafts folder.

5. Click the message area above the original message. Key **What is the value of the airfare and weekend at Resort Adventures?**
6. [Press **Enter** twice.] Key **[your name]**, as shown in Figure 2-14.

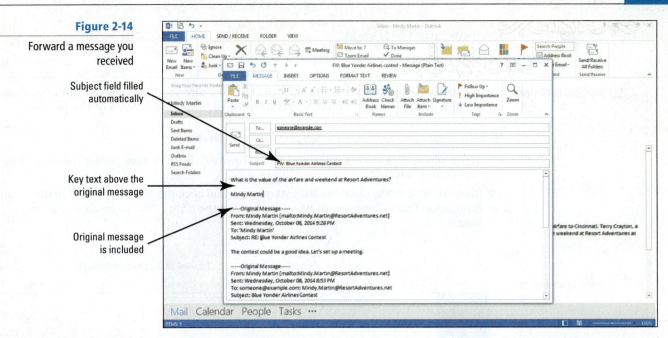

Figure 2-14

Forward a message you received

Subject field filled automatically

Key text above the original message

Original message is included

CERTIFICATION READY? 2.1.2

How do you forward a message?

7. Click the **Send** button. The Message window closes, and the message is moved to the Outbox. The message is sent when your computer is connected to the Internet.

PAUSE. LEAVE Outlook open to use in the next exercise.

When a message has been forwarded, the icon next to the original message changes to an arrow pointing right, as shown in Figure 2-15, indicating that you forwarded the message.

Figure 2-15

Icon indicates the message was forwarded

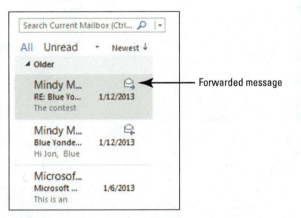

Forwarded message

Printing an Email Message

In Outlook 2013, each message is actually a document. As with any other documents you create or receive, you might want to have a hard copy of the information. You can use the tools on the Print page in Backstage view to preview and print the selected message. The Print page includes a preview pane that shows you how the message will look when printed so you can make any necessary changes before sending it to the printer. The Print page also contains the various printing options you can select, such as the number of copies and the range of pages to print. You can choose unique printing options each time or simply print using the default options. In this exercise, you'll print a message.

STEP BY STEP   **Print an Email Message**

⚠️ **Troubleshooting**   Before printing your document, you will need to make sure you have selected a printer. If your computer is already set up to print, you will not need to complete step 5 of this exercise.

USE the message you created in the previous exercises.

1. In the Inbox, click the message with the subject **RE: Blue Yonder Airlines Contest**. The message is selected.
2. Click the **FILE tab** to open the Backstage view and click the **Print** command in the Navigation Pane. The preview pane appears on the right of the page, as shown in Figure 2-16.

Figure 2-16

Printing a message

Preview of the selected message

Click to print message using the current settings

Click to select a printer

Click to see additional settings

Message printing styles

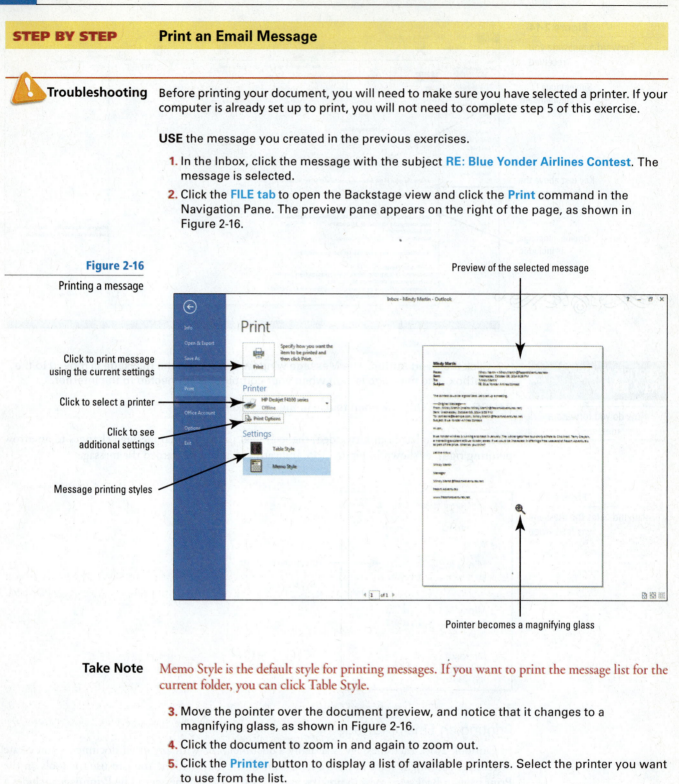

Pointer becomes a magnifying glass

Take Note   Memo Style is the default style for printing messages. If you want to print the message list for the current folder, you can click Table Style.

3. Move the pointer over the document preview, and notice that it changes to a magnifying glass, as shown in Figure 2-16.
4. Click the document to zoom in and again to zoom out.
5. Click the **Printer** button to display a list of available printers. Select the printer you want to use from the list.

⚠️ **Troubleshooting**   You may need to set up a new printer before you can proceed.

6. Click the **Print Options** button to display the Print dialog box, as shown in Figure 2-17. Notice the available printing options.

Figure 2-17

Print options dialog box

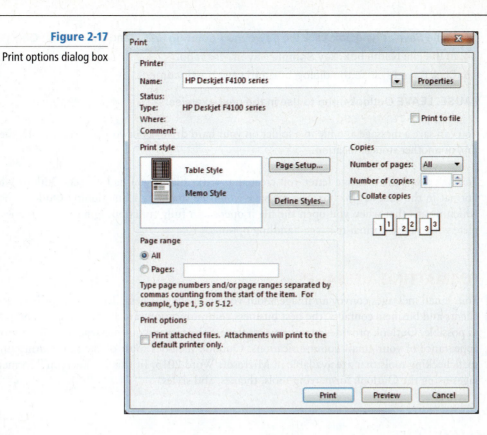

Another Way

If you already have a printer selected and want to use the default settings, you can simply click the large Print button at this time.

7. In the Copies area, click the **upward-pointing arrow** next to the *Number of copies* box to change it to **2**.
8. Click **Print** to print two copies of the letter.

PAUSE. LEAVE Outlook open to use in the next exercise.

CERTIFICATION
READY?   **1.3.1**

How do you print a message?

You printed two copies of the message in this activity. If the message were longer, you could have chosen other options, such as printing a range of pages, collating the pages, or printing multiple pages per sheet.

🔍 **Cross Ref**

You will learn more about printing multiple messages in Lesson 3.

Saving a Message in an External Format

Outlook stores a copy of every message you write or receive in one of its folders until you delete it. Saving messages in the Outlook folder structure in Outlook Message Format is often all you need. However, if you need a message to be available in a different format, you can choose to save it as a .txt file or as a fully formatted .html file. In this exercise, you'll save a copy of a message as a text file.

STEP BY STEP   **Save a Message in an External Format**

USE the message you created in the previous exercises.

1. Click the **FILE tab** to open the Backstage view; then click **Save As**. The Save As dialog box is displayed, showing the Documents folder.
2. Navigate to the **Outlook Lesson 2** folder. You can also choose a different folder in which to store the file from the folders list.

Take Note   To create a new folder in the folders list to store your message, click the New Folder button in the menu bar.

Another Way
You can also choose any of the other types listed. If the message is in the default HTML format, saving it as an HTML document will also be a choice.

CERTIFICATION READY?   **1.3.7**

How do you save a message in an alternate format?

The Bottom Line

3. In the *Save as type* box, click the downward-pointing arrow and choose Text Only (*.txt).
4. In the File Name box, key Sample Saved Message.
5. Click Save to close the dialog box and save the document.

PAUSE. LEAVE Outlook open to use in the next exercise.

You can save a message as a file in a folder on your hard drive, a network location, a CD, the desktop, or another storage location.

You just saved the message letter you created as a .txt file. If you had chosen Outlook Message Format in the *Save as type* box, the message would be stored as a functioning Outlook message, which means that when you open the file it opens as a fully functioning message window, complete with all the normal message handling options.

FORMATTING MESSAGES

Your email messages convey an image about you and your business. To present the best image to clients and business contacts, the best business communications are as eye-catching and polished as possible. Outlook provides many ways to format the text in your message so as to improve the appearance of your email communications. Outlook includes most of the same formatting and spellchecking tools that are available in Microsoft Word 2013. In this section, you'll format messages using the Outlook formatting tools, themes, and styles.

SOFTWARE ORIENTATION

Formatting Outlook Messages

As you learn to format messages, it is important to become familiar with the tools you will use. The FORMAT TEXT tab displayed in Figure 2-18 contains the formatting commands that you will use to enhance the appearance of the messages you create.

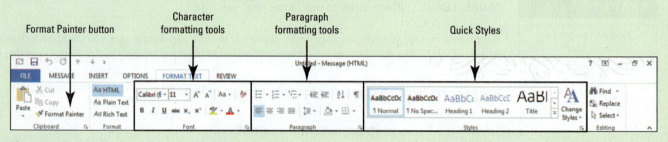

Figure 2-18

Message window's FORMAT TEXT tab

You will use commands from every group on the FORMAT TEXT tab as you learn to apply formatting to text, copy formatting, and apply styles and themes.

Using Formatting Tools

Microsoft has a variety of **fonts** and font sizes to help you communicate your intended message, whether it is casual for your personal life or formal for the workplace. In addition to changing the font and font size, you can apply special **formatting attributes**, such as bold or italic, to characters within your text to give them special emphasis. A **character** can be a letter, number, punctuation mark, or symbol. In this exercise, you'll use the Outlook formatting tools to enhance the appearance of a message.

You can use the **Format Painter** to copy formats, including font, font size, font style, font color, alignment, indentation, number formats, borders, and shading. To copy formatting from one location to another, select text whose formatting you want to copy. Click the Format Painter button in the Clipboard group. The mouse pointer turns into a white plus sign with the paintbrush beside it. Drag the mouse pointer across the text you want to format.

To copy formatting to several locations, double-click the Format Painter button, and then drag the mouse pointer across each text item you want to format. When you're done, click the Format Painter again or press Esc to turn off the Format Painter.

STEP BY STEP	Use Formatting Tools

GET READY. LAUNCH Outlook if it is not already running.

1. If necessary, click the **Mail** button in the Navigation bar to display the Mail folder.
2. Click the **New Email** button on the HOME tab. The Message window is displayed, as shown in Figure 2-1.
3. Open the *Promotional Flyer* document in the data files for this lesson, and select all the text.
4. Right-click and click **Copy** on the shortcut menu.
5. Close the *Promotional Flyer* document, navigate back to your new message, and click the message area.
6. Click **Paste** in the Clipboard group on the MESSAGE tab. The text of the Promotional Flyer is pasted into the message.
7. Select all the text in the message area.
8. Click the **FORMAT TEXT** tab to display the Font group, as shown in Figure 2-19.

Figure 2-19

The Font group

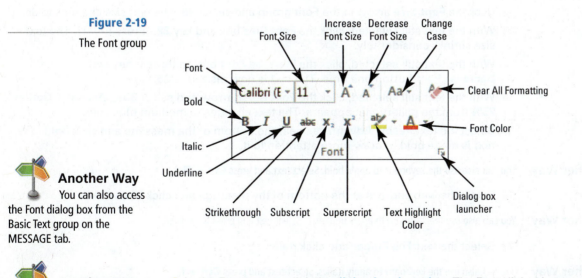

Another Way
You can also access the Font dialog box from the Basic Text group on the MESSAGE tab.

Another Way
You could also key the name of the font in the Font box.

9. In the Font group, click the **dialog box launcher**. The Font dialog box appears.
10. Click the **down arrow** in the selection pane under the Font box to scroll through the list to select **Verdana**, as shown in Figure 2-20. Notice that the Preview area displays how your selected text will look with each font selected.

Figure 2-20

Font dialog box

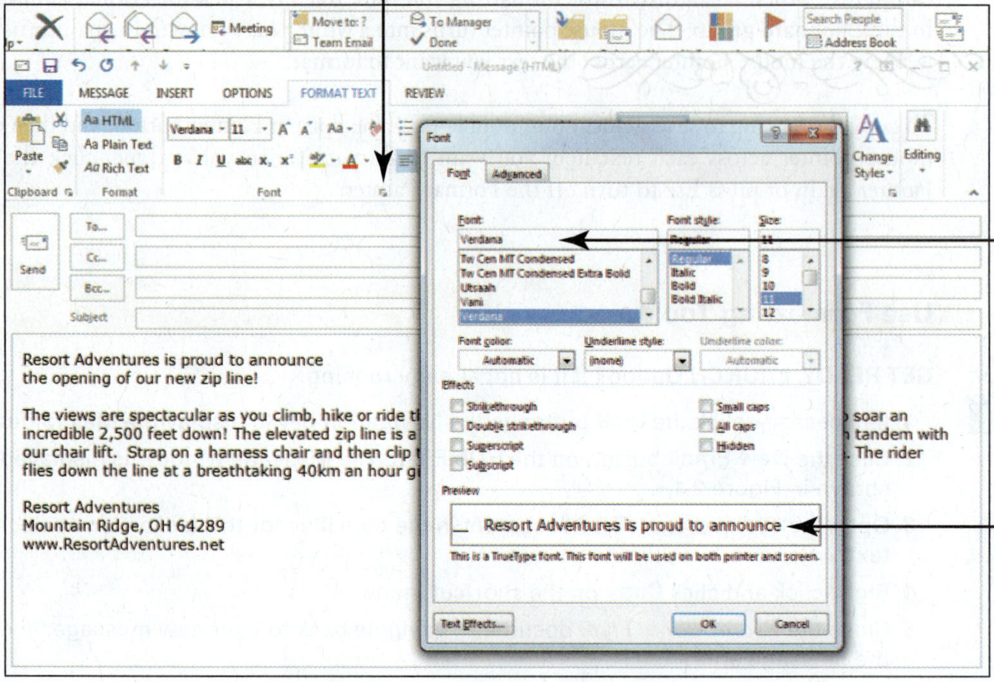

Dialog box launcher

Font box

Sample of the font applied to the selected text

Resort Adventures is proud to announce the opening of our new zip line!

The views are spectacular as you climb, hike or ride t... incredible 2,500 feet down! The elevated zip line is a... our chair lift. Strap on a harness chair and then clip... flies down the line at a breathtaking 40km an hour gi...

Resort Adventures
Mountain Ridge, OH 64289
www.ResortAdventures.net

Resort Adventures is proud to announce

This is a TrueType font. This font will be used on both printer and screen.

11. Click **OK** to close the dialog box and apply the format.

Another Way   You can also click the Font arrow button on the Ribbon to open a menu that you can use to change the font of the selected text.

12. Select the first sentence in the message area (be sure to select both lines).

13. Click the **Font Size** arrow in the Font group and select **36**. The text size changes to 36.

14. With the text still selected, click the **Font Size** box and key **22**. [Press **Enter**]. The text size shrinks considerably.

15. With the text still selected, click the **Increase Font** button three times and then the **Decrease Font** button one time. The text is now resized to 26.

16. With the text still selected, click the **Font Color** arrow and select **Blue, Accent 1, Darker 25%** from the gallery that appears. The text changes to medium blue color.

17. Select the text **Resort Adventures** near the bottom of the message and click **Bold**. The text is made bold to draw more attention to it.

Another Way   You can also use the keyboard to apply bold. Select text and press **Ctrl + B**.

18. Select the web address at the bottom of the message and click **Underline**.

Another Way   You can also use the keyboard to apply underline. Select text and press **Ctrl + U**.

19. Select the text **The Zipper** and click **Italic**.

Another Way   You can also use the keyboard to apply italics. Select text and press **Ctrl + I**.

20. Select the text **Resort** near the bottom of the message, and click the **Format Painter** button in the Clipboard group. The formatting details are stored in the clipboard.

Another Way   The Format Painter is available in the Clipboard group.

21. Click one of the zeros in 2,500 in the main paragraph. The text 500 becomes bold, but the rest of the number doesn't. The Format Painter applies the format to the entire word, but because there is a comma in this number, Format Painter interprets it as two different words.

Another Way   You can use the Format Painter to change multiple selections. With the source formatting selected, double-click the Format Painter button. You can click any text to change it. Double-click to turn off the Format Painter.

22. Click the **Format Painter** button again to copy the format, and this time click and drag the cursor across the entire number 2,500. The format is applied to the entire number.
23. In the *Subject* field, key **Come Fly with Us.** Your message should look like the one shown in Figure 2-21.

Figure 2-21

A formatted message

FORMAT TEXT tab

CERTIFICATION READY? 2.2.1

How do you format text in a message?

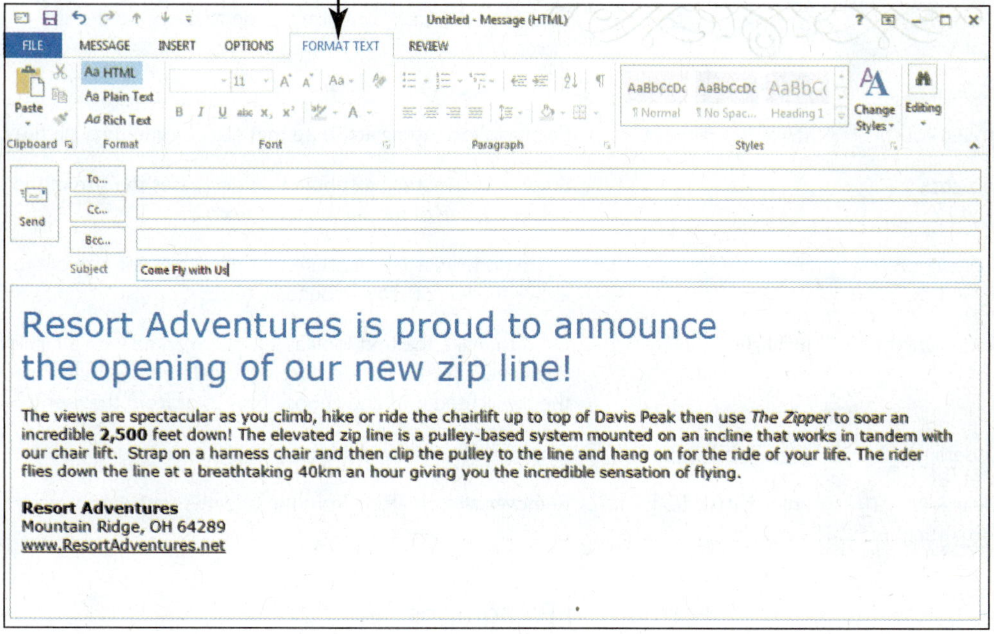

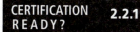

PAUSE. LEAVE the Outlook Message window open to use in the next exercise.

The Font group in the FORMAT TEXT tab contains the Font menu for changing the font, and the Font Size menu for changing its size. You can also access these commands on the Mini toolbar. Table 2-3 provides extra information about each character formatting tool.

Table 2-3

Formatting Tools

Button	Example	Description
Bold	**bold text**	Emphasis formatting attribute that makes the selected text look darker and thicker.
Change Case	Hello world hello world HELLO WORLD Hello World hELLO wORLD	The Change Case menu in the Font group has five options for changing the capitalization of text.
Font	Calibri Times New Roman Comic Sans	A font is a set of characters that have the same design. Each font has a unique name.
Font Color	font color	Changes the color of the selected text. Click the down arrow next to the button to select a different font color.
Font Size	Size 8 Size 10 Size 12	Font sizes are measured in points. Point sizes refer to the height of text characters, with one point equaling approx. 1/72 of an inch.
Increase Font Size	Grow Grow Grow	Click the Increase Font Size button to increase the size of the selected text by one increment.

(Continued)

Table 2-3

Continued.

Button	Example	Description
Italic	*italic text*	Emphasis formatting attribute that makes the selected text look lighter and tilted to the right.
Decrease Font Size	Shrink Shrink Shrink	Click the Decrease Font Size button to decrease the size of the selected text by one increment.
Strikethrough	~~strikethrough text~~	Emphasis formatting attribute that places a line through the center of the selected text.
Subscript	subscript	Emphasis formatting attribute that decreases the size of the selected text and places it just below the line of the surrounding text.
Superscript	superscript	Emphasis formatting attribute that decreases the size of the selected text and places it just above the line of the surrounding text.
Text Highlight Color	highlight	Used to make the text look as if it was marked with a highlighting pen. Click the down arrow next to the button to select a different highlight color. To remove highlighting select the highlighted text and choose No Color from the menu.
Underline	underlined text	Emphasis formatting attribute that places an underline beneath the selected text.
Clear All Formatting	unformatted text	Removes all formatting from the selected text.

Formatting Paragraphs

Depending on the type of information you want to convey in your message, you might want to apply paragraph formatting to make your message more understandable. Outlook contains a number of tools that you can use to change the appearance of paragraphs. You can change alignment and line spacing, create numbered and bulleted lists, sort paragraphs, and use shading and borders. To apply paragraph formatting, place the insertion point anywhere in a paragraph. Outlook will apply the formatting you chose to the entire paragraph. In this exercise, you will try out the different paragraph formatting options.

STEP BY STEP   **Format Paragraphs**

USE the message you created in the previous exercise.

1. If necessary, open the **Come Fly with Us** message that you worked on in the previous exercise and click at the top of the message area.
2. Click the **FORMAT TEXT** tab to display the Paragraph group, as shown in Figure 2-22.

Figure 2-22

The Paragraph group

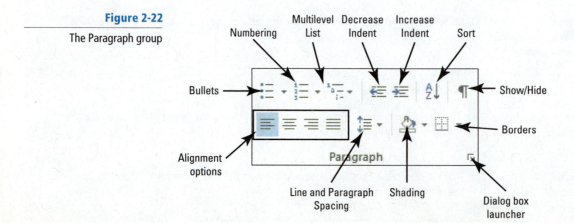

3. Click the **Show/Hide** button in the Paragraph group of the FORMAT TEXT tab. The paragraph symbol (¶) appears at the end of each paragraph.

4. Select the paragraph symbol (¶) after the word *announce* at the end of the first line and press **Delete**.

5. Press **Spacebar**. The first sentence becomes one paragraph.

6. Click after the word *opening* and press **Shift + Enter** to create a manual line break.

7. Click anywhere in the first line, and click the **Paragraph group dialog box launcher**. The Paragraph dialog box is displayed, as shown in Figure 2-23.

Figure 2-23

Paragraph dialog box

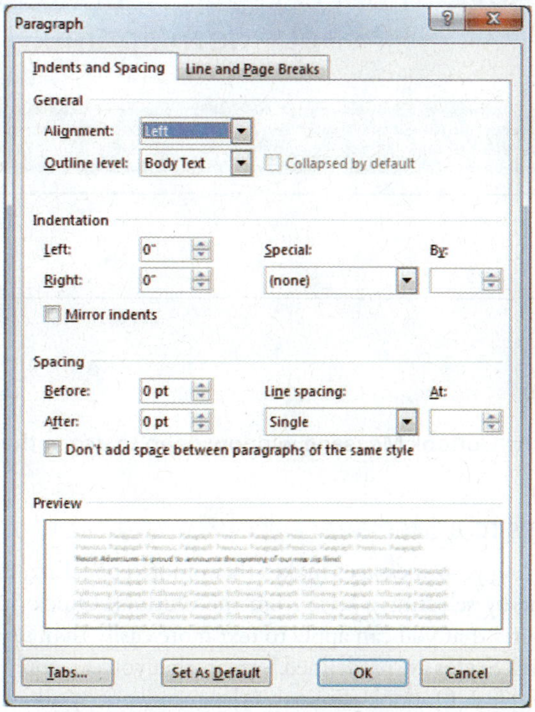

8. Key **18** in the After box in the Spacing area.

9. Click **OK** to close the dialog box. The spacing between the first paragraph and the second paragraph is increased.

10. Click the **Center** button in the Paragraph group of the FORMAT TEXT tab. The paragraph where the insertion point is located is centered at the top of the message.

11. Click anywhere in the main paragraph, and then click the **Shading button arrow** and select **Dark Blue**. Dark blue shading appears behind the main paragraph. Notice that Outlook automatically changes the font color to white to make text more readable.

12. Click the **Shading button arrow** again, and select **Green, Accent 6, Lighter 40%**. Since you've applied a lighter shading option, the font color automatically changes back to black to make text more readable.

13. Select the last three lines of text and click **Align Right**.

14. Click anywhere in the bolded text *Resort Adventures,* and click the **Borders button arrow**. A menu of border styles is displayed.

15. Click the **Top Border** button in the menu. A thin line appears above the text. Your message should look like the one in Figure 2-24.

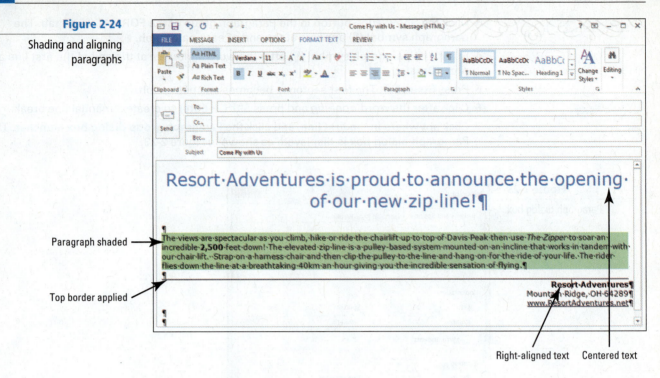

Paragraph shaded →

Top border applied →

Right-aligned text   Centered text

PAUSE. LEAVE the Outlook Message window open to use in the next exercise.

Applying Styles to a Message

Although formatting your messages makes them more appealing, it can also be time consuming. You can save time by selecting a style from the Outlook Quick Style gallery. A **style** is a set of formatting attributes that you can apply to text more easily than setting each formatting attribute individually. **Quick Styles** are predefined formats that you can apply to your document to instantly change its look and feel. Outlook eliminates the guesswork by allowing you to preview the formatting changes in your message before you commit to a style. In this exercise, you will apply Quick Styles to a message.

STEP BY STEP   **Apply Styles to a Message**

USE the message you created in the previous exercise.

1. If necessary, open the **Come Fly with Us** message that you worked on in the previous exercise and click the **FORMAT TEXT** tab to display the Styles group, as shown in Figure 2-25.

Figure 2-25   The Styles Gallery   Change Styles

The Styles group

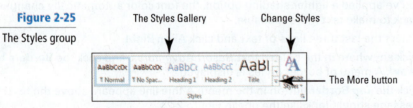

The More button

2. Click anywhere in the first sentence (the title), and click the **More** button in the Styles group to display the Quick Styles gallery, as shown in Figure 2-26.

Figure 2-26

Quick Styles gallery

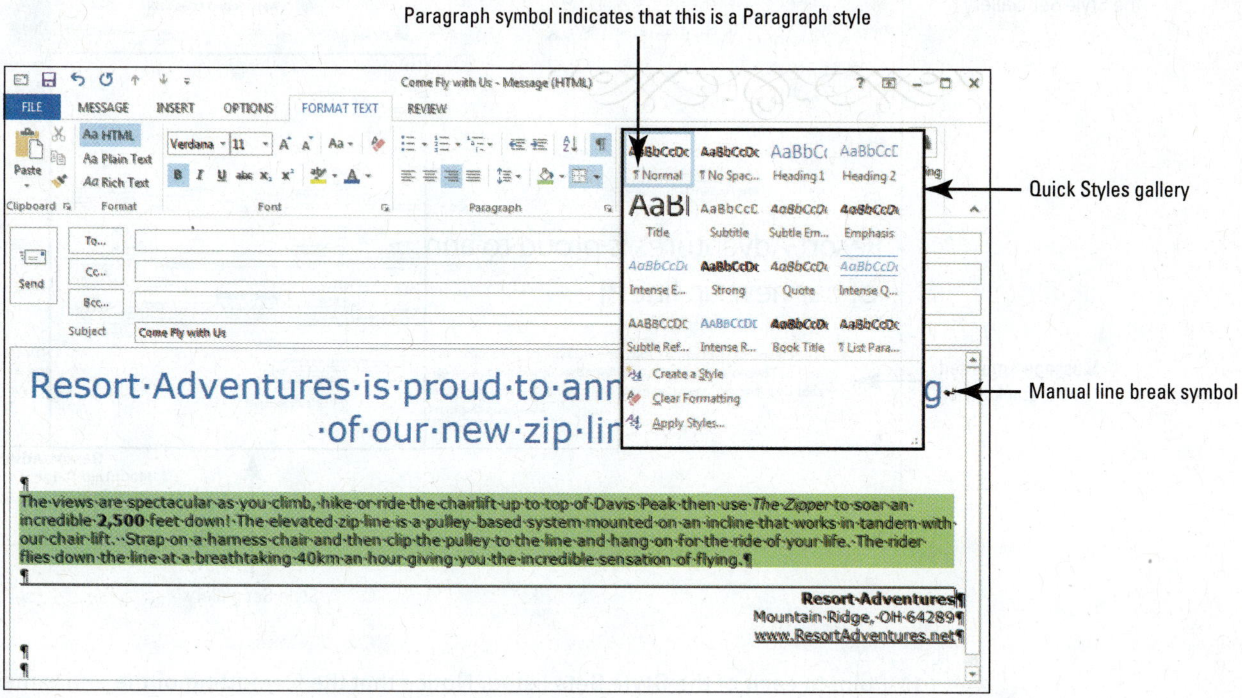

Paragraph symbol indicates that this is a Paragraph style

Quick Styles gallery

Manual line break symbol

3. Place your pointer over any choice on the Quick Styles gallery, and notice that your message changes to show you a preview of that style.

4. Click **Title**. The text changes font, color, and alignment to reflect the Title style.

5. Select the body paragraph that begins *"The views are spectacular..."*

6. Click the **More** button to open the Quick Styles gallery again.

7. Place your pointer over any thumbnail in the gallery, and notice that the paragraph changes to show you a preview of that style.

Take Note   You will notice that some of the thumbnails remove the background formatting and some do not. When you select a paragraph style, all the previous formatting for the paragraph is replaced with the new style.

8. Click the **Quote** thumbnail. Notice that the style is applied to the paragraph you selected.

9. Click the **Change Styles** button in the Styles group, and point to **Style Set**. A gallery of additional Style Sets is displayed, as shown in Figure 2-27.

Figure 2-27

Working with Quick Styles and the Style Set Gallery

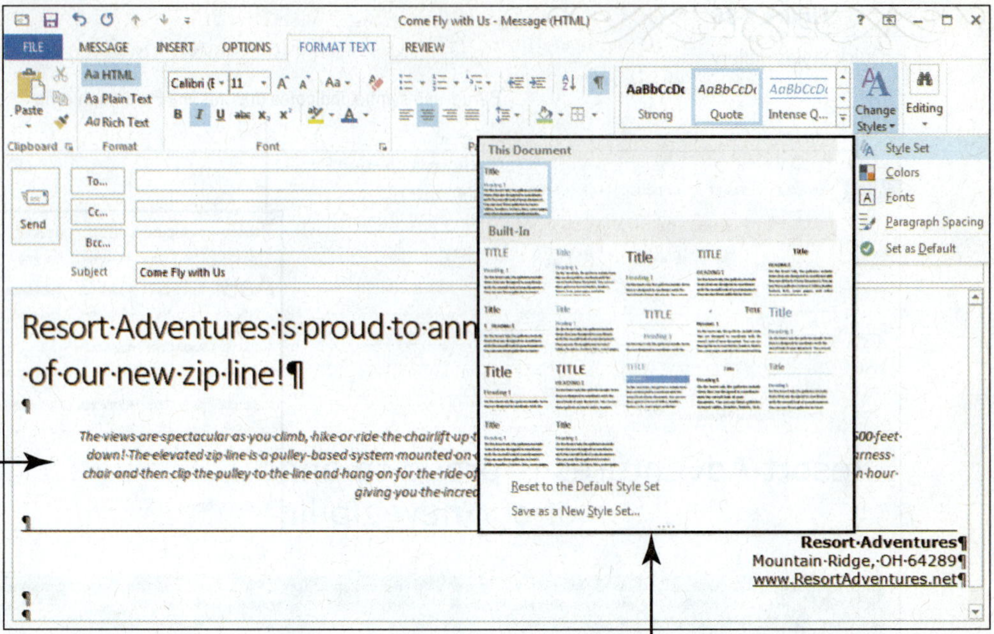

Message formatted with Quick Styles →

Style Set gallery

10. Point to each of the Style Sets listed. Notice that the formatting of the entire message changes to reflect the style set.

11. Click on **Lines (Distinctive)**. The message changes to reflect the new style, as shown in Figure 2-28.

Figure 2-28

Message formatted with a Style Set

PAUSE. LEAVE the Outlook Message window open to use in the next exercise.

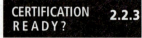

CERTIFICATION READY?   **2.2.3**

How do you apply styles to message text?

There are two kinds of Quick Styles—paragraph styles and character styles. A paragraph mark to the left of the style's name denotes a style created for paragraphs. When you choose paragraph styles, the formats are applied to all the text in the paragraph in which your insertion point is located, whether or not you have it all selected. Character styles are applied to individual characters you have selected within a paragraph rather than affecting the entire paragraph.

Style Sets are collections of Quick Style formats that go well together. When you select a Style Set from the Change Styles button, the entire message is changed to reflect the combination of styles in the set.

Creating Styles

Outlook allows you to create custom styles that you can save to the Styles list. You can then apply the custom style to future messages. You can also modify Quick Styles to suit your needs. In this exercise, you'll create a custom style.

STEP BY STEP   **Create Styles**

USE the message you created in the previous exercise.

1. If necessary, open the **Come Fly with Us** message that you worked on in the previous exercise, and click the **FORMAT TEXT** tab to display the Styles group (refer to Figure 2-25).

2. If necessary, click the **Show/Hide** button on the FORMAT TEXT tab to hide the paragraph marks.

3. Select the first two lines of text, and click the **dialog box launcher** for the Styles group. The Styles list is displayed as a floating box in the Message window.

4. Click the top of the **Styles** list, and drag it to the left edge of the message window. The Styles list is docked to the side of the message window, as shown in Figure 2-29.

Figure 2-29

Docked Styles list

Styles list →

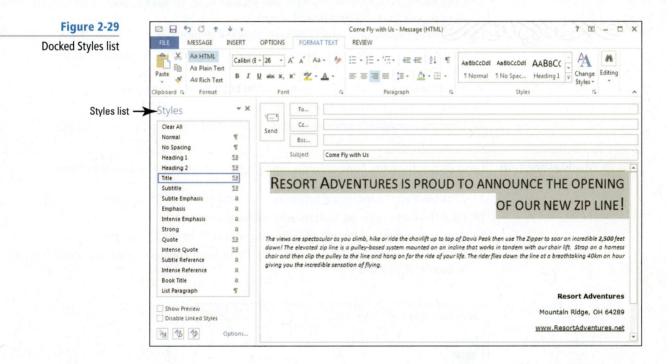

5. Hover over the word **Title** in the Styles list. An arrow appears to the right of the style name.

6. Click the **arrow** to the right of the Title style to display the shortcut menu.

7. Click **Modify**. The Modify Style dialog box appears.

8. Click the **Format** button in the dialog box and select **Font**. The Font dialog box opens, as shown in Figure 2-30.

Figure 2-30

Modify Style and Font dialog boxes

Style shortcut arrow →

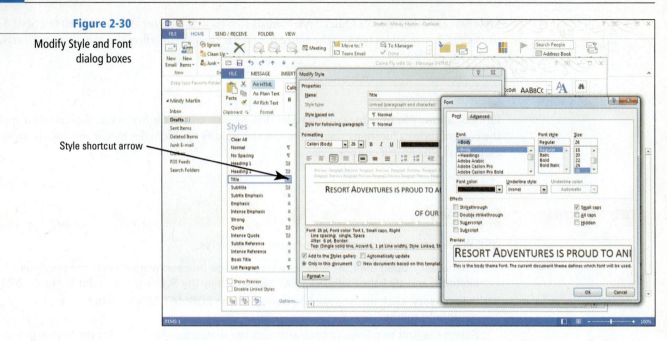

9. Deselect the **Small Caps** check box in the dialog box.

10. Click **Italic** in the Font Style box. Notice that the preview in the dialog box changes.

11. Click the **Font Color down arrow** and click **Blue-Gray, Text 2, Darker 25%**. Notice that the preview in the dialog box changes.

12. Click **OK** to apply your changes and close the dialog box.

13. Click **OK** again to close the Modify Style dialog box. The appearance of the selected text changes.

14. Select the text **Resort Adventures** at the bottom of the message.

15. Click the **Italic** button in the Font group.

16. Click the **Font down arrow** and select **Cooper Black**.

⚠️ **Troubleshooting** If you do not have this font, select a similar one from your list of available fonts.

17. Click the **Font Color down arrow** and select **Blue-Gray, Text 2, Darker 25%**.

18. Click the **Increase Font** button until the font size is **14**.

19. With the text still selected, click the **More** button in the Styles group.

20. Select **Create a Style**. The Create New Style from Formatting dialog box opens, as shown in Figure 2-31.

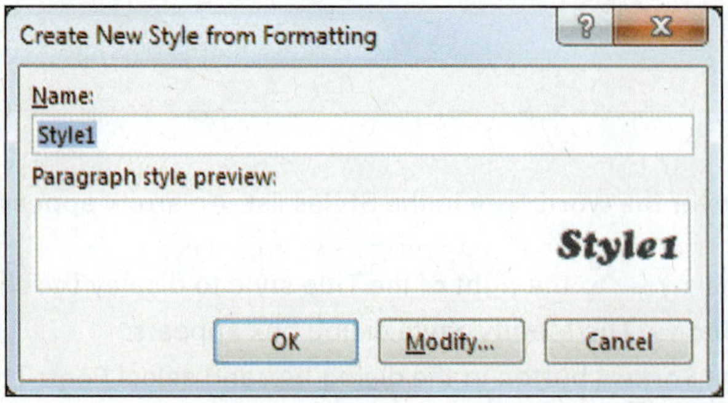

Figure 2-31

Create New Style from Formatting dialog box

Create New Style from Formatting

Name:

Style1

Paragraph style preview:

Style1

OK   Modify...   Cancel

21. Key **Resort Adventures** in the Name box and click **OK**. The Resort Adventures style is displayed in the Styles list, as shown in Figure 2-32. Notice it has also been placed in the Quick Styles gallery.

Figure 2-32

Creating a custom style

New style
added to the list →

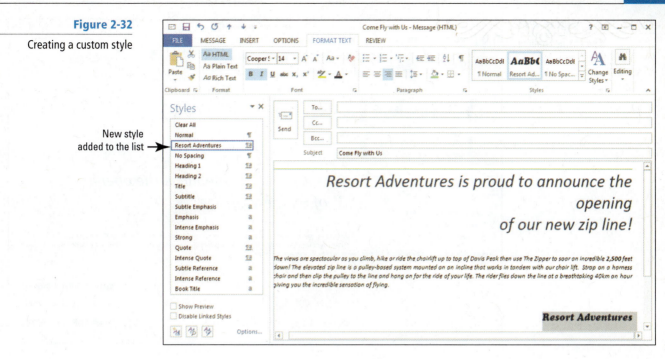

22. Close the **Come Fly with Us** message window. Be sure to allow Outlook to save a copy of the message.

PAUSE. LEAVE Outlook open to use in the next exercise.

You just learned that the Modify Style dialog box has basic formatting commands like the Font menu; Font Size menu; Bold, Italic, and Underline buttons; and Font Color menu. When you modify paragraph fonts, you can also change alignment indents and spacing.

Applying a Message Theme

Message themes are another way to quickly change the overall design of your document using formatting choices that are predefined in Outlook. A **theme** is a predefined set of colors, fonts, and lines that can be applied to an entire message. Outlook contains the same collection of themes that are available in the rest of Microsoft Office. You can apply an entire theme to your message or choose from a variety of theme fonts, colors, and effects. In this exercise, you'll use a theme to format an email message.

STEP BY STEP **Apply a Message Theme**

GET READY.

1. Click **Drafts** in the Folder Pane.
2. Open the **Come Fly with Us** message that you worked on in the previous exercise by double clicking on it.
3. Click anywhere in the first line of text, and click the **Center** button in the Basic Text group on the MESSAGE tab.
4. Click the **OPTIONS** tab to display the Themes group.
5. In the Themes group, click **Page Color**. The Page Color gallery is displayed.
6. Select the **Gold, Accent 4, Lighter 60%** color from the Theme colors area.
7. In the Themes group, click **Themes** as shown in Figure 2-33.

Figure 2-33

The Themes gallery

CERTIFICATION READY? **2.2.3**

How do you apply a theme to message text?

8. Place your pointer over any built-in theme and notice that the document changes to show you a preview of that theme.

9. Click **Facet**. The colors, fonts, and effects for that theme are applied to your message. Notice that the text using your new custom styles does not change.

PAUSE. LEAVE the Outlook Message window open to use in the next exercise.

Creating a New Theme

Although you used a theme to change the overall design of the entire message, you can also change individual elements by using the Theme Colors, Theme Fonts, and Theme Effects buttons. If you make any changes to the colors, fonts, or effects of the current theme, you can save it as a custom message theme and then apply it to other messages.

STEP BY STEP **Create a New Theme**

USE the message you created in the previous exercise.

1. If necessary, open the **Come Fly with Us** message that you worked on in the previous exercise, and click the **OPTIONS** tab to display the Themes group.

2. In the Themes group, click **Theme Fonts** as shown in Figure 2-34.

Figure 2-34

The Theme Fonts gallery

Figure 2-34

The Theme Fonts gallery

3. Place your pointer over any of the theme fonts and notice that the document changes to show you a preview of that theme.

4. Click the **Trebuchet MS** theme font. The fonts for that theme are applied to your message.

5. In the Themes group, click **Theme Colors** as shown in Figure 2-35.

Figure 2-35

The Theme Colors gallery

6. Click the **Slipstream** theme color. The colors for that theme are applied to your message.

7. In the Themes group, click **Themes**.

8. Click the **Save Current Theme** option at the bottom of the Themes gallery. The Save Current Theme dialog box is displayed with the text Theme1 already displayed in the *File name* box, as shown in Figure 2-36.

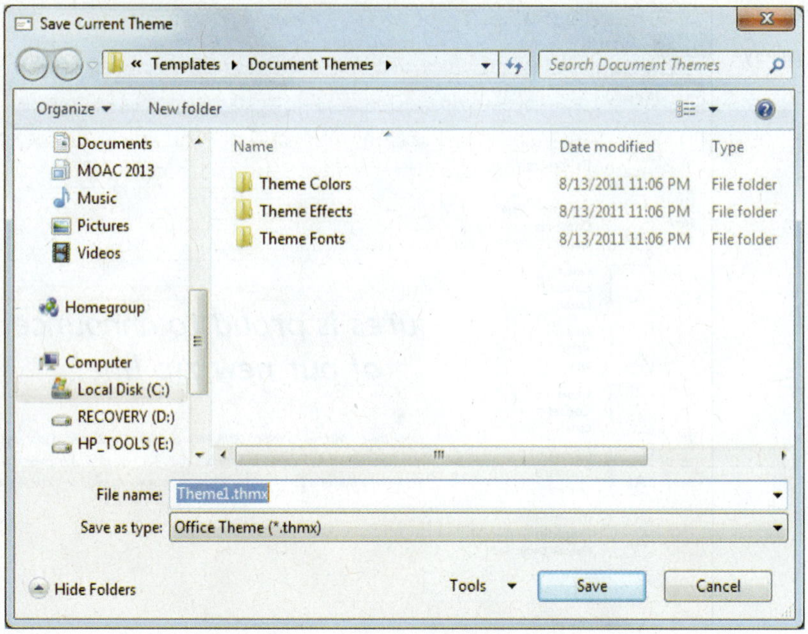

Figure 2-36

The Save Current
Theme dialog box

9. In the *File name* box, select the existing text and key **Resort Adventures**, and click **Save**.

10. In the Themes group, click **Themes**. The new custom theme appears in the Custom area of the Themes gallery, as shown in Figure 2-37.

Figure 2-37

The Resort Adventures
theme is displayed in the
Themes gallery

New theme added
to the gallery →

PAUSE. LEAVE the Outlook Message window open to use in the next exercise.

Take Note   You can share your custom theme throughout all Office programs, so all of your Office documents can have the same look and feel. Try opening Word and clicking on Themes on the DESIGN tab. You should see your custom theme in the gallery.

Document themes can contain the following elements:

- Theme colors contain four text and background colors, six accent colors, and two hyperlink colors. Click the Theme Colors button to change the colors for the current theme (refer to Figure 2-35).
- Theme fonts contain a heading font and a body text font. Click the Theme Fonts button to change the fonts for the current theme (refer to Figure 2-34).
- Theme effects are sets of lines and fill effects. Click the Theme Effects button to change the effects for the current theme (see Figure 2-38).

Figure 2-38

The Theme Effects gallery

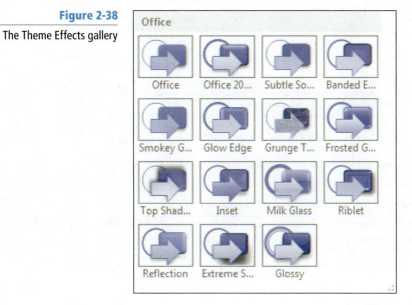

Using Paste Special

When you copy something from one source and paste it into an Outlook message, Outlook assumes you want to keep the source formatting. Sometimes this formatting works with your existing formatting, but often the pasted text clashes with the existing message. You can use the Paste Special feature to have more control over how the text appears. In this exercise, you'll use the Paste Special feature to copy and paste text into your message.

STEP BY STEP **Use Paste Special**

USE the message you created in the previous exercise.

1. If necessary, open the **Come Fly with Us** message that you worked on in the previous exercise, and click the **MESSAGE** tab to display the Clipboard group.
2. Place the insertion point at the end of the main paragraph in the message. Press **Enter** twice to add some space.
3. In your Internet browser, open the *Zipper Rates* web page document in the data files for this lesson.
4. Scroll down the web page. Select the text **Some Highlights You Could Experience:** and the bulleted list that follows. Press **Ctrl + C**, which is the keyboard shortcut for the Copy command.

Take Note The Ctrl + C keyboard shortcut is a powerful tool. Using the shortcut allows you to copy text in almost any application and then paste it (by using the Paste button or the keyboard shortcut Ctrl + V) into Outlook.

5. Back in Outlook, click the message area one line below the main paragraph.

6. In the Clipboard group, click the **Paste** button. The copied text is pasted into the message using the original formatting from the web page and the Paste Options button appears at the end of the text. In this case, the new text does not match the text in the original message, as shown in Figure 2-39.

Figure 2-39

Pasting into a message

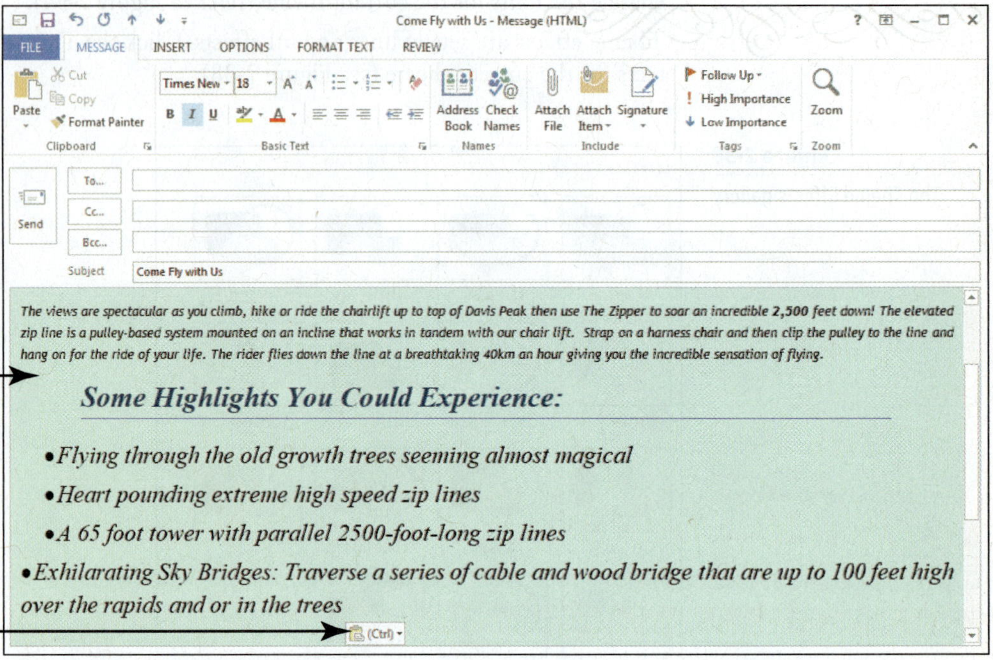

The pasted text →

The Paste Options button →

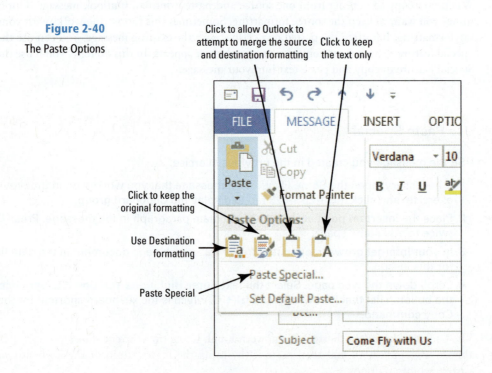

7. Click the **Undo** button.

8. In the Clipboard group, click the **Paste down arrow**. The Paste Options are listed beneath the Paste button, as shown in Figure 2-40.

Figure 2-40

The Paste Options

9. Select **Paste Special**. The Paste Special dialog box is displayed, as shown in Figure 2-41.

Figure 2-41

The Paste Special dialog box

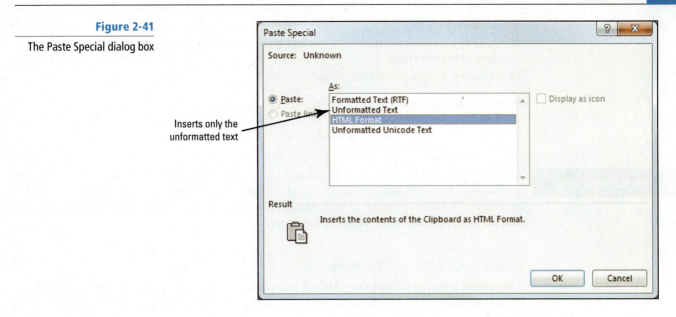

Figure 2-41

The Paste Special dialog box

Inserts only the
unformatted text

10. Select **Unformatted Text** and click **OK**. The dialog box closes and the text is pasted into the message without any formatting.

11. Click the **FORMAT TEXT** tab.

12. Select the text **Some Highlights You Could Experience:** and select **Heading 1** from the Style gallery in the Styles group to apply the Heading 1 Quick Style to just this text selection.

13. Select the pasted list under the heading. Click the **Bullets** button in the Paragraph group. The new text is bulleted as it was in the browser window.

14. Click the **More** button to open the Style gallery. Select **Emphasis** from the Style gallery to give the bulleted items a style that blends well with the rest of the message.

15. Click the **Bullets down arrow** and select the **large circle** from the Bullet Library to change the bullets in the list.

16. Delete the extra line between the bulleted items. The bulleted list should look like the one shown in Figure 2-42.

Figure 2-42

Formatting the pasted text

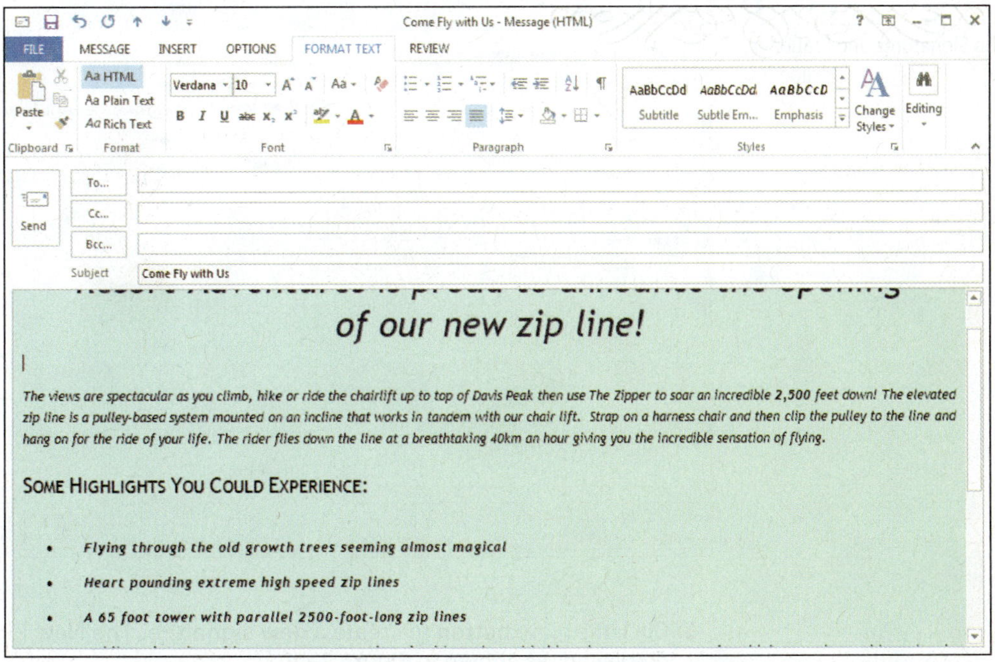

of our new zip line!

The views are spectacular as you climb, hike or ride the chairlift up to top of Davis Peak then use The Zipper to soar an incredible 2,500 feet down! The elevated zip line is a pulley-based system mounted on an incline that works in tandem with our chair lift. Strap on a harness chair and then clip the pulley to the line and hang on for the ride of your life. The rider flies down the line at a breathtaking 40km an hour giving you the incredible sensation of flying.

SOME HIGHLIGHTS YOU COULD EXPERIENCE:

•   *Flying through the old growth trees seeming almost magical*

•   *Heart pounding extreme high speed zip lines*

•   *A 65 foot tower with parallel 2500-foot-long zip lines*

17. In the *To* field, key [your email address].

18. Close the Come Fly with Us – Message window. Be sure to allow Outlook to save a copy of the message.

19. Close the *Zipper Rates* Web page.

PAUSE. LEAVE Outlook open to use in the next exercise.

PERSONALIZING MESSAGES

The Bottom Line

You can personalize your messages in many ways. Formatting, colors, and images probably come to mind first. However, the signature is one of the best places to personalize your messages. In this section, you'll create a personal signature and attach it to a message. You'll also look into attaching your personal signature to all outgoing messages.

Creating a Personal Signature

A **signature** is text or images that Outlook automatically places at the end of your outgoing messages. A signature can be as fancy or as plain as you like. In this exercise, you'll create a personal signature.

STEP BY STEP   **Create a Personal Signature**

GET READY. LAUNCH Outlook if it is not already running.

1. If necessary, click the **Mail** button in the Navigation bar to display the Mail folder.

2. Click the **New Email** button on the HOME tab. The Message window is displayed.

3. Click the **Signature** button in the Include group on the Ribbon.

4. In the dropdown list, click **Signatures**. The Signatures and Stationery dialog box is displayed, as shown in Figure 2-43.

Take Note   If you share your email account with other users or if additional Outlook profiles have been created, signatures created by other users may be listed in the Signatures and Stationery dialog box.

Figure 2-43

The Signatures and Stationery dialog box

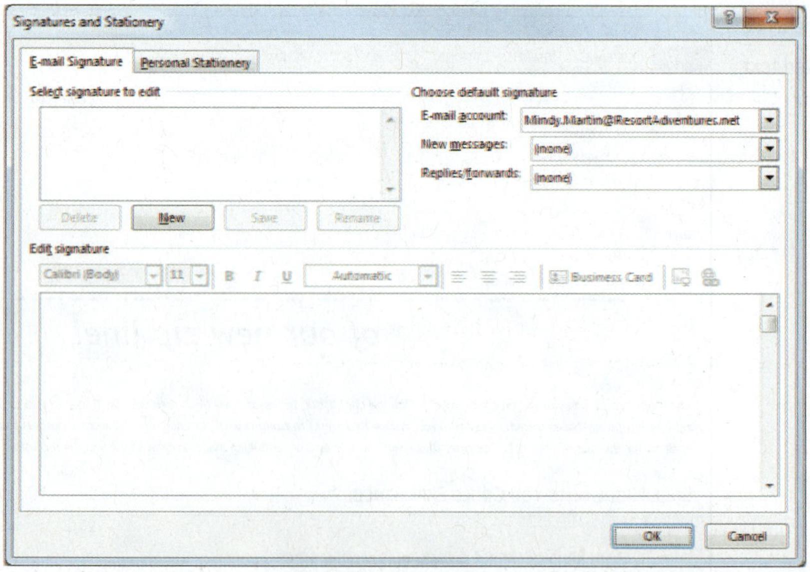

5. Click the **New** button to create a new signature. The New Signature dialog box is displayed, as shown in Figure 2-44.

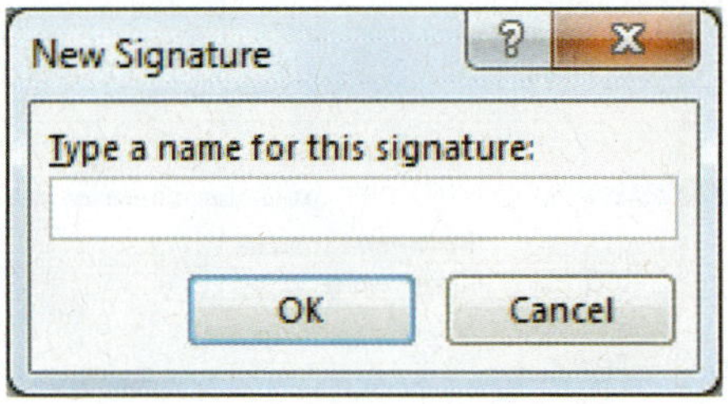

Figure 2-44

The New Signature dialog box

Figure 2-44

The New Signature dialog box

New Signature

Type a name for this signature:

OK   Cancel

CERTIFICATION   1.2.2
READY?

How do you create a
signature?

6. To name the new signature, key **Lesson 2** into the *Type a name for this signature* field.

7. Click **OK**. The New Signature dialog box is closed, and Lesson 2 is highlighted in the *Select signature to edit* list box.

8. Click in the empty **Edit signature** box. Any changes you make here are applied to the selected Lesson 2 signature. If additional signatures were listed, you could select a different signature and make changes to it.

9. Key [**your name**]. [Press **Enter**.]

   Key [**your title**]. [Press **Enter**.]

   Key [**your email address**]. [Press **Enter** twice.]

   Key [**the name of your company**]. [Press **Enter**.]

   Key [**the web address of your company**]. [Press **Enter**.]

   If you do not have a title, company, or company website, key the information that appears in Figure 2-45.

10. Select all the text in the signature.

11. In the toolbar above the *Edit Signature* box, click the **Font dropdown box arrow**, and select **Arial** from the list.

12. In the Font Size box on the toolbar, key **10**.

13. Click the **Font Color dropdown box arrow** (the current selection is Automatic) to open a palette of Font colors, as shown in Figure 2-45.

Figure 2-45

Editing a signature

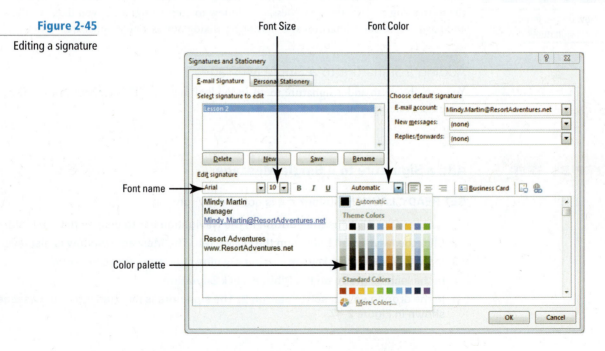

14. Select the color **Blue** from the Standard Colors Palette.

15. Click in the **Edit Signature** box to deselect the text.

16. Now select just your name in the Edit Signature box.

17. Click **Bold** and **Italic** to apply those formatting attributes to the selected text.

18. Change the font size to 12, as shown in Figure 2-46.

Figure 2-46

New signature

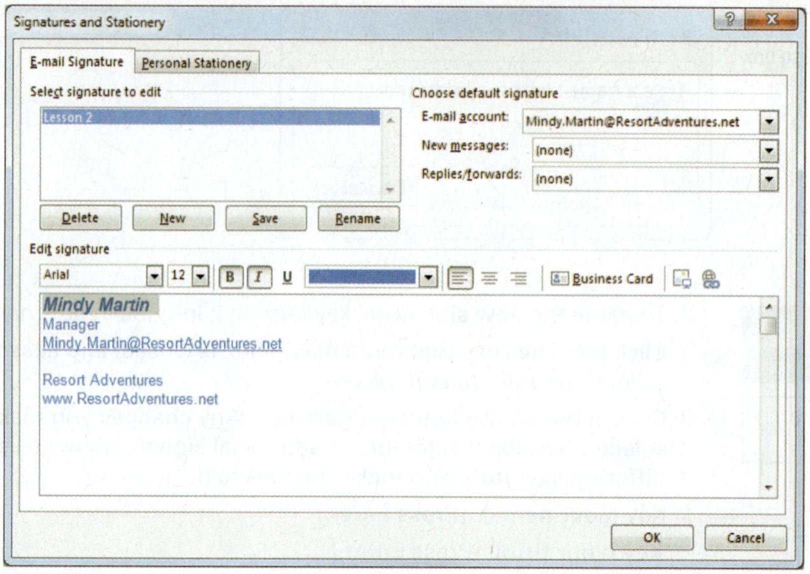

Signatures and Stationery

E-mail Signature | Personal Stationery

Select signature to edit

Lesson 2

[Delete] [New] [Save] [Rename]

Choose default signature

E-mail account: Mindy.Martin@ResortAdventures.net

New messages: (none)

Replies/forwards: (none)

Edit signature

Arial   12   B *I* U

Mindy Martin
Manager
Mindy.Martin@ResortAdventures.net

Resort Adventures
www.ResortAdventures.net

[OK] [Cancel]

19. Verify that (none) is still selected in the *New Messages* and *Replies/Forwards* fields. Click **OK**. The dialog box is closed, and the signature is saved.

20. Close the message window.

PAUSE. LEAVE Outlook open to use in the next exercise.

Cross Ref

You can find more information on creating signatures in Lesson 7.

CERTIFICATION READY?   **2.2.6**

How do you format a signature?

Although you can include images and more complicated formatting in a signature, the formatting you can apply in the Signatures and Stationery dialog box is limited. For example, you can't resize an image in the Signatures and Stationery dialog box. However, you can open a new message, use the formatting tools in the new Message window to create a signature you like, cut the signature, and paste it into the Signatures and Stationery dialog box as a new signature.

Adding a Signature to a Single Message

You can choose to add a signature to an individual message. This enables you to create and use more than one signature.

STEP BY STEP   **Add a Signature to a Single Message**

GET READY. LAUNCH Outlook if it is not already running.

1. If necessary, click the **Mail** button in the Navigation bar to display the Mail folder.
2. Click the **New Email** button on the HOME tab. The Message window is displayed.
3. In the message area, key **I'm testing my new signature.** Press **Enter** twice.
4. In the Include group on the Ribbon, click **Signature**.
5. In the dropdown list, select **Lesson 2**. The signature is inserted into the message, as shown in Figure 2-47.

Figure 2-47

Message using the
new signature

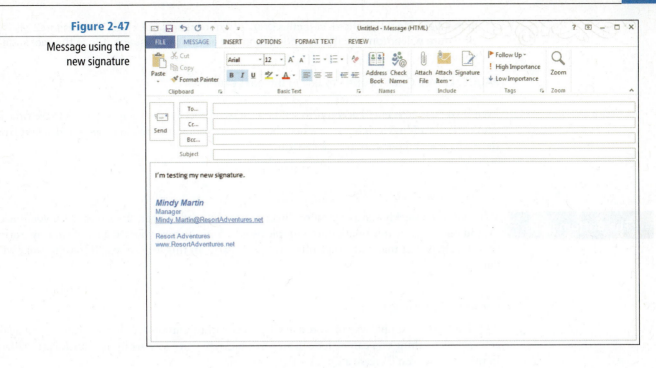

6. Click the **To** field and key your email address.

7. Click the **Subject** field and key **Testing Signature in a Single Message**. Click the **Send** button.

8. If the message has not been received, click the **Send/Receive All Folders** button.

9. Click the message in the message list, and click the **FILE tab** and select the **Save As** option. The Save As dialog box is displayed.

10. Navigate to the folder where you want to save the file and click the **Save** button. The message is saved as *Testing Signature in a Single Message.msg*.

PAUSE. LEAVE Outlook open to use in the next exercise.

Troubleshooting If formatting has been applied to your email messages or other signatures, the same formatting may be applied to the signature as you key the text. You can change the formatting after you key the signature.

CERTIFICATION READY?   **2.2.5**

How do you add a signature to a message?

You might want to create several signatures. This enables you to select the signature to match the message. When you send a personal message, use a signature that includes a picture from your favorite sport or a photo of your new puppy. When you send a business message, use a signature that includes your business information.

Adding a Signature to All Outgoing Messages

If you primarily use your email account for the same type of email (business or personal), you can select a signature that is automatically inserted into every outgoing message. This gives you a quick, consistent way to insert your signature.

STEP BY STEP   **Add a Signature to All Outgoing Messages**

GET READY. LAUNCH Outlook if it is not already running.

1. If necessary, click the **Mail** button in the Navigation bar to display the Mail folder.

2. Click the **New Email** button on the HOME tab. The Message window is displayed.

3. Click the **Signature** button in the Include group on the Ribbon. In the dropdown list, click **Signatures**. The Signatures and Stationery dialog box is displayed.

4. In the *New Messages* field, select **Lesson 2**, if necessary. Click **OK**. The Lesson 2 signature will automatically be added to every outgoing message. Close the message window.

PAUSE. LEAVE Outlook open to use in the next exercise.

Even if you use your email account to send business and personal messages, you can save time by automatically adding a signature. When the automatic signature isn't appropriate, delete it from the message and insert the correct signature.

WORKING WITH QUICK PARTS

The Bottom Line

Whether it is a weekly status report or directions to your office, there are times when you'll need to send out the same information to multiple people. You can save yourself a lot of time by storing these blocks of text that you repeat often as Quick Parts. In this section, you'll learn to work with quick parts.

Creating a Quick Part

A **Quick Part** is a simple way to store a block of text within Outlook so that you can reuse it again and again. Anything you can include in an email message you can store in the Quick Parts gallery. In this exercise, you'll create a Quick Part.

STEP BY STEP   **Create a Quick Part**

GET READY. LAUNCH Outlook if it is not already running.

1. If necessary, click the **Mail** button in the Navigation bar to display the Mail folder.
2. Click the **New Email** button on the HOME tab to display a new Message window.
3. In the message area above the signature, key **Thanks for your interest in working for Resort Adventures for the summer season. Your resume has been forwarded to our human resources department for processing. If you have any questions, you can send them to HR@ResortAdventures.net.** [Press **Enter**].
4. Select all the message text (including the signature) and click the **INSERT tab**.
5. In the Text group, click **Quick Parts**.
6. In the drop list, hover over the **AutoText** option. A collection of general text blocks are displayed.
7. Click **Save Selection to AutoText Gallery**. The Create New Building Block dialog box is displayed, as shown in Figure 2-48.

Figure 2-48

The Create New Building Block
dialog box

Click to Create or add a Quick Part

Give a name to
your text block

Select the text you want to
include in the Quick Part

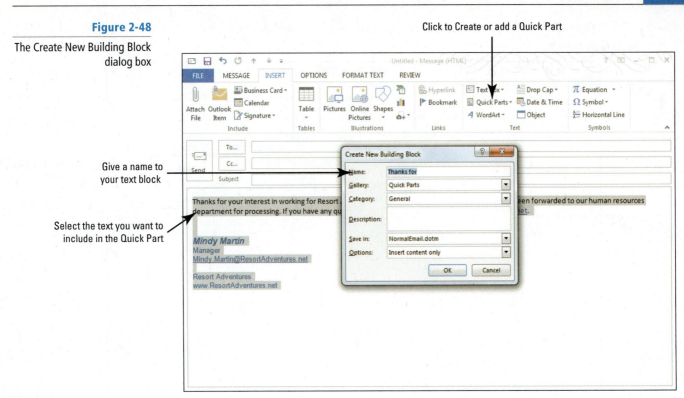

CERTIFICATION
READY?   2.2.7

How do you create a
Quick Part?

8. In the **Name** box, key **HR Reply** as the name for your Quick Part.

9. Click **OK** to save the Quick Part. Close the email message without saving it.

PAUSE. LEAVE Outlook open to use in the next exercise.

Using Quick Parts

Once you've stored something as a building block, it will be added to the Quick Parts gallery. You can add these building blocks in much the same way that you add a signature to a message. In this exercise, you'll use a Quick Part.

STEP BY STEP   **Use Quick Parts**

GET READY. LAUNCH Outlook if it is not already running.

1. If necessary, click the **Mail** button in the Navigation bar to display the Mail folder.

2. Click the **New Email** button on the HOME tab to open a new message window and click in the message area.

3. On the **INSERT tab**, click **Quick Parts** in the Text group. The HR Reply Quick Part appears in the gallery, as shown in Figure 2-49.

Figure 2-49

The HR Reply Quick Part

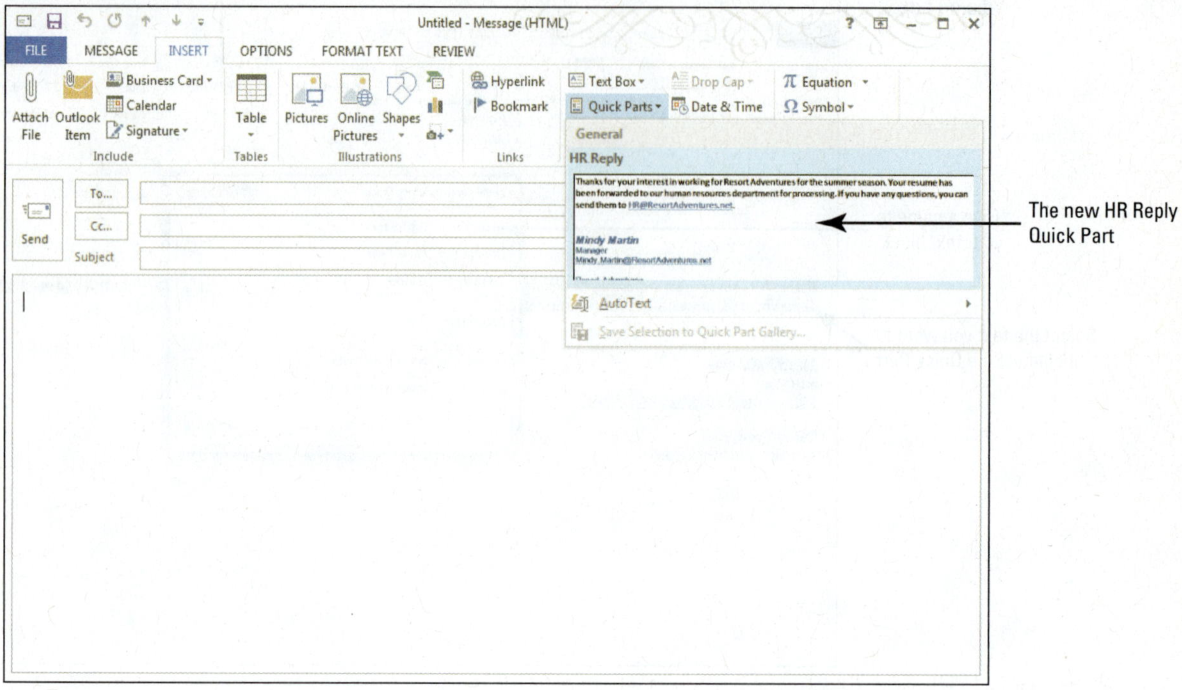

The new HR Reply Quick Part

4. Click the **HR Reply** Quick Part. The text appears in the message window. In this case, Mindy put her signature in the QuickPart (to save time), but her signature is also added to all new messages. When she places the QuickPart in a new message, her signature will appear twice. If the signature appears twice in a message, be sure to delete one of them before sending.

PAUSE. LEAVE Outlook open to use in the next exercise.

CERTIFICATION READY?   2.2.7

How do you use a Quick Part?

Managing Quick Parts

Quick Parts are a convenient way to automate the messages that you send out frequently. You can add any text that you repeat to your Quick Parts gallery. Because it can be used for so many different things, the gallery can quickly become quite large. Once you've added a number of building blocks, you'll find it easier to manage your Quick Parts if you organize them into groups. In this exercise, you'll organize your Quick Parts and learn how to delete them.

STEP BY STEP   **Manage Quick Parts**

GET READY. USE the message created in the previous exercise.

1. On the **INSERT tab**, click **Quick Parts** in the Text group. The Quick Parts gallery is displayed.

2. Right-click the **HR Reply** Quick Part and select **Organize and Delete**. The Building Blocks Organizer is displayed.

3. Click **Edit Properties**. The Modify Building Block dialog box is displayed, as shown in Figure 2-50.

Figure 2-50

Organizing the Quick
Parts Gallery

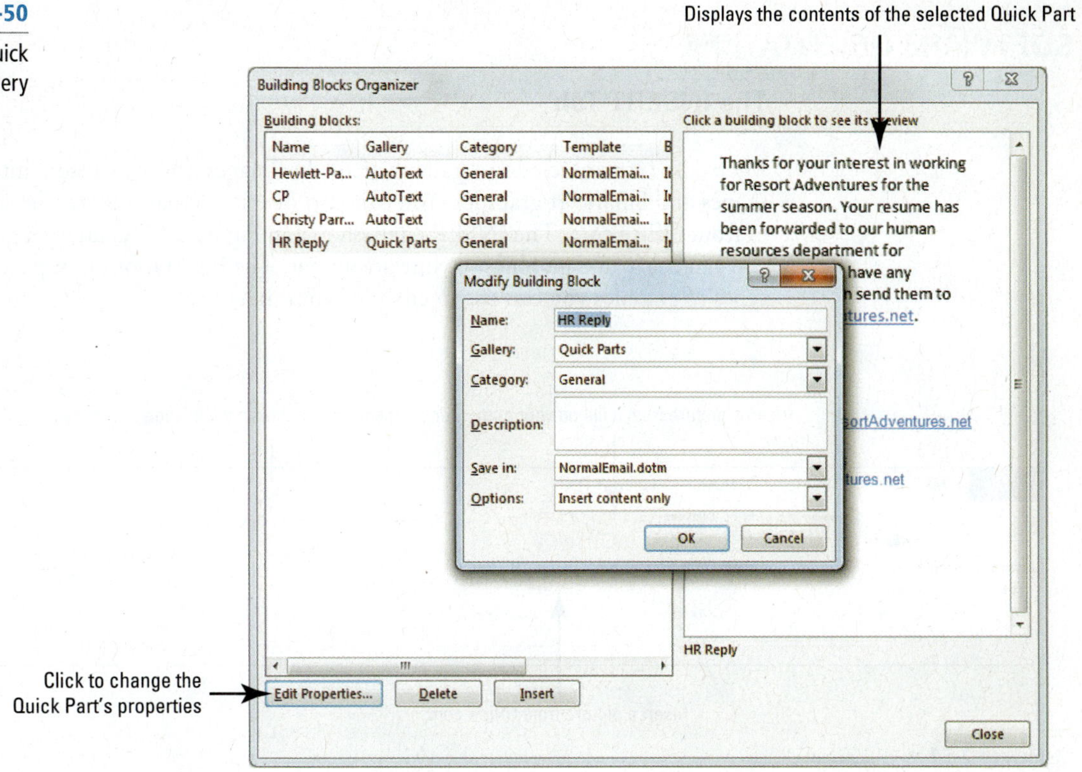

Displays the contents of the selected Quick Part

Click to change the
Quick Part's properties

4. Click the **Category** drop arrow.

5. Select **Create New Category**. The Create New Category dialog box is displayed.

6. In the Name box, key **Staffing**. Click **OK** twice to close both dialog boxes. A warning box prompts you to verify that you want to make the change.

7. Click **Yes**. The message box closes and the HR Reply Quick Part is now categorized as a Staffing Quick Part.

8. With the HR Reply Quick Part still selected, click **Delete**, and click **Yes** to confirm.

9. Click **Close** to exit out of the Building Blocks Organizer.

10. Click the **Signature** button (on the MESSAGE tab) in the Include group on the Ribbon. In the dropdown list, click **Signatures**. The Signatures and Stationery dialog box is displayed.

11. In the *New Messages* field, select **(none)**. Click **OK**. The Lesson 2 signature will no longer be added to every outgoing message.

12. Close the message window and save the changes to your Drafts folder.

PAUSE. LEAVE Outlook open to use in the next exercise.

INSERTING AND FORMATTING GRAPHIC MESSAGE CONTENT

The Bottom Line

Adding a chart, picture, or other illustration to a message captures attention and immediately portrays an idea of what the message is all about. In this section, you'll add hyperlinks and graphics to a message.

SOFTWARE ORIENTATION

The INSERT Tab

Microsoft Office includes a gallery of media images you can insert into messages such as shapes and SmartArt graphics. You can also insert external picture files from your computer or from Office.com. The INSERT tab, shown in Figure 2-51, contains a group of features that you can use to add graphics to your document. The Illustrations group has options for several types of graphics you can use to enhance your messages.

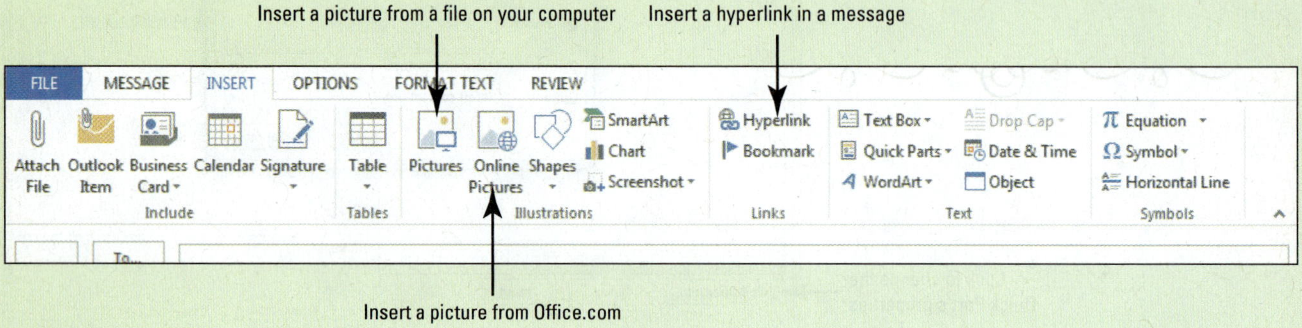

Insert a picture from a file on your computer   Insert a hyperlink in a message

[FILE | MESSAGE | INSERT | OPTIONS | FORMAT TEXT | REVIEW]

Attach File | Outlook Item | Business Card | Calendar | Signature | Table | Pictures | Online Pictures | Shapes | SmartArt | Chart | Screenshot | Hyperlink | Bookmark | Text Box | Quick Parts | WordArt | Drop Cap | Date & Time | Object | Equation | Symbol | Horizontal Line

Include | Tables | Illustrations | Links | Text | Symbols

To...

Insert a picture from Office.com

Figure 2-51
The INSERT tab

Use this figure as a reference through out this section as you become skilled in inserting and formatting illustrations within a message.

Inserting a Graphical Element

While the old adage "A picture is worth a thousand words" is perhaps an exaggeration, a visual element adds interest and calls attention to your messages. Unlike a message background that is displayed but does not print, pictures and other graphic objects are included in message printouts.

Graphics can be an integral part of creating a compelling message. You can insert or copy pictures into a message from image providers, such as Office.com, or files on your computer. A well-chosen picture can portray a powerful message. In this exercise, you will insert a graphic element into a message.

Insert a Graphical Element

USE the Come Fly with Us message you created in a previous exercise.

1. If necessary, click the **Mail** button in the Navigation bar to display the Mail folder. In the last exercise, you saved and closed the message window. Outlook automatically places messages that you've worked on but haven't sent in the Drafts folder.
2. Click on the **Drafts** folder; then open the **Come Fly with Us** message that you worked on in a previous exercise.
3. Click the **INSERT tab** to display the Illustrations group, as shown in Figure 2-51.
4. Place the insertion point at the end of the main paragraph in the message. Press **Enter** twice to add two lines of blank space.
5. In the Illustrations group, click **Pictures**. The Insert Picture dialog box is displayed.

6. Select the *Vista.jpg* file in the data files for this lesson.

7. Click **Insert**. A large picture of a landscape near the resort is displayed in the message and the PICTURE TOOLS FORMAT tab is displayed in the Ribbon, as shown in Figure 2-52.

Figure 2-52

Inserting a graphic in a message window

PICTURE TOOLS FORMAT tab

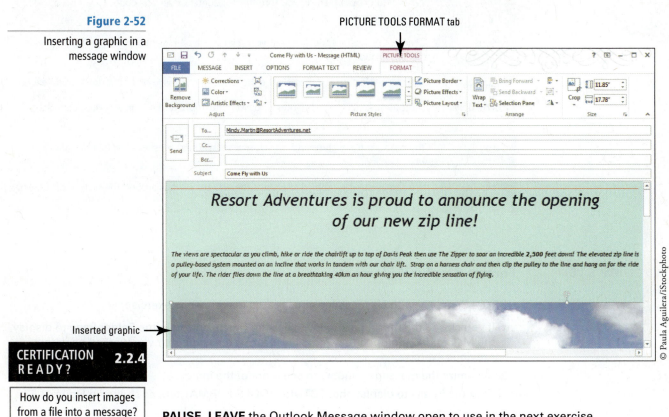

Inserted graphic

CERTIFICATION READY? **2.2.4**

How do you insert images from a file into a message?

PAUSE. LEAVE the Outlook Message window open to use in the next exercise.

The Insert Picture technique enables you to customize a message with selected photographs. The picture you inserted in this exercise is a digital photograph.

You can also insert clip art images in your messages. **Clip art** refers to illustrated picture files available from Office.com and other online resources. The easiest way to find online images is using the Online Pictures button on the INSERT tab. At Office.com, you can also search for photographs, movies, and sounds. To include any of those media types, click on the image to open a larger view of the image. Click the Copy button and then click Paste in your message window.

You can also insert SmartArt graphics. **SmartArt graphics** are visual representations of information that can help communicate your message or ideas more effectively.

Formatting Graphical Elements

Once you've inserted a graphic, you can alter it using the PICTURE TOOLS FORMAT tab. There are many options for changing the graphic. For example, you can change the shape of the graphic, alter its direction, change the layout, and change the colors. In this exercise, you make multiple formatting changes to the picture in an email message. The same formatting options are available when you work with clip art, SmartArt, and shapes. You can quickly make adjustments to a picture or graphic that has been inserted into a message by using the tools in Table 2-4.

Table 2-4

Formatting Tools for Graphics

Tool	Description
Crop	When you **crop** a picture, you trim the horizontal or vertical edges to get rid of unwanted areas.
Resize	Change the size or scale of a graphic using the Shape Height and Shape Width tools in the Size group.
Picture Style	You can use Picture Styles to change the shape of the image or add borders or 3D effects.
Corrections	You can make an image brighter or darker and improve the sharpness and contrast of the image.
Color	You can turn the picture into a grayscale, sepia-toned, washed-out, or black-and-white version.
Wrap Text	You can use text wrapping to change the way text wraps around the picture or drawing object.

STEP BY STEP   **Format Graphical Elements**

USE the Come Fly with Us message you created in a previous exercise.

1. If you closed the message window, click the **Drafts** button in the Folder Pane to display the Mail folder and open the **Come Fly with Us** message that you worked on in the previous exercise.

2. Maximize the message window to see more of the image.

3. Click the **image** to display the PICTURE TOOLS FORMAT tab, as shown in Figure 2-53.

Figure 2-53

The PICTURE TOOLS FORMAT tab

Click to access image correction tools

Delete current picture and insert a new one

Add a border to the image

Set picture height

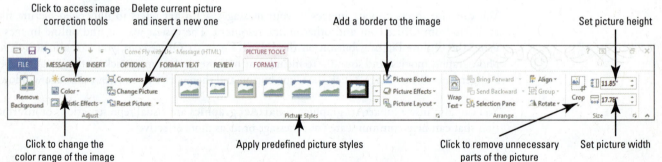

Click to change the color range of the image

Apply predefined picture styles

Click to remove unnecessary parts of the picture

Set picture width

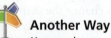

Another Way
You can also crop an image by selecting the image and clicking Crop in the Size group on the PICTURE TOOLS FORMAT tab.

4. Click the **Width** box in the Size group, and key **6.5** and press **Enter**. The image width changes to 6.5", and the image height changes as needed to avoid warping the image. The image height and width change together only if the lock aspect ratio box is selected. This setting is located in the Layout dialog box that appears when you click the Size group's dialog box launcher.

5. Right-click the image, and click the **Crop** button that appears with the shortcut menu. Crop handles appear at each corner and side of the image.

6. Drag each of the crop handles toward the center of the image, as shown in Figure 2-54.

Figure 2-54

Cropping an image

Click to remove unnecessary parts of the picture   Set picture height

Set picture width

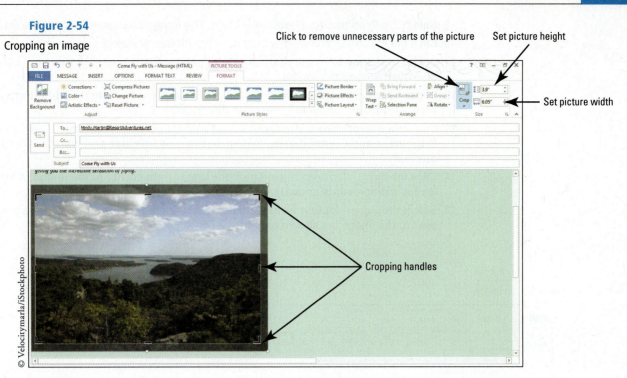

Cropping handles

Another Way

You can also apply a style to an image by clicking the image and selecting a thumbnail within the Picture Styles Gallery.

7. Click the **Crop** button on the PICTURE TOOLS FORMAT tab to save your changes.
8. Right-click the image, and select the **Style** button that appears with the shortcut menu. A selection of available picture styles is displayed, as shown in Figure 2-55.

Figure 2-55

Applying Picture Styles to an image

Click to add a picture border

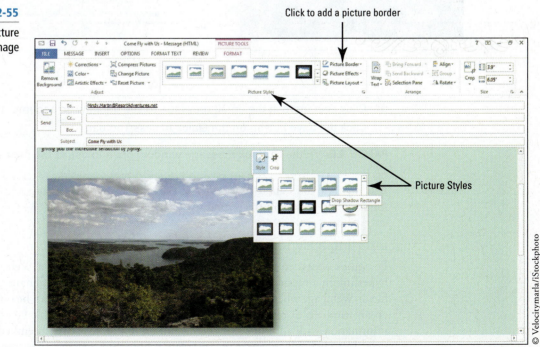

Picture Styles

9. Select the **Drop Shadow Rectangle** style. The image changes to match the style.

10. Click the **Picture Border** arrow button in the Picture Styles group.

11. Select **Dark Blue** from the Standard Color palette that appears. A thin blue border is displayed around the image.

12. In the Adjust group, click **Color** and select **Saturation: 200%** in the Color Saturation area. The image is now brighter than the original.

13. Click the **Corrections** button and select **Brightness: 0%**, **Contrast: +20%** in the Brightness and Contrast area. The image is now brighter and warmer than the original.

14. Click the **Layout Options** button near the upper right corner of the image. A selection of layout arrangements appears in a menu.

15. Select the **Square** option from the list. The remaining text for the message moves up next to the image, as shown in Figure 2-56.

Figure 2-56

Adjusting an image

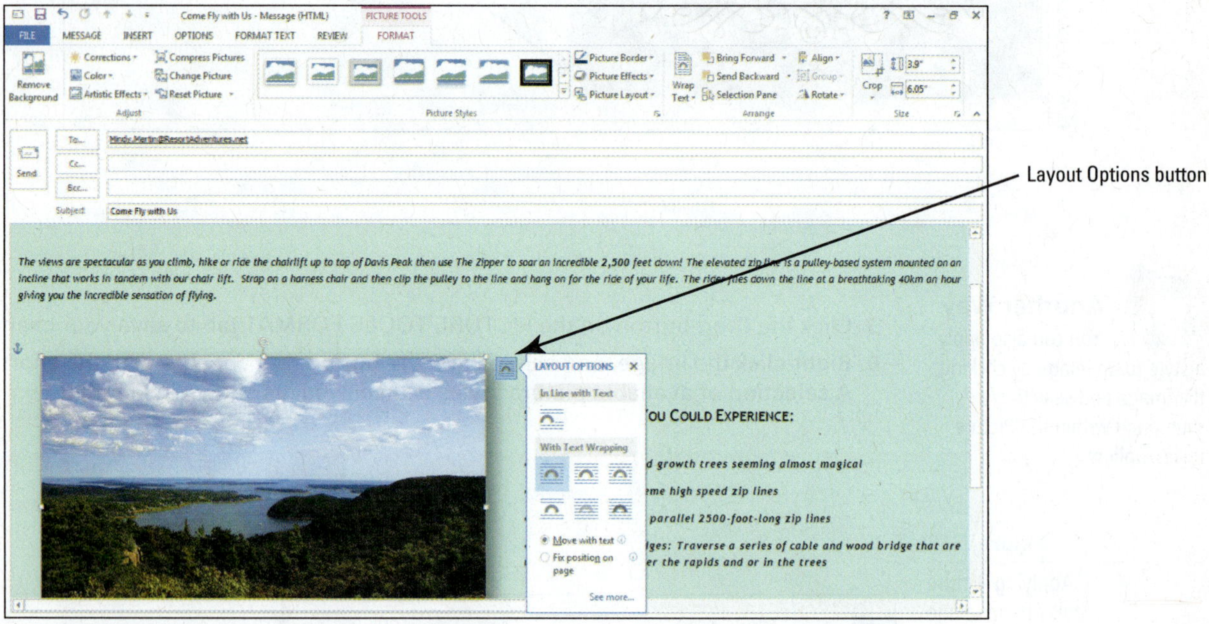

Layout Options button

© Velocitymarla/iStockphoto

16. Click anywhere in the email message to see the new arrangement.

17. Click the **Save** button on the Quick Access Toolbar.

PAUSE. LEAVE the Outlook message window open to use in the next exercise.

Take Note   If at any time you want to revert back to the original graphic, click the Reset Picture button in the Adjust group to discard the formatting changes you have made.

Inserting a Hyperlink

For quick access to related information in another file or on a Web page, you can insert a hyperlink in a message. A **hyperlink** is an image or sequence of characters that opens another file or Web page when you click it. The target file or Web page can be on the World Wide Web, on an Intranet, or on your personal computer. Hyperlinks enable you to supplement message information with additional materials and resources. It is easy to embed a hyperlink in a message. Just click where you want to create a hyperlink or select the text or object you want to become a hyperlink, and click the Hyperlink button on the INSERT tab. In this exercise, you'll insert a hyperlink into a message.

Insert a Hyperlink

USE the Come Fly with Us message you created in a previous exercise.

1. If necessary, click the **Mail** button in the Navigation bar to display the Mail folder. Open the **Come Fly with Us** message that you worked on in the previous exercise. It should be in the Drafts folder.

2. If necessary, click the **image** in the message, and click the **INSERT tab**.

3. Click **Hyperlink** in the Links group. The Insert Hyperlink dialog box opens, as shown in Figure 2-57.

Figure 2-57

The Insert Hyperlink dialog box

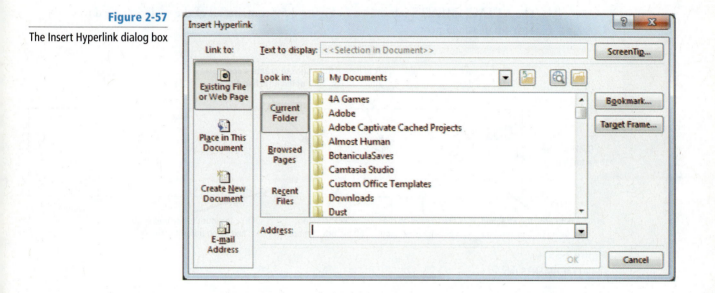

4. Navigate to the *Zipper Rates.mht* file in the data files for this lesson.

5. Click **ScreenTip** in the upper-right corner of the Insert Hyperlink dialog box. The Set Hyperlink ScreenTip dialog box is displayed, as shown in Figure 2-58.

Figure 2-58

The Set Hyperlink ScreenTip dialog box

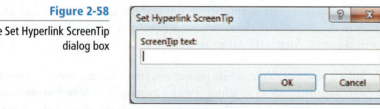

6. Key **For more information click here** in the ScreenTip Text textbox. Click **OK** twice to apply your changes and close the dialog boxes.

7. Click the message window's **Send** button to send the message to yourself.

8. If the message has not been received, click the **Send/Receive All Folders** button.

9. Click the message in the message list. Click the **FILE tab** and select the **Save As** option. The Save As dialog box is displayed.

10. In the *File name* box, key **Come Fly with Us**.

11. Navigate to the folder where you save your solution files and click the **Save** button. The message is saved as *Come Fly with Us.msg*.

PAUSE. LEAVE Outlook open to use in the next exercise.

WORKING WITH ATTACHMENTS

The Bottom Line

Attachments are files sent as part of an email message. An attachment is a convenient way to send pictures, spreadsheets, and other types of files to an email recipient. In this section, you'll attach files and items to email messages. You'll then preview, save, and print an attachment.

SOFTWARE ORIENTATION

The ATTACHMENTS Tab

The ATTACHMENTS tab shown in Figure 2-59 contains all of the tools you need to work with email attachments.

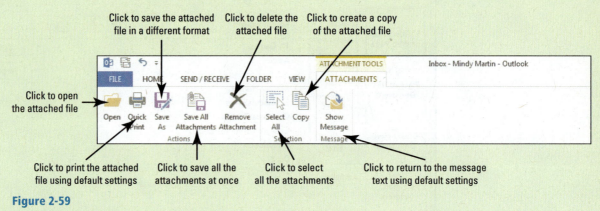

Figure 2-59

The ATTACHMENTS tab

The tools on the ATTACHMENTS tab are the same tools available when you right-click on an attachment icon in the Reading Pane.

Attaching an External File to a Message

Do you need to submit a five-page report to your supervisor at the home office? Perhaps you have a new product brochure to distribute to all the sales representatives, or you want to share a picture of your new puppy with a friend. Attach the file to an email message and send it.

Outlook 2013 also includes a new tool that can help protect you from making one of the most common email mistakes: forgetting to include an attachment with a message. The **Attachment Reminder** tool will scan each message you create to see whether it mentions something that should be attached. If you attempt to send the message without the attachment, Outlook displays a warning message asking whether you meant to include an attachment.

When you attach a file to a message, the filename, size, and an icon representing the file are displayed in the *Attached* field. If you attach more than one file, the files are listed separately in the *Attached* field. In this exercise, you'll attach a file to a message.

STEP BY STEP   **Attach an External File to a Message**

GET READY. LAUNCH Outlook if it is not already running.

1. If necessary, click the **Mail** button in the Navigation bar to display the Mail folder.
2. Click the **New Email** button on the HOME tab. The Message window is displayed.

3. In the *To* field, key [your email address]. You will send this message to yourself, so you can use the attachment in the following exercises.

4. In the *Subject* field, key Zipper Coupon Attached.

5. Click the message area. Key Hi Jon, [Press Enter twice].

6. Key the following note: I attached a copy of the coupon for the new Zipper attraction. I'd like to get your opinion of it before sending it with the Come Fly with Us promotional message we discussed earlier. [Press Enter twice.]

7. Key Thanks, [press Enter].

8. Key [your name].

9. Click Send. An Attachment Reminder message appears asking you whether you want to send the message without the attachment you mentioned in the text, as shown in Figure 2-60.

Figure 2-60

An Attachment Reminder

The Include group

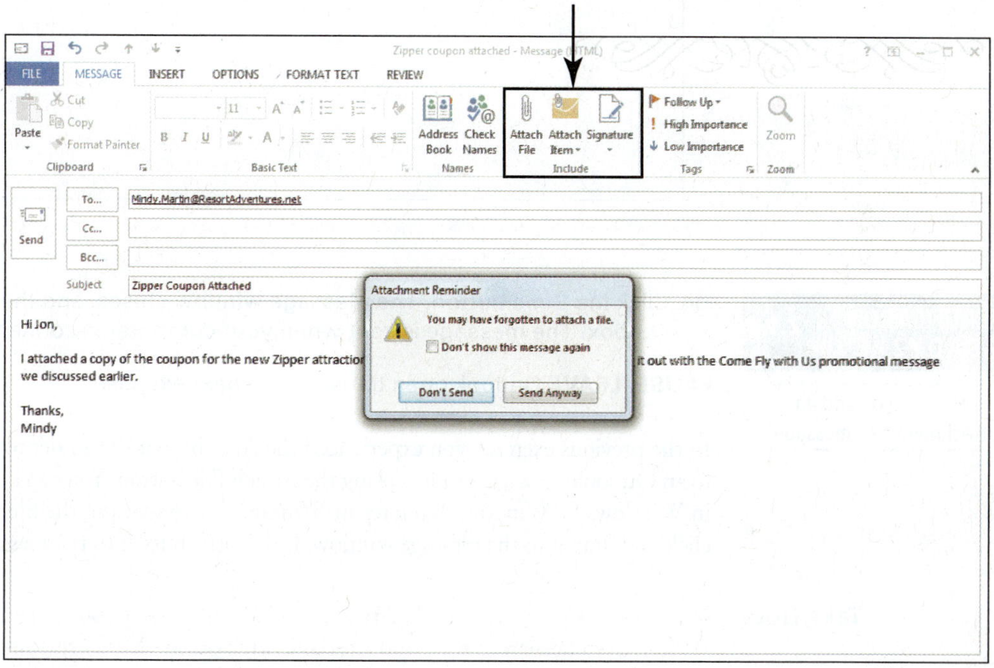

10. Click Don't Send to go back to the message window.

11. Click the Attach File button in the Include group on the Ribbon. The Insert File dialog box is displayed.

12. Navigate to the data files for this lesson.

13. Click the *Zipper Coupon* file and click Insert. The Insert File dialog box is closed, and the file is listed in the *Attached* field, as shown in Figure 2-61.

Figure 2-61

Sending an attachment

Attach File button

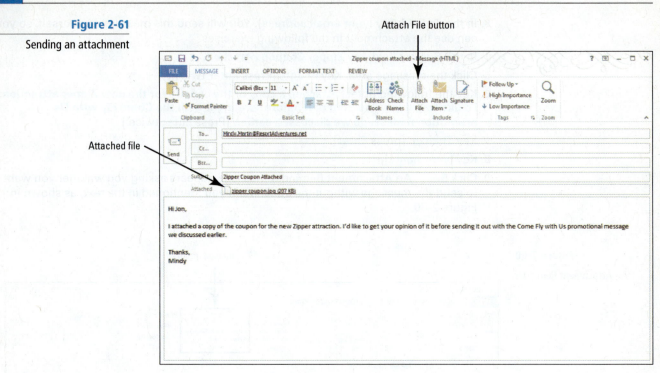

Attached file

14. Click the **Send** button. The Message window closes, and the message is moved to the Outbox. The message is sent when your computer is connected to the Internet.

PAUSE. LEAVE Outlook open to use in the next exercise.

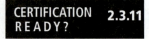

CERTIFICATION READY?   2.1.4

How do you add an attachment to a message?

In the previous exercise, you experienced the Attachment Reminder tool and attached an external file to an Outlook message window using the Attach File button. You can also open a File Explorer window in Windows 8 (Windows Explorer in Windows 7) containing the file you want to attach and simply click and drag it to the message window. It will attach itself to the message, and you're ready to share.

Take Note   If you would prefer to not get Attachment Reminders as you create messages you can turn off the option. Scroll down to the Send messages area on the Mail Options page of the Outlook Options dialog box. Locate the *Warn me when I send a message that may be missing an attachment* option, and deselect it.

CERTIFICATION READY?   2.3.11

How do you modify Attachment Reminder settings?

Attaching an Outlook Item to a Message

An attachment can also be an Outlook item, such as a contact, a note, or a task. In this exercise, you'll attach an Outlook message to another message.

STEP BY STEP   **Attach an Outlook item to a Message**

GET READY. LAUNCH Outlook if it is not already running.

1. If necessary, click the **Mail** button in the Navigation bar to display the Mail folder.
2. Click the **New Email** button on the HOME tab. The Message window is displayed.
3. In the *To* field, key [**your email address**].
4. In the *Subject* field, key **Promotional Message Attached**.
5. Click the message area. Key **Hi Jon,** [Press **Enter** twice.]
6. Key the following note: **I attached a copy of the Come Fly with Us promotional message we discussed.** [Press **Enter** twice.]
7. Key **Let me know what you think.** [Press **Enter**.]

8. Key [**your name**].
9. Click the **Attach Item** button in the Include group on the Ribbon.
10. Select **Outlook Item**. The Insert Item dialog box is displayed, as shown in Figure 2-62.

Figure 2-62

Attaching an Outlook item to a message

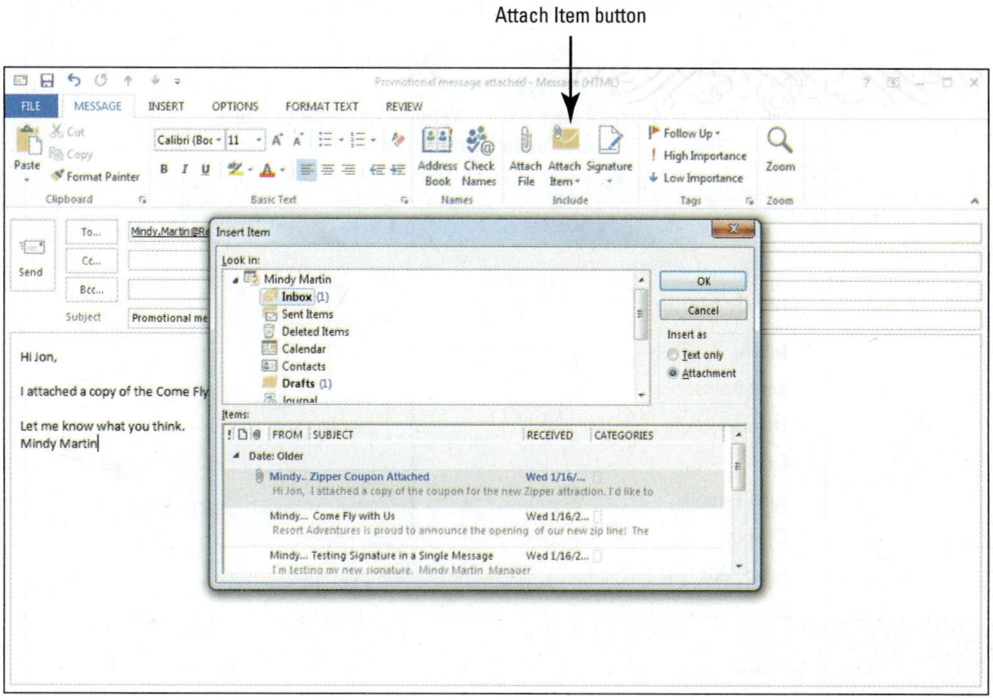

Attach Item button

11. If necessary, click **Inbox** in the *Look in* window.
12. In the Items window, select **Come Fly with Us**.
13. Make sure that Attachment is selected in the *Insert As* area. Click **OK**. The Insert Item dialog box is closed, and the file is listed in the *Attached* field.
14. Click the **Send** button. The Message window closes, and the message is moved to the Outbox. The message is sent when your computer is connected to the Internet.

PAUSE. LEAVE Outlook open to use in the next exercise.

Previewing an Attachment in Outlook

The Attachment Previewer enables you to view attachments in the Reading Pane. Without needing to save and open an attachment, you can make critical decisions quickly and efficiently. In this exercise, you'll preview an attachment in Outlook.

STEP BY STEP   **Preview an Attachment in Outlook**

USE the Zipper Coupon Attached message with the attachment you sent to yourself in an earlier exercise.

1. If the message with the coupon attachment has not arrived yet, click the **Send/Receive All Folders** button on the SEND/RECEIVE tab to check for new messages. The paper clip icon with the message, as shown in Figure 2-63, indicates that the message has an attachment.

Figure 2-63

Message with attachment
received

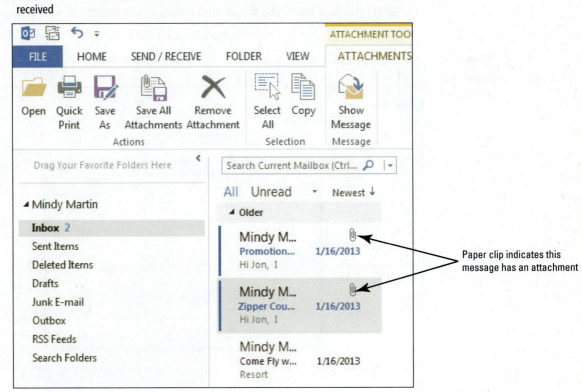

Paper clip indicates this
message has an attachment

2. Click the **Zipper Coupon Attached** message. The message is displayed in the Reading
   Pane, as shown in Figure 2-64.

Figure 2-64

Reading Pane containing the
message with attachment

Click to view the attached file

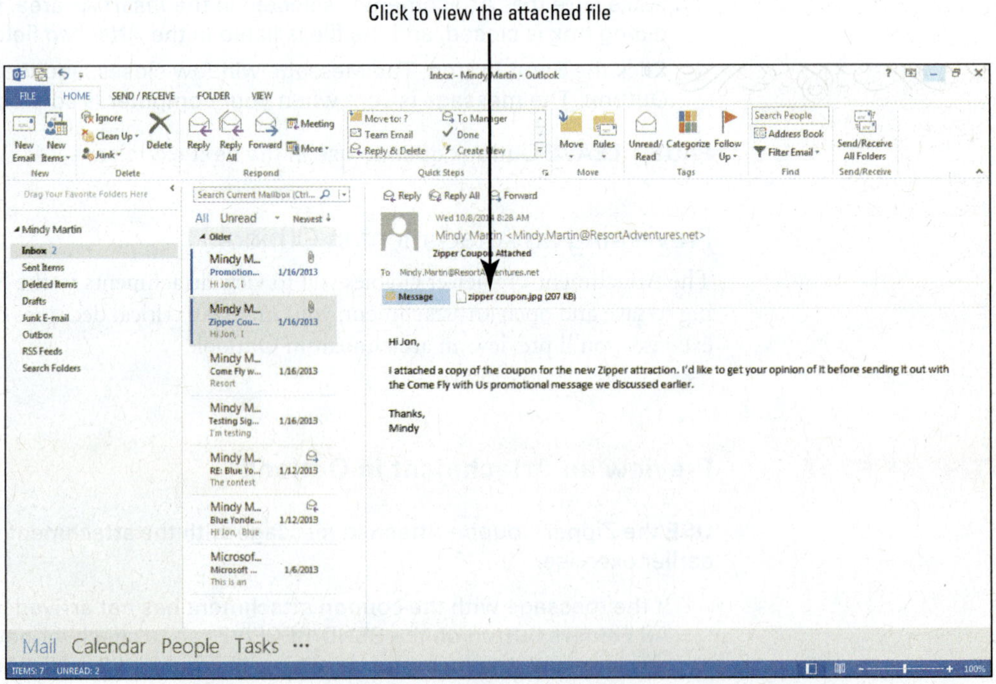

3. In the Reading Pane, click the attachment's filename. The attachment is displayed in the Reading Pane, as shown in Figure 2-65.

Figure 2-65

Attachment displayed in the Reading Pane

Click to view the attached file

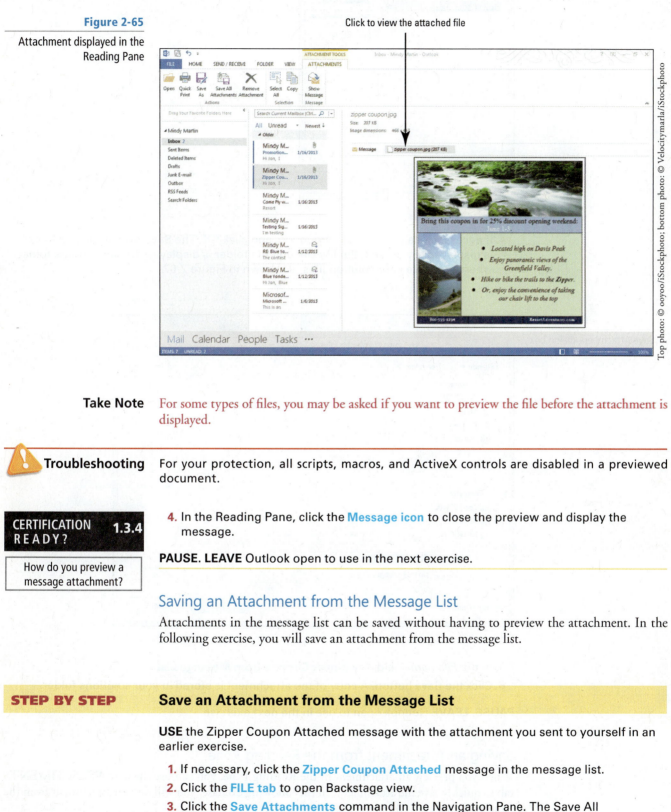

Top photo: © ooyoo/iStockphoto; bottom photo: © Velocitymarla/iStockphoto

Take Note   For some types of files, you may be asked if you want to preview the file before the attachment is displayed.

Troubleshooting   For your protection, all scripts, macros, and ActiveX controls are disabled in a previewed document.

CERTIFICATION READY?   1.3.4

How do you preview a message attachment?

4. In the Reading Pane, click the **Message icon** to close the preview and display the message.

PAUSE. LEAVE Outlook open to use in the next exercise.

Saving an Attachment from the Message List

Attachments in the message list can be saved without having to preview the attachment. In the following exercise, you will save an attachment from the message list.

STEP BY STEP   **Save an Attachment from the Message List**

USE the Zipper Coupon Attached message with the attachment you sent to yourself in an earlier exercise.

1. If necessary, click the **Zipper Coupon Attached** message in the message list.
2. Click the **FILE tab** to open Backstage view.
3. Click the **Save Attachments** command in the Navigation Pane. The Save All Attachments dialog box is displayed, as shown in Figure 2-66.

Figure 2-66

Save All Attachments
dialog box

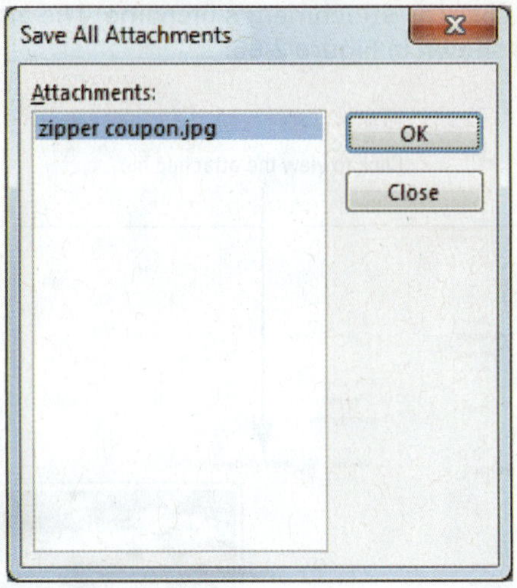

Save All Attachments

Attachments:

zipper coupon.jpg

OK

Close

4. If necessary, select *Zipper Coupon.jpg*, and click **OK**. The Save Attachment dialog box is displayed. By default, the My Documents folder is displayed. Navigate to the folder where you save your solution files, as shown in Figure 2-67.

Figure 2-67

Save Attachment dialog box

Save Attachment

« Less... ▸ Lesson 02 Instructor Solution ...   Search Lesson 02 Instructor Sol...

Organize ▾   New folder

- Documents
- MOAC 2013
- Music
- Pictures
- Videos

- Homegroup

- Computer
  - Local Disk (C:)
  - RECOVERY (D:)
  - HP_TOOLS (E:)

Name	Date modified	Type
No items match your search.		

File name: zipper coupon.jpg

Save as type: HPTSMSMVP.JPG (*.jpg)

Hide Folders   Tools ▾   Save   Cancel

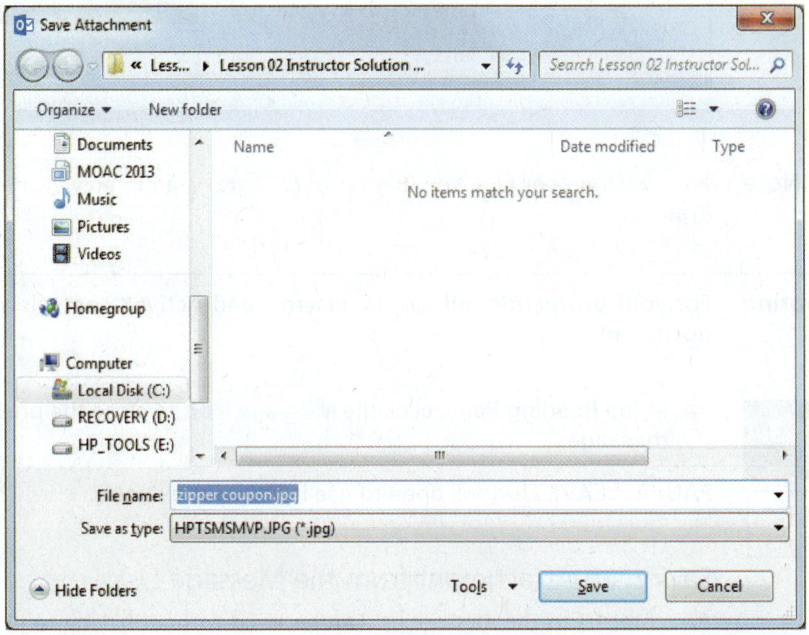

5. In the *File name* field, key **Zipper Coupon from Message List**.
6. Click the **Save** button. A copy of the attachment is stored in your solutions folder.

PAUSE. LEAVE Outlook open to use in the next exercise.

Saving an Attachment from the Reading Pane

When you preview an attachment in the Reading Pane, you can use the new ATTACHMENTS tab to quickly save the attachment. In the following exercise, you will save an attachment from the Reading Pane.

STEP BY STEP   **Save an Attachment from the Reading Pane**

USE the Zipper Coupon Attached message with the attachment you sent to yourself in an earlier exercise.

1. Click the **Zipper Coupon Attached** message in the message list.
2. In the Reading Pane, click the *Zipper Coupon.jpg* attachment. The ATTACHMENTS tab is displayed, as shown in Figure 2-68.

Figure 2-68

Saving an attachment using the ATTACHMENTS tab

Click to save the attached file

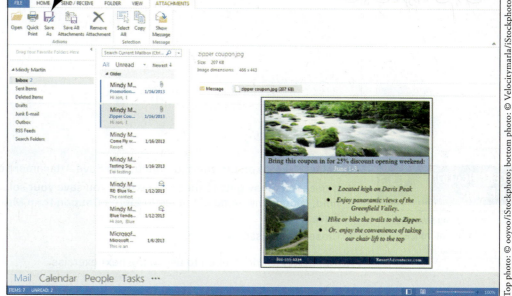

3. Click the **Save As** button on the ATTACHMENTS tab. The Save Attachment dialog box is displayed, as shown in Figure 2-67.
4. If necessary, navigate to the folder where you save your solution files. In the *File name* field, change the name of the file to **Zipper Coupon from Reading Pane**.
5. Click the **Save** button.

PAUSE. LEAVE Outlook open to use in the next exercise.

Another Way

If the message contains multiple attachments, click Save All Attachments to save them all in one step.

Saving an Attachment from an Open Message

It is easy to save an attachment from an open message window. You can use the Save Attachments option on the FILE tab, but you can also save the attachment from the attachment's shortcut menu. In the following exercise, you will save an attachment from an open message window.

STEP BY STEP   **Save an Attachment from an Open Message**

USE the Zipper Coupon Attached message with the attachment you sent to yourself in an earlier exercise.

1. Double-click the **Zipper Coupon Attached** message in the message list. The message is opened in a new window.
2. In the new window, right-click the *Zipper Coupon.jpg* attachment. The attachment's shortcut menu is displayed, as shown in Figure 2-69.

Figure 2-69

Figure 2-69

Attachment's shortcut menu

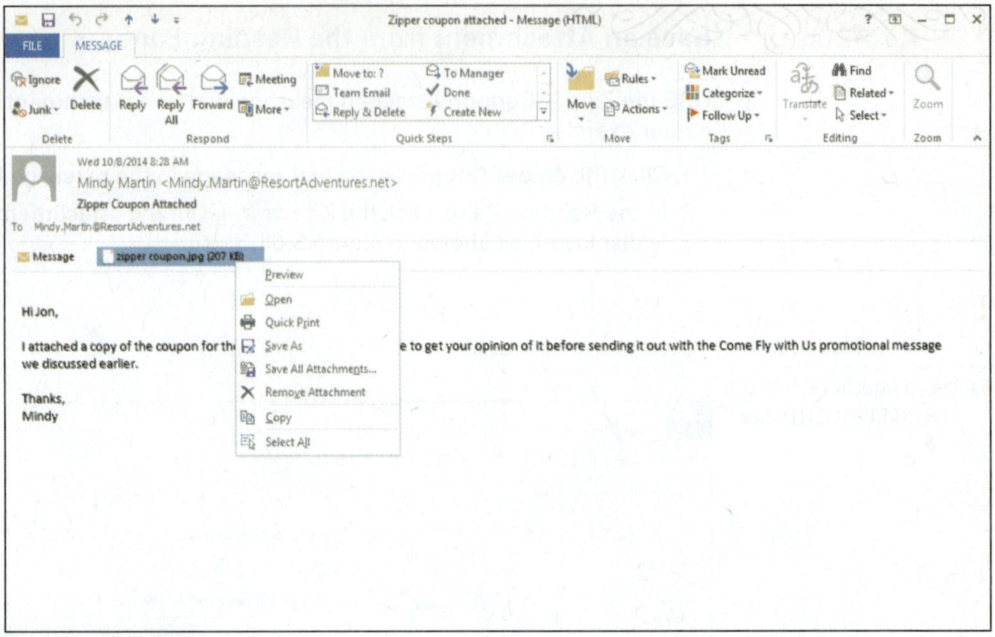

CERTIFICATION READY? 1.3.3

How do you save an attachment from a message?

3. Select **Save As** on the shortcut menu. The Save Attachment dialog box is displayed.

4. If necessary, navigate to the folder where you save your solution files. In the *File name* field, change the name of the file to **Zipper Coupon from Message Window**. Click the **Save** button.

5. Close the message window.

PAUSE. LEAVE Outlook open to use in the next exercise.

Opening an Email Attachment

You can open an attachment from the Reading Pane or from an open message. In the following exercise, you will open an attachment from each location.

STEP BY STEP   **Open an Email Attachment**

USE the *Promotional Message Attached* message and the *Zipper Coupon Attached* message with the attachment that you sent to yourself in an earlier exercise.

1. Click the **Promotional Message Attached** message in the message list.

2. In the Reading Pane, click the **Come Fly with Us** attachment icon. The Come Fly with Us message window is displayed in the Reading Pane.

⚠️ **Troubleshooting**   It is safer to save an attachment and scan the file with an antivirus software program before opening an attachment. Do not open attachments from unknown sources.

3. In the Reading Pane, double-click the **Come Fly with Us** attachment. The Come Fly with Us - Message window is displayed.

4. Close the message window.

5. In the message list, click on the **Zipper Coupon Attached** message.

6. In the Reading Pane, click the **Zipper Coupon attachment icon** once, and click **Open** on the ATTACHMENTS tab. The zipper coupon.jpg file opens in the default image viewing program, as shown in Figure 2-70.

Figure 2-70

Opening an attachment

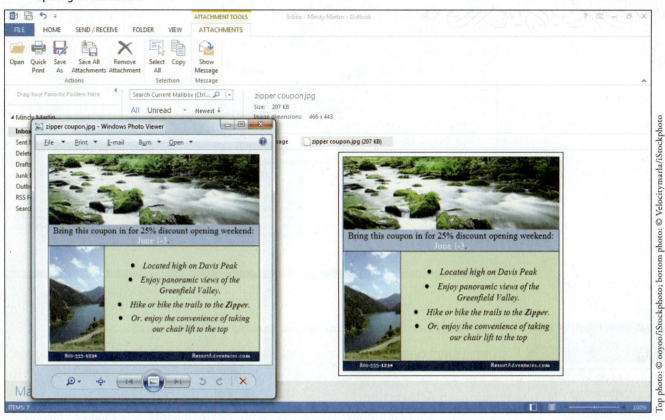

Figure 2-70

Opening an attachment

7. Close the image viewer.

PAUSE. LEAVE Outlook open to use in the next exercise.

Removing an Attachment

Removing an attachment is an easy process using the ATTACHMENTS tab. In this exercise, you'll remove an attachment from a message you received.

STEP BY STEP	Removing an Attachment

USE the *Promotional Message Attached* message with the attachment you sent to yourself in an earlier exercise.

1. In the message list, click the **Promotional Message Attached** message.
2. In the Reading Pane, click the **Come Fly with Us** attachment to display it in the Reading Pane.
3. Click the **Remove Attachment** button on the ATTACHMENTS tab. A confirmation dialog box is displayed, as shown in Figure 2-71.

Figure 2-71

Removing an attachment

Click to remove
the attached file

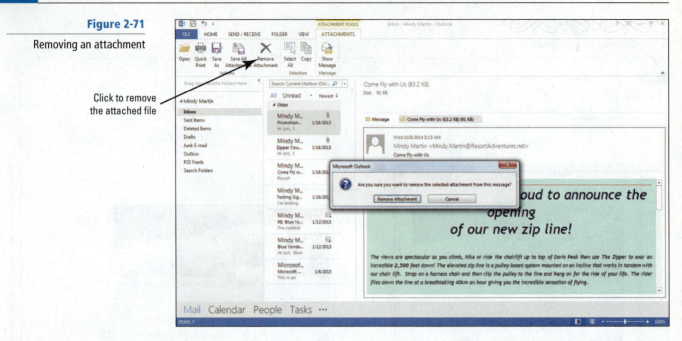

Figure 2-71

Removing an attachment

4. Click the **Remove Attachment** button. The attachment is deleted.

PAUSE. LEAVE Outlook open to use in the next exercise.

Printing an Attachment

Printing an attachment is simple once you've set up your default printer in Outlook. Just use the Quick Print tool on the ATTACHMENTS tab. In this exercise, you'll print an attachment from a message you received.

STEP BY STEP   **Printing an Attachment**

USE the *Zipper Coupon Attached* message with the attachment you sent to yourself in an earlier exercise. You need to have set up the printer in a previous exercise to complete this exercise.

1. Click the **Zipper Coupon Attached** message in the message list.
2. In the Reading Pane, click the ***Zipper Coupon.jpg*** attachment to display it in the Reading Pane.
3. Click the **Quick Print** button on the ATTACHMENTS tab.

PAUSE. LEAVE Outlook open to use in the next exercise.

If you have not set up a printer previously, you can still print an attachment. Just click the attachment icon in the Reading Pane, and click the Open button on the ATTACHMENTS tab to open the attachment in a new window. From there, click the FILE tab, and click the Print button in the Navigation Pane. In the Printer area, click the Printer dropdown arrow, and select the printer you would like to use.

SKILL SUMMARY

In This Lesson You Learned How To:	Exam Objective	Objective Number
Create Messages	Create messages	2.1.1
	Change text formats for all outgoing messages	1.1.2
Send a Message	Add cc and bcc to messages	2.1.5
Read and Respond to Messages	Reply to sender only	2.1.8
	Reply to all	2.1.7
	Forward messages	2.1.2
	Print messages	1.3.1
	Save messages in alternate formats	1.3.7
Format Messages	Format text	2.2.1
	Apply themes and styles	2.2.3
Personalize Messages	Create and assign signatures	1.2.2
	Format signatures	2.2.6
	Add a signature to specific messages	2.2.5
Work with Quick Parts	Create and use Quick Parts	2.2.7
Insert and Format Graphic Message Content	Insert images	2.2.4
	Insert hyperlinks	2.2.2
Work with Attachments	Add/remove message	2.1.4
	Set attachment reminder options	2.3.11
	Preview attachments	1.3.4
	Save message attachments	1.3.3

Knowledge Assessment

Multiple Choice

Select the letter of the text that best completes the following statements.

1. The _____ command can be used to save a copy of a message with a new file type and a new location.
   a. Print Preview
   b. Save New
   c. Save As
   d. Save

2. The _____ feature enables you to respond to messages from the Reading Pane.
   a. Instant Reply
   b. AutoReply
   c. Rapid Response
   d. Quick Response

3. Before a message can be sent, the _____ field(s) must be filled in.
   a. To
   b. From
   c. Cc
   d. A and C

4. You can quickly add a saved section of text to a message by selecting it from the _____.
   a. Quick Parts gallery
   b. Drafts Organizer
   c. Data Blocks Organizer
   d. Text Parts gallery

5. Text or images that are automatically placed at the end of your outgoing messages are called _____.
   a. signatures
   b. stationery
   c. templates
   d. Quick Parts

6. The _____ describes what the message is about.
   a. Reference
   b. Reply
   c. Subject
   d. Topic

7. To preview a style or theme _____.
   a. It is not possible to preview a style or theme.
   b. print the document
   c. place your pointer over the choice
   d. use Print Preview

8. A file sent as part of an email message is called a(n) _____.
   a. add on
   b. attachment
   c. enclosure
   d. supplement

9. A theme includes sets of _____.
   a. Effects
   b. Fonts
   c. Colors
   d. All of the above

10. Use the _____ tab to alter the look of a graphic in a message.
    a. Graphic Tools Format tab
    b. PICTURE TOOLS FORMAT tab
    c. Format
    d. Format Images tab

True/False

Circle T if the statement is true or F if the statement is false.

T F **1.** The PICTURE TOOLS FORMAT tab only appears when a picture is selected.

T F **2.** Use the Message window to compose and send an email message.

T F **3.** The Attachment Reminder reminds you to follow up on an attachment that you received.

T F **4.** You can add clip art to a message by clicking the Online Pictures button on the INSERT tab and then entering a search term.

T F **5.** You can restore a picture to its original formatting without reverting to a saved file.

T F **6.** Use the Building Blocks feature to insert a block of saved text or images to the body of a message.

T F **7.** If you have a personal signature, it can be used as the default mailbox to save time.

T F **8.** To send a message to several recipients, key a semicolon (;) after a name before adding the next addressee.

T F **9.** When you make changes to the colors, fonts, or effects of the current theme, you permanently change the original theme.

T F **10.** A Quick Response button allows you to reply to a message from the Reading Pane.

Project 2-1: Create an Email Message

Send an email message to a friend inviting him to lunch next Friday.

GET READY. LAUNCH Outlook if it is not already running.

1. On the HOME tab, click the New Email button to open a new Message window.
2. Key [a friend's email address] in the *To* field. If you are not completing these exercises with a friend or coworker, key [your email address] in the *To* field. This will give you a message to reply to in the next exercise.
3. In the *Subject* field, key Lunch tomorrow?
4. Click in the message area. Key Hi, [press Enter twice].
5. Key How about lunch next Friday? [Press Enter twice]. Key [your first name].
6. Click the Send button.

LEAVE Outlook open for the next project.

Project 2-2: Reply to a Friend's Email Message

Reply to a friend's lunch request.

USE the email you received at the end of Project 2-1 before starting this project.

1. If the message sent in Project 2-1 has not arrived, click the Send/Receive All Folders button on the SEND/RECEIVE tab.
2. In the message list, click the message sent in Project 2-1.
3. Click the Reply button in the Respond group.
4. Key Sure. Let's eat at the plaza. Could you pick me up here at 11:30? [Press Enter twice.] Key [your name] [press Enter twice].
5. Key We are conveniently located in Rustic Oaks, OH at the corner of Beecher Lane and Route 92.
6. Select the text typed in step 5 and on the FORMAT TEXT tab, click Center in the Paragraph group and Italic in the Font group.
7. With the text still selected, click Quick Parts in the Text group on the INSERT tab.
8. Select Save Selection to Quick Part Gallery.
9. In the Create New Building Block dialog box, in the Name box, key Directions and click OK.
10. Click the Send button.
11. Click the Send/Receive All Folders button.
12. In the message list, select the reply message.
13. Click the FILE tab and select the Save As option. The Save As dialog box is displayed.
14. Navigate to your solutions folder for Lesson 2, and save the message as *RE Lunch tomorrow.htm*.

LEAVE Outlook open for the next project.

Proficiency Assessment

Project 2-3: Insert Pictures and Clip Art

Resort Adventures is in the process of putting together a new brochure to publicize the resort's ski facilities. Create a new email message to a colleague containing two pictures and two clip art images.

GET READY. LAUNCH Outlook if it is not already running.

1. Create a new email message and address it to yourself.
2. In the *Subject* field, key **Ski Images**.
3. On the INSERT tab, click **Pictures**.
4. Navigate to the data files for Lesson 2 and insert *Ski 1.jpg*. Press **Enter** twice.
5. On the INSERT tab, click **Online Pictures**. The Insert Pictures dialog box opens.
6. Key **skiing** in the *Search Office.com* field, and click the **magnifying glass** icon.
7. Scroll through the search results, click a drawing you like that represents skiing, and click **Insert**.
8. Save the message to your Drafts folder in Outlook and close the message.

LEAVE Outlook open for the next project.

Project 2-4: Format and Reset a Picture to Its Original State

Apply formatting to the images in your Ski Images message. You'll then reset one of the images back to its original state.

USE the email you created at the end of Project 2-4 in this lesson.

1. Open the **Ski Images** message in the Drafts folder.
2. Click the first picture. On the PICTURE TOOLS FORMAT tab, in the Picture Styles group, select the Simple Frame, Black picture style.
3. Change the height to **4"**.
4. Click the **Picture Border** button, and select **Red** in the Standard Colors.
5. In the Picture Border menu, select **Weight** and click **2¼ pt**.
6. Click **Crop** and crop excess from each side of the image. Place the crop tool at the lower-right corner and drag up into the picture. Click **Crop** to complete the crop.
7. Select the second picture. In the Picture Styles group, select a style with a Drop Shadow.
8. Click **Color** and select **Blue, Accent color 1 Light**.
9. Save the message as *Ski Images.htm*.
10. Select the second picture and click **Reset Picture**.
11. Send the message.

LEAVE Outlook open for the next project.

Project 2-5: Create a Custom Theme

Blue Yonder Airlines has decided to give all their documents a branded look by creating a new custom theme to be used for all client-facing business documents.

GET READY. LAUNCH Outlook if it is not already running.

1. Open a new email message, and address it to **someone@example.com**.
2. In the *Subject* field, key **Custom Theme for Blue Yonder Airlines**.
3. On the OPTIONS tab, choose a custom set of colors, fonts, and/or effects that you feel would be a good choice for Blue Yonder Airlines.
4. Save the theme as **Custom_xxx** (where *xxx* are your initials).
5. Key a short paragraph explaining that you are creating a custom theme. Include a bulleted list outlining which colors, fonts, or effects you used. Format the paragraph with your custom theme.
6. Create a custom signature named **Blue Yonder**, and insert it into the message.
7. **SAVE** the message in Outlook Message Format as **Custom Theme for Blue Yonder Airlines**, and then click **Send**.

LEAVE Outlook open for the next project.

Project 2-6: Send an Attachment

The last guest in the best suite at Resort Adventures accidentally broke the stained-glass window. You must replace the window before you can accept any reservations for the suite.

GET READY. LAUNCH Outlook if it is not already running.

1. Create a new email message to Nancy Anderson at the Graphic Design Institute. Nancy's email address is Nancy@graphicdesigninstitute.com.
2. Ask Nancy if she can design a window similar to the stained-glass window that was broken. Ask Nancy how long the project will take and how much it will cost.
3. Attach the *Window.jpg* file located in the data files for this lesson.
4. Be sure to include the signature you created earlier in this lesson (not the signature from Project 2-5).
5. At the bottom of the message, insert the **Directions** Quick Part.
6. Save a copy of the message in Outlook Message format; then send the message.

CLOSE Outlook.

3 Advanced E-mail Tools

LESSON SKILL MATRIX

Skill	Exam Objective	Objective Number
Managing Automatic Message Handling	Set Outlook options	1.1.7
	Include original messages with all reply messages	1.1.1
Automating Message Format	Change quoted text colors	1.2.1
	Change text formats for all outgoing messages	1.1.2
Using Message Options	Prioritize messages	2.1.9
	Configure reminders	3.3.3
	Manage multiple accounts	1.1.6
	Request delivery/read receipt	2.1.11
	Redirect replies	2.1.12
Working with Voting Options	Add voting options to messages	2.1.6
Working with Security	Mark as private	2.1.10
Locating Messages	Sort messages	2.3.1
	Search for messages	1.4.2
	Use search by location	1.4.7
Printing Multiple Messages	Print messages	1.3.1

KEY TERMS

- **attribute**
- **delivery receipt**
- **digital ID**
- **digital signature**
- **encryption**
- **InfoBar**
- **Instant Search**
- **private key**
- **public key**
- **read receipt**
- **sensitivity**
- **theme**

© Gorfer/iStockphoto

© Gorfer/iStockphoto

Business is booming. Mindy and Jon have accepted reservations for several major events to be held at Resort Adventures. Two weddings, a company retreat, and a confidential marketing meeting for a major toy company have been scheduled for next month. As the dates for the events get closer, e-mail messages have been flying. The toy company insists on using security features, such as a digital ID, for all e-mail communications. One of the ways that Outlook 2013 helps you save time is by allowing you to automate how Outlook creates and processes messages. In this lesson, you'll use some of the advanced Microsoft Outlook e-mail tools to take advantage of this capability as you finalize arrangements for the new clients.

SOFTWARE ORIENTATION

The Microsoft Outlook Mail Options

Many of the advanced e-mail options in Microsoft Outlook are set through the Mail Options page of the Outlook Options dialog box, as shown in Figure 3-1.

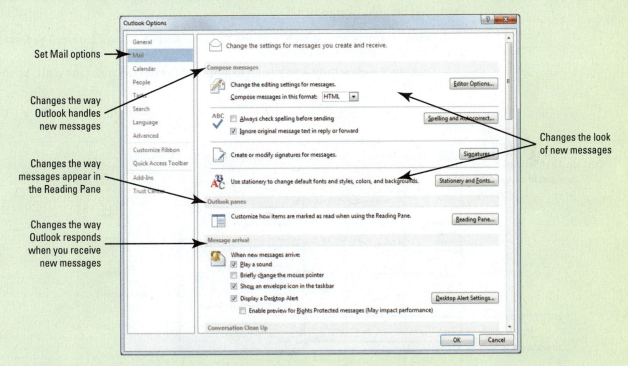

Figure 3-1

The Mail Options page of the Outlook Options dialog box

The advanced mail options in Microsoft Outlook enable you to change the way Outlook formats each message so that it best suits you and your business.

MANAGING AUTOMATIC MESSAGE HANDLING

The Bottom Line

You can use Outlook Options dialog box to control many of the settings and options that Outlook uses to determine how to handle e-mail messages you create and receive. You can use these options to control how messages are sent and received, as well as how they are tracked and saved.

Setting Mail Options

When you open the Outlook Options dialog box and click Mail in the Navigation Pane, the Mail Options page is displayed. You can adjust the Mail Options to have Outlook automatically save your messages, notify you when new mail arrives, check spelling in messages, and more. In this exercise, you'll learn how to set Outlook Mail options.

STEP BY STEP   **Set Mail Options**

GET READY. LAUNCH Outlook if it is not already running.

1. Click the **FILE** tab to open the Backstage view, then select **Options** on its Navigation Pane to display the Outlook Options dialog box.

2. Click **Mail** on the left Navigation Pane. The Mail Options page of the Outlook Options dialog box is displayed, as shown in Figure 3-1.

Take Note   Steps 3–7 only apply to users running Windows 7. Desktop alert options are not displayed in Outlook 2013 on Windows 8 operating system; instead, the defualt Windows 8 notification is used to alert of incoming e-mail messages. If you are running Windows 8 (or don't see the Desktop Alert Setting), skip to step 8.

3. In the Message arrival area, click the **Desktop Alert Settings** button. The Desktop Alert Settings dialog box is displayed.

4. Click the **Preview** button to see an example of the default message alert, as shown in Figure 3-2.

Figure 3-2

Desktop Alert Settings dialog box and Message Alert preview

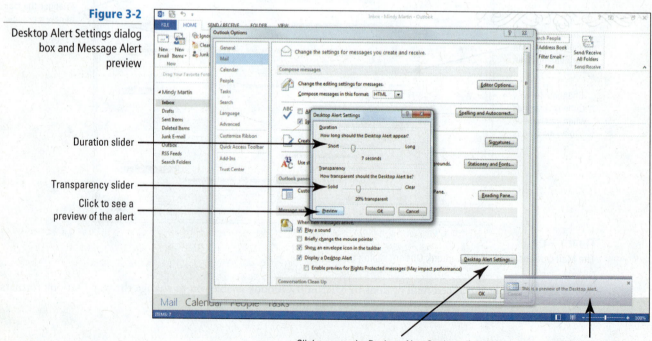

Duration slider

Transparency slider

Click to see a preview of the alert

Click to open the Desktop Alert Settings dialog box

Message alert

5. Change the alert Duration slider to **10 seconds** and change the alert Transparency slider to **15% transparent**.

6. Click the **Preview** button to see how your changes affected the message alert box.

7. Click **OK** to apply your changes and close the Desktop Alert Settings dialog box.

8. Scroll down to the Save messages area of the Mail Options page and change the Automatically save items that have not been sent after this many minutes option to reflect **1 minute**.

9. Click **OK** to save your changes, close the Outlook Options dialog box, and return to the main Mail window.

10. Click the **New E-mail** button on the HOME tab. The Untitled – Message (HTML) window is displayed.

11. In the *To* field, key **someone@example.com**. In the *Subject* field, key **This is a Timed Test** and press **Tab**.

12. Minimize the *This is a Timed Test – Message* window.

13. Click **Drafts** in the Folders List to open the Drafts folder. After a minute the *This is a Timed Test* message will appear in the Drafts folder.

14. Close the *This is a Timed Test* message window, and click **No** when prompted whether to save changes. Notice that the message disappears from the Drafts folder.

15. Click the **FILE tab** to open the Backstage view, and open the Mail Options page of the Outlook Options dialog box.

16. In the Save messages area, change the Automatically save items that have not been sent after this many minutes option back to **3 minutes**.

17. Click **OK** to save your changes.

PAUSE. LEAVE Outlook open to use in the next exercise.

Specifying Options for Replies and Forwards

You can also use the Mail Options page to control how Outlook handles messages when you send replies or when you forward a message to someone. These options include things like determining whether you want Outlook to include the text of an original message when you send a reply and where you want Outlook to store your reply messages. In this exercise, explore the default way that Outlook handles replies and forwards.

STEP BY STEP **Specify Options for Replies and Forwards**

GET READY. LAUNCH Outlook if it is not already running.

1. Click **Inbox** in the Folders List to open the default Mail folder.

2. Double-click on your **Microsoft Outlook Test Message**. The Microsoft Outlook Test Message window is displayed.

⚠ **Troubleshooting** If you don't have a Microsoft Outlook Test Message in your inbox, you can open any received message for this exercise.

3. Click **Reply** on the MESSAGE tab. By default, when you reply to a message or forward it to someone else, Outlook keeps the original message open and includes the text from the original message at the bottom of the new message window. A new RE: Microsoft Outlook Test Message window is displayed on top of the original message, as shown in Figure 3-3.

Figure 3-3

Outlook's default reply handling

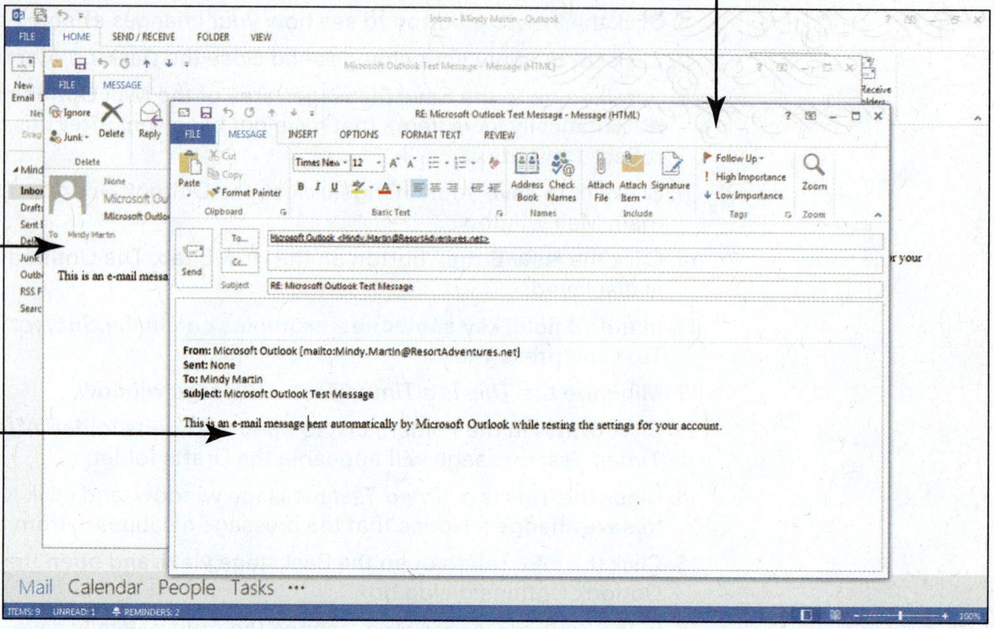

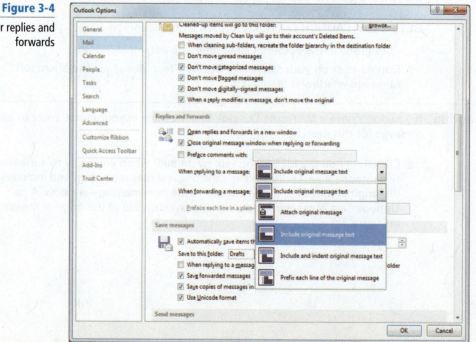

New message window for replies

Original message

Text from the original message

> **Troubleshooting**   If you see a Bcc button on the Microsoft Outlook Text Message – Message (HTML) window, don't be surprised. Since you added the Bcc button in Lesson 2, Outlook will remember to keep adding it to each Message window until you turn this option off on the Message window's OPTIONS tab.

4. Close the open message windows.

5. Click the **FILE tab** to open Backstage view, and select **Options** on its Navigation Pane to display the Outlook Options dialog box.

6. Click **Mail** on the left Navigation Pane. The Mail options page of the Outlook Options dialog box is displayed. Scroll down to see the options for Replies and Forwards.

7. In the Replies and Forwards area, click the **Close original message window when replying or forwarding** check box to activate this option.

8. Click the **When forwarding a message** dropdown arrow. A list of options is displayed, as shown in Figure 3-4.

Figure 3-4

Setting options for replies and forwards

9. Select **Attach original message** and click **OK** to apply your changes and close the Outlook Options dialog box.

10. Double-click the **Microsoft Outlook Test Message** window to display it again.

11. Click the **Forward** button on the MESSAGE tab. The original message window closes and the FW: Microsoft Outlook Test Message – Message window is displayed. Notice that the original message now appears as an attachment. Close the window without saving changes.

12. Click the **FILE tab** to open the Backstage view. Open the Outlook Options dialog box, and click **Mail** in the Navigation Pane.

13. In the Replies and Forwards area of the Mail page, deselect the **Close original message window when replying or forwarding** option.

14. Click the **When forwarding a message** dropdown arrow. Select **Include original message text**.

15. Click **OK** to restore the default settings.

PAUSE. LEAVE Outlook open to use in the next exercise.

AUTOMATING MESSAGE FORMAT

You can use the Microsoft Outlook Mail Options to create a format for all new messages, complete with background, colors, and fonts. Creating a default format for all messages provides continuity and a professional finish to your messages without requiring you to spend time formatting each message.

Specifying the Default Font for New Messages

In the previous lesson, you learned how to format your message content to make it more appealing and professional looking. You may want to streamline that process by choosing a default font for all new messages. You can also set options to change the color of text for replies and forwards. In this exercise, you'll specify the font to use for new messages.

Specify the Default Font for New Messages

GET READY. LAUNCH Outlook if it is not already running.

1. Click the **FILE tab** and select **Options** in the Backstage view Navigation Pane to display the Outlook Options dialog box.

2. Click **Mail** on the left Navigation Pane. The Mail Options page of the Outlook Options dialog box is displayed.

3. In the Compose Messages area, click the **Stationery and Fonts** button. The Signatures and Stationery dialog box is displayed, as shown in Figure 3-5.

Figure 3-5

The Signatures and Stationery dialog box

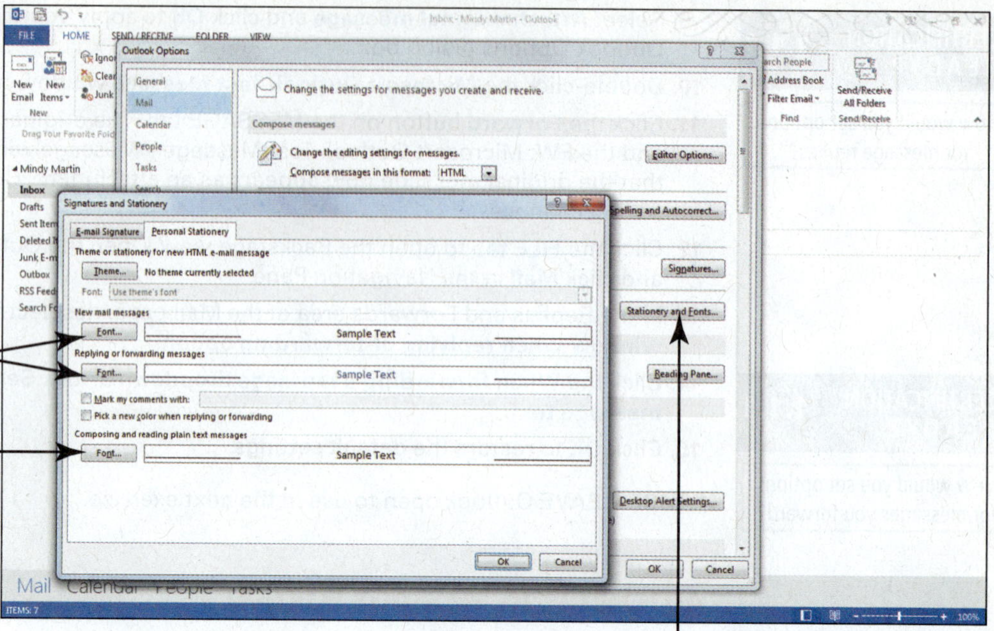

Set default font for HTML messages

Set default font for Plain Text messages

Click to open the Signatures and Stationery dialog box

4. In the *New Mail Messages* area, click the **Font** button. The Font dialog box is displayed.
5. In the Font box, select **Century Schoolbook**.
6. Click the **Font Color** dropdown arrow and select **Green, Accent 6, Darker 50%**.
7. Click **OK** to apply your changes and close the Font dialog box.
8. In the *Replying or Forwarding Messages* area of the Signatures and Stationery dialog box, click the **Font** button. The Font dialog box is displayed. The settings you change here will affect the way the text that is quoted from the original message appears when you reply to a message or forward it. It only affects the way that original message text appears in your new message; it does not affect the original message itself.
9. Click the **Font Color** dropdown arrow and select **Dark Red**. Click **OK**.
10. In the *Composing and reading plain text messages* area, click the **Font** button and select **Arial**. Click **OK**.
11. Notice the change in the *Sample Text* boxes.
12. Click **Cancel** to close both dialog boxes without saving the changes.

CERTIFICATION READY? 1.2.1

How would you change the color of quoted text?

PAUSE. LEAVE Outlook open to use in the next exercise.

CERTIFICATION READY? 1.1.7

How would you change the default font of a new message?

Setting a Default Theme for All New HTML Messages

In Outlook 2013, you can specify a default theme for all the new HTML messages you create. In Outlook, **themes** are a set of formatting choices that include colors, fonts (including heading and body text fonts), and theme effects (including lines and fill effects). In this exercise, you'll specify a new default theme to use for future messages and create a test message to see how your new theme looks.

STEP BY STEP **Set a Default Theme for All New HTML Messages**

GET READY. LAUNCH Outlook if it is not already running.

1. Select **Options** on the Backstage view Navigation Pane to display the Outlook Options dialog box.
2. Click **Mail** on the left Navigation Pane to display the Mail options page of the Outlook Options dialog box.

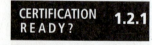

3. In the Compose Messages area, click the **Stationery and Fonts** button. The Signatures and Stationery dialog box is displayed (refer to Figure 3-5).

4. In the *Theme or stationery for new HTML e-mail message* area, click the **Theme** button. The Theme or Stationery dialog box is displayed.

5. Click **Garden (Stationery)** in the *Choose a Theme* box. Notice the change in the Sample window. Selecting one of the options marked by *(Stationery)* will set the default background, or stationery, for all of your future HTML messages.

6. Scroll through a variety of options and then select the **Afternoon** theme, as shown in Figure 3-6. Selecting one of the options without *(Stationery)* will set the default theme for all of your future HTML messages.

Figure 3-6

The Theme or Stationery dialog box

Specifies the default theme

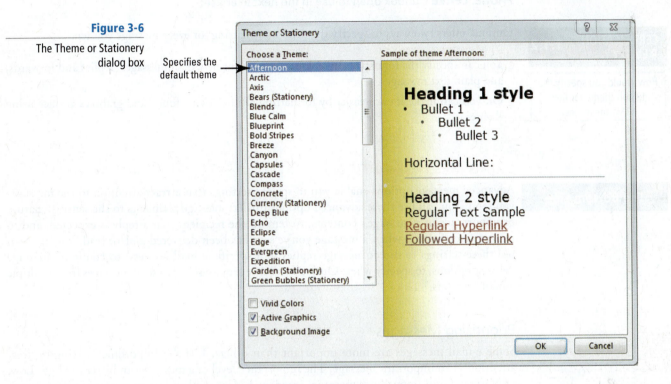

7. Click **OK** to apply the new theme and close the Theme or Stationery dialog box. Click **OK** to close the Signatures and Stationery dialog box, and click **OK** again to close the Outlook Options dialog box.

Take Note Each theme has an associated font. If you want to override the theme's font, you can select *Use my font when replying and forwarding messages* or *Always use my fonts* from the Font dropdown under the selected Theme in the Signatures and Stationery dialog box.

8. In the main Mail window, click the **New E-Mail** button on the HOME tab. The Untitled—Message window is displayed.

Take Note Throughout this chapter you will see information that appears in black text within brackets, such as [Press **Enter**], or [**your e-mail address**]. The information contained in the brackets is intended to be directions for you rather than something you actually type word for word. It will instruct you to perform an action or substitute text. Do **not** type the actual text that appears within brackets.

9. In the *To* field, key [**your e-mail address or the address of someone you know**]. In the Subject field, key **Sample Theme**.

10. In the Message area, key **This is a sample of the Afternoon theme**.

11. Click the **FILE tab** to open the Backstage view and then click **Save As**. The Save As dialog box is displayed, showing the Documents folder.

12. Navigate to the Outlook Lesson 3 folder. You can also choose a folder in which to store the file from the Folders List.

13. In the *Save As type* box, click the **downward-pointing arrow** and choose **HTML (*.htm, *.html)**. Click **Save**.

14. Click the **FILE tab** and select **Options**, then **Mail**. The Mail options page is displayed.

15. Click the **Stationery and Fonts** button. Click the Theme . . . button in the Signatures and Stationery dialog box, and then select (No Theme) in the Choose a Theme box in the Theme or Stationery dialog box.

16. Click **OK** three times to close all the open dialog boxes and restore the default settings.

17. Close the sample theme window. Click No when asked to save changes.

PAUSE. LEAVE Outlook open to use in the next exercise.

Outlook offers two ways to specify the default formatting for every message you send.

CERTIFICATION READY?   **1.1.2**

How would you specify the default theme for new HTML messages?

- You can specify the font style and color to be used for new mail messages, replies and forwards, and plain text messages.
- Or, you can make it even easier by formatting all the colors, fonts, and graphics at once using themes.

USING MESSAGE OPTIONS

The Bottom Line

Advanced message options enable you to specify settings that attract attention to the messages you send. You can use these advanced options to alert message recipients to the sensitive nature or importance of a message's contents, to remind the recipient that a reply is expected, and to trigger a notification when a message you've sent has been delivered and/or read. You also can use these settings to direct message replies to a specific e-mail address, to configure message delivery options, to specify where Outlook will save sent items, or to send messages from multiple e-mail accounts.

Prioritizing Messages

Some e-mail messages are more important than others. Use the Importance setting to draw attention to an important message. The importance level of a message can be set to High, Low, or Normal. High-importance messages are identified by a red exclamation point in the message list and noted in the message InfoBar. An **InfoBar** is a banner containing information added automatically at the top of a message. Low-importance messages are marked with a blue down arrow in the message list and noted in the InfoBar. Normal-importance messages are not marked. In this exercise, you'll create a sample message with a high importance level.

STEP BY STEP   **Prioritize Messages**

GET READY. LAUNCH Outlook if it is not already running.

1. If necessary, click the **Mail** button in the Navigation Pane to display the Mail folder.

2. Click the **New E-mail** button on the HOME tab. The Message window is displayed. By default, the MESSAGE tab is selected.

3. Click the **High Importance** button in the Tags group.

4. In the message area, key **Sample important message**.

5. In the *To* field, key **[your e-mail address]**. In the *Subject* field, key **Sample Important Message**, as shown in Figure 3-7.

Another Way
Select the importance in the message Properties dialog box.

Figure 3-7

Creating an important message

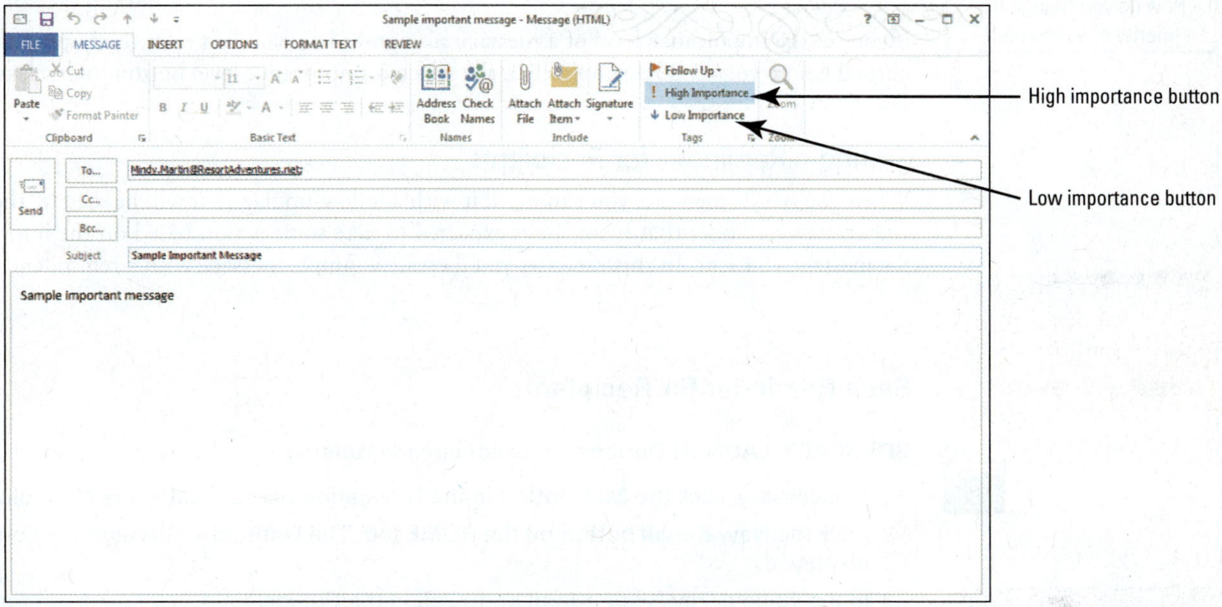

High importance button

Low importance button

6. Click the **Send** button. The message is moved to the Outbox, and it is sent when your computer is connected to the Internet.

7. Return to your Inbox, and click the **Send/Receive All Folders** button if the message has not arrived yet.

8. Select the new message, which is flagged with a red exclamation mark in your Inbox list. The text *This message was sent with High importance* appears in the InfoBar at the top of the message in the Reading Pane, as shown in Figure 3-8.

Figure 3-8

Important message received

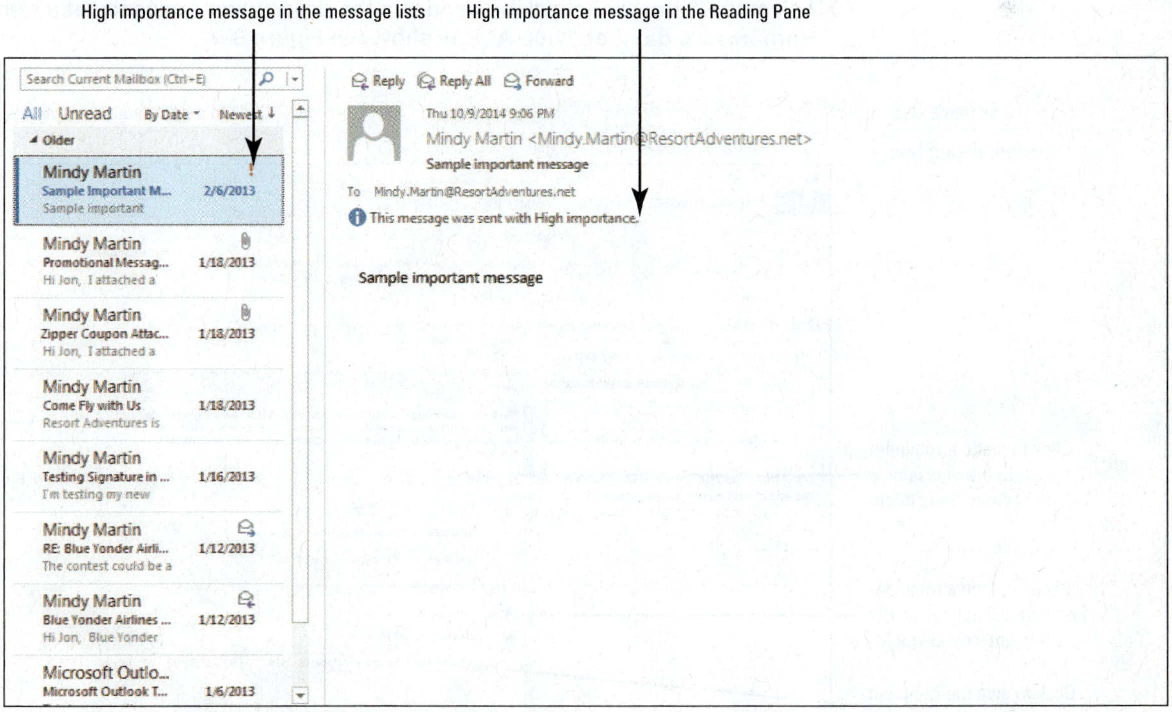

High importance message in the message lists   High importance message in the Reading Pane

PAUSE. LEAVE Outlook open to use in the next exercise.

CERTIFICATION
READY?   **2.1.9**

How do you change the
priority of a message?

In this exercise, you saw that an InfoBar was added to the High Importance message. The messages are handled the same as any other message you send—the text in the InfoBar is the only difference (in addition to the red exclamation mark).

If you set the importance level of a message to high or low, you can reset the importance level to normal before you send it. Simply click the selected Importance level button to deselect it.

Setting a Reminder for Recipients

When you send a message, you can mark it with a follow-up flag that will be seen by the recipient and act as a reminder that he or she is expected to take some action based on the information in the message you sent. In this exercise, you'll create a sample message with a reminder.

STEP BY STEP   **Set a Reminder for Recipients**

GET READY. LAUNCH Outlook if it is not already running.

1. If necessary, click the **Mail** button in the Navigation bar to display the Mail folder.

2. Click the **New E-mail** button on the HOME tab. The Untitled – Message window is displayed.

3. In the *To* field, key [**your e-mail address**]. In the *Subject* field, key **Lunch Tomorrow with Alan Brewer**.

4. In the message area, key the following message: **Don't forget lunch tomorrow with Alan Brewer from Fabrikam, Inc. He wants to discuss arrangements for the conference scheduled for our Blue Conference Room at the end of next month. Come prepared!**

Take Note   No all e-mail accounts in Outlook 2013 will have the Custom option. If you don't see the custom option, you are likely using an IMAP or Exchange e-mail account that doesn't support this option. If you don't see the Custom option, skip ahead to the end of this exercise.

5. In the Tags group on the MESSAGE tab, click the **Follow Up** dropdown button and select **Custom** from the dropdown menu to select additional options.

6. Click the **Flag for Recipients** option.

7. Select the **Reminder** check box and use the drop-down boxes to set a reminder for [**tomorrow's date**] at **11:00 AM**, as shown in Figure 3-9.

Figure 3-9

Custom dialog box

Click to select reminder options

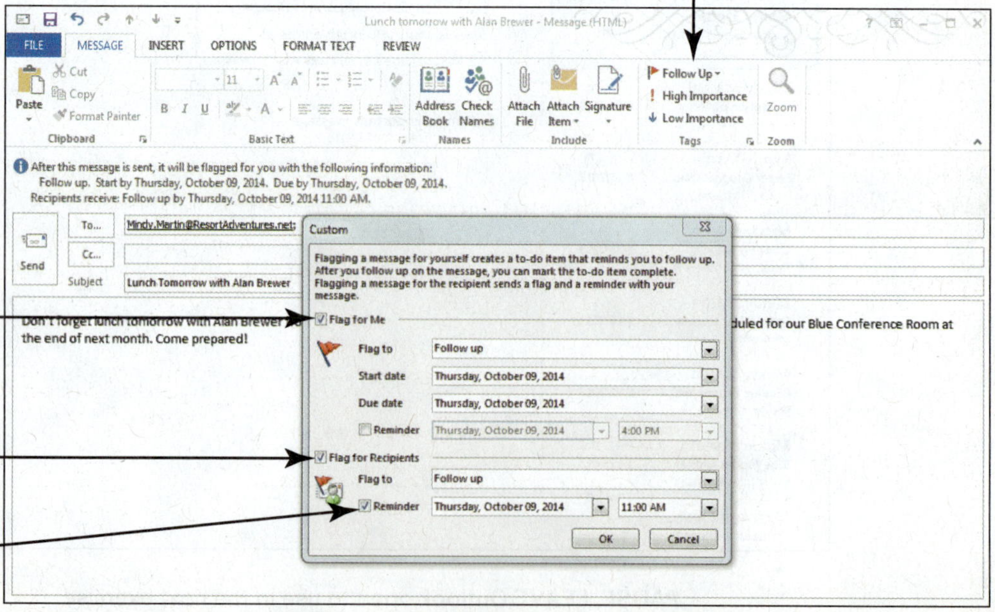

Click to place a reminder flag on the message in your Sent Items folder

Click to place a reminder flag that will appear on the recipient's message list

Click to give the recipient a Reminder window

8. Click **OK** to save the settings. The dialog box is closed. As shown in Figure 3-10, the InfoBar in the message you're creating indicates that the recipient will receive the Follow-Up flag.

Figure 3-10

Creating a message with reminder for a recipient

InfoBar indicates that this message will be flagged for follow-up for the recipient

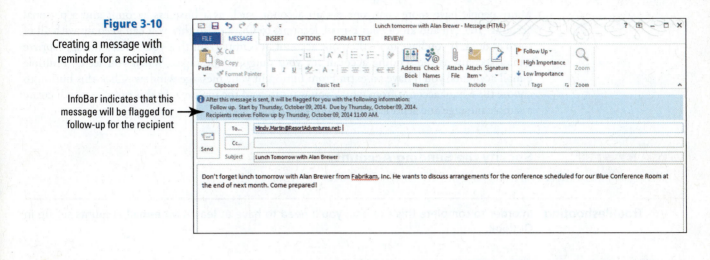

> **Troubleshooting** The text *After this message is sent, it will be flagged for you with the following information* in the InfoBar appears while the message is being composed. This text is not displayed to the recipient.

9. Click the **Send** button. The message is moved to the Outbox and it is sent when your computer is connected to the Internet.

PAUSE. LEAVE Outlook open to use in the next exercise.

When the computer is connected to the Internet and a message is sent, the message in the Sent Items folder will have a flag, as shown in Figure 3-11.

Figure 3-11

Sent message with follow-up flag for the recipient

Icon indicates that the sent message contains a flag

Follow up flag for the message

Follow up message in Reading Pane

How do you configure a reminder for the recipient of a message?

When the message arrives in the recipient's Inbox, the message is marked by a flag, as shown in Figure 3-12. This draws attention to the message and indicates that some action might be required. A flag set by a sender contains a small silhouette, making it look different from a flag you set for yourself. If the recipient clicks the flag in the message list, it is added to the recipient's task list.

Figure 3-12

Received message with follow-up flag set by the sender

Indicates that message was sent with a flag

Cross Ref   You can find more information about tasks in Lesson 11.

Specifying the Sending Account

Many people have more than one e-mail account, such as a business account and a personal account. You can add all of your e-mail accounts to Outlook so that you can keep up with all of them at once. If you have more than one account, it is important that you specify the appropriate e-mail account as the sending account for your outgoing messages. When you set up multiple e-mail accounts, you'll have an extra From button in your message window. Click this button to choose the e-mail account from which you want to send the message. In this exercise, you'll create a sample message and send it from an alternate e-mail address.

STEP BY STEP   **Specify the Sending Account**

⚠️ **Troubleshooting**   In order to complete this exercise, you'll need to have at least two e-mail accounts set up in Outlook.

GET READY. LAUNCH Outlook if it is not already running and be sure that you have more than one e-mail account set up.

1. Click the **New E-mail** button on the HOME tab. The Message window is displayed.
2. Click the **From** button shown in Figure 3-13. A dropdown list is displayed showing each of your e-mail accounts.

Figure 3-13

Selecting a sending account

The sending email address

Click to select an alternate sending account

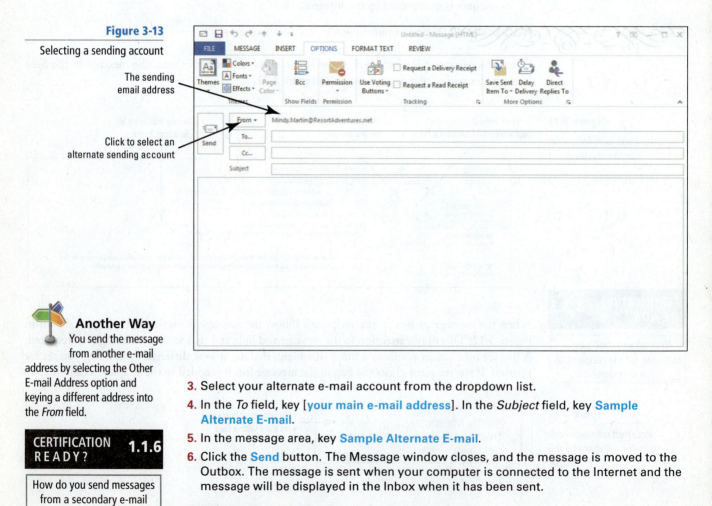

Another Way
You send the message from another e-mail address by selecting the Other E-mail Address option and keying a different address into the *From* field.

3. Select your alternate e-mail account from the dropdown list.
4. In the *To* field, key [**your main e-mail address**]. In the *Subject* field, key **Sample Alternate E-mail**.
5. In the message area, key **Sample Alternate E-mail**.
6. Click the **Send** button. The Message window closes, and the message is moved to the Outbox. The message is sent when your computer is connected to the Internet and the message will be displayed in the Inbox when it has been sent.

CERTIFICATION READY?   **1.1.6**

How do you send messages from a secondary e-mail account?

PAUSE. LEAVE Outlook open to use in the next exercise.

SOFTWARE ORIENTATION

The Microsoft Outlook Message OPTIONS Tab

The mail component in Microsoft Outlook 2013 can do more than just send basic e-mail messages. Many of the advanced e-mail options in Microsoft Outlook are set through the New Message window's OPTIONS tab, shown in Figure 3-14.

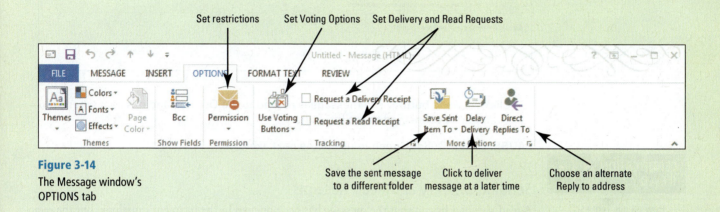

Figure 3-14
The Message window's OPTIONS tab

The advanced options in Microsoft Outlook enable you to change the message settings, address security issues, vote for selected items, set tracking options, and determine delivery options.

Requesting Delivery and Read Receipts

Did your client get that important message? Requesting delivery and read receipts takes the mystery out of sending a message because you will know that the message was delivered to the recipient and opened for reading. A **delivery receipt** tells you that the message has arrived in the recipient's mailbox; the message has been delivered. A delivery receipt does not guarantee that the recipient has opened or read the message. A **read receipt** tells you that the message has been opened in the recipient's mailbox. In this exercise, you'll send a sample message with a delivery and read receipt request.

Request Delivery and Read Receipts

GET READY. LAUNCH Outlook if it is not already running.

1. If necessary, click the **Mail** button on the Navigation bar to display the Mail folder.
2. Click the **New E-mail** button on the HOME tab. The Message window is displayed. By default, the MESSAGE tab is selected.
3. In the *To* field, key [**your e-mail address**]. In the *Subject* field, key **Sample Delivery Receipt and Read Receipt**.
4. In the message area, key **Sample delivery receipt and read receipt**.
5. Click the **OPTIONS** tab on the Ribbon.
6. In the Tracking group, click the **Request a Delivery Receipt** and the **Request a Read Receipt** check boxes, as shown in Figure 3-15.

Another Way
Click the Request a delivery receipt for this message check box and click the Request a read receipt for this message check box in the Properties dialog box.

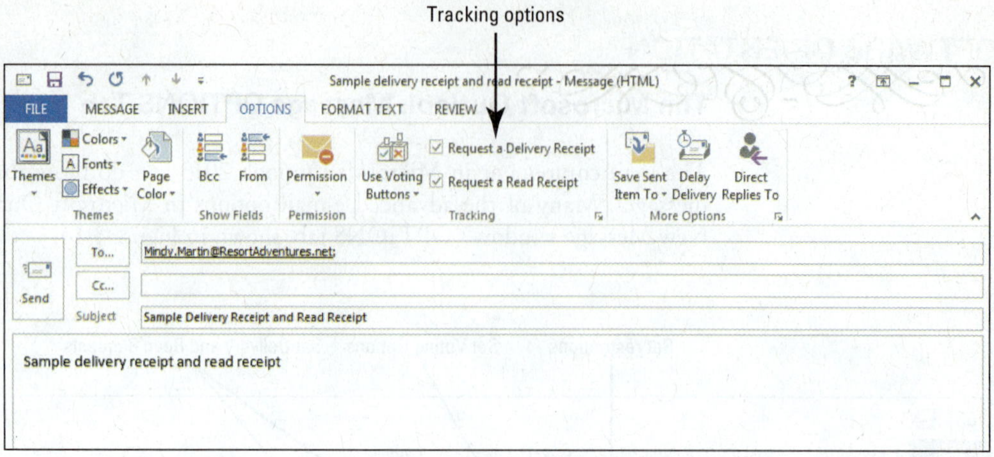

Figure 3-15

Creating a message requesting
a delivery receipt and
a read receipt

Tracking options

7. Click the **Send** button. The message is moved to the Outbox, and it is sent when your computer is connected to the Internet.

PAUSE. LEAVE Outlook open to use in the next exercise.

CERTIFICATION
READY? **2.1.11**

How do you request a
delivery or read receipt?

Sending Delivery and Read Receipts

A read receipt tells you that the message has been opened in the recipient's mailbox, but the recipient can choose whether to send a read receipt or not. In this exercise, you'll send a read receipt and a delivery receipt.

STEP BY STEP **Sending Delivery and Read Receipts**

GET READY. LAUNCH Outlook if it is not already running.

1. If necessary, click the **Mail** button on the Navigation bar to display the Mail folder. If you have not received the *Sample Delivery Receipt and Read Receipt* message, click the **Send/Receive All Folders** button on the Quick Access Toolbar.

2. Double click on the **Sample Delivery Receipt and Read Receipt** e-mail in the message list. Outlook displays a message notifying you that the sender requested a read receipt and asking whether you would like to send one, as shown in Figure 3-16.

Figure 3-16

Recipient can choose to send a
read receipt

3. Click **Yes** to send the read receipt. The warning message closes and the Sample Delivery Receipt and Read Receipt message window opens.

4. Click on the **Read: Sample Delivery Receipt and Read Receipt** e-mail in the message list. If you have not received the message, click the **Send/Receive All Folders** button on the Quick Access Toolbar. The read receipt appears in the Reading Pane notifying you when your message was received and opened, as shown in Figure 3-17.

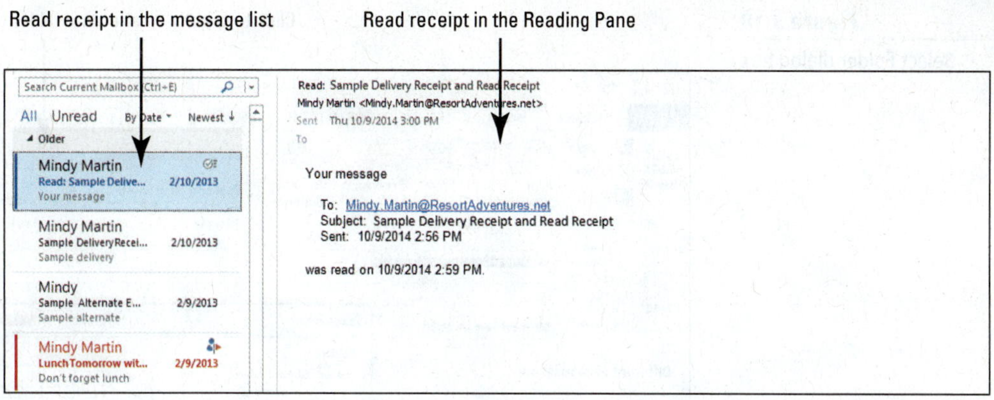

Figure 3-17

Read receipt received in mailbox

Read receipt in the message list   Read receipt in the Reading Pane

PAUSE. LEAVE Outlook open to use in the next exercise.

Saving a Sent Item to a Specific Folder

By default, sent messages are saved in the Sent Items folder, which is fine for most of your messages. However, you might want to save a copy of a message in a different location. For example, you can keep messages about a specific project in a different folder, or you can keep correspondence with a specific individual in a separate folder. Organizing your messages this way can help you stay on top of a hectic day. In this exercise, you'll create a sample message and change the options to have the sent message saved in a specific folder.

STEP BY STEP	Save a Sent Item to a Specific Folder

GET READY. LAUNCH Outlook if it is not already running.

1. Click the **New E-mail** button on the HOME tab. The Untitled – Message (HTML) window is displayed.

2. Click the **To** field. Key [**the e-mail address of a friend or coworker**].

3. Click the **Subject** field. Key **Different Save Location**. In the message area, key **Different Save Location**.

4. Click the **OPTIONS tab** on the Ribbon.

5. Click the **Save Sent Item To** button and select the **Other Folder** option from the drop down list. The Select Folder dialog box is displayed, as shown in Figure 3-18.

Figure 3-18

Select Folder dialog box

Click to specify an alternate folder to store the sent message

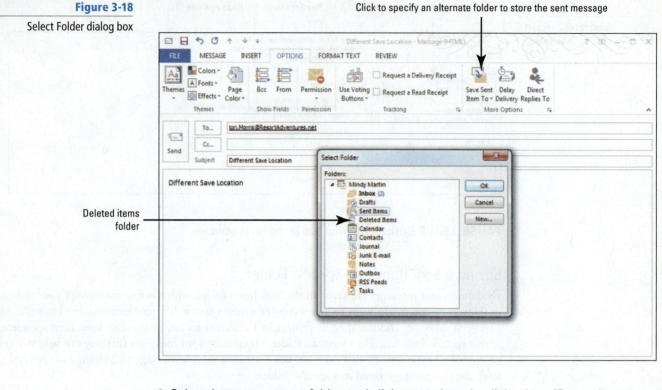

Deleted items folder

6. Select the **Deleted Items** folder, and click **OK** to close the dialog box. (Depending upon the e-mail account type you have set up in Outlook, you might see a Trash folder instead of Deleted Items).

 Troubleshooting   Normally, you will create a new folder or save the message to a folder you created earlier, but that isn't necessary for this exercise.

7. Click the **Send** button. The Message window closes, and the message is moved to the Outbox. The message is sent when your computer is connected to the Internet.

8. In the main Outlook window, click the **Deleted Items** folder in the Folders List. The message will be displayed in the Deleted Items folder when it has been sent.

Cross Ref   You will learn more about creating and using folders in Lesson 4.

9. Click the **Inbox** in the Folders List.

PAUSE. LEAVE Outlook open to use in the next exercise.

Saving sent messages in different folders determined by the message content or addressee is a great way to keep your mailbox organized. Later, you will learn to create rules that automatically move messages to different folders.

SOFTWARE ORIENTATION

Advanced Message Options

Some Microsoft Outlook 2013 options require more detail than is available on the OPTIONS tab. You can access the Properties dialog box, shown in Figure 3-19, by clicking on the More Options dialog box launcher on the Message window's OPTIONS tab.

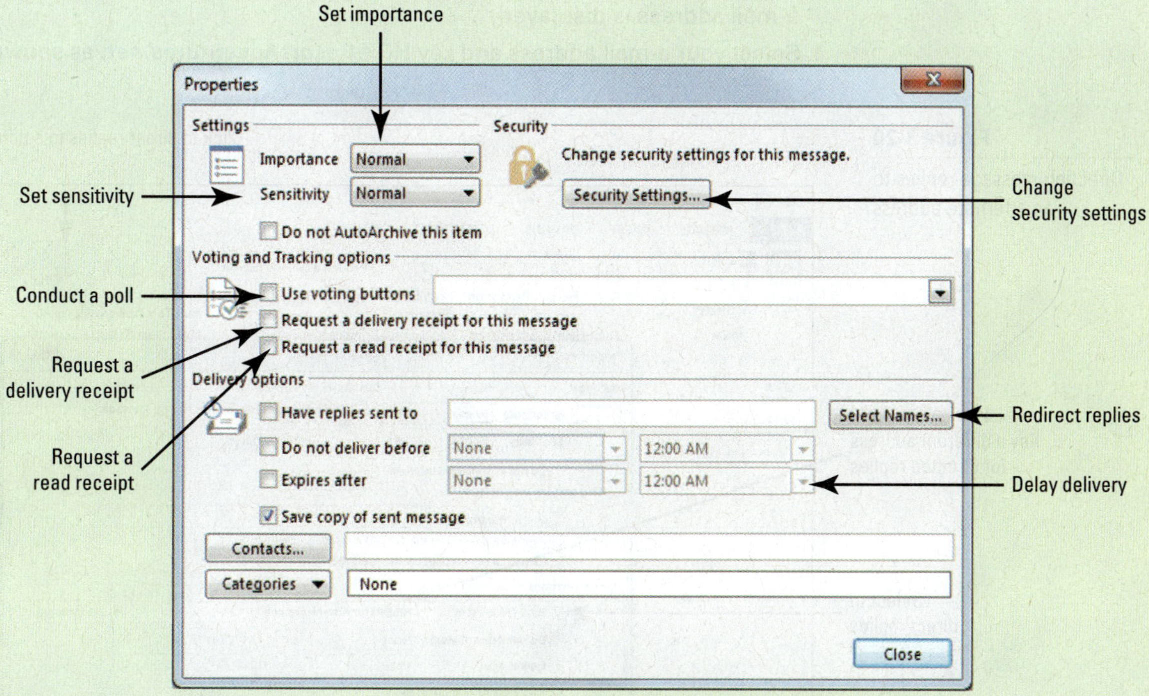
Set importance
Properties
Settings
Security
Importance
Normal
Change security settings for this message.
Set sensitivity
Sensitivity
Normal
Security Settings...
Change security settings
Do not AutoArchive this item
Voting and Tracking options
Conduct a poll
Use voting buttons
Request a delivery receipt for this message
Request a read receipt for this message
Request a delivery receipt
Delivery options
Have replies sent to
Select Names...
Redirect replies
Request a read receipt
Do not deliver before
None
12:00 AM
Expires after
None
12:00 AM
Delay delivery
Save copy of sent message
Contacts...
Categories
None
Close

Figure 3-19
The Properties dialog box

In the message Properties dialog box, you can make decisions about these options for the message you are creating. These changes affect only the current message; they do not affect all messages you send.

Directing Replies to a Specific Address

Directing replies to an e-mail address other than the sending account can be a surprisingly useful tool. By sending a message with the replies directed elsewhere, you prevent your inbox from being flooded with messages that you'll need to forward to someone else. For example, the president of a company could send out a message about an upcoming event, but direct any replies to the message to the event coordinator. Or, a human resources manager might want to send out an announcement of a job opening and direct the replies to her assistant for processing. In this exercise, you'll create a sample message and direct the replies to go to HR@ResortAdventures.net.

STEP BY STEP   Direct Replies to a Specific Address

GET READY. LAUNCH Outlook if it is not already running.

1. In the Mail folder, click the **New E-mail** button on the HOME tab. The Message window is displayed, with the MESSAGE tab selected.

2. Click the **OPTIONS** tab in the Ribbon and click the **Direct Replies To** button in the More Options group. The Properties dialog box is displayed.

3. In the *Delivery Options* area, the Have replies sent to check box is selected, and your e-mail address is displayed.

4. Select your e-mail address and key **HR@ResortAdventures.net**, as shown in Figure 3-20.

Figure 3-20

Directing message replies to an alternate address

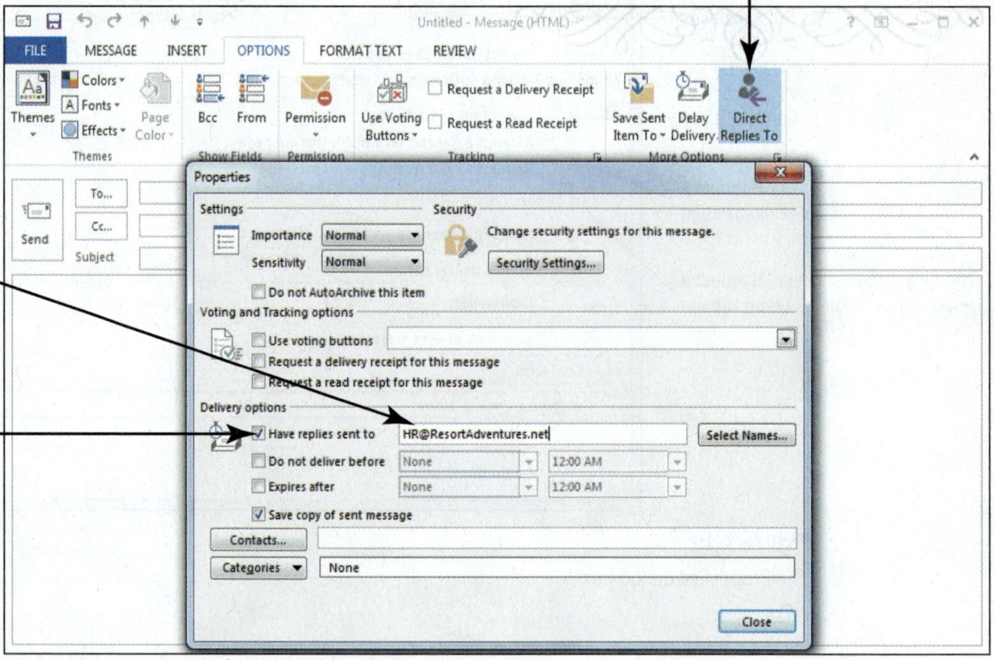

Click to direct replies to a different address

Key a different address for directed replies

Select to direct replies

5. Click **Close** to close the Properties dialog box; then close the message window without saving or sending a message.

PAUSE. LEAVE Outlook open to use in the next exercise.

CERTIFICATION READY? 2.1.12

How do you direct the replies to a message to a specific e-mail address?

When you send an e-mail message, the message header includes information about where to send replies. This information tells the recipient's e-mail application what e-mail address to use in the *To* field of a reply message. (When you request replies to be directed to a different address, Outlook replaces your Reply To information in the message coding with the alternate address you requested.)

Take Note   Some spam filters interpret messages with a different sender and reply to address as spam. If you are going to use this technique, you should also add a delivery receipt to ensure that your recipients receive your message.

If you have contacts entered in Outlook, you can choose a contact for the *Have replies sent to* field rather than keying an address. Using contact information in Outlook simplifies the process of directing replies to a different address.

Cross Ref   You can find more information about contacts in Lesson 6.

Configuring Message Delivery Options

Occasionally, you might want to delay the delivery of a message. For example, a Human Resources specialist can write a message explaining a change in benefits, but delay sending the message until the announcement is made later in the day. Delayed messages are held in the Outbox until the specified time, regardless of how often you click the Send/Receive All Folders button during the day. In this exercise, you learn how to specify details about a delivery delay using the message Properties dialog box.

STEP BY STEP   **Configure Message Delivery Options**

GET READY. LAUNCH Outlook if it is not already running.

1. Click the **New E-mail** button on the HOME tab. The Message window is displayed. By default, the MESSAGE tab is selected.

2. Click the **OPTIONS** tab in the Ribbon, and click the **Delay Delivery** button. The message Properties dialog box is displayed and the *Do not deliver before* check box is selected. The *current date* and *5:00 PM* are selected.

3. Click the **Time dropdown arrow**. Select the next available time from the dropdown list, as shown in Figure 3-21.

Another Way
Click the More Options dialog box launcher to open the message Properties dialog box.

Figure 3-21

Message Properties dialog box with delayed delivery selected

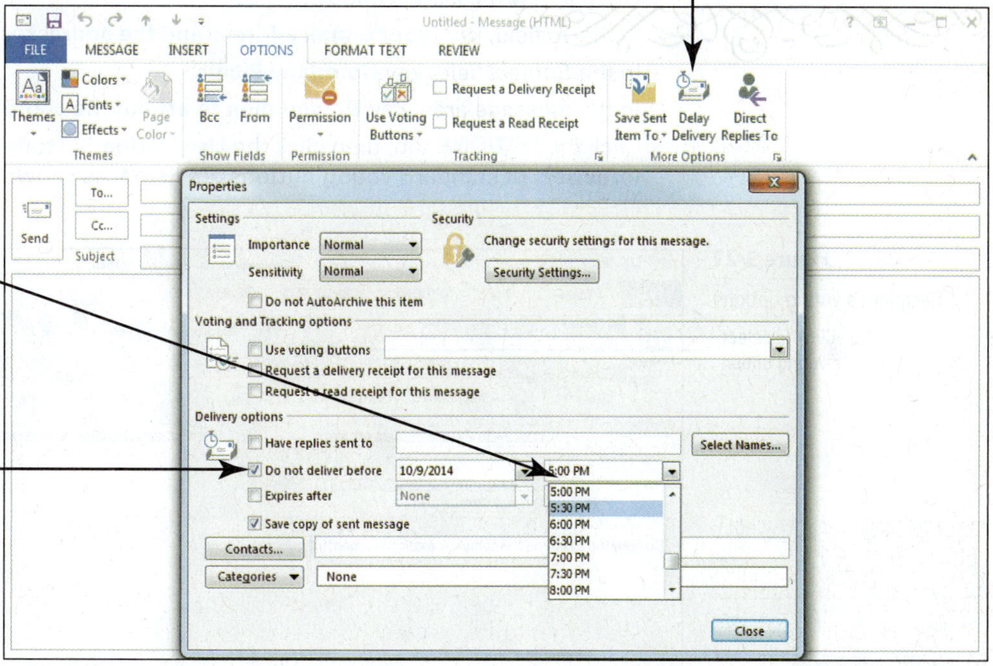

Click to delay delivery of a message

Select the date and time to send the message

Select to delay delivery of a message

4. Do not change the date. Click the **Close** button at the bottom of the dialog box. Note that the Delay Delivery button is highlighted.

5. In the *To* field, key [**the e-mail address of a coworker or friend**]. In the *Subject* field, key **Delayed Delivery**.

Troubleshooting If you are using a POP3 e-mail account rather than an internal company network, you must have Outlook open and the computer connected to the Internet at the time specified for delivery.

6. In the message area, key **Sample delayed delivery**.

7. Click the **Send** button. The message is moved to the Outbox. The message is sent at the specified time if your computer is connected to the Internet.

PAUSE. LEAVE Outlook open to use in the next exercise.

Be sure that Outlook is running and your computer is connected to the Internet at the specified delivery time in order to send the delayed message at the scheduled time.

WORKING WITH VOTING OPTIONS

The Bottom Line

Often the most time-consuming part of planning a project or event is getting everyone's consensus on specific aspects of the activity at hand. You can use the voting options to poll message recipients. If the standard voting buttons do not meet your need, you can create customized voting buttons.

⚠️ **Troubleshooting** Microsoft Exchange Server is required to use voting buttons.

Using Standard Voting Buttons

The standard sets of voting buttons include Approve and Reject; Yes and No; and Yes, No, and Maybe. These three standard voting options can handle most of your voting needs. In this exercise, you'll create a sample message containing a standard set of voting buttons.

STEP BY STEP **Use Standard Voting Buttons**

GET READY. LAUNCH Outlook if it is not already running.

1. Open a new message window.
2. In the *To* field, key [**your e-mail address and the addresses of two friends or coworkers**].
3. In the *Subject* field, key **Company Picnic**.
4. In the message area, key **Do you plan to attend the company picnic next month?**
5. Click the **OPTIONS** tab, then click the **Use Voting Buttons** button on the Ribbon. The three sets of standard voting buttons are listed, as shown in Figure 3-22.

Figure 3-22

Recipient's voting options

Click to select a voting option

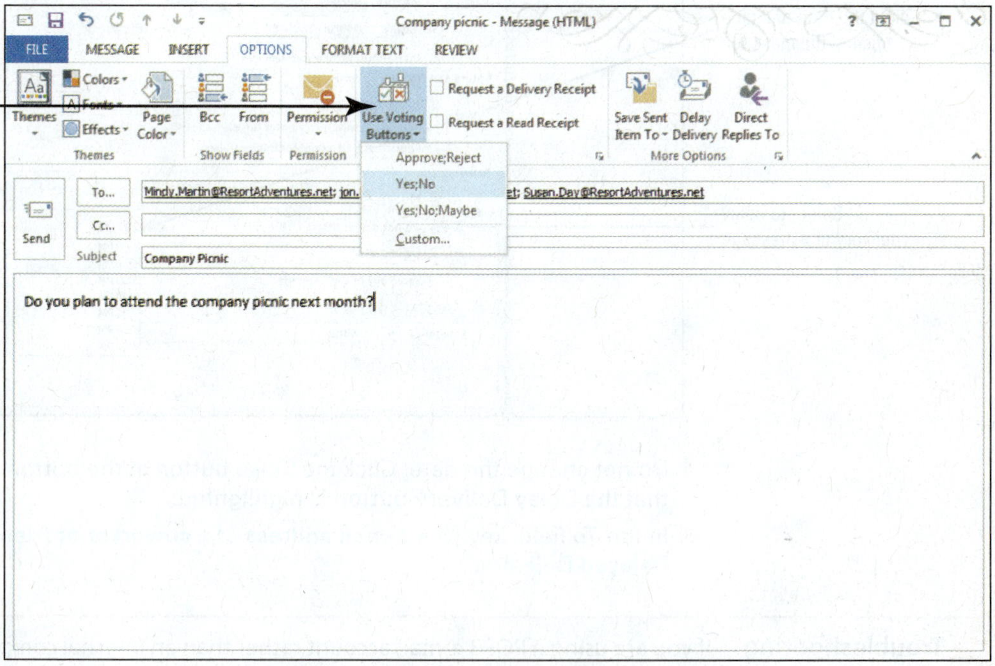

Another Way

Click the Use voting buttons check box in the message Properties dialog box. To display the message Properties dialog box, click the dialog box launcher in the Tracking group on the OPTIONS tab.

6. Click the **Yes;No** option.

7. Click the **Send** button. The message is moved to the Outbox, and it is sent when your computer is connected to the Internet.

PAUSE. LEAVE Outlook open to use in the next exercise.

When the message arrives in a recipient's mailbox, the InfoBar in the Reading Pane displays the text "This message includes voting buttons. Click here to vote." When the recipient clicks the InfoBar, a drop down showing the voting options is displayed. The recipient simply clicks the choice he or she wants.

Another Way

If you double click the message to open it in a separate window, the InfoBar will display the text "Vote by clicking Vote in the Respond group above." The recipient can click the Vote button in the Respond group to display the voting options. The recipient simply clicks the choice she wants.

A dialog box asks the recipient to confirm the choice, as shown in Figure 3-23. When the recipient confirms his or her choice, a message is automatically sent to the source of the poll. In this case, you are the source of the poll.

Figure 3-23

Responding to a message with voting options

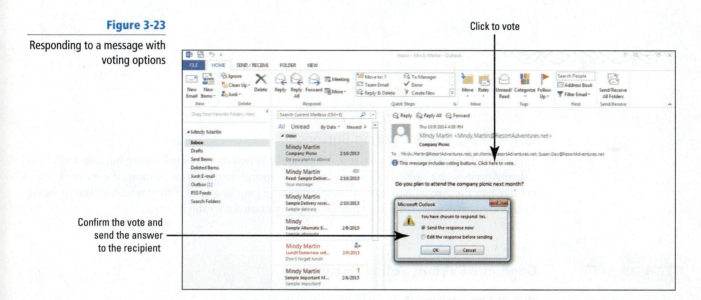

As replies arrive, the votes are tracked in the original sent message containing the poll question. The message used to send the poll is saved in the Sent Items folder like other sent messages. However, it is identified in the message list by the Tracking icon (see Figure 3-24), which resembles the Tracking button.

Figure 3-24

Sent message with voting options

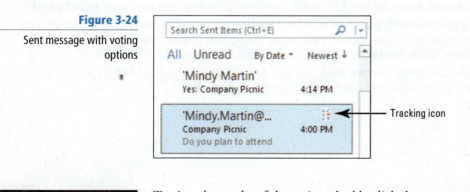

To view the results of the voting, double-click the message to open it. Click the Tracking button in the Ribbon, as shown in Figure 3-25.

CERTIFICATION READY? **2.1.6**

How do you create a poll using standard voting buttons?

Figure 3-25

Viewing poll results

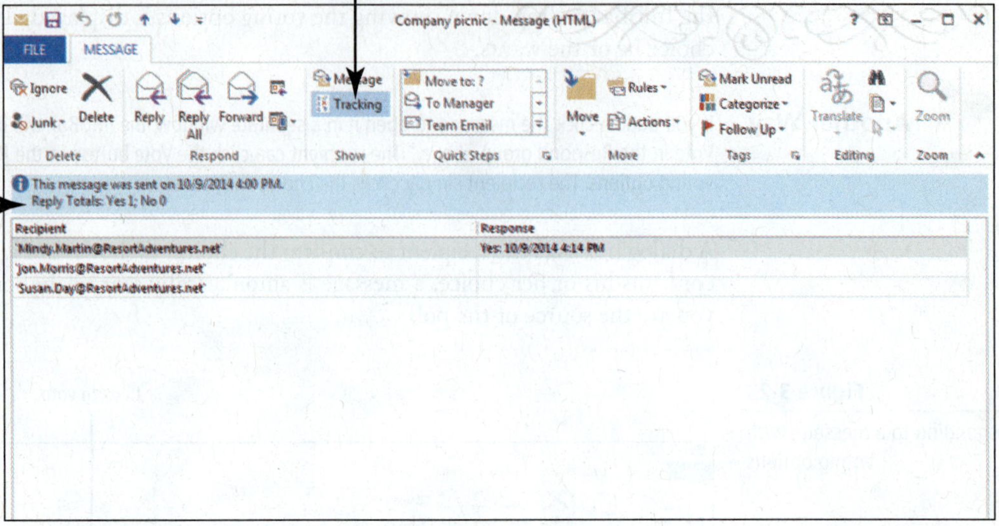

Click to view poll results

Results tallied on the InfoBar

Configuring Custom Voting Buttons

Sometimes a simple Yes/No answer is not enough. When the standard voting buttons don't provide the options you need, you can create custom voting buttons. For example, if your company's holiday party is catered, you can ask employees who plan to attend if they want chicken or steak. In this exercise, you'll create a sample message with custom voting buttons.

STEP BY STEP   **Configure Custom Voting Buttons**

GET READY. LAUNCH Outlook if it is not already running.

1. Open a new message window.
2. In the *To* field, key [**your e-mail address and the addresses of two friends or coworkers**].
3. In the *Subject* field, key **Company Holiday Dinner**.
4. In the message area, key **Select the meal you prefer for the company holiday party**.
5. Click the **OPTIONS** tab, then click the **Use Voting Buttons** button on the Ribbon, and click the **Custom** option. The Properties dialog box is displayed. The *Use voting buttons* option is selected and *Approve; Reject* is displayed in the field.
6. In the *Use voting buttons* field, key **Chicken;Steak**, as shown in Figure 3-26. Always insert a semicolon between the custom button labels.

Another Way
You could also click the Tracking group dialog box launcher to open the Properties dialog box.

Figure 3-26

Message Properties dialog box with *Use voting buttons* selected

Click to choose voting buttons

Key custom options separated by semicolons

Select to use voting buttons

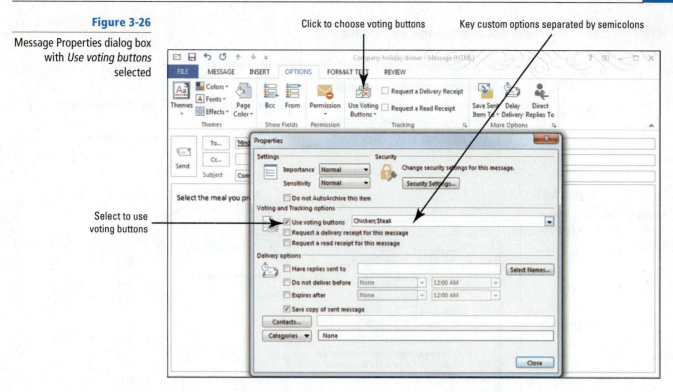

7. Click the **Close** button at the bottom of the dialog box to close the dialog box and return to the message.

8. Click the **Send** button. The message is moved to the Outbox, and it is sent when your computer is connected to the Internet.

PAUSE. LEAVE Outlook open to use in the next exercise.

Customized buttons provide flexibility when conducting polls. Choosing dinner is only one of the many types of polls you can create. Any time you need to gather opinions from several people, consider using a poll.

WORKING WITH SECURITY

The Bottom Line

Microsoft Outlook provides several security features to protect your e-mail correspondence. These features include everything from alerting message recipients to the sensitive nature or importance of a message's contents, encryption, and using a digital signature. In this section, you'll create sample messages using each of these security features.

Marking a Message as Private

The **sensitivity** level of a message is an indicator of how private the message's contents are. Although sensitivity does not affect how the message is sent or received, it does suggest how the recipient should treat the message and the type of information it contains. You set the Sensitivity settings Normal, Personal, Private, and Confidential—in the Properties dialog box. In this exercise, you'll create a message and mark the message as private.

Mark a Message as Private

GET READY. LAUNCH Outlook if it is not already running.

1. Open a new message window.

2. Click the **More Options dialog box launcher** on the OPTIONS tab. The message Properties dialog box is displayed.

3. In the Settings area, click the **Sensitivity setting** dropdown arrow, as shown in Figure 3-27.

Figure 3-27

Setting the Sensitivity level of a message

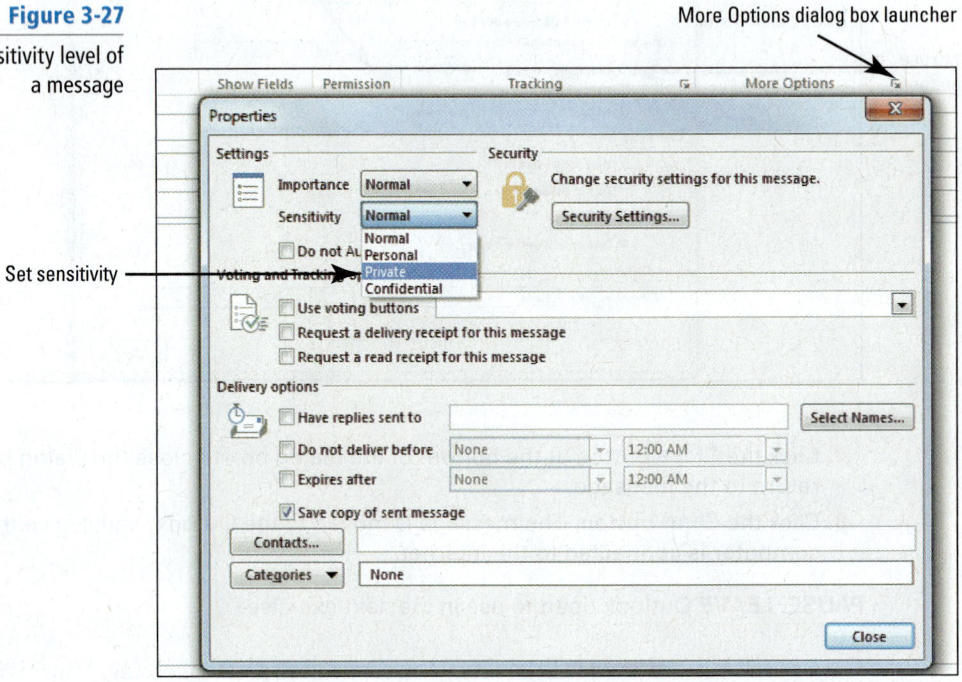

More Options dialog box launcher

Set sensitivity

4. Then select **Private** from the dropdown list.

5. Click the **Close** button to accept the Private setting and return to the message window.

6. In the message area, key **Sample private message**.

7. In the *To* field, key [**your e-mail address**]. In the *Subject* field, key **Sample Private Message**.

8. Click the **Send** button. The message is moved to the Outbox, and it is sent when your computer is connected to the Internet.

9. When your computer is connected to the Internet, click the **Send/Receive All Folders** button on the SEND/RECEIVE tab if the message has not arrived yet.

10. When the new message appears in your Inbox, click the received message to select it. The message has the text *Please treat this as Private* in the InfoBar at the top of the message, as shown in Figure 3-28.

Figure 3-28

Private message received

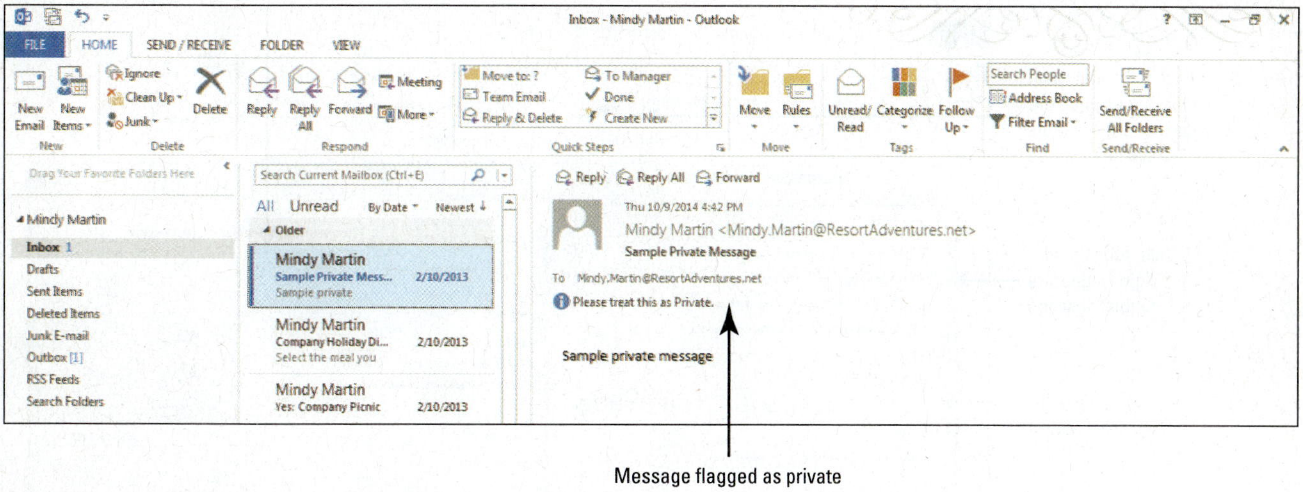

Message flagged as private

PAUSE. LEAVE Outlook open to use in the next exercise.

The default sensitivity is normal. The InfoBar is not added to messages with a normal sensitivity.
An InfoBar is added for personal, private, and confidential messages.

Using a Digital Signature

A **digital ID**, also called a **digital signature**, is a way to authenticate that a message is coming from
you and to add a level of encryption to the message. Digital IDs enable a recipient to verify that a
message is really from you and decrypt any encrypted messages received from you. A digital ID
contains a **private key** that remains on your computer and a **public key** you give to your correspondents. When you give a recipient a digital ID, you are giving their computer the codes to unlock
your encrypted messages. In this exercise, you'll create a sample message and add a digital signature.

⚠ **Troubleshooting**   To use a digital signature or encrypt a message, you must have a digital ID. If you do not have
a digital ID, consult your system administrator or purchase a digital ID from a certificate
authority.

STEP BY STEP   **Use a Digital Signature**

GET READY. LAUNCH Outlook if it is not already running.

1. Open a new message window.
2. In the *To* field, key [the address of a friend or coworker].
3. In the *Subject* field, key Digitally Signed Message.
4. On the OPTIONS tab, click the More Options dialog box launcher. The message
   Properties dialog box opens.
5. Click the Security Settings button. The Security Properties dialog box is displayed, as
   shown in Figure 3-29.

Figure 3-29

Security Properties dialog box

Click to open the Security Properties dialog box

Click to digitally sign messages once the initial security settings have been set up

Select to add your digital signature to this message

Click to select your Digital ID from the list

Another Way
Once you've set up your Security Settings with your Digital ID, you can simply click the Digitally Sign Message button on the OPTIONS tab to sign future messages.

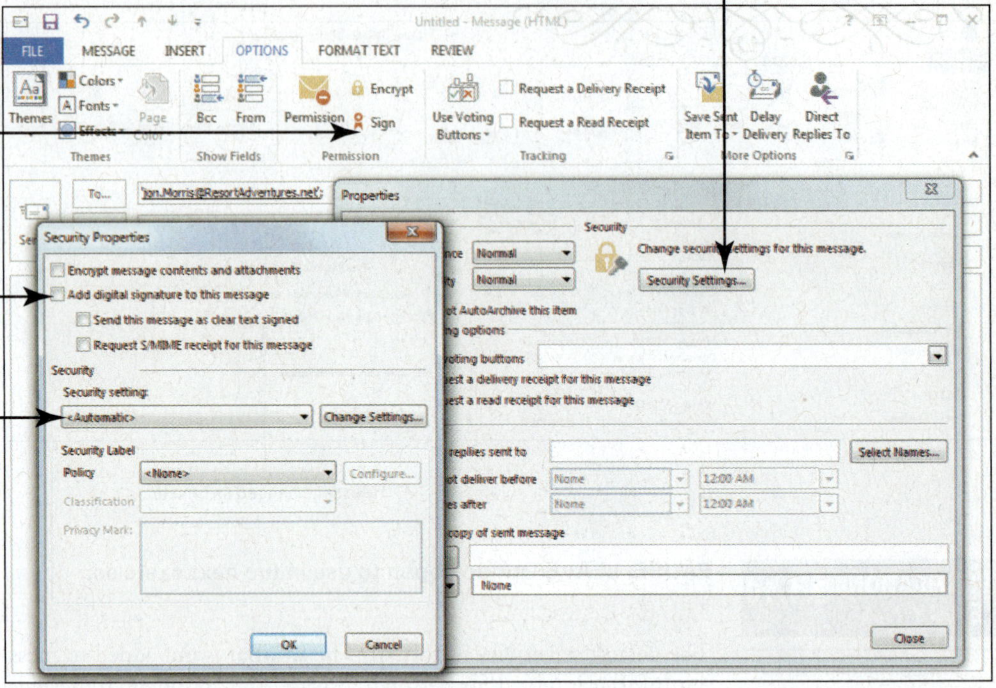

6. Click the **Add digital signature to this message** check box.

7. Click the **Security setting** dropdown box and select your Digital ID from the list.

8. Click **OK** to close the dialog box. Click the **Close** button to close the message Properties dialog box.

9. In the message area, key **Sample digitally signed message**. Click the **Send** button. The message is moved to the Outbox and it is sent when your computer is connected to the Internet.

10. Depending on how the security is set up on your PC, you might get a *Request for Permission to Use a Key* message asking you to confirm that it is OK to allow Outlook to use your Digital ID for this message. If you see this message, select **Grant Permission** and click **OK**.

PAUSE. LEAVE Outlook open to use in the next exercise.

When a digitally signed message arrives in the Inbox, an icon in the message list indicates that the message is digitally signed, as shown in Figure 3-30. The message header also contains a digital signature icon. The recipient can click on the icon to see additional information about the digital signature.

Figure 3-30

Digitally signed message

Icon indicates a digitally signed message

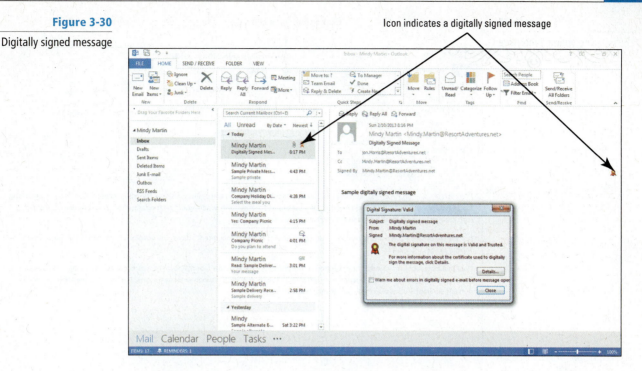

Remember that messages with a digital ID contain the codes you will need to unlock encrypted messages from that person. So the first time you receive a digitally signed message for any sender, you should use the digital ID to add the person to your contact list or to update existing contact information so that their private key information is added to their contact record.

Cross Ref

You can find more information about contacts in Lesson 6.

Using Encryption

Encryption is a great way to protect the privacy of important messages. When you use **encryption**, your message contents are scrambled so that only a recipient with the encryption key can decipher the message. To send an encrypted message and decrypt an encrypted message, you must have exchanged digital ID certificates with the recipient. In other words, both you and the recipient need to send each other a digitally signed message and add each other's digital ID to the Contacts list. In this exercise, you'll create a sample encrypted message.

STEP BY STEP | **Use Encryption**

GET READY. LAUNCH Outlook if it is not already running.

Take Note   Before you exchange encrypted messages, both you and the recipient need to send each other a digitally signed message and add each other's digital ID to the Contacts list.

1. Open a new message window.
2. In the *To* field, key [the address of the friend or coworker who has exchanged digital ID certificates with you].
3. In the *Subject* field, key Sample Encrypted Message.
4. Open the *Content* file in the data files for this lesson. Select and copy all the text and close Microsoft Word. Paste it in the message area.
5. On the OPTIONS tab, click the Encrypt button, as shown in Figure 3-31.

Figure 3-31

Encrypting a message

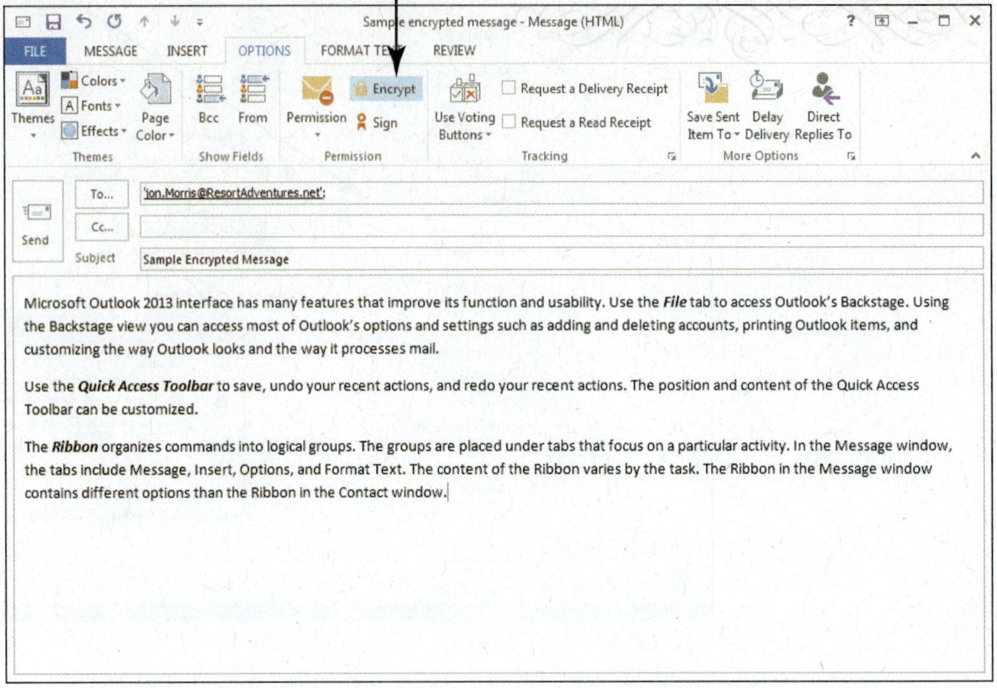

Click to encrypt a message

Troubleshooting If you do not have a digital ID, you might not see the Encrypt button.

6. Click the **Send** button. The message is moved to the Outbox, and it is sent when your computer is connected to the Internet.

LEAVE Outlook open to use in the next exercise.

When an encrypted message arrives in the Inbox, an icon in the message list indicates that the message is encrypted, as shown in Figure 3-32. An encrypted message cannot be viewed in the Reading Pane. It must be opened to be read.

Figure 3-32

Encrypted message

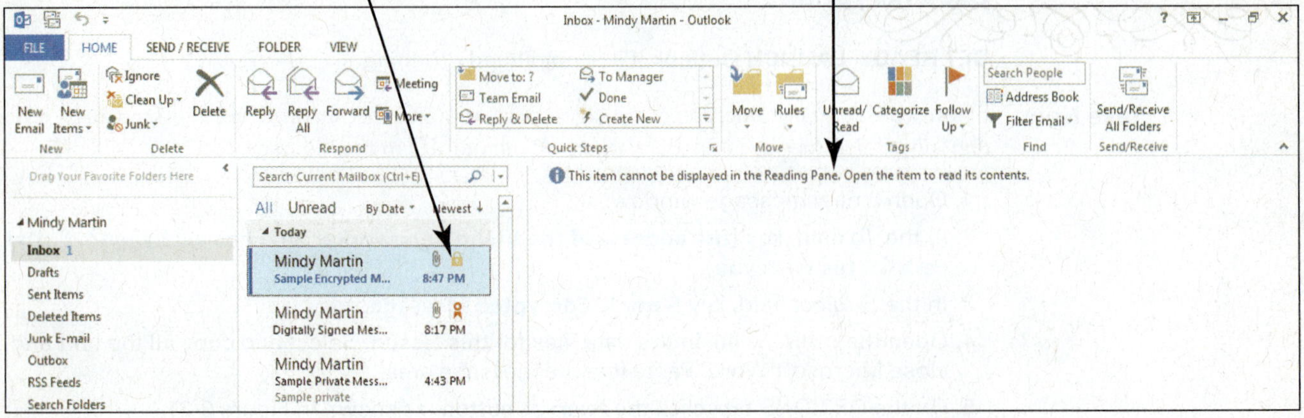

Icon indicates encrypted message   Encrypted messages cannot be viewed in the Reading Pane

LOCATING MESSAGES

The Bottom Line

What was the cost of that item? When is the project deadline? Important information is often exchanged through e-mail messages, and finding that information again can be critical. Outlook 2013 has several powerful tools that make it easy to locate the right message when you need it.

You can sort Mail folders by any attribute. You can easily locate messages with specific attributes using the Filter E-mail tool, or you can filter search results using Instant Search with its companion SEARCH TOOLS tab. If you find that you need to perform the same search on a regular basis, you can create a custom search folder that will always contain your filtered items.

Sorting Messages by Attributes

In the message list, e-mail messages are usually listed by date. The newest messages are displayed at the top of the message list. By default, messages are sorted by the date they are received. One of the easiest ways to locate messages is by sorting the message list by another **attribute** such as size, subject, or sender. In this exercise, you'll sort the message list by different file attributes.

STEP BY STEP **Sort Messages by Attributes**

GET READY. LAUNCH Outlook if it is not already running.

1. If necessary, click the **Mail** button in the Navigation bar of the main Outlook window.
2. Click **By Date** above the message list. A list of available sort parameters is displayed, as shown in Figure 3-33.

Figure 3-33

Sorting message by attribute

Email Sorting Attributes

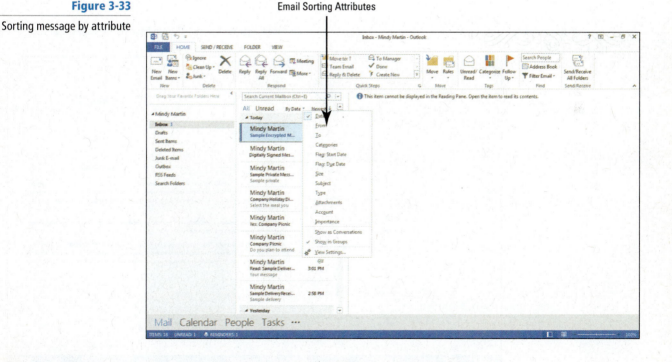

⚠️ **Troubleshooting** If you don't see the By Date heading above the message list, you can click the right edge of the message list and drag it a little to the right.

Another Way

To sort messages, click the VIEW tab, and select an attribute in the Arrangement gallery.

CERTIFICATION READY? | **2.3.1**

How do you sort messages by a specific attribute?

---

3. Select the **Size** option. Messages are grouped by the size of the message.

4. Click **By Size** above the message list.

5. Select the **Date** option. Messages are grouped by date. Groups are listed in chronological order.

PAUSE. Leave Outlook open to use in the next exercise.

In the previous exercise, you used attributes to change the order of items in the message list. Another great way to locate specific messages is by limiting the number of messages in the message list by filtering out all the messages that don't have the attributes you are looking for using the Filter E-mail button.

Filtering E-mail Messages

Over time the number of messages that we exchange can make it difficult to locate the ones for which we're looking. You can reduce the number of messages you need to wade through with the click of a button by using the Filter E-mail button. The Filter E-mail button offers a list of the most common search refining options. In this exercise, you'll filter the messages in the message list.

STEP BY STEP | **Filter E-mail Message**

GET READY. LAUNCH Outlook if it is not already running.

1. If necessary, click the **Mail** button in the Navigation bar.

2. Click the **Filter E-mail** button in the Find group on the HOME tab. A drop down list of the most common search filter options is displayed, as shown in Figure 3-34.

Figure 3-34

The Filter E-mail tool

Sort messages by   Click to filter the messages in a folder

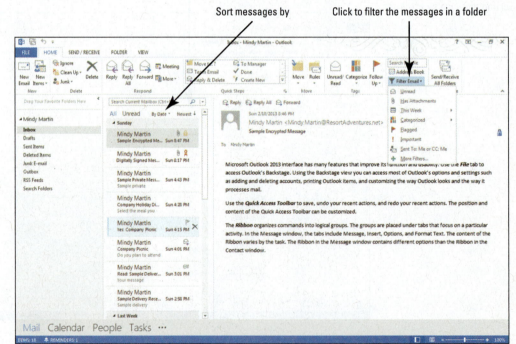

3. Select **Important** from the Filter E-mail list. Notice that the SEARCH TOOLS tab appears and only messages that have been prioritized as Important are displayed.

4. Click **Inbox** in the Folders List to clear the search.

PAUSE. Leave Outlook open to use in the next exercise.

Using Instant Search

One of the biggest problems with searching through e-mail messages over time is that the searches usually produce far too many results. **Instant Search** now includes two features that you can use to filter through the results: Search Suggestions list and the SEARCH TOOLS content aware tab. As you begin typing a keyword in the Instant Search box, results are immediately displayed in the mail list rather than waiting to complete the search to display the results. In this exercise, you'll locate an Outlook item using Instant Search to filter your results.

STEP BY STEP   **Use Instant Search**

GET READY. LAUNCH Outlook if it is not already running.

1. If necessary, click the **Mail** button in the Navigation bar of the main Outlook window.
2. If necessary, click the **Inbox** folder in the Folders List. The Instant Search box is displayed at the top of the message list.

Take Note   The Instant Search feature works in every Outlook folder.

3. In the Instant Search box, start to slowly key **Sample**. As you key the search text, three things happen. Outlook displays the messages that match the text; the Search Suggestions list appears, allowing you to choose which part of the message includes the keyword; and the SEARCH TOOLS tab appears, as shown in Figure 3-35.

Figure 3-35

Instant Search features

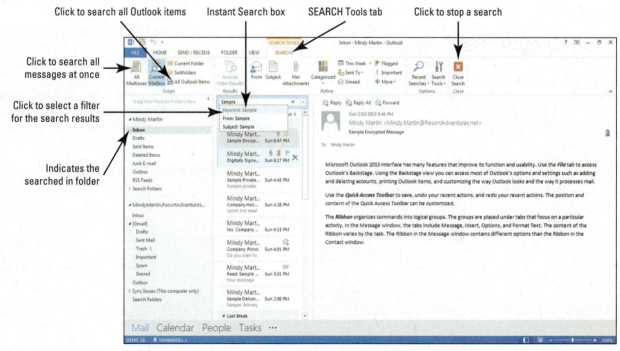

Take Note   Instant Search searches all the folders in the mailbox you're currently viewing. You can search everywhere in Outlook at the same time by clicking the All Outlook Items button.

4. Click the **Subject: Sample** from the Search Suggestions list. Only messages that include the word Sample in the subject line are displayed.
5. Click the **Close Search** button in the Instant Search box to clear the search.

PAUSE. Leave Outlook open to use in the next exercise.

Selecting one of the options in the Search Suggestions list, you can filter the results based on where the keyword appears in the message. You can further reduce the number of items in a search list by clicking one or more items in the Refine group.

Searching Multiple Accounts

If you are one of the many people with more than one e-mail account, then the problem of searching through e-mail messages is compounded. You can expand your search to include all of your e-mail accounts by clicking All Mailboxes in the SEARCH TOOLS tab. You can also limit your search to a specific mailbox by selecting Locations to Search from the Search Tools list on the SEARCH TOOLS tab. In this exercise, you'll locate an Outlook item using Instant Search to filter your results.

⚠️ **Troubleshooting** In order to complete this exercise, you'll need to have at least two e-mail accounts set up in Outlook.

STEP BY STEP   **Search Multiple Accounts**

GET READY. LAUNCH Outlook if it is not already running and be sure that you have more than one e-mail account set up.

1. If necessary, click the **Mail** button in the Navigation bar of the main Outlook window, and click the **Inbox** folder in the Folders List.
2. Click in the **Instant Search** box to open the SEARCH TOOLS tab.
3. Click the **Sent To** button in the Refine group. A drop down list of options is displayed.
4. Select **Not Sent Directly to Me** from the list.
5. Click **All Mailboxes** on the SEARCH TOOLS tab to expand the search to all of your e-mail accounts.
6. Click the **Search Tools** button in the Options group to expand a list of advanced search options.
7. Select **Locations to Search** from the Search Tools drop list. A fly-out menu appears listing the e-mail accounts you have set up within Outlook. Accounts with a checkmark indicate accounts that will be searched, as shown in Figure 3-36.

Figure 3-36

Locations to Search

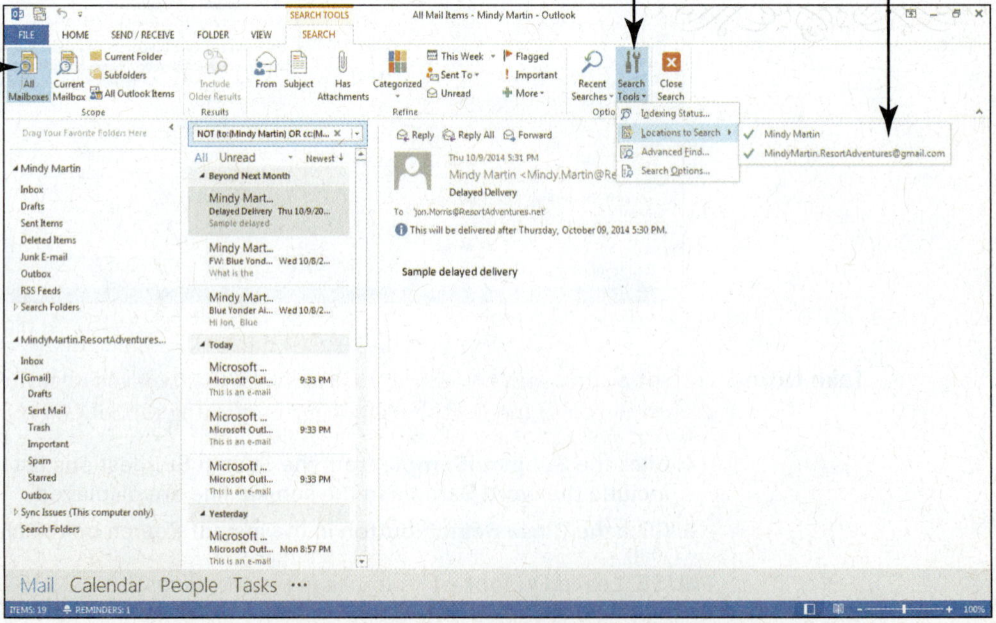

Click to search all mailboxes at once

Click to select a location to search   Set up email accounts

CERTIFICATION
READY? **1.4.7**

How would you search for a message in a different Outlook data file?

8. Select your primary e-mail account. The checkmark will disappear, and the search results from that e-mail account will be filtered out of the Message list.

9. Click the Search Tools button and select Locations to Search and then your primary e-mail account to restore the checkmark and include your primary e-mail account in future searches. Click **Close Search**.

PAUSE. Leave Outlook open to use in the next exercise.

Using Built-in Search Folders

If you find that you need to perform the same kind of search on a regular basis, you can save time by using a built-in Search folder. Search folders are virtual folders stored in the Folders List. A virtual folder looks and acts like a normal folder, but a virtual folder is really just a collection of links to messages that are stored in other folders. This allows you to maintain your folder organization while still offering you easy access to messages that fit your search needs. For example, you can access every unread e-mail message from every folder using the Unread Mail search folder.

STEP BY STEP **Use Built-in Search Folders**

GET READY. LAUNCH Outlook if it is not already running.

1. If necessary, click the **Mail** button in the Navigation bar.

2. On the FOLDER tab, click **New Search Folder** in the New group. The New Search Folder dialog box is displayed, as shown in Figure 3-37.

Figure 3-37

New Search Folder dialog box

Click to create a new search folder

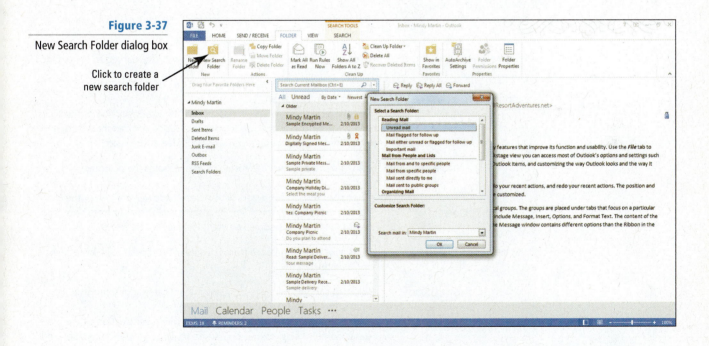

3. In the *Select a Search Folder* section of the dialog box, select **Mail flagged for follow up** in the *Reading Mail* portion of the list.

4. Click **OK** to close the dialog box. Outlook displays a new folder at the bottom of the Folders List called Search Folders. The For Follow Up folder appears within Search Folders, as shown in Figure 3-38.

Figure 3-38

For Follow Up search folder

Figure 3-38

For Follow Up search folder

New search folder

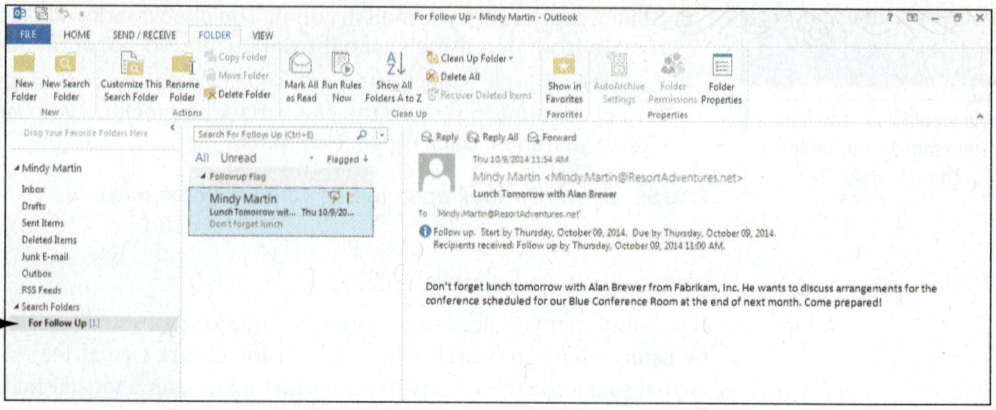

PAUSE. LEAVE Outlook open to use in the next exercise.

Outlook provides a number of built-in search folders (see Table 3-1) for everything from unread mail to mail containing specific keywords. You can also create a custom search folder containing any criteria you want.

Table 3-1

Built-in Search Folders

Search Folder	What Items Will Appear in the Search Folder
Unread mail	Holds links to any message from any folder that is marked as unread.
Mail flagged for follow up	Holds links to any message from any folder that has been flagged.
Mail either unread or flagged for follow-up	Holds links to any message from any folder that is marked as unread or flagged.
Important mail	Holds links to any message from any folder that is marked as important.
Mail from and to specific people	Holds links to any message from any folder that is either from or to contact(s) you choose. When selected, a new box is displayed in the lower portion of the New Search Folder dialog box. Click Choose to open your address book and select the names of people you want included in the search.
Mail from specific people	Holds links to any message from any folder that is from contact(s) you choose. When selected, a new box is displayed in the lower portion of the New Search Folder dialog box. Click Choose to open your address book and select the names of people you want included in the search.
Mail sent directly to me	Holds links to any message from any folder that specifically lists you in the *To* field.
Mail sent to public groups	Holds links to any message from any folder that is addressed to a contact group or distribution list chosen by you. When selected, a new box is displayed in the lower portion of the New Search Folder dialog box. Click Choose to open your address book and select the contact group(s) you want included in the search.
Categorized mail	Holds links to any message from any folder that you've organized using categories. When selected, a new box is displayed in the lower portion of the New Search Folder dialog box. By default, any category is included, but you can click Choose to open a new window in which you can specify the categories you want included in your search.

Search Folder	What Items Will Appear in the Search Folder
Large mail	Holds links to any message from any folder that is at least a specified size. When selected, a new box is displayed in the lower portion of the New Search Folder dialog box. By default, the size limit is 100 KB, but you can click Choose to open a new window in which you can specify the size limit you want.
Old mail	Holds links to any message from any folder that is older than a specific date. When selected, a new box is displayed in the lower portion of the New Search Folder dialog box. By default, anything older than one week is included, but you can click Choose to open a new window in which you can specify the number of days, weeks, or months you want to include.
Mail with attachments	Holds links to any message from any folder that has an attachment.
Mail with specific words	Holds links to any message from any folder that contains words that you specify. When selected, a new box is displayed in the lower portion of the New Search Folder dialog box. Click Choose to open a new window in which you can specify the words you want included in your search.
Create a custom Search Folder	Holds any message from any folder that is marked as unread. When selected, a new box is displayed in the lower portion of the New Search Folder dialog box. Click Choose to open a new window in which you can specify the name for the folder and the specific criterion you want to use.

 Cross Ref You can find more information about custom search folders in Lesson 7.

PRINTING MULTIPLE MESSAGES

The Bottom Line

With Outlook 2013, printing multiple messages is just as easy as printing one. Printed messages include the header and the body of the message. You can control all the printing settings in Backstage view.

Printing Multiple Messages

In this exercise, you learn how to print multiple messages in Outlook 2013.

STEP BY STEP **Print Multiple Messages**

GET READY. LAUNCH Outlook if it is not already running.

1. If necessary, click the **Mail** button in the Navigation bar of the main Outlook window, and click the **Inbox** folder in the Folders List.
2. Select the three most recent e-mail messages.
3. Press **Ctrl** and then click the next message in the list to select.
4. Click the **FILE tab** to open Backstage view.
5. Click **Print** in the Navigation Pane to open the Print page. The preview pane on the right displays a message saying that it might take a few moments to display the preview of multiple messages, as shown in Figure 3-39.

Click to see a preview of multiple messages

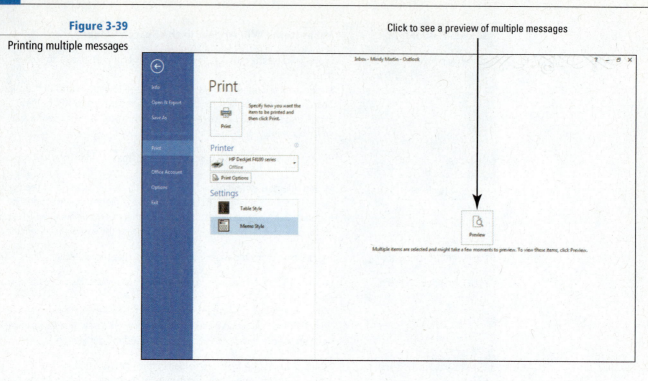

Figure 3-39

Printing multiple messages

6. Click the **Preview** button. A preview of the first of the selected message is displayed, as shown in Figure 3-40.

Figure 3-40

Print Settings in Backstage view

Previous Page   Next Page

7. Click the **Next Page** button to see the next selected message.
8. Click the **Table Style** button. Click **Print Options**, under Print range click **Only selected rows**. Click **Preview**. The preview changes to a single table listing of the three messages.
9. Click the **Printer** dropdown arrow and select your printer from the list.
10. Click **Print** to print the selected messages and turn them in to your instructor.

CLOSE Outlook.

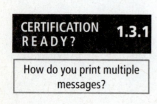

CERTIFICATION READY?   1.3.1

How do you print multiple messages?

SKILL SUMMARY

In This Lesson You Learned To:	Exam Objective	Objective Number
Manage Automatic Message Handling	Set Outlook options	1.1.7
	Include original messages with all reply messages	1.1.1
Automate Message Format	Change quoted text colors	1.2.1
	Change text formats for all outgoing messages	1.1.2
Use Message Options	Prioritize messages	2.1.9
	Configure reminders	3.3.3
	Manage multiple accounts	1.1.6
	Request delivery/read receipt	2.1.11
	Redirect replies	2.1.12
Work with Voting Options	Add voting options to messages	2.1.6
Work with Security	Mark as private	2.1.10
Locate Messages	Sort messages	2.3.1
	Search for messages	1.4.2
	Use search by location	1.4.7
Print Multiple Messages	Print messages	1.3.1

Knowledge Assessment

Multiple Choice

Select the best response for the following statements.

1. What Options page in the Outlook Options dialog box contains the controls for how Outlook handles message replies and forwards?
   a. Mail Options
   b. General Options
   c. Advanced Options
   d. Message Options

2. What scrambles the text so that only the recipient with a key can decipher the message?
   a. blending
   b. digital remixing
   c. encryption
   d. encoding

3. Use the Location to Search option to search through multiple?
   a. folders
   b. accounts
   c. Contact locations
   d. Both A and B

4. A _____ assures the recipient the identity of the sender of a message.
   a. secure ID
   b. message header
   c. digital ID
   d. All of the above

5. What is the name of the banner containing information added automatically at the top of a message?
   a. InfoBar
   b. ScreenTip
   c. Context bar
   d. Message header

6. Which of the following tells you that the message has been opened in the recipient's mailbox?
   a. Delivered flag
   b. Delivery receipt
   c. Read receipt
   d. Message Tracking

7. Which of the following allows you to filter search results?
   a. Arrange by field
   b. Search Suggestions list
   c. Filter E-mail button
   d. All of the above

8. Which of the following contains a private key that remains on your computer and a public key you give to your correspondents to verify that you are the message sender?
   a. digital ID
   b. confidential e-mail
   c. same server transfer
   d. encryption

9. Which of the following is not a standard voting option?
   a. Approve
   b. Maybe
   c. Reject
   d. Okay

10. Which of the following tells you that the message has arrived in the recipient's mailbox?
    a. Delivered flag
    b. Delivery receipt
    c. Read receipt
    d. Read flag

True/False

Circle T if the statement is true or F if the statement is false.

T F 1. Plain text is the default format for all messages.

T F 2. When you delay the delivery of a message, it is held in the Outbox until it is time to be sent.

T F 3. A red exclamation point is the icon used in the message list to indicate that a message is confidential.

T F 4. An encrypted message can be previewed in the Reading Pane when the message arrives.

T F 5. An InfoBar is a banner containing information added automatically at the top of a message.

T F 6. To search through multiple e-mail accounts you can use the Filter E-mail feature.

T F 7. "Maybe" is one of the standard voting buttons.

T F 8. The Instant Search feature displays items matching the search criterion before the search is complete.

T F 9. A delivery receipt indicates that the message has been opened by the recipient.

T F 10. When you create custom voting buttons, insert a colon between the options.

Competency Assessment

Project 3-1: Create a Confidential Message

Doug Hite is the personal assistant for a well-known actress. The actress has reservations for next weekend. To avoid publicity, the actress will use the alias "Julie Kenan" when she registers. Create a confidential message confirming the reservation.

GET READY. LAUNCH Outlook if it is not already running.

1. Click the **New E-mail** button to create a new message.
2. In the *To* field, key [**your e-mail address**].
3. In the *Subject* field, key **Reservation Confirmation**.
4. In the message area, key the following message.

   [**Today's date**] [Press **Enter** twice.]

   Mr. Hite, [Press **Enter** twice.]

   This message confirms the reservation for Julie Kenan, arriving after 5 PM on Friday and leaving Sunday afternoon. As you requested, five pounds of dark chocolate nonpareils have been placed in the suite's refrigerator. [Press **Enter** twice.]

   Please contact me if you need any further assistance. [Press **Enter** twice.]

   Mindy Martin [Press **Enter**.]

   Resort Adventures

5. Click the **Tags dialog box launcher**. Change the Sensitivity option to **Confidential**. Close the message Properties dialog box.
6. Click the **FILE** tab and select the **Save As** option. Save the message in Outlook Message Format as *Confidential Confirmation* in the location specified by your instructor.
7. Close the message without sending it. Let Outlook save a copy.

LEAVE Outlook open for the next project.

Project 3-2: Create a Message with a Read Request

Mindy Martin, co-owner of Resort Adventures, is supervising the arrangements for a family reunion scheduled for next spring at the resort. She needs to send them a message confirming the date and notifying them of the cancellation policy. Because she doesn't want any question as to whether the message was read, she is going to send the message with a read receipt.

GET READY. LAUNCH Outlook if it is not already running.

1. On the HOME tab, click the **New E-mail** button to create a new message.
2. In the *Subject* field, key **Smithfield Reunion Confirmation**.
3. In the message area, key the following message.

   [**Today's date**] [Press **Enter** twice.] **Mrs. Smithfield,** [Press **Enter** twice.]

   As per our conversation of today, I am pleased to confirm the date of April 26 for the Smithfield reunion. [Press **Enter** twice.]

   Please be advised that our policy requires a four-week notice for cancellations. Any cancellations after that date will result in forfeiture of your down payment. [Press **Enter** twice.]

   Please let me know if you have any additional questions, [Press **Enter** twice.]

   Mindy Martin [Press **Enter**.]

   Resort Adventures

4. On the MESSAGE tab, click the **High Importance** option.
5. Click the **OPTIONS tab**. Select the **Request a Read Receipt**.

6. Click the **FILE tab** and select the **Save As** option. Save the message in Outlook Message Format as *Smithfield Reunion Confirmation*.

7. Close the message without addressing or sending it.

LEAVE Outlook open for the next project.

Proficiency Assessment

Project 3-3: **Specify a Default Theme and Create a Message with Voting Options**

You work for Resort Adventures. Mindy Martin, one of the owners, asked you to select a default theme to be used for the resort. You need to select a theme and send a message to Mindy for her review.

GET READY. LAUNCH Outlook if it is not already running.

1. Open the Signatures and Stationery dialog box from the Mail Options page in the Outlook Options dialog box.

2. Open the Theme or Stationery dialog box, and select the **Sumi Painting** theme.

3. Close the open dialog boxes, saving your changes, and open a new message. The new theme will be applied.

4. In the *To* field, key [**your e-mail address**].

5. In the *Subject* field, key **Proposed theme**.

6. In the message area, key the following message using the same line spacing between paragraphs and signature lines that you've used in the previous projects.

[**Today's date**] [Press **Enter** twice.]

Mindy,

I think Water might be a good theme for our stationery as it meets the requirements we discussed.

It is brighter than the previous theme proposed.

It is colorful without being too intense.

Please let me know what you think.

[**Your Name**]

Resort Adventures

7. Select the two sentences that begin with *It is* and make them bullet points.

8. Add the Approve; Reject voting option to the message.

9. Save the message in HTML format as *Proposed theme* in the location specified by your instructor.

10. Click **Send**.

11. Go back to the Mail Options page in the Outlook Options dialog box and select (**No Theme**) from the Theme or Stationery dialog box.

PAUSE. LEAVE Outlook open to use in the next exercise.

Project 3-4: **Locate and Print Messages**

Mindy Martin, co-owner of Resort Adventures, received your message containing the proposed theme; however, before she votes on it, she would like to sit down with you and Jon to discuss the pros and cons of each. You need to locate each of the theme styles that have been proposed (be sure to include the themed message that you created in Lesson 2). Print a copy of all three messages and bring them to the meeting.

GET READY. LAUNCH Outlook if it is not already running.

1. Click the **Sent Items** folder.

2. In the *Instant Search* field, key **theme**.

3. From the Search Suggestions list, select **subject: theme**.

4. Select the three messages that remain in the search results list.

5. Click the **FILE tab** to open Backstage view and select **Print** on the Navigation Pane.

6. Click **Memo Style**, if necessary, then click the **Preview** button.

PAUSE. LEAVE Outlook open to use in the next exercise.

Mastery Assessment

Project 3-5: Press Announcement

Its natural surroundings, luxurious facilities, and exceptional reputation have made Resort Adventures a hometown favorite location for weddings. Later today, another well-known local couple will send wedding invitations to a few close friends and the press. Mindy wants to provide her contact information for the press, but it will be a busy afternoon. She decides to write the message, but delay the delivery of the message until the couple announces the wedding date and location an hour from now.

GET READY. LAUNCH Outlook if it is not already running.

1. Open a new message window.

2. In the *To* field, key [**your e-mail address**].

3. In the *Subject* field, key **Mello-Stevens Wedding**.

4. In the message area, write a brief message stating that you are confirming that the Mello-Stevens wedding will be held at Resort Adventures. Provide a link to your website at www.resortadventures.net and your contact information at 800-555-1234. Don't forget to include your name at the end of the message.

5. Set the delivery delay for **2** minutes from now. (You must be able to leave the computer running and connected to the Internet until the specified time.)

6. Send the message.

7. Locate the message in the Sent Items folder and save it in Outlook Message Format.

PAUSE. LEAVE Outlook open to use in the next exercise.

Project 3-6: Send Your Digital Signature

A large corporation in a nearby city has decided to hold its fall sales convention at Resort Adventures. However, the Marketing Department in charge of the convention requires digital signatures on every message. You must exchange your digital signature with the marketing team member in charge of the convention.

GET READY. LAUNCH Outlook if it is not already running.

1. Open a new message window.

2. In the *To* field, key the [**address for a friend or coworker**].

3. In the *Subject* field, key **Fall Conference**.

4. In the message area, write a brief message stating that your digital signature has been added to the message.

5. Add your digital ID to the message.

6. Send the message.

CLOSE Outlook.

Circling Back

Fabrikam, Inc. is an older company. This family business was established by Rob Caron in 1973 to sell, install, and maintain swimming pools. As the second generation has taken over management of the company, Fabrikam has expanded by increasing the Fabrikam line of products. Fabrikam now sells patio furniture, house awnings, and hot tubs. Over time, they plan to add almost every product that makes your back yard more fun or more comfortable.

Project 1: Signature Message

Marian Cole, the Marketing Manager, has asked you to create a signature for her e-mail messages. She asked you to use a graphic she likes.

GET READY. Outlook should not be running.

1. Launch Outlook from a desktop shortcut.
2. Click the New E-mail button. A new message window is opened.
3. In the *To* field, key Marian@fabrikam.com. In the *Subject* field, key New Signature.

Take Note Throughout this Circling Back you will see information that appears in black text within brackets, such as [Press Enter] or [your e-mail address]. The information contained in the brackets is intended to be directions for you rather than something you actually type word for word. It will instruct you to perform an action or substitute text. Do **not** type the actual text that appears within brackets.

4. Click the OPTIONS tab and click Bcc to display the Bcc field. In the *Bcc* field, key [your e-mail address].
5. Click in the message area. Key Hi Marian, do you like this signature? [Press Enter three times.]
6. On the INSERT tab, click the Table button in the Tables group. Click the second square in the fifth row of boxes in the dropdown list. An empty table with two columns and five rows is inserted in the message area.
7. Select all the cells in the first column of the table and click the LAYOUT tab. Because table cells are selected, the displayed layout options apply to tables.
8. Click the Merge Cells button in the Merge group. The cells in the first column are merged.
9. Click in the merged cell. Click the INSERT tab.

10. Click the Pictures button in the Illustrations group. Select the *Pool.jpg* file in the Data files. Click the Insert button in the dialog box. The image is inserted, but it will likely be much too large to use in a signature. The image is automatically selected in the table. (If your image looks to be about the right size for a signature, you can skip ahead to step 14.)
11. With the picture still selected, click the Dialog Box Launcher in the Size group on the Picture Tools FORMAT tab. The Layout dialog box is displayed.

Take Note Hint: The dialog box launcher is the small arrow in the bottom-right corner of a group.

12. In the *Scale* area, click the Lock aspect ratio check box to select the option if necessary. This option will keep the image in proportion as you resize it.
13. Click in the Height box. Key 5% and [press Tab]. Click the OK button to return to the message window. The pool image has been resized.
14. Drag the vertical center border of the table to the left so the first column is barely wider than the pool image.
15. Click in the first row of the second column and enter the following information in that column:

First row	Marian Cole
Second row	Marketing Manager
Third row	Fabrikam, Inc.

Fourth row	**www.fabrikam.com**
Fifth row	**800-555-8734 or Marian@fabrikam.com**.

[Press **Enter**.]

16. Select all the text in the table. Click the **MESSAGE** tab if necessary. In the Basic Text group, change the font to **Century Gothic**. (Use *Arial* font if you don't have Century Gothic.)

17. Select **Marian Cole** in the first row of the second column. Change the font to **Lucida Handwriting**. (If you don't have Lucida Handwriting, use any font that looks like handwriting or leave the font unchanged.)

18. Increase the font size of Marian's name to **20** and click the **Bold** button.

19. Select the text in the first row of the table. Click the **Font Color** arrow. In the displayed colors, click a medium blue shade that coordinates with the color of the pool image.

20. Drag the right border of the table to the left so that the second column is barely wider than the widest text in the column.

21. Click the **pool image**. Click the **TABLE TOOLS LAYOUT** tab. Click the **Align Center** button in the Alignment group.

22. Select the table. Click the **TABLE TOOLS DESIGN** tab. In the Borders group, click the **Borders** arrow. Click the **No Border** option.

23. In the message area, select the new signature table.

24. In the Text group on the INSERT tab, click the **Quick Parts** drop button. Click **Save Selection to Quick Part Gallery**.

25. In the Name box, key **CB 1-1** as the name for your Quick Part. Click **OK**.

26. Click the **FILE** tab and select **Save As**. The Save As dialog box is displayed.

27. In the *File name* field, key **CB Project 1-1**. In the *Save as type* field, select **HTML**. Click **Save**.

28. Click **Send**.

LEAVE Outlook and the message window open for the next project.

Project 2: Send a Digital ID with a Default Theme

Marian likes the new signature and has asked you to create a default theme to go with the "look" you are designing. Create and send a message using the new signature and theme. Mark the message as High Importance and flag the message for the recipient to follow up. If you have a digital ID, include your digital ID in the message.

GET READY. Outlook must be running for this project.

1. Click the **FILE** tab and select **Options**. The Outlook Options dialog box is displayed.

2. Click **Mail** in the Navigation Pane. In the *Compose messages* area, click the **Stationery and Fonts** button. The Signatures and Stationery dialog box opens.

3. Click the **PERSONAL STATIONERY** tab. Click the **Theme** button to display the Theme or Stationery dialog box.

4. In the list of themes and stationery, scroll down and click **Soft Blue**. Click **OK** to close the Theme or Stationery dialog box.

5. Click the **Font** dropdown arrow, select **Use theme's fonts**.

6. Click **OK** to close the Signatures and Stationery dialog box. Note that changes to the theme or stationery are not displayed until you open a new message window. Click **OK** again to close the Outlook Options dialog box.

7. On the HOME tab, click the **New E-mail** button. A new message window is opened and the MESSAGE tab is selected.

8. Click in the message area. Key **Hi Jon,** and [press **Enter** twice]. Notice that the theme you selected changed the fonts used in the message area.

9. Key **I'm looking forward to our lunch appointment tomorrow.** [Press **Enter** twice.]

10. In the *To* field, key [**the e-mail address of a friend or coworker**].

11. In the *Subject* field, key **CB Project 1-2**.

12. In the Tags group, click the **Follow Up** button. Click the **Custom** option. The Custom dialog box is displayed.

13. Click the **Flag for Recipients** check box so the option is selected. Click **OK** to close the dialog box.

14. In the Tags group, click the **High Importance** button.

15. If necessary, in the Show Fields group, click **Bcc** to select it. In the *Bcc* field, key [**your e-mail address**].

16. Click in the message area of the window. On the INSERT tab, click **Quick Parts** in the Text group. Click the **CB 1-1** Quick Part.

17. Click the **Send** button. Click **Send/Receive All Folders** on the HOME tab.

18. In the Instant Search box, key **CB Project 1-1**. Click the **All Mailboxes** button on the SEARCH TOOLS tab to locate the message.

19. Double-click the **CB Project 1-2** message. In the Move group, click the **Actions** button and select **Resend This Message** in the dropdown list. If you don't have a digital ID account, simply click **Send**.

Take Note   If you have already set up a digital ID account, proceed with the steps below. If you do not have digital ID, proceed to step 23.

20. If you have already set up a digital ID account, click at the end of the message and key **I'm sending my digital ID**.

21. In the Permission group, click the **Sign** button.

22. Click **Send** to send the message a second time.

23. In the Show Fields group on the OPTIONS tab, click **Bcc** to deselect it. Close the original message window, if it is still open.

LEAVE Outlook open for the next project.

Project 3: Send Voting Message with Attachments

When the New signature message arrives, Marian previews it and saves the signature table as a personal signature. Afterward, she needs to create and send a message with two attachments asking the recipient to vote on which of the two images should be included in the upcoming brochure.

USE the New Signature message you created in Project 1.

1. Click the **Folders** button on the Navigation bar.

Take Note   Hint: Click the *** on the Navigation bar to locate the Folders button.

2. Click the **Minimize the Folder Pane** button at the top right of the Folders List. The Navigation Pane collapses to a bar along the left side of the screen.

3. On the VIEW tab, click the **To-Do Bar** button in the Layout group. Select **Calendar** in the dropdown list if it isn't already selected.

4. Click in the **Instant Search** box, and key **Cole**. Messages to Marian Cole appear in the message list.

5. Click once on the **New Signature** message to select it. The Reading Pane displays a preview of the message.

6. From the Reading Pane, select the table containing the signature for Marian Cole and [press **Ctrl + C**] to copy the table.

7. Click the **New E-mail** button. A new message window is opened.

8. On the MESSAGE tab in the Include group, click the **Signature** button. Click the **Signatures** option to display the Signatures and Stationery dialog box.

9. Click the **New** button. The New Signature dialog box is displayed.

10. Key **CB Project 1-3** and click **OK** to return to the Signatures and Stationery dialog box.

11. Click in the *Edit signature* area. [Press **Ctrl + V**] to paste the new signature into the box. Click the **OK** button to return to the message window.

12. In the *To* field, key [the e-mail address of a friend or coworker]. In the *Cc* field, key [your e-mail address]. In the *Subject* field, key New brochure photo.

13. Click in the message area. Key Please view the two attached images and vote on whether they will be okay to use in the new brochure. [Press Enter three times.]

14. In the Include group, click the Signature button. Click the CB Project 1-3 option to insert the signature.

15. In the Illustrations group on the INSERT tab, click the Pictures button. The Insert Picture dialog box is displayed.

16. Select the *Porch.jpg* file in the Data files for this activity. [Press Ctrl] and click the *Patio.jpg* file that is also in the data files. Click Insert.

17. Click the OPTIONS tab. Click Use Voting Buttons and select Yes; No; Maybe. An InfoBar appears at the top of the message to notify you that voting buttons have been added to the message.

18. Click the Send button. The message is moved to the Outbox and sent when the computer is connected to the Internet. Click Send/Receive All Folders on the HOME tab.

19. If necessary, click the Mail button on the Navigation bar to return to the Inbox.

20. Save the New brochure photo message in Outlook Message Format.

21. Select the New Signature and New brochure photo messages.

22. Click the FILE tab and select Print in the Navigation Pane. Click the Preview button to view the messages in the Preview pane.

23. If you have a printer connected to your PC, click Print to print the messages using your default settings.

24. Click the FILE tab and select Options. Click Mail in the Navigation Pane.

25. Click the Stationery and Fonts button and click the PERSONAL STATIONERY tab. Click the Theme button to display the Theme or Stationery dialog box.

26. In the list of themes and stationery, click No Theme. Click OK to close the dialog box and click OK again to restore the default theme. Click OK to close the Outlook Options dialog box.

CLOSE Outlook.

4 Managing E-mail Messages

LESSON SKILL MATRIX

Skills	Exam Objective	Objective Number
Working with Folders	Add new local folders	2.3.3
	Move messages between folders	2.3.2
Using Conversation View	Sort by conversation	2.3.10
	Ignore messages	2.3.9
Managing the Mailbox	Mark as read/unread	2.3.7
	Delete messages	2.1.3
	Flag messages	2.3.8
	Configure reminders	3.3.3
Using the Outlook Cleanup Tools	Cleanup messages	2.3.6
Managing Junk Mail	Configure junk e-mail settings	2.3.5
	Block specific addresses	1.1.4

KEY TERMS

- archive
- AutoArchive
- Blocked Senders list
- Conversation
- Deleted Items folder
- Drafts folder
- Inbox folder
- Junk E-mail folder
- Outbox
- Really Simple Syndication (RSS)
- restore
- retention rules
- Safe Senders List
- Sent Items folder
- spam

© webphotographeer/iStockphoto

148

Mindy Martin, co-owner of Resort Adventures, started using Outlook 2013 a couple of months ago. She was amazed to see that her Inbox already contained 180 messages. Clearly, she needs some way to organize them. After a bit of thought, she decides to mimic the organizational method she uses with her paper documents. She begins creating folders for the main categories of vendors, events, and guests. If you don't take the time to organize and maintain your mailbox, things can quickly get out of hand. In this lesson, you'll learn how to manage your mailbox to organize and maintain your information.

SOFTWARE ORIENTATION

The Folders List

The Folders List, shown in Figure 4-1, provides a complete list of the initial Outlook 2013 folders. It includes a folder for each Outlook 2013 component, such as the Calendar and Notes.

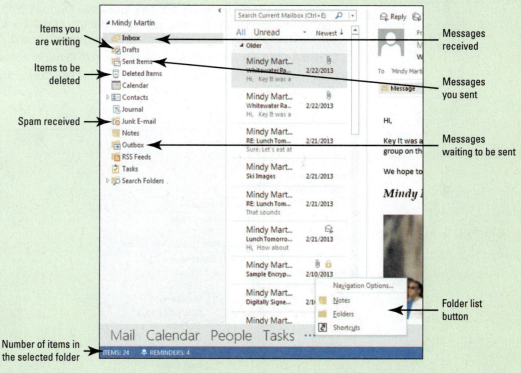

Figure 4-1

The Outlook Folders List

Although the Folders List includes every component, you will normally work only with the mail folders identified in Figure 4-1. The status bar at the bottom of the Outlook 2013 window displays the number of items in the selected folder. Create new folders to organize Outlook 2013 items by projects or individuals.

WORKING WITH FOLDERS

The Bottom Line

How often do you wander around your house looking for your car keys? If your answer is "rarely," you are already in the habit of putting things away, so you know where to find them later. Organize your Outlook 2013 items in folders for the same reason. Items are easier to find when you put them away. In this section, you'll work with Outlook 2013 folders by creating, moving, deleting, and restoring them. You'll also move mail items from folder to folder.

Creating and Moving a Mail Folder

In your office, new documents arrive in your Inbox regularly. You look at the document, perform the associated tasks, and file the paper in a folder you labeled for that type of item. You don't place it back in your Inbox. If you piled up all your documents in your Inbox, in a few weeks or months you would have a stack of paper that was several inches tall. In the same way, you don't want to keep all your messages in your Inbox in Microsoft Outlook 2013. In this exercise, you'll create and move Outlook 2013 folders.

STEP BY STEP   **Create and Move a Mail Folder**

GET READY. LAUNCH Outlook 2013 if it is not already running.

1. Click the icon at the end of [•••] the Navigation bar and select **Folders** to display the Folders List shown in Figure 4-1. The four main Outlook 2013 folders (Inbox, Drafts, Sent Items, and Deleted Items) appear at the top of the list with the remaining Outlook 2013 folders appearing in alphabetical order beneath them.

2. Click the **FOLDER tab** to display the Outlook 2013 folder tools.

3. Click the **New Folder** button in the New group. The Create New Folder dialog box is displayed, as shown in Figure 4-2.

Figure 4-2

Create New Folder dialog box

Key a name for the new folder →

Select the location for the new folder →

4. In the *Name* field, key **Lesson 4** to label the new folder. When creating a folder, use a name that identifies its contents. Don't use abbreviations that you won't remember next week or six months from now.

5. Click the **Outlook Data Files** folder in the Select Where to Place the Folder list. This determines the location where the new folder will be placed when it is created. If you do not have the correct location selected, you can move the new folder later.

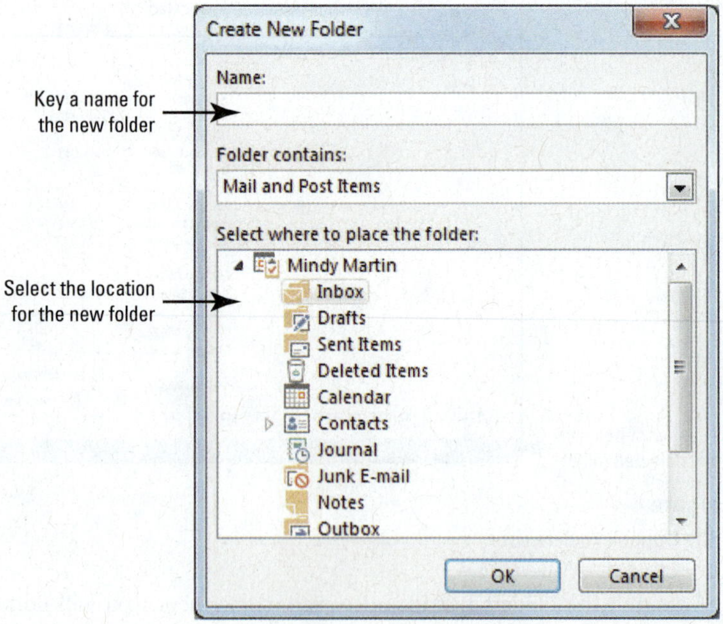

Another Way

To create a new folder, right-click any folder in the Folders List and select New Folder.

⚠️ **Troubleshooting**   For this exercise, you want to select the top-level folder. It's the folder that holds your Inbox, Sent Items folder, and so on. Depending on the settings on your computer and the type of e-mail account you have, this might be called Outlook Data Files, Personal Folders, your name, or simply your e-mail address.

6. Click the **OK** button to close the dialog box and create the folder. The new folder is added to the Folders list alphabetically below the Junk E-mail folder.

7. In the Folders list, click the **Lesson 4 folder** to select it and then drag the folder down to the Notes folder. When the Notes folder is highlighted, drop the folder. An expand arrow is displayed next to the Notes folder, indicating that it contains a folder, as shown in Figure 4-3.

Figure 4-3

New folder created and moved into the Notes folder

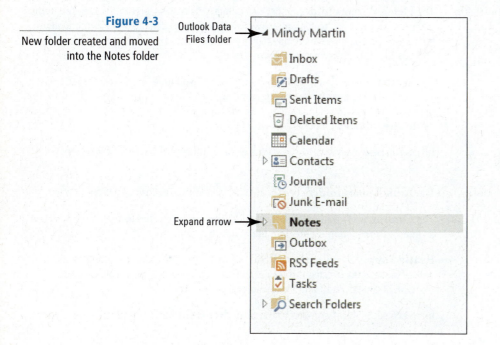

8. Click the **expand arrow** next to the Notes folder. The Folders list expands to display the Lesson 4 folder, as shown in Figure 4-4.

Figure 4-4

The expanded Notes folder

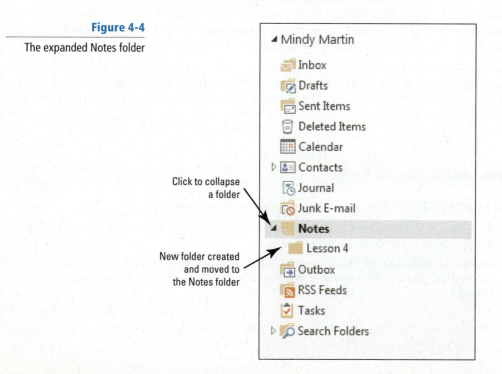

9. Drag the Lesson 4 folder and drop it just below the Outlook Data Files folder in the Folders list. The Lesson 4 folder is placed back on the Folders List, but it is now at the top of the list, and the expand arrow is removed from the Notes folder.

CERTIFICATION READY?   2.3.3

How do you add a new local folder?

PAUSE. LEAVE Outlook 2013 open to use in the next exercise.

Outlook 2013 provides several default mail folders that meet your most basic organizational needs. Table 4-1 identifies the default mail folders and describes their content.

Table 4-1

Default Mail Folders

Folder	Description
Deleted Items	The **Deleted Items folder** holds your deleted messages. Items in the Deleted Items folder can be restored to full use. However, if the item is deleted while in the Deleted Items folder, it will be permanently deleted from your computer. Emptying the Deleted Items folder permanently removes every item in the folder.
Drafts	The **Drafts folder** holds Outlook 2013 messages you have written but haven't sent. You can return to a draft later to complete and send the message. If you close a message without sending it, a dialog box will ask if you want to save the draft. Click Yes to save the draft. Click No to discard the draft.
Inbox	By default, new messages you receive are placed in the **Inbox folder** when they arrive.
Junk E-mail	The **Junk E-mail folder** contains messages identified as spam when they arrive.
Outbox	The **Outbox** holds outgoing messages until you are connected to the Internet. When an Internet connection is detected, the message is sent.
RSS Feeds	**Really Simple Syndication (RSS)** allows you to subscribe to content from a variety of websites offering the service. RSS is not covered in this book. Use The Outlook Help feature to find more information on RSS.
Sent Items	Items are automatically moved to the **Sent Items folder** after they have been sent.

Deleting and Restoring a Folder

You can delete an Outlook 2013 folder you no longer need. When you delete a folder, it is moved to the Deleted Items folder. Items in the Deleted Items folder are still on your computer. You can **restore** these items, that is, make them available for use again, by moving them out of the Deleted Items folder. In this exercise, you'll delete the Lesson 4 folder and restore it.

⚠️ **Troubleshooting**   Use caution. If you *delete* an item that is stored in the Deleted Items folder instead of moving the item to another folder, such as the Outlook Data File, the item is permanently removed from your computer and can no longer be restored.

STEP BY STEP   **Delete and Restore a Folder**

GET READY. USE the folder you created in the previous exercises.

1. If necessary, click the icon at the end of the Navigation bar and select **Folders** to display the complete list of Outlook 2013 folders.
2. Right-click the **Lesson 4 folder** created in the previous exercise, and select **Delete Folder** from the shortcut menu. A warning dialog box is displayed, as shown in Figure 4-5.

Figure 4-5

Deleting a folder

The Lesson 4 folder
is being deleted

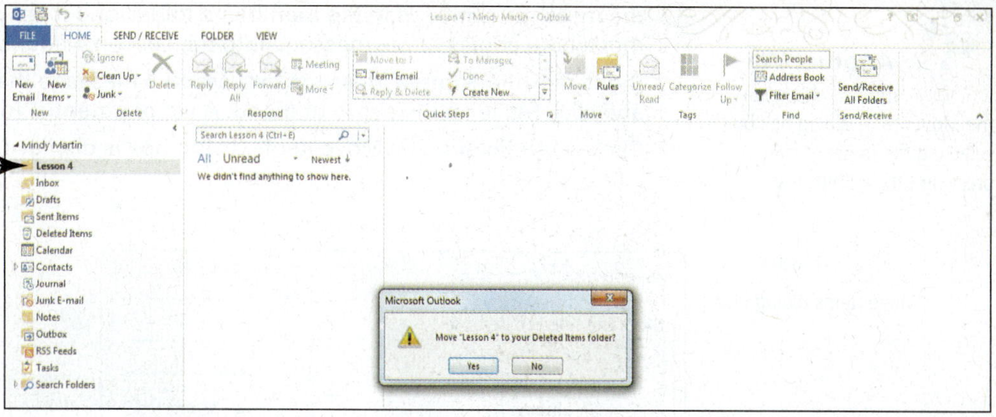

3. Click **Yes** to close the warning dialog box. The Lesson 4 folder is moved to the Deleted Items folder. It will not be removed from your computer until you empty the Deleted Items folder.

4. In the Folders list, click the **expand arrow** next to the Deleted Items folder. The Lesson 4 folder is displayed in the Deleted Items folder.

5. Drag the Lesson 4 folder and drop it on the Outlook Data Files folder again. The Lesson 4 folder is placed in the Outlook Data Files folder, and the expand arrow is removed from the Deleted Items folder. The Lesson 4 folder has been restored, and it is now available for use.

PAUSE. LEAVE Outlook 2013 open to use in the next exercise.

Moving Messages to a Different Folder

Outlook 2013 uses folders to organize Outlook 2013 items. Messages arrive in the Inbox. Messages you send are stored in the Sent Items folder. To effectively organize your messages, create new folders for projects or individuals and move the related messages into the new folders. In this exercise, you'll start organizing your mailbox by moving messages to different folders.

STEP BY STEP   **Move Messages to a Different Folder**

GET READY. LAUNCH Outlook 2013 if it is not already running, and complete the previous exercises.

1. If necessary, click the **Mail** button in the Navigation bar to display the Inbox.

Cross Ref In Lesson 5, you will create and use rules to automatically move messages.

2. Click the **New E-mail** button on the HOME tab. The Message window is displayed. By default, the MESSAGE tab is selected.

3. In the *To* field, key [**your e-mail address**]. In the *Subject* field, key **Sample Message for Lesson 4**.

Take Note Throughout this chapter you will see information that appears in black text within brackets, such as [Press **Enter**] or [**your e-mail address**]. The information contained in the brackets is intended to be directions for you rather than something you actually type word for word. It will instruct you to perform an action or substitute text. Do **not** type the actual text that appears within brackets.

4. In the message area, key **Sample Message for Lesson 4**.

5. Click the **Send** button. The message is moved to the Outbox, and it is sent when your computer is connected to the Internet.

6. Return to your Inbox in the Folders list. Click the **Send/Receive All Folders** button if the message has not arrived yet. Because the message was sent to your e-mail address,

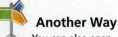

Another Way
You can also open the Move Items dialog box by selecting the message and pressing Ctrl + Shift + V.

the message is moved to the Sent Items folder, and it arrives in your Inbox. You will move both copies of the message into the Lesson 4 folder.

7. Right-click the **Sample Message for Lesson 4** message that just arrived in your Inbox, and click **Move** on the shortcut menu. A list of potential folders is displayed.

8. Click **Other Folder**. The Move Items dialog box is displayed, as shown in Figure 4-6.

Figure 4-6

Move Items dialog box

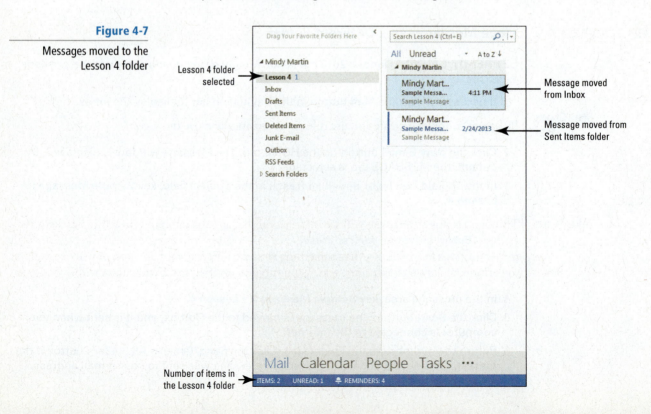

9. Click the **Lesson 4 folder** in the dialog box, if necessary; then click the **OK** button to close the dialog box and move the received message from the Inbox to the Lesson 4 folder.

10. Click the **Sent Items folder** in the Folders list. A list of the messages you have sent is displayed in the message list.

11. Click the **Sample Message for Lesson 4** message and drag it to the Lesson 4 folder. The message is moved from the Sent Items folder to the Lesson 4 folder.

12. Click the **Lesson 4 folder** in the Folders list. The two messages you moved are displayed in the message list, as shown in Figure 4-7.

Figure 4-7

Messages moved to the Lesson 4 folder

CERTIFICATION	2.3.2
READY?	

How would you move
messages between folders?

PAUSE. LEAVE Outlook 2013 open to use in the next exercise.

USING CONVERSATION VIEW

The Bottom Line

In Outlook 2013, using Conversation view enables you to organize every e-mail message you send or receive about the same subject together into one **Conversation** group right there in your Inbox. In this section, you will turn on Conversation view and learn how to work with it. You'll also learn how to ignore a Conversation that you no longer want to follow.

SOFTWARE ORIENTATION

Conversation View

Outlook 2013 allows you to streamline your Inbox into Conversation view, shown in Figure 4-8. Conversation view groups all related messages (based on the Subject line) in one convenient location.

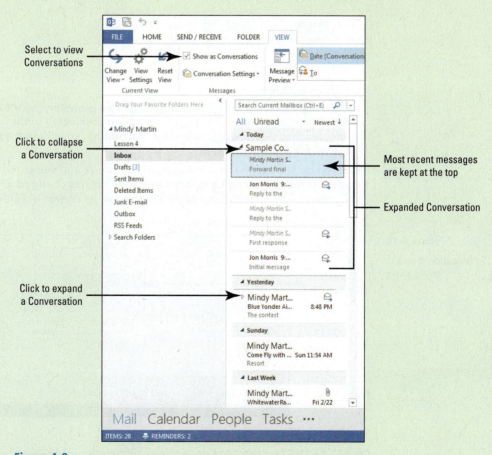

Figure 4-8

Message list in Conversation view

Conversation view lets you know the status of each message in the Conversation. Every related message is included in the Conversation group, even if it has been stored in a different folder. Use this figure as a reference throughout this lesson as well as the rest of this book.

Turning on Conversation View

Conversations are a great way to organize your messages. They can greatly reduce the clutter in your Inbox by grouping like information together. For example, you send an e-mail called *Lunch Tomorrow* to four friends asking what restaurant they want to go to for lunch. All replies are grouped into a single Conversation along with the original message you sent, as well as any other messages that the five of you send back and forth as replies or forwards to the original e-mail message. To let you know that more information is available, Outlook 2013 displays an expansion arrow beside the message. In this lesson, you will turn on Conversation view.

STEP BY STEP   **Turn on Conversation View**

USE the *Blue Yonder Airlines contest* messages you created in Lesson 2.

1. If necessary, click the **Mail** button in the Navigation bar to display the mailbox and select **Inbox** in the Folders List.

2. Click the **VIEW** tab and select **Show as Conversations** in the Messages group. A message box is displayed, as shown in Figure 4-9.

Figure 4-9

Turning on Conversation view

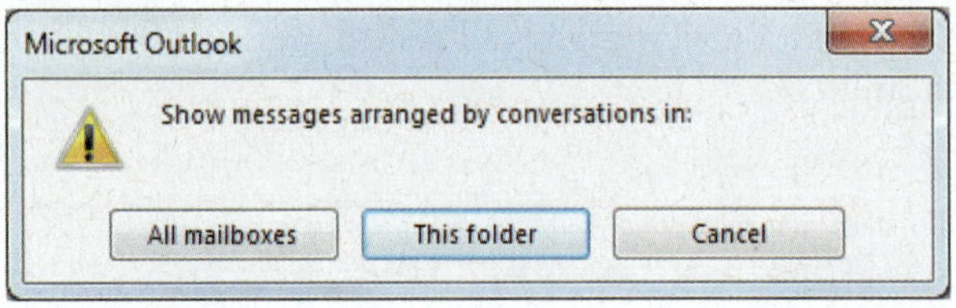

3. Click **This Folder**.

4. Click **Conversation Settings** in the Messages group on the VIEW tab, and verify that the **Show Messages from Other Folders** option is selected in the menu that appears. This ensures that Outlook 2013 will show you entire Conversations regardless of the folder the messages are stored in.

5. Scroll back through the messages in your Inbox and select the **Blue Yonder Airlines contest** message. Notice that the message list has changed to show that it is a Conversation by adding an expansion arrow, as shown in Figure 4-10.

Figure 4-10

Conversation shown in Message list

Click to expand a Conversation

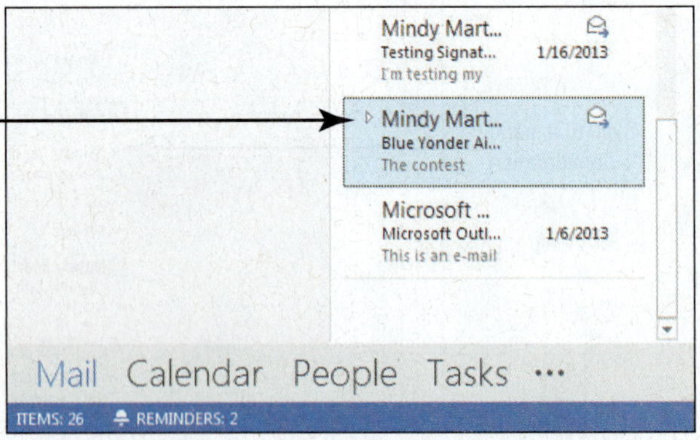

PAUSE. LEAVE Outlook 2013 open to use in the next exercise.

Working with Conversations

Conversations can grow to hold dozens of messages. When you click the header of the Conversation message, the most recent message received appears in the Reading Pane. When you click the expansion arrow next to the Conversation, it expands to show all the related messages from the Inbox as well as any related messages in other folders. In this exercise, you will practice working with Conversations.

Take Note   Because Conversations are typically with two or more people, you should try to complete this exercise with a friend or coworker. If none is available, you can complete the exercise by sending and receiving messages to yourself.

Work with Conversations

GET READY. LAUNCH Outlook 2013 if it is not already running.

1. If necessary, click the **Mail** button in the Navigation bar to display the Inbox. On the VIEW tab, ensure that Show as Conversations is selected.

2. Click the **New E-mail** button on the HOME tab to open a new message window.

3. In the *To* field, key [**the e-mail address of a friend who is also working on this lesson**]. Then type a semicolon and key **someone@example.com**.

4. In the *Subject* field, key **Sample Conversation**. In the message area, key **Initial message**.

5. Click **Send**. Click the **Send/Receive All Folders** button on the Quick Access toolbar.

6. When the Sample Conversation message with the text *Initial message* arrives from your friend, select it and click the **Reply Quick Response** button.

7. In the message area, key **First response**. Click **Send**.

8. Click the **Send/Receive All Folders** button on the HOME tab. Notice that an expansion arrow appears next to the Sample Conversation message to let you know that it is now a Conversation, as shown in Figure 4-11.

Figure 4-11

Identifying a Conversation

A closed conversation

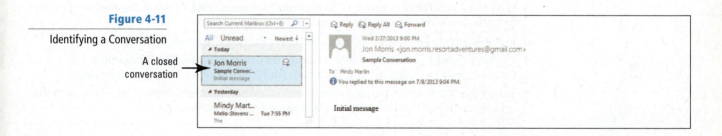

9. Click the **expansion arrow** to expand the Conversation. The conversation expands to show the two related messages, as shown in Figure 4-12. Notice that the sender information is italicized on the First Response message.

Figure 4-12

An expanded conversation in the Message list

Most recent message

Conversation

Original message

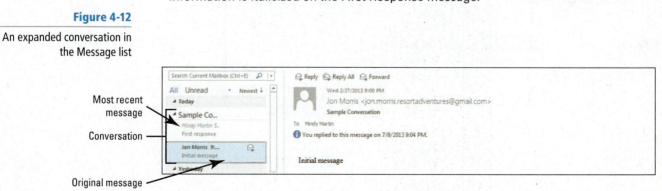

10. Hover over the **RE: Sample Conversation message** in the Conversation. A ScreenTip appears indicating the folder where the message is stored, as shown in Figure 4-13.

Figure 4-13

Viewing messages from other folders in the Conversation

Folder where this message is stored

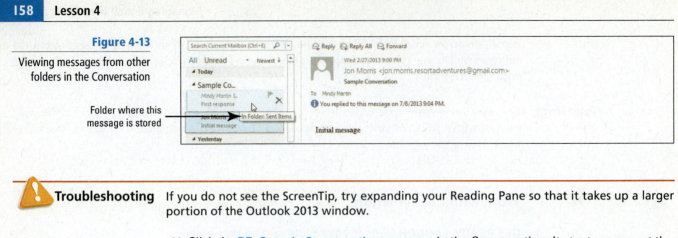

Troubleshooting If you do not see the ScreenTip, try expanding your Reading Pane so that it takes up a larger portion of the Outlook 2013 window.

11. Click the **RE: Sample Conversation message** in the Conversation. Its text appears at the top of the Reading Pane (as shown in Figure 4-14). Notice that there is now a thin grey line that divides the two messages.

Figure 4-14

Viewing the next message in the Conversation

Collapse button

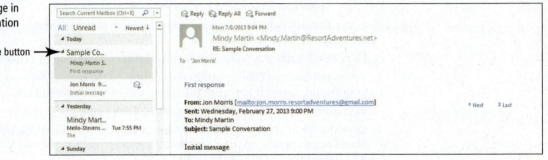

12. With the *RE: Sample Conversation* message selected, click **Reply** in the Respond group to open a new RE: Sample Conversation message window.

13. In the message area, key **Reply to the "first response" message**. Click **Send**.

14. Click the **Send/Receive All Folders** button on the HOME tab. The RE: Sample Conversation message arrives from your friend and is added to the Conversation.

15. Select the **RE: Sample Conversation message** when it arrives from your friend with the text *Reply to the "first response" message*, as shown in Figure 4-15.

Take Note You can read and respond to any of the messages in a Conversation just as you would any other message.

Figure 4-15

Continuing the Conversation

Newly received message added to the list

Messages within the Conversation are stacked in the Reading Pane

16. Click **Forward** in the Respond group to open a FW: Sample Conversation message window.

17. In the *To* field, key [**the e-mail address of a different friend**]. In the message area, key **Forward final message to a friend**. Click **Send**.

18. Click the **Send/Receive All Folders** button on the HOME tab. The message that you sent appears at the top of the expanded Conversation.

19. Select the **FW: Sample Conversation** message.

20. In the Reading Pane, point above the right end of the grey line that appears below the *"Forward final message to a friend"* message. Two navigation buttons appear just above the line, as shown in Figure 4-16.

Figure 4-16

Completing the Conversation

Reading Pane now shows the selected message

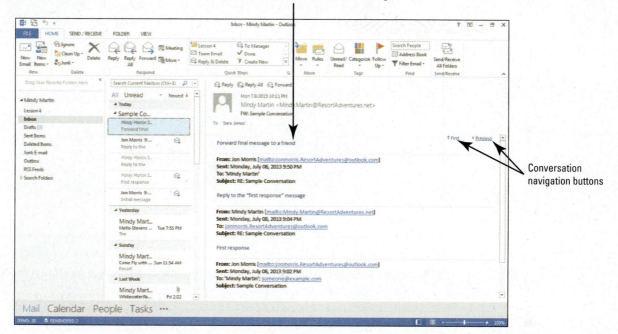

Conversation navigation buttons

21. Click the **Previous** button. As you can see by the arrow on the button, clicking the Previous button jumps you back through the previous messages in the Conversation.

Take Note   Remember that because Conversations flow from newest to oldest, the Next button takes you forward through the messages.

22. Click the black **collapse arrow** next to the Conversation heading. The Conversation compresses down to one item in the message list with an expansion arrow.

PAUSE. LEAVE Outlook 2013 open to use in the next exercise.

CERTIFICATION READY? 2.3.10

How do you sort your messages by Conversation?

One of the convenient things about working with Conversations is that no matter how you organize your messages, you can still see them in one convenient place. When Outlook 2013 displays a message from another folder, the message information appears grey and italicized in the message list.

Ignoring a Conversation

Although Conversations are a great organizing tool, you might find that you no longer want to be included in a particular Conversation. You can stop following a Conversation by selecting the Conversation header and clicking Ignore in the Delete group on the HOME tab. All future messages related to this Conversation (as indicated by the Subject line) will automatically move to your Deleted Items folder. In this exercise, you will ignore a Conversation.

STEP BY STEP   **Ignore a Conversation**

USE the *Lunch Tomorrow* messages you sent to yourself in Lesson 2.

1. If necessary, click the **Mail** button in the Navigation bar to display the mailbox and click the **Lunch Tomorrow?** Conversation in the message list.

2. Click the **HOME tab** to display the Delete group.

3. Click **Ignore** in the Delete group. Outlook 2013 asks you to confirm that you want to ignore the entire Conversation, as shown in Figure 4-17.

Figure 4-17

Ignoring a Conversation

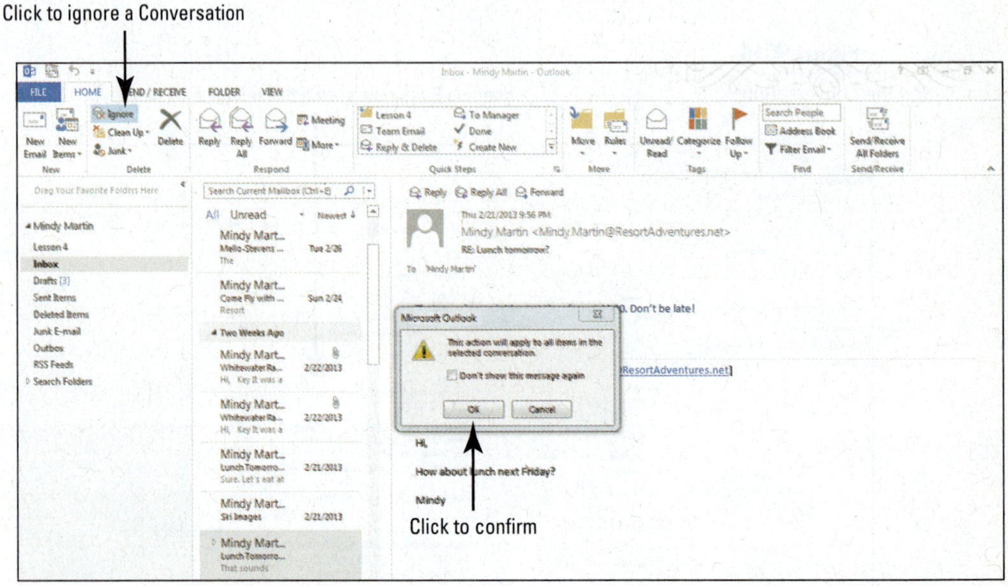

Click to ignore a Conversation

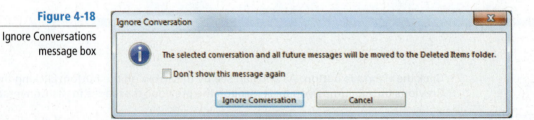

Click to confirm

4. Click **OK**. The Ignore Conversation message box is displayed, as shown in Figure 4-18.

Figure 4-18

Ignore Conversations message box

> **Ignore Conversation**
>
> The selected conversation and all future messages will be moved to the Deleted Items folder.
>
> ☐ Don't show this message again
>
> [Ignore Conversation]   [Cancel]

5. Click **Ignore Conversation**. The Conversation moves out of the Inbox and into the Deleted Items box. Outlook 2013 will move all future messages related to this Conversation to your Deleted Items folder as soon as they are received by your e-mail account.

6. Click the **VIEW** tab and deselect **Show as Conversations** in the Messages group. A message box is displayed asking whether you want to stop using Conversations view.

7. Click **All Mailboxes** to turn off Conversation view.

PAUSE. LEAVE Outlook 2013 open to use in the next exercise.

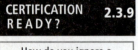

CERTIFICATION READY?   **2.3.9**

How do you ignore a Conversation?

Take Note   When you receive replies or forwards, the text from the previous e-mail appears at the end. This is the same text that is in some of the messages in the Conversation. To get rid of even more clutter, you can click Clean Up in the Delete group and select Clean Up Conversation. The extra messages will be deleted.

MANAGING THE MAILBOX

The Bottom Line

Although organizing your messages into folders and Conversations is a good way to cut down the clutter in your mailbox, you still need to manage the items that remain. Managing your messages means keeping track of what you have or have not read, deleting messages that you no longer need, and following up on messages that require a response or action from you in a timely fashion. In this section, you will learn to manually mark items as read or unread, add follow-up reminders for yourself, and work with the Reminder windows that Outlook 2013 uses to keep you on your toes.

Marking a Message as Read or Unread

Have you ever been called away in the middle of reading an e-mail message? Once you've opened a message or even paused on it for a few seconds, Outlook 2013 considers it read (whether or not you actually finished reading it) and displays it as such in the Inbox listing. When the Inbox shows no unread messages, it can be easy to forget which messages you need to read more completely. To help you avoid this confusion, you can manually mark a message as read or unread. In this exercise, you will mark messages as read and unread.

STEP BY STEP   **Mark a Message as Read or Unread**

USE the *Blue Yonder Airlines contest* messages you sent to yourself in Lesson 2.

1. If necessary, click the **Mail** button in the Navigation bar to display the mailbox, and click the **Blue Yonder Airlines contest** message in the message list. Because you sent a reply to this message, Outlook 2013 shows the message as read.

2. In the message list, click the left side of the message preview item. The message status changes to Unread and a blue bar appears along the left edge; the subject line also turns blue in the message list, as shown in Figure 4-19.

Figure 4-19

Marking a message as unread in the message list

Click to mark a message as read or unread →

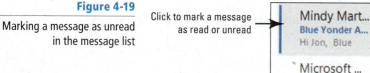

Another Way

You can also mark a message as unread by selecting the message in the message list; then clicking Unread/Read in the Tags group on the HOME tab.

3. With the message still selected in the message list, click the blue bar on the left edge of the message list. The message status changes to Read, and its subject is no longer blue in the message list.

PAUSE. LEAVE Outlook 2013 open to use in the next exercise.

CERTIFICATION READY?   **2.3.7**

How do you mark a message as read or unread?

Deleting an E-mail Message

Some messages require you to act on them or respond to them, and some messages need to be saved until the end of a project. Once you are finished with messages, however, it is best to delete them so that the clutter is eliminated. This makes it easier to find and work with the messages you still need. In this exercise, you'll delete a finished message.

Delete an E-mail Message

USE the *Sample delivery receipt and read receipt* messages you sent to yourself in Lesson 3.

1. If necessary, click the **Mail** button in the Navigation bar to display the mailbox.
2. Hover your mouse over the **Sample delivery receipt and read receipt** message in the message list. A black x appears on the right side of the message item, as shown in Figure 4-20.

Figure 4-20

Using the Delete icon in the message list

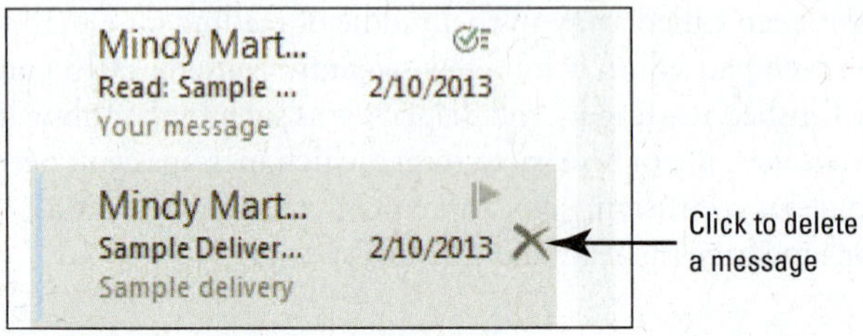

Click to delete a message

3. A red x appears on the right side of the message item when you point to it, as shown in Figure 4-21. Click the red **X** to delete the message.

Figure 4-21

Deleting a message in the message list

Click to delete a message

 Another Way
You can also delete a message by selecting the message in the message list and then clicking Delete in the Delete group on the HOME tab.

PAUSE. LEAVE Outlook 2013 open to use in the next exercise.

CERTIFICATION READY?   2.1.3

How would you delete a message you no longer needed?

Setting a Flag as a Reminder for a Message

The easiest way to keep track of messages that you need to follow up on is to mark them with a flag. When you see a flag, you know that there is still something that you need to do in regard to that message. You can choose whether or not you want Outlook 2013 to give you a Reminder window at a specified time to remind you of your deadline. Once you've completed the required task or response, you can clear the flag to remove the reminder. In this exercise, you'll add a reminder flag to a message.

Set a Flag as a Reminder for a Message

GET READY. USE the Sample Important Message message you sent to yourself in Lesson 3. Because this is an important message, you want to be sure to follow up.

1. If necessary, click the **Mail** button in the Navigation bar to display the mailbox.
2. Hover your mouse over the **Sample Important Message** item in the message list. A grey flag appears in the upper right corner of the message item.
3. Hover your mouse over the **flag**. The flag turns red and a ScreenTip appears, as shown in Figure 4-22. (Depending upon the type of e-mail accounts you have installed, the ScreenTips will differ slightly).

Figure 4-22

Flagging a message in the message list

Another Way

The Follow Up button is also available on the HOME tab in the Tags group.

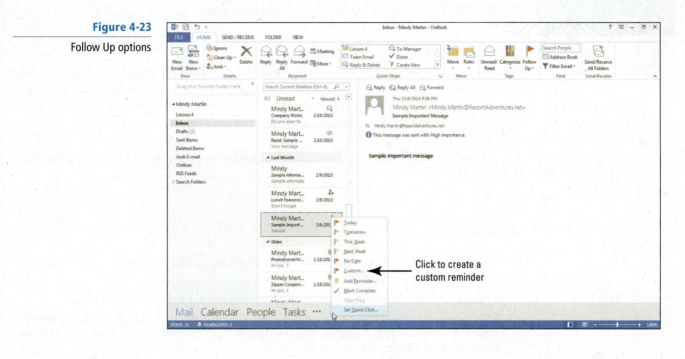

4. Right-click the flag icon. A list of options is displayed beneath the button, as shown in Figure 4-23.

Figure 4-23

Follow Up options

Take Note The color of the flag becomes darker the closer you get to the deadline.

Take Note If you don't see the Custom option, it is because Outlook does not support this option in the type of e-mail account you're running. If you don't see this option, skip ahead to the end of this exercise.

5. Click **Custom** in the dropdown menu to open the Custom dialog box, as shown in Figure 4-24. (Depending upon the type of e-mail account you have installed in Outlook, you might not see the Custom option; in that case, skip steps 5–8).

Figure 4-24

The Custom dialog box

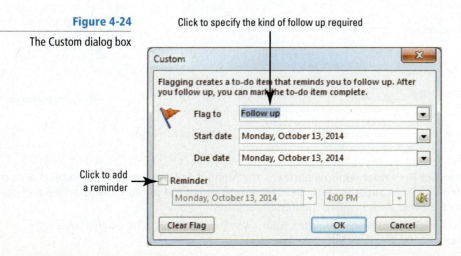

6. Click the **Flag To** down arrow, and select **Review** from the list.

7. Click the **Reminder** check box near the bottom of the dialog box.

8. Set a reminder for five minutes from now. Click **OK** to close the dialog box. The message list now shows the message with a reminder flag in the far-right column, as shown in Figure 4-25.

Figure 4-25

A reminder flag in the message list

Dark reminder flag indicating that the action is due today

PAUSE. LEAVE Outlook 2013 open to use in the next exercise.

Working with Reminder Windows

Once you've set a reminder flag for a message, Outlook 2013 uses the Reminder window as a way to prompt you that a due date is approaching. Outlook 2013 uses the same Reminder window to remind about tasks and calendar appointments. In this exercise, you'll open an Outlook 2013 item from the Reminder window, dismiss the reminder, and clear the flag on a message.

 Cross Ref You can read more about setting reminders for Calendar appointments in Lesson 8 and for tasks in Lesson 11.

STEP BY STEP   **Work with Reminder Windows**

GET READY. USE the Sample Important Message message and complete the preceding exercise, if you haven't already.

1. If necessary, click the **Mail** button in the Navigation bar to display the mailbox.

2. A Reminder window is displayed at the time you indicated in the Custom dialog box in step 8 of the preceding exercise. The window lists all reminders that have not yet been completed, as shown in Figure 4-26.

Figure 4-26

Reminder window

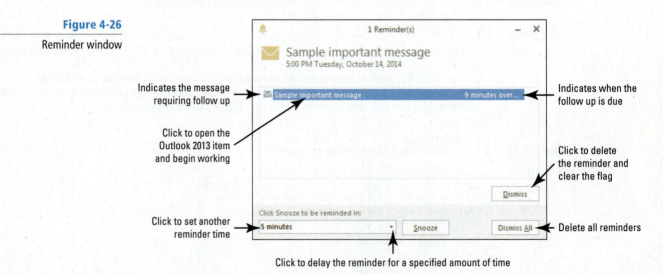

Indicates the message requiring follow up

Click to open the Outlook 2013 item and begin working

Click to set another reminder time

Indicates when the follow up is due

Click to delete the reminder and clear the flag

Delete all reminders

Click to delay the reminder for a specified amount of time

When your Reminder window appears, the highlighted entry within the Subject area of the window indicates the Outlook 2013 item to which the reminder is attached and how much time has passed since the Reminder time.

3. Double click the highlighted entry, **Sample important item**. The original message window is displayed for your review.

4. Click the **Close** button in the top-right corner of the message window to close the message and return to the Reminder window.

5. Click **Dismiss**. The reminder item is deleted from the Subject area. If that was the only item in the Reminder window, the window closes as well.

6. Click the **flag** in the message list. The flag disappears and a check mark takes its place, indicating that you've already followed up, as shown in Figure 4-27. (Depending upon your e-mail account type, Outlook might not display a check mark, but instead the flag just disappears.)

Figure 4-27

A completed reminder
in the message list

Indicates that you've already
followed up on the message

PAUSE. LEAVE Outlook 2013 open to use in the next exercise.

The Reminder window is a great way to stay on top of all your obligations. When the Reminder window appears, it might not be a convenient time to complete the follow-up. If this occurs, click the *Click Snooze to be reminded in:* down arrow and select the amount of time you want before the next reminder. Then click Snooze. You'll get another Reminder window at the appointed time.

USING THE OUTLOOK CLEANUP TOOLS

The Bottom Line

To maintain your folders, you should delete or archive old items. This prevents you from keeping old items past the date when they are useful. In this section, you'll delete and archive older messages. Microsoft Outlook 2013 makes it easy to maintain a neat and organized mailbox by consolidating its Cleanup tools in one convenient location in Backstage view. In this section, you'll work with the Outlook Cleanup tools to reduce the size of your mailbox.

Viewing Mailbox Size and Cleanup Tools

Outlook 2013 stores all of your items in one large .pst file on your computer. Over time, this file can become huge. Rather than saving every single item, it makes more sense to remove any item that you no longer need. You can use the Mailbox Cleanup option within the Cleanup Tools in Backstage view. In the Mailbox Cleanup window, you can view the mailbox size and choose options to delete items, archive items, and find large e-mails with attachments. In this exercise, you'll view the mailbox size and explore the Mailbox Cleanup tools.

STEP BY STEP   **View Mailbox Size and Cleanup Tools**

GET READY. LAUNCH Outlook 2013 if it is not already running.

1. Click the **FILE tab** to open the Backstage view.

2. Click **Cleanup Tools** in the Mailbox Cleanup section. A list of available cleanup tools is displayed, as shown in Figure 4-28.

Figure 4-28

The Outlook Mailbox
Cleanup tools

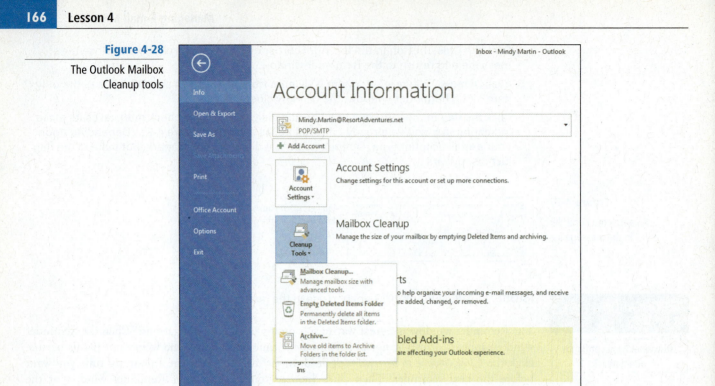

3. Click **Mailbox Cleanup**. The Mailbox Cleanup dialog box is displayed, as shown in Figure 4-29.

Figure 4-29

Mailbox Cleanup dialog box

Click to view the
size of each folder
in your mailbox

Click to find
the oldest or
largest messages

Click to archive
all of the older
messages

4. Click **View Mailbox Size** in the top section of the dialog box. The Folder Size dialog box is displayed, as shown in Figure 4-30.

Figure 4-30

Folder Size dialog box

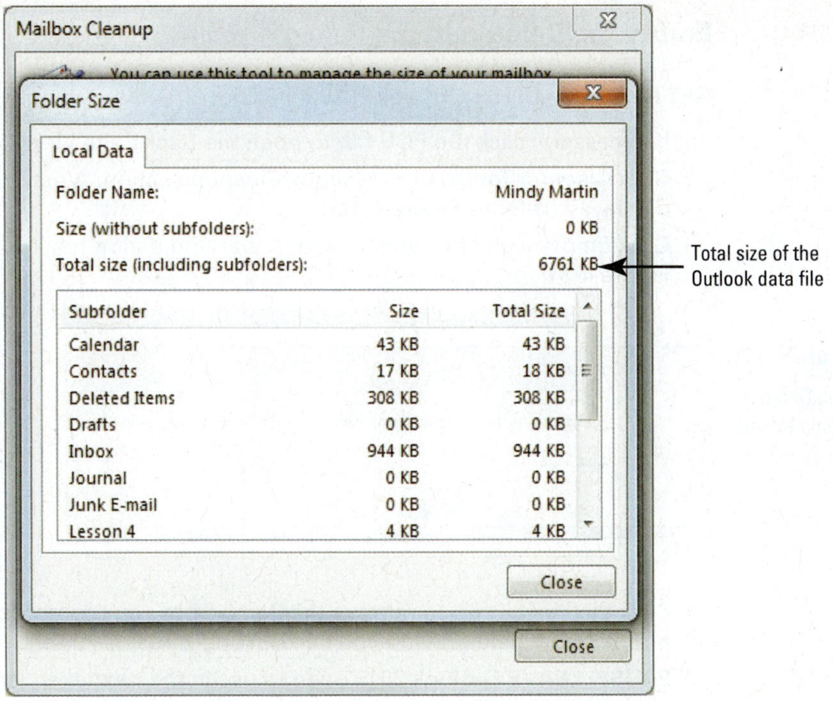

Total size of the
Outlook data file

5. Locate the Total Size item to see the total size of your mailbox file.

Troubleshooting Remember that your mailbox size might differ substantially from the one in the picture depending on the mailbox items that you've created or received.

6. Scroll through the list of folders in the dialog box to see which are the largest.
7. Click **Close** twice to close the Folder Size dialog box and the Mailbox Cleanup dialog box and return to Backstage view.

CERTIFICATION
READY?   **2.3.6**

How would you cleanup
messages in your mailbox?

PAUSE. LEAVE Outlook 2013 open to use in the next exercise.

The Mailbox Cleanup dialog box contains several useful tools to help you keep a handle on your mailbox size.

- **View Mailbox Size** Enables you to see which folders are using up the most space.
- **Find** Helps you to locate either the largest or oldest messages in the mailbox. These are the messages that can make the biggest difference when cleaning up your mailbox.
- **AutoArchive** Uses the Outlook 2013 default AutoArchive settings to take the oldest items out of your mailbox and store them in a separate archive file.
- **Empty** Empties the items in the Deleted Items folder.

Emptying the Deleted Items Folder

When you delete an Outlook 2013 item, it is moved to the Deleted Items folder. It is held in the Deleted Items folder indefinitely. Items in the Deleted Items folder can be moved to another folder or permanently deleted from the computer. Rather than deleting each item manually, you can use the Empty Folder tool to permanently delete every item from the Deleted Items folder at the same time. When you use the Empty Folder tool, the contents of the folder are removed from your computer and can no longer be restored. The same procedure can be used to empty the Junk E-mail folder. In this exercise, you'll empty the Deleted Items folder.

Empty the Deleted Items Folder

GET READY. LAUNCH Outlook 2013 if it is not already running.

1. If necessary, click the **FILE tab** to open the Backstage view.
2. Click **Cleanup Tools** in the Mailbox Cleanup section. A list of available cleanup tools is displayed (refer to Figure 4-28).
3. Click **Empty Deleted Items Folder**. A warning dialog box is displayed, as shown in Figure 4-31.

Figure 4-31

Emptying the Deleted Items folder

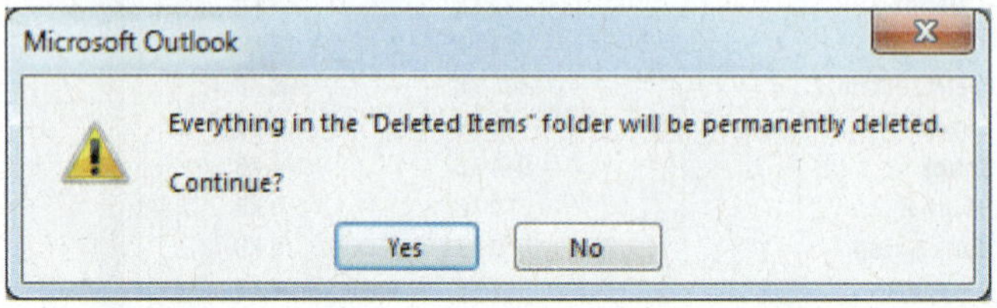

4. Click the **Yes** button to remove the items from your computer; those items are now permanently deleted, and you can no longer restore them.
5. **PAUSE. LEAVE** Outlook 2013 open to use in the next exercise.

Archiving Outlook Items

It is easy to accumulate messages. Some messages are no longer related to your current projects, but you don't want to delete them. Some companies or departments also have to follow **retention rules** that specify the length of time correspondence must be kept. When you **archive** a message, you store it in a separate folder, reducing the number of messages in the folders you use most often. You can still access archived messages in Outlook 2013. By default, items are archived automatically using the **AutoArchive** function, but you can change the AutoArchive settings and archive items manually. In this exercise, you'll manually archive Outlook 2013 items.

Archive Outlook Items

GET READY. LAUNCH Outlook 2013 if it is not already running.

1. If necessary, click the **FILE** tab to open the Backstage view.
2. Click **Cleanup Tools** in the Mailbox Cleanup section. A list of available cleanup tools is displayed (refer to Figure 4-28).
3. Click **Archive**. The Archive dialog box is displayed, as shown in Figure 4-32. This dialog box displays the AutoArchive options that are currently active.

Figure 4-32

Archive dialog box

Select the folder to be archived

Click to select the date for the archive to end

Click to select a location for the archive file

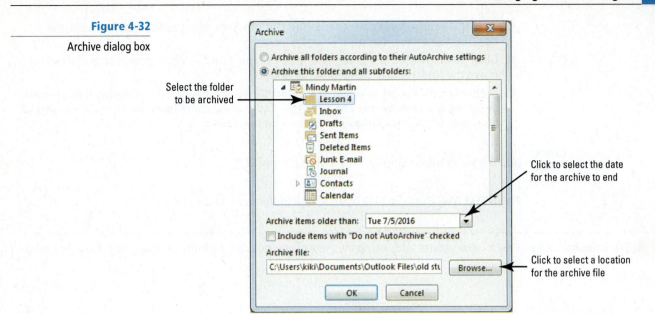

4. Ensure that the *Archive this folder and all subfolders* option is selected, and click the **Lesson 4 folder** in the dialog box.

⚠ **Troubleshooting** Be careful! If you select the wrong folder, whatever folder you click will be emptied of items.

5. Click the **Archive Items older than** down arrow, and select [**tomorrow's date**].

6. Click **Browse** and select the **Solutions** folder for this lesson.

7. In the File name box, key **Archive_xxx** (where *xxx* is your initials).

8. Click **OK** twice.

9. Outlook 2013 warns you that because the date you've chosen is in the future, all items will be archived. Click **Yes**. The items are automatically moved to the Archives file you created and the dialog box closes.

10. Click the **Back arrow** at the top left of the screen. Notice that the Lesson 4 folder you created earlier in this lesson is now empty and that a new Archives folder appears at the bottom of the Folders list.

11. Click the **Archives folder expansion arrow** to open the archive. The Archives folder includes the Lesson 4 folder, in addition to a Search folder and a Deleted Items folder. These two folders are automatically created whenever you archive folders.

12. Click the **Lesson 4 folder** within the Archives folder. It now contains the messages removed from the original Lesson 4 folder, as shown in Figure 4-33.

Figure 4-33

The new Archives folder

Lesson 4 folders

The messages from the Lesson 4 folder have moved to the archive

The new Archives folder

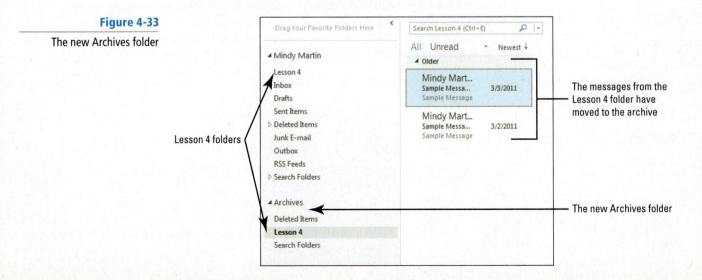

13. Click the empty **Lesson 4 folder** in the Outlook Data Files folder and then click the **FOLDER** tab on the Ribbon.

14. Click **Delete Folder** to delete the empty Lesson 4 folder. When prompted, click **Yes** to move the folder to the Deleted Items folder.

15. Right-click the **Archives** folder and select **Close "Archives"** from the shortcut menu to close the Archives folder. The Archives folder disappears from the Folders List and is stored as an Outlook Data File in the Solutions folder.

Cross Ref You'll learn more about using data files in Lesson 12.

PAUSE. LEAVE Outlook 2013 open to use in the next exercise.

⚠ Troubleshooting Check your state and company retention policies before deleting any business-related messages.

MANAGING JUNK MAIL

The Bottom Line

Nearly every day, the average inbox receives **spam**—unwanted junk mail messages from advertisers and con artists. Aside from the nuisance factor, many junk mail messages are designed to plant viruses on your computer or lure you into divulging your identity information. In this section, you'll learn to spot and manage junk mail messages.

Viewing Message Properties

Having your mailbox flooded with ads is annoying, but falling prey to someone who is misrepresenting himself in a spam message is downright dangerous. Some spammers format and design their messages to look as though they are coming from someone else. You can spot most of these "spoofing" messages by examining the message header to ensure that its properties are in keeping with the content of the message. The message header is text that is encoded into every e-mail message. Though not visible when reading the actual message, it contains detailed information about the sender, the sender's domain, and the sender's e-mail service. In this exercise, you'll examine a message header's properties.

STEP BY STEP   **View Message Properties**

GET READY. LAUNCH Outlook 2013 if it is not already running.

1. If necessary, click the **Mail** button in the Navigation bar and display the Inbox.

2. Double-click a message that you sent to yourself. The message window opens, displaying the selected message.

3. Click the **FILE tab**, and click **Properties** in Backstage view. The Properties dialog box is displayed, as shown in Figure 4-34.

Figure 4-34

Properties dialog box

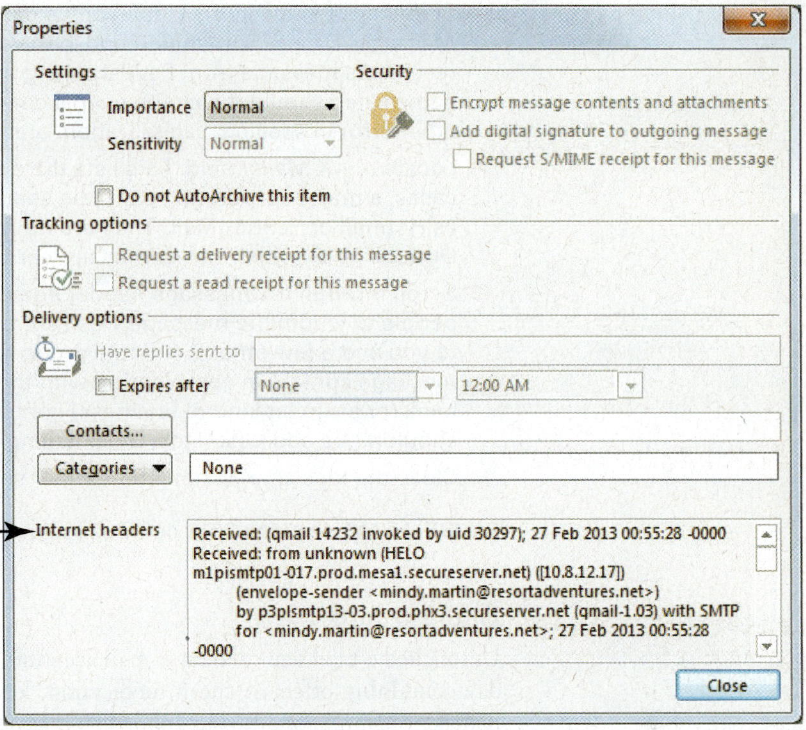

The Internet headers contain information about the person who sent the message

4. Click anywhere in the **Internet Headers** area at the bottom of the dialog box. The Internet Headers area can contain a lot of information that can be hard to read. To make it easier to locate the information you're looking for, it helps to copy the header information and paste it into a blank document or message window.

5. [Press **Ctrl+A**] to select all the information listed there.

6. [Press **Ctrl+C**] to copy it.

7. Click **Close** to close the Properties dialog box.

8. On the MESSAGE tab, click **Reply**.

9. In the message area, [press **Ctrl+V**] to paste the information about the message header into your Reply message, as shown in Figure 4-35.

Figure 4-35

Reading a message header

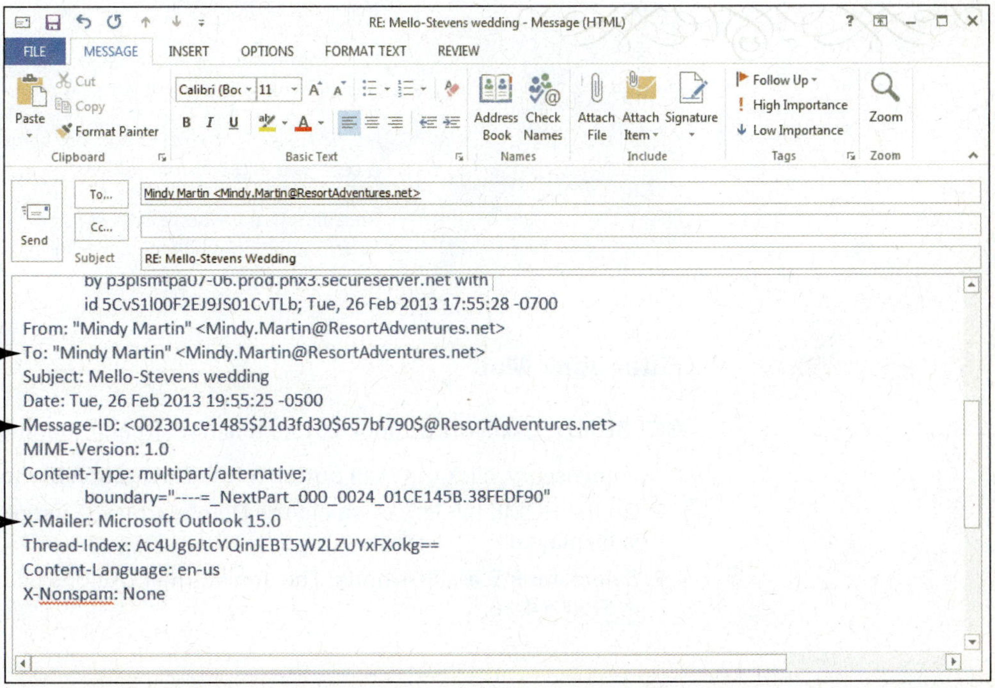

To: field

Message-ID field

X-mailer field

10. Scroll through the information you've pasted in the Reply message area. Locate the *Message-ID* field. This should end in the domain name of the sender. For example, if you received a message from PayPal asking to confirm your account settings, the domain name listed should match the paypal.com that the official PayPal site uses. If you see any other error in spelling, capitalization, or suffix, you know the message is a fake.

11. Locate the *X-Mailer* field. This lists the e-mail software used by the sender. In most cases, a major corporation won't be sending messages from a webmail system, such as Hotmail or Yahoo! Mail. They are more likely to use a business e-mail program like Outlook 2013 (which sometimes appears as Microsoft Outlook 15.0).

12. Scroll through the message header again and locate the *To:* field. This field lists all the people to whom the message was sent. Now obviously you'll receive messages to you, to you and a few others, and to a group to which you belong. The key is to look at the message content in combination with the To: field. For example, messages from your bank (or a similar kind of business) containing supposedly confidential information shouldn't be addressed to a bulk mailing list.

13. Close the message without sending or saving.

PAUSE. LEAVE Outlook 2013 open to use in the next exercise.

Filtering Junk Mail

Unsolicited e-mail sent to many e-mail accounts is spam or junk e-mail. It arrives at all times of the day containing offers of cheap medication, knock-off jewelry, and bad stock tips. If you don't manage the junk e-mail, your Inbox could easily be buried in spam. Outlook 2013 has a streamlined junk e-mail filtering process that makes it easier than ever to keep your Inbox free from spam. In this exercise, you'll explore the Outlook 2013 options for filtering junk e-mail and learn how to add someone to your **Blocked Senders list**.

By default, there is no automatic filtering applied to e-mail. Increasing the level of protection decreases the amount of spam that will be directed to your Inbox. However, it increases the chance that a non-spam message will be delivered to the Junk E-mail folder. The Outlook 2013 Junk E-mail options are described in Table 4-2.

Table 4-2

Junk E-mail Options

Option	Description
No Automatic Filtering	Mail from blocked senders is sent to the Junk E-mail folder.
Low	Mail from obvious junk e-mail is sent to the Junk E-mail folder.
High	Mail from most junk e-mail is sent to the Junk E-mail folder but some non-junk messages might get sent there as well.
Safe Lists Only	Any message that is received from someone not on your Safe Senders List is sent to the Junk E-mail folder.
Permanently delete	Messages that Outlook 2013 considers Junk are sent to the Deleted Items folder. Some non-junk messages might get deleted as well.

STEP BY STEP **Filter Junk Mail**

GET READY. LAUNCH Outlook 2013 if it is not already running.

1. If necessary, click the **Mail** button in the Navigation bar to display the Inbox.
2. On the HOME tab, click **Junk** in the Delete group. A list of options for handling junk mail is displayed.
3. Select **Junk E-mail Options**. The Junk E-mail Options dialog box is displayed, as shown in Figure 4-36.

Figure 4-36
Junk E-mail Options dialog box

Current security level →

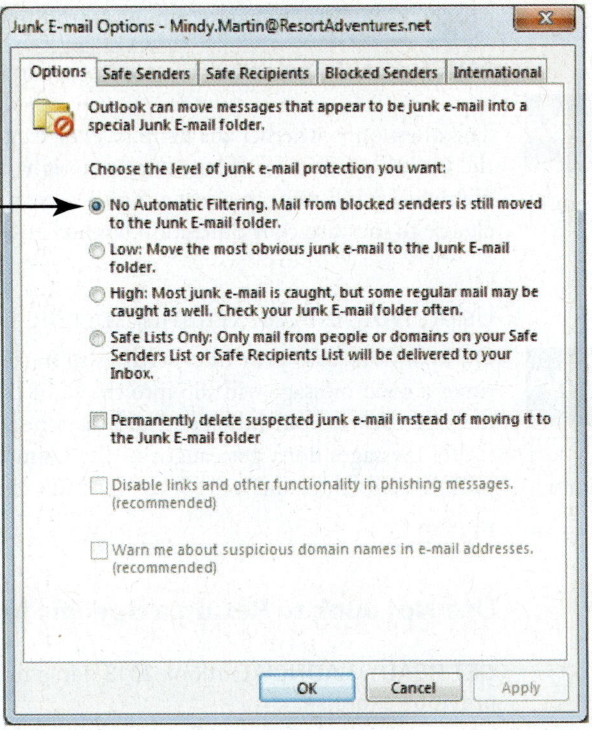

> **Junk E-mail Options - Mindy.Martin@ResortAdventures.net**
>
> Options | Safe Senders | Safe Recipients | Blocked Senders | International
>
> Outlook can move messages that appear to be junk e-mail into a special Junk E-mail folder.
>
> Choose the level of junk e-mail protection you want:
>
> ○ **No Automatic Filtering.** Mail from blocked senders is still moved to the Junk E-mail folder.
>
> ○ **Low:** Move the most obvious junk e-mail to the Junk E-mail folder.
>
> ○ **High:** Most junk e-mail is caught, but some regular mail may be caught as well. Check your Junk E-mail folder often.
>
> ○ **Safe Lists Only:** Only mail from people or domains on your Safe Senders List or Safe Recipients List will be delivered to your Inbox.
>
> ☐ Permanently delete suspected junk e-mail instead of moving it to the Junk E-mail folder
>
> ☐ Disable links and other functionality in phishing messages. (recommended)
>
> ☐ Warn me about suspicious domain names in e-mail addresses. (recommended)
>
> [OK] [Cancel] [Apply]

Figure 4-36
Junk E-mail Options dialog box

4. Review each level of junk e-mail protection. The Outlook 2013 Junk E-mail options are described in Table 4-2.

5. For now, you will leave the setting where it is, so you don't miss any important messages. Click the **Cancel** button to close the dialog box and return to the main Outlook 2013 window.

6. If a message from a friend or coworker is in your Inbox, right-click the message in the message list. Point to Junk on the shortcut menu. A list of Junk E-mail options is displayed, as shown in Figure 4-37.

Figure 4-37
Selecting a Junk E-mail option

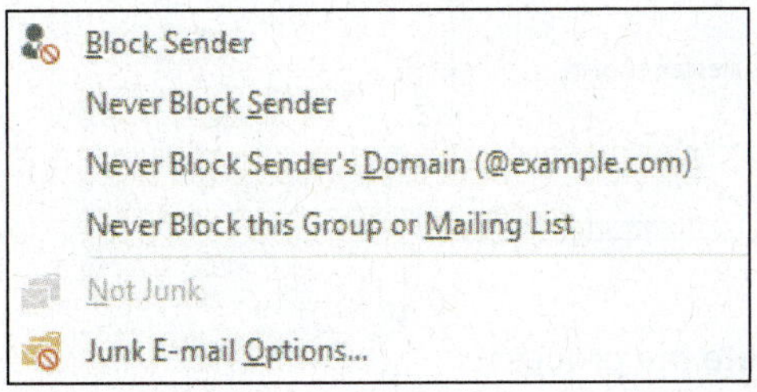

> Block Sender
> Never Block Sender
> Never Block Sender's Domain (@example.com)
> Never Block this Group or Mailing List
> Not Junk
> Junk E-mail Options...

7. Click the **Block Sender** option. A message is displayed notifying you that the sender has been added to your Blocked Senders List, as shown in Figure 4-38.

Figure 4-38
Blocking a specific message

> **Microsoft Outlook**
>
> ⚠ The sender of the selected message has been added to your Blocked Senders List, and the message has been moved to the Junk E-mail folder.
>
> ☐ Don't show this message again
>
> [OK]

8. Click **OK**. The message moves from the Inbox to the Junk E-mail folder.

PAUSE. LEAVE Outlook 2013 open to use in the next exercise.

CERTIFICATION
READY?   **2.3.5**

How do you filter junk mail?

The question is whether the extra level of security is worth the hassle of hunting for messages in the Junk E-mail folder. There is no one right answer. However, if you are receiving a lot of junk messages, you'll want to select a higher security level than the default. Just remember that if you choose to increase your protection level, check your Junk E-mail folder frequently.

Using Not Junk to Return a Specific Message to the Inbox

CERTIFICATION
READY?   **1.1.4**

How do you block all messages from a particular sender?

Outlook 2013 uses your filter settings to make a guess as to what is spam and what isn't. Sometimes a good message will slip into the Junk E-mail list. If this happens, you can easily move the message back to your Inbox and add the sender to your **Safe Senders list**, which will ensure that future messages don't get caught in the spam filter. In this exercise, you'll find a message in the Junk E-mail folder and mark it as Not Junk to return it to the Inbox.

STEP BY STEP   **Use Not Junk to Return a Specific Message to the Inbox**

GET READY. LAUNCH Outlook 2013 if it is not already running and complete the previous exercise.

1. If necessary, click the **Mail** button in the Navigation bar to display the mailbox.
2. Click the **Junk E-mail folder** in the Folders list, and right-click on the message. Point to Junk in the shortcut menu. A list of Junk E-mail options is displayed as a fly-out menu.
3. In the Junk E-mail options list, select **Never Block Sender**. Outlook 2013 notifies you that it will move the selected message's Sender e-mail address to the Safe Senders List, as shown in Figure 4-39.

Figure 4-39

Using Never Block Sender to add a person to your Safe Senders List

Microsoft Outlook

⚠ The sender of the selected message has been added to your Safe Senders List.

☐ Don't show this message again

OK

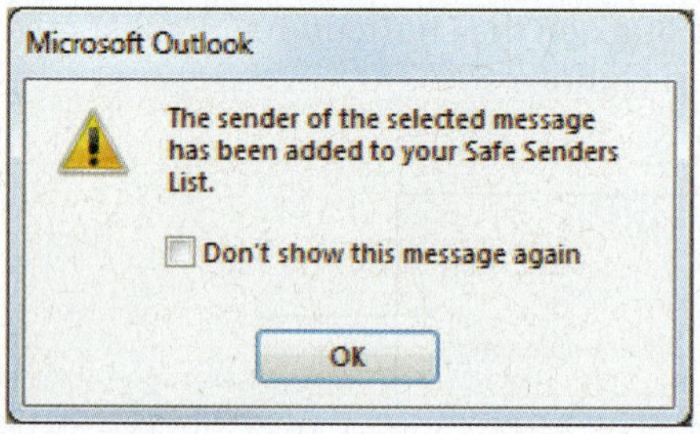

4. Click **OK** to complete the process.
5. Your friend's e-mail address is now considered safe, but the message remains in the Junk E-mail folder.
6. Right-click the message again and click **Junk** in the shortcut menu to open the list of options.
7. Click **Not Junk**. The Mark as Not Junk message box is displayed, as shown in Figure 4-40.

Figure 4-40

Mark as Not Junk message box

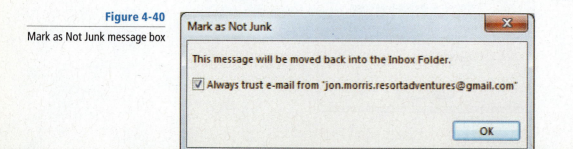

Mark as Not Junk   ✕

This message will be moved back into the Inbox Folder.

☑ Always trust e-mail from "jon.morris.resortadventures@gmail.com"

OK

8. Click the **Always trust e-mail from . . .** option to deselect it.

9. Click **OK**. The message moves back to the Inbox.

CLOSE Outlook 2013.

The Outlook 2013 Junk E-mail filtering options are outlined in Table 4-3 below.

Table 4-3

Junk E-mail Filtering Options

Option	Description
Block Sender	Add the sender to the Blocked Senders List. All future messages from this sender's e-mail address will go straight to the Junk E-mail folder.
Never Block Sender	Add the sender to the Safe Senders List. Future messages from this sender will be regarded as safe.
Never Block Sender's Domain	Add the sender's domain to the Safe Senders List. Future messages from anyone at the same domain will be considered safe.
Never Block this Group or Mailing List	Add the mailing list or contact group to the Safe Senders List. Future messages from the group will be considered safe.
Not Junk	Regardless of other settings, Not Junk marks the message as safe and returns it to the inbox.

As you receive messages from people you want to correspond with, add their e-mail addresses to the Safe Senders List. Messages from senders on the Safe Senders List are never directed to the Junk E-mail folder.

SKILL SUMMARY

In This Lesson You Learned How To:	Exam Objective	Objective Number
Work with Folders	Add new local folders	2.3.3
	Move messages between folders	2.3.2
Use Conversation View	Sort by conversation	2.3.10
	Ignore messages	2.3.9
Manage the Mailbox	Mark as read/unread	2.3.7
	Delete messages	2.1.3
	Flag messages	2.3.8
	Configure reminders	3.3.3
Use the Outlook Cleanup Tools	Cleanup messages	2.3.6
Manage Junk Mail	Configure junk e-mail settings	2.3.5
	Block specific addresses	1.1.4

Knowledge Assessment

Multiple Choice

Select the best response for the following statements.

1. In a message header, the _____ field contains the sender's domain name.
   a. Message-ID
   b. X-Mailer
   c. Domain ID
   d. Sender ID

2. By default, where does e-mail arrive?
   a. Inbox
   b. Outbox
   c. Junk E-mail
   d. Sent Items

3. By default, what attribute does AutoArchive use to determine which messages should be archived?
   a. Attachments
   b. Sender
   c. Size
   d. Date

4. In Conversation view, the Conversation _____ when more than one person responds to the same e-mail.
   a. grows
   b. expands
   c. breaks
   d. splits

5. If you want to stop following a Conversation, you can select it and click _____.
   a. Delete
   b. Ignore
   c. Stop
   d. Block

6. If you want to remember to go back to reading a message again later, you can _____.
   a. flag it
   b. mark it as read
   c. mark it as unread
   d. Both a and c

7. How do you remove an Outlook 2013 item from your computer?
   a. Delete the item and then delete again from within the Deleted Items folder
   b. Move the item to the Deleted Items folder
   c. Select the item and press the **Delete** key
   d. Delete the item and close Outlook 2013

8. How do you restore a folder?
   a. Delete the folder
   b. Archive the folder
   c. Move the folder from the Deleted Items folder to the Outlook Data Files folder in the Folders list
   d. Delete items from the folder

9. When you receive a junk e-mail message, select the message and click the _____ button in the Delete group.
   a. Spam
   b. Delete
   c. Block Sender
   d. Junk

10. The Outlook Mailbox Cleanup tools are accessed _____.
   a. on the Tools menu
   b. in the Options dialog box
   c. in Backstage view
   d. in the Outlook data file

Fill in the Blank

Complete the following sentences by writing the correct word or words in the blanks provided.

1. Messages are automatically moved to the _____ after they are sent.
2. To permanently remove deleted items from your Outlook data file, use the _____ tool.
3. To eliminate clutter in your mailbox, _____ your older and no longer relevant messages to a separate folder.
4. In _____ view, Outlook 2013 groups all the related messages together.
5. Set a _____ so that Outlook 2013 will prompt you when a deadline approaches.
6. Messages you send are stored in the _____ until your computer is connected to the Internet.
7. _____ determine(s) the length of time correspondence should be kept.
8. Spam is stored in the _____ folder.
9. Messages from senders on the _____ are immediately delivered to the Junk E-mail folder.
10. The _____ contains messages you have written but not sent yet.

Competency Assessment

Project 4-1: Use Junk Mail Options

Add your own name to the Safe Senders List using the Never Block Sender option.

GET READY. LAUNCH Outlook 2013 if it is not already running.

1. Return to your Inbox if necessary. Select a message you sent to yourself.
2. Click the **Junk** button on the HOME tab and select **Block Sender**. Click **OK**. Outlook moves the selected message to the Junk E-mail folder and future messages you send to yourself will be blocked.
3. Open the **Junk E-mail** folder and right-click the message to yourself to open the shortcut menu.
4. Point to **Junk** on the shortcut menu and select **Never Block Sender** from the menu that appears. Click **OK**.
5. Right-click the message to yourself in the **Junk E-mail** folder again and point to **Junk** on the shortcut menu. Select **Not Junk** from the shortcut menu.
6. Click **OK** to move the message back to the Inbox.

LEAVE Outlook 2013 open for the next project.

Project 4-2: Create a Mail Folder

The Alpine Ski House is just a brisk walk away from Resort Adventures. Joe Worden, Mindy Martin's cousin, is the owner of the Alpine Ski House, which sells ski equipment. To attract and hold local customers when it isn't ski season, Joe started a ski club for local residents. During the off season, club members meet to hike, bike, and exercise together to stay in shape for skiing. Since the ski club has recently become more active and gained more members, Joe decided that he needs to organize his ski club messages.

Create a folder to store ski club messages and send a message to the club notifying them about an upcoming hike.

GET READY. LAUNCH Outlook 2013 if it is not already running.

1. Click the icon at the end of the Navigation bar and select the Folders list button to display the Folders list.

2. On the FOLDER tab, click the **New Folder** button. The Create New Folder dialog box is displayed.

3. In the *Name* field, key **Ski Club** to identify the new folder.

4. Click the **Outlook Data Files** folder at the top of the Folders List to place the folder in the main level of folders.

5. Click the **OK** button to close the dialog box and create the folder.

6. Click the **Ski Club** folder in the Folders List and drag it above the Outbox folder in the Folders list.

7. Click the **New E-mail** button on the HOME tab. The Message window is displayed.

8. In the *To* field, key **[your e-mail address]**. In the *Subject* field, key **Ski Club Hike Saturday!**

9. In the message area, key the following message:

   Hi Ski Club members! [Press **Enter** twice.]

   This is just a reminder. We'll be hiking the Mountain Dancer trail this Saturday. Meet in the Mountain Dancer camp site. Bring sandwiches for lunch and plenty of water for the hike. The weather forecast says it will be hot, hot, hot! Be sure you stay hydrated! [Press **Enter** twice.]

   I'll see you Saturday at 9 AM! Call by Friday afternoon if you can't make it for the hike! [Press **Enter** twice.]

   Joe Worden [Press **Enter**.]

   Alpine Ski House

10. Click the **Send** button. The message is moved to the Outbox, and it is sent when your computer is connected to the Internet.

LEAVE Outlook 2013 open for the next project.

Proficiency Assessment

Project 4-3: Ski Club Conversation

Joe Worden of the Alpine Ski House is planning a hike for the ski club members this weekend. He sent a message about the hike and wants to use Conversation view to monitor the responses more efficiently.

GET READY. LAUNCH Outlook 2013 if it is not already running.

1. If necessary, click the **Mail** button in the Navigation bar to display the Inbox.

2. Select the **Ski Club Hike Saturday!** message and click the **Reply** Quick Response button in the Reading Pane.

3. In the message area, key **Great!** and click **Send**.

4. Select the **Ski Club Hike Saturday!** message and click the **Reply** Quick Response button in the Reading Pane.

5. In the message area, key **Sorry, I can't make it.** Click **Send**.

6. On the VIEW tab, select **Show as Conversations**. When prompted, select **All Mailboxes** to apply the Conversation view everywhere.

7. If the new messages haven't arrived, click **Send/Receive All Folders** on the HOME tab.

8. Click the **expansion arrow** beside the Conversation to see all the messages.

LEAVE Outlook 2013 open for the next project.

Project 4-4: Organize Ski Club E-mails

Now that more e-mails have arrived, it's time to organize them. Move the messages to the Ski Club folder and set up a reminder so you don't forget about Saturday's hike.

GET READY. LAUNCH Outlook 2013 if it is not already running.

1. If necessary, click the **Mail** button in the Navigation bar to display the inbox.
2. Right-click the **Ski Club Hike Saturday!** Conversation header and select **Move** on the shortcut menu.
3. Select **Ski Club** from the list of folders. Click **OK**.
4. Click the **Ski Club** folder and expand the Conversation.
5. Click the blue bar on the left edge of all the new reply messages to mark them as **Read**.
6. Select the replies in the conversation that are stored in the Sent Items folder and click **Unread/Read** in the Tags group on the HOME tab.
7. Select the original message and right-click the **Follow Up Flag** in the message list. Select **Custom** from the list.
8. In the *Start Date* box, key [**Saturday's date**].
9. Select the *Reminder* box, and change the time to **6:00 AM**. Click **OK**.

LEAVE Outlook 2013 open for the next project.

Mastery Assessment

Project 4-5: Manually Archive the Ski Club Folder

GET READY. LAUNCH Outlook 2013 if it is not already running.

1. If necessary, click the **Mail** button in the Navigation bar to display the inbox.
2. On the VIEW tab, deselect **Show as Conversations**. Click **All mailboxes**.
3. Click the **Ski Club** folder in the list of mail folders, and click the **FILE tab**.
4. Click **Cleanup Tools,** and select **Archive** from the list. The Archive dialog box is displayed.
5. If necessary, click the **Archive this folder and all subfolders** option.
6. Select the **Ski Club** folder. If necessary, change the *Archive Items Older Than* date to [**tomorrow's date**].
7. Click **Browse**. Select the solution folder for this lesson and key **Project 4-5_xxx** (where *xxx* is your initials). Click **OK**.
8. Click **OK**. Click **Yes** to initiate the Archive process.

LEAVE Outlook 2013 open for the next project.

Project 4-6: Permanently Delete the Ski Club Folder

Joe Worden thought about the ski club while he sipped his coffee. With only one event per month, perhaps it wasn't necessary to create a folder just for the ski club. Delete the Ski Club folder and empty the Deleted Items folder.

GET READY. LAUNCH Outlook 2013 if it is not already running.

1. If necessary, click the icon at the end of the Navigation bar and the Folders list option to display the complete list of Outlook 2013 folders.

2. Right-click the **Ski Club** folder created in a previous project. Click **Delete Folder** from the shortcut menu. A warning dialog box is displayed.

3. Click **Yes** to close the warning dialog box.

4. Right-click the **Deleted Items** folder. Select **Empty Folder** from the list. Click **Yes** to confirm.

CLOSE Outlook 2013.

LESSON SKILL MATRIX

Skills	Exam Objective	Objective Number
Creating and Running Rules	Create and manage rules	1.2.4
Managing Rules	Create and manage rules	1.2.4
Working with Automated Microsoft Exchange Tools	Create auto-replies Delegate access	1.2.5 2.1.13
Using Quick Steps	Apply Quick Steps	1.2.3

KEY TERMS

- action
- condition
- exception
- Quick Steps
- rule
- template
- wizard

© GVision/iStockphoto

Mindy Martin is a co-owner of Resort Adventures, a luxury resort. As in any business, a steady stream of information goes in and out of her office. Reservations, schedules, vendor orders, maintenance requests, and menus for the resort's restaurant are only a small sample of the information flying in and out of Mindy's e-mail folders. To keep things straight, Mindy uses message rules to organize her messages as they arrive.

© GVision/iStockphoto

SOFTWARE ORIENTATION

The Rules and Alerts Dialog Box

Message rules are displayed in the Rules and Alerts dialog box, as shown in Figure 5-1. You can refer to this figure as you work through this lesson and throughout the book.

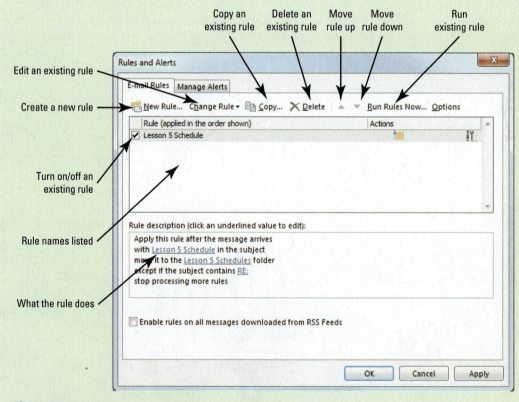

Figure 5-1

The Rules and Alerts dialog box

The rules that help you organize your messages are displayed in the Rules and Alerts dialog box. In this dialog box, you can edit existing rules, create new rules, enable rules, and disable rules.

CREATING AND RUNNING RULES

The Bottom Line

A **rule** defines an action that happens automatically when messages are received or sent. Rules can be created in a number of different ways. Using a template is the easiest method for creating a new rule. A **template** is an existing rule provided by Outlook that contains specific pieces of information that can be customized to create new rules. You also can create a rule from an existing message or copy an existing rule and edit one or more of the rule's components. If a rule is simple, you can create it quickly from scratch. In this section, you'll use a variety of methods to create rules.

Creating a Rule Using the Rules Wizard

One of the best ways to organize your mailbox is to move messages out of the Inbox and into folders that group related messages together. For example, you can place messages about your active projects in project folders and messages from vendors in separate vendor folders. Create and use as many folders as you need to keep yourself organized. Manually locating and moving a lot of messages can be time consuming and prone to errors. Instead, automate the process by creating a rule to move the messages for you. The simplest method of creating rules is to let the Rules Wizard help you create a rule from a template. A **wizard** consists of steps that walk you through completing a process in Microsoft Office applications. In this exercise, you'll use a template to create a rule for moving messages.

A rule consists of three parts: a *condition*, an *action*, and an *exception*. In simple terms, a rule says if A happens (the condition), then B (the action) occurs unless C (the exception) exists. Table 5-1 describes these parts of a rule.

Table 5-1

Parts of a Rule

Part	Description
Condition	The **condition** identifies the characteristics used to determine the messages affected by the rule. Use caution when you define the conditions. If your conditions are too broad, the rule will affect more messages than intended. If your conditions are too narrow, the rule will not identify some of the messages that should be affected.
Action	The **action** determines what happens when a message meets the conditions defined in the rule. For example, the message can be moved, forwarded, or deleted.
Exception	The **exception** identifies the characteristics used to exclude messages from being affected by the rule.

STEP BY STEP | **Creating a Rule Using the Rules Wizard**

GET READY. LAUNCH Outlook if it is not already running.

1. If necessary, click the **Mail** button in the Navigation bar to display the mailbox. If necessary, click **Inbox** in the Folders List to display your standard mailbox.

2. Right-click **Outlook Data Files** in the Folders List, and click **New Folder** in the shortcut menu. A small box appears at the top of the Folders List, as shown in Figure 5-2.

Troubleshooting For this exercise, you want to select the top-level folder. It's the folder that holds your Inbox, Sent Items folder, and so on. Depending on the settings on your computer and the type of e-mail account you have, this might be called Outlook Data Files, Personal Folders, or simply your e-mail address.

Figure 5-2

Creating a folder in the
Folders List

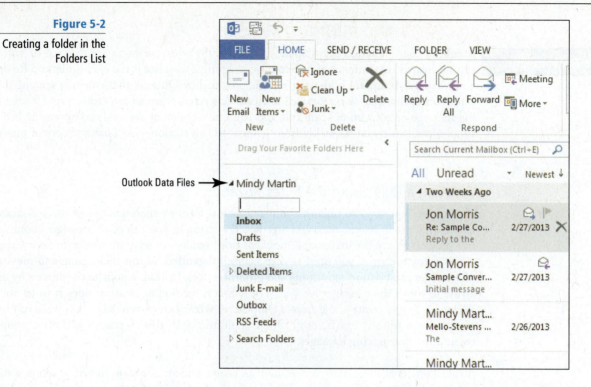

3. In the box, key **Lesson 5 Schedules** [Press **Enter**]. You will create a rule to move messages into this folder.

Take Note   Throughout this chapter you will see information that appears in black text within brackets, such as [Press **Enter**] or [**your e-mail address**]. The information contained in the brackets is intended to be directions for you rather than something you actually type word for word. It will instruct you to perform an action or substitute text. Do **not** type the actual text that appears within brackets.

4. Click the **FILE** tab. In Backstage view, click the **Manage Rules & Alerts** option. The Rules and Alerts dialog box shown in Figure 5-1 is displayed.

Figure 5-3

Rules Wizard dialog box with
default selections

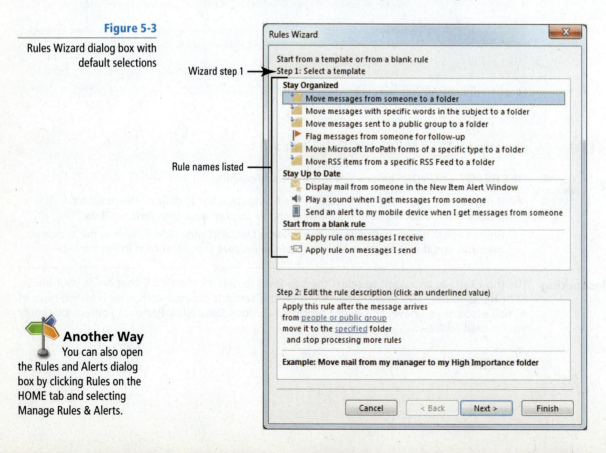

Another Way
You can also open the Rules and Alerts dialog box by clicking Rules on the HOME tab and selecting Manage Rules & Alerts.

5. Click the **New Rule** button. The Rules Wizard dialog box is displayed, as shown in Figure 5-3. Step 1 of this wizard involves choosing a template or blank rule.

6. In *Step 1: Select a template,* select **Move messages with specific words in the subject to a folder** in the Stay Organized category templates list. This rule will move messages about the selected topic. The rule description in the lower area of the dialog box changes, as shown in Figure 5-4.

Figure 5-4

Rules Wizard dialog box with template to move messages selected

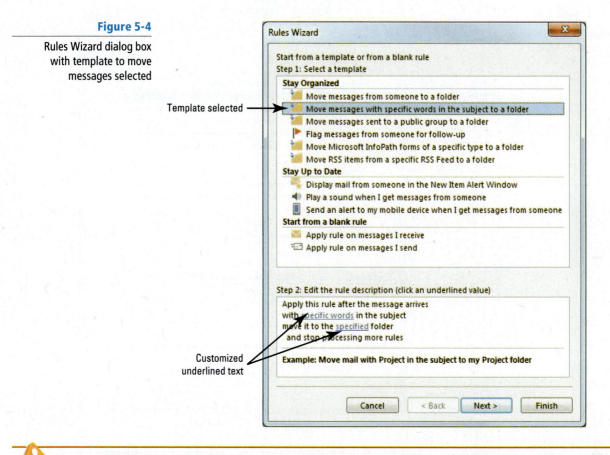

7. In the *Step 2: Edit the rule description* area, click **specific words**. The Search Text dialog box is displayed, as shown in Figure 5-5.

Troubleshooting To ensure that a rule looking for a specific subject moves the messages, the subject line must contain the exact words shown in the editing area of the Rules Wizard dialog box.

Figure 5-5

Search Text dialog box

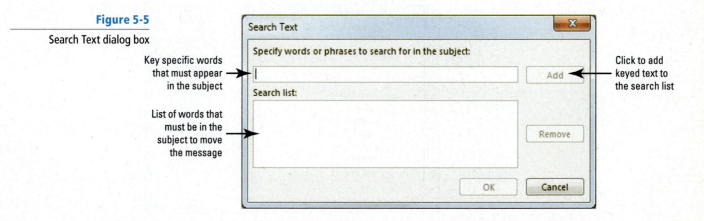

Take Note In this exercise, you will use a single phrase as the search text. To add more words or phrases to the search list, key the text into the Search Text dialog box and click the Add button.

8. In the *Specify words or phrases to search for in the subject* field, key **Lesson 5 Schedule**. Click the **Add** button. The Lesson 5 Schedule phrase is enclosed by quotation marks and added to the search list for this rule.

9. Click **OK** to close the Search Text dialog box. The Rules Wizard dialog box is displayed. The Lesson 5 Schedule search phrase is identified, as shown in Figure 5-6.

Figure 5-6

Rules Wizard dialog box with the search phrase identified

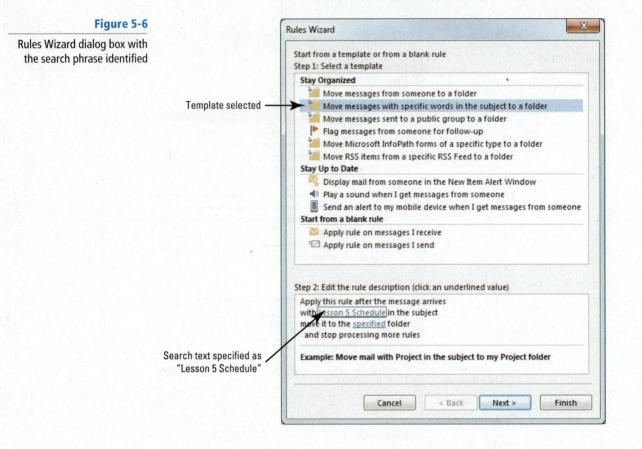

10. In the Step 2 area of the Rules Wizard dialog box, click **specified** to identify the destination folder. The Folders List is displayed in the Rules and Alerts dialog box, as shown in Figure 5-7.

Figure 5-7

Select the destination folder

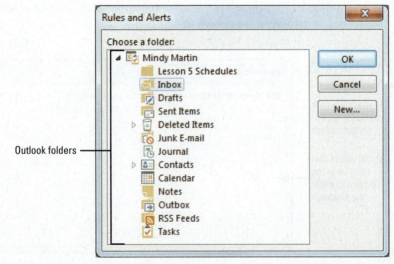

11. Click the **Lesson 5 Schedules** folder in the Choose a Folder list, and click **OK**. The specified destination folder is identified in the Rules Wizard dialog box, as shown in Figure 5-8.

Figure 5-8

Rules Wizard dialog box with the destination folder identified

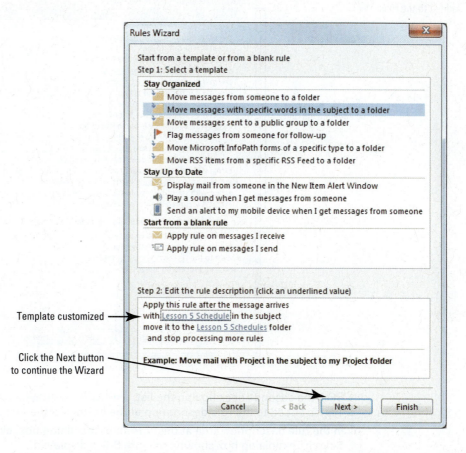

Template customized →

Click the Next button
to continue the Wizard

12. Click the **Next** button to continue. The next page of the Rules Wizard displays a number of conditions that you can add to the rule.

13. Click the **Next** button because you don't need to add any more conditions to this rule. The third wizard page is displayed. Under *Step 1: Select action(s)*, you will see a list of actions that can be taken if the conditions selected on the previous wizard page are met.

14. Click the **Next** button to continue to the next page of the wizard. Because you didn't select any special conditions on the previous wizard page, you don't want to add actions to this rule. A list of exceptions to the rule is displayed, as shown in Figure 5-9.

Exceptions that can
be added to the rules

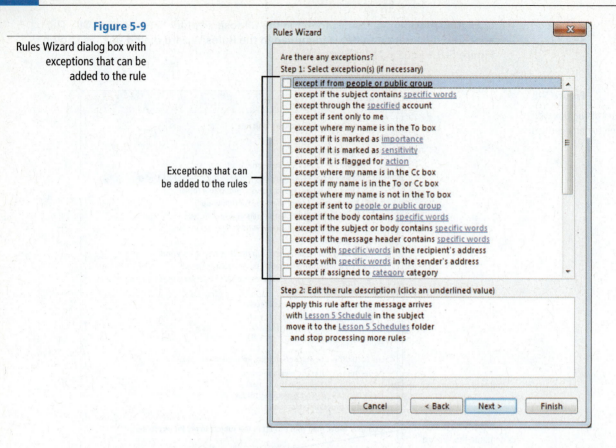

15. Click the second check box on the list: **except if the subject contains specific words**. Text is added to the rule description at the bottom of the Rules Wizard dialog box.

16. In the rule description area at the bottom of the dialog box, click **specific words**. The Search Text dialog box shown in Figure 5-5 is displayed.

17. In the *Specify words or phrases to search for in the subject* field, key **RE:**. Making RE: an exception prevents replies to the Lesson 5 Schedule messages from being moved to the destination folder.

18. Click the **Add** button. The RE: text is enclosed by quotation marks and added to the search list for this rule.

19. Click **OK** to close the Search Text dialog box. The Rules Wizard dialog box is displayed. The exception is added to the rule, as shown in Figure 5-10.

Figure 5-10

Rules Wizard dialog box with exception added to the rule

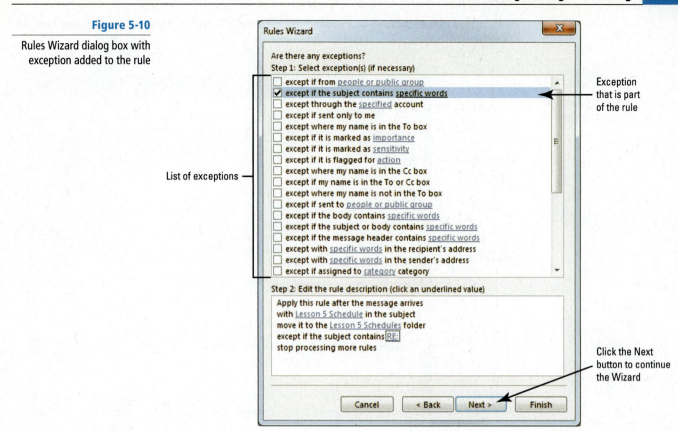

List of exceptions

Exception that is part of the rule

Click the Next button to continue the Wizard

20. Click the **Next** button to continue the Wizard. The rule is displayed for your approval, as shown in Figure 5-11. Examine the rule carefully to verify that it is correct.

Figure 5-11

Rules Wizard dialog box with rule displayed for approval

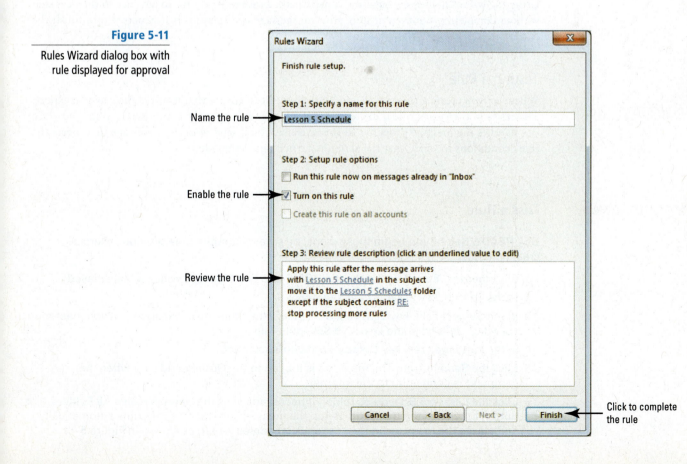

Name the rule

Enable the rule

Review the rule

Click to complete the rule

21. Click the **Finish** button. The new rule is displayed in the Rules and Alerts dialog box, as shown in Figure 5-12.

Rules and Alerts dialog box with the new rule displayed

New rule created

Description of the new rule

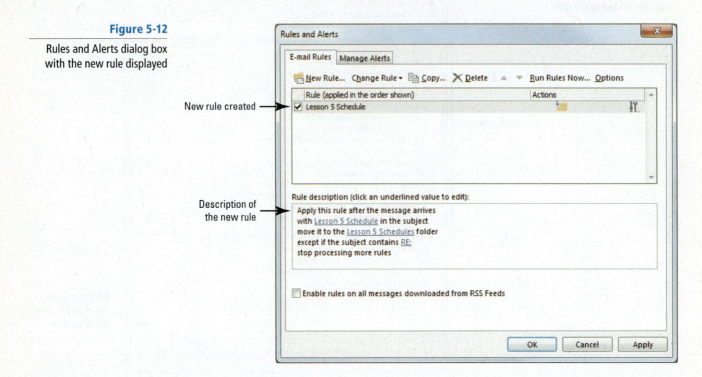

22. Click the **OK** button to close the Rules and Alerts dialog box.

PAUSE. LEAVE Outlook open to use in the next exercise.

Using the wizard to create a new rule simplifies the process. If you try to advance to the next step without completing the current step, an error message is displayed. It instructs you to finish the current step.

Testing a Rule

Whenever you create a rule, it is a good idea to test it to ensure that it works the way you expect. The easiest way to test a rule is to create a message that will meet the conditions of your rule to see if it handles the message properly. In this exercise, you'll send yourself a message that meets the rule's conditions to verify that the action is carried out as intended.

STEP BY STEP   **Test a Rule**

GET READY. Before you begin these steps, be sure to complete the previous exercise creating a rule.

1. Click the **New E-mail** button on the HOME tab. The Message window is displayed.

2. In the *To* field, key [**your e-mail address**].

3. In the *Subject* field, key **Lesson 5 Schedule**. When this message arrives, it will meet the condition defined in the Lesson 5 Schedule rule.

4. In the message area, key **Lesson 5 Schedule rule test**.

5. Click the **Send** button. The message is moved to the Outbox and sent when the computer is connected to the Internet.

6. Click the **Lesson 5 Schedules** folder. If necessary, click the **Send/Receive All Folders** button to receive the message. When the message arrives, the rule runs automatically and places the message in the Lesson 5 Schedules folder, as shown in Figure 5-13.

Figure 5-13

Figure 5-13

Rule moved the received message

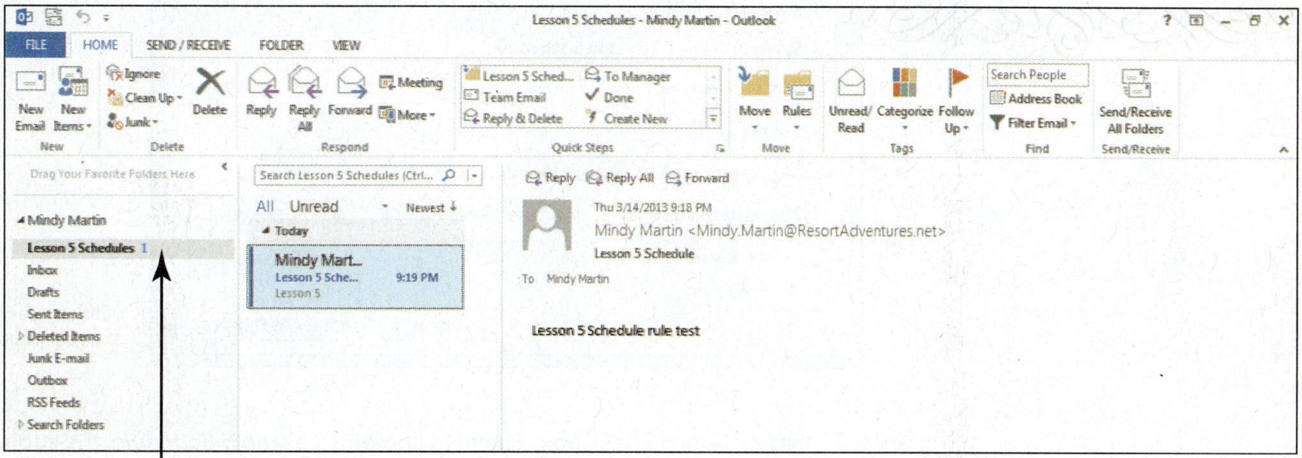

Message move to the specified folder

PAUSE. LEAVE Outlook open to use in the next exercise.

CERTIFICATION READY?   1.2.4

How do you create a rule to move messages?

Every time you create a rule, you should test the rule to verify that it works. For example, to test the rule created in the previous exercise, you sent a message with *Lesson 5 Schedule* as the subject to yourself. Over time, you might need to add conditions to the rule because not everyone who sends schedules to you uses the correct subject. You can add a condition such as the *Lesson 5 Schedule* phrase in the body of the message or add a condition identifying any message with the word *schedule* in the subject.

Creating a Rule from a Selected Message

Repeating the same action over and over is one of the most common reasons for creating a rule. For example, another common organizational tool that requires repetitive tasks is categorizing messages. When you categorize messages, you assign messages about related topics a specific color code so that they are easy to locate. Categorizing messages is a common organizational task that you can automate by creating a rule. The next time you select a message on which you plan to perform an often-repeated action, use the message to create a rule. In this exercise, you'll create a rule from an existing message. The rule will categorize messages by color.

STEP BY STEP   **Create a Rule from a Selected Message**

USE the message you sent in the previous exercise.

1. If necessary, click the **Mail** button in the Navigation bar to display the mailbox.
2. In the Folders List, click the **Lesson 5 Schedules** folder. One message is highlighted in the Message List.
3. Right-click the message. Click on **Rules**, and select **Create Rule** on the shortcut menu. The Create Rule dialog box is displayed, as shown in Figure 5-14. The conditions of the selected message are displayed in the dialog box.

Figure 5-14

Create Rule dialog box

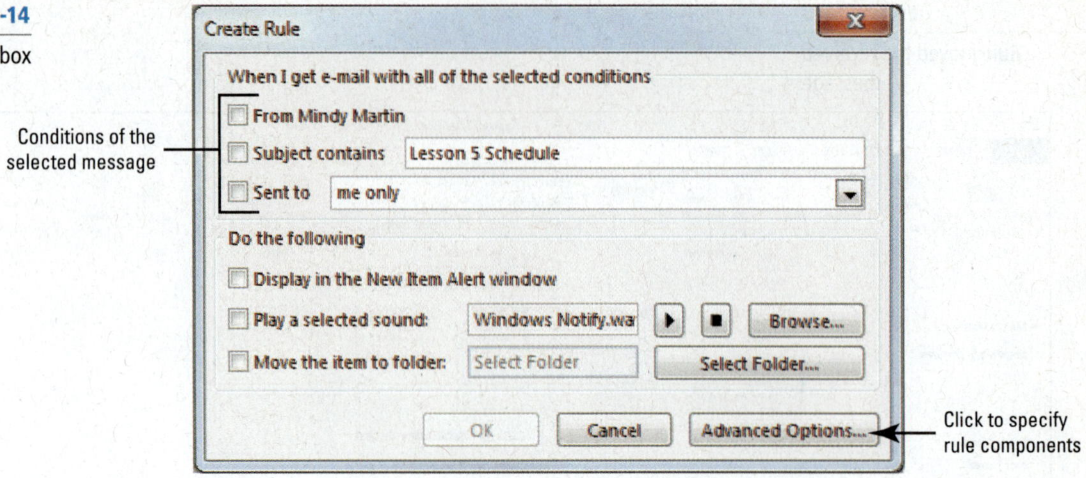

Conditions of the
selected message

Click to specify
rule components

4. Click the **Subject contains** check box. The field contains *Lesson 5 Schedule*, the subject of the selected message.

5. Click the **Advanced Options** button to specify additional rule components. The Rules Wizard dialog box is displayed. The condition about the message's subject is already selected in the first Rules Wizard page.

6. Click the **Next** button. The Rules Wizard dialog box lists the available actions for the rule. Actions based on the selected message are displayed at the top of the list.

7. Click the **assign it to the category category** check box. The selected action is moved to the lower area of the dialog box, as shown in Figure 5-15.

Figure 5-15

Rules Wizard dialog box with
available actions based on the
selected message

Characteristics of the
selected message

Click to specify
the category

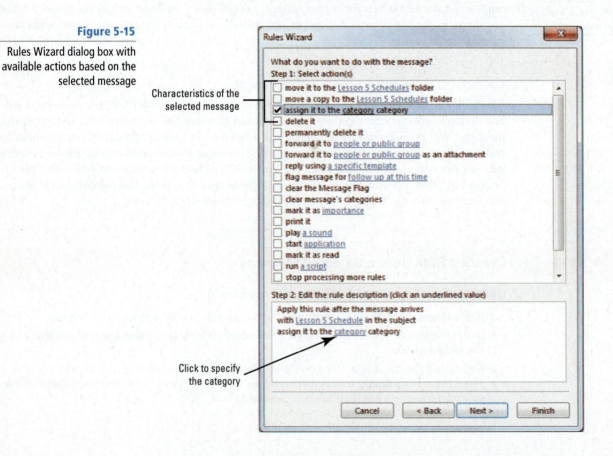

8. In the *Step 2: Edit the rule description* area, click the underlined **category**. The Color Categories dialog box is displayed, as shown in Figure 5-16.

Figure 5-16

Color Categories dialog box

Select the
category

Click to close
the dialog box

Figure 5-16

Color Categories dialog box

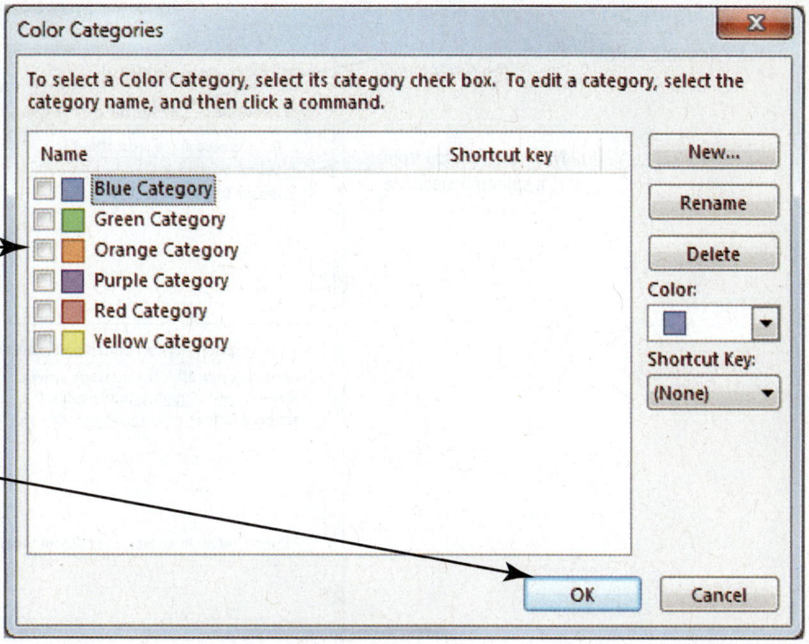

9. Click the **Orange Category** check box; then click **OK**. When you complete the exercise and run the rule, messages that match the conditions you've outlined will be highlighted with orange, making them easier to spot in a message list.

Cross Ref You can find more information on Color Categories in Lesson 12.

10. If a Rename Category dialog box is displayed, click the **No** button. The Color Categories dialog box is closed, and you are returned to the Rules Wizard dialog box.

Take Note You can rename categories, but it isn't necessary in this lesson.

11. The condition and action for the rule are complete. You don't want to identify any exceptions. Click the **Finish** button. The rule is saved. The Rules Wizard dialog box is closed, and you are returned to the main Outlook window. In the following steps, you will rename and test the new rule.

Another Way
You can also access the Rules and Alerts dialog box by right-clicking a message, pointing to Rules, and selecting Manage Rules & Alerts.

12. On the HOME tab, click **Rules** in the Move group, and select the **Manage Rules & Alerts** option. The Rules and Alerts dialog box is displayed. The new rule you just created is identified as Lesson 5 Schedule (1). The name was inherited from the rule already applied to the message when you selected the message.

13. If necessary, select only the **Lesson 5 Schedule (1)** rule or de-select the other rule. Click the **Change Rule** button, and click the **Rename Rule** option. The Rename dialog box is displayed, as shown in Figure 5-17.

Figure 5-17

Rename a Rule

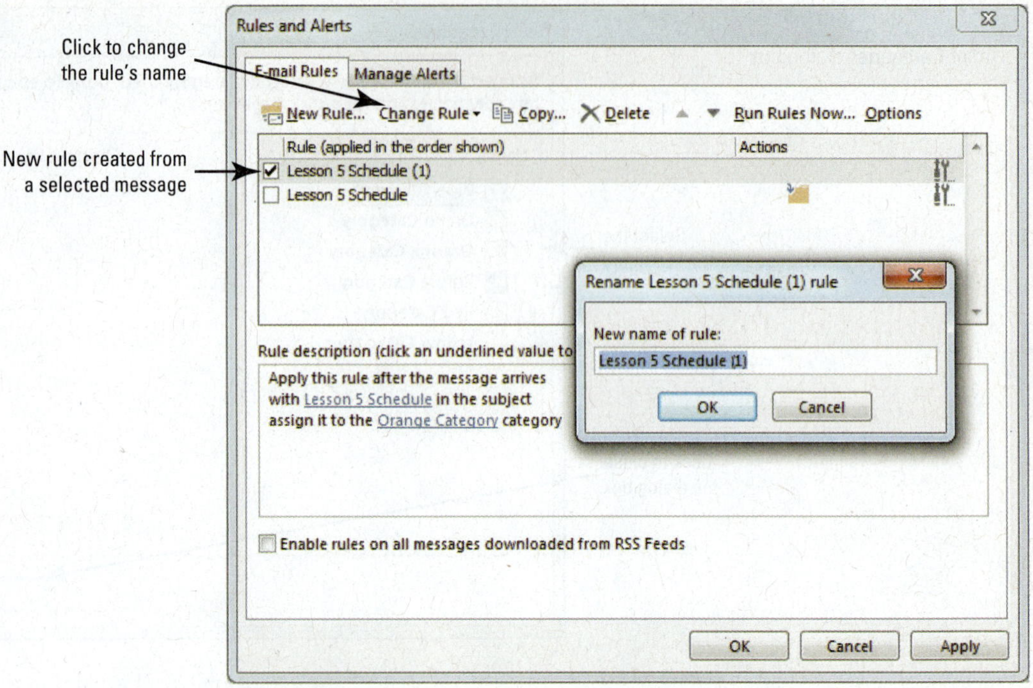

Click to change
the rule's name

New rule created from
a selected message

14. In the *New name of rule* field, key **Orange Lesson 5 Schedule**; then click **OK**. The Rename dialog box is closed. The name of the rule has been changed.

15. Click **OK** to close the Rules and Alerts dialog box.

PAUSE. LEAVE Outlook open to use in the next exercise.

Running a Rule

Rules run automatically when new messages arrive, so what happens to the mail that is already in your mailbox? You can run a rule manually. When you run a rule, it scans the mailbox as if it were new mail and applies the rule's actions on any messages that meet your conditions. In this exercise, you'll run a rule so that it processes your existing messages.

STEP BY STEP   **Run a Rule**

GET READY. LAUNCH Outlook if it is not already running.

1. If necessary, click the **Mail** button in the Navigation bar to display the mailbox. If necessary, click **Inbox** in the Folders List to display your standard mailbox.

2. Click the **FILE** tab to return to Backstage view. Click **Manage Rules & Alerts**.

3. Click the **Run Rules Now** button. The Run Rules Now dialog box is displayed.

4. In the *Select rules to run* section, click the **Orange Lesson 5 Schedule** check box, as shown in Figure 5-18.

Figure 5-18

Run Rules Now dialog box

Select the rule

Select the folder

Run the rule

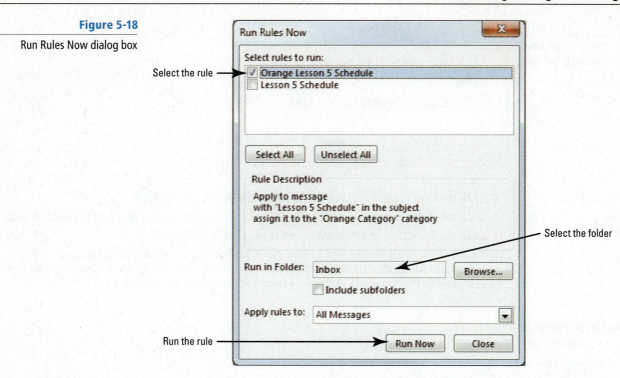

5. Click the **Browse** button in the Run in Folder section. The Select Folders list is displayed in the Select Folder dialog box, as shown in Figure 5-19.

Figure 5-19

The Select Folders list

Outlook Data File

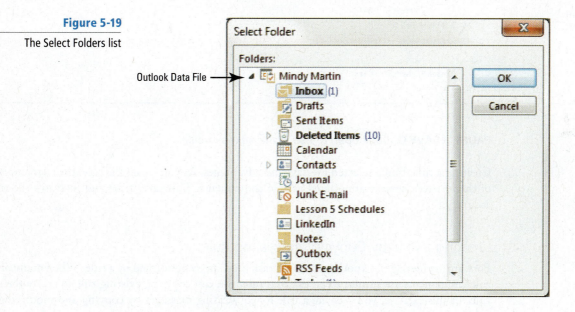

6. Click the **Outlook Data File** folder and click **OK**.

7. Click the **Include subfolders** check box.

8. Click the **Run Now** button. The rule runs quietly in the background. Because you are running the new rule against the entire Outlook Data File folder, Outlook presents the message shown in Figure 5-20 asking you to verify that you only want to run the rule against mail items.

Figure 5-20

The Run Rules Now
message window

9. Click the **Don't show this message again** checkbox and click **OK**.

10. Click the **Close** button, and click the **OK** button to return to the Outlook Backstage view.

11. Click the **Back** button to return to the main Outlook window.

12. Click the **Lesson 5 Schedules** folder. Because you have a message in the Lesson 5 Schedules folder that matches the conditions of this rule, the Orange Category has been assigned to the message in the message list, as shown in Figure 5-21.

Figure 5-21

Orange Category assigned
to a message

Orange Category assigned

PAUSE. LEAVE Outlook open to use in the next exercise.

Creating a rule from a selected message has advantages. As you create the rule, the characteristics of the selected message are offered as rule components. This saves time and increases the rule's accuracy.

Creating a Rule by Copying an Existing Rule

Forwarding messages is another common task that can be performed by a rule. When many of the rule components are similar to an existing rule, you can copy the existing rule to create the new rule. In this exercise, you'll create a rule for forwarding messages by copying and modifying an existing rule.

STEP BY STEP | **Create a Rule by Copying an Existing Rule**

USE the message and the rule created in a previous exercise.

1. If necessary, click the **Mail** button in the Navigation bar to display the mailbox.

2. On the HOME tab, click the **Rules** command in the Move group. Select the **Manage Rules & Alerts** option from the menu that appears. The Rules and Alerts dialog box is displayed.

3. Select the **Orange Lesson 5 Schedule** rule, and click the **Copy** button in the Rules and Alerts dialog box. The Copy Rule To dialog box is displayed, as shown in Figure 5-22. The Folder listing in this dialog box identifies the Inbox as being affected by the rule.

Figure 5-22

Copying a rule

> **Copy rule to...**
>
> **Folder:**
>
> Inbox [Mindy.Martin@ResortAdventures.net]
>
> OK   Cancel

Take Note If your Outlook profile accesses more than one e-mail account, you can choose the Inbox to be affected by the rule. Refer to the Outlook Help tool for more information about Outlook profiles.

4. Click **OK** to accept the Folder listing and close the dialog box. A copy of the selected rule is created and added to the list of rules, as shown in Figure 5-23.

Figure 5-23

Copied rule created

Click to change the rule's name

Copy of rule is turned off

Copy of rule created

> **Rules and Alerts**
>
> **E-mail Rules** | Manage Alerts
>
> New Rule... Change Rule ▼ Copy... ✕ Delete ▲ ▼ Run Rules Now... Options
>
> Rule (applied in the order shown) | Actions
> ☑ Orange Lesson 5 Schedule
> ☐ Lesson 5 Schedule
> ☐ Copy of Orange Lesson 5 Schedule
>
> Rule description (click an underlined value to edit):
> Apply this rule after the message arrives
> with Lesson 5 Schedule in the subject
> assign it to the Orange Category category
>
> ☐ Enable rules on all messages downloaded from RSS Feeds
>
> OK   Cancel   Apply

5. Select the **Copy of Orange Lesson 5 Schedule** rule, if necessary, and de-select the other rules. Click the **Change Rule** button, and click **Rename Rule**. The Rename dialog box is displayed.

6. In the *New name of rule* field, key **Forward Lesson 5 Schedule**; then click **OK**. The dialog box is closed, and the rule's name is changed.

7. With the *Forward Lesson 5 Schedule* rule selected, click the **Change Rule** button, and click the **Edit Rule Settings** option. The Rules Wizard dialog box is displayed.

8. The condition about the message's subject is already selected. Click the **Next** button. The Rules Wizard dialog box lists the available actions for the rule.

9. Click the **assign it to the category category** check box to deselect the action.

10. Click the **forward it to people or public group** check box. The action is moved to the rule description in the lower area of the Rules Wizard dialog box.

11. In the *Step 2: Edit the rule description* area, click the underlined **people or public group** text. The Rule Address dialog box is displayed.

 Cross Ref Rather than keying an e-mail address into the *To* field, you can select a person from your Outlook Contacts. You will learn more about contacts in Lesson 6.

12. In the *To* field at the bottom of the dialog box, key [the e-mail address of a friend or coworker]. Click the **OK** button to close the dialog box. The Rules Wizard dialog box is updated, as shown in Figure 5-24.

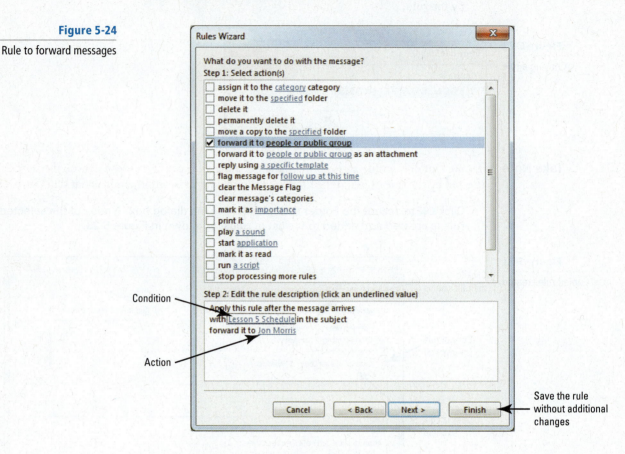

Condition

Action

Save the rule without additional changes

13. This rule does not have exceptions. Click the **Finish** button to save the rule and return to the Rules and Alerts dialog box.

14. If necessary, click the **Forward Lesson 5 Schedule** check box to turn on the rule.

15. Click the **Run Rules Now** button. The Run Rules Now dialog box is displayed.

16. Click the **Forward Lesson 5 Schedule** check box and the **Include subfolders** check box.

17. Click the **Run Now** button. Outlook looks through your mailbox for messages that meet the conditions you set and forwards them on to the e-mail address you specified in the Rule Address dialog box.

18. Click the **Close** button. Click **OK** to return to the main Outlook window. The forwarded message is listed in the Sent Items folder.

PAUSE. LEAVE Outlook open to use in the next exercise.

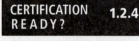

CERTIFICATION READY?   1.2.4

How do you modify a rule?

So far, you have created a rule to move a message, a rule to assign a category, and a rule to forward messages. Rather than creating three separate rules, you could create a single rule that performs all three actions.

When you combine actions into a single rule, keep in mind that you can't simply turn off individual actions. If you turn off a rule with several actions, none of the actions are performed. If one part of the rule or conditions is likely to change periodically, consider keeping that part as a unique rule.

Alternatively, if you do combine it into a single rule and conditions change, you can go in and manually alter the actions within a rule, but you'll have to remember to go back in and alter the actions again when conditions change. Although this is certainly doable, it is time consuming and could easily be forgotten. If an action is likely to change, it is better practice to leave it as a separate rule that you can simply turn on and off.

Let's put that in terms of a real-life situation. Suppose that Jon, the addressee of the forwarded messages you just created, goes on a two-week business trip followed by a two-week vacation in Hawaii. He asked you to stop forwarding schedules to him for four weeks. If the three actions were combined into one rule, you would need to create new rules or edit the combined rule so that the messages are still moved and categorized, but not forwarded to Jon. Then when Jon returns, you'll need to go back in and edit the rule again to add back the third step. If you keep the forwarded action in a separate rule, you just need to deselect the rule in the Rules and Alerts dialog box to turn off the forwarding rule until Jon returns with a tan and too many vacation photos. When he gets back, just select the action again.

Creating a Rule from Scratch

Some rules are simple to write. You want to find messages that meet one condition and perform one action without exceptions. For example, a simple rule might be "Delete all the messages in the Orange Category." As you learn in this exercise, you can quickly create simple rules like this from scratch. This is the best method to create simple rules with one condition, one action, and no exceptions.

STEP BY STEP   **Create a Rule from Scratch**

USE the message you sent in the previous exercise.

1. If necessary, click the **Mail** button in the Navigation bar to display the mailbox.
2. Click the **Rules** button on the HOME tab and click the **Manage Rules & Alerts** option. The Rules and Alerts dialog box is displayed.
3. Click the **New Rule** button. The Rules Wizard dialog box is displayed, as shown in Figure 5-25.

Figure 5-25

Creating a rule from scratch

Select options in this category to write a rule from scratch →

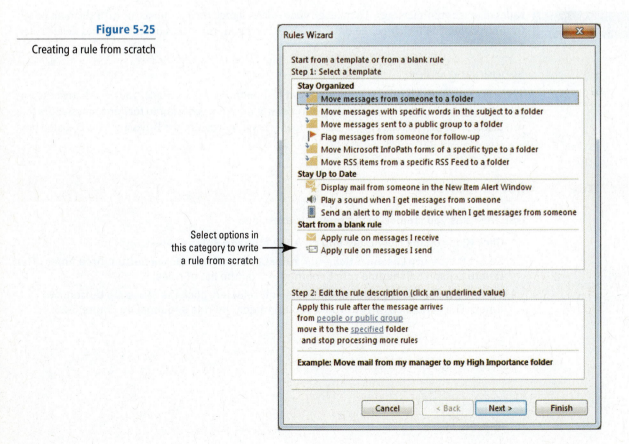

Another Way

If you wanted to delete all messages from a specific sender instead, select the *from people or public group* condition in the *Step 1* area of this first Rules Wizard dialog box. In the *Step 2* area, click *people or public group*. At the Rules Address page, you can key or click the sender's e-mail address into the *From* field and click OK to continue creating the rule.

4. In the *Start from a blank rule* section, click **Apply rule on messages I receive**. This identifies when the rule will run automatically.

5. Click the **Next** button to continue creating the rule.

6. In this Rules Wizard dialog box, you identify the conditions of the rule. Click **with specific words in the subject**. This rule will identify messages about the selected topic.

7. In the *Step 2* area, click **specific words**. The Search Text dialog box is displayed.

8. In the *Specify words or phrases to search for in the subject* field, key **Lesson 5 Schedule**.

9. Click the **Add** button. The *Lesson 5 Schedule* phrase is enclosed by quotation marks and added to the search list for this rule.

10. Click **OK** to close the Search Text dialog box. The Rules Wizard dialog box is displayed. The *Lesson 5 Schedule* search phrase is identified.

11. Click the **Next** button to continue creating the rule.

12. Available actions are listed in the Rules Wizard dialog box. Click the **delete it** check box.

13. You don't want to add any additional conditions, actions, or exceptions, so click the **Finish** button. The rule is complete: When a message arrives with Lesson 5 Schedule in the subject, delete it.

14. Select the **Lesson 5 Schedule (1)** rule, if necessary. Click the **Change Rule** button, and click **Rename Rule**. The Rename dialog box is displayed.

15. In the *New name of rule* field, key **Delete Lesson 5 Schedule**. Click **OK**. The dialog box is closed, and the rule's name is changed.

16. Click the **Delete Lesson 5 Schedule** check box to clear it. Click the **OK** button to close the Rules and Alerts dialog box.

PAUSE. LEAVE Outlook open to use in the next exercise.

MANAGING RULES

The Bottom Line

Rules manage your messages. To manage your rules, change their sequence or turn them on or off. In this section, you'll change the order in which rules run, turn rules on and off, and delete rules.

Sequencing Rules

The sequence in which rules are processed can be important. For example, you can change the importance of a message before forwarding it to a coworker. Also, you want to forward a message before you delete it. In this exercise, you'll change the sequence of rules in the Rules and Alerts dialog box.

STEP BY STEP   **Sequence Rules**

USE the rules you created in the previous exercises.

1. Click **Rules** on the HOME tab and click the **Manage Rules & Alerts** option.

2. Select the **Delete Lesson 5 Schedule** rule. Click the **Move Down** button three times. The Delete Lesson 5 Schedule rule becomes last on the list of rules.

3. With the Delete Lesson 5 Schedule rule still selected, click the **Move Up** button two times. The sequence of your rules should match the rule sequence in Figure 5-26.

Figure 5-26

Sequenced rules

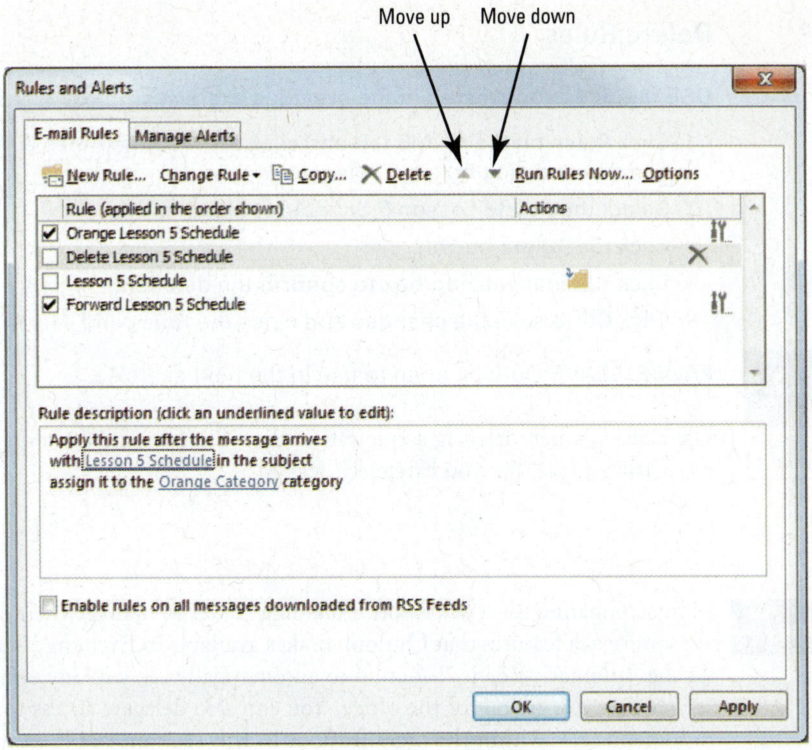

Move up   Move down

Rules and Alerts

E-mail Rules   Manage Alerts

New Rule... Change Rule ▾ 📋 Copy... ✕ Delete ▲ ▾ Run Rules Now... Options

Rule (applied in the order shown)	Actions	
☑ Orange Lesson 5 Schedule		⸙
☐ Delete Lesson 5 Schedule		✕
☐ Lesson 5 Schedule		📁
☑ Forward Lesson 5 Schedule		⸙

Rule description (click an underlined value to edit):

Apply this rule after the message arrives
with Lesson 5 Schedule in the subject
assign it to the Orange Category category

☐ Enable rules on all messages downloaded from RSS Feeds

OK   Cancel   Apply

4. Click **OK** to save the changes and close the Rules and Alerts dialog box.

PAUSE. LEAVE Outlook open to use in the next exercise.

Turning Off a Rule

In the Rules and Alerts dialog box, the check box in front of the rule's name controls its status. A rule is either on or off. If a rule is on, the check box in front of the rule is checked. If a rule is off, the check box is empty. Turning off a rule rather than deleting it enables you to turn on the rule if you need it later. It also enables you to keep a rule turned off and run it at a time of your choice. In this exercise, you'll turn off a rule.

STEP BY STEP   **Turn Off a Rule**

USE the rules you created in the previous exercises.

1. Click **Rules** on the HOME tab and click the **Manage Rules & Alerts** option. The Rules and Alerts dialog box is displayed.

2. Click the **Forward Lesson 5 Schedule** check box so the check box is empty and no rules are selected.

3. Click **OK** to save the changes and close the Rules and Alerts dialog box.

PAUSE. LEAVE Outlook open to use in the next exercise.

Deleting Rules

If you created a rule that you will not use again, delete it. This keeps your list of rules organized and reduces confusion caused by a long list of old rules that are not used. In this exercise, you'll delete a rule.

Delete Rules

USE the rules you created in the previous exercises.

1. Click **Rules** on the HOME tab and click the **Manage Rules & Alerts** option. The Rules and Alerts dialog box is displayed.
2. Select the **Delete Lesson 5 Schedule** rule.
3. Click the **Delete** button.
4. Click **Yes** in the dialog box to confirm the deletion.
5. Click **OK** to save the changes and close the Rules and Alerts dialog box.

CERTIFICATION READY? 1.2.4

How do you delete a rule?

PAUSE. LEAVE Outlook open to use in the next exercise.

Use caution when deleting a rule rather than disabling it. You don't want to have to spend time re-creating a rule that you carelessly deleted.

WORKING WITH AUTOMATED MICROSOFT EXCHANGE TOOLS

The Bottom Line

Many companies use a Microsoft Exchange Server to manage their e-mail communication. There are some extra features that Outlook makes available to Exchange Server e-mail accounts. You can set the Automatic Replies function to automatically reply to any e-mail you receive informing the sender that you are out of the office. You can also delegate access to parts of your e-mail account to someone else within the organization. In this section, you'll create an Auto-reply message and work with the delegating access tool.

Creating an Auto-reply Message

When you're out of the office, you will still receive e-mail messages. If you use a Microsoft Exchange Server e-mail account, you can use the improved Automatic Replies tool to send an internal message informing coworkers that you are out of the office. Internal messages are ones that are sent to and from other individuals in the same Exchange Server. By the same token, you can use the same tool to send a similar message to people outside your organization. In this section, you'll create an Auto-reply message.

Create an Auto-reply Message

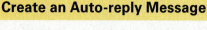

GET READY. You must use a Microsoft Exchange Server account to complete this exercise. If you do not have a Microsoft Exchange Server account, read through the exercise and use it as a reference when preparing for your certification exam.

1. If necessary, click the **Mail** button in the Navigation bar to display the mailbox.
2. Click the **FILE** tab and click the **Automatic Replies (Out of Office)** option. The Automatic Reply dialog box is displayed.

⚠ **Troubleshooting** If you don't have an Exchange Server account, this option won't be visible.

3. Click the **Send automatic replies** option.
4. Select the **Only send during this time range** option. Select **12:00 AM** [tomorrow] as the Start time. Select **12:00 AM** [the following day] as the End time.
5. Click the **Inside My Organization** tab, if necessary.

Take Note For the Automatic Replies function, Microsoft defines *organization* as people who share an Exchange Server account on your e-mail system.

6. Click the **Outside My Organization** tab, and select the **Auto-reply to people outside my organization** check box.
7. Select **My Contacts only**.

Take Note

Another Way
If you want the reply sent to everyone who e-mails you, select *Anyone outside my organization* instead of *My contacts only*.

CERTIFICATION READY? 1.2.5

How do you create an Auto-reply message?

For the Automatic Replies function, Microsoft defines My Contacts only as the people listed in your Exchange Server contact list.

8. In the text entry area, key **I am out of the office today. I'll respond to your message tomorrow**.
9. Click **OK**. The dialog box is closed. The Auto-reply message will be sent when you receive messages during this time period.

PAUSE. LEAVE Outlook open to use in the next exercise.

Delegating Access to Your Account

Microsoft Office 2013 includes another new feature for use with a Microsoft Exchange Server e-mail account. You can delegate access to your account to someone else within your organization. This means that the delegate can view your incoming messages and meeting requests and then respond to them in your place. Not only is this useful if you're planning to be away from the office for an extended period, it can also be used to allow an assistant to review the day-to-day items and keep you informed of important items that warrant your personal attention. In this section, you'll make someone else your delegate.

STEP BY STEP **Delegate Access to Your Account**

GET READY. You must use a Microsoft Exchange Server account to complete this exercise. If you do not have a Microsoft Exchange Server account, read through the exercise and use it as a reference when preparing for your certification exam.

1. If necessary, click the **Mail** button in the Navigation bar to display the mailbox.
2. Click the **FILE** tab and click the **Account Settings** option. A group of Account Setting options displays.
3. Click the **Delegate Access** option.

Troubleshooting If you don't have an Exchange Server account, this option won't be visible.

Another Way
If necessary, search for their name in the address list.

4. Click the **Add** button. Type the name of a person who is in the Global Access List for your organization's Exchange.
5. Click **Add** again and then click **OK**. The Delegate Permissions dialog box is displayed showing each of the primary Outlook components. By default, the scroll bar next to the Calendar component has been changed to Editor, which will allow the delegate to read, create, and modify Calendar items.
6. Click the **Automatically send a message to delegate summarizing these permissions** checkbox.
7. Click **OK**. The dialog box is closed. The delegate that you granted access to your Calendar will receive an e-mail notifying them of the change.
8. Click **OK**. The dialog box is closed.

CERTIFICATION READY? 2.1.13

How do you delegate access to your e-mail account?

PAUSE. LEAVE Outlook open to use in the next exercise.

As the owner of the account, you can limit how much access you want to grant to your delegate. Table 5-2 describes these parts of a rule.

Delegate Permissions	Description
Send on Behalf	The Send on Behalf permission is the lowest level of access that you can delegate. It gives the recipient permission to read and respond to meeting requests only. It is particularly useful if you have someone else managing your schedule.
Reviewer	The Reviewer permission level allows the delegate to read mail items in your Outlook Data File, but not make any changes to them.
Author	The Author permission level allows the delegate to read any mail items and authorizes them to create new items on your behalf. They can also modify or delete any items that they personally created.
Editor	The Editor permission level means that the delegate can do anything that you can do. They have all the permissions available at the Author level, but they can also modify or delete items that you created.

Modifying and Removing Delegate Access

Allowing some access to your mailbox items can be a convenient tool. However, if circumstances or personnel changes, you need to go back and make changes to the permission level that you have granted your delegate. In this section, you'll change a delegate's permission level and then remove it altogether.

STEP BY STEP   **Modify and Remove Delegate Access**

GET READY. You must use a Microsoft Exchange Server account to complete this exercise. If you do not have a Microsoft Exchange Server account, read through the exercise and use it as a reference when preparing for your certification exam.

1. If necessary, click the **Mail** button in the Navigation bar to display the mailbox.
2. Click the **FILE** tab, and click the **Account Settings** option. A group of Account Setting options displays.
3. Click the **Delegate Access** option.

⚠ **Troubleshooting**   If you don't have an Exchange Server account, this option won't be visible.

4. Select the person that you delegated access to your account in the previous exercise. Click the **Permissions** button. The Delegate Permissions dialog box is displayed showing each of the primary Outlook components similar to the one displayed in the last section.
5. Click the Inbox drop bar and select **Author** from the displayed list to give the person permission to create and send e-mails from you.
6. Deselect the **Automatically send a message to delegate summarizing these permissions** checkbox, if necessary.
7. Click **OK**. The dialog box is closed.
8. In the Delegates box, select the name of the delegate again, and click the **Remove** button. The name disappears from the list.
9. Click **OK** to close the dialog box having no one selected as a delegate.

PAUSE. LEAVE Outlook open to use in the next exercise.

USING QUICK STEPS

Outlook Quick Steps brings the computer power of macros to Outlook. They enable you to perform a series of tasks with the click of a button. Unlike Rules, you choose when and where to apply the Quick Steps. **Quick Steps** are a type of customizable shortcut that you can use to perform several functions at the same time.

Outlook comes with a set of several default Quick Steps that you can program with your personal information. For example, you can program the Team E-mail Quick Step with the contact information for the people on your team. When you click the Team E-mail Quick Step, a new message window opens already addressed to your team. In this section, you'll get to know the new Quick Step feature by creating, editing, deleting, performing, duplicating, and resetting Quick Steps.

SOFTWARE ORIENTATION

The Quick Steps Group

The Quick Steps feature (see Figure 5-27) allows you to set up a group of custom shortcuts to perform your common message management. The Quick Steps group contains six default Quick Steps for the most commonly performed tasks in Outlook. You can also click the Create New button in the Quick Steps group to create your own custom Quick Step shortcuts.

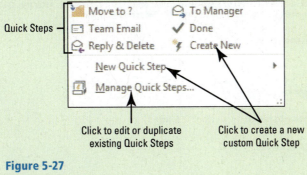

Figure 5-27

The Quick Steps group

Use this figure as a reference throughout this lesson as well as the rest of this book.

Performing Quick Steps

Quick Steps are easier to run than traditional rules, because they are right there at your fingertips on the HOME tab. To perform a Quick Step, you simply select a message and then click the Quick Steps icon for the action you want. The first time you perform most Quick Steps, you are asked to add information to personalize the action. For example, if you click the Move to ? Quick Step, you are asked to specify which folder you want the message moved to. Once you set up the Quick Step, it will always move mail items to the folder you designated during setup unless you go back in and edit the settings. In this exercise, you'll perform a couple of Quick Steps.

STEP BY STEP	**Perform Quick Steps**

GET READY. LAUNCH Outlook if it is not already running.

1. If necessary, click the **Mail** button in the Navigation bar to display the mailbox.

2. Select the **Sample Private Message** in the message list. If you don't have this message, choose any message with the word *Sample* in the subject.

3. On the HOME tab, click the **Reply & Delete** button in the Quick Steps group shown in Figure 5-27. A *RE: Sample Private Message* window is displayed and the original is moved to the Deleted Items folder. Note that like any other message reply, the *To* field is automatically filled with the name of the person who sent the original message to you.

4. Click **Send**.

5. Click **Send/Receive All Folders** on the HOME tab.

6. Select the newly arrived message and click the Flag icon in the message list to flag it for follow up.

7. Click **Done** in the Quick Steps group. The First Time Setup dialog box for the Done Quick Step is displayed, as shown in Figure 5-28. The Done Quick Step can perform three actions: mark the message as read, mark it as complete, and move it to a folder you choose.

Figure 5-28

First Time Setup dialog box for Done Quick Step

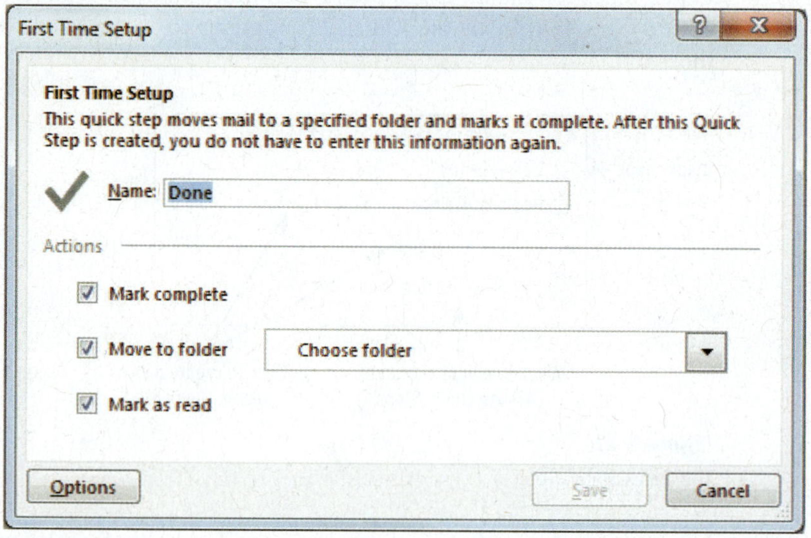

First Time Setup	?	X

First Time Setup
This quick step moves mail to a specified folder and marks it complete. After this Quick Step is created, you do not have to enter this information again.

✓ **Name:** Done

Actions

☑ Mark complete

☑ Move to folder   Choose folder   ▼

☑ Mark as read

Options		Save	Cancel

Another Way

You can also perform a Quick Step by right-clicking on a message, pointing to Quick Steps in the shortcut menu, and selecting the desired Quick Step from the fly-out list.

8. In the Name field, key **Completed Events**. After the setup process, the Quick Step button will be called Completed Events.

9. Click the **Choose Folder** down arrow and select the **Lesson 5 Schedules** folder.

10. Click **Save**. The First Time Setup dialog box closes and the Completed Events button appears in the Quick Steps group, as shown in Figure 5-29.

Figure 5-29

Newly formatted Quick Step

11. With the message still selected, click the new **Completed Events** button in the Quick Steps group. The message is moved to the Lesson 5 Schedules folder and is marked as read and completed.

12. Click the **Lesson 5 Schedules** folder in the Folder List, as shown in Figure 5-30.

Figure 5-30

The completed message in its new location

Message moved and categorized

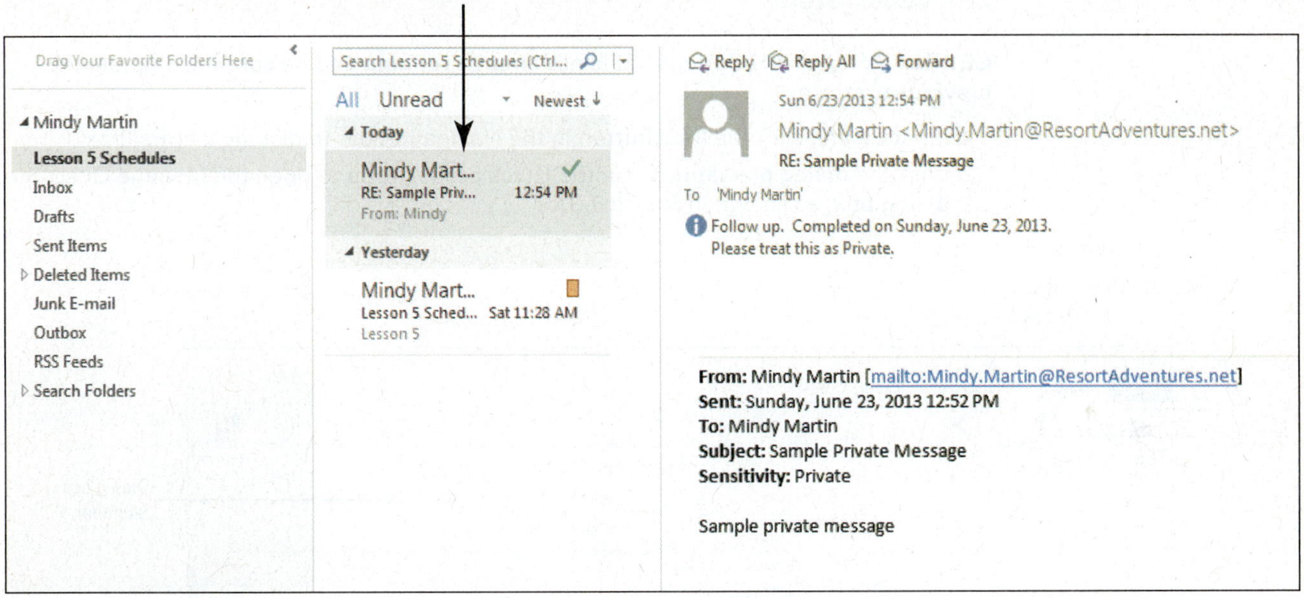

PAUSE. LEAVE Outlook open to use in the next exercise.

CERTIFICATION READY?   1.2.3

How do you perform a Quick Step?

Outlook Quick Steps (see Table 5-3) is a combination of rules and customized Ribbon buttons. By using Quick Steps, you can perform multiple different actions with a single click.

Table 5-3

Default Quick Steps

Quick Steps	Description
Move to ?	The Move to Quick Step marks the select message as read and moves it to the assigned folder.
To Manager	The To Manager Quick Step forwards the selected message to your manager. If you use Microsoft Exchange Server, Outlook determines your manager's name from Active Directory. If you don't use the Exchange Server, you can key the correct e-mail address in the *To* field.
Team E-mail	The Team E-mail Quick Step creates a new message to the members of your team. If you use Microsoft Exchange Server, Outlook determine the names of your team members from Active Directory. If not, you can key the correct e-mail addresses in the *To* field.
Done	The Done Quick Step marks the selected message as read and complete and moves it to the selected folder.
Reply & Delete	The Reply & Delete Quick Step creates a reply to the selected message and deletes it.
Create New	The Create New Quick Step allows you to create an entirely custom Quick Step.

Editing Quick Steps

Although the default Quick Steps covers many of the most common tasks, you can easily modify them to suit your needs. Using the Manage Quick Steps dialog box, you can rename a Quick Step, change or eliminate actions, or add additional steps to the process. In this exercise, you'll edit a Quick Step.

STEP BY STEP | **Edit Quick Steps**

GET READY. LAUNCH Outlook if it is not already running and be sure to complete the previous exercise.

1. If necessary, click the **Mail** button in the Navigation bar to display the mailbox.
2. Click the **dialog box launcher** in the Quick Steps group to open the Manage Quick Steps dialog box, as shown in Figure 5-31.

Figure 5-31

Manage Quick Steps dialog box

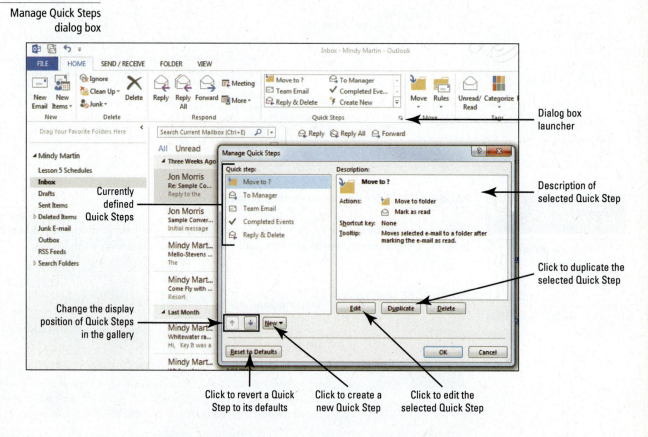

Dialog box launcher

Currently defined Quick Steps

Change the display position of Quick Steps in the gallery

Description of selected Quick Step

Click to duplicate the selected Quick Step

Click to revert a Quick Step to its defaults

Click to create a new Quick Step

Click to edit the selected Quick Step

3. In the *Quick step* area, select **Completed Events**. The Description area changes to define the actions performed by this Quick Step, as shown in Figure 5-32.

Figure 5-32

Manage Quick Steps dialog box with Completed Events selected

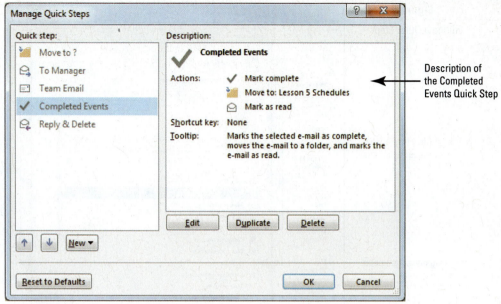

Description of the Completed Events Quick Step

4. Click the **Edit** button. The Edit Quick Step dialog box is displayed, as shown in Figure 5-33.

Figure 5-33

Edit Quick Step dialog box

Click to an action box to see a list of available actions →

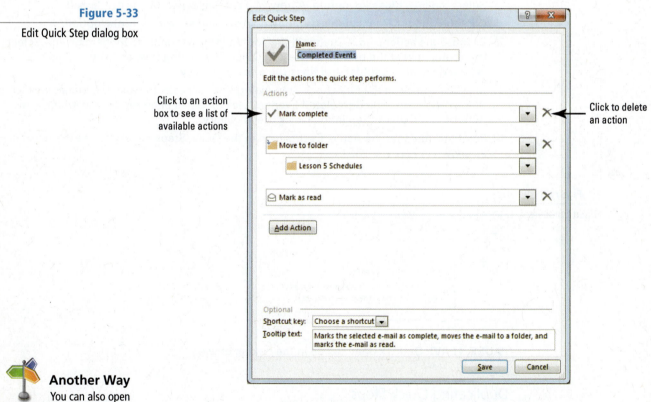

Click to delete an action

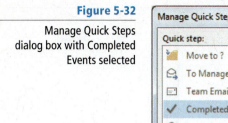

Another Way
You can also open the Edit Quick Step dialog box by right-clicking the desired Quick Step in the Quick Steps gallery and selecting Edit Quick Step from the shortcut menu.

5. In the *Name* field, select the existing text and key **Active Events**.
6. Click the **Delete** button next to the Mark Complete action.
7. Click the **Mark as Read** action's dropdown arrow. A dropdown list of options is displayed, as shown in Figure 5-34.

Figure 5-34

Editing a Quick Step

Figure 5-34

Editing a Quick Step

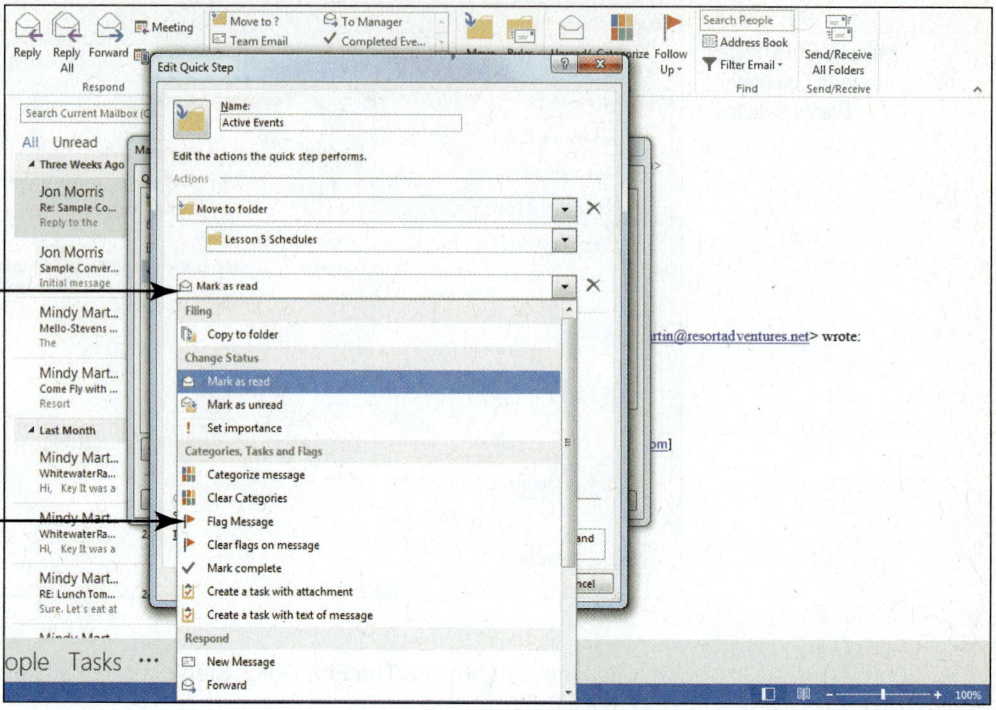

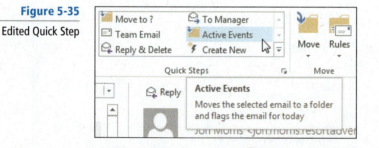

8. Select the **Flag Message** option. A new Choose flag action box is displayed.

9. Click the **Choose Flag** action's dropdown arrow, and select the **Today** option.

10. Because the actions have changed, the Tooltip information is no longer correct. Select the Tooltip text at the bottom of the Edit Quick Step dialog box, and key **Moves the selected email to a folder and flags the email for today**.

11. Click **Save** to close the Edit Quick Step dialog box. Click **OK** to close the Manage Quick Steps dialog box. The Completed Events Quick Step has been replaced with the new Active Events Quick Step in the Quick Steps gallery.

12. Point the cursor at the Active Events icon in the Quick Steps gallery to see the new tip, as shown in Figure 5-35.

Figure 5-35

Edited Quick Step

PAUSE. LEAVE Outlook open to use in the next exercise.

Duplicating Quick Steps

In many cases, you'll find yourself needing multiple Quick Steps that perform similar functions. For example, you might want to use one Team E-mail Quick Step to send an e-mail to members of your marketing project, another to send e-mails to the members of the Employee Softball team, and another to send e-mails to members of your book club. The easiest way to create new Quick Steps that perform similar actions is by duplication. In this exercise, you'll duplicate a Quick Step.

STEP BY STEP **Duplicate Quick Steps**

GET READY. LAUNCH Outlook if it is not already running.

1. If necessary, click the Mail button in the Navigation bar to display the mailbox.

2. Right-click Outlook Data Files in the Folders List, and click New Folder in the shortcut menu. A New Folder name box appears in the Folders List.

3. Key Pending Reservations and [Press Enter]. The new folder is displayed in the Folders List.

4. On the HOME tab, in the Quick Steps group, click the More button to open the Quick Steps gallery.

5. Select Manage Quick Steps. The Manage Quick Steps dialog box is displayed (refer to Figure 5-31). Note: This is the same dialog box that is opened when you click on the dialog box launcher in the Quick Steps group.

6. Click Active Events in the Quick Step list in the Manage Quick Steps dialog box; then click Duplicate. The Edit Quick Step dialog box is displayed. The text *Copy of Active Events* is automatically entered into the *Name* field, as shown in Figure 5-36.

Figure 5-36

Duplicating a Quick Step

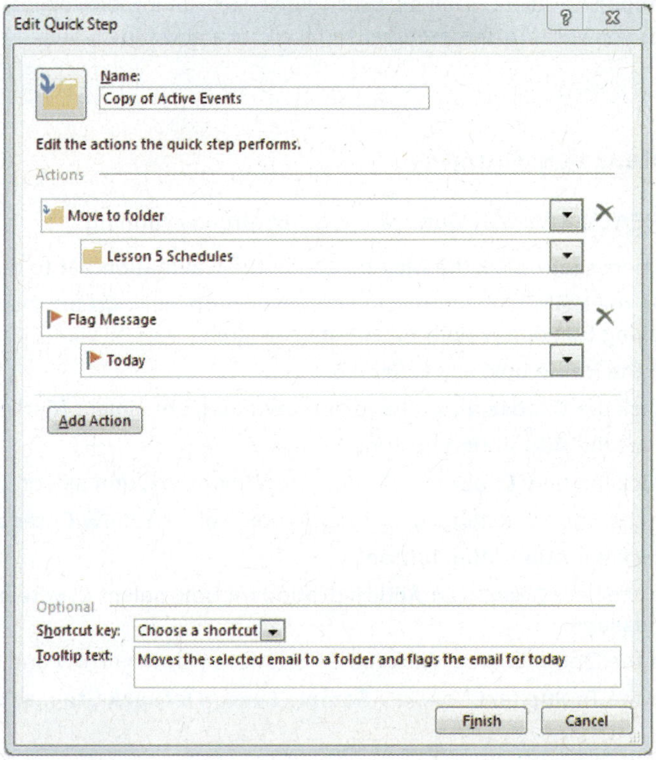

Another Way
You can also duplicate a Quick Step by right-clicking the desired Quick Step in the Quick Steps gallery and selecting Duplicate Quick Step from the shortcut menu.

7. Click the Lesson 5 Schedules dropdown box. A dropdown list of available folders appears.

8. Select the Pending Reservations folder. The list collapses.

Troubleshooting If necessary, click Other Folder to open the Select Folder dialog box. Select Pending Reservations and click OK.

9. In the Name field, key **Pending Projects**.

10. Click **Finish**. Click **OK**. The new Quick Step appears in the Quick Steps gallery, as shown in Figure 5-37.

PAUSE. LEAVE Outlook open to use in the next exercise.

Creating Quick Steps

Although the default Quick Steps handle many of the most common tasks in Outlook, you may want to create a unique Quick Step that performs different tasks or a combination of actions. When you click the New button in the Manage Quick Steps dialog box and select Custom from the dropdown menu, a blank Edit Quick Step dialog box opens, allowing you to choose any actions you wish. In this exercise, you'll create a new Quick Step.

STEP BY STEP   **Create Quick Steps**

GET READY. LAUNCH Outlook if it is not already running.

1. If necessary, click the **Mail** button in the Navigation bar to display the mailbox.

2. On the HOME tab, in the Quick Steps group, click **Create New**. The Edit Quick Step dialog box opens with no actions selected.

3. In the Name box, key **Lesson 5**.

4. Click the **Choose an Action** dropdown box, and select **Mark as Unread**.

5. Click the **Add Action** button.

6. Click the new **Choose an Action** dropdown box, and select **Categorize message**.

7. In the Choose category dropdown box, select **Yellow Category**.

8. Click the **Add Action** button.

9. In the new **Choose an Action** dropdown box, select **Create a task with text of message**.

10. In the Optional area, click the **Shortcut key** down arrow and select [**Ctrl + Shift + 1**].

11. In the Tooltip text box, key **Sample Lesson 5 Quick Step**, as shown in Figure 5-38.

Another Way

You can also create a new Quick Step by clicking the New button in the Manage Quick Steps dialog box and selecting Custom from the dropdown menu.

Figure 5-38

Creating a custom Quick Step

Figure 5-38

Creating a custom Quick Step

Click to add
an action

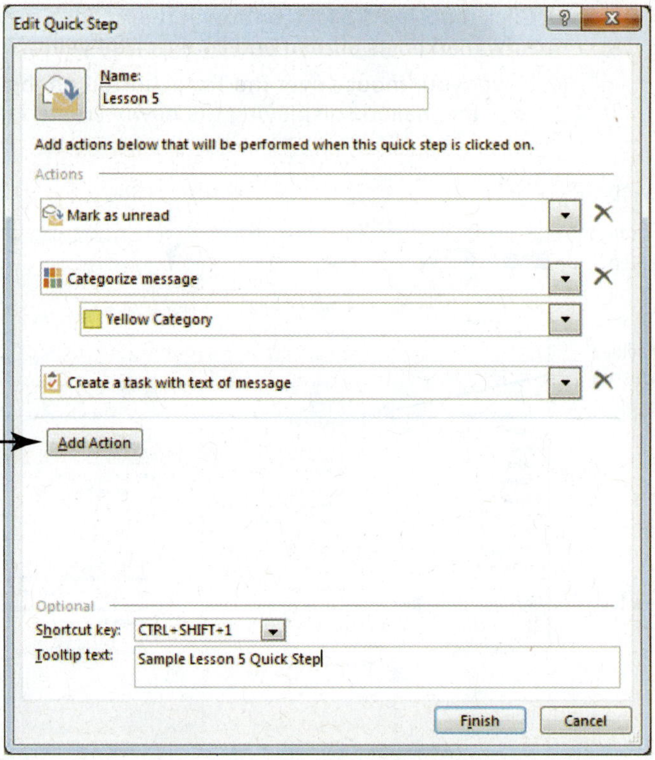

12. Click **Finish**. The new Quick Step appears in the Quick Steps gallery.

13. Open the **Lesson 5 Schedules** folder.

14. Select the completed private message, and click the new **Lesson 5 Quick Step** in the Quick Steps gallery. A Sample private message Task window is displayed showing the contents of the e-mail message in the body of the task, as shown in Figure 5-39.

Figure 5-39

Lesson 5 Quick Step created task

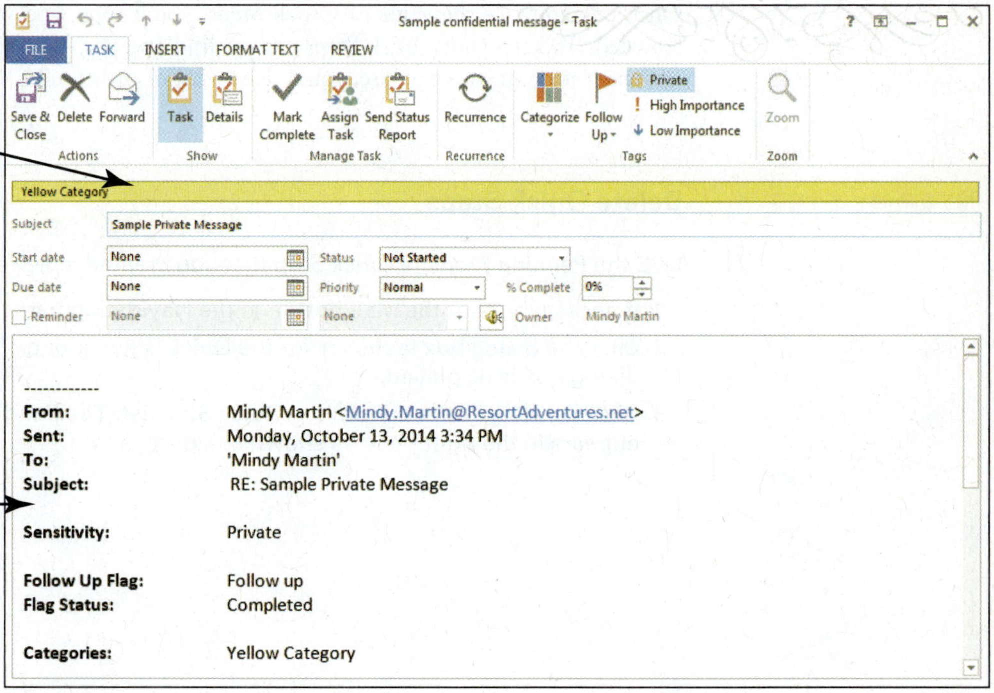

Quick Step categorized
the task Yellow

Original
message text

15. Click the **Save & Close** button in the Actions group on the TASK tab. The message is now marked as unread and categorized yellow.

16. Hover your mouse over the Tasks button on the Navigation bar. The Tasks peek opens over the mailbox displaying the newly created task, as shown in Figure 5-40.

Figure 5-40

Newly created task from Lesson 5 Quick Step

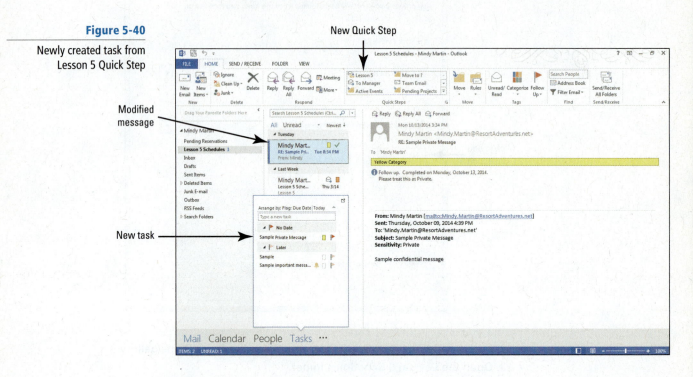

PAUSE. LEAVE Outlook open to use in the next exercise.

Deleting Quick Steps

Once you embrace the value of Quick Steps, you'll soon find your Quick Steps gallery getting crowded. To keep your Quick Steps easy to find and use, be sure to delete Quick Steps that you no longer need. In this exercise, you'll delete one of your Quick Steps.

STEP BY STEP   **Delete Quick Steps**

USE the Pending Projects Quick Step that you created in a previous exercise.

1. If necessary, click the **Mail** button in the Navigation bar to display the mailbox.

2. Click the **dialog box launcher** for the Quick Steps group. The Manage Quick Steps dialog box is displayed.

3. Click **Pending Projects** from the Quick Step list. The Pending Projects description appears in the right pane as shown in Figure 5-41.

Figure 5-41

Manage Quick Steps dialog
box with Pending Projects
selected

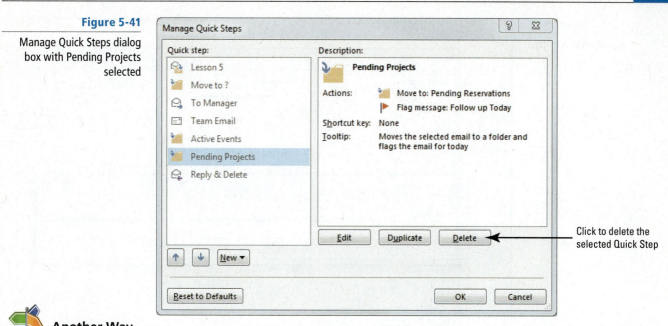

Figure 5-41

Manage Quick Steps dialog
box with Pending Projects
selected

Click to delete the
selected Quick Step

Another Way
You can also delete
a Quick Step by right-clicking a
Quick Step and selecting
Delete.

4. Click the **Delete** button. The Pending Projects Quick Step is immediately removed from the Quick Step list.
5. Click **OK** to close the dialog box.

PAUSE. LEAVE Outlook open to use in the next exercise.

Resetting Quick Steps to Default

If your Quick Steps gallery gets overfilled with items that you no longer need, you might find it easier to simply reset your Quick Steps gallery and start over. In this exercise, you'll reset your Quick Steps.

STEP BY STEP   **Reset Quick Steps to Default**

GET READY. LAUNCH Outlook if it is not already running.

1. If necessary, click the **Mail** button in the Navigation bar to display the mailbox.
2. Click the **dialog box launcher** in the Quick Steps group to open the Manage Quick Steps dialog box.
3. Click the **Reset to Defaults** button. A message is displayed warning you that any changes will be lost, as shown in Figure 5-42.

Figure 5-42

Resetting Quick Steps

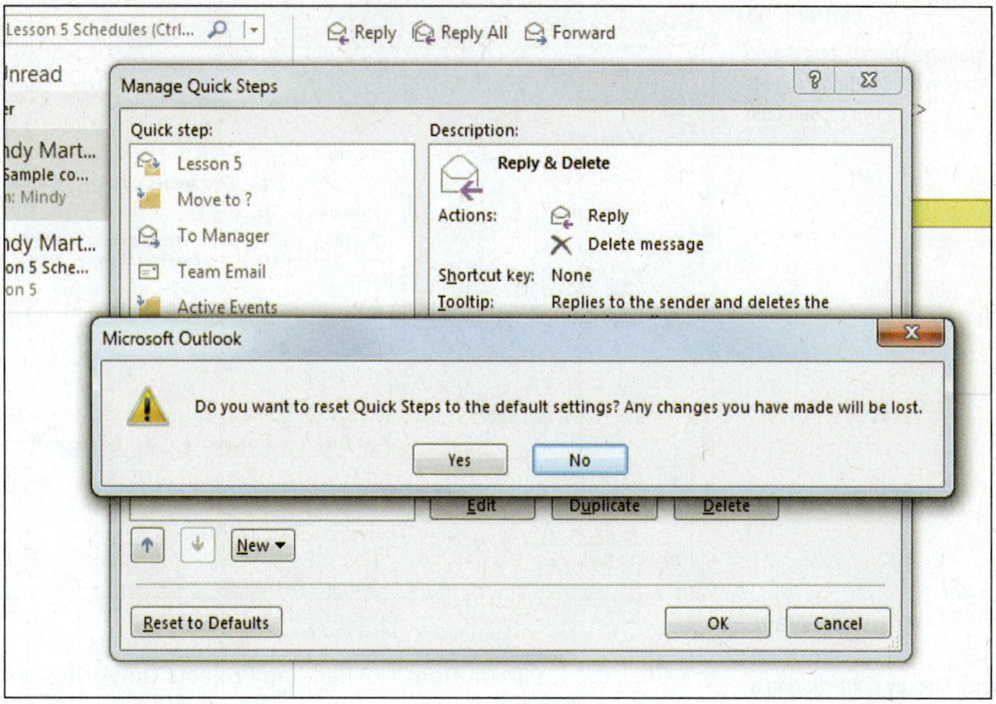

4. Click **Yes**. The Quick Steps in the Manage Quick Steps dialog box revert back to the original list.

5. Click **OK** to close the dialog box.

CLOSE Outlook.

Many people complain that the reason they don't organize their mailboxes and manage their messages is because it is time-consuming. Quick Steps has the power to change all that.

SKILL SUMMARY

In This Lesson You Learned How To:	Exam Objective	Objective Number
Create and Run Rules	Create and manage rules	1.2.4
Manage Rules	Create and manage rules	1.2.4
Work with Automated Microsoft Exchange Tools	Create auto-replies Delegate access	1.2.5 2.1.13
Use Quick Steps	Apply Quick Steps	1.2.3

Knowledge Assessment

Multiple Choice

Select the best response for the following statements.

1. Which Quick Step moves a message to specific folder and marks it as read?
   a. Move to
   b. To folder
   c. Done
   d. Both a and c

2. The _____ Delegate Access permission level allows a delegate to do everything in your mailbox that you can do.
   a. Send on Behalf
   b. Editor
   c. Author
   d. Manager

3. Why would you turn off a rule?
   a. The rule is no longer needed.
   b. The rule should only be run periodically.
   c. You don't want the rule to run automatically.
   d. All of the above

4. Why would you change the sequence of your rules?
   a. Rules should be in alphabetic order.
   b. Short rules should be processed first.
   c. Some actions should be performed before others.
   d. Rules should be processed in the order they were created.

5. What happens if a rule's conditions are too broad?
   a. The rule will affect more messages than intended.
   b. The rule will affect fewer messages than intended.
   c. The rule will not run.
   d. The affected messages are deleted.

6. How does a rule identify the messages it affects?
   a. Actions
   b. Cues
   c. Conditions
   d. Phrases

7. What dialog box allows you to modify Quick Steps?
   a. Define Quick Steps
   b. Edit Quick Step
   c. Modify Quick Steps
   d. Manage Quick Steps

8. What dialog box enables you to add steps in a rule?
   a. Rules and Alerts
   b. Rules Wizard
   c. Steps
   d. New Rule

9. Why would you duplicate an existing Quick Step to create a new rule?
   a. Many of the new Quick Step's characteristics are similar to the existing rule.
   b. The new Quick Step replaces the existing Quick Step.
   c. The existing Quick Step does not work correctly.
   d. This process tests the existing Quick Step.

10. How do you decide which actions can be combined in a single rule?
   a. The conditions are the same for all of the actions.
   b. The exceptions are the same for all of the actions.
   c. A rule with combined actions is easier to write.
   d. The actions won't need to be turned off separately.

Fill in the Blank

Complete the following sentences by writing the correct word or words in the blanks provided.

1. When you perform a Quick Step for the first time, you must complete the _____.

2. A(n) _____ walks you through a process.

3. You can use _____ to help you manage your messages automatically.

4. A Quick Step can be _____ to create a new one.

5. You should only _____ a rule if you are sure you won't need it again.

6. A(n) _____ is taken only if the conditions of a rule are met.

7. You must have _____ in order to set up an Auto-reply message.

8. The _____ of the rules changes when you move a rule up or down.

9. A(n) _____ provides structure for a rule.

10. The _____ Quick Step creates a new message with the addressees automatically entered.

Competency Assessment

Project 5-1: Modify an Existing Rule

Julie Reynolds owns a small Internet-based gift shop with a big name. World-Wide Importers sells a variety of crafted objects created by small crafters across the country and by one vendor in Canada, justifying the "World-Wide" portion of her company's name. Julie regularly receives pictures of crafted items from her suppliers and sends invoices to customers who buy her products. Julie decided to modify an existing rule to manage her messages automatically.

GET READY. LAUNCH Outlook if it is not already running.

1. If necessary, click the **Mail** button in the Navigation bar to display the mailbox.

2. On the HOME tab, click the **Rules** command in the Move group and select the **Manage Rules & Alerts** option.

3. Select the **Orange Lesson 5 Schedule** rule.

4. Click the **Change Rule** button; then click the **Edit Rule Settings** option.

5. In the *Step 2: Edit the rule description* area, click the underlined **Lesson 5 Schedule** text.

6. Key **New Product** and click **Add**.

7. Select the **"Lesson 5 Schedule"** text in the *Search list* box, and click **Remove**; then click **OK**.

8. In the *Step 2: Edit the rule description* area, click the underlined **Orange Category** text.

9. In the Color Categories dialog box, select **Blue Category** and deselect **Orange Category**.

10. Click **OK** and then **No** to close the Rename Category dialog box.

11. Click **Finish** and then click **OK** to close the Rules and Alerts dialog box.

12. Click the **New E-mail** button on the HOME tab. The Message window is displayed.

13. Click the *To* field. Key [**your e-mail address**].

14. Click the *Subject* field. Key **New Product!**

15. In the message area, key **Take a look at this new birdfeeder! It's sure to be a big hit!**

16. Click the **Attach File** button on the Ribbon. Navigate to the data folders for this lesson, click the **Birdfeeder** file, and click the **Insert** button.

17. Click the **Send** button. The message is moved to the Outbox and sent when the computer is connected to the Internet. Click the **Send/Receive All Folders** button on the HOME tab.

18. Locate the New Product! message in the Inbox.

19. Click the FILE tab and select the Save As option. Save the message in Outlook Message Format as *New Blue Rule* in the location specified by your instructor.

LEAVE Outlook open for the next project.

Project 5-2: Create Folders and Test Rules and Quick Steps

To begin her organization, Julie needs to create two folders and a message. Suppliers frequently send pictures of new products to Julie. She wants to move these messages to one of her new folders.

GET READY. LAUNCH Outlook if it is not already running.

1. If necessary, click the Mail button in the Navigation bar to display the mailbox.

2. Right-click Outlook Data Files in the Folders List. Click New Folder in the shortcut menu. A box is displayed in the Folders List.

3. Key P5 Products and [press Enter].

4. Right-click Outlook Data Files in the Folders List. Click New Folder in the shortcut menu. A box is displayed in the Folders List.

5. Key P5 Invoices and [press Enter].

6. Click the More button in the Quick Steps group to open the Quick Steps gallery.

7. Click New Quick Step and select Move to Folder from the list of available Quick Steps. The First Time Setup dialog box is displayed.

8. In the *Name* field, key P5 Products.

9. Click the Move to Folder box, and select P5 Products. Click Finish.

10. Locate the New Product! message in the message list.

11. Click the P5 Products Quick Step.

LEAVE Outlook open for the next project.

Proficiency Assessment

Project 5-3: Duplicate a Quick Step

Julie wants to move messages about invoices into the P5 Invoices folder. Complete Project 5-2 before starting this project.

USE the message and folders you created in Project 5-2 for this project.

1. If necessary, click the Mail button in the Navigation bar to display the mailbox.

2. Click the Quick Steps group's dialog box launcher to open the Manage Quick Steps dialog box.

3. Select P5 Products and click Duplicate to open the Edit Quick Step dialog box.

4. Change the Name to Project 5-3.

5. Click the P5 Products box and select P5 Invoices.

6. Click Finish and OK to close the boxes.

7. Click the P5 Products folder to display the message you moved in the previous project.

8. If necessary, select the message and click the Project 5-3 Quick Step to move the message.

9. Click the P5 Products folder in the Folder List to see the messages that were moved there using the Quick Steps.

LEAVE Outlook open for the next project.

Project 5-4: Create and Run a Rule that Moves Messages

Julie wants to create a rule that will automatically move messages about invoices into the P5 Invoices folder. To test the Invoice rule, Julie will send a message to herself with the word "Invoice" in the *Subject* field. Complete Project 5-2 before starting this project.

GET READY. LAUNCH Outlook if it is not already running.

1. Click the **FILE** tab. In Backstage view, click the **Manage Rules & Alerts** option to display the Rules and Alerts dialog box.
2. Click the **New Rule** button. The Rules Wizard dialog box is displayed.
3. In the Stay Organized category, click **Move messages with specific words in the subject to a folder**.
4. In the *Step 2 area*, click **specific words**. The Search Text dialog box is displayed.
5. In the *Specify words or phrases to search for in the subject* field, key **Invoice**.
6. Click the **Add** button; then click **OK** to close the Search Text dialog box.
7. In the *Step 2 area*, click **specified** to identify the destination folder.
8. Click the **P5 Invoices** folder, and click **OK**.
9. Click the **Finish** button.
10. In the Rules and Alerts dialog box, click **Change Rule,** and click the **Rename Rule** option. Key **Move Invoices** in the *New name of rule* field. Click **OK**.
11. Click **OK** to close the Rules and Alerts dialog box and return to the main Outlook window.
12. Create a message addressed to yourself. Use **Invoice** for the *Subject* field and **Testing** for the message body. Click **Send**.
13. If necessary, click the **Send/Receive All Folders** button on the HOME tab. The rule is run automatically when messages are received.
14. Click the **P5 Invoices** folder to verify that the received Invoice message was moved to the P5 Invoices folder.

LEAVE Outlook open for the next project.

Mastery Assessment

Project 5-5: Manage Rules

Julie has made several rules lately. Because she knows that it is important to keep her rules organized, she needs to go back and manage the rules in the Rules and Alerts dialog box. Complete Projects 5-2 and 5-3 before starting this project.

GET READY. LAUNCH Outlook if it is not already running.

1. Click **Rules** on the HOME tab and click **Manage Rules & Alerts** to open the **Rules and Alerts** dialog box.
2. Select the **Orange Lesson 5 Schedule** rule and use the **Move Up arrow** to move this rule to the top.
3. Click the **Lesson 5 Schedule** rule and use the **Move Down** arrow to move it to the bottom of the list.
4. Select the **Move Invoices** rule to deselect it and click the **Delete** button. Click **Yes** to confirm.
5. Close the dialog box and return to the mailbox.

LEAVE Outlook open for the next project.

Project 5-6: Create a Quick Step from Scratch to Assign a Category

Julie wants to create a rule that categorizes the messages she sends with "Invoice" in the *Subject* field to assign the messages to the Yellow category. Complete Project 5-2 before starting this project.

GET READY. LAUNCH Outlook if it is not already running.

1. If necessary, click the **Mail** button in the Navigation bar to display the mailbox.
2. In the Quick Steps gallery, click **Create New** to open the Edit Quick Step dialog box.
3. In the *Name* field, key **Project 5-6**.
4. Add the following actions:

Move to folder	select	**P5 Invoices**
Categorize message	select	**Yellow Category**

5. Change the Tooltip text to read:

   Categorizes selected message Yellow and moves it to the P5 Invoices folder.

6. Click **Finish**. To test the Quick Step, select the message in the P5 Invoices folder and click **Reply & Delete** in the Quick Steps gallery. Click **Send** in the message window.
7. Click **Send/Receive All Folders** on the HOME tab.
8. Select the new message in the Inbox, and click the **Project 5-6** Quick Step. Confirm that the message has moved to the P5 Invoices folder and is categorized as Yellow.
9. Move the **P5 Products** folder to inside the **P5 Invoices** folder.
10. Use the Archive tool to archive the **P5 Invoices** folder as follows:

    change the *Archive Items Older Than* date to [**tomorrow's date**]

    Save the archive file to the solution folder for this lesson

    Name the archive file **P5 Invoices_xxx** [**your initials**]

11. Return to the mailbox, and delete the folders you created in this lesson (*P5 Invoices*, *Pending Reservations*, and *Lesson 5 Schedules*).

CLOSE Outlook.

6 Working with Contacts

LESSON SKILL MATRIX

Skills	Exam Objective	Objective Number
Creating and Modifying Contacts	Create new contacts	4.1.1
	Edit contact information	4.1.4
	Attach notes to contacts	3.4.3
	Attach an image to contacts	4.1.5
	Add tags to contacts	4.1.6
Sending and Receiving Contacts	Create new contacts	4.1.1
	Share contacts	4.1.7
Viewing and Deleting Contacts	Configure views	1.1.5
	Delete contacts	4.1.2
Creating and Manipulating Contact Groups	Create new contact groups	4.2.1
	Delete group members	4.2.6
	Add contacts to existing groups	4.2.2
	Update contacts within groups	4.2.4
	Add notes to a group	4.2.3
	Share contacts	4.1.7
	Delete groups	4.2.5
Sending a Message to a Contact Group		

KEY TERMS

- contact
- Contact Group
- Contact Index
- Contacts folder
- duplicate contact
- message header
- People Hub
- spoofing

© lisafx/iStockphoto

© lisafx/iStockphoto

Like many business executives, Mindy Martin will tell you that *who* you know is just as important as *what* you know. Mindy refers to the contact information dozens of times every day. She calls, writes, and sends messages to suppliers, guests, and other business organizations. Direct contact with the right people can avoid problems or solve small problems before they become catastrophes. Mindy and Jon have decided to create an outdoor adventure video game based on some of their more popular programs. Mindy needs to set up contact information for her contacts in the software industry so that their information will be readily available. In this lesson, you will learn how to create contacts and Contact Groups, edit and modify contact information, and send a message to a Contact Group.

SOFTWARE ORIENTATION

The Microsoft Outlook People Hub

In Outlook 2013, the **People Hub** is the main view of the Contacts folder, as shown in Figure 6-1.

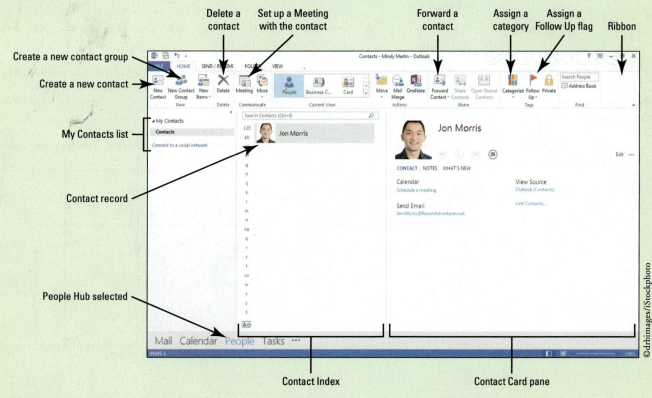

Figure 6-1

The Outlook People Hub

The **Contacts folder** enables you to organize and maintain information about the individuals and businesses you communicate with regularly. In this window, you can select a contact record, create a new contact record, view appointments, view tasks, send a message to a contact, call a contact, assign a contact to a category, and assign a follow-up flag to a contact.

CREATING AND MODIFYING CONTACTS

The Bottom Line

A **contact** record is a collection of information about a person or company. The Outlook Contacts feature is essentially an electronic organizer that you can use to create, view, and edit contact information. In this section, you'll learn a number of ways to create new contacts and modify existing contact information.

 Cross Ref

Contacts can be added in many different ways, for example, by exchanging digital signatures. If you exchanged digital signatures with a coworker or friend in Lesson 3, your Contacts list contains a contact for that individual.

Creating a Contact from Scratch

You can use a variety of methods to create contacts. The most basic method of creating a contact is opening a new contact window and keying the necessary information. The blank Contact window has its own Ribbon and command groups. Once a contact has been created, its information is stored in the Outlook Address Book and displayed in the People Hub. In this exercise, you'll create a contact using the New Contact button on the HOME tab.

STEP BY STEP | **Create a Contact from Scratch**

GET READY. Before you begin these steps, be sure to turn on or log on to your computer and start Outlook 2013.

1. Click the **People** button on the Navigation bar to display the Outlook People Hub shown in Figure 6-1.

Take Note The Ribbon options look different in each of the Outlook tools. The Ribbon options now reflect the most commonly used commands for working with contacts.

Another Way
You can also open the People Hub by clicking Contacts in the Folders List.

2. Click **New Contact** on the HOME tab. The Untitled—Contact window is displayed, as shown in Figure 6-2. The blank Contact window is ready to store data for a new contact.

Figure 6-2

Untitled - Contact window

Quick Access Toolbar   Picture placeholder   Business card   Free text notes   Ribbon

FILE tab

(Figure shows the Untitled - Contact window with FILE, CONTACT, INSERT, FORMAT TEXT, REVIEW tabs; Actions, Show, Communicate, Names, Options, Tags, Zoom groups; and fields for Full Name, Company, Job title, File as, Internet E-mail, Display as, Web page address, IM address, Phone numbers (Business, Home, Business Fax, Mobile), Addresses (Business), Notes.)

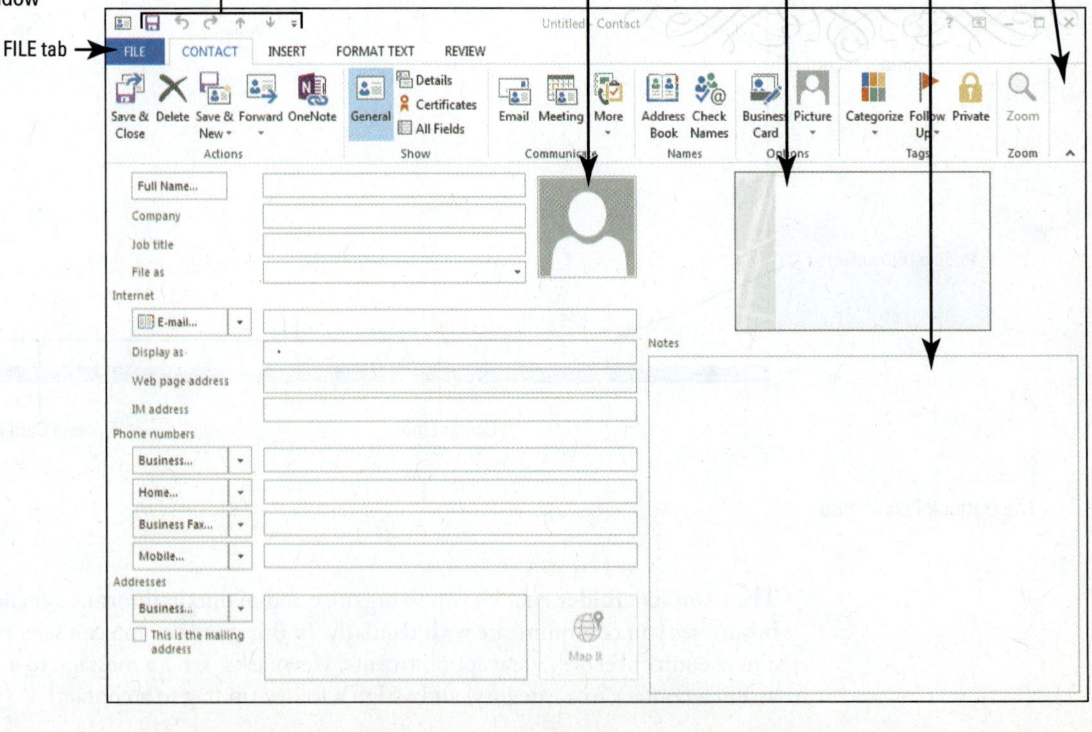

3. Click the *Full Name* field, if your cursor isn't already positioned there.

4. Key Gabe Mares and [press Tab]. The insertion point moves to the *Company* field. The *File as* field is automatically filled with *Mares, Gabe,* and *Gabe Mares* is displayed in the business card. The name of the window is changed to Gabe Mares–Contact.

Take Note Throughout this chapter you will see information that appears in black text within brackets, such as [Press Enter] or [next Friday's date]. The information contained in the brackets is intended to be directions for you rather than something you actually type word for word. It will instruct you to perform an action or substitute text. Do **not** type the actual text that appears within brackets.

5. In the *Company* field, key Wingtip Toys and [press Tab]. The insertion point moves to the *Job title* field. The company's name is added to the business card.

6. In the *Job title* field, key Sales Support Manager and [press Tab]. Gabe's job title is added to the business card. The insertion point moves to the *File as* field, highlighting the current value.

7. Click the dropdown arrow in the *File as* field. A short list of alternative ways of filing the contact is displayed. Some methods use the company name to file the contact. Other alternatives file the contact by the contact's first name.

8. Release the mouse button. When you click another field, the *File as* field will return to the default selection, which files contacts by last name.

⚠ Troubleshooting The e-mail addresses provided in these exercises belong to unused domains owned by Microsoft. When you send a message to these addresses, you will receive an error message stating that the message could not be delivered. Delete the error messages when they arrive.

9. Click the *E-mail* field, and key Gabe@wingtiptoys.com and [press Tab]. The *Display as* field is automatically filled, and Gabe's e-mail address is added to the business card.

10. You don't want to change the way Gabe's e-mail address is displayed, so [press Tab]. The insertion point moves to the *Web page address* field.

11. In the *Web page address* field, key www.wingtiptoys.com.

12. Below the *Phone numbers* heading, click the *Business* field. When you move the insertion point out of the *Web page address* field, the Web page address is automatically added to the business card.

13. Key 6155551205 in the *Phone Numbers* field.

Take Note It isn't necessary to key spaces or parentheses in phone numbers. Outlook automatically formats phone numbers when the insertion point leaves the field.

14. Below the Addresses heading, click the *Business* field, and key 7895 First Street. [Press Enter]. Key Nashville, TN 76534. [Press Tab]. The business card is automatically updated, and the Map It button is undimmed, as shown in Figure 6-3.

Take Note In a contact record, using the postal abbreviation for a state makes it easier to use the information in a mailing list or other data exports.

Figure 6-3

Gabe Mares—Contact window

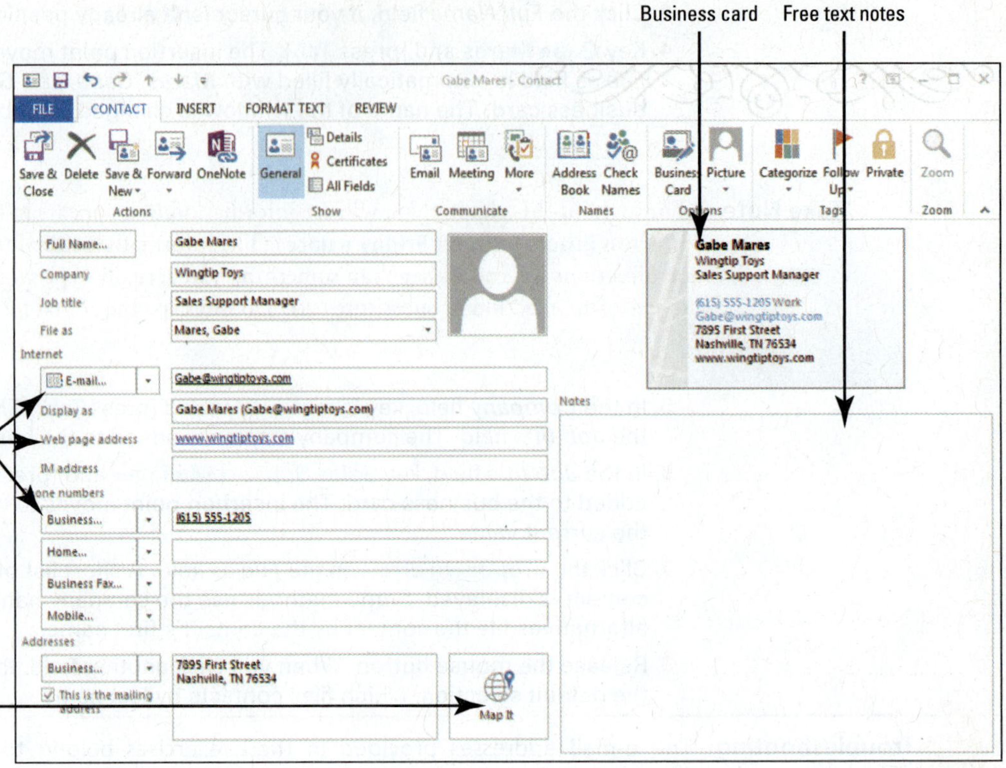

Business card   Free text notes

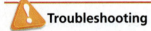

Outlook automatically formats phone numbers, e-mails, and web addresses

Click to open a web page containing a map to the address shown

---

Troubleshooting If you press Tab in the *Address* field before keying at least two lines of text, the Check Address dialog box is displayed. Because Outlook expects at least two lines of text in an address, the text you have already keyed might be displayed in the wrong fields in the Check Address dialog box. Click the Cancel button to close the dialog box and continue keying the address.

15. In the Actions group on the Ribbon, click the **Save & Close** button. Gabe Mares' contact information is saved and stored in the Outlook Address Book, and you are returned to the main People Hub.

16. Double click a blank area in the Contacts Index. A new Untitled—Contact window is displayed.

17. Click the following fields and key the new values.

Name	Susan Davis
Company Name	Example Company
E-mail	someone@example.com

The name of the contact record window changes to Susan Davis—Contact.

18. In the Actions group on the Ribbon, click the **Save & Close** button. The Susan Davis contact information is saved, and you are returned to the main People Hub.

PAUSE. LEAVE Outlook open to use in the next exercise.

Take Note You do not have to key information into every field. To save contact information, you should have a value in the *File As* field. If the *File As* field is empty when you try to save the contact, Outlook displays a warning message asking if you want to save the contact with an empty *File As* field. If you save the contact, it will be placed before any other contacts saved with a value in the *File As* field, because a blank is sorted as a value that occurs before any other value.

In the previous exercise, you keyed the basic information for a contact.

Creating a Contact from an Existing Contact

Often, you will have several contacts who work for the same company. Rather than keying the same data for a new contact, you can create the new contact from the existing contact. When you create a new contact for a person from the same company, the company name, File As, website, phone number, and address are carried over to the new contact. The name, job title, and e-mail address are not carried over to the new contact because these fields will usually differ between contacts, even if they work for the same company. In this exercise, you'll learn how to create a new contact from an existing contact's record.

STEP BY STEP   **Create a Contact from an Existing Contact**

GET READY. Before you begin these steps, be sure to complete the previous exercise.

1. If necessary, click the **People** button in the Navigation bar to open the People Hub.
2. Click the **Gabe Mares** contact record. The Gabe Mares—Contact window is displayed in the Contact Card pane. In the New group on the Ribbon, click **New Items** to display a list of options, as shown in Figure 6-4.

Figure 6-4

Create a Contact from an Existing Contact

[screenshot of Outlook Contacts window showing the New Items dropdown menu with options: E-mail Message, Appointment, Meeting, Contact, Task, Contact Group, Contact from the Same Company, More Items; Gabe Mares contact card displayed showing Sales Support Manager, Wingtip Toys]

Click to create a contact from an existing contact

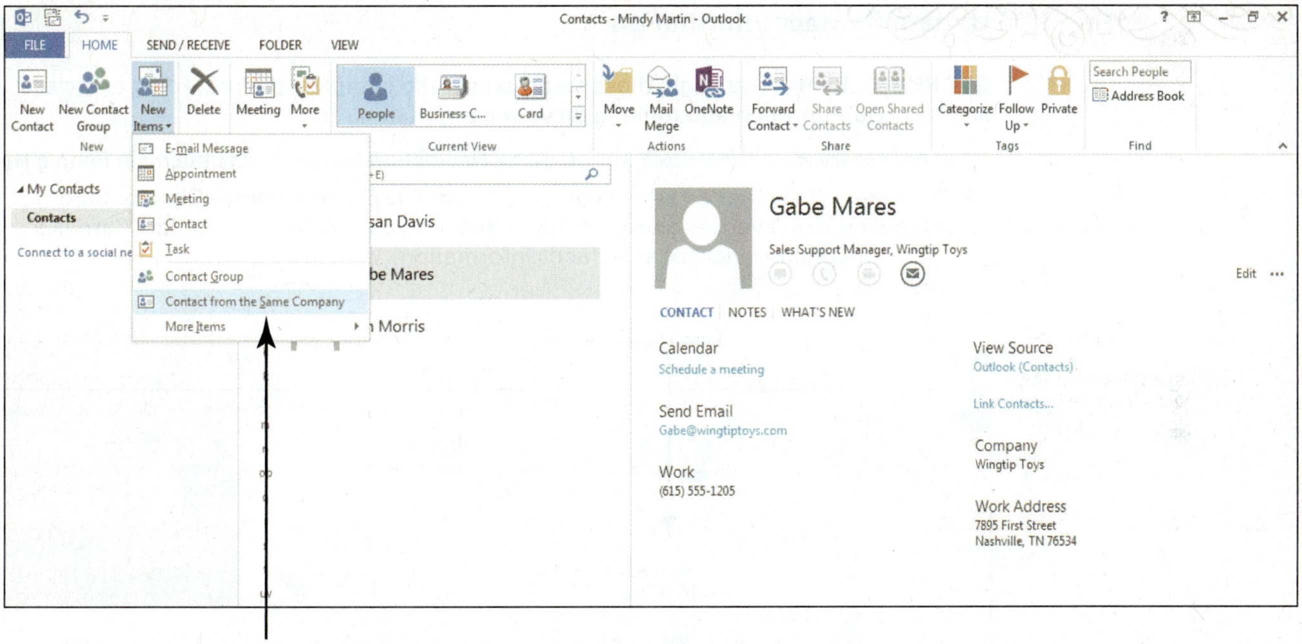

3. In the dropdown list of options, click **Contact from the Same Company**. A new window titled Wingtip Toys—Contact is displayed.
4. Click the *Full Name* field if necessary. Key **Diane Tibbott** and [press **Tab**]. The insertion point moves to the *Company* field. The *File As* field is automatically filled with *Tibbott, Diane*, and *Diane Tibbott* is displayed in the business card. The name of the window is changed to Diane Tibbott—Contact.
5. Click the *Job title* field. Key **Marketing Representative** and [press **Tab**]. Diane's job title is added to the business card. The insertion point moves to the *File As* field, highlighting the current value.
6. Click the *E-mail* field. Key **Diane@wingtiptoys.com** and [press **Tab**]. The *Display As* field is automatically filled, and Diane's e-mail address is added to the business card.
7. In the Actions group on the Ribbon, click the **Save & Close** button. Diane Tibbott's contact information is saved and her Contact window closes.

PAUSE. LEAVE Outlook open to use in the next exercise.

Updating Contact Information

To keep the information in your Contacts list current, you often need to modify the information for existing contacts. After a contact has been created, you can modify the contact's information using either the Contact Card or the contact record. For each contact we have, there are many kinds of information that we need to track. The information that we use to actually reach our contacts is stored on the General page of the Contact window and the Contact Card. However, there are often other pieces of information that we collect about our contacts over time, such as their birth date or their spouse's name. We may not need this kind of information to set up a meeting with them, but this information helps us to relate to them to make a stronger connection. In the following exercise, you'll change the following contact information:

- Gabe Mares left Wingtip Toys. He was hired by Tailspin Toys as the Software Development Manager. Most of his contact information has changed.
- Diane Tibbott was promoted to Software Support Manager. Her e-mail address and phone number remain the same. Only her title has changed. The corner office with a view that came with the promotion is not part of her contact information.
- Susan Davis's contact record needs to be updated with her photo and some background information, and notes will be added to her contact record.

STEP BY STEP   **Update Contact Information**

GET READY. Before you begin these steps, be sure to complete the preceding exercises and have Outlook open and running on your computer.

1. If necessary, click the **People** button in the Navigation bar to display the main People Hub.
2. Double-click the **Diane Tibbott** contact record. The Diane Tibbott—Contact Card window is displayed, as shown in Figure 6-5. As you can see, the Contact Card is a more streamlined view of a contact's information.

Figure 6-5

Editing a Contact in the Contact Card

Contact Card

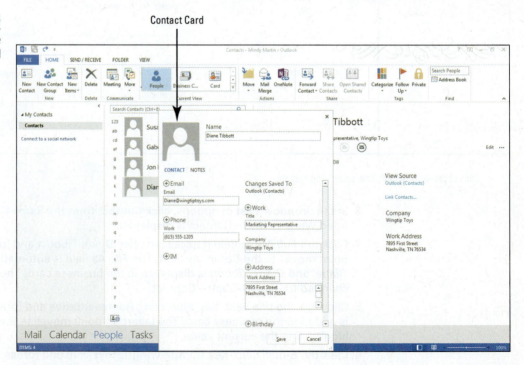

3. Click the **Title** field. Select the existing value, key **Software Support Manager**, and [press **Tab**]. Diane's job title is modified on the People Hub.
4. Click the **Save** button. The modified contact information is saved, and the Contact Card pop out is displayed, as shown in Figure 6-6.

Figure 6-6

Modified Contact Card

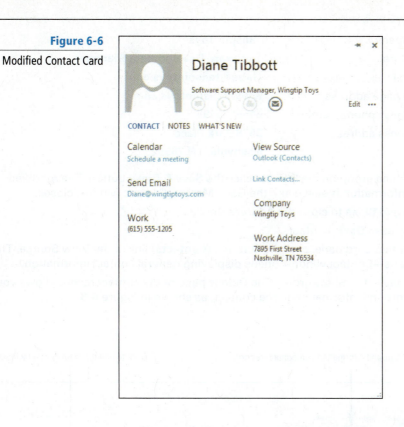

5. Click the **X** in the upper right corner to close the card.
6. In the Find group on the HOME tab, click **Address Book**. The Address Book: Contacts window is displayed, as shown in Figure 6-7.

Figure 6-7

Address Book: Contacts window

Outlook contacts sorted alphabetically

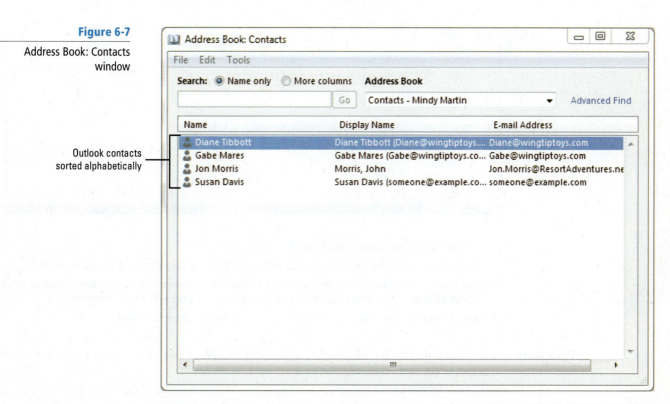

7. In the list of contacts, double-click the **Gabe Mares** contact. The full Gabe Mares—Contact window opens.
8. Click the following fields and replace the existing values with the new values.

Company	Tailspin Toys
Job title	Software Development Manager
E-mail	Gabe@tailspintoys.com
Web page address	www.tailspintoys.com
Business phone number	6155550195
Business address	5678 Park Place
	Nashville, TN 76502

9. In the Actions group on the Ribbon, click the **Save & Close** button. The modified contact information is saved and the Gabe Mares—Contact window closes.

10. Click **File** and **Close** to close the Address Book.

11. Click the **Susan Davis** contact.

CERTIFICATION READY?   4.1.4

How do you edit contact information?

12. In the Contact Card pane, click the **Outlook (Contacts)** link under View Source. The Susan Davis—Contact window opens displaying general contact information.

13. Click **Details** in the Show group. The Details page of the contact record allows you to add background information to the contact, as shown in Figure 6-8.

Figure 6-8

The Details page of the Contact window

Click to add background information to a contact record   Click to edit the main contact window

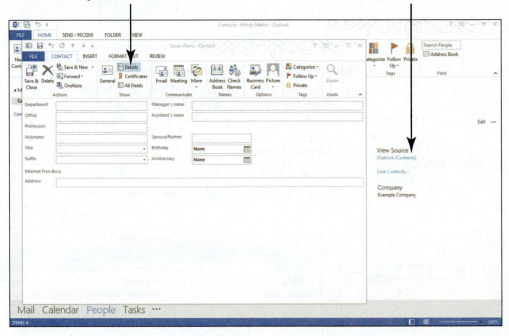

14. In the Assistant's name field, key **Michael**.

15. Click **General** in the Show group to return to the primary Contact window view.

16. Click in the **Notes** block in the lower right corner of the window. Use the Notes area to enter additional information about the contact that you want to remember.

17. Key **Susan is interested in working on the New Horizons project.**

Take Note   When you send contact information, any text in the *Notes* area of the contact record and items attached to the contact record are not sent.

CERTIFICATION READY?   3.4.3

How do you add a note to a contact record?

18. Click the **picture placeholder** in the center of the window. The Add Contact Picture dialog box is displayed.

19. Navigate to the data files for this lesson and select the *Susan.jpg* file and click **OK**. The Add Contact Picture dialog box closes, and you return to the Susan Davis—Contact window, as shown in Figure 6-9.

Click to add an image to a contact   Photo appears in default business card

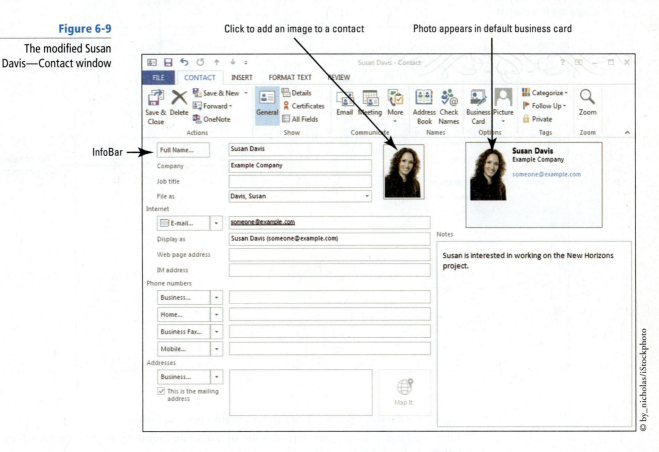

InfoBar →

20. In the Actions group on the Ribbon, click the **Save & Close** button. The modified contact information is saved, and the Susan Davis—Contact window closes to return to the main People Hub.

PAUSE. LEAVE Outlook open to use in the next exercise.

In the previous exercise, you updated the information for three contacts.

Setting Reminders for a Contact Record

When you have a busy office and a lot of contacts, it can be easy for things to slip by the wayside. An easy way to keep track of important reminders about your contacts is to use tags. You can use the tools in the Tags group to categorize a contact for a specific project or mark a contact as private so that it won't be viewed by other people who have access to your contact list. But the most common use of tags with contacts is reminders. You can use the Follow Up tool to remind yourself to follow up with them on an issue, schedule a meeting, or give them a call. In this exercise, you'll add tags to a contact.

STEP BY STEP   **Set Reminders for a Contact Record**

GET READY. Before you begin these steps, be sure to complete the preceding exercises and have Outlook open and running on your computer.

1. If necessary, click the **People** button in the Navigation bar to display the main People Hub.

2. Select the **Diane Tibbott** contact record, and click the **Outlook (Contacts)** link under the View Source heading. The Diane Tibbott—Contact window is displayed.

3. Click **Follow Up** in the Tags group, as shown in Figure 6-10.

Figure 6-10

Adding a tag to a contact

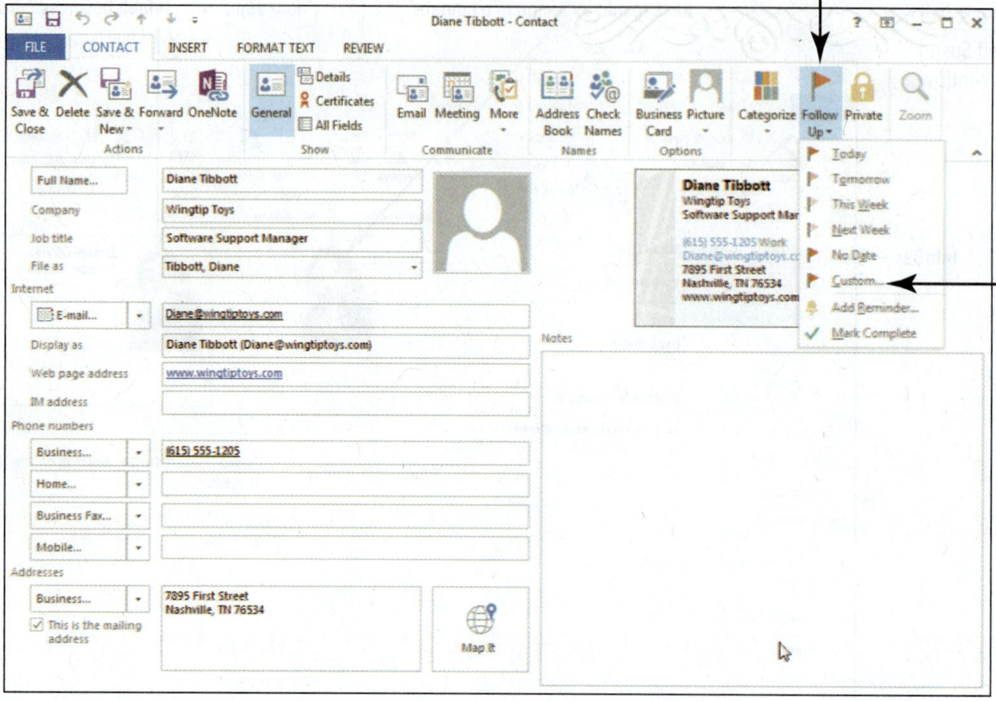

Tags group

Click to select a
Custom reminder

4. Select the **Custom** option. The Custom dialog box is displayed.

5. Click the **Flag to** dropdown arrow. A list of available follow up tags is displayed, as shown in Figure 6-11.

Figure 6-11

Selecting the type
of reminder needed

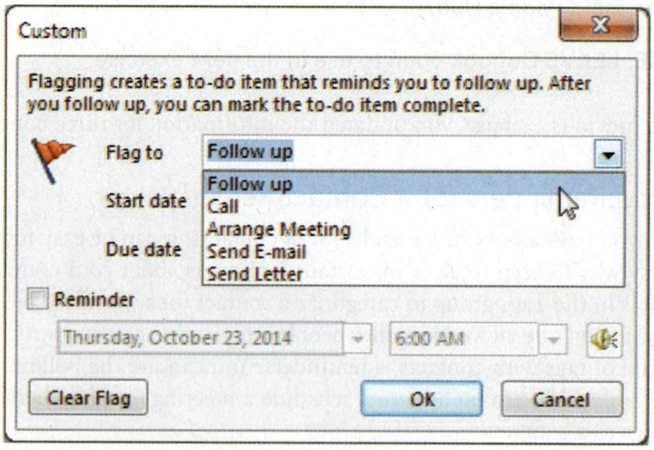

6. Select the **Arrange Meeting** tag.

7. In the *Start date* field, select a date that is two weeks from today. Set the same date for the *Due date* field.

8. Click **OK**. An InfoBar appears at the top of the contact record reminding you to set up a meeting with Diane in two weeks, as shown in Figure 6-12.

Figure 6-12

Click to add a tag a contact

Figure 6-12

An InfoBar reminder
of your tag

InfoBar →

9. Click **Save & Close** to return to the main Contacts folder.

10. Hover over the Tasks button on the Navigation bar to display the Tasks Peek. Notice that Diane Tibbot has been added to the Task list.

PAUSE. LEAVE Outlook open to use in the next exercise.

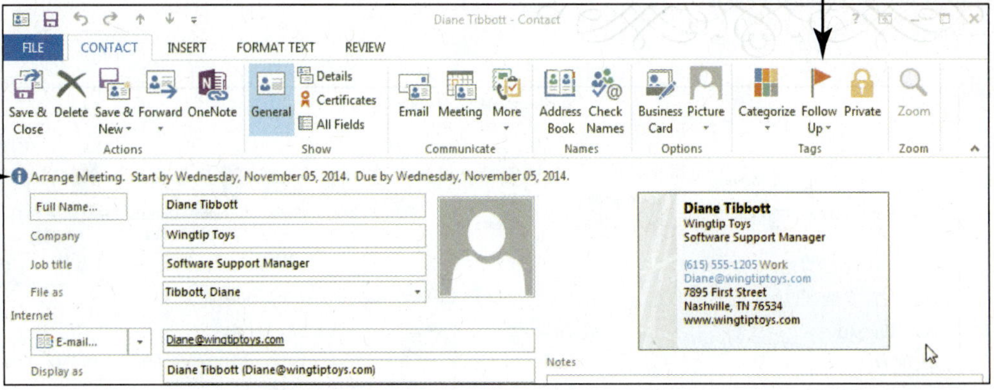

CERTIFICATION READY? 4.1.6

How do you add tags to a contact record?

SENDING AND RECEIVING CONTACTS

The Bottom Line

It is easy to exchange contact information via e-mail. You can send and receive contacts as attachments. Every time you send a message, you are also sending your contact information. In Outlook, you can create a contact for the sender of any message you receive, and you can create a contact from a message header.

Creating a Contact from a Message Header

Every message you send automatically contains your contact information in the message header. The **message header** is the text automatically added at the top of a message. The message header contains the sender's e-mail address, the names of the servers used to send and transfer the message, the subject, the date, and other basic information about the message. In this exercise, you'll learn how to use a message header to create a contact record in your Contacts list for the message's sender.

STEP BY STEP   **Create a Contact from a Message Header**

GET READY. Before you begin these steps, be sure that Microsoft Outlook is running and that you have completed the preceding exercises in this lesson.

1. Click the **Mail** button in the Navigation bar to display the Mail folder.

2. Click on a message you sent to yourself. The message is displayed in the Reading Pane.

3. In the Reading Pane, point to the sender's name or e-mail address. An information pane appears above the e-mail address, as shown in Figure 6-13.

Figure 6-13

Outlook's sender information

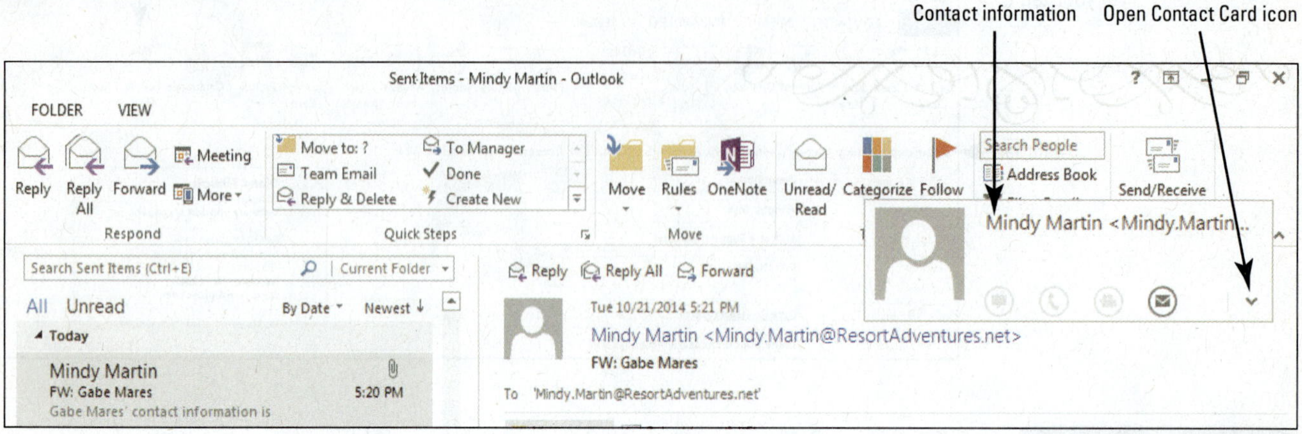

Contact information   Open Contact Card icon

4. Click the **Open Contact Card** icon on the contact information pane. A Contact Card containing the sender's information is displayed, as shown in Figure 6-14.

Figure 6-14

Creating a contact from a message header

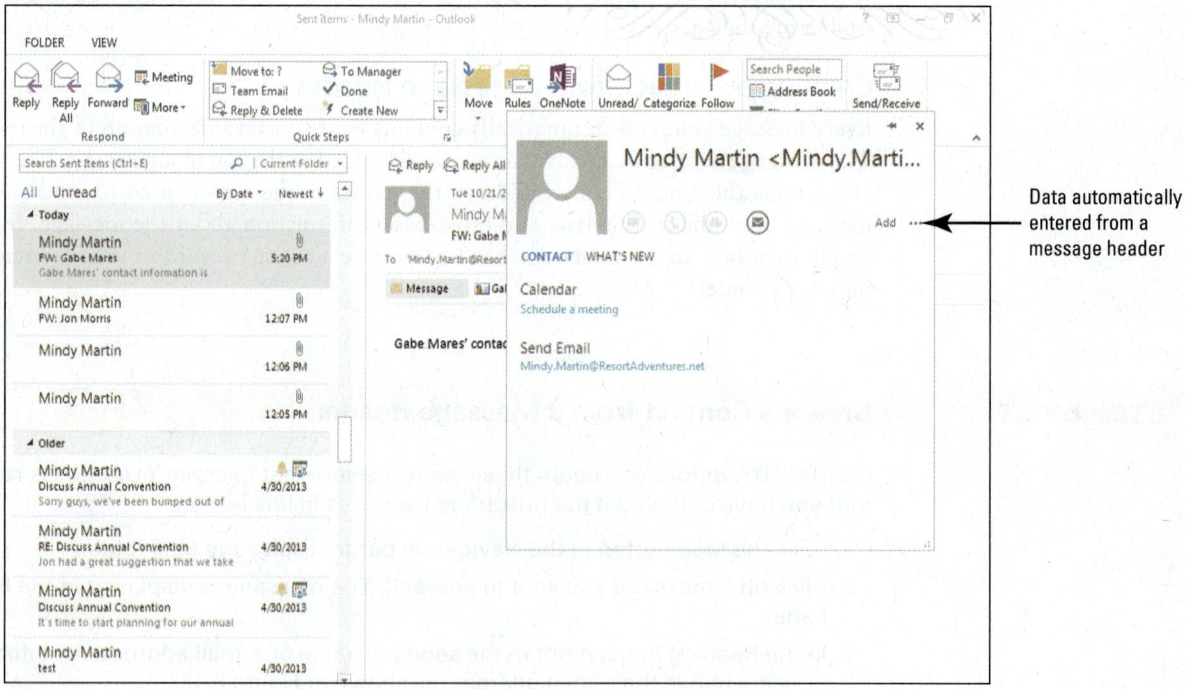

Data automatically entered from a message header

5. Click **Add** on the Contact Card to add your contact information to your Address Book. The Contact Card changes to an Edit Contact Card window.

6. Click the **Save** button. The contact record is created.

7. Click the **People** button in the Navigation bar to display the People Hub. Notice that you are now listed in the Contact Index.

PAUSE. LEAVE Outlook open to use in the next exercise.

CERTIFICATION READY? 4.1.1

How do you create a contact from a message header?

In the previous exercise, you created a contact from a message header. Although a message header contains important information, it is important to note that false information can be provided in the message header. This is known as **spoofing**. Many junk messages contain false information in the message header.

Forwarding a Contact as an Attachment

You already know that you can send documents and files as attachments. You can also send contacts as attachments. These attachments can be formatted as Outlook contacts, business cards, or plain text. When you send a contact as an Outlook contact, recipients who use Outlook will easily be able to see all the information they need to add the contact to their records. However, if you are unsure what e-mail program the recipient uses, it is safest to send the contact as a business card. Recipients who have Outlook will see it as a contact record, and everyone else will see it as an image of the business card. In this exercise, you learn how to send a contact as an attachment in Outlook 2013.

STEP BY STEP   **Forward a Contact as an Attachment**

GET READY. Before you begin these steps, be sure to complete the preceding exercises and have Outlook 2013 open and running on your computer.

1. If necessary, click the **People** button in the Navigation bar to display the main People Hub.
2. Click the **Susan Davis** contact record. Susan Davis' contact information is displayed in the Contact Card pane.
3. In the Share group on the Ribbon, click the **Forward Contact** button. In the dropdown menu that appears, click the **As a Business Card** option. A new message window is displayed. In the *Subject* field, the topic is automatically identified as *Susan Davis*, Susan's contact record is attached to the message as a .vcf file, and a copy of her business card appears in the body of the message, as shown in Figure 6-15.

Figure 6-15

Sending a contact as an attachment

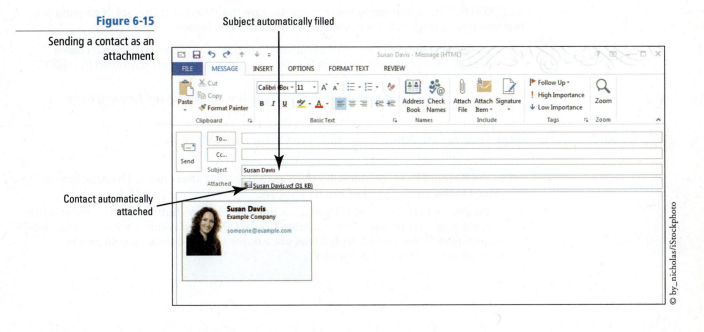

Subject automatically filled

Contact automatically attached

© by_nicholas/iStockphoto

⚠️ **Troubleshooting**   If a message is displayed stating that you must save the original item, click OK to continue.

4. In the *To* field, key [**your e-mail address**].

5. Click the **Send** button. The message is moved to the Outbox, and it is sent when your computer is connected to the Internet.

PAUSE. LEAVE Outlook open to use in the next exercise.

In the previous exercise, you sent contact information directly from the Contacts folder as an attachment to a message. This enables you to send contact information without keying it as text in a message.

Troubleshooting   If the recipient does not use Outlook 2007 or newer, the contact information might not be displayed correctly, and the recipient might not be able to create a contact from the attachment.

CERTIFICATION READY?   4.1.7

How do you share a contact with someone?

Saving a Contact Received as a Contact Record

When you request contact information from a coworker's Contacts list, the coworker can send the information as a business card or a contact record in Outlook format. If the contact record is sent in Outlook format, you can open the attachment, view the information, and save it as a contact record. When you try to save a contact with an address that is already in your Address Book, Outlook automatically detects it as a **duplicate contact** and gives you an opportunity to add the new contact or to update the existing contact. However, once a duplicate is detected, you should always combine the information onto one record and delete the duplicate. This eliminates errors that can occur when one record is updated and the other is not. In this exercise, you learn how to save a received contact as a contact record and how to deal with duplicate contacts.

 Cross Ref   You will learn more about electronic business cards in Lesson 7.

STEP BY STEP   **Save a Contact Received as a Contact Record**

GET READY. Before you begin these steps, be sure that Microsoft Outlook is running and that you have completed the preceding exercises in this lesson.

1. Click the **Mail** button in the Navigation bar to display the Inbox. If the *Susan Davis* message has not arrived yet, click the **Send/Receive All Folders** button on the HOME tab.

2. Click the **Susan Davis** message. The message is displayed in the Reading Pane.

Troubleshooting   If the Reading Pane is not visible, click Reset View on the VIEW tab.

3. In the Reading Pane, double-click the **Susan Davis.vcf** attachment. The attachment opens in the Susan Davis—Contact window.

4. In the Actions group on the Ribbon, click the **Save & Close** button. Outlook detects that this is a duplicate contact. The Duplicate Contact Detected window shown in Figure 6-16 is displayed. If the contact record was not a duplicate, the contact would be saved without any further action needed.

Figure 6-16

Duplicate Contact
Detected window

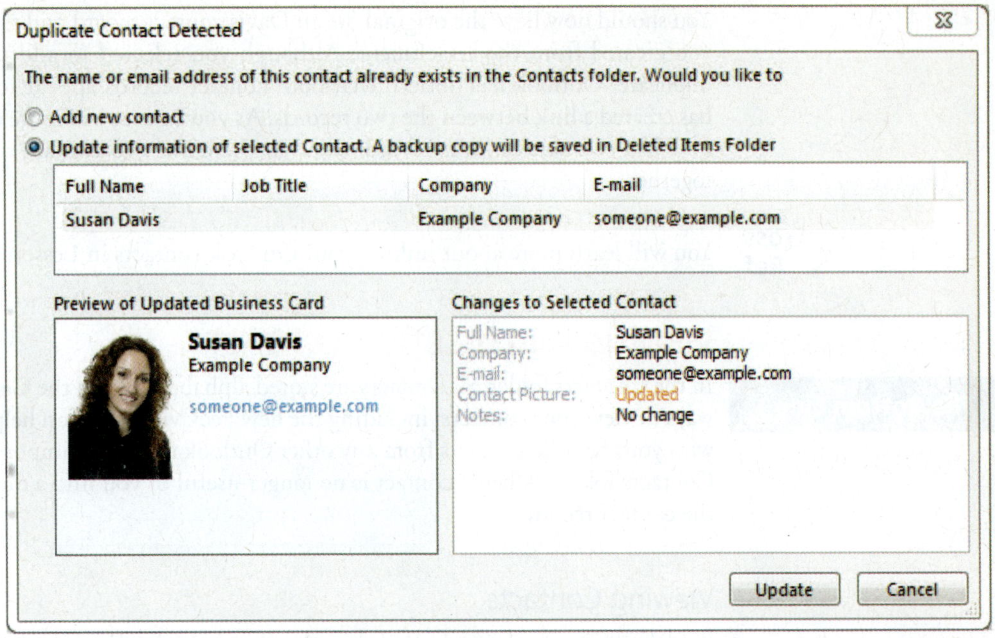

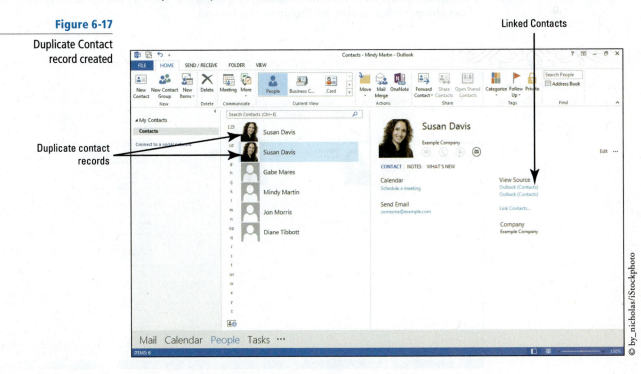

> **Duplicate Contact Detected**
>
> The name or email address of this contact already exists in the Contacts folder. Would you like to
>
> ○ Add new contact
> ● Update information of selected Contact. A backup copy will be saved in Deleted Items Folder
>
> | Full Name | Job Title | Company | E-mail |
> | --- | --- | --- | --- |
> | Susan Davis | | Example Company | someone@example.com |
>
> **Preview of Updated Business Card**
>
> **Susan Davis**
> Example Company
>
> someone@example.com
>
> **Changes to Selected Contact**
>
> Full Name: Susan Davis
> Company: Example Company
> E-mail: someone@example.com
> Contact Picture: Updated
> Notes: No change
>
> [Update] [Cancel]

© by_nicholas/iStockphoto

Take Note   As mentioned at the beginning of this exercise, creating duplicate contact records frequently leads to inaccurate information and is not a good practice. You are creating a duplicate record here only so that you can learn additional techniques for eliminating duplicate records in a later exercise.

5. You want to create a new contact, so select the **Add new contact** option at the top of the window, and click the **Add** button at the bottom of the window. The Duplicate Contact Detected window is closed, the contact record is created, and you are returned to the Mail folder.

6. Click the **People** button in the Navigation bar to display the main People Hub. Now, you have the original Susan Davis contact record you created by keying the data and the Susan Davis contact record you created from the attachment. Your Contacts folder should be similar to Figure 6-17. In your Contacts folder, Jon Morris's contact record is replaced by the individual with whom you exchanged digital signatures in Lesson 3.

Figure 6-17

Duplicate Contact
record created

Linked Contacts

Duplicate contact
records

© by_nicholas/iStockphoto

PAUSE. LEAVE Outlook open to use in the next exercise.

You should now have the original Susan Davis contact record and the Susan Davis contact record you created from the attachment. Although you selected to add the Susan Davis contact as a duplicate, Outlook has noticed that both contact records appear to be related. Consequently, it has created a link between the two records. As you can see in Figure 6-17, the Susan Davis contact now has two source links to indicate that there are two contact records that have been linked together.

 Cross Ref You will learn more about linking your Outlook contacts in Lesson 7.

VIEWING AND DELETING CONTACTS

The Bottom Line

In the Contacts folder, all contacts are stored alphabetically in the **Contact Index**. There are many ways to view your contacts, including the new Peek view that can help you to see what's happening with your favorite contacts from any other Outlook folder. It's important to prevent clutter in your Contacts folder. When a contact is no longer useful or you find a duplicate contact, delete or link the contact records.

Viewing Contacts

By default, contacts are displayed in the People Hub, which includes the Contact Index and a Contact Card pane that includes detailed information about the client. However, you can select other views that allow you to focus on specific kinds of information. In this exercise, you'll explore some Contact window views.

STEP BY STEP | **View Contacts**

GET READY. Before you begin these steps, be sure that Microsoft Outlook is running and that you have completed the preceding exercises in this lesson.

1. If necessary, click the **People** button in the Navigation bar to open the People Hub.
2. Click **Business Card** in the Current View group of the HOME tab. The views are displayed as business cards including any graphics, such as the contacts photo, as well as contact information, as shown in Figure 6-18.

Figure 6-18

The Contact List in Business Card view

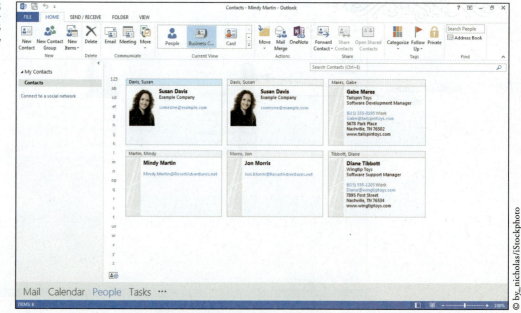

3. Click the **Card** button in the Current View group of the HOME tab. The view is modified as shown in Figure 6-19. The cards are lined up in narrow columns, and any graphics are hidden, but notes are shown.

Figure 6-19

The Contact List in Card view

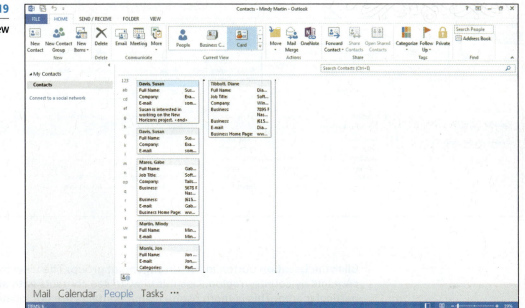

4. Click the **More** button to open the Current View gallery on the HOME tab. Select the **Phone** option to view the contacts as a phone list as shown in Figure 6-20. Use this view if you need to call several contacts in your Contacts folder.

Figure 6-20

Contacts in Phone List view

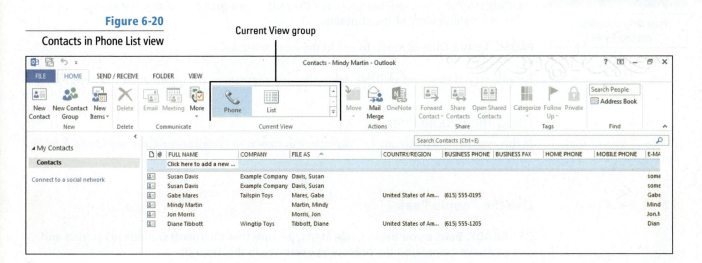

5. Click the **VIEW** tab to see additional viewing options. In the Arrangement group, you can select to organize the list by category, company name, or location.

6. Click the **Categories** button. The view is modified to group the contacts by category. At this point we haven't categorized any of the contacts, but this view can be helpful if you use categories to organize your Outlook Data File.

 Cross Ref   You will learn more about organizing your Outlook items using categories in Lesson 12.

7. Click the **Company** button in the Arrangement group on the VIEW tab. The view is modified to sort the contacts by company name, as shown in Figure 6-21. Use this view to see all the contacts working for a specific company. The List view is similar but it breaks the contacts into groups by company.

Figure 6-21

Contacts sorted by company name

Reset view to its default settings

Arrangement group

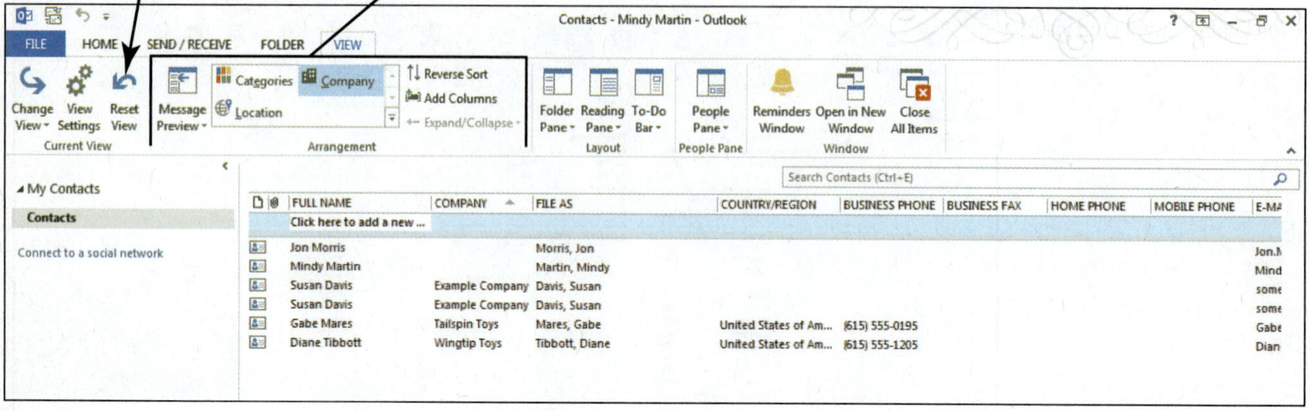

8. Click the **Location** button in the Arrangement group. The view is modified to group the contacts by country/region. Use this view to see contacts with an address in a particular area. This is more useful if your contacts are not located in the same geographic area.

9. Click the **Reset View** button in the Current View group to return the phone list to its default view. Outlook will display a warning box asking you to verify that you want to reset the view.

10. Click **Yes** to continue.

11. Click the **Change View** button in the Current Views group, and select **People** to return to the default view of the contacts.

PAUSE. LEAVE Outlook open to use in the next exercise.

Because several views are available, select the view that targets the information you need to see.

CERTIFICATION READY?   1.1.5

How do you configure contact views?

Using the People Peek

In this exercise, you'll explore the People peek to view your favorite contacts in any Outlook folder.

STEP BY STEP   **Use the People Peek**

GET READY. Before you begin these steps, be sure that Microsoft Outlook is running and that you have completed the preceding exercises in this lesson.

1. If necessary, click the **People** button in the Navigation bar to open the People Hub.

2. Hover over the word **People** in the Navigation bar to view the new People peek view of your contacts, as shown in Figure 6-22. Notice that most, if not all, of your contacts are not listed here. The only contacts that appear in the peek are ones that you've added to your favorites.

Figure 6-22

The People peek

Contact index

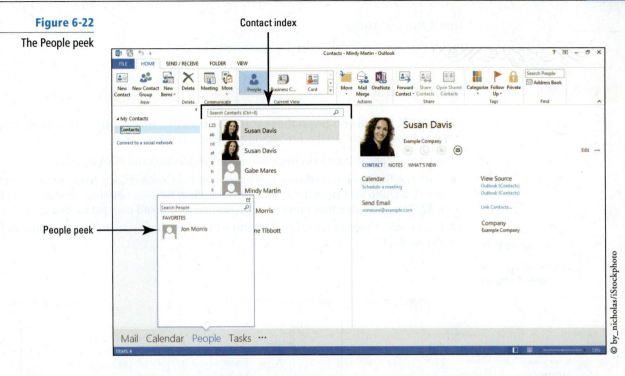

People peek

3. Right-click the linked **Susan Davis** contact record in the Contact Index. Select **Add to Favorites** in the shortcut menu.

4. Click the **Mail** button in the Navigation bar to open the Inbox.

5. Hover over the word **People** in the Navigation bar again to view Susan Davis' contact record added to the People peek.

6. Click on **Susan Davis** in the People peek. A fly out of the contact information pane appears, as shown in Figure 6-23. You can send an e-mail to the contact by clicking the message icon. You can also click the Open Contact Card down arrow to view all of Susan's contact information.

Figure 6-23

Adding a contact to the People peek

Click to send an e-mail to the contact

Click to view the full Contact Card

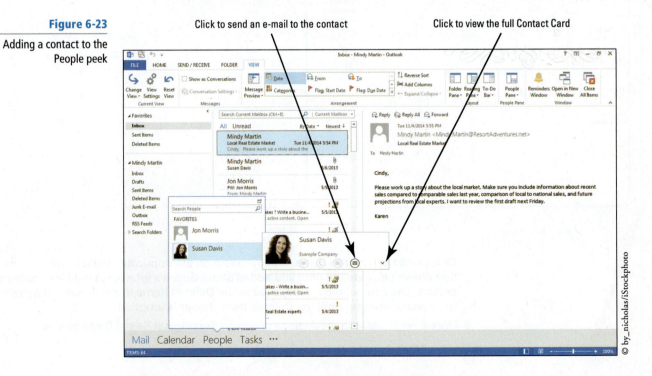

PAUSE. LEAVE Outlook open to use in the next exercise.

The People peek is a great way to keep your favorite contacts always at your fingertips.

© by_nicholas/iStockphoto

Deleting Contacts

In this exercise, you'll delete the duplicate contact record.

Delete Contacts

GET READY. Before you begin these steps, be sure that Microsoft Outlook is running and that you have completed the preceding exercises in this lesson.

1. Click the People button in the Navigation bar to open the People Hub.
2. Click the first Susan Davis contact record. In the Contact Card pane, notice that there are two Outlook (Contacts) links under the View Source heading, as shown in Figure 6-17. This indicates that there are two unique but linked contact records.
3. Click each of these two source links to view the two contact records, as shown in Figure 6-24.

Figure 6-24

Viewing duplicate contact sources

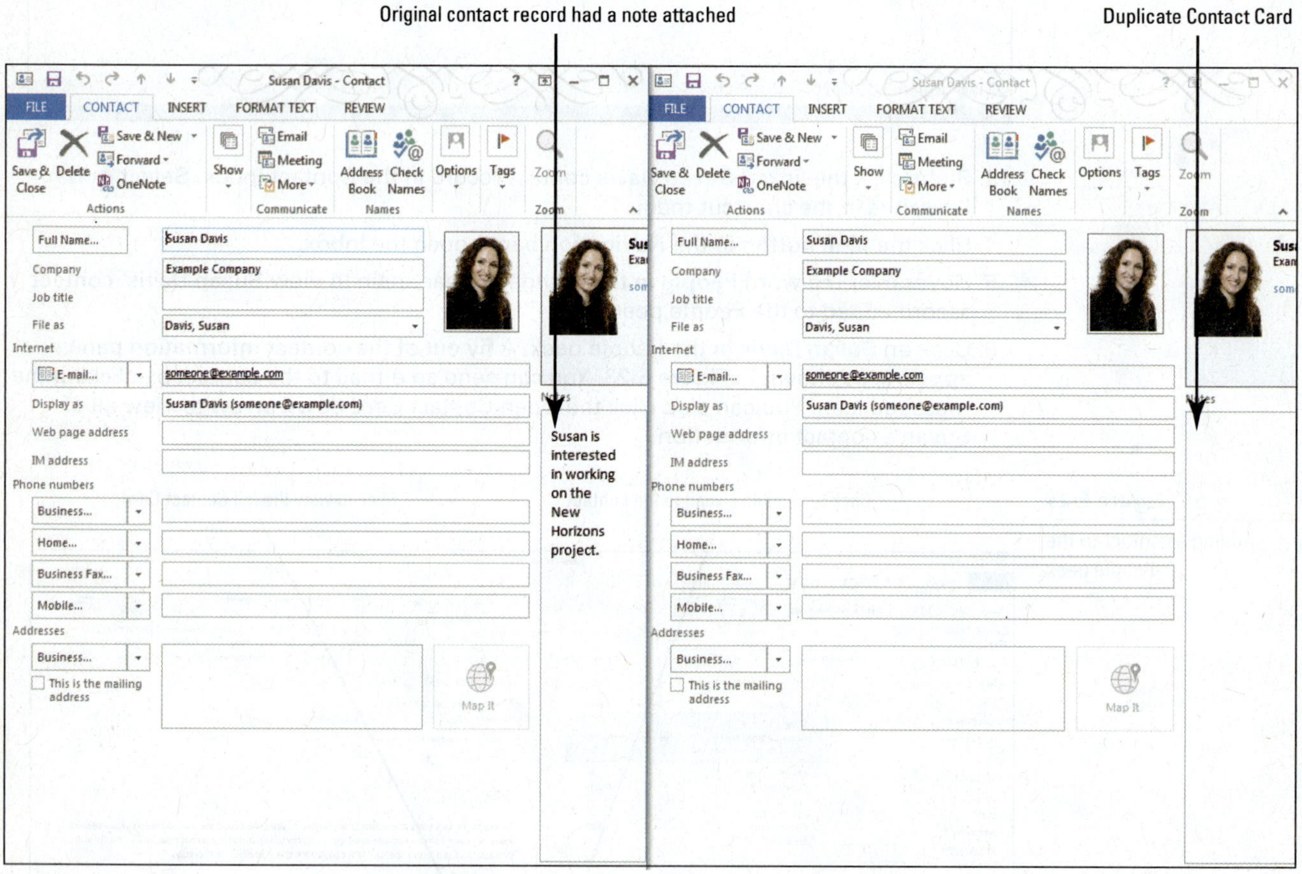

Original contact record had a note attached   Duplicate Contact Card

© by_nicholas/iStockphoto

4. Click the Delete button in the Actions group on the duplicate contact, which is the one that doesn't include the note you added about Susan's interest in the New Horizon project. The contact record is moved to the Deleted Items folder. It will not be removed from your computer until the Deleted Items folder is emptied.
5. Click Save & Close in the Actions group on the original Susan Davis contact.

PAUSE. LEAVE Outlook open to use in the next exercise.

When you are viewing contact records, you can minimize clutter by deleting contacts that are no longer useful or duplicates that have been accidentally created. In addition to the method used in this exercise, you can also delete contacts by selecting the record in the Contacts folder and doing one of the following:

CERTIFICATION READY?   **4.1.2**

How do you delete a contact?

• Clicking the Delete button in the Delete group on the HOME tab.
• Right-clicking the contact and selecting Delete on the shortcut menu.

CREATING AND MANIPULATING CONTACT GROUPS

The Bottom Line

A **Contact Group** is a group of individual contacts saved together as a single contact. A Contact Group simplifies the task of regularly sending the same message to a group of people. If you create a Contact Group, you can make one selection in the *To* field to send the message to all members of the Contact Group. In this section, you'll create a Contact Group, create notes to be stored with it, and change who is in the group. Then you'll forward the Contact Group as an attachment and send a message to the members of the Contact Group.

Creating a Contact Group

To create a Contact Group, you create a contact record that is identified as a Contact Group. Then you select the members of the Contact Group and save the Contact Group. In this exercise, you'll create a Contact Group and add members to it.

STEP BY STEP   **Create a Contact Group**

GET READY. Before you begin these steps, be sure that Microsoft Outlook is running and that you have completed the preceding exercises in this lesson.

1. If necessary, click the **People** button in the Navigation bar to display the People Hub.
2. In the New group on the HOME tab, click **New Contact Group**. The Untitled—Contact Group window is displayed, as shown in Figure 6-25. The Members button in the Show group on the Ribbon is selected.

Figure 6-25

Untitled - Contact Group window

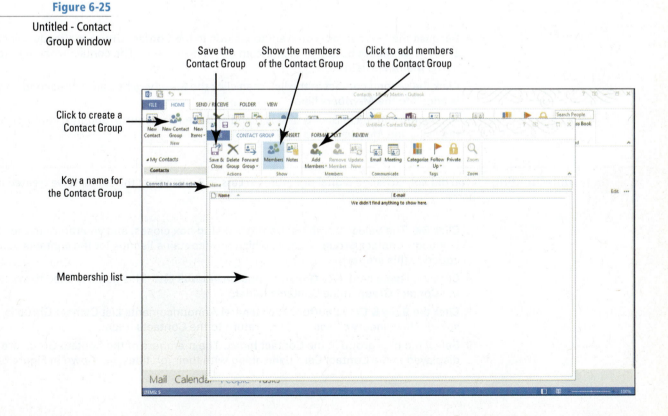

Save the Contact Group

Show the members of the Contact Group

Click to add members to the Contact Group

Click to create a Contact Group

Key a name for the Contact Group

Membership list

3. In the Members group on the Ribbon, click the **Add Members** button and select the **From Outlook Contacts** option. The Select Members: Contacts dialog box is displayed, as shown in Figure 6-26. Your Outlook contacts are listed. The first contact is already selected.

Figure 6-26

Select Members: Contacts
window

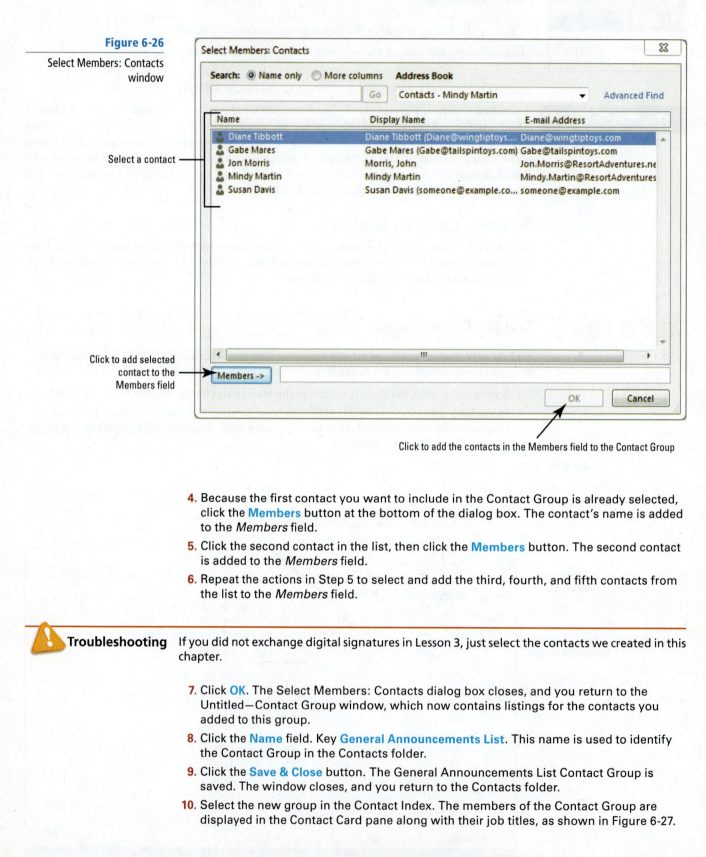

Select a contact

Click to add selected
contact to the
Members field

Click to add the contacts in the Members field to the Contact Group

4. Because the first contact you want to include in the Contact Group is already selected, click the **Members** button at the bottom of the dialog box. The contact's name is added to the *Members* field.

5. Click the second contact in the list, then click the **Members** button. The second contact is added to the *Members* field.

6. Repeat the actions in Step 5 to select and add the third, fourth, and fifth contacts from the list to the *Members* field.

⚠️ **Troubleshooting** If you did not exchange digital signatures in Lesson 3, just select the contacts we created in this chapter.

7. Click **OK**. The Select Members: Contacts dialog box closes, and you return to the Untitled—Contact Group window, which now contains listings for the contacts you added to this group.

8. Click the **Name** field. Key **General Announcements List**. This name is used to identify the Contact Group in the Contacts folder.

9. Click the **Save & Close** button. The General Announcements List Contact Group is saved. The window closes, and you return to the Contacts folder.

10. Select the new group in the Contact Index. The members of the Contact Group are displayed in the Contact Card pane along with their job titles, as shown in Figure 6-27.

Figure 6-27

Contact Group created

Contact Group added to Contacts folder   Click to edit the group

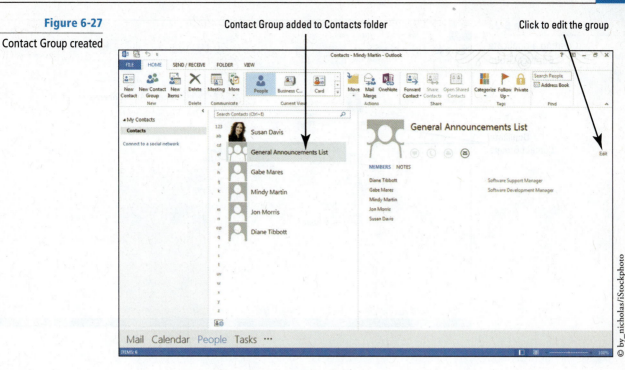

PAUSE. LEAVE Outlook open to use in the next exercise.

In the previous exercise, you created a Contact Group that contains all of your contacts. However, Contact Groups are typically limited to just the contacts working on a specific project.

Creating a Contact Group from an Existing Contact Group

You already know how to create a Contact Group from scratch, but you can also create a Contact Group by duplicating another group and then modifying it. In this exercise, you'll create a new Contact Group by duplicating an existing group.

STEP BY STEP   **Create a Contact Group from an Existing Contact Group**

GET READY. Before you begin these steps, be sure that Microsoft Outlook is running and that you have completed the preceding exercises in this lesson.

CERTIFICATION READY?   **4.2.1**

How do you create a new contact group?

1. If necessary, click the **People** button in the Navigation bar to display the People Hub.
2. Right-click the **General Announcements List** contact record and select **Copy** from the shortcut menu that appears.
3. [Press **Ctrl + V**]. A duplicate Contact Group record is displayed in the People Hub, as shown in Figure 6-28.

Figure 6-28

Creating a duplicate
Contact Group

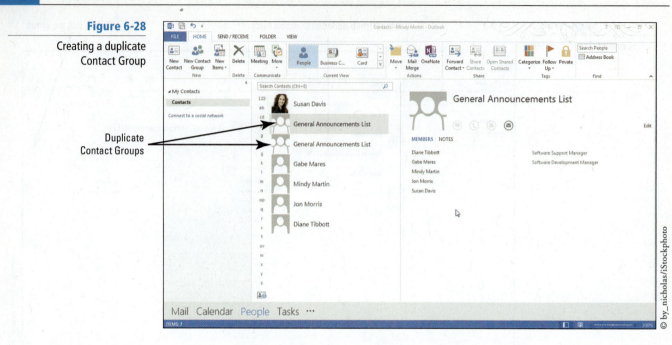

Duplicate
Contact Groups

4. Click the **Edit** link on one of the *General Announcements List* contact records to display the General Announcements List—Contact Group window.

5. Select the text in the *Name* field. Key **Wingtip Toys**. This name is used to identify the name of the project this group is working on.

6. Click the **Save & Close** button. The Wingtip Toys List Contact Group is saved. The window is closed, and you are returned to the People Hub.

PAUSE. LEAVE Outlook open to use in the next exercise.

Another Way
You can also double click on the group in the Contact list to open the contact record.

In the previous exercise, you created a Contact Group for the Wingtip Toys project you are working on. However, because the Contact Group was created from a Contact Group that contained all of your contacts, you'll need to modify the Contact Group's membership to reflect the members of the project team.

Managing Contact Group Membership

Any Contact Group used over time will eventually require changes. In this case, Mindy has decided to add Katie Mathews, the resort's new PR specialist, to the Wingtip Toys project. In this exercise, you'll learn how to add and remove a member from a Contact Group list and edit the contact information.

STEP BY STEP   **Manage Contact Group Membership**

GET READY. Before you begin these steps, be sure that Microsoft Outlook is running and that you have completed the preceding exercises in this lesson.

1. If necessary, click the **People** button in the Navigation bar to display the default People Hub.

2. Double-click the **Wingtip Toys** contact. The Wingtip Toys—Contact Group window is displayed.

3. Click Gabe's name in the lower area of the window.

4. In the Members group on the Ribbon, click the **Remove Member** button. Gabe is removed from the Contact Group.

5. Click the **Add Members** button and select New E-mail Contact. The Add New Member dialog box is displayed, as shown in Figure 6-29.

**CERTIFICATION   4.2.6
READY?**

How do you delete group members?

Figure 6-29

Adding a new e-mail contact
to a Contact Group

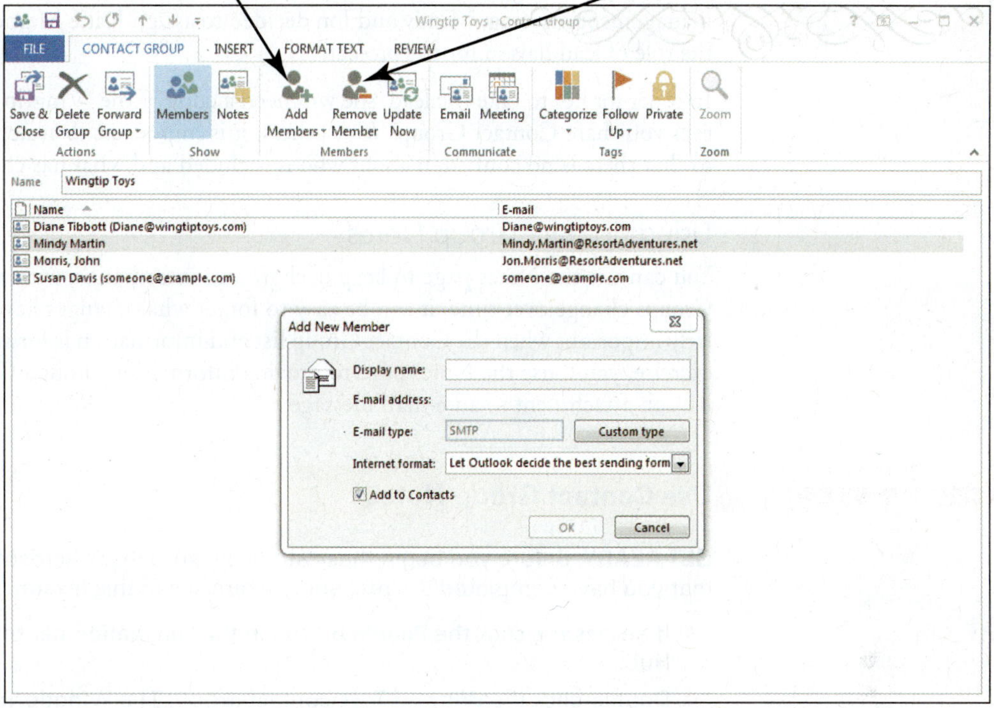

Click to add members to the Contact Group   Click to remove members from the Contact Group

CERTIFICATION READY? 4.2.2

How do you add contacts to
an existing group?

CERTIFICATION READY? 4.2.4

How do you update contacts
within groups?

6. In the *Display name* field, key Katie Mathews. In the *E-mail address* field, key Katie.Mathews@ResortAdventures.net. Click OK to add her to the list.

7. In the list of members, double-click your own name. Your contact record is displayed.

8. Click the *Company* field. Key [the name of your company].

9. Click the Save & Close button in your Contact window. Your modified contact record is saved and closed.

10. Click the Save & Close button in the Contact Group window. The Contact Group is saved. The window is closed, and you are returned to the People Hub, as shown in Figure 6-30.

Figure 6-30

Wingtip Toy's modified
membership

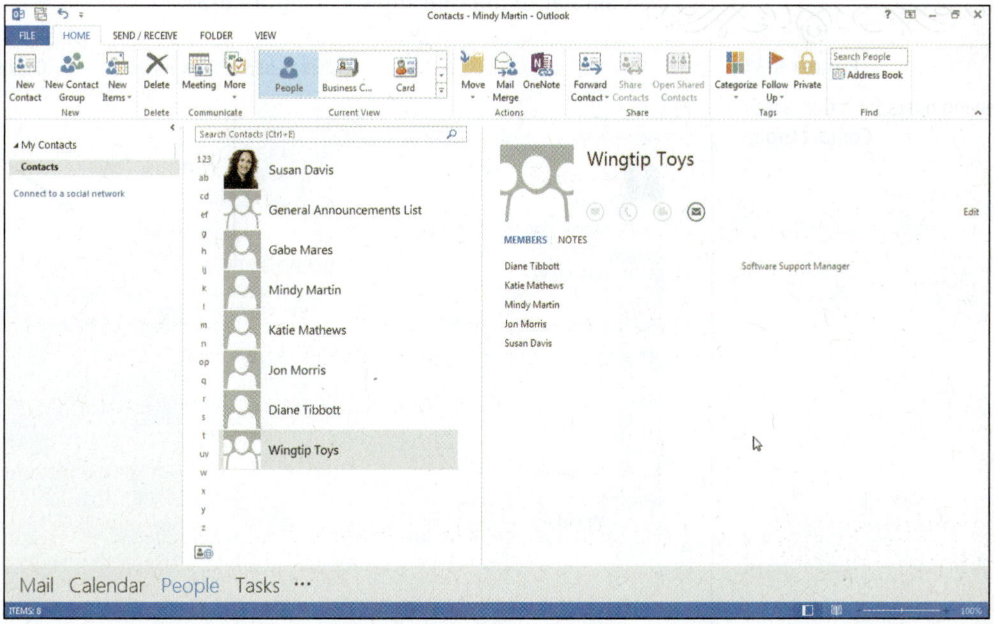

PAUSE. LEAVE Outlook open to use in the next exercise.

In the previous exercises, you modified the Wingtip Toys Contact Group so that it only contains the people working on the Outdoor Adventure software development project. During the weekly management meeting, Mindy and Jon decided to assign Katie Mathews, the resort's PR specialist, the role of lead liaison for the project.

In order for her to take the lead, she will need a copy of the Wingtip Toys Contact Group. Whenever you share Contact Groups with others, it is important to attach notes to the Contact Group so that there is no confusion about who is included and what has changed.

Using Contact Group Notes

You can use the Notes page to keep background information with a Contact Group. As Contact Groups change over time, it can be easy to forget what changes have been made. This is particularly important when the Contact Group list and information is forwarded to someone else. In this exercise, you'll use the Notes page to provide information about a Contact Group before sending it as an attachment to an e-mail message.

STEP BY STEP   **Use Contact Group Notes**

GET READY. Before you begin these steps, be sure that Microsoft Outlook is running and that you have completed the preceding exercises in this lesson.

1. If necessary, click the **People** button in the Navigation bar to display the default People Hub.
2. Double-click the **Wingtip Toys** contact group. The Wingtip Toys—Contact Group window is displayed with the Contact Group tab opened on the Ribbon.
3. Click the **Notes** button in the Show group to show the notes about a Contact Group. The Notes page for this Contact Group is displayed.
4. In the empty text area, key **The group includes everyone working on the Outdoor Adventure game project, including Susan Davis, an independent storyboard consultant.**
5. Click the **Save & Close** button in the Contact Group window. The Contact Group is saved. The window is closed, and you are returned to the People Hub.
6. Select the **Wingtip Toys** Contact Group in the Contact Index to display the information about the Contact Group in the Contact Card pane.
7. Click **Notes** in the Contact Card to show the notes for this group. Your screen should look similar to the one shown in Figure 6-31.

Figure 6-31

Viewing notes for a Contact or Contact Group

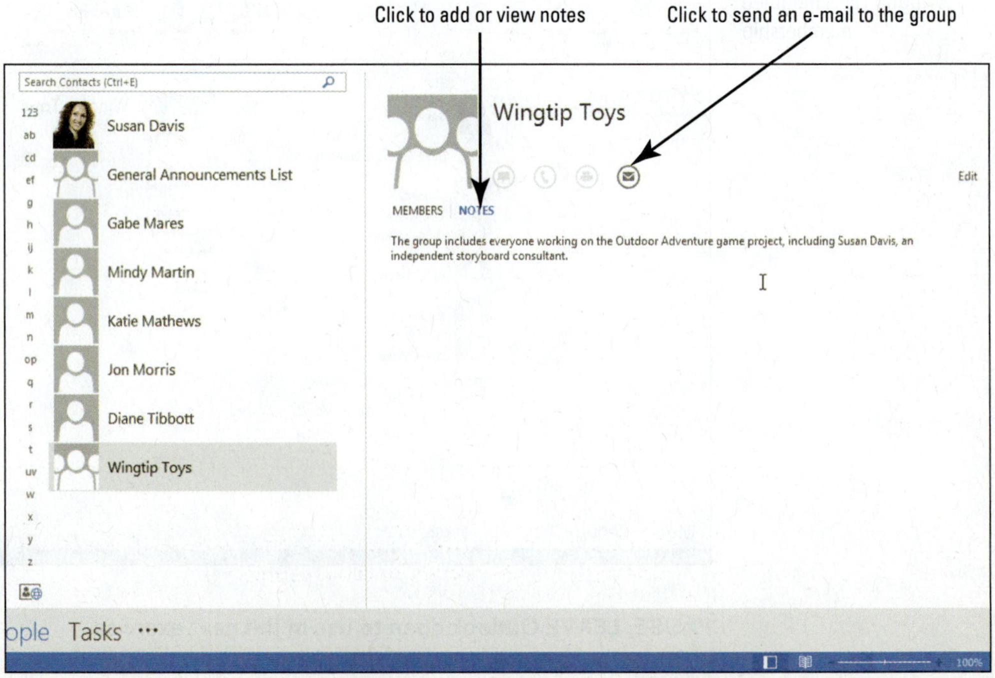

Click to add or view notes

Click to send an e-mail to the group

© by_nicholas/iStockphoto

PAUSE. LEAVE Outlook open to use in the next exercise.

CERTIFICATION
READY?   4.2.3

How do you add notes to a
contact group?

In the previous exercise, you added an informative note about the Wingtip Toys Contact Group. You are now ready to send the Contact Group to Katie.

Forwarding a Contact Group

Sending a Contact Group to someone as an e-mail attachment is just as easy as sending a contact. You can forward a Contact Group just by selecting the group's contact record and clicking Forward Contact in the Share group of the People Hub's HOME tab. In this exercise, you'll forward a Contact Group to an e-mail recipient.

STEP BY STEP   **Forward a Contact Group**

GET READY. Before you begin these steps, be sure that Microsoft Outlook is running and that you have completed the preceding exercises in this lesson.

1. If necessary, click the **People** button in the Navigation bar to display the default People Hub.
2. Click the **Wingtip Toys** contact record and then click **Forward Contact** in the Share group of the HOME tab.
3. In the dropdown menu that appears, select the **As an Outlook Contact** option. A new FW: Wingtip Toys—Message window is displayed.
4. In the *To* field, key **Katie.Mathews@ResortAdventures.net**. Because Katie is in your Contacts list, you will not need to type the entire address. Outlook will complete it for you.
5. In the message area, key **Hi Katie, here is the Contact Group for the game project.**, as shown in Figure 6-32.

Figure 6-32

Sending a Contact Group
as an attachment

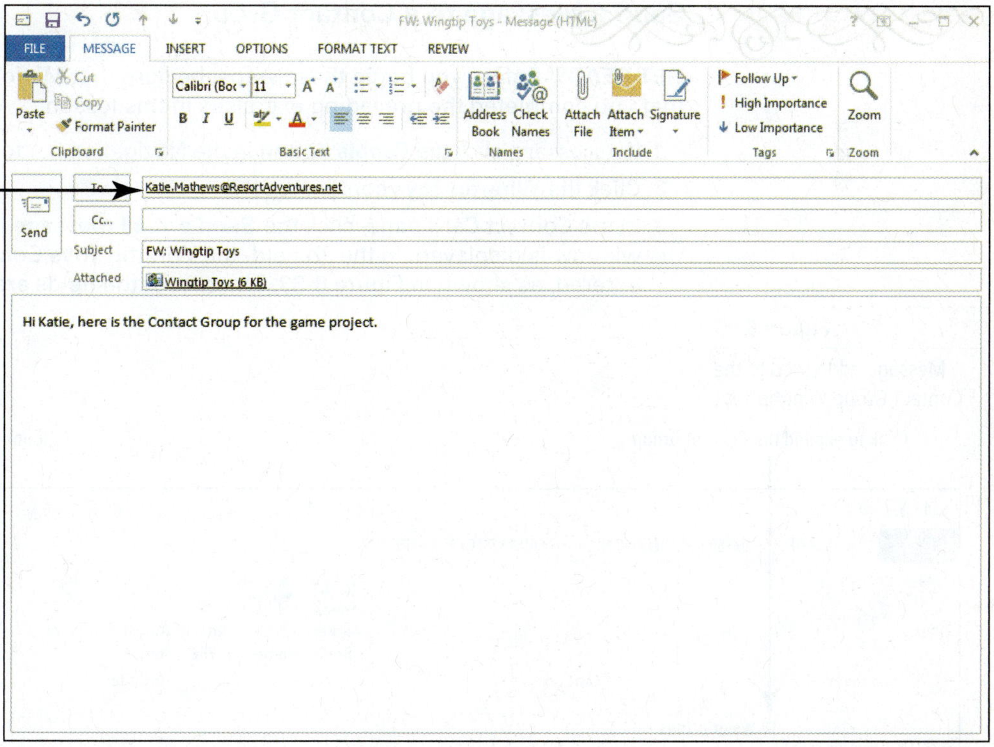

Contact Group
attachment →

6. Click the **Send** button. The message is moved to the Outbox, and it is sent when your computer is connected to the Internet.

PAUSE. LEAVE Outlook open to use in the next exercise.

Deleting a Contact Group

Contact Groups are a great way to help you keep your contacts organized, but when you no longer need a Contact Group, you should delete it so you don't accidentally send messages to the group. Fortunately, deleting a Contact Group is just as easy as deleting a contact. In this exercise, you'll delete the General Announcements List Contact Group.

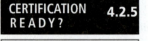

STEP BY STEP   **Delete a Contact Group**

GET READY. Before you begin these steps, be sure that Microsoft Outlook is running and that you completed the preceding exercises in this lesson.

1. If necessary, click the **People** button in the Navigation bar to display the main People Hub.
2. Click the **General Announcements List** contact record. On the HOME tab, click the **Delete** button in the Delete group. The Contact Group record is moved to the Deleted Items folder. It will not be removed from your computer until the Deleted Items folder is emptied.

PAUSE. LEAVE Outlook open to use in the next exercise.

Now that you've sent the Wingtip Toys Contact Group to Katie, you want to send a message to the members of the team to introduce her.

SENDING A MESSAGE TO A CONTACT GROUP

The Bottom Line

Sending an e-mail message to a Contact Group is a simple process. By adding the Contact Group's name in the *To* field, the e-mail message will go to each member of the group. In this exercise, you'll create an e-mail message to be sent to a Contact Group.

STEP BY STEP   **Send a Message to a Contact Group**

GET READY. Before you begin these steps, be sure that Microsoft Outlook is running and that you completed the preceding exercises in this lesson.

1. If necessary, click the **People** button in the Navigation bar to display the main People Hub.
2. Click the **Wingtip Toys** contact record.
3. In the Contact Card pane, click the **Send e-mail message to:** icon. A blank Message window is displayed. In the *To* field, the Wingtip Toys Contact Group is automatically entered, as shown in Figure 6-33. The rest of the fields are empty.

Figure 6-33

Message addressed to the Contact Group Wingtip Toys

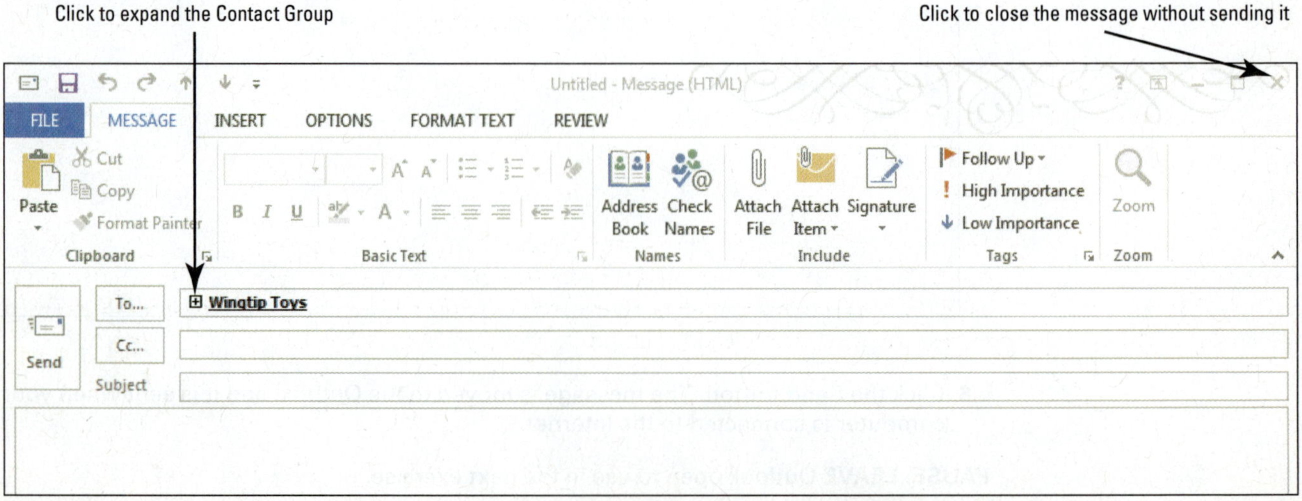

Click to expand the Contact Group   Click to close the message without sending it

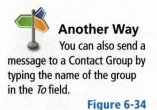

Another Way
You can also send a message to a Contact Group by typing the name of the group in the *To* field.

Figure 6-34

The Expand List dialog box

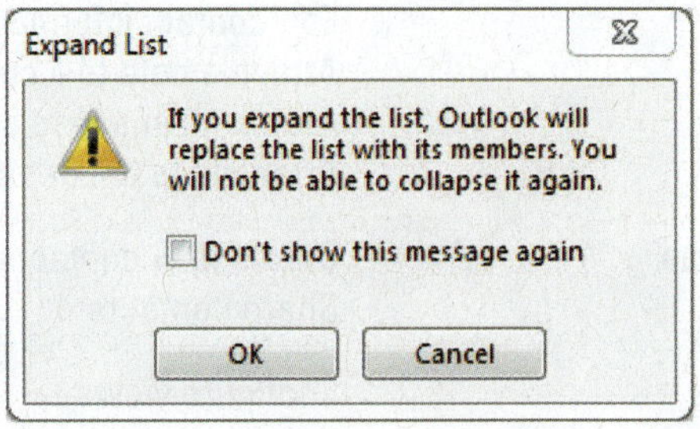

4. Click the plus sign (+) in the *To* field. A warning box is displayed stating that the group name will be replaced with the names of the group's members, as shown in Figure 6-34.

> ⚠ **Expand List** ☒
>
> ⚠ If you expand the list, Outlook will replace the list with its members. You will not be able to collapse it again.
>
> ☐ Don't show this message again
>
> [OK]   [Cancel]

5. Click **OK**. The individual addressees are displayed in the *To* field, as shown in Figure 6-35.

Figure 6-35

The contact group expanded in the To: field

Click to close the message without sending it →

FILE   MESSAGE   INSERT   OPTIONS   FORMAT TEXT   REVIEW

Paste — Cut, Copy, Format Painter | Clipboard
B I U | A | Basic Text
Address Book Check Names | Names
Attach File Attach Item Signature | Include
Follow Up ▾ ! High Importance ↓ Low Importance | Tags
Zoom | Zoom

To... | Diane Tibbott (Diane@wingtiptoys.com); John Morris; Katie Mathews; Mindy Martin; Susan Davis (someone@example.com)

Cc...

Subject

Send

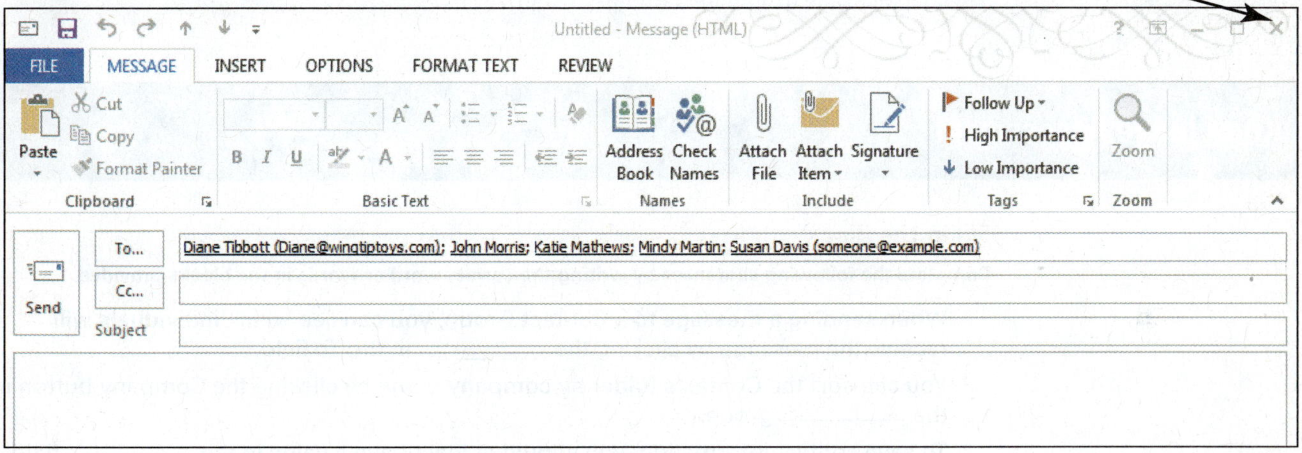

⚠ **Troubleshooting** It is not necessary to expand the Contact Group in a message. You expanded the Contact Group in this exercise merely for demonstration purposes.

6. Click the **Close** button to close the message without sending it. Do not save changes to the message.

CLOSE Outlook.

When you created the Wingtip Toys Contact Group, you included Gabe Mares. However, he works for Tailspin Toys now. In a previous exercise, you removed Gabe from the Contact Group. You also accessed and modified your contact record through the Contact Group. Finally, you created a message that could be sent to the members of the Contact Group.

SKILL SUMMARY

In This Lesson You Learned How to:	Exam Objective	Objective Number
Create and Modify Contacts	Create new contacts	4.1.1
	Edit contact information	4.1.4
	Attach a note to a contact	3.4.3
	Attach an image to contacts	4.1.5
	Attach tags to contacts	4.1.6
Send and Receive Contacts	Create new contacts	4.1.1
	Share contacts	4.1.7
View and Delete Contacts	Configure views	1.1.5
	Delete contacts	4.1.2
Create and Manipulate Contact Groups	Create new contact groups	4.2.1
	Delete group members	4.2.6
	Add contacts to existing groups	4.2.2
	Update contacts within groups	4.2.4
	Add notes to a group	4.2.3
	Share contacts	4.1.7
	Delete groups	4.2.5
Send a Message to a Contact Group		

Knowledge Assessment

Fill in the Blank

Complete the following sentences by writing the correct word or words in the blanks provided.

1. When sending a message to a Contact Group, you can see which individuals will receive the message by clicking the _____ in the *To* field.
2. You can sort the Contacts folder by company name by clicking the Company button in the _____ group.
3. To save contact information, you should at least have a value in the _____ field.
4. You can use the _____ to keep background information with a Contact Group record.
5. A(n) _____ simplifies the task of regularly sending the same message to a group of people.
6. Providing false information in a message header is called _____.
7. If you try to add a contact that already exists in your Contacts folder, Outlook detects a(n) _____.
8. The default view in the Contacts folder is the _____ view.
9. You can add or delete individuals in a Contact Group using the _____ page.
10. Like documents and files, contact information can be sent as a(n) _____.

True or False

Circle T if the statement is true or F if the statement is false.

T F 1. When keying phone numbers in the Contact window, it is important to format the number by including the parentheses, spaces, and dashes.

T F 2. Every time you send a message, you are also sending your contact information.

T F 3. When you create a new contact for a person from the same company, the company name, File as, e-mail domain, and address are carried over to the new contact.

T F 4. When you select a contact from the Contact Index in the People Hub, Outlook displays a peek of the contact record in the right pane of the window.

T F 5. If you are unsure what e-mail program the recipient uses, it is safest to send the contact in plain text format.

T F 6. You can forward a Contact Group just by selecting the group's contact record and clicking the Share button on the HOME tab.

T F 7. Many junk messages contain false information in the message header.

T F 8. After a contact has been created, you can modify the contact's information using either the main Contact window or the Outlook Address Book.

T F 9. A listing of members is visible when you view the Contact Group in the Contacts folder.

T F 10. Once a duplicate record is detected, you should always combine the information into one record and delete the duplicate.

Competency Assessment

Project 6-1: Create Contacts from Scratch

Gabe Mares recently started a new job at Tailspin Toys. As part of the training program, he will be traveling to different divisions to examine their procedures. At his first stop in Pittsburgh, PA, Gabe collected contact information for the team leader.

GET READY. LAUNCH Outlook if it is not already running.

1. Click the **People** button in the Navigation bar to display the People Hub.
2. Click **New Contact** on the HOME tab. The Untitled—Contact window is displayed.
3. In the *Full Name* field, key **Mandar Samant** and [press **Tab**].
4. In the *Company* field, key **Tailspin Toys** and [press **Tab**].
5. In the *Job Title* field, key **Software Development Team Lead** and [press **Tab**].
6. Click the *E-mail* field. Key **Mandar@tailspintoys.com** and [press **Tab**].
7. In the *Web Page Address* field, key **www.tailspintoys.com**.
8. Below the Phone Numbers heading, click the *Business* field. Key **4125551117**. [Press **Tab**].
9. Below the Addresses heading, click the *Business* field. Key **4567 Broadway**. [Press **Enter**]. Key **Pittsburgh, PA 14202**.
10. In the Actions group on the Ribbon, click the **Save & Close** button.

LEAVE Outlook open for the next project.

Project 6-2: Create a Contact from a Contact at the Same Company

While Gabe was in Pittsburgh, he interviewed a software developer in Mandar Samant's team. Although Gabe doesn't usually contact developers directly, he wants to save her contact information in case an opening occurs as a team leader.

GET READY. LAUNCH Outlook if it is not already running.

1. If necessary, click the **People** button in the Navigation bar to display the People Hub.
2. Select the **Mandar Samant** contact, and In the New group, click **New Items**.
3. Select the **Contact from the Same Company** option. The Contact window is displayed.
4. Click in the **Full Name** field if necessary. Key **Jamie Reding** and [press **Tab** twice].
5. In the *Job title* field, key **Software Developer**.

6. In the *E-mail* field, key **Jamie@tailspintoys.com**.

7. In the *Notes* field, key **Potential team lead**.

8. In the Actions group on the Ribbon, click the **Save & Close** button.

LEAVE Outlook open for the next project.

Proficiency Assessment

Project 6-3: Modify Contact Information

Two months later, Jamie Reding was promoted to a team leader in the Pittsburgh office. Gabe modified her contact information.

GET READY. LAUNCH Outlook if it is not already running.

1. If necessary, click the **People** button in the Navigation bar to display the People Hub.

2. Double-click the **Jamie Reding** contact in the Contact Index. The Contact Card is displayed.

3. Select **Title**. Change her title to **Software Development Team Lead**. If Title is not showing, click the **plus sign** next to the **Work** heading.

4. Click **Notes**. Change the text to **Monitor her progress**.

5. At the bottom of the card, click the **Save** button. Close the Contact Card.

LEAVE Outlook open for the next project.

Project 6-4: Send a Contact as an Attachment

Gabe's manager asked for information about the team leader for a new project. Gabe sends Jamie's contact record.

GET READY. LAUNCH Outlook if it is not already running.

1. If necessary, click the **People** button in the Navigation bar to display the People Hub.

2. Select the **Jamie Reding** contact in the Contact Index. The Contact Card pane is displayed.

3. In the Share group on the Ribbon, click the **Forward Contact** button. Select the **As an Outlook Contact** option. If a message is displayed stating that you must save the original item, click **OK** to continue.

4. Click the **To** button. In the *Select Names: Contacts* window, click your contact record. Click the **To** button. Click **OK**.

5. Click in the message area. Key **The contact information you requested is attached.**

6. Click the **Send** button.

LEAVE Outlook open for the next project.

Mastery Assessment

Project 6-5: Create a Contact Group

Gabe sends several messages to the team leaders each day. To simplify the task, Gabe creates a Contact Group.

GET READY. LAUNCH Outlook if it is not already running.

1. If necessary, click the **People** button in the Navigation bar to display the People Hub.
2. On the HOME tab, click the **New Contact Group** button.
3. In the Members group on the Ribbon, click the **Add Members** button and select **From Outlook Contacts**.
4. Add all the Tailspin Toys employees to the *Members* field, including Gabe, and click **Members**. Click **OK**.
5. Name the Contact Group **Tailspin Team Leaders**.
6. Click the **Save & Close** button.

LEAVE Outlook open for the next project.

Project 6-6: Modify a Contact Group

Gabe realized that he needs to change the Tailspin Team Leaders Contact Group. Gabe needs to remove himself from the Contact Group and add Diane Tibbott. Diane just accepted the position of Software Development Team Lead for Tailspin Toys. She will work in the Nashville office with Gabe.

GET READY. LAUNCH Outlook if it is not already running.

1. If necessary, click the **People** button in the Navigation bar to display the People Hub.
2. Use Gabe's contact record to create a new contact record from the same company for Diane Tibbott. Use the following information:

    Full Name   **Diane Tibbott**
    Job title   **Software Development Team Lead**
    E-mail   **Diane@tailspintoys.com**
3. Update Diane's contact record with the new information.
4. Open the **Tailspin Team Leaders** contact record.
5. Click **Gabe Mares** in the list of members and click the **Remove Member** button.
6. Add **Diane Tibbott** to the *Members* field.
7. **SAVE** the changes to the Contact Group.

CLOSE Outlook.

LESSON SKILL MATRIX

Skills	Exam Objective	Objective Number
Using Electronic Business Cards	Edit contact information	4.1.4
	Share contacts	4.1.7
	Create new contacts	4.1.1
	Create and assign signatures	1.2.2
Finding Contact Information	Search for contacts	1.4.4
	Create new search folders	1.4.1
Managing Multiple Address Books	Manage multiple address books	4.1.8
	Import contacts from external sources	4.1.3
Printing Contacts	Print contacts	1.3.5

KEY TERMS

- address book
- custom Search Folders
- electronic business cards
- import
- secondary address book
- Social Connector
- virtual folders

© adventtr/iStockphoto

© adventtr/iStockphoto

The marketing department at Tailspin Toys is holding a contest that is open to all employees. To compete, employees must design an electronic business card. Gabe Mares, the Software Development Manager, wasn't planning to enter the contest. Nevertheless, he had an idea for an electronic business card that he couldn't resist. He thumbed through the Tailspin Toys catalog until he found the perfect picture for his design. After all, who can resist a teddy bear?

Outlook is an ideal tool for customizing a business card. The Edit Business Card dialog box is specifically designed to help you design a custom business card. All you need to do is determine what information you want to include and the Outlook business card template makes it fit. In this lesson, you'll customize a business card and use it as a digital signature. You'll also practice searching for contacts and create a second address book.

SOFTWARE ORIENTATION

The Edit Business Card Dialog Box

Outlook 2013 is more graphic than ever. The default view in the Contacts window is now the People Hub, in which Outlook displays the information about your contacts along with an image of each. However, many businesses frequently use the Business Card view, which allows them to see multiple contacts at a time as business cards. By default, the text appears to the right of a wide, gray bar that borders the left side of the card, as shown in Figure 7-1. In this lesson, you'll learn how to customize your business card so that it stands out from the crowd.

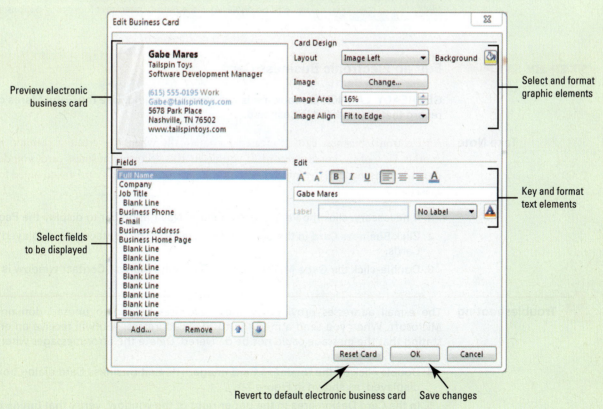

Figure 7-1

The Edit Business Card dialog box

Use the Edit Business Card dialog box to create an electronic business card that fits your company image. Refer to Figure 7-1 as you complete the following exercises.

USING ELECTRONIC BUSINESS CARDS

Electronic business cards are the digital version of paper business cards. They can be sent as attachments, used as signatures, and used to create a contact record. Although the default Contacts view is now the People Hub, electronic business cards are still an important tool. Designing an electronic business card that is memorable makes it easy to find whenever several electronic business cards are displayed on the screen, as when contacts are displayed in Business Card view. In this section, you'll edit a default business card by adding an image to it, sending it to a coworker, and using it as a digital signature.

Editing an Electronic Business Card

The Edit Business Card dialog box has four separate areas, as identified in Table 7-1. The four areas work together to provide a flexible tool that can create an amazing variety of customized business cards. In this exercise, you'll customize the default Outlook contact record to create a unique electronic business card that is just as eye-catching as a paper business card.

Table 7-1

Edit Business Card dialog box

Area	Description
Preview	View the effects of the changes you make.
Fields	Identify the fields you want to display on the electronic business card. Use the Add button to insert a new field. Select a field in the list and click the Remove button to delete a field. To move a field up or down on the card, select the field and click the Move Field Up (Up arrow) button or the Move Field Down (Down arrow) button.
Card Design	Insert and position a graphic or select a background color for the card. Position the image and define the amount of the card that can be used for the graphic. Although you can edit graphics in Outlook 2013, you cannot edit graphics in the Edit Business Card dialog box.
Edit	Key the value to be displayed in the field. Limited text formatting options are available.

STEP BY STEP   **Edit an Electronic Business Card**

GET READY. LAUNCH Outlook if it is not already running. Use the Gabe Mares contact record that you created in Lesson 6.

Take Note   An electronic business card is created automatically when you create a contact. It is basically another view of the contact record. If you delete the electronic business card, you delete the contact. Changes made to the information on the electronic business card are changed for the contact as well.

1. If necessary, click the **People** button in the Navigation bar to display the People Hub.
2. Click **Business Card** in the Current View Gallery. The contacts are displayed as Business Cards.
3. Double-click the **Gabe Mares** contact. The Gabe Mares—Contact window is displayed.

Troubleshooting   The e-mail addresses provided in these exercises belong to unused domains owned by Microsoft. When you send a message to these addresses, you will receive an error message stating that the message could not be delivered. Delete the error messages when they arrive.

4. Double click on the **Business Card** image. The Edit Business Card dialog box is displayed, as shown in Figure 7-1.
5. In the Card Design area in the upper right of the window, verify that **Image Left** is selected in the *Layout* field and **Fit to Edge** is selected in the *Image Align* field. This defines the position of the graphic. Currently, the graphic is the default gray bar.
6. Click the **Change** button. The Add Card Picture dialog box is displayed.

7. Navigate to the data files for this lesson. Click the *Bear Side.jpg* image file, and click **OK**. The bear image is added to the card preview.

8. In the Card Design area, click the **Image Align** field. In the dropdown list, click **Bottom Center**. In the card preview, the image is repositioned to appear at the bottom of the card.

9. In the Card Design area, click the **Image Align** field. In the dropdown list, click **Fit to Edge**. In the card preview, the image is resized and fills the entire side of the card.

10. Click the **Add** button. In the dropdown menu, point to **Internet Address** and then click **IM Address**. IM Address is added to the list of fields. The *IM Address* field is used for an instant messaging address.

11. With IM Address selected in the list of fields, click the empty field in the Edit area. Key **GabeTailspinToys**, as shown in Figure 7-2. The IM address is now added to the business card.

Figure 7-2

Modified Edit Business Card dialog box

© burnbank/iStockphoto

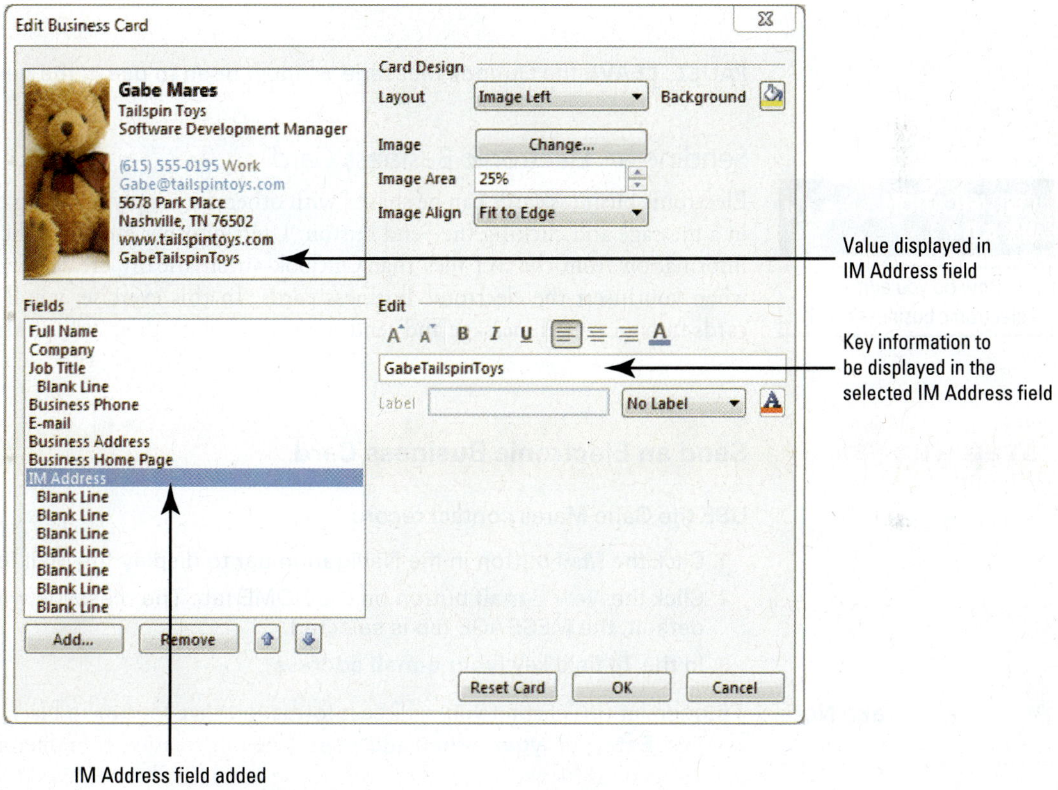

Edit Business Card

Gabe Mares	**Card Design**	
	Layout	Image Left ▼ Background 🎨
Tailspin Toys		
Software Development Manager	Image	Change...
(615) 555-0195 Work	Image Area	25% ▲▼
Gabe@tailspintoys.com	Image Align	Fit to Edge ▼
5678 Park Place		
Nashville, TN 76502		
www.tailspintoys.com		→ Value displayed in IM Address field
GabeTailspinToys		

Fields
- Full Name
- Company
- Job Title
  - Blank Line
- Business Phone
- E-mail
- Business Address
- Business Home Page
- **IM Address**
  - Blank Line
  - Blank Line
  - Blank Line
  - Blank Line
  - Blank Line
  - Blank Line
  - Blank Line

[Add...] [Remove] [↑] [↓]

Edit

A^ Å **B** *I* <u>U</u> ≡ ≡ ≡ A

GabeTailspinToys   → Key information to be displayed in the selected IM Address field

Label [ ] No Label ▼ A

[Reset Card] [OK] [Cancel]

↑ IM Address field added

12. Click **OK**. The Edit Business Card dialog box is closed. Click the **Save & Close** button. Gabe's business card is displayed, as shown in Figure 7-3.

Figure 7-3

Modified business card

© by_nicholas/iStockphoto; © burnbank/iStockphoto

PAUSE. LEAVE the Outlook Message window open to use in the next exercise.

Sending an Electronic Business Card

CERTIFICATION
READY?   4.1.4

How do you edit an
electronic business card?

Electronic business cards can be shared with others by simply inserting one or more business cards in a message and clicking the Send button. Users of other e-mail applications can get the contact information from the .vcf files that Outlook automatically creates and attaches to the message when you insert the electronic business cards. In this exercise, you'll insert electronic business cards into an e-mail message and send them along with their .vcf file attachments to a colleague.

STEP BY STEP **Send an Electronic Business Card**

USE the Gabe Mares contact record.

1. Click the **Mail** button in the Navigation bar to display the Mail folder.
2. Click the **New E-mail** button on the HOME tab. The Message window is displayed. By default, the MESSAGE tab is selected.
3. In the *To* field key [**your e-mail address**].

Take Note   Throughout this chapter you will see information that appears in black text within brackets, such as [Press **Enter**] or [**your e-mail address**]. The information contained in the brackets is intended to be directions for you rather than something you actually type word for word. It will instruct you to perform an action or substitute text. Do **not** type the actual text that appears within brackets.

4. In the *Subject* field key **Business cards attached**.
5. Click in the message area. Key **I attached the electronic business cards you requested.** [Press **Enter** twice] to add a bit of space between your text and the business card that you're about to attach.
6. On the **INSERT** tab in the Include group, click the **Insert Business Card** button. A dropdown list is displayed.
7. Click **Other Business Cards** in the dropdown list. The Insert Business Card dialog box is displayed, as shown in Figure 7-4.

Figure 7-4

Insert Business Card dialog box

Click to attach business cards to a message

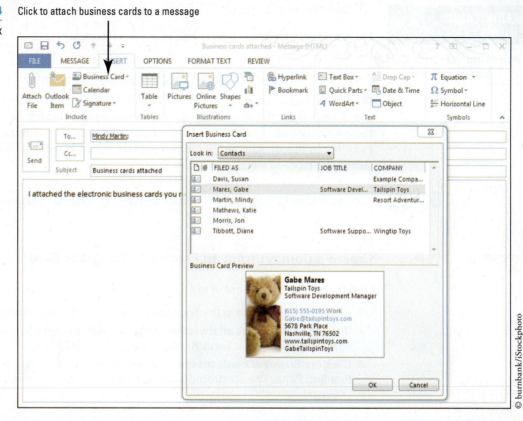

Another Way

If the contact name is displayed in the dropdown list, you can click the name to insert the electronic business card.

8. Click the **Gabe Mares** contact. A Preview pane at the bottom of the dialog box shows you an image of the business card you have chosen to send with the message.

9. With the contact still selected, [press and hold **Ctrl**]. This allows you to select multiple contacts.

10. Click the **Diane Tibbott** contact. Click **OK**. The electronic business cards are inserted into the message. In the *Attached* field, the contact records are attached as .vcf files, as shown in Figure 7-5.

Figure 7-5

Electronic business cards inserted into a message

Attached .vcf files

Inserted electronic business cards

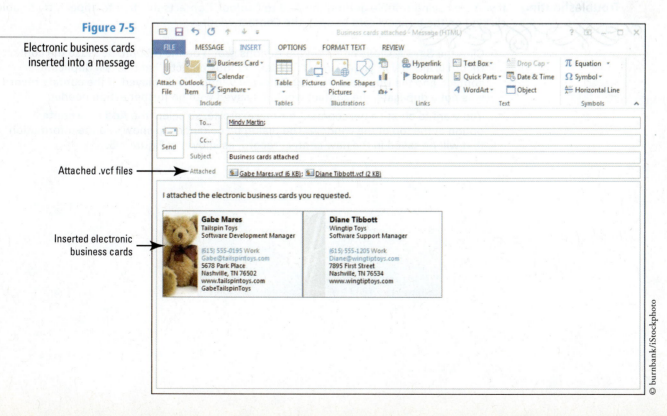

11. Click the **Send** button.

PAUSE. LEAVE Outlook open to use in the next exercise.

Creating a Contact from an Electronic Business Card

When you receive an electronic business card, Outlook allows you to add the contact record to your Contacts list either by using the .vcf file or by right-clicking on the business card itself. All the information on the electronic business card and the card's appearance are saved in your Contacts list. In this exercise, you'll create a contact record based on an electronic business card attached to a received e-mail message.

 Cross Ref   You can find more information on other methods of creating contacts in Lesson 6.

STEP BY STEP   **Create a Contact from an Electronic Business Card**

USE the message you sent in the previous exercise.

1. Click the **Mail** button in the Navigation bar to display the mailbox.
2. If the *Business cards attached* message has not arrived yet, click the **Send/Receive All Folders** button in the Send/Receive group of the HOME tab.
3. Click the **Business cards attached** message in the message list to display it in the Reading Pane. The electronic business cards are displayed in the message body.

⚠ **Troubleshooting**   If the Reading Pane Is not visible, click the Reading Pane button in the Layout group of the VIEW tab and select Right.

4. Right-click the **Gabe Mares** electronic business card in the message body. Click the **Add to Outlook Contacts** option in the shortcut menu. A Gabe Mares—Contact window is displayed that contains the information from the electronic business card, including the preview image of the card.

⚠ **Troubleshooting**   If you are having trouble getting the Add to Outlook Contacts shortcut to appear, try double clicking on the business card to open the Contact window.

5. Click the **Save & Close** button in the Actions group on the Ribbon. Because the contact record is already in your Contacts folder, Outlook detects that this is a duplicate contact, and the Duplicate Contact Detected window is displayed. If the contact record was not a duplicate, the contact would be saved with no further action needed.
6. You want to create a new contact for this exercise, so select the **Add new contact** option at the top of the window. The dialog box changes to show you the information that will be saved in the new contact record, as shown in Figure 7-6.

Figure 7-6

Duplicate Contact Detected window

Add new contact →

Click to add the electronic business card

Troubleshooting Normally, when you receive a duplicate record you will use the received information to update the contact in your *Contacts* folder. This exercise simply gives you the scenario for adding a new contact record. You can compare the information in your contact record with the information sent to you in the message. Before you update contact information, be sure that the new data is accurate.

7. Click the **Add** button at the bottom of the window. The Duplicate Contact Detected window is closed, the contact record is created, and you are returned to the Mail folder.

CERTIFICATION READY? 4.1.1

How do you create a contact from an electronic business card?

8. Click the **People** button in the Navigation bar to display the People Hub. Now, you have the original Gabe Mares contact record and the Gabe Mares contact record you created from the electronic business card in the message.

9. Click the first **Gabe Mares** contact record and click the **Delete** button on the HOME tab. The contact record is moved to the Deleted Items folder. It will not be removed from your computer until the Deleted Items folder is emptied.

PAUSE. LEAVE Outlook open to use in the next exercise.

Using an Electronic Business Card in a Signature

As you learned in Lesson 2, a signature can be added automatically in every message you send. You can also include your electronic business card in your signature to provide an easy way for the recipient to add the contact to the Contacts window. In this exercise, you'll change settings to set an electronic business card as a default digital signature and send an e-mail to test it.

Use an Electronic Business Card in a Signature

 Cross Ref   You can find more information on creating signatures in Lesson 2.

USE the Gabe Mares electronic business card you modified in a previous exercise.

1. If necessary, click the **People** button in the Navigation bar to display your contacts.

2. Click the **New Items** button in the New group, and select **E-mail Message** to open the Message window with the MESSAGE tab selected.

3. Click the **Signature** button in the Include group on the Ribbon. In the dropdown list, click **Signatures**. The Signatures and Stationery dialog box is displayed.

4. Click the **New** button to create a new signature. The New Signature dialog box is displayed.

5. To name the new signature, key **Gabe** into the *Type a name for this signature* field. Click **OK**. The New Signature dialog box is closed, and Gabe is highlighted in the *Select signature to edit* list box.

6. Click in the empty **Edit signature** box. Key the following text, [pressing **Enter**] at the end of each line.

   Gabe Mares

   Software Development Manager

   Tailspin Toys

   Gabe@tailspintoys.com

Take Note   Outlook automatically recognizes the e-mail address as a link and formats it as a hyperlink.

7. Click the **Business Card** button above the Edit Signature box. The Insert Business Card window is displayed.

8. Click the **Gabe Mares** contact record and click **OK**. The electronic business card is inserted into the signature, as shown in Figure 7-7.

Figure 7-7

Signature containing an electronic business card

Business card inserted in the signature

Business Card button

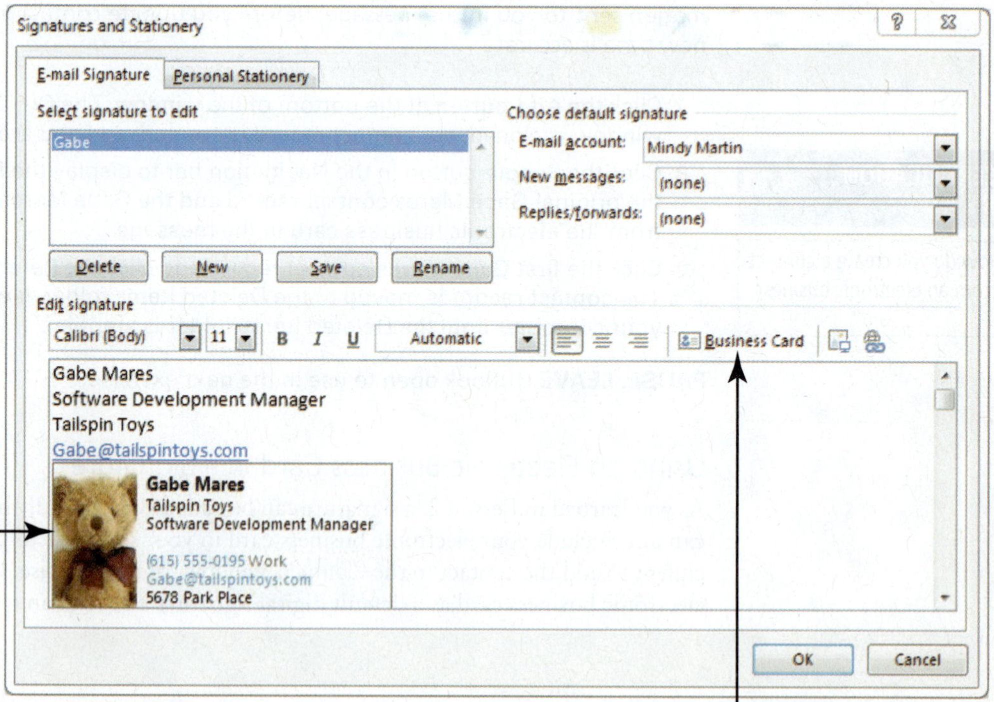

© burnbank/iStockphoto

9. Click **OK** to accept your changes and close the Signatures and Stationery dialog box.

10. In the Message window, key [**your e-mail address**] in the *To* field.

11. In the *Subject* field, key **New Signature Test**.

12. In the message body, key **Testing new signature** and [press **Enter** twice].

13. In the Include group on the Ribbon, click the **Signature** button and then click **Gabe** in the dropdown list of signatures that appears. The signature is inserted into the message, as shown in Figure 7-8.

Figure 7-8

Message containing Gabe's signature

Attachment containing information in the business card added automatically

Signature

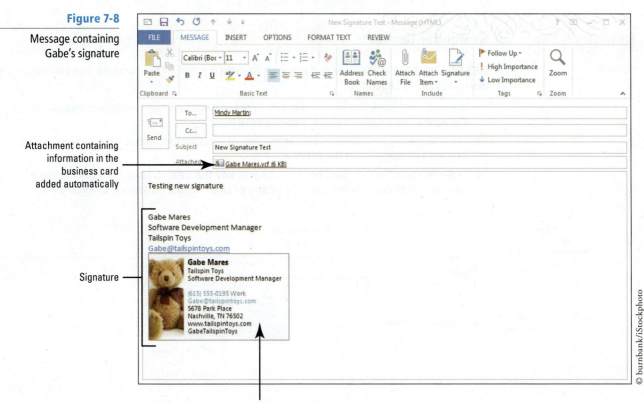

Electronic business card included in the signature

14. Click the **Send** button.

PAUSE. LEAVE Outlook open to use in the next exercise.

CERTIFICATION READY? 1.2.2

How do you use an electronic business card as a signature?

Recipients using other e-mail programs might not be able to view the electronic business card or save it as a contact record. However, almost all e-mail programs can read .vcf files. This is why Outlook automatically attaches a .vcf file containing the contact information to messages containing business cards.

Take Note Remember that for added security, some people avoid opening messages with attachments. You can delete the .vcf attachment before sending the message. Deleting the attachment doesn't remove the signature from the message, but prevents the recipient's spam filter from deleting your message simply because it has an attachment.

FINDING CONTACT INFORMATION

The Bottom Line

The search features in Outlook can help you search your stored contacts for information so you don't have to rely on your memory. You can use the Instant Search tool to conduct a quick search, or you can create a custom Search Folder to conduct more detailed searches for contact information as well as other Outlook items, such as messages and Calendar events, related to specific contacts. In this section, you'll use the Outlook search tools to locate messages associated with a contact.

Searching for Contacts

Outlook 2013 has enhanced search tools with a separate SEARCH TOOLS tab that contains a variety of tools for filtering the search results. The improved search and filter tools allow you to use any information in a contact record as the search parameter. For example, you can search for contacts containing text such as Diane, Pittsburgh, or Lead. As you begin keying text into the Instant Search box, Outlook starts searching your contacts list and begins populating the results list with matching contacts as they are found. In this exercise, you'll use Instant Search to find a contact.

STEP BY STEP   **Search for Contacts**

GET READY. LAUNCH Outlook if it is not already running. The contacts used in this exercise were created in Lesson 6.

1. If necessary, click the **People** button in the Navigation bar and select **People** in the Current View group to display the People Hub.

2. Click in the **Instant Search** box at the top of the Contact Index. The new SEARCH TOOLS tab appears in the Ribbon.

3. In the Instant Search box, key **toy**. As you key the search text, Outlook displays all the contacts that contain the text *toy* in any of their fields, as shown in Figure 7-9.

Figure 7-9

Search for contacts

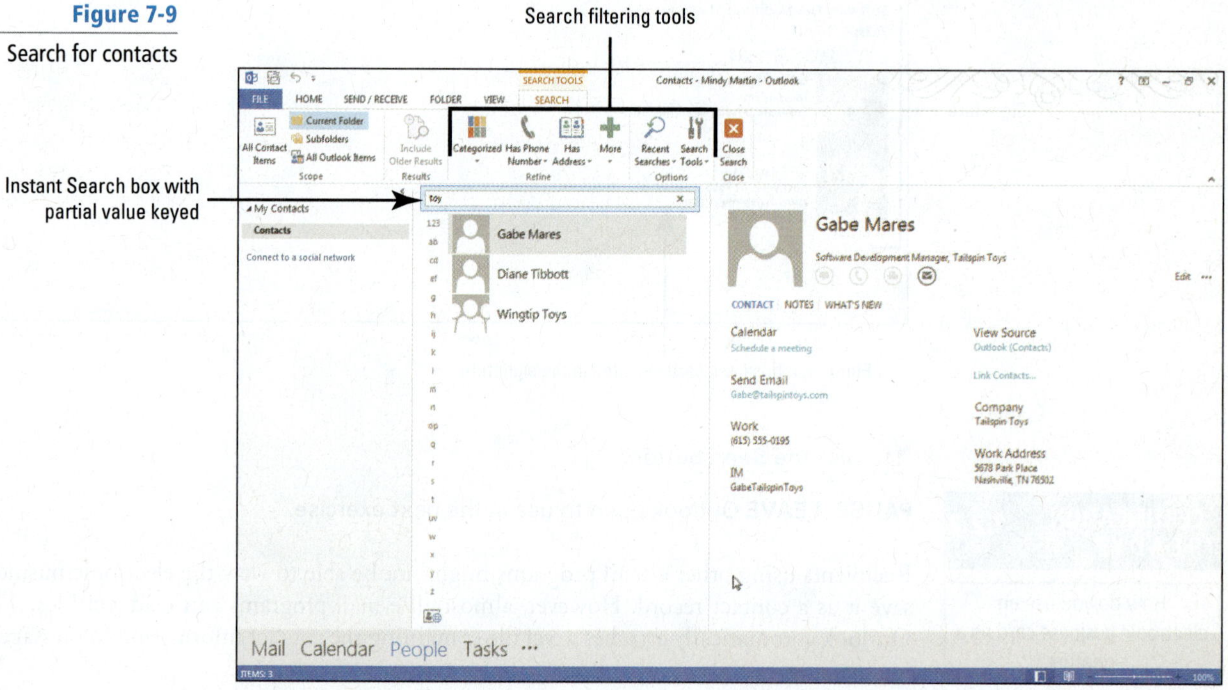

4. Click the **More** button in the Refine group of the SEARCH TOOLS tab. A menu of additional search fields is displayed, as shown in Figure 7-10.

Figure 7-10

The More Search Criteria
dropdown list

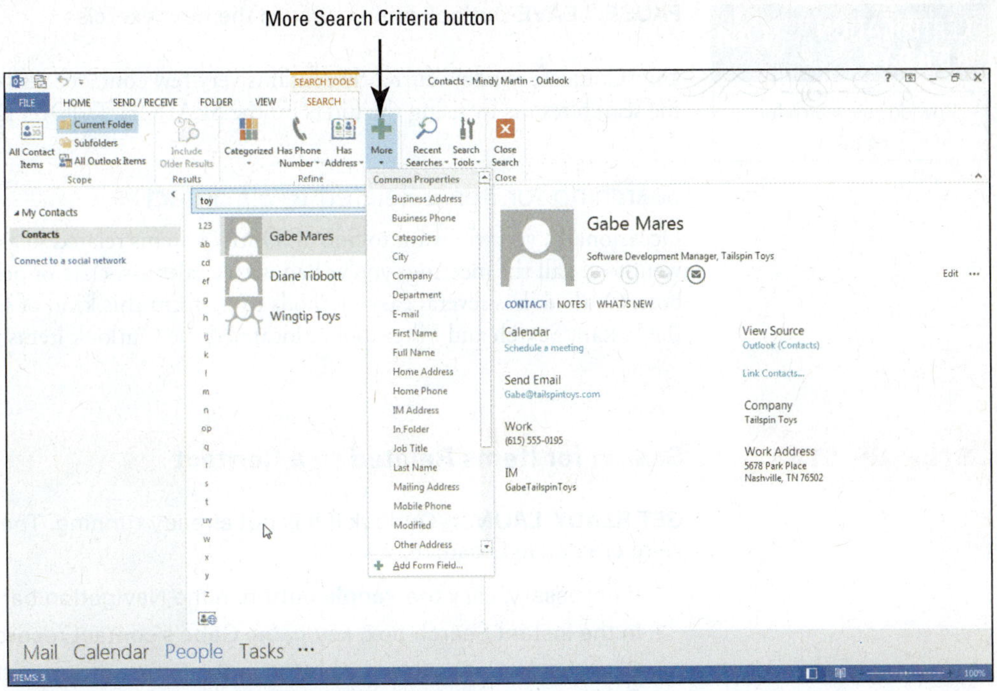

More Search Criteria button

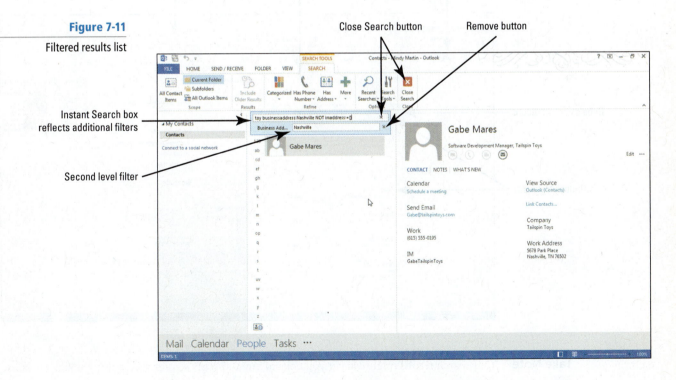

5. Select **Business Address** from the list.

6. In the *Business Address* field, key **Nashville**. Outlook refines the results list to show only the two contacts that both contain the word toy and are located in Nashville.

7. Click the **Has Address** button to open a list of additional filters. Click **Has IM Address**. Outlook refines the search results again to find the only one of the contacts that meets the previous search parameters and has an IM address listed, as shown in Figure 7-11.

Figure 7-11

Filtered results list

Close Search button

Remove button

Instant Search box
reflects additional filters

Second level filter

8. Click the **Remove** button next to the Business Address field. Click the **Close Search** button on the SEARCH TOOLS SEARCH tab.

CERTIFICATION
READY?   1.4.4

How do you search for a
contact?

PAUSE. LEAVE Outlook open to use in the next exercise.

Your Contacts window currently contains very few contacts. As you add contacts, you can narrow the search results by using the filters on the SEARCH TOOLS tab.

Searching for Items Related to a Contact

Occasionally, you will want to find all Outlook items related to a contact. For example, you might want to see all the meetings you've had with a sales associate or perhaps all the messages from your boss. Outlook has several easy methods to perform this kind of search. In this exercise, you'll use the Instant Search and Filter tool to locate all the Outlook items related to a contact.

STEP BY STEP   **Search for Items Related to a Contact**

GET READY. LAUNCH Outlook if it is not already running. The contacts used in this exercise were created in Lesson 6.

1. If necessary, click the **People** button in the Navigation bar to display the People Hub.
2. In the Instant Search box, key **gabe**. Gabe's contact record is displayed.
3. Click the **All Outlook Items** button in the Scope group of the SEARCH TOOLS tab. Outlook displays the matching Outlook items.
4. The Gabe Mares contact record and the related messages are displayed. Notice that Outlook highlights the term *Gabe* wherever it appears in the results list, as shown in Figure 7-12.

Figure 7-12

Outlook items related to Gabe

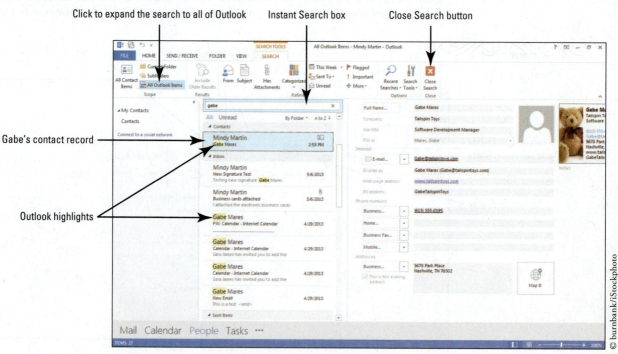

Click to expand the search to all of Outlook   Instant Search box   Close Search button

Gabe's contact record ───→

Outlook highlights ───→

Take Note   Your search results might vary if you deleted any messages sent or received in previous lessons.

5. Click the **Close Search** button to clear the search criterion.

PAUSE. LEAVE Outlook open to use in the next exercise.

Creating a Custom Search Folder

Instant Search quickly finds Outlook items, but it requires you to key the search text every time you want to perform a search. That's all well and good when you need to find a specific item for a one-time need. But there are many times in business where you might need to perform the same search more than once. For example, as an assistant sales manager you might need to submit a weekly status report to your manager that gives her an update on each salesman's progress. Each week you need to search through your messages to locate the progress reports from each of the five salesmen. You can certainly use the Instant Search feature to locate the needed information, but why set up a search each week when you can set it up once and save your search parameters?

In Outlook 2013, **custom Search Folders** are essentially searches saved in a virtual folder. When you create the custom Search Folder with your specific search parameters, Outlook adds a virtual folder to your Folders Pane under the Search Folders folder. Whenever you click one of these **virtual folders**, you can see all the items that meet the search parameters you specified. Although your search results look like items in a normal Outlook mail folder, the items are actually still stored in their original location (you're seeing a link to the original location). Using virtual folders gives you the convenience of working with items as you would in any folder and the ability to keep the original item in a more appropriate folder based on your mailbox organization. In this exercise, you'll create a custom Search Folder.

STEP BY STEP	**Create a Custom Search Folder**

GET READY. LAUNCH Outlook if it is not already running. The contacts used in this exercise were created in Lesson 6.

1. Click the **Mail** button in the Navigation bar to display the mailbox.
2. On the FOLDER tab, click the **New Search Folder** button to display the New Search Folder dialog box.
3. Scroll to the bottom of the *Select a Search Folder* list and click **Create a custom Search Folder**, as shown in Figure 7-13.

Figure 7-13

New Search Folder dialog box

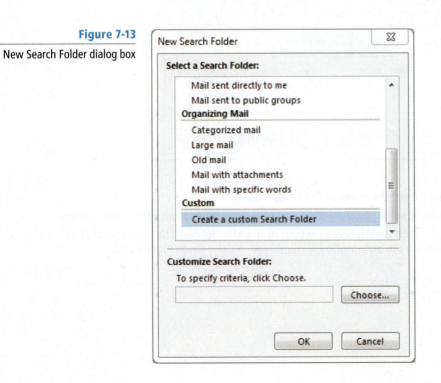

Cross Ref You learned about using the built-in Search Folders in Lesson 3.

4. Click the **Choose** button to display the Custom Search Folder dialog box shown in Figure 7-14.

Figure 7-14

Custom Search Folder dialog box

Custom Search Folder	☒

📁 Name: [   ] ← Key a name for the new Search Folder

Select "Criteria" to specify what items this Search Folder contains.   [Criteria...] ← Click to specify search criteria

Mail from these folders will be included in this Search Folder:

[Mindy Martin   ]   [Browse...]

[OK]   [Cancel]

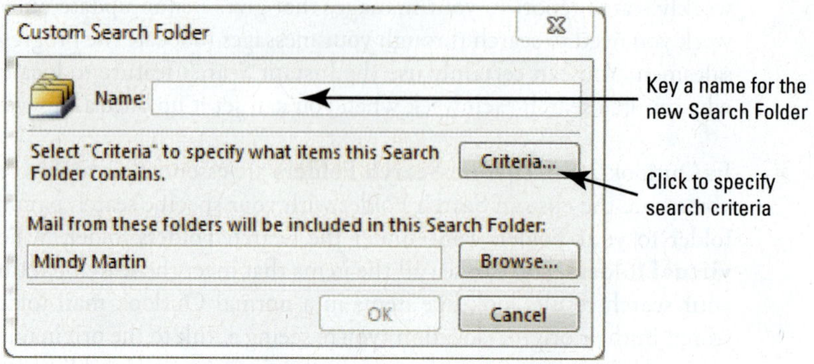

5. In the *Name* field, key **Messages about Susan**. When naming a Search Folder, create a name that reflects the search criteria.
6. Click the **Criteria** button to display the Search Folder Criteria dialog box shown in Figure 7-15.

Figure 7-15

Search Folder Criteria dialog box

Search Folder Criteria	☒

Messages | More Choices | Advanced

Search for the word(s): [▼] ← Search for this text

In: [subject field only   ▼] ← Search in this location

[From...]   [   ]
[Sent To...]   [   ]
☐ Where I am: [the only person on the To line ▼]

Time: [none ▼] [Anytime ▼]

[OK]   [Cancel]   [Clear All]

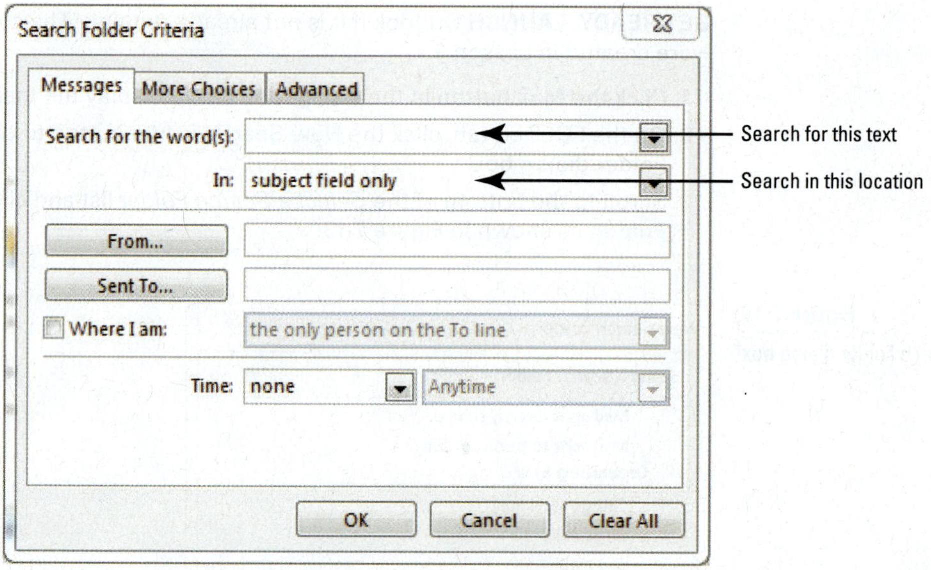

7. In the *Search for the word(s)* field, key **Susan**.
8. In the *In* field, select **subject field and message body** from the dropdown list.
9. Click **OK** in each dialog box to return to the Mail folder. The new Search Folder and the search results are automatically displayed, as shown in Figure 7-16.

Figure 7-16

Search Folder created

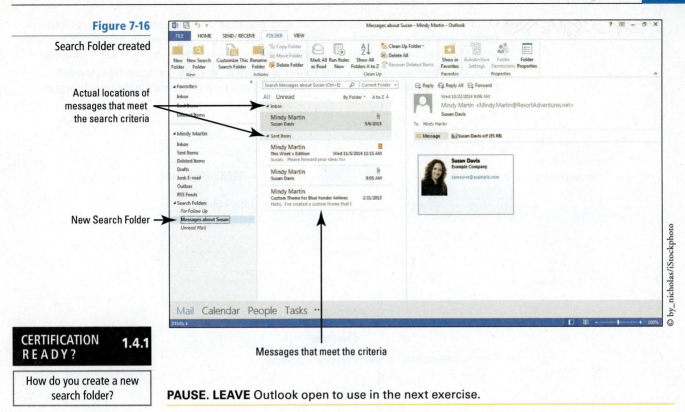

Actual locations of
messages that meet
the search criteria

New Search Folder →

Messages that meet the criteria

CERTIFICATION
READY?   1.4.1

How do you create a new
search folder?

PAUSE. LEAVE Outlook open to use in the next exercise.

Take Note   Search Folders are virtual folders. You can delete a Search Folder without deleting the displayed messages because the messages are actually located in other folders. However, because Search Folders lets you work with messages as if it were a real folder, if you delete a message within a Search Folder, the original message is really moved into the Deleted Items folder.

MANAGING MULTIPLE ADDRESS BOOKS

The Bottom Line

Every Contacts folder has its own Outlook <mark>address book</mark> that stores contact information, such as names and e-mail addresses. To keep your personal contacts separate from your business contacts, you can create an additional Contacts folder that has its own address book. For example, it is usually a good idea to keep your personal contacts in a <mark>secondary address book</mark> to keep them separate from the main Contacts list. A secondary address book has all the functionality of the familiar *Contacts* folder. This helps eliminate errors that can occur if you think you're sending a personal e-mail to a friend named Cathy, but you actually send the message to Cathy Reynolds, Regional Sales Manager.

Creating a Personal Address Book

Each Outlook Contacts folder has an associated Outlook address book. In this exercise, you will create a new Contacts folder to hold your secondary address book for personal contacts.

STEP BY STEP   **Create a Personal Address Book**

GET READY. LAUNCH Outlook if it is not already running.

1. Click the **People** button in the Navigation bar to display the People Hub.
2. On the FOLDERS tab, click **New Folder** in the New group. The Create New Folder dialog box is displayed.

3. In the *Name* field, key **Personal Contacts**. Because you selected the *Contacts* folder before creating a new folder, Contact Items is already displayed in the *Folder contains* field and the Contacts folder is selected in the *Select where to place the folder* list.

4. Click **OK**. The Personal Contacts folder is created. The My Contacts heading now contains the following folders: *Contacts* and the new *Personal Contacts* folders, as shown in Figure 7-17.

Figure 7-17

Personal Contacts
folder created

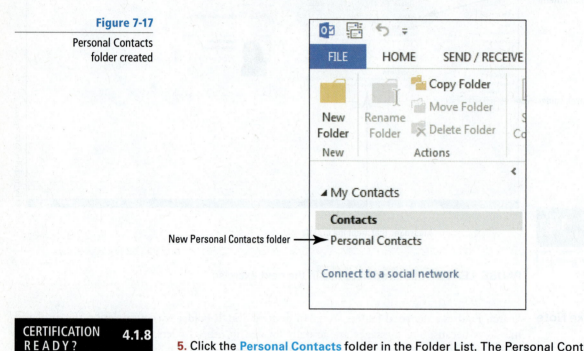

New Personal Contacts folder ——→

5. Click the **Personal Contacts** folder in the Folder List. The Personal Contacts window is blank because you don't have any contacts for this folder yet.

PAUSE. LEAVE Outlook open to use in the next exercise.

Importing an Address Book from a File

Manually keying a large number of contacts can be tedious. It's much easier to import the contact information. When you **import** a file, you bring information into a file from an external source. Most e-mail programs offer the option of exporting your contacts. Outlook 2013 can only import contacts in a few formats, the most common of which is .csv (comma-separated value). In this exercise, you import contact information from a Microsoft Excel file.

STEP BY STEP   **Import a Secondary Address Book from a File**

USE the Personal Contacts folder you created in the previous exercise.

1. Click the **FILE** tab to open the Backstage view.
2. Click **Open & Export** in the Navigation Pane.
3. Click the **Import/Export** option. The Import and Export Wizard is displayed, as shown in Figure 7-18.
4. Click **Import from another program or file**, if necessary, in the list of available actions.

Figure 7-18

Import and Export Wizard

Import and Export Wizard

Choose an action to perform:

Export RSS Feeds to an OPML file
Export to a file
Import a VCARD file (.vcf)
Import an iCalendar (.ics) or vCalendar file (.vcs)
Import from another program or file
Import RSS Feeds from an OPML file
Import RSS Feeds from the Common Feed List

Description

Import data from other files, such as Outlook data files (.PST) and text files.

Select to Import from another program or file

< Back   Next >   Cancel

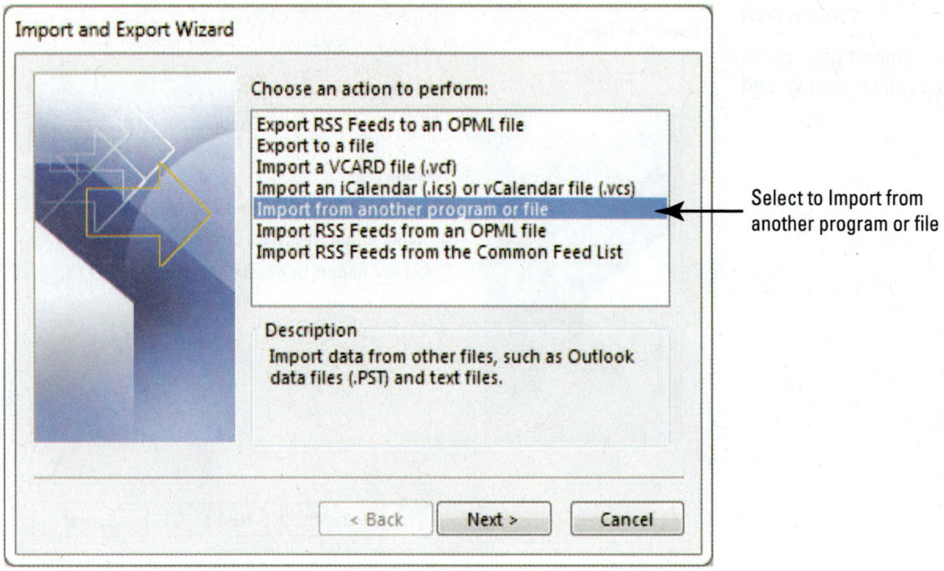

5. Click the **Next** button.
6. In the *Select file type to import from* list box, click **Comma Separated Values** in the list of available import file types, as shown in Figure 7-19; then click the **Next** button.

Figure 7-19

The Select file type to import from page of the Import and Export Wizard

Import a File

Select file type to import from:

Comma Separated Values
Outlook Data File (.pst)

Select the Comma Separated Values file type

< Back   Next >   Cancel

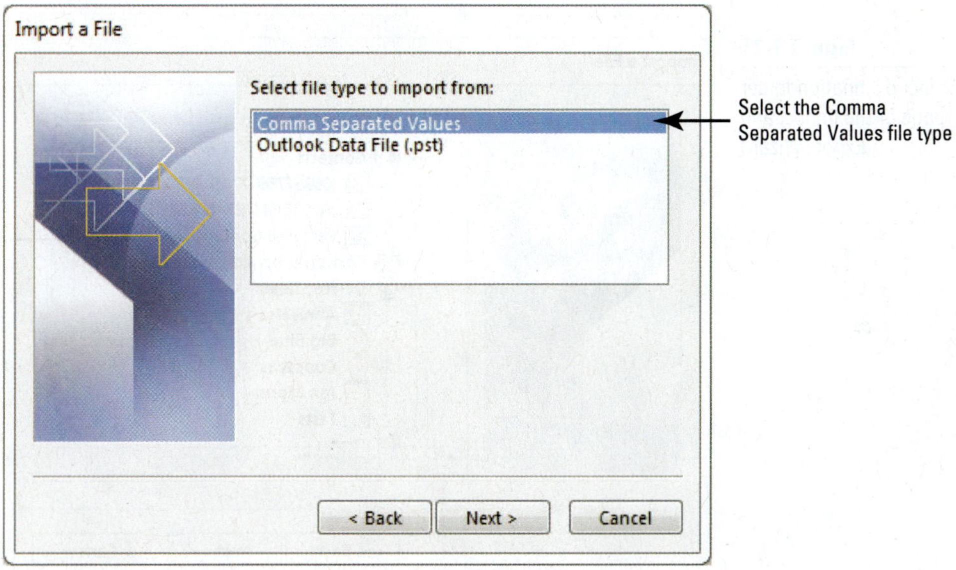

7. Click the **Browse** button. The Browse dialog box is displayed.
8. Navigate to the data files for this lesson and click the **Source Personal Contacts** file.
9. Click **OK** to apply your choices and close the Browse dialog box to return to the Import a File dialog box, as shown in Figure 7-20.

Figure 7-20

The File to import page of the Import and Export Wizard

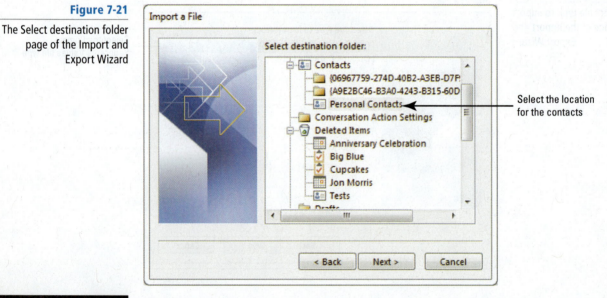

Name and location of the source file

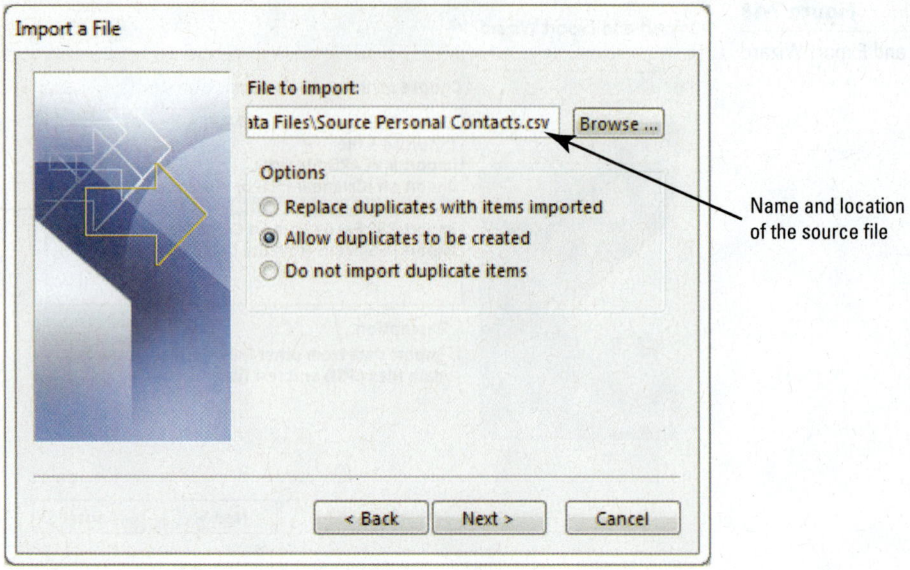

10. Back at the Import a File dialog box, click the **Next** button. The *Select destination folder* list is displayed.

11. Verify that **Personal Contacts** is selected as the destination folder, as shown in Figure 7-21.

Figure 7-21

The Select destination folder page of the Import and Export Wizard

Select the location for the contacts

CERTIFICATION READY?   4.1.3

How do you import contacts from external sources?

12. Click the **Next** button; then click the **Finish** button. The contacts are imported and displayed in the Personal Contacts folder.

PAUSE. LEAVE Outlook open to use in the next exercise.

 **Troubleshooting**   If you plan to import an address book from an Excel file, make sure that the file contains only one worksheet. You must also make sure that the file is saved in the CSV format.

By default, when you key an address in the *To*, *Cc*, or *Bcc* field in a new message, the address book displays potential matches from the default *Contacts* folder. If the name is a match, you can click the displayed name to fill the address field.

Alternatively, if you click the *To*, *Cc*, *Bcc*, or *Address Book* buttons, Outlook displays the Select Names: Contacts window. To work with a different address book, click the *Address Book* down arrow and select the address book you want, as shown in Figure 7-22.

Figure 7-22

The Select Names: Contacts window

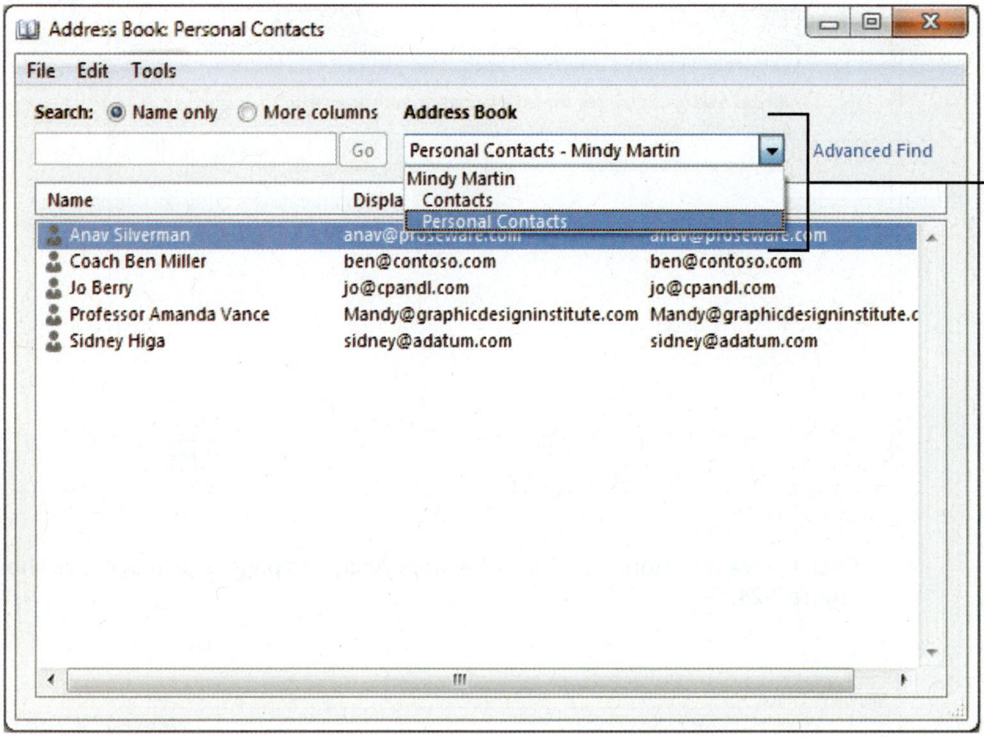

Not only is importing contact information much easier than keying the data into the fields, it also avoids keying errors. One typographical error could result in calling a complete stranger instead of Great-Grandma Mabel on her birthday.

Using the Social Connector

If you have contacts stored in social networking sites like LinkedIn or Facebook, you can use the **Social Connector** to sync Outlook to your external sites. This gives you access to the contact information for each of your connections and allows you to keep up with their status updates. In this exercise, you import contact information using the Social Connector.

STEP BY STEP   **Use the Social Connector**

USE the Personal Contacts folder you created in the previous exercise.

1. Click the **People** button in the Navigation bar to open the People Hub.
2. Click **Connect to a social network** in the Folders Pane. The Social Connector Wizard is displayed, as shown in Figure 7-23.

Figure 7-23

The Social Connector Wizard

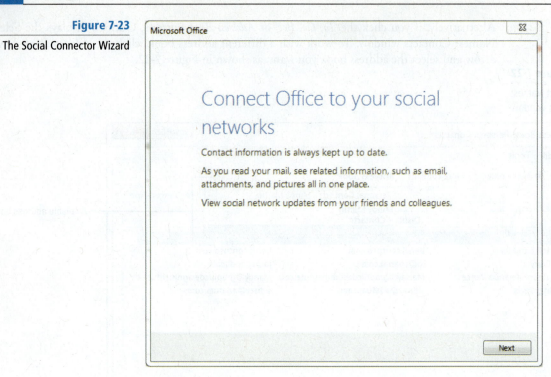

Microsoft Office

Connect Office to your social networks

Contact information is always kept up to date.

As you read your mail, see related information, such as email, attachments, and pictures all in one place.

View social network updates from your friends and colleagues.

Next

3. Click the **Next** button. The Social Network Accounts page is displayed, as shown in Figure 7-24.

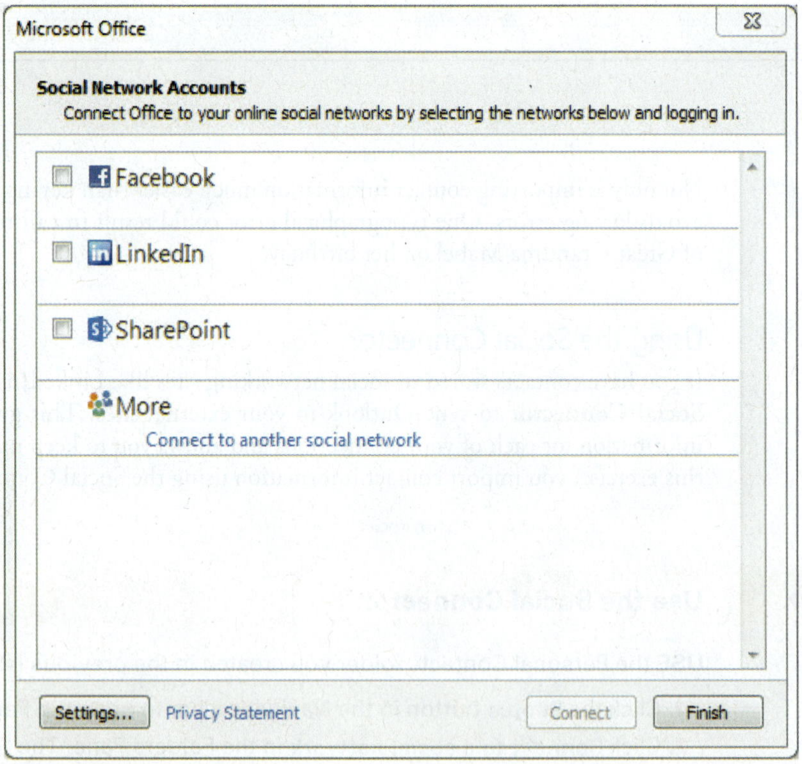

Figure 7-24

Select a social network

Microsoft Office

Social Network Accounts

Connect Office to your online social networks by selecting the networks below and logging in.

☐ **f** Facebook

☐ **in** LinkedIn

☐ **S** SharePoint

More
Connect to another social network

Settings...   Privacy Statement   Connect   Finish

4. Select a social network, as shown in Figure 7-25.

Figure 7-25

Enter your account information

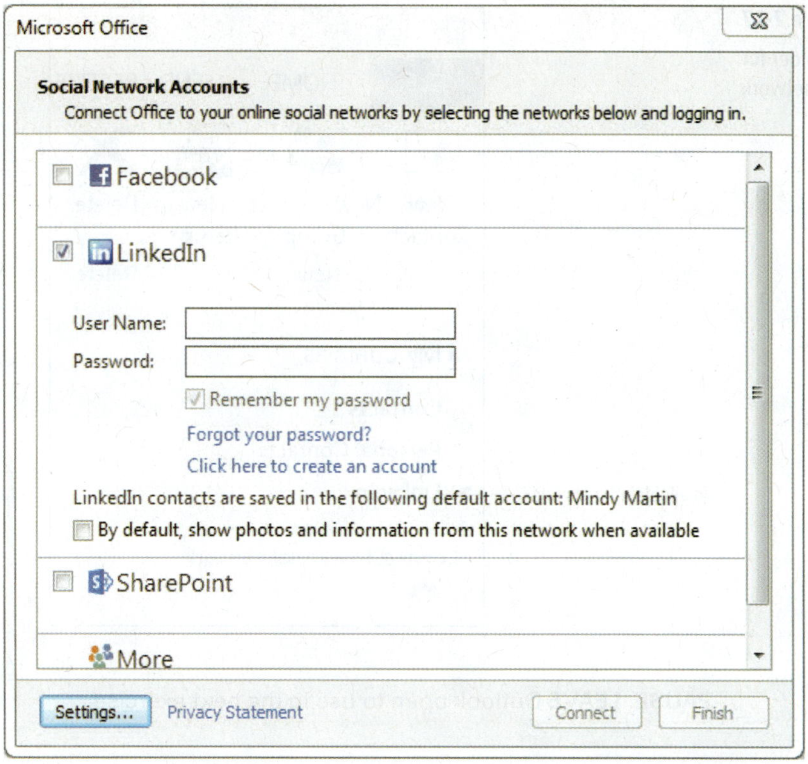

Microsoft Office

Social Network Accounts
Connect Office to your online social networks by selecting the networks below and logging in.

☐ 📘 Facebook

☑ 🔵 LinkedIn

User Name: [_____]
Password: [_____]

☑ Remember my password

Forgot your password?

Click here to create an account

LinkedIn contacts are saved in the following default account: Mindy Martin

☐ By default, show photos and information from this network when available

☐ 🟦 SharePoint

👥 More

[Settings...] Privacy Statement   [Connect] [Finish]

5. Key in [**your User Name and Password**]. If you want it, select the **By default, show photos and information from this network when available** option.

6. Click **Connect**. After a moment, the Social Network accounts page is displayed again, indicating the newly connected account, as shown in Figure 7-26.

Figure 7-26

Completing the connection

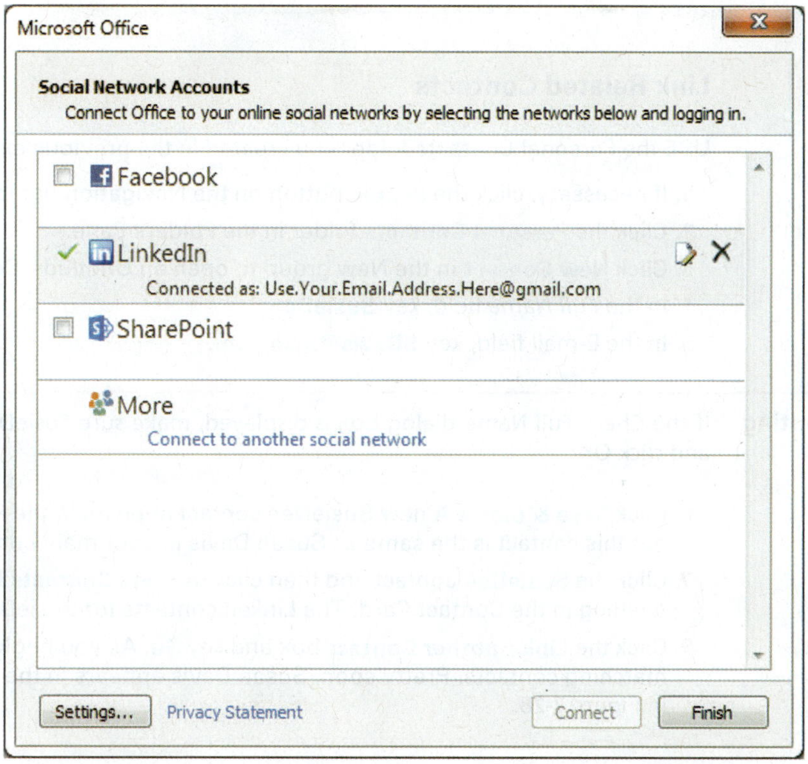

Microsoft Office

Social Network Accounts
Connect Office to your online social networks by selecting the networks below and logging in.

☐ 📘 Facebook

✓ 🔵 LinkedIn   📝 ✕
Connected as: Use.Your.Email.Address.Here@gmail.com

☐ 🟦 SharePoint

👥 More
Connect to another social network

[Settings...] Privacy Statement   [Connect] [**Finish**]

7. Click **Finish**. Outlook congratulates you on your new connection.

8. Click **Close** to complete the process. A new contacts folder appears in your Folders Pane for your new network, as shown in Figure 7-27.

Figure 7-27

The new contacts folder for
the social network

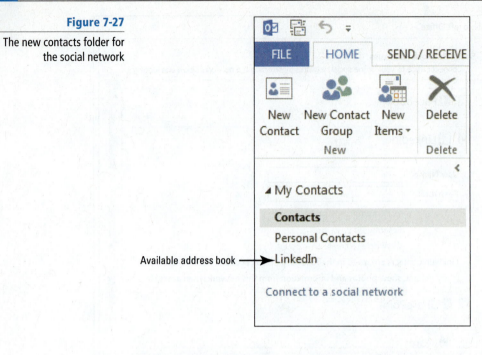

Available address book ⟶ LinkedIn

PAUSE. LEAVE Outlook open to use in the next exercise.

Linking Related Contacts

Whenever you have more than one contact record for the same person, Outlook automatically links the contacts together to eliminate clutter. However, Outlook can't always tell that contacts from different sources refer to the same person. When this happens, you can manually link the contacts together. In this exercise, you link contact information using the Social Connector.

STEP BY STEP | **Link Related Contacts**

USE the Personal Contacts folder you created in the previous exercise.

1. If necessary, click the **People** button on the Navigation bar to open the People Hub.
2. Click the **Personal Contacts** folder in the Folders Pane.
3. Click **New Contact** in the New group to open an Untitled—Contact window.
4. In the *Full Name* field, key **SusieDee**.
5. In the E-mail field, key **SDavis@msn.com**.

⚠ **Troubleshooting** If the Check Full Name dialog box is displayed, make sure SusieDee appears in the First field and click OK.

6. Click **Save & Close**. A new SusieDee contact appears in the Personal Contacts folder, but this contact is the same as Susan Davis in your main contacts folder.
7. Click the **SusieDee** contact and then click the **Link Contacts** link under the *View Source* heading in the Contact Card. The Linked contacts for SusieDee window is displayed.
8. Click the **Link Another Contact** box and key **Su**. As you begin to type, Outlook supplies matching contacts. Pretty soon, Susan Davis appears in the search results, as shown in Figure 7-28.

Figure 7-28

Searching for related contacts

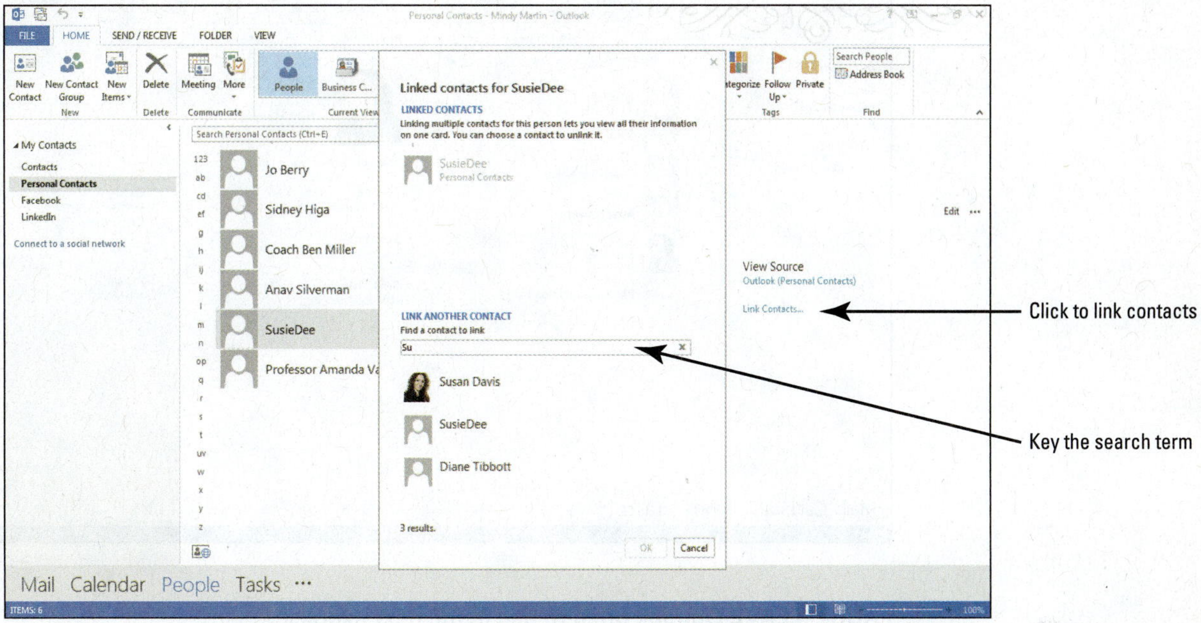

© by_nicholas/iStockphoto

9. Click **Susan Davis** in the results list. The Susan Davis contact and Favorite move to the Linked contacts list, as shown in Figure 7-29.

Figure 7-29

Linking related contacts

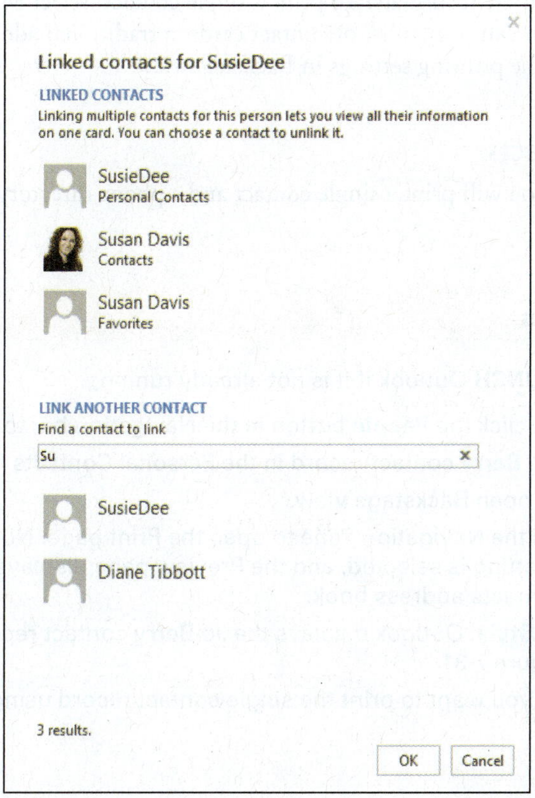

© by_nicholas/iStockphoto

10. Click **OK**. The SusieDee contact record in the Personal Contacts folder is updated with Susan's image and contact information, as shown in Figure 7-30.

Figure 7-30

The updated contact record

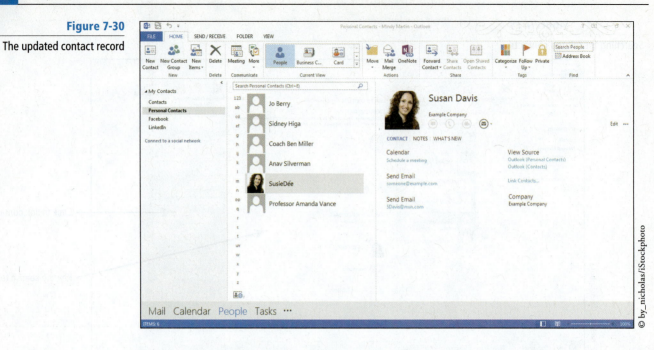

PAUSE. LEAVE Outlook open to use in the next exercise.

PRINTING CONTACTS

The Bottom Line

In Outlook 2013 it is easy to print a single contact or an entire address book. Outlook can print contacts in five different formats. To print a single contact, select Memo Style. For printing multiple contacts, you can print a list of contact cards, a traditional address book, or a phone listing. You can control the printing settings in Backstage view.

Printing Contacts

In this exercise, you will print a single contact and a phone directory.

STEP BY STEP   **Print Contacts**

GET READY. LAUNCH Outlook if it is not already running.

1. If necessary, click the **People** button in the Navigation bar to open the People Hub.

2. Select the **Jo Berry** contact record in the Personal Contacts folder.

3. Click **FILE** to open Backstage view.

4. Click **Print** in the Navigation Pane to open the Print page. Notice that by default the Card Style setting is selected, and the Preview pane displays all of the contacts in the Personal Contacts address book.

5. Click **Memo Style**. Outlook displays the Jo Berry contact record in the Preview pane, as shown in Figure 7-31.

6. Click **Print** if you want to print the single contact record using the default printer.

Figure 7-31

A Memo Style contact record

Click to print using
the default settings

Click to print a single
contact record

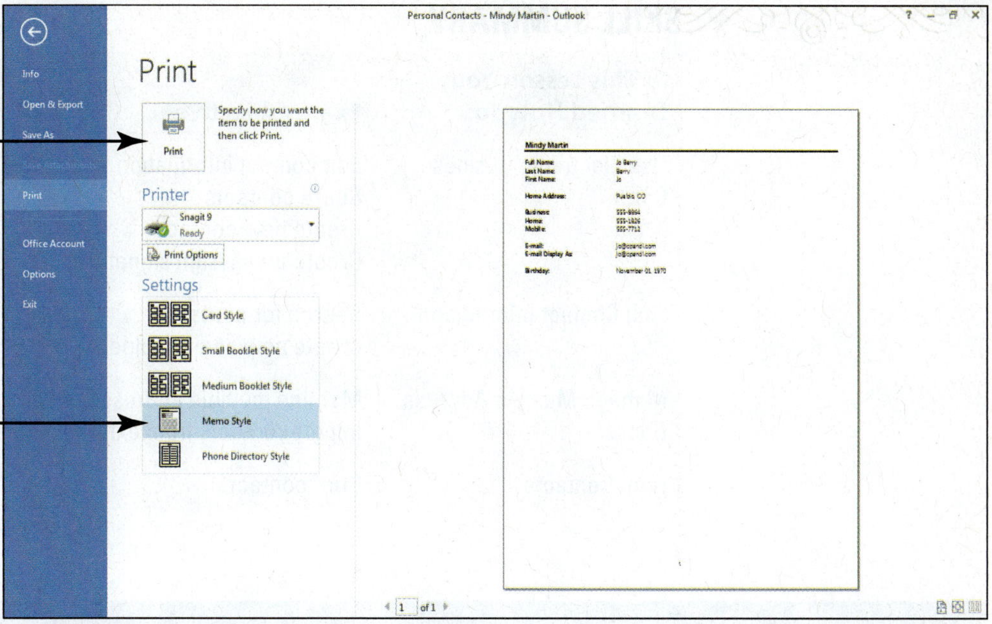

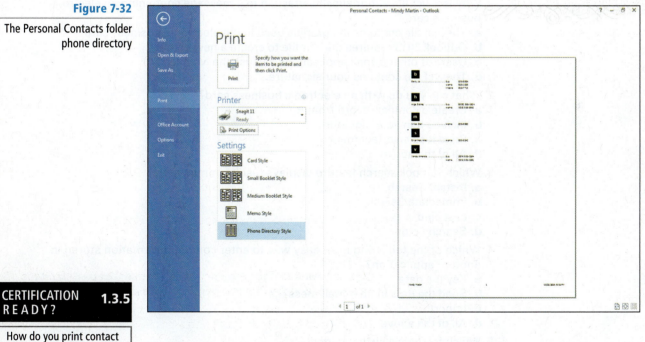

7. Click **Phone Directory Style**. Outlook displays a preview of the entire phone directory for the Personal Contacts, as shown in Figure 7-32.

8. Click **Print** if you want to print a phone directory for all of the contacts in the selected folder using the default printer.

Figure 7-32

The Personal Contacts folder
phone directory

CERTIFICATION
READY?   **1.3.5**

How do you print contact
records?

CLOSE Outlook.

SKILL SUMMARY

In This Lesson You Learned How To:	Exam Objective	Objective Number
Use Electronic Business Cards	Edit contact information	4.1.4
	Share contacts	4.1.7
	Create new contacts	4.1.1
	Create and assign signatures	1.2.2
Find Contact Information	Search for contacts	1.4.4
	Create new search folders	1.4.1
Manage Multiple Address Books	Manage multiple address books	4.1.8
	Import contacts from external sources	4.1.3
Print Contacts	Print contacts	1.3.5

Knowledge Assessment

Multiple Choice

Select the best response for the following statements.

1. Why is a .vcf file automatically attached to a message containing an electronic business card?
   a. The .vcf file contains the graphic used in the electronic business card.
   b. Outlook 2013 requires the .vcf file to create a new contact.
   c. Users of other e-mail applications can use the .vcf file.
   d. The .vcf file contains your signature.

2. What can you do with an electronic business card?
   a. Create a contact record from it
   b. Include it in your signature
   c. Send it as an attachment
   d. All of the above

3. Which Outlook search feature displays results immediately?
   a. Instant Search
   b. Immediate Search
   c. Fast Find
   d. Search Folder

4. Which of the following is an easy way to enter contact information stored in another application?
   a. Key the data
   b. Send the data in an e-mail message
   c. Import
   d. All of the above

5. Which folder is a virtual folder?
   a. Secondary Contacts folder
   b. Sent Items folder
   c. Search Folder
   d. Contacts folder

6. When is an electronic business card created?
   a. When the electronic business card is viewed
   b. When the electronic business card is modified
   c. When the contact record is created
   d. When the electronic business card is sent with a message

7. You can use the Social Connector to synchronize your Outlook 2013 contacts with:
   a. LinkedIn
   b. Google +
   c. Facebook
   d. Both A and C

8. How many different styles can you use to print a single contact record?
   a. One
   b. Two
   c. Three
   d. Five

9. Where can you store personal contacts in Outlook 2013?
   a. Search Folder
   b. Secondary address book
   c. Private address book
   d. Default address book

10. How many areas are in the Edit Business Card dialog box?
    a. One
    b. Three
    c. Four
    d. Eight

Fill in the Blank

Complete the following sentences by writing the correct word or words in the blanks provided.

1. To print a single contact, select the _____ print option.
2. Electronic business cards can be shared with others by simply inserting one or more business cards in a message and clicking the _____ button.
3. It is usually a good idea to keep your personal contacts in a(n) _____.
4. The _____ dialog box has four separate areas: Preview, Fields, Card Design, and Edit.
5. When you create the custom Search Folder with your specific search parameters, Outlook adds a(n) _____ to your Folders Pane under the Search Folders folder.
6. Contact records can be deleted by clicking the _____ button on the HOME tab.
7. Outlook automatically creates and attaches a(n) _____ file when you insert an electronic business card to a message.
8. Use Outlook's _____ to sync Outlook to external sites like LinkedIn or Facebook.
9. You import contact information from a .csv file using the _____.
10. _____ are the digital version of paper business cards.

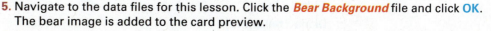

Competency Assessment

Project 7-1: Edit an Electronic Business Card

Diane Tibbott was recently hired by Tailspin Toys. She decided to use a teddy-bear image to brighten up her electronic business card also.

GET READY. LAUNCH Outlook if it is not already running.

1. Click the **People** button on the Navigation bar. If necessary, display the People Hub.
2. Select the **Diane Tibbott** contact, and click **Outlook (Contacts)** in the Contact Card pane. The Diane Tibbott—Contact window is displayed.
3. In the Options group on the Ribbon, click the **Business Card** button to display the Edit Business Card dialog box.
4. Click the **Change** button. The Add Card Picture dialog box is displayed.
5. Navigate to the data files for this lesson. Click the *Bear Background* file and click **OK**. The bear image is added to the card preview.

6. In the **Card Design** area in the upper right of the window, select **Background Image** in the *Layout* field.

7. In the Card Design area, click the **Image Align** field. Change the value to **Center**.

8. Click **Business Phone** in the Fields list. Click the **Add** button. In the dropdown menu, point to **Phone** and then click **Mobile Phone**.

9. With Mobile Phone selected in the list of fields, click the empty field in the Edit area. Key **6155550197**.

10. Click the **No Label** button and select **Right**. In the Label box, key **Mobile**.

11. Click **OK** to close the Edit Business Card dialog box. Click the **Save & Close** button to return to the People Hub.

LEAVE Outlook open for the next project.

Project 7-2: Send an Electronic Business Card

Diane Tibbott wants to stay in touch with her friends at Wingtip Toys. She decided to send her new electronic business card to her former supervisor.

GET READY. LAUNCH Outlook if it is not already running.

1. Display the Mail folder.

2. Click the **New E-mail** button on the HOME tab.

3. Key **Molly@wingtiptoys.com** in the *To* field of the message window.

4. Key **Let's keep in touch!** in the *Subject* field.

5. Click in the message area. Key the following message: **I attached my new electronic business card. Write when you have time**. [Press **Enter** twice].

6. Click the **INSERT** tab. In the Include group, click the **Insert Business Card** button.

7. Click **Diane Tibbott** in the dropdown list.

8. Click the **Send** button.

LEAVE Outlook open for the next project.

Proficiency Assessment

Project 7-3: Use an Electronic Business Card in a Signature

Management has decided that every message sent to clients must include an electronic business card. Rather than manually inserting the electronic business card into every message, Diane decided to create a signature containing her new electronic business card.

GET READY. LAUNCH Outlook if it is not already running.

1. Open a new Message window.

2. Click the **Signature** button on the Ribbon, and then click **Signatures** in the dropdown list.

3. In the Signatures and Stationery dialog box, click the **New** button to display the New Signature dialog box.

4. Key **Diane** into the *Type a name for this signature* field. Click **OK**.

5. Click the empty **Edit signature** box. Key in the following:

Diane Tibbott
Software Development Team Lead
Tailspin Toys
Diane@tailspintoys.com

6. [Press **Enter** twice]. Click the **Business Card** button above the Edit Signature box to display the Insert Business Card window.

7. Insert Diane Tibbott's electronic business card into the signature.

8. Click **OK** to close the Signatures and Stationery dialog box and return to the Message window.

9. On the MESSAGE tab, click the **Signature** button, and then click **Diane**.

10. **CLOSE** the message without saving or sending it.

LEAVE Outlook open for the next project.

Project 7-4: Create a Custom Search Folder

Diane wants to monitor messages about the team's new software development project. The project has been nicknamed 007 for the fictional character James Bond. All messages about the project must contain "007" in the *Subject* field. Diane decided to create a custom Search Folder to collect messages about the project.

GET READY. LAUNCH Outlook if it is not already running.

1. Click the **Mail** button in the Navigation bar to display the Mail folder.

2. From the Inbox, use the tools on the FOLDER tab to create a **New Search Folder**.

3. Create a custom Search Folder called **Project 007**.

4. Set the Project 007 Search Folder criterion to be the word **007** in the **subject field only**.

5. Test the new Search Folder by creating a new message that contains the word *007* in the subject field. In the message body, key **Testing Search Folder**. Click the **Send** button.

6. After the message arrives, click the **Project 007** folder to view its contents. It should contain the 007 message in the Sent Items folder and the 007 message in the Inbox.

LEAVE Outlook open for the next project.

Mastery Assessment

Project 7-5: Create a Secondary Address Book

Diane works for a new company, but she wants to stay in touch with friends she made at Wingtip Toys. Diane decided to create a secondary address book before she imports personal contacts for her friends.

GET READY. LAUNCH Outlook if it is not already running.

1. Display the People Hub.

2. Create a New Folder.

3. In the *Name* field, key **Diane's Contacts**. Click **OK**.

LEAVE Outlook open for the next project.

Project 7-6: Import a Secondary Address Book from a File

After creating the Diane's Contacts folder, Diane can import contact records for her friends at Wingtip Toys.

GET READY. LAUNCH Outlook if it is not already running.

1. Open the Backstage view and select **Open & Export** in the Navigation Pane.
2. Click **Import/Export** to open the Import and Export Wizard.
3. Follow the steps of the wizard to import the Microsoft Excel CSV file ***Source Diane's Contacts*** from the data files for this lesson into the Diane's Contacts folder. Use the default options.
4. Open the **Diane's Contacts** folder to view the new contacts.
5. Use the **Print** page in Backstage view to preview the **Small Booklet Style**.
6. Print the Diane's Contacts folder in **Card Style**.

CLOSE Outlook.

Circling Back

Kim Ralls was promoted to Shift Supervisor and transferred to the downtown office at City Power & Light. Although Kim was transferred, her computer and other equipment did not move with her. She needs to set up Outlook 2013 with new rules and contacts to help her manage her new responsibilities. She also needs to update her electronic business card to display her new title and contact information.

Project CB2-1: Create Mail and Contacts Folders and Import Contacts

Kim starts the process of customizing Outlook 2013 to meet her needs by creating new folders. One mail folder will contain messages about requests for new service. A contact folder will contain Kim's CP & L contacts and a second folder will contain her secondary address book.

Take Note   The folders and contacts you create in this project will be used in Projects CB2-2 and CB2-3.

GET READY. LAUNCH Outlook if it is not already running.

1. If necessary, click the **Mail** button in the Navigation bar to display the Inbox.
2. Right-click the **Outlook Data File**, and select **New Folder** from the shortcut menu. A blank box is displayed on the Folders Pane.

Troubleshooting   For this exercise, you want to select the top-level folder. It's the folder that holds your Inbox, Sent Items folder, and so on. Depending on the settings on your computer and the type of e-mail account you have, this might be called Outlook Data Files, Personal Folders, or simply your e-mail address.

3. Key **New Service** in the box and [press **Enter**] to identify the new folder.
4. Click the **FOLDER** tab. In the New group, click the **New Folder** button. The Create New Folder dialog box is displayed.
5. In the *Name* field, key **CP & L** to identify the new folder. Select **Contact Items** in the *Folder contains* field. If necessary, click **Contacts** in the *Select where to place the folder* list. Click **OK** to create the folder.
6. Click the `...` on the Navigation bar. Select the **Folders** option.
7. Right-click the **Contacts** folder in the Folders Pane and select **New Folder** from the shortcut menu. The Create New Folder dialog box is displayed.
8. In the *Name* field, key **Project CB 2-1** to identify the new folder. Select **Contact Items** in the *Folder contains* field. Click **CP & L** in the *Select where to place the folder* list. Click **OK** to create the folder.
9. Click the **FILE** tab. Click **Open & Export** in the Backstage view's Navigation Pane and select **Import/Export**. The Import and Export Wizard is displayed.
10. Click **Import from another program or file**, if necessary, in the list of available actions. Click the **Next** button.
11. Click **Comma Separated Values** in the list of available import file types. Click the **Next** button. Click the **Browse** button. The Browse dialog box is displayed.

12. Navigate to the data files for this lesson and click the *Kim Ralls Contacts* file. Click **OK** to apply your choices and close the Browse dialog box and return to the Import a File dialog box. Click the **Next** button.

13. In the *Select destination folder* box, select **Project CB 2-1**. Click the **Next** button.

14. Click the **Finish** button. Click the **Project CB 2-1** folder to see that the imported contacts are located there.

15. Click **File** to open Backstage view.

16. Click **Print** in the Navigation Pane to open the Print page. Notice that the Preview pane displays all of the contacts in the Project CB 2-1 address book in the Card Style.

17. Click **Phone Directory Style**. Select your printer in the Printer area and click **Print**.

LEAVE Outlook open for the next project.

Project CB2-2: Create Contact Records and a Contact Group

Kim needs to create contact records for herself and the two new Service Technicians in her department. She also needs to create a Contact Group containing the Service Technicians in her department.

Take Note   The contacts you create in this project will be used in Project CB2-3.

GET READY. LAUNCH Outlook if it is not already running.

1. Click the **People** button in the Navigation bar to display the main Contacts window. Click the **Contacts** folder in the Folder List.

2. Click **New Contact** on the HOME tab to display a blank Contact window.

Take Note   Throughout this chapter you will see information that appears in black text within brackets, such as Press **Enter** or [your e-mail address]. The information contained in the brackets is intended to be directions for you rather than something you actually type word for word. It will instruct you to perform an action or substitute text. Do **not** type the actual text that appears within brackets.

3. Click the **Full Name** field, if necessary. Key **Kim Ralls**. [Press **Tab**.]

4. In the *Company* field, key **City Power & Light**. [Press **Tab**.]

5. In the *Job title* field, key **Shift Supervisor**. [Press **Tab**.]

⚠ Troubleshooting   The e-mail addresses provided in these projects belong to unused domains owned by Microsoft. When you send a message to these addresses, you will receive an error message stating that the message could not be delivered. Delete the error messages when they arrive.

6. In the *E-mail* field, key **Kim@cpandl.com**. [Press **Tab**.]

7. In the *Web page address* field, key **www.cpandl.com**.

8. Below the Phone numbers heading, in the *Business* field, key **2175559821**. Outlook formats the number as a phone number when you move to another field.

9. Below the Addresses heading, in the *Business* field, key **324 Main Street**. [Press **Enter**.] Key **Springfield, IL 68390**. [Press **Tab**.]

10. In the Actions group on the Ribbon, click the **Save & New** arrow. In the dropdown list of options, click **Contact from the Same Company**. A new contact record window is displayed containing the same company information as the previous contact.

11. Click the **Full Name** field, if necessary. Key **Jay Henningsen**. [Press **Tab**.] Click the **Job title** field. Key **New Service Technician**. [Press **Tab**.] Click the **E-mail** field. Key **Jay@cpandl.com**. [Press **Tab**.]

12. In the Actions group on the Ribbon, click the **Save & New** arrow. In the dropdown list of options, click **Contact from the Same Company**. A new contact record window is displayed containing the same company information as the previous contact.

13. Click the **Full Name** field, if necessary. Key **Julia Moseley**. [Press **Tab**.] Click the **Job title** field. Key **New Service Technician**. [Press **Tab**.] Click the **E-mail** field. Key **Julia@cpandl.com**. [Press **Tab**.]

14. In the Actions group on the Ribbon, click the **Save & Close** button. Close any open contact records, saving changes if prompted.

15. Click the **VIEW** tab. In the Current View group, click **Change View** and select **List**. In the Arrangement group, click **Company**. The appearance of the Contacts window changes to a simple list of contacts sorted by company name.

16. Click the **HOME** tab. Click the **New Contact Group** button to display a blank Contact Group window.

17. In the *Name* field, key **New Service Technicians**.

18. In the Members group of the CONTACT GROUP tab, click the **Add Members** button. Click **From Outlook Contacts** from the dropdown list that appears. The Select Members: Contacts dialog box is displayed.

19. Select the two New Service Technician contact records. Click **Members** and click **OK**. Click **Save & Close**.

20. Select the **New Service Technicians** Contact Group and drag it to the **CP & L** folder in the Folders List.

LEAVE Outlook open for the next project.

Project CB2-3: Edit an Electronic Business Card

Now that Kim has created new contact records, she wants to make sure that all the CP & L contacts are located in the CP & L folder. Finally, she wants to dress up her electronic business card so that she can send it out to the Contact Group.

GET READY. USE the Kim Ralls contact record and the Contact Group created in the previous project.

1. If necessary, click the **People** button in the Navigation bar to display the Contacts window. If necessary, click the **Contacts** folder. If necessary, click **People** in the Current View group to display the People Hub.

2. Click the **Kim Ralls** contact. The Kim Ralls – Contact Card is displayed in the Contact Card Pane.

3. Click the **Outlook (Contacts)** link in the Contact Card Pane.

4. In the Options group on the Ribbon, click the **Business Card** button. The Edit Business Card dialog box is displayed.

5. In the *Card Design* area in the upper right of the dialog box, verify that **Image Left** is selected in the *Layout* field.

6. Also in the *Card Design* area, click the **Change** button. The Add Card Picture dialog box is displayed. Navigate to the data files for this project. Click the *Lights on* file and click **OK**.

7. In the Card Design area, click the **Image Area** field. Change the value to **20%**.

8. In the Card Design area, click the **Image Align** field. In the dropdown list, click **Fit to Edge**.

9. In the Card Design area, click the **Background** button. The Color dialog box is displayed. Click the **Define Custom Colors** button and select [a **medium soft gold**] shade. Click **OK**.

10. In the *Fields* area, click **E-mail** in the list of fields. Click the **Bold** button.

11. Click **OK**. The Edit Business Card dialog box is closed. Click **Save & Close** to save the business card.

12. On the HOME tab, click the **Forward Contact** button in the Share group. Select **As a Business Card**. A new message window is displayed with Kim's business card attached.

13. In the *To* field, key **New Service Technicians**. In the *Cc* field, key [**your e-mail address**].

14. In the message area, key the following text above the business card:

    Here is my new business card. Feel free to forward it to clients as needed. [Press **Enter** twice.]

15. Click the **Send** button. The message is moved to the Outbox and sent when the computer is connected to the Internet.

16. In the **Instant Search** box at the top of the Contact Index, key **cpandl**. Because this is the domain for the e-mail address you added in Project CB2-1, the three new addresses appear in the results list.

17. Click the **All Contact Items** button in the Scope group of the SEARCH TOOLS tab. One more contact record appears in the results list.

18. On the SEARCH TOOLS SEARCH tab, click the **More** button and select **City**.

19. In the *City* field, key **Springfield**.

20. Select the four contact records and click **Move** on the HOME tab – Actions group. A dropdown list of folders is displayed. Click **Other Folder**. The Move Items dialog box is displayed.

⚠️ **Troubleshooting** If you did not do all of the exercises in lesson 7, you will only have four contact records to move.

21. Click the **CP & L** folder and click **OK**. The contacts are moved to the CP & L folder but they still remain in the search results list onscreen.

22. Click the **Mail** button on the Navigation bar and select the **Kim Ralls** message you just sent. If necessary, click **Send/Receive All Folders** on the HOME tab.

23. Click the **Junk** button in the Delete group and select **Never Block this Group or Mailing List**. Select all the checkboxes and click **OK**.

LEAVE Outlook open for the next project.

Project CB2-4: **Manage Your Mailbox**

Now that her contacts are in place, Kim decides it's time to manage her mailbox. Kim knows that she will be receiving a lot of messages requesting new service from the Customer Service department. Messages could come from a dozen different Customer Service Representatives. However, the *Subject* field for every message contains the words "New Service Request." Kim decides to create a rule moving all of the requests to the New Service folder. After testing the rule, she sets up an archive of the New Service folder.

GET READY. USE the folders, contacts, and message you created in previous exercises. Your computer must be connected to the Internet to test the rule at the end of this project.

1. Click the **FILE** tab, then click **Manage Rules & Alerts**. The Rules and Alerts dialog box is displayed. Turn off all rules by deselecting the check boxes.

2. Click the **New Rule** button. The Rules Wizard dialog box is displayed.

3. In the Stay Organized category, click **Move messages with specific words in the subject to a folder**.

4. In the Step 2 area, click **specific words**. The Search Text dialog box is displayed.

5. In the *Specify words or phrases to search for in the subject* field, key **New Service Request**. Click the **Add** button. Click **OK** to close the Search Text dialog box and return to the Rules Wizard dialog box.

6. In the Step 2 area of the Rules Wizard dialog box, click **specified** to identify the destination folder. The Folders List is displayed in a new Rules and Alerts dialog box.

7. Click the **New Service** folder, and click **OK**. The specified destination folder is identified in the Rules Wizard dialog box.

8. Click the **Next** button three times to continue the Wizard without modifying conditions or actions.

9. Under Select exceptions, click the **except if the subject contains specific words** check box. Text is added to the rule description at the bottom of the Rules Wizard dialog box.

10. In the rule description area, click **specific words**. The Search Text dialog box is displayed.

11. In the *Specify words or phrases to search for in the subject* field, key **RE:**. Click the **Add** button. The *RE:* text is enclosed by quotation marks and added to the search list for this rule. Click **OK** to close the Search Text dialog box. The Rules Wizard dialog box is displayed.

Troubleshooting Be sure to include the colon in the specified words or any message subject containing the letters "re" will be an exception.

12. Click the **Next** button to continue the Wizard. The rule is displayed for your approval. Examine the rule carefully to verify that it is correct. Click the **Finish** button. The new rule is displayed in the Rules and Alerts dialog box. Click the **OK** button to close the Rules and Alerts dialog box.

13. On the HOME tab, click the **New Items** button and select **E-mail Message** to display a new Message window.

14. Address the message to [**your e-mail address**]. In the *Subject* field, key **New Service Request**. In the message area, key **Kim**. Send the message.

15. Create and send a second message to your e-mail address using **RE: New Service Request** in the *Subject* field. In the message area, key **Kim**. Click **Send**.

16. Click the **SEND/RECEIVE** tab and click **Send/Receive All Folders**, if necessary, to receive the messages. Verify that the New Service Request message was moved to the New Service folder and the RE: New Service Request message remained in the Inbox.

17. On the HOME tab, click **Rules** and select **Manage Rules & Alerts**. The Rules and Alerts dialog box is displayed. Turn off all rules. Click **OK** to close the Rules and Alerts dialog box.

18. If necessary, click the **Inbox** in the Folders Pane. Click the **Instant Search**, and key **Kim**. The message list is replaced with the messages containing the word *Kim*.

19. Select the messages that you sent in Projects CB2-1-CB2-4 and click **More** in the Quick Steps gallery on the HOME tab. Point to **New Quick Step** and select **Move to folder** from the fly out menu.

20. Click **Choose Folder** and select **New Service**. Click **Finish**. Now redo the search for "Kim" and then click the **New Service Quick Step** in the gallery to get all of the messages to move to the New Service folder.

21. Click the **New Service** folder. Mark the two e-mails with the business card attached as **Unread** by clicking the bar on the left of the message in the message list.

22. Click the **FILE** tab, click **Cleanup Tools** and select **Archive**. In the *Archive this folder and all subfolders* list, select **New Service**.

23. In the *Archive items older than* box, key **[tomorrow's date]**.

24. Click **Browse** and navigate to your solutions folder. Key **Project CB2-4_xx** (where *xx* is your initials). Click **OK** to select the archive location. Click **OK** to close the Archive dialog box.

25. Right click on the **Archives Outlook Data File** and select **Close "Archives"**.

CLOSE Outlook.

LESSON SKILL MATRIX

Skills	Exam Objective	Objective Number
Creating Appointments	Create calendar items	3.2.1
	Set calendar item times	3.2.5
	Create calendar items from messages	3.2.4
Setting Appointment Options	Configure reminders	3.3.3
	Change availability status	3.2.8
	Create recurring calendar items	3.2.2
	Mark as private	2.1.10
	Forward calendar items	3.3.2
Creating an Event		
Printing Appointment Details	Print Calendars	1.3.2

KEY TERMS

- appointment
- availability indicator
- banner
- Busy
- event
- Free
- iCalendar
- meeting
- Out of Office
- private
- recurring appointment
- tasks
- Tentative

© Thomas_EyeDesign/iStockphoto

As a marketing assistant, Terry Eminhizer knows the value of time. Terry manages her schedule and the schedules of two marketing representatives who are constantly on the road. By setting up travel arrangements and confirming appointments with clients, Terry gives the marketing reps more time to make bigger sales. Time is money. In this lesson, you will create and manage appointments and events in Outlook 2013.

© Thomas_EyeDesign/iStockphoto

SOFTWARE ORIENTATION

The Appointment Window

The Appointment window displayed in Figure 8-1 enables you to schedule an appointment. Scheduled appointments and events are displayed on your calendar, calendar peeks, and in your To-Do Bar.

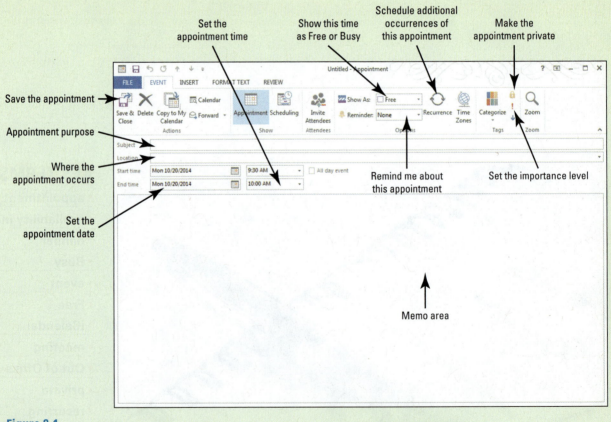

Figure 8-1

The Appointment window

Use the Appointment window to create an appointment or event. Refer to Figure 8-1 as you complete the following exercises.

CREATING APPOINTMENTS

The Bottom Line

In Outlook 2013, an appointment is a scheduled activity that does not require the user to invite other people or resources to attend. This might occur because the appointment only pertains to the user, such as recording a doctor's appointment that will keep the user out of the office. However, an appointment could also be created for occasions in which multiple people are going to attend but the other attendees don't use Outlook 2013 or the user isn't responsible for inviting the others. An appointment can occur once or at regularly scheduled intervals. In this section, you will create different kinds of appointments.

Creating a One-Time Appointment

Appointments that don't involve other people can include such activities as doctor's appointments and picking up your daughter after soccer practice. In this exercise, you will create a basic one-time appointment.

STEP BY STEP

Create a One-Time Appointment

GET READY. Before you begin these steps, be sure to launch Microsoft Outlook 2013.

1. Click the **Calendar** button in the Navigation bar to display your Calendar.
2. Click the **Month** button in the Arrange group on the Ribbon to display the Month view, if necessary.
3. Click [**next Friday's date**] on the monthly calendar.

Take Note

Throughout this chapter you will see information that appears in black text within brackets, such as [Press **Enter**], or [**next Friday's date**]. The information contained in the brackets is intended to be directions for you rather than something you actually type word for word. It will instruct you to perform an action or substitute text. Do **not** type the actual text that appears within brackets.

Another Way

You can also select the date in the Appointment window. If the date is displayed in the monthly calendar, it is easier to select the date in the calendar. For appointments that occur several months in the future, it is easier to select the date in the Appointment window.

Another Way

You can key text in the Start time and End time fields rather than a date. Outlook 2013 translates the text into a date.

4. On the HOME tab, click the **New Appointment** button. The Untitled – Appointment window in Figure 8-1 is displayed. The date selected in the monthly calendar is already displayed in the *Start time* and *End time* fields.
5. In the *Subject* field, key **Blood Drive**.
6. In the *Location* field, key **Van in the South parking lot**.
7. In the *Start time* fields, click the **Time down arrow**. A list of possible starting times appears.
8. Select **2:00 PM**. By default, each appointment is 30 minutes long, so the time in the *End time* field changes to 2:30 PM.
9. Select an *End Time* of **3:00 PM**. You need to fill out forms before donating and eat a few cookies after donating, so give yourself a bit more time.
10. Click the **Save & Close** button in the Actions group on the Ribbon. The appointment is displayed on the calendar, as shown in Figure 8-2.

Figure 8-2

Figure 8-2

The appointment scheduled on the calendar

The scheduled appointment

PAUSE. LEAVE the Outlook 2013 Calendar open to use in the next exercise.

CERTIFICATION READY?   3.2.1

How do you create a calendar item?

In Outlook 2013, there are three different kinds of calendar items that can be created: appointments, meetings, and events. Table 8-1 explains when to use each of these items.

Table 8-1

Calendar Items

Calendar Item	Description
Appointment	An appointment is an activity with a specific start and end time that does not involve inviting any other attendees.
Meeting	A meeting is an activity that has a specific start and end time and that does involve inviting various attendees. Attendees can be either resources or people, and meeting attendance can be either required or optional.
Event	An event is an activity that does not have a specific start and end time (and is therefore blocked out for the entire day) and that, like an appointment, does not involve inviting any other attendees.

By default, when you select a future date in the calendar, the displayed time of the appointment in the Appointment window will be the start of the workday.

Creating an Appointment from a Message

CERTIFICATION READY?   3.2.5

How do you set calendar item times?

Sometimes, a message can lead to an appointment. For example, your son's cross-country running coach sends you a message about the awards banquet or you receive a message that a farewell lunch will be held Thursday for a coworker in your department. When you create an appointment from a message you received, the message text is saved automatically in the Appointment window's memo area. This stores the related message with the appointment. In this exercise, you will simply use an e-mail message to create an appointment.

STEP BY STEP   **Create an Appointment from a Message**

GET READY. Before you begin these steps, be sure to launch Microsoft Outlook 2013.

1. If necessary, click the **Calendar** button on the Navigation bar to display the Calendar feature.

2. Click the **New Items** button on the HOME tab. A list of available items is displayed.

3. Click **E-mail Message** in the list to display a new Message window.

4. In the *To* field, key [**your e-mail address**]. In the *Subject* field, key **Vice President Duerr Visiting Thursday afternoon**. In the message area, key **Vice President Bernard Duerr is visiting this division on Thursday. An employee meeting will be held in the company cafeteria from 2:00 PM to 4:00 PM. Attendance is mandatory.**

5. Click the **Send** button.

6. Click **Mail** on the Navigation bar to return to your Inbox.

7. Click the **Send/Receive All Folders** button if the message has not arrived yet.

8. Click the **Vice President Duerr Visiting Thursday afternoon** message to select it.

9. Click the **Move** button in the Move group on the HOME tab.

10. In the dropdown list, click **Other Folder**. The Move Items dialog box is displayed, as shown in Figure 8-3.

Figure 8-3

Move Items dialog box

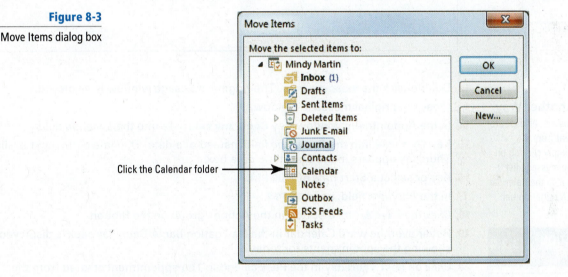

Click the Calendar folder →

11. In the Move Items dialog box, click **Calendar** and then click **OK**. An Appointment window is opened. The message subject is displayed in the *Subject* field in the Appointment window. A link to the original message is displayed in the Memo area of the Appointment window, as shown in Figure 8-4.

Figure 8-4

Creating an appointment from
a message

Subject created
automatically from
message subject →

Link to the original
message used to
create the appointment →

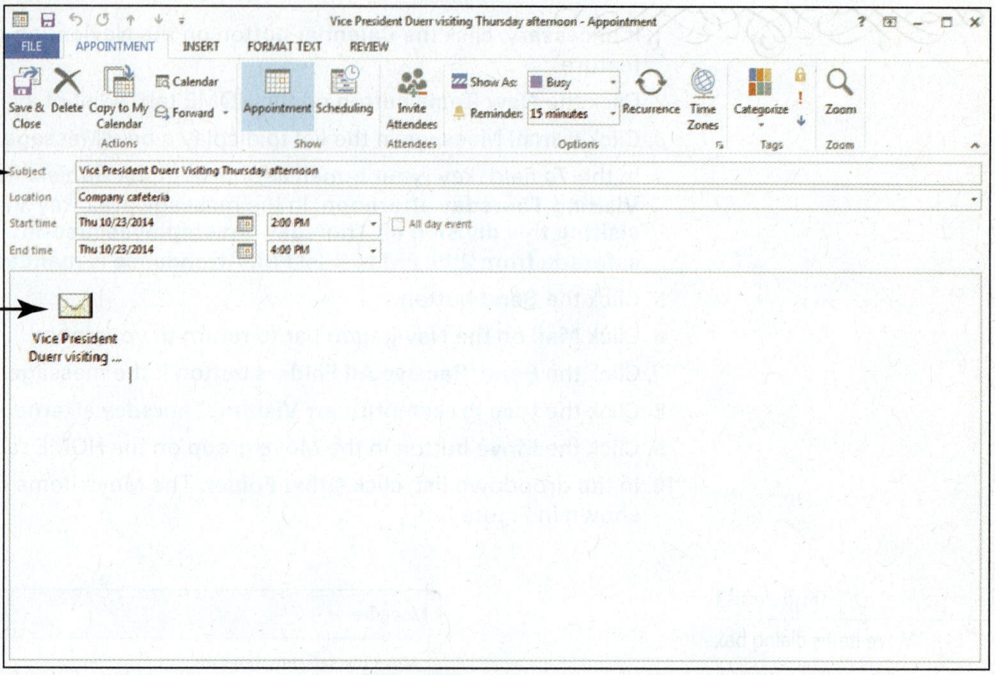

Vice President
Duerr visiting ...

Another Way

You can also create
an appointment from a
message by simply clicking on
the item in the message list
and dragging it to the Calendar
button in the Navigation bar.

CERTIFICATION
READY?   **3.2.4**

How do you create an
appointment from a
message?

12. Double-click the **message icon**. The original message window is displayed.

13. Close the original message window.

14. In the Appointment window, key **Company cafeteria** into the *Location* field.

15. Key **Thursday** into the *Start time* field instead of a date. The date of the next available Thursday appears in the Start time date box.

16. Key or select a *Start time* of **2:00 PM**.

17. In the *End time* field, key **4:00 PM**.

18. Click the **Save & Close** button in the Actions group on the Ribbon.

19. Hover over the word Calendar in the Navigation bar. A Calendar peek is displayed showing the appointments for today.

20. Click on **next Thursday** in the Peek calendar. The appointment created from the message is displayed, as shown in Figure 8-5.

Figure 8-5

Viewing an appointment from a message in a peek

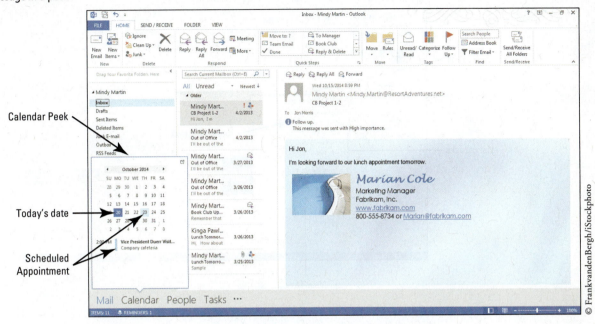

© Frank van den Bergh/iStockphoto

PAUSE. LEAVE Outlook 2013 open to use in the next exercise.

Creating an Appointment from a Task

Tasks describe activities you have to do. Appointments tell you when activities are performed. Tasks frequently become appointments when the time to perform a task is scheduled. The task text is saved automatically in the Appointment window's memo area, storing the information with the appointment. In this exercise, you will create an appointment from a task.

STEP BY STEP   **Create an Appointment from a Task**

GET READY. Before you begin these steps, be sure to launch Microsoft Outlook 2013.

1. If necessary, click the **Calendar** button on the Navigation bar to display the Calendar feature.

2. Hover over the **Tasks** button in the Navigation bar to display the Tasks peek.

 Cross Ref   You can find more information on tasks in Lesson 11.

3. Click the *Type a new task* field, and key **Lunch with Vice President Duerr**. [Press **Enter**]. The task is created, as shown in Figure 8-6.

Figure 8-6

Viewing a new Task on the peek

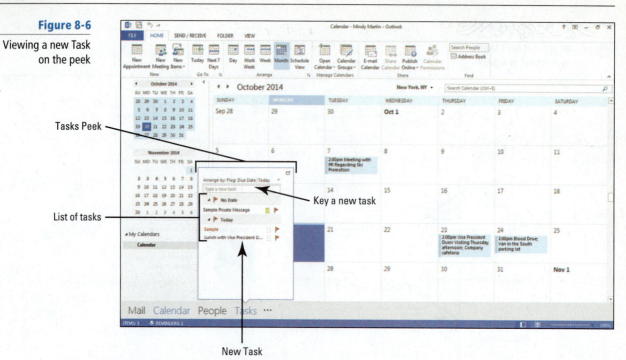

Tasks Peek

List of tasks

Key a new task

New Task

4. Click the **Lunch with Vice President Duerr** task.

5. Drag it to Thursday's date on the calendar. You already have an appointment for the employee meeting from 2:00 PM to 4:00 PM for that date.

6. Double-click the **Lunch with Vice President Duerr** item in the calendar. The Lunch with Vice President Duerr – Event window containing the task information is displayed. Because our task did not specify a specific start and end time, Outlook 2013 interprets the task as an event, which is a meeting or appointment that lasts all day long. You'll need to change that so that you can add the appropriate times.

7. Click the **All day event** check box to clear the check box. The time fields become available.

8. Key a *Start time* of **12:30 PM** and an *End time* of **1:45 PM**. The Appointment window should be similar to Figure 8-7.

Figure 8-7

Creating an appointment from a task

Task used to create appointment

Subject:	Lunch with Vice President Duerr
Start Date:	Monday, October 20, 2014
Due Date:	Monday, October 20, 2014
Status:	Not Started
Percent Complete:	0%
Total Work:	0 hours
Actual Work:	0 hours
Owner:	Mindy Martin

9. Click the **Save & Close** button in the Actions group on the Ribbon. The appointment created from the task is displayed on the calendar.

PAUSE. LEAVE Outlook 2013 open to use in the next exercise.

SETTING APPOINTMENT OPTIONS

The Bottom Line

Creating a basic appointment is one thing, but many appointments don't fit a cookie-cutter mold. For example, you might need to create an appointment that occurs every other Friday, mark an appointment as private, or forward an appointment on to a colleague. You can use the appointment options to customize the details of each appointment. In this section, you will set some appointment options to create a recurring, private meeting.

Creating and Customizing Appointments

Outlook 2013 offers many different kinds of options that you can use to set appointments. Appointment options are located in both the Options and Tags groups on the APPOINTMENT tab. The Time Zones option allows you to establish the time zone for an appointment, which can be very helpful when planning appointments with people in multiple time zones. The Show As option allows you to let others know whether you can be disturbed during a meeting. You can set the Reminder tool to give you an alert when an appointment approaches. In this exercise, you will create an appointment and customize it with tools in the Options group.

STEP BY STEP **Create and Customize an Appointment**

GET READY. Before you begin these steps, be sure to launch Microsoft Outlook 2013.

1. If necessary, click the **Calendar** button on the Navigation bar to display the Calendar feature.

2. Double-click **next Wednesday's date** on the monthly calendar. A new Event window is displayed.

Take Note   In the Month view, double-click on a date square to open a new Untitled – Event window. Double-clicking on the date in the upper left corner of the square changes the calendar arrangement to Day view for the selected date.

3. In the *Subject* field, key **Customizing Appointment Options**.

4. In the *Location* field, key **Training Center**.

5. Click the **All day event** check box to clear the check box because this appointment has a start and end time. The window changes to an appointment window.

6. Key a *Start time* of **1:00 PM** and an *End time* of **1:45 PM**.

7. Click the **Reminder** dropdown arrow in the Options group and select **1 hour** from the list of available times that appears.

8. Click the **Time Zones** button in the Options group on the Ribbon. New Time Zone boxes appear next to the Start and End time boxes.

9. Select **Pacific Time** from the list because the appointment is going to be conducted via a video feed from California.

CERTIFICATION READY? **3.3.3**

How do you set appointment options to remind you of an appointment?

 Cross Ref   You can find more information about using time zones and how they affect your calendar in Lesson 11.

10. Click the **Show As down arrow** in the Options group to display the Show As options, as shown in Figure 8-8.

Figure 8-8

Setting Appointment options

Select an option to indicate your availability

Time Zone boxes

11. Select **Tentative**.

12. Click the **Save & Close** button in the Actions group on the Ribbon. The appointment is displayed on the calendar. Notice that the Show As indicator on the left side of the appointment is striped to match the appearance of the Tentative option in the Show As drop list shown in Figure 8-8.

PAUSE. LEAVE Outlook 2013 open to use in the next exercise.

The *Show As* field in the Appointment window determines how the time is displayed on your calendar. When others look at your calendar, this **availability indicator** tells others if you are available and how definite your schedule is for a specific activity. You can choose from four options displayed in Table 8-2.

Table 8-2

Availability Indicator Options

Show As	Description
Free	No activities are scheduled for this time period. You are available.
Busy	An activity is scheduled for this time period. You are not available for other activities.
Tentative	An activity is scheduled for this time period, but the activity might not occur. You might be available for other activities.
Out of Office	An activity is scheduled for this time period, and you are not available because you are out of the office.

Scheduling a Recurring Appointment

A **recurring appointment** is an appointment that occurs at regular intervals. Recurring appointments are common in many calendars. Weekly soccer games, monthly lunch dates with an old friend, and semi-annual company dinners are examples of recurring appointments. Recurrences can be scheduled based on daily, weekly, monthly, and yearly intervals. In this exercise, you set a recurring appointment.

Schedule a Recurring Appointment

GET READY. Before you begin these steps, be sure to launch Microsoft Outlook 2013.

1. If necessary, click the Calendar button in the Navigation bar to display your Calendar.
2. Click the Month button to display the Month view, if necessary.
3. Double-click the [fourth Monday of this month] on the monthly calendar. If the fourth Monday of this month has passed, click the fourth Monday of next month.
4. In the *Subject* field, key Engineering Lunch.
5. In the *Location* field, key Company cafeteria.
6. Click the All day event check box to clear the check box.
7. Key a *Start time* of 12:15 PM and an *End time* of 1:15 PM.
8. Click in the Memo area, and key New techniques and troubleshooting.
9. Click the Recurrence button in the Options group. The Appointment Recurrence dialog box is displayed, as shown in Figure 8-9.

Figure 8-9

Appointment Recurrence dialog box

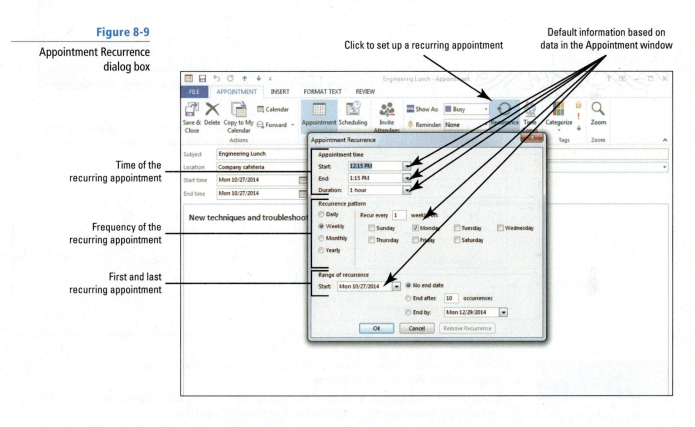

Click to set up a recurring appointment

Default information based on data in the Appointment window

Time of the recurring appointment

Frequency of the recurring appointment

First and last recurring appointment

10. In the Appointment Recurrence dialog box, click Monthly in the Recurrence Pattern area. Selecting a different frequency changes the available patterns.
11. On the right side in the Recurrence Pattern area, click the button to select The fourth Monday of every 1 month(s). Because the date of the first recurring appointment was the fourth Monday of the month, the fourth Monday of every month is offered as a likely pattern (as is the selected date in each month), as shown in Figure 8-10.

Figure 8-10

Setting the recurrence pattern

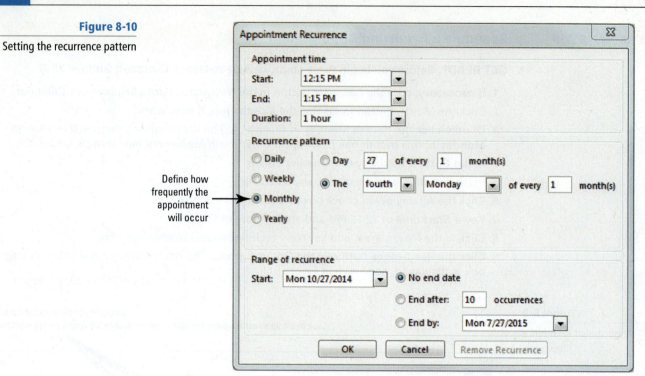

Define how
frequently the
appointment
will occur →

12. Click **OK** to set the recurrence pattern and return to the Appointment window. The recurrence pattern is displayed in the Appointment window, as shown in Figure 8-11.

Figure 8-11

Recurring appointment

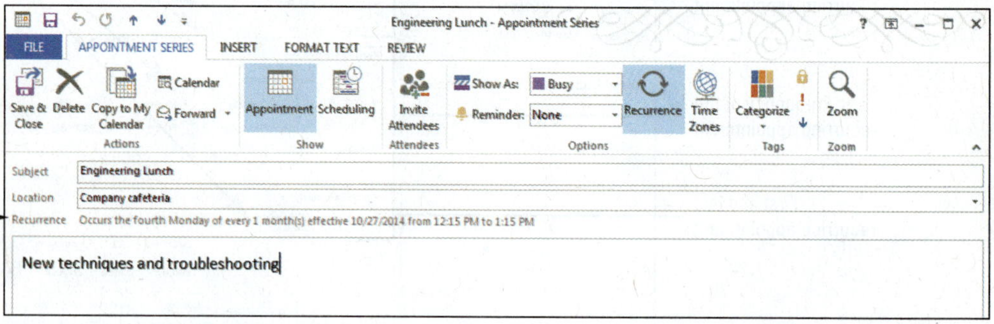

Recurring pattern →

13. Click the **Save & Close** button in the Actions group on the Ribbon. The appointment is displayed on the monthly calendar.

14. Click the **Forward** arrow button at the top of the monthly calendar to verify that the recurring appointment is displayed in next month's calendar.

15. Click the **Today** button in the Go To group on the HOME tab to return to the current month.

PAUSE. LEAVE the Outlook 2013 Calendar open to use in the next exercise.

CERTIFICATION READY? 3.2.2

How do you create a recurring appointment or event?

Marking an Appointment as Private

You can also choose to mark an appointment as **private**. This feature blocks the details of an activity from anyone whom you've delegated access to read your Calendar account using Microsoft Exchange Server. When you've marked an appointment as private, you can change the way your schedule prints so that the details of private appointments don't print out. In this exercise, you will mark an appointment as private. At the end of the lesson, you'll print the exercises for the week and see how a private appointment appears when printed.

 Cross Ref

In Lesson 5, you learned more about delegating access to your e-mail account.

STEP BY STEP   **Mark an Appointment as Private**

GET READY. Before you begin these steps, be sure to launch Microsoft Outlook 2013.

1. Show the Calendar in Month view.

2. Click [next Friday's date] on the monthly calendar. The Blood drive is already scheduled for 2:00 PM on that date.

3. On the HOME tab, click the New Appointment button. The Appointment window in Figure 8-1 is displayed. The date selected in the monthly calendar is already displayed in the *Start time* and *End time* fields.

4. In the *Subject* field, key Interview Rebecca Laszlo for Receptionist.

5. In the *Location* field, key My office.

6. In the *Start time* field, key or select a time of 4:30 PM and an End time of 5:00 PM, if necessary.

7. Click the Private button in the Tags group on the Ribbon.

8. Click the Save & Close button in the Actions group on the Ribbon. The appointment is displayed on your monthly calendar.

9. Hover over the new appointment. A flyout window appears displaying details about the appointment. Outlook 2013 displays a lock next to the private appointment, as shown in Figure 8-12.

Figure 8-12

A private appointment

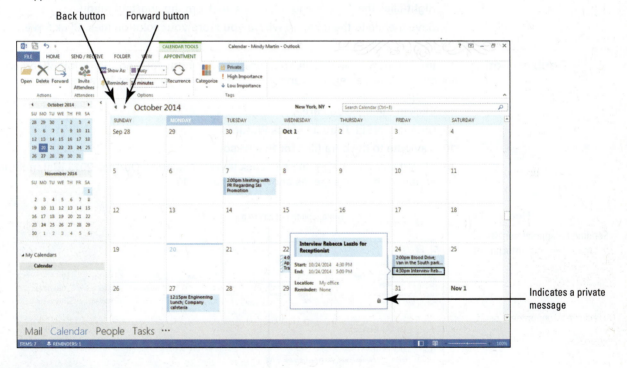

PAUSE. LEAVE Outlook 2013 open to use in the next exercise.

<table>
<tr><td>**CERTIFICATION READY?** 2.1.10</td></tr>
<tr><td>How do you mark an appointment as private?</td></tr>
</table>

In the previous exercise, you marked an appointment as Private by clicking the Private button before saving the appointment. You also can open an existing appointment and click the Private button to turn on or off the Private feature for that appointment. Be sure to save the modified appointment after changing the Private status.

Take Note   Although marking appointments and events as private hides the details from the casual viewer, it does not ensure privacy. Any person who has Read privileges to your calendar could access the information by a variety of methods.

Forwarding an Appointment

Forwarding an appointment to someone allows you to invite someone to join you or notifies them of your schedule. You can forward an appointment to another Outlook 2013 user as an attached Outlook 2013 item. Or, if you want to send the appointment to someone that may not be using Outlook 2013, you can send it in an iCalendar file format. The **iCalendar** *(.ics)* format is interchangeable between most calendar and e-mail applications, which makes it a versatile tool. When you click on an iCalendar attachment, Outlook 2013 automatically adds the appointment to your calendar. In this exercise, you will forward an appointment as an attachment.

STEP BY STEP   **Forward an Appointment**

GET READY. Before you begin these steps, be sure to launch Microsoft Outlook 2013.

1. Show the Calendar in the Month view.
2. Select the **Lunch with Vice President Duerr** appointment. If necessary, click the **CALENDAR TOOLS APPOINTMENT** tab.
3. Click the **Forward** down arrow in the Actions group. Select **Forward as iCalendar**. The FW: Lunch with Vice President Duerr message window is displayed with the appointment attached as an .ics file.
4. In the *To* field, key [**your e-mail address**].
5. In the message area, key **Come and join us at McCarty's.** [Press **Enter** twice.]
6. Right-click the **.ics file** and click **Save As** from the shortcut menu.
7. Save the file to the location where you store your solution files. Click **Save**.

⚠️ **Troubleshooting** It is important to save the file to a location that both you and the recipient can access. If you are on the same server, you can save it there. If not, you might try a website.

8. Click in the message area.
9. Click the **INSERT** tab and click **Pictures**.
10. Navigate to the data files for this lesson.
11. Click the **iCalendar.jpg** file and click **Insert**. The stock Outlook 2013 iCalendar image is added to the message, as shown in Figure 8-13.

Figure 8-13

Sending an appointment as an attachment

The appointment saved as an .ics file

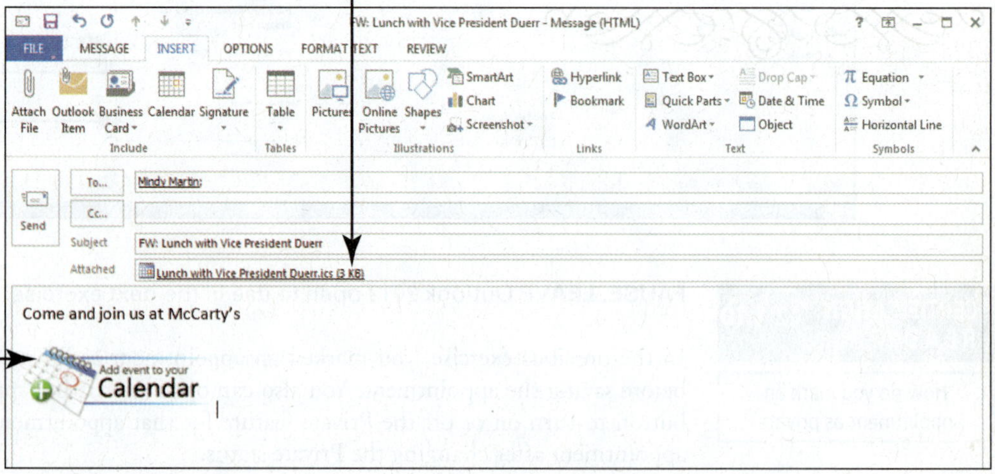

Turn the image into a link to the appointment

12. Right-click the image and select **Hyperlink**. The Insert Hyperlink dialog box is displayed.

13. Select **Existing File or Web Page**, then use the Look In directory to navigate to the solution folder where you stored the appointment, as shown in Figure 8-14.

Figure 8-14

Insert Hyperlink dialog box

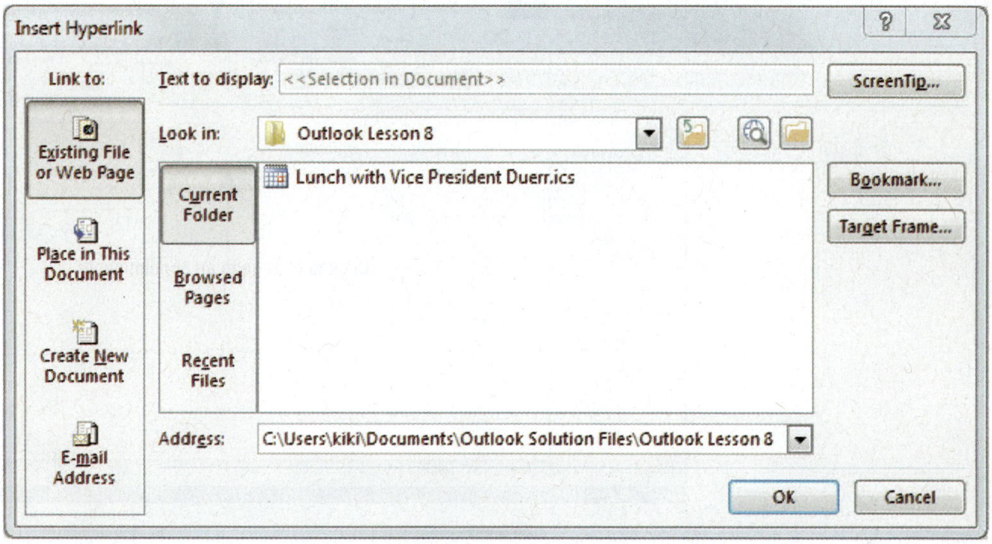

14. Select the appointment and click **OK**.

15. Click **Send**.

16. Click the **Mail** button on the Navigation bar to return to the Inbox. If the message hasn't arrived, click the **Send/Receive All Folders** button.

17. Click the **FW: Lunch with Vice President Duerr message** in the message list. The message appears in the Reading Pane.

18. Click the **iCalendar image**. The original Lunch with Vice President Duerr – Appointment window opened.

19. Close the Appointment window. Save changes when prompted.

PAUSE. LEAVE Outlook 2013 open to use in the next exercise.

CERTIFICATION READY?   3.3.2

How do you send an appointment as an iCalendar attachment?

CREATING AN EVENT

The Bottom Line

An event is an activity that lasts one or more days. In your calendar, an event is displayed as a **banner** text prominently displayed at the top of the day window that indicates an activity is going to require the entire day. For scheduling purposes, an event is displayed as free time, meaning that you are still available for appointments and meetings. In this exercise, you will create an event in Outlook 2013.

STEP BY STEP   **Create an Event**

GET READY. Before you begin these steps, be sure to launch Microsoft Outlook 2013.

1. Show the Calendar in Month view.

2. On the HOME tab, click the **New Items** button and select the **All Day Event** option. The Untitled — Event window is displayed (see Figure 8-15).

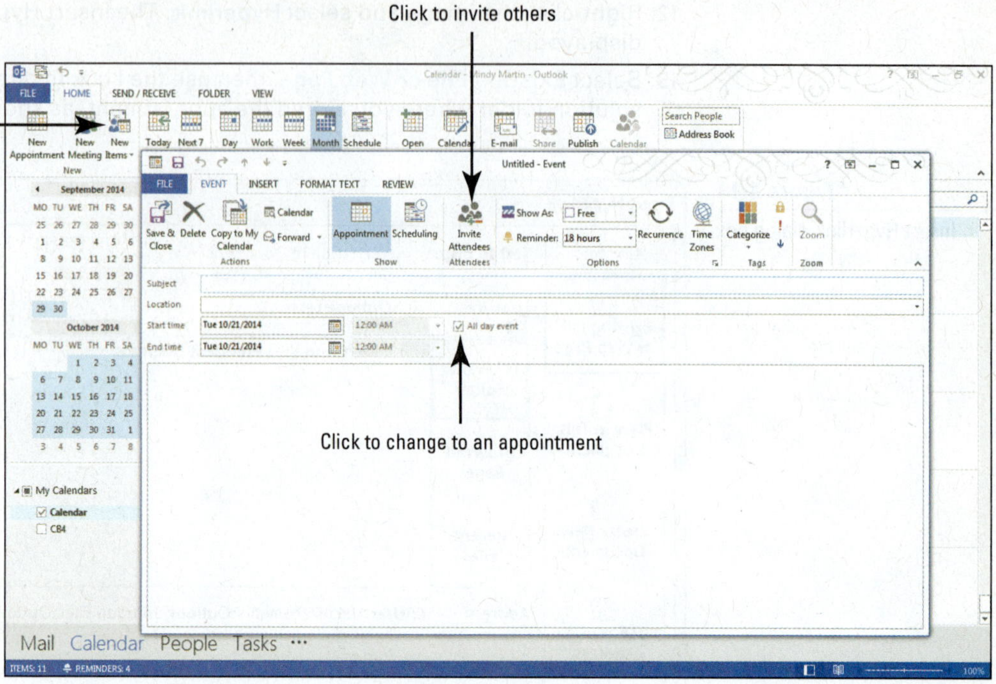

Figure 8-15

Creating an Event

Click to create an Event →

Click to invite others

Click to change to an appointment

Mail   Calendar   People   Tasks   ···

3. In the *Subject* field, key **Anniversary**.

4. In the *Start time* field, key [**the date of your anniversary or a family member's anniversary.**]

5. Click the **Private** button in the Tags group on the Ribbon.

6. Click the **Recurrence** button in the Options group on the Ribbon. The Appointment Recurrence dialog box is displayed.

7. In the Appointment Recurrence dialog box, click **Yearly** in the *Recurrence pattern* area. Selecting a different frequency changes the patterns available for selection on the right side in the Recurrence pattern area.

8. On the right side in the *Recurrence pattern* area, click the button to select **On [month] [date]**.

9. Click **OK** to set the recurrence pattern and return to the Event window. The recurrence pattern is displayed in the Event window.

10. Click the **Reminder** dropdown list arrow. Click the **1 week** option, to schedule Outlook 2013 to remind you one week in advance of the scheduled event.

Another Way
The methods of creating new appointments from messages or tasks that you performed in the earlier exercises in this lesson can also be used to create events.

11. Click the **Save & Close** button in the Actions group on the Ribbon. The appointment is added to your calendar.

12. Click the **Forward** button at the top of the monthly calendar to verify that the recurring event is displayed on the correct date. Click the **Back** button at the top of the monthly calendar to return to the current month.

PAUSE. LEAVE Outlook 2013 open to use in the next exercise.

PRINTING APPOINTMENT DETAILS

The Bottom Line

In Outlook 2013, it is easy to print out the details about an appointment or even print out a calendar. The Memo Style format allows you to print the selected appointment. You can use settings in the Print dialog box to select the print style and the range of dates to include.

Printing Appointment Details

In this section, you will print the details about one of your appointments.

Print Appointment Details

GET READY. Before you begin these steps, be sure to launch Microsoft Outlook 2013.

1. Show the Calendar in Month view.
2. Click **FILE** to open Backstage view and click **Print** in the Navigation Pane to open the Print settings page.
3. Click the **Print Options** button. The Print dialog box is displayed, as shown in Figure 8-16.

Figure 8-16

Print dialog box

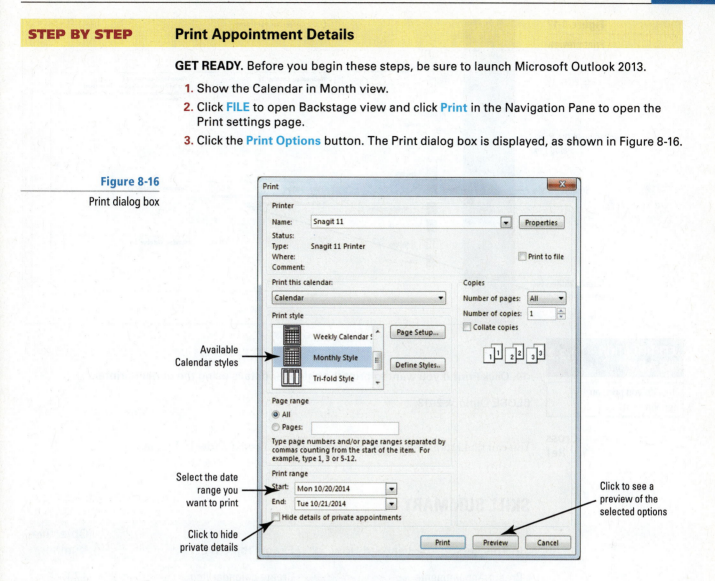

Available Calendar styles

Select the date range you want to print

Click to hide private details

Click to see a preview of the selected options

4. In the *Print Style* area, click **Weekly Agenda Style**.
5. In the *Start* box of the Print range area, key today's date.
6. In the *End* box, key [**next Friday's date**].
7. Click the **Hide details of private appointments** check box.
8. Click the **Preview** button. The Print dialog box is closed, and the print page of Backstage view is displayed showing a preview of the new settings.
9. Click the Preview to zoom in on the print out, as shown in Figure 8-17.

Figure 8-17

Print preview

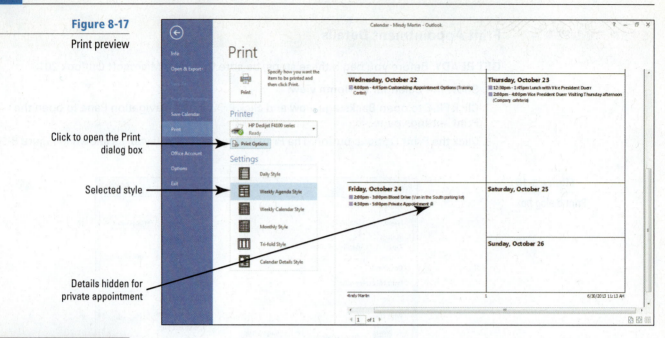

Click to open the Print dialog box →

Selected style →

Details hidden for private appointment →

CERTIFICATION
READY?   1.3.2

How do you print an appointment?

10. Click **Print** if you want to print the calendar details using the default printer.

CLOSE Outlook 2013.

🔍 **Cross Ref**

You can find more information about using the Calendar folder in Lesson 10.

SKILL SUMMARY

In This Lesson You Learned How To:	Exam Objective	Objective Number
Create Appointments	Create calendar items	3.2.1
	Set calendar item times	3.2.5
	Create calendar items from messages	3.2.4
Set Appointment Options	Configure reminders	3.3.3
	Change availability status	3.2.8
	Create recurring calendar item	3.2.2
	Mark as private	2.1.10
	Forward calendar items	3.3.2
Create an Event		
Print Appointment Details	Print Calendars	1.3.2

Knowledge Assessment

Multiple Choice

Select the letter beside the term that best completes each of the following statements.

1. An event is displayed as
   a. a lock.
   b. an exclamation point.
   c. a seal.
   d. a banner.

2. The _____ setting indicates that an activity is scheduled for this time period, but the activity might not occur.
   a. Show As: Possible
   b. Show As: Free
   c. Show As: Saved
   d. Show As: Tentative

3. An activity that lasts one or more days is referred to as a(n)_____.
   a. extended activity
   b. session
   c. event
   d. All of the above

4. A _____ appointment is one that occurs at regular intervals.
   a. recurring
   b. regular
   c. routine
   d. repeating

5. In Outlook 2013, an activity that has to be performed is a(n) _____.
   a. duty
   b. task
   c. event
   d. chore

6. The _____ contains an option to print appointments from selected dates.
   a. Appointment Options dialog box
   b. Print dialog box
   c. Edit Settings box
   d. Layout dialog box

7. For scheduling purposes, an event is displayed as _____ time.
   a. busy
   b. free
   c. tentative
   d. out of office

8. The _____ enables you to create a schedule.
   a. calendar
   b. appointment book
   c. weekly organizer
   d. ledger

9. The _____ tag protects the details of an activity from a casual observer.
   a. private
   b. secure
   c. encrypted
   d. lock

10. A(n) _____ is a scheduled activity that does not require sending invitations to other people or resources.
   a. private meeting
   b. solo meeting
   c. closed event
   d. appointment

True/False

Circle T if the statement is true or F if the statement is false.

T F 1. You are not available for other activities when your time is displayed as Busy.

T F 2. By default, each appointment is one hour long.

T F 3. Recurrences can be scheduled based on daily, weekly, monthly, and yearly intervals.

T F 4. A task cannot be used to create an appointment unless the task is private.

T F 5. Appointments require invitations sent through Outlook 2013.

T F 6. Marking an appointment as private ensures that users who can view your calendar cannot view the details of the private appointment.

T F 7. You can key text in the *Start time* and *End time* fields rather than a date.

T F 8. Selecting a different frequency changes the available recurrence patterns displayed.

T F 9. A message is deleted automatically when it is used to create an appointment.

T F 10. An event is displayed as a banner in your calendar.

Competency Assessment

Project 8-1: Create a One-Time Appointment

You have been selected to create a presentation about a new product your company will sell in the coming year. You will deliver the presentation at a company dinner on Wednesday. Schedule the time to prepare the presentation.

GET READY. LAUNCH Outlook 2013 if it is not already running.

1. Click the **Calendar** button in the Navigation bar to display your Calendar.
2. Click the **Month** button to display the Month view, if necessary.
3. Click [**next Tuesday's date**] on the monthly calendar.
4. On the HOME tab, click the **New Appointment** button. The Appointment window is displayed.
5. In the *Subject* field, key **Prepare New Product Presentation**.
6. In the *Start time* fields, key or select the time of **9:30 AM**. Key or select the *End time* of **2:00 PM**.
7. Click the **Save & Close** button in the Actions group on the Ribbon. The appointment is added to the calendar.

LEAVE Outlook 2013 open for the next project.

Project 8-2: Schedule Vacation

Your boss has finally approved your vacation request for July. Now that it's official, it's time add your vacation to the calendar.

GET READY. LAUNCH Outlook 2013 if it is not already running.

1. Click the **Calendar** button in the Navigation bar to display the Calendar folder.
2. Click the **Forward** arrow button until the calendar displays the next July.
3. Double-click the first **Monday** in July. An Event window is displayed.
4. In the *Subject* field, key **Vacation**.
5. In the *End time* field, key **Friday** as the end of your vacation.

6. Click the **Show As** drop down arrow to adjust the availability indicator. Select the **Out of Office** option.

7. Click the **All day event** check box to select the option, if necessary. The time fields are dimmed.

8. Click the **Save & Close** button in the Actions group on the Ribbon. The Event is added to your calendar.

LEAVE Outlook 2013 open for the next project.

Proficiency Assessment

Project 8-3: Create an Appointment from a Message

A friend sent you a message about a concert in November. Create an appointment from the message.

GET READY. LAUNCH Outlook 2013 if it is not already running.

1. Click the **Calendar** button in the Navigation bar if necessary to display the Calendar folder.

2. Click the **New Items** button on the HOME tab to display the available options. Select **E-mail Message**.

3. In the *To* field, key [**your e-mail address**]. In the *Subject* field, key **Concert!** In the message area, key [**the name of your favorite musical performer**] **is coming to** [**the name of local the concert hall**]**! Mark November 15 on your calendar! I've already bought our tickets!** Click the **Send** button.

4. Return to your **Inbox**, if necessary. Click the **Send/Receive All Folders** button if the message has not arrived yet.

5. Click the **Concert!** message and drag it to the Calendar button on the Navigation bar to open a Concert! – Appointment window.

6. Key **November 15** in the *Start time* field. Key or select **7:00 PM**.

7. Key or select an *End time* of **11:00 PM**.

8. Click the **Save & Close** button in the Actions group on the Ribbon.

LEAVE Outlook 2013 open for the next project.

Project 8-4: Schedule a Recurring Appointment

Every week, you collect information to track the difference between goals and actual sales. Create a recurring appointment every Monday to gather the previous week's information and post it for the managers to review.

GET READY. LAUNCH Outlook 2013 if it is not already running.

1. Click the **Calendar** button in the Navigation bar to display the Calendar folder, if necessary.

2. Click the **first Monday of next month** on the monthly calendar.

3. On the HOME tab, click the **New Appointment** button. The Appointment window is displayed.

4. In the *Subject* field, key **Prepare Sales Report**.

5. In the *Start time* field, key or select **8:30 AM**. Key or select an *End time* of **9:30 AM**.

6. Click the **Recurrence** button in the Options group on the Ribbon. The Appointment Recurrence dialog box is displayed.

7. Click **OK** to accept the suggested recurrence pattern and return to the Appointment window.
8. Click the **Save & Close** button in the Actions group on the Ribbon. The appointment is added to the calendar.

LEAVE Outlook 2013 open for the next project.

Mastery Assessment

Project 8-5: Mark an Appointment as Private

In Project 8-3, you created an appointment for the concert. Your taste in music might not be appreciated by everyone who views your calendar. Make the appointment private. Note: You should only print this assignment if your instructor has asked you to.

GET READY. LAUNCH Outlook 2013 if it is not already running.

1. Click the **Calendar** button in the Navigation bar to display the Calendar folder.
2. Display the **November** calendar.
3. Double-click the **Concert!** appointment to open it.
4. Click the **Private** button in the Tags group.
5. Click the **Save & Close** button in the Actions group. The private appointment is added to the calendar.
6. Click the **FILE** tab and select **Print** in the Navigation Pane.
7. Select the **Calendar Details Style** and click the **Print Options** button.
8. Set the Print Range to *Start* and *End* on **November 15**.
9. Click the **Print** button. Turn the printout in to your instructor.

LEAVE Outlook 2013 open for the next project.

Project 8-6: Create and Print an Appointment from a Task

Last week, a coworker asked you to review a new marketing presentation that he finished yesterday. Turn the task into an appointment to review the presentation tomorrow after lunch. Note: You should only print this assignment if your instructor has asked you to.

GET READY. LAUNCH Outlook 2013 if it is not already running.

1. Switch back to the current month in the calendar. Display the Tasks peek on the Navigation bar.
2. Click the *Type a new task* field, and key **Review presentation for Gary Tambor**. [Press **Enter**]. The task is created.
3. Click the **Review presentation for Gary Tambor** task. Drag it to [**tomorrow's date**] on the calendar.
4. Double-click the **Review presentation for Gary Tambor** item in the calendar. An Event window is displayed.
5. Click the **All day event** check box to clear the check box. The time fields become available.
6. Key or select a *Start time* of **3:30 PM** and an *End time* of **5:00 PM**.
7. Set the appointment as **High Importance**.
8. Click the **Save & Close** button in the Actions group on the Ribbon. The appointment is added to the calendar.
9. With the appointment selected, click the **FILE** tab and select **Print** in the Navigation Pane.
10. Select **Memo Style** in the Settings area and click **Print**. Turn the printout in to your instructor.

CLOSE Outlook 2013.

LESSON SKILL MATRIX

Skills	Exam Objective	Objective Number
Creating a Meeting Request	Create calendar items	3.2.1
	Use the scheduling assistant	3.2.7
	Utilize Room Finder	3.2.10
	Create calendar items from messages	3.2.4
	Set calendar item importance	3.3.1
	Configure reminders	3.3.3
Responding to a Meeting Request	Respond to invitations	3.3.5
Managing a Meeting		
Updating a Meeting Request	Update calendar items	3.3.6
	Schedule resources	3.2.9
	Add participants	3.3.4
	Cancel calendar items	3.2.3
Managing a Recurring Meeting	Create recurring calendar items	3.2.2
Sharing Meeting Notes	Share meeting notes	3.3.7

KEY TERMS

- cancel
- mandatory attendee
- meeting
- meeting organizer
- meeting request
- occurrence
- optional attendee
- recurring meeting
- resource

© Chimpinski/iStockphoto

© Chimpinski/iStockphoto

Tailspin Toys has been working with Resort Adventures on a new adventure sports game. The project is scheduled to move into its final phase next month. Gabe Mares, Software Development Manager for Tailspin Toys, just finished reviewing the latest bug reports for Project Snow. Unfortunately, the list is much longer than it should be at this stage in the software development cycle. If the problems don't get resolved quickly, they won't be able to meet their deadline. It is obviously time to call a meeting to identify the reason for the long list of problems and determine how the problems could be resolved to meet the project deadlines. The Outlook 2013 Calendar feature is a great tool for managing your meetings because of the flexibility and control it gives you. You can use Outlook 2013 to invite guests to a meeting, schedule your resources, and check the availability of attendees. In this lesson, you will work on all the different aspects of using meetings in the Outlook 2013 calendar. You will create, modify, and cancel meetings. You'll also respond to meetings set by others.

SOFTWARE ORIENTATION

The Meeting Window

The Meeting window displayed in Figure 9-1 enables you to create a meeting involving other people or resources. Scheduled meetings are displayed on your calendar.

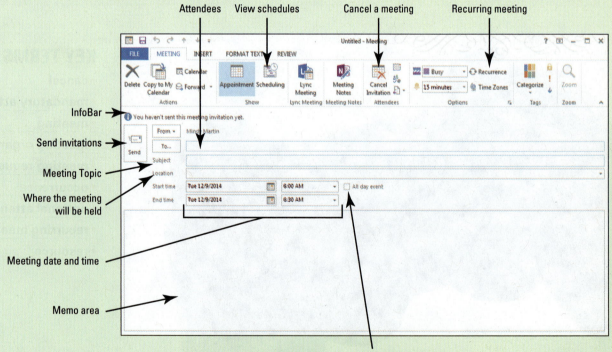

Figure 9-1

The Meeting window

Use the Meeting window to create a meeting. Refer to Figure 9-1 as you complete the following exercises.

CREATING A MEETING REQUEST

In Outlook 2013, a **meeting** is a scheduled appointment that requires sending invitations to other people or resources. Therefore, the Meeting window, shown in Figure 9-1, is very similar to the Appointment window. However, the Meeting window also includes the *To* field to invite attendees and the *Send* button to send the invitations. A meeting can occur once or at regular intervals.

 Cross Ref

For more information about appointments, refer to Lesson 8.

Creating a One-Time Meeting

Meeting a goal often requires more than one person. Working with others to accomplish a goal usually requires meetings. Use Outlook 2013 to start planning a meeting by selecting the right time, the right place, and the right people to accomplish the goal. A **meeting request** is an Outlook 2013 item that creates a meeting and invites attendees. In this exercise, you will start the process of creating a one-time meeting.

Create a One-Time Meeting

GET READY. LAUNCH Outlook 2013 if it is not already running.

1. Click the **Calendar** button in the Navigation bar to display the Calendar window.
2. Use the *Date Navigator* in the Folder Pane to select [**the second Tuesday of December**].

Take Note   Throughout this chapter you will see information that appears in black text within brackets, such as [Press **Enter**], or [**next Friday's date**]. The information contained in the brackets is intended to be directions for you rather than something you actually type word for word. It will instruct you to perform an action or substitute text. Do not type the actual text that appears within brackets.

 Cross Ref

You can find more information on the Calendar folder in Lesson 10.

⚠️ **Troubleshooting**   If you completed Lesson 8, a recurring appointment for the Engineering Lunch is scheduled for 12:15 PM to 1:15 PM on the fourth Monday of every month. If you did not complete Lesson 8, the busy times shown on your schedule will differ.

3. On the HOME tab, click **New Meeting** in the New group. The Meeting window shown in Figure 9-1 is displayed. Outlook 2013 selects a default time for the meeting.

Another Way   You can schedule a meeting from within the Contact features as well. Select a contact's name and click Meeting in the Communicate group.

4. Click the *Subject* field and key **Discuss Annual Convention**.

 Cross Ref

You can find more information on scheduling meeting locations later in this lesson.

PAUSE. LEAVE the Meeting window open to use in the next exercise.

Inviting Mandatory and Optional Attendees

A **mandatory attendee** is a person who must attend the meeting. An **optional attendee** is a person who should attend the meeting, but whose presence is not required. When planning a meeting, you should always invite at least one mandatory attendee. If a mandatory attendee is not needed to accomplish a goal at the meeting, you might not need a meeting at all. When you select a meeting time, choose a time slot when all mandatory attendees are available. It is helpful to use the message area to provide information about the meeting, including an agenda. In this exercise, you will select the right people to make this meeting a success. You will add both a mandatory attendee and an optional attendee and write a brief note to the attendees.

Invite Mandatory and Optional Attendees

Troubleshooting When creating messages, you must send and receive the requests and responses from two different e-mail accounts. So, for the exercises in this lesson, you will need to either work with a friend or coworker or have access to a separate e-mail account.

GET READY. USE the meeting request you began in the preceding exercise. The mandatory attendee used in this exercise must have a different active e-mail account from you and be able to respond to your meeting invitation.

1. Click the **Scheduling** (or **Scheduling Assistant**) button in the Show group on the Ribbon. A scheduling grid is displayed showing the scheduling information for all of the attendees, as shown in Figure 9-2.

Figure 9-2

Scheduling information

Icon identifies meeting organizer

Your name and schedule shown in this row

Additional names and schedules shown in remaining rows

Add attendees

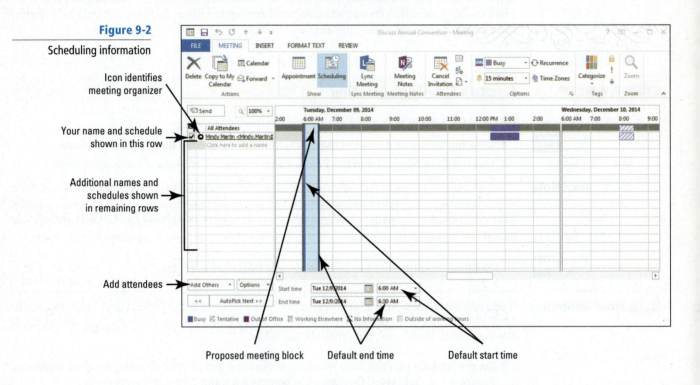

Proposed meeting block   Default end time   Default start time

2. Click the **Options** button located below the All Attendees pane and select the *Show Only My Working Hours* option, if necessary. The scheduling information updates to show your work hours.

Troubleshooting If you are using Microsoft Exchange, the Scheduling button is called Scheduling Assistant and should include free/busy information for your contacts.

3. Click **Add Others** and then click **Add from Address Book** from the dropdown list that appears. The Select Attendees and Resources: Contacts window appears, as shown in Figure 9-3.

Figure 9-3

Select Attendees and
Resources: Contacts window

Change Address Book if desired attendees are in a different Contacts folder

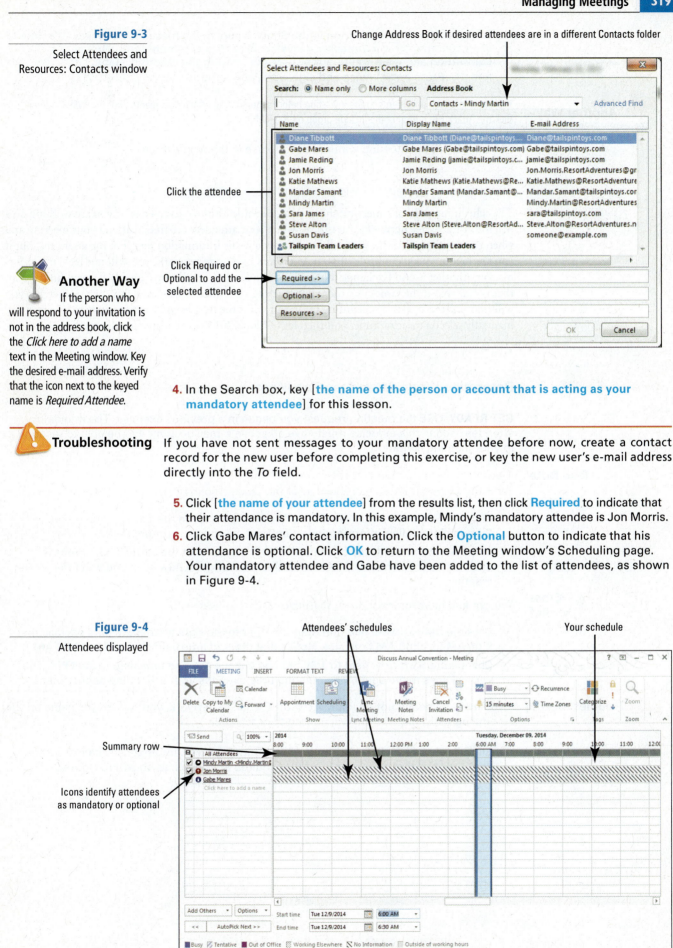

Click the attendee

Click Required or
Optional to add the
selected attendee

Another Way

If the person who
will respond to your invitation is
not in the address book, click
the *Click here to add a name*
text in the Meeting window. Key
the desired e-mail address. Verify
that the icon next to the keyed
name is *Required Attendee*.

4. In the Search box, key [**the name of the person or account that is acting as your mandatory attendee**] for this lesson.

Troubleshooting

If you have not sent messages to your mandatory attendee before now, create a contact record for the new user before completing this exercise, or key the new user's e-mail address directly into the *To* field.

5. Click [**the name of your attendee**] from the results list, then click **Required** to indicate that their attendance is mandatory. In this example, Mindy's mandatory attendee is Jon Morris.

6. Click Gabe Mares' contact information. Click the **Optional** button to indicate that his attendance is optional. Click **OK** to return to the Meeting window's Scheduling page. Your mandatory attendee and Gabe have been added to the list of attendees, as shown in Figure 9-4.

Figure 9-4

Attendees displayed

Attendees' schedules

Your schedule

Summary row

Icons identify attendees
as mandatory or optional

7. Click the **Appointment** button in the Show group. In the message body, key: **It's time to start planning for our annual convention. Bring the comments from last year's convention and we'll create our project plan during the meeting. Gabe, I hope you can join us**. [Press **Enter**] twice and sign with your name.

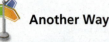

Another Way   You can also attach documents to the invitation before sending it. To attach documents, click the INSERT tab and click the Attach File button in the Include group on the Ribbon.

PAUSE. LEAVE the meeting window open to use in the next exercise.

Determining When Attendees Can Meet

The scheduling page of a meeting shows your schedule for the selected day. If you are working on a Microsoft Exchange network, you can see when your attendees are free to attend your meeting and when they are busy. Ideally, you will be able to view this information for all of the attendees, but if you are inviting people outside of your Microsoft Exchange network, you will not have this information. Another useful Exchange tool is the Room Finder. The Room Finder helps you find a room that is available at the same time that your meeting's attendees are all available. In this exercise, you will examine the available scheduling information for the people you want to invite to the meeting, manually select a meeting time, and then let Outlook 2013 select a time for the meeting.

STEP BY STEP   **Determine When Attendees Can Meet**

GET READY. USE the meeting request you began in a previous exercise. The mandatory attendee used in this exercise must have an active e-mail account and be able to respond to your meeting invitation.

Take Note   The directions below require that you are operating on a Microsoft Exchange network. If you are not using Microsoft Exchange, take note of the Troubleshooting alerts throughout this exercise.

1. Click the **Scheduling** (or **Scheduling Assistant**) button in the Show group on the Ribbon. Scheduling information is displayed, as shown in Figure 9-4.

2. In the *Start time* field, key or select **9:00 AM**. Notice that the vertical bars move to enclose the 9:00 AM to 9:30 AM time slot reflecting the new start and end time for the meeting.

 Cross Ref   You can find more information on sharing calendars in Lesson 10.

3. Click the **right vertical line** and drag it farther to the right so that the bars enclose the 9:00 AM to 10:00 AM time slot. Notice that the *End time* field changed to 10:00 AM.

4. Change the *Start time* field to **1:00 PM** and change the *End time* field to **2:00 PM**. The vertical lines move again. The meeting time overlaps your scheduled appointment.

Troubleshooting   If you invite someone not on your Microsoft Exchange network, you will see the name on the Scheduling Assistant, but you will not see their schedule.

5. Click the **AutoPick Next** button to allow Outlook 2013 to automatically search for the next time slot that is free for all of the required attendees, as shown in Figure 9-5.

Updated schedule grid

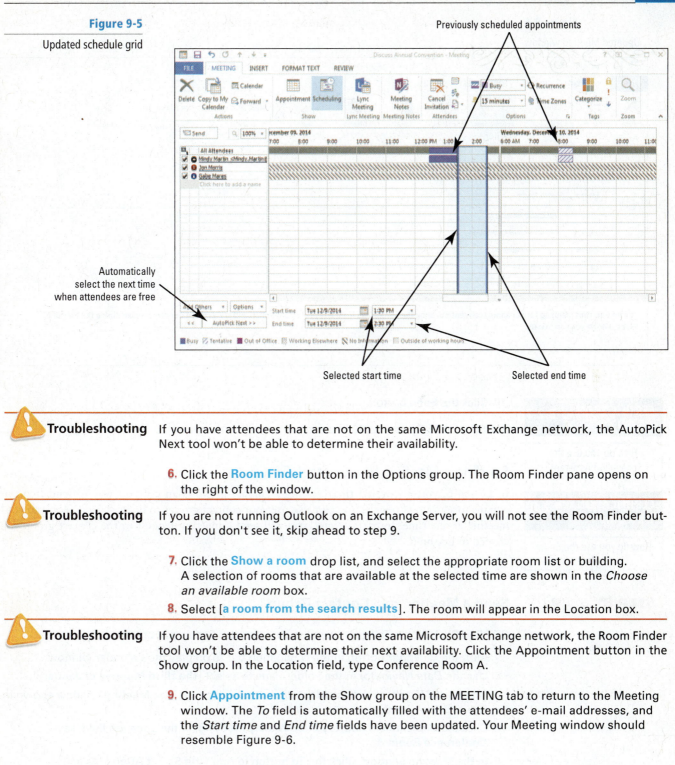

Previously scheduled appointments

Automatically select the next time when attendees are free

Selected start time

Selected end time

⚠️ **Troubleshooting**   If you have attendees that are not on the same Microsoft Exchange network, the AutoPick Next tool won't be able to determine their availability.

6. Click the **Room Finder** button in the Options group. The Room Finder pane opens on the right of the window.

⚠️ **Troubleshooting**   If you are not running Outlook on an Exchange Server, you will not see the Room Finder button. If you don't see it, skip ahead to step 9.

7. Click the **Show a room** drop list, and select the appropriate room list or building. A selection of rooms that are available at the selected time are shown in the *Choose an available room* box.

8. Select [**a room from the search results**]. The room will appear in the Location box.

⚠️ **Troubleshooting**   If you have attendees that are not on the same Microsoft Exchange network, the Room Finder tool won't be able to determine their next availability. Click the Appointment button in the Show group. In the Location field, type Conference Room A.

9. Click **Appointment** from the Show group on the MEETING tab to return to the Meeting window. The *To* field is automatically filled with the attendees' e-mail addresses, and the *Start time* and *End time* fields have been updated. Your Meeting window should resemble Figure 9-6.

Figure 9-6

Updated Meeting window

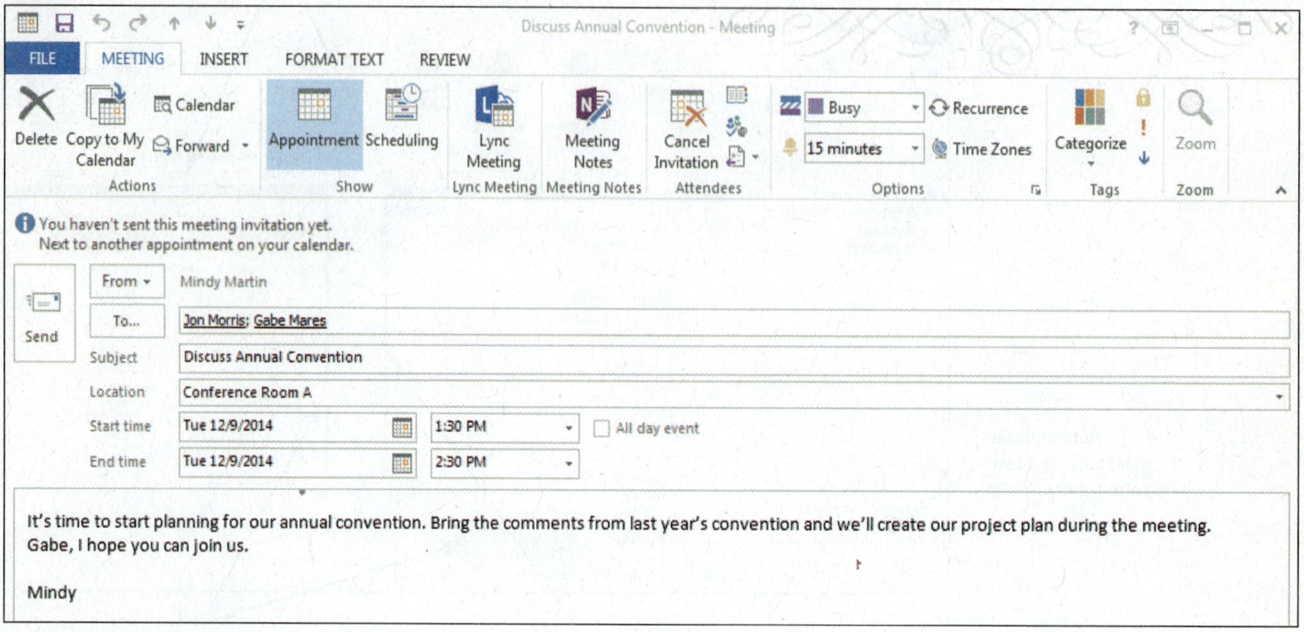
Discuss Annual Convention - Meeting
FILE
MEETING
INSERT
FORMAT TEXT
REVIEW
Delete
Copy to My Calendar
Calendar
Forward
Actions
Appointment
Scheduling
Show
Lync Meeting
Lync Meeting
Meeting Notes
Meeting Notes
Cancel Invitation
Attendees
Busy
15 minutes
Recurrence
Time Zones
Options
Categorize
Tags
Zoom
Zoom
You haven't sent this meeting invitation yet.
Next to another appointment on your calendar.
Send
From
Mindy Martin
To...
Jon Morris; Gabe Mares
Subject
Discuss Annual Convention
Location
Conference Room A
Start time
Tue 12/9/2014
1:30 PM
All day event
End time
Tue 12/9/2014
2:30 PM
It's time to start planning for our annual convention. Bring the comments from last year's convention and we'll create our project plan during the meeting. Gabe, I hope you can join us.
Mindy

10. Click the **Send** button.

PAUSE. LEAVE Outlook 2013 open to use in the next exercise.

CERTIFICATION READY? 3.2.7

How do you use the Scheduling Assistant?

CERTIFICATION READY? 3.2.10

How do you use the Room Finder?

Sending a Meeting to a Contact Group

In Lesson 6, you discovered that creating a contact group is an efficient way to send frequent e-mails to a group of people. You can also use your contact groups to invite several people to your meeting at one time. In this exercise, you will send a meeting request to the contact group you created in Lesson 6.

STEP BY STEP **Send a Meeting to a Contact Group**

GET READY. USE the Tailspin Team Leaders Contact Group you created in Lesson 6.

1. Click the **Calendar** button in the Navigation bar to display the Calendar window.
2. Use the *Date Navigator* in the Folder Pane to select [**the third Monday of January**].
3. On the HOME tab, click **New Meeting** in the New group. The Meeting window shown in Figure 9-1 is displayed.
4. Click the *Subject* field and key **First Weekly Meeting**. In the *Location* field, key **Conference Room A**.
5. In the Meeting window, click the **To** button to open the Select Attendees and Resources: Contacts window. Select the **Tailspin Team Leaders Contact Group** you created in Lesson 6 and click the **Required** button to indicate that their attendance is mandatory.
6. Click **OK** and return to the Meeting window's Scheduling page. Click the **plus sign** in front of the contact group name. The Expand List dialog box is displayed asking if you want to replace the Contact Group name with the names of the individual members, as shown in Figure 9-7.

Figure 9-7

Expand List dialog box

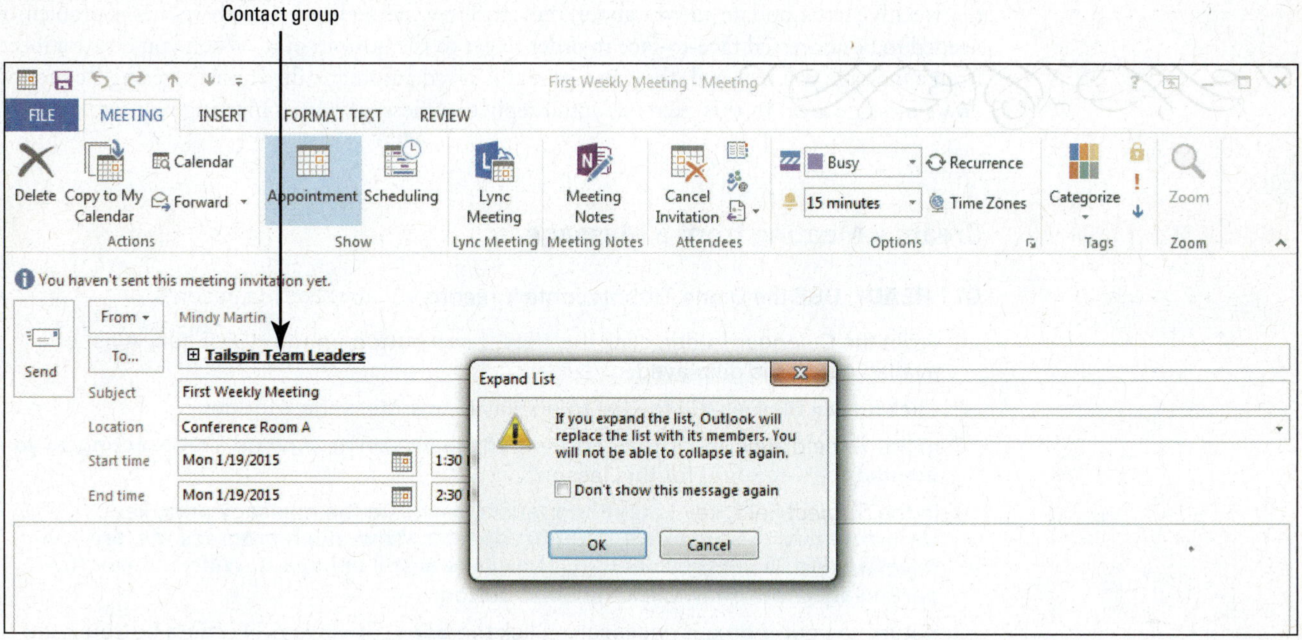

Contact group

7. Click **OK** to close the dialog box and return to the Meeting window. The *To* field now shows the name of each of the Contact Group's members, as shown in Figure 9-8.

Figure 9-8

Meeting invitation to Contact Group

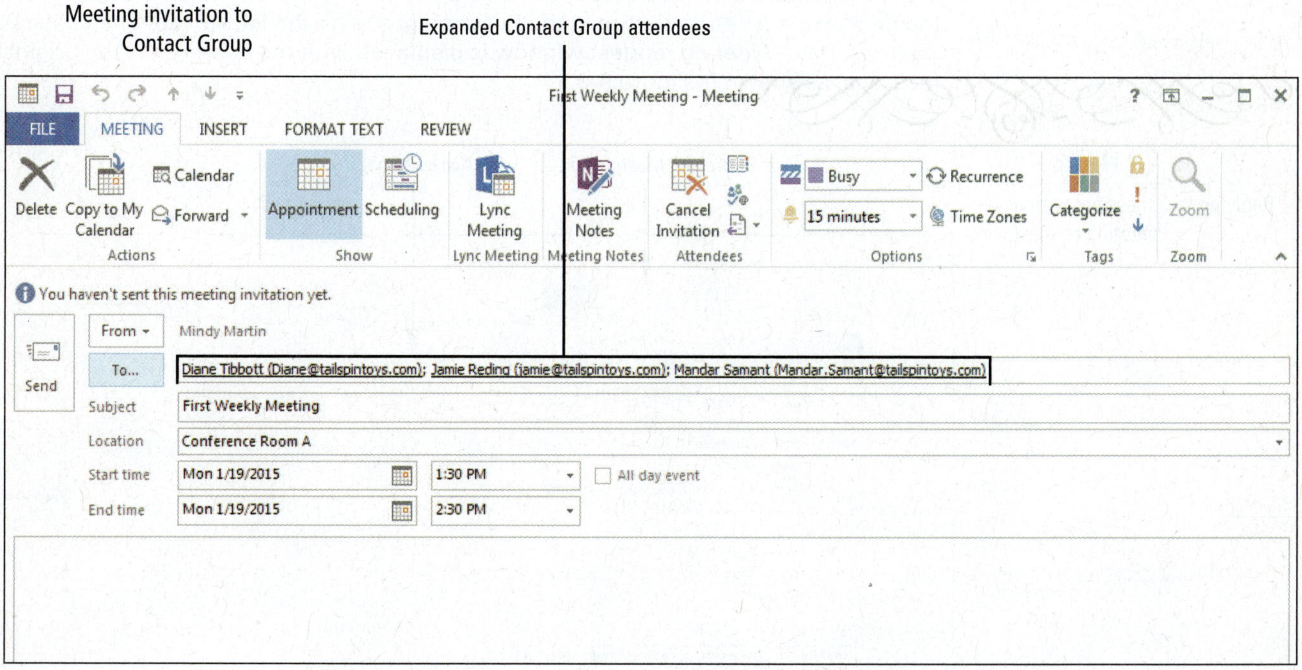

Expanded Contact Group attendees

8. Change the *Start time* field to **2:00 PM** and change the *End time* field to **3:00 PM**, if necessary.

9. In the message body, key **Agenda: Create project plan**. [Press **Enter**]. **Assign project roles**. [Press **Enter** twice] and sign with [**your name**].

10. Click **Send**.

PAUSE. LEAVE Outlook 2013 open to use in the next exercise.

Creating a Meeting from a Message

Sometimes, a message can lead to a meeting. For example, when Gabe received the bug report in the weekly status update memo about Project Snow, he realized that there was a problem that needed to be addressed face-to-face in order to get to the bottom of it. When you create a meeting from a message you received, the message text is saved automatically in the Meeting Request window's message area. In this exercise, you'll reply to a message with a meeting request.

STEP BY STEP | **Create a Meeting from a Message**

GET READY. USE the Diane Tibbott contact record you created in Lesson 6.

1. From the Calendar folder, click the **New Items** button on the HOME tab. A list of available items is displayed.
2. Click **E-mail Message** in the list to display a new Message window.
3. In the *To* field, key [**the e-mail address of the person or account that is acting as your mandatory attendee**] for this lesson.
4. In the *Subject* field, key **Latest bug report issues**. In the message area, key **Unfortunately, this week's bug report doesn't show much progress. We are still experiencing 20 glitches per unit. The cause is still unknown. Will send you the particulars later today.** Click the **Send** button.
5. Return to your **Inbox**, if necessary. Click the **Send/Receive All Folders** button if the message has not arrived yet.

⚠ **Troubleshooting** If you are not working with a friend or coworker on this lesson, switch to the mandatory attendee account that you are using.

6. In the mandatory attendee account, click the **Latest bug report issues** message. Click the **Reply with Meeting** button in the Respond group on the HOME tab. The *Latest bug report issues – Meeting* request window is displayed with the contents of the original message, as shown in Figure 9-9.

Figure 9-9

Replying to a message with a meeting request

Reply with Meeting button   Address Book

Text of the original message

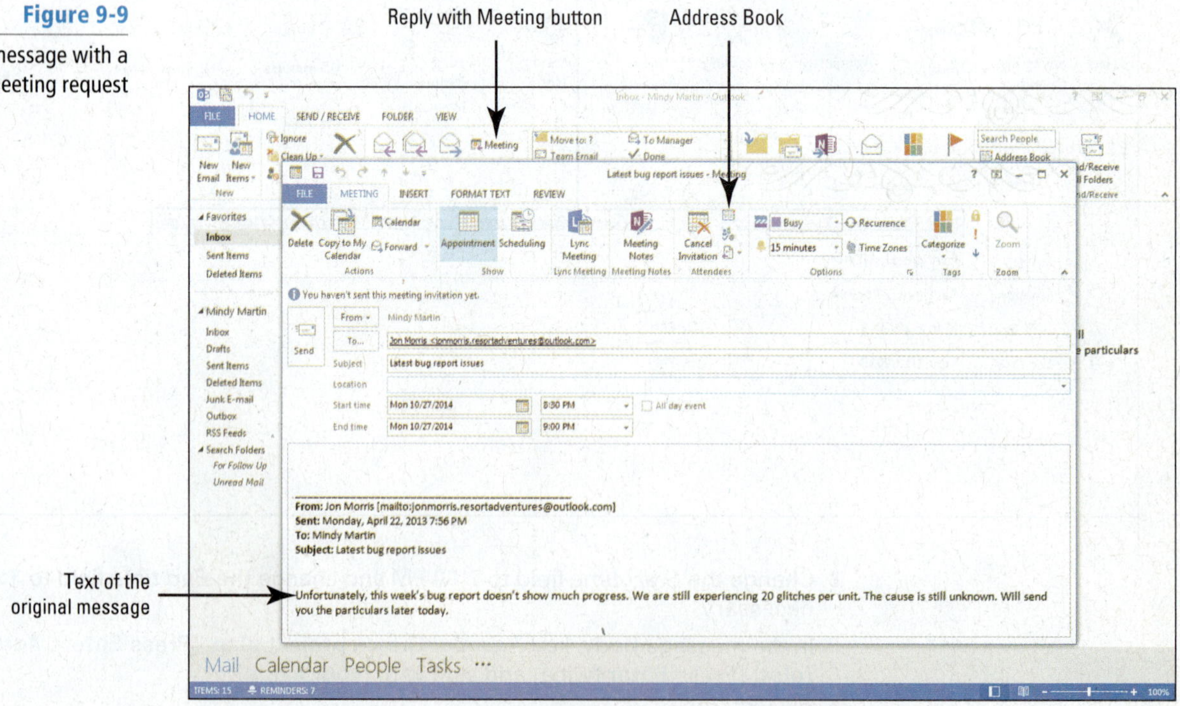

CERTIFICATION READY? 3.2.4

How do you create a meeting from a message?

CERTIFICATION READY? 3.3.1

How do you set the importance of a meeting?

7. Key **Wednesday** into the *Start time* field instead of a date. Key or select a start time of **9:00 AM**.
8. In the *End time* field, key **11:00 AM**.
9. Click **High Importance** in the Tags group. In the Location field, key **Design Center 2**.
10. Click the **Address Book** button in the Attendees group. Select **Diane Tibbott**, **Jamie Reding**, and **Mandar Samant** from the address book. Click **Required** and click **OK**.

PAUSE. LEAVE Outlook 2013 open to use in the next exercise.

Setting Response Options for a Meeting Request

By default, when you create a meeting in Outlook 2013, there are two response options selected: Request Responses and Allow New Time Proposals. The Request Responses option adds response buttons to the meeting request. These buttons allow attendees to respond to the request by letting you know whether they will attend. The Allow New Time Proposals option allows recipients to propose a different time to hold the meeting. As the meeting organizer, you still have final say about the meeting time; you can also choose to turn off one or both options. In this exercise, you will reply to a message with a meeting request, but will not give anyone the option of changing the meeting time.

STEP BY STEP

Set Response Options for a Meeting Request

GET READY. USE the meeting request you have started in the preceding exercise.

1. In the *Latest bug report issues – Meeting* window, click the message area. Key **This continuing problem is unacceptable. Bring all your data to this meeting. No one leaves until we have some answers.**
2. In the Attendees group, click the **Response Options** button. A dropdown list is displayed, as shown in Figure 9-10.

Figure 9-10

Setting Response options

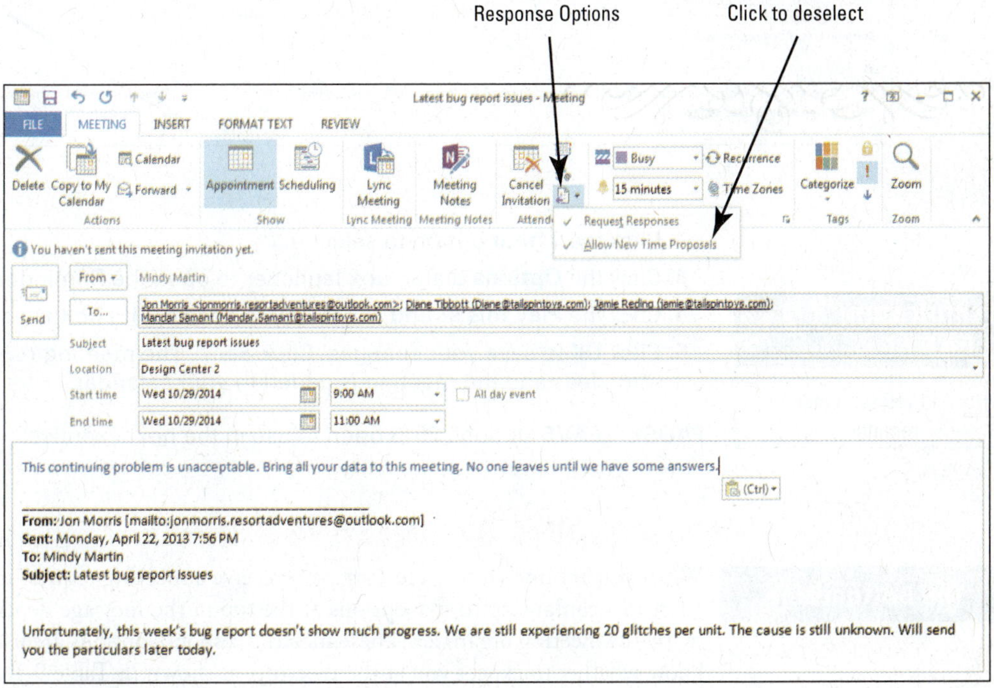

3. Click the **Allow New Time Proposals** option to deselect it.

PAUSE. LEAVE Outlook 2013 open to use in the next exercise.

Configuring Meeting Reminders

When you create a meeting, Outlook 2013 automatically creates a reminder for 15 minutes prior to the meeting start time. However, you do have the option to customize a message reminder. In this exercise, you will change the reminder time and even the sound used.

STEP BY STEP   **Configure Meeting Reminders**

> **GET READY. USE** the meeting request you have started in the preceding exercise.
>
> 1. In the *Latest bug report issues – Meeting* window, click the **Reminder** drop down arrow, as shown in Figure 9-11.

Figure 9-11

Configuring meeting reminders

Reminder Options

Click to change the reminder alarm sound

> 2. Click the **1 hour** option to select it.
> 3. Click the **Options** dialog box launcher to open the Reminder Sound box.
> 4. Click the **Play this sound** check box to deselect it and turn off the alarm sound.
> 5. Click **OK** to save your changes. Click **Send**. The meeting request is sent to your attendees and the meeting is added to your calendar.

PAUSE. LEAVE Outlook 2013 open to use in the next exercise.

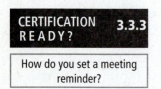

CERTIFICATION READY?   3.3.3

How do you set a meeting reminder?

RESPONDING TO A MEETING REQUEST

The Bottom Line

When you are invited to a meeting, you receive a meeting request in your Inbox. The meeting request can contain up to five options at the top of the message depending on the response options set by the meeting organizer. These meeting response options are used to let the meeting organizer know whether to expect you at the meeting, as shown in Table 9-1.

Table 9-1

Meeting Response Options

IOptions	Description
Accept	Indicates that you *accepted* the invitation and marks your calendar as busy.
Decline	Indicates that you *will not* attend the meeting and leaves your calendar free at the requested time.
Tentative	Indicates that you *might* attend the meeting, but does not commit you. Your calendar is marked as tentative with diagonal stripes.
Propose New Time	Indicates that you *might* be able to attend the meeting if the organizer were to *change the time* of the meeting to something that better fits your schedule.
Please Respond	Allows you to *ask a question* of the meeting organizer, perhaps asking for clarification, without accepting or declining the actual invitation. This link appears in the InfoBar, not at the top of the message.

Responding to a Meeting Request

Response options are set by the meeting organizer. The invitee must choose one of these options to let the meeting organizer know that invitee's intentions. In this exercise, you will tentatively accept a meeting invitation.

STEP BY STEP   **Respond to a Meeting Request**

GET READY. LAUNCH Outlook 2013 if it is not already running and complete the previous exercises. The mandatory attendee used in this exercise must have a different active e-mail account from yours and be able to respond to your meeting invitation.

1. In the mandatory attendee's account, click the **Mail** button in the Navigation bar to display the Mail folder, if necessary.

2. Locate the Discuss Annual Convention message in the message list. If it has not arrived, click the **Send/Receive All Folders** button on the HOME tab. The Discuss Annual Convention message is identified in the message list by the Meeting icon, shown in Figure 9-12, which resembles the New Meeting button on the Calendar's HOME tab.

3. Click the **Discuss Annual Convention** message in the message list. The message is displayed in the Preview pane, as shown in Figure 9-12.

Figure 9-12

Previewing a meeting request in the Reading Pane

Message is sent with a reminder to encourage a prompt response

Meeting icon

Response Options

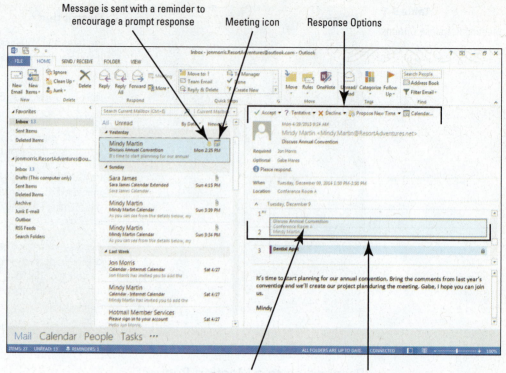

Requested meeting

Preview of your schedule for the requested time

4. Click the **Tentative** button. A dropdown list of options is displayed, offering you the options to send your response now, add a comment before sending the response, or choose to not send a response, as shown in Figure 9-13.

Figure 9-13

Sending a Tentative response to a meeting request

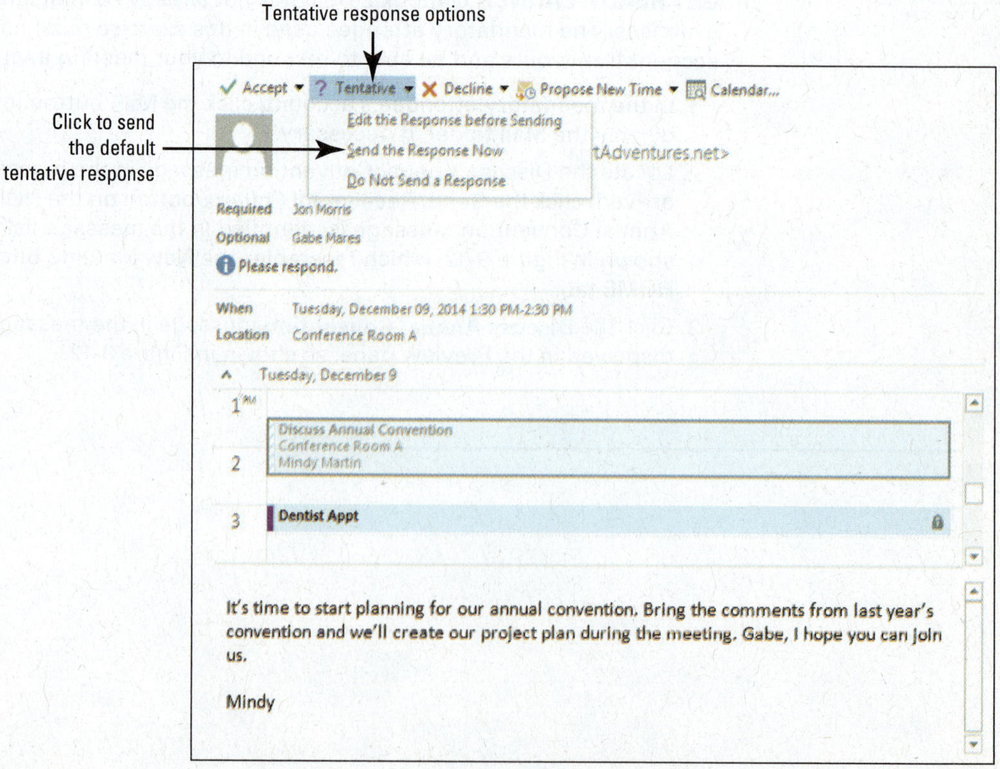

Tentative response options

Click to send the default tentative response

✓ Accept ▾   ? Tentative ▾   ✗ Decline ▾   🗓 Propose New Time ▾   📅 Calendar...

　　　Edit the Response before Sending
　　　Send the Response Now　　　　　tAdventures.net>
　　　Do Not Send a Response

Required   Jon Morris

Optional   Gabe Mares

ℹ Please respond.

When   Tuesday, December 09, 2014 1:30 PM-2:30 PM

Location   Conference Room A

∧   Tuesday, December 9

1 ᴬᴹ

　　　Discuss Annual Convention
　　　Conference Room A
2　　Mindy Martin

3   **Dentist Appt**   🔒

It's time to start planning for our annual convention. Bring the comments from last year's convention and we'll create our project plan during the meeting. Gabe, I hope you can join us.

Mindy

Another Way
You can also right-click on a meeting request in the message list to access the different response options.

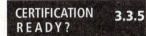

CERTIFICATION READY? 3.3.5

How do you respond to a meeting invitation?

5. Click the **Send the Response Now** option. The meeting request is removed from your Inbox, and the meeting is added to your calendar.

LEAVE Outlook 2013 open to use in the next exercise.

Proposing a New Time for a Meeting

Meeting times are set by the <mark>meeting organizer</mark>, the person who creates the meeting and sends meeting invitations. In most cases, when a meeting invitation is received, an attendee can suggest a different time for the meeting that better fits the attendee's schedule as long as the organizer has enabled the setting on the meeting invitation. In this exercise, you will propose a new meeting time for a meeting invitation.

STEP BY STEP   **Propose a New Time for a Meeting**

GET READY. Before you begin these steps, complete the previous exercises. The mandatory attendee used in this exercise must have a different active e-mail account from yours and be able to respond to your meeting invitation.

1. In the mandatory attendee's account, click the **Mail** button in the Navigation bar to display the Mail feature, if necessary.

2. Click the **Deleted Items** folder and locate the Discuss Annual Convention message. Because you already responded *Tentatively* to the meeting request, the message has been moved to the Deleted Items folder.

3. Double-click the **Discuss Annual Convention** deleted meeting request. The Discuss Annual Convention – Meeting window is displayed. Notice that the InfoBar reminds you that you have already responded to this request using the *Tentatively* option, as shown in Figure 9-14.

Figure 9-14

Discuss Annual Convention – Meeting window

Response Options

InfoBar →

Striped bar indicates that the time on the calendar has been marked as tentative

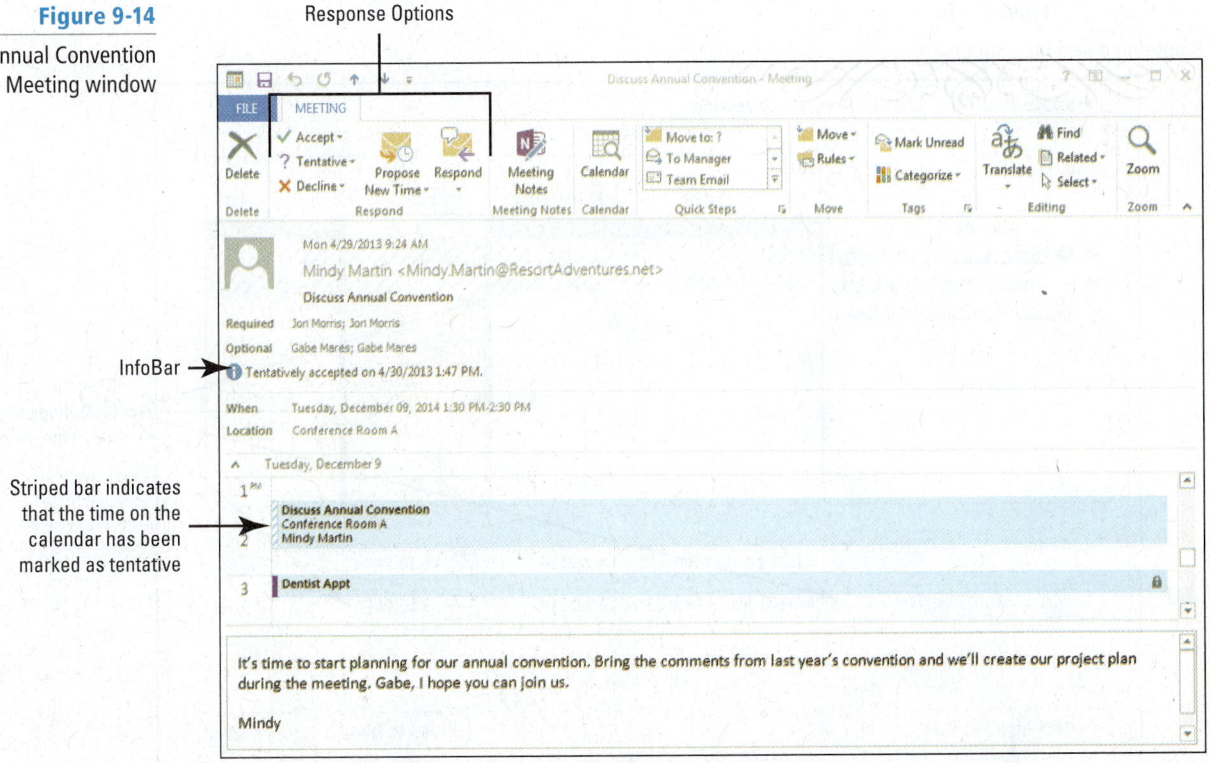

4. Click the **Propose New Time** button in the Ribbon. The Propose New Time window is displayed, as shown in Figure 9-15. The meeting time is indicated with a yellow bar.

Figure 9-15

Propose New Time: Discuss
Annual Convention window

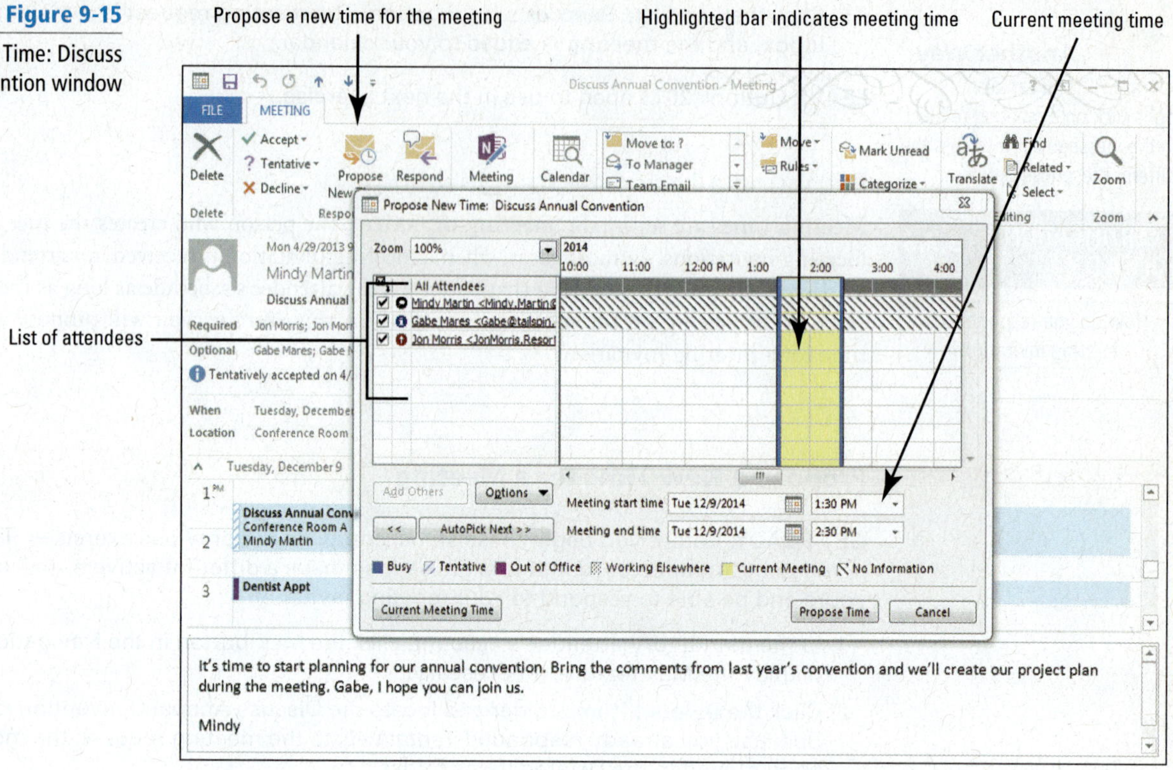

Propose a new time for the meeting — Highlighted bar indicates meeting time — Current meeting time

List of attendees

5. Verify that 1:30 is in the *Start time* field. Click the *End time* field. Key **3:00 PM**. The right vertical line indicating the meeting's end time has moved to 3:00, as shown in Figure 9-16.

Figure 9-16

Proposing a new meeting time

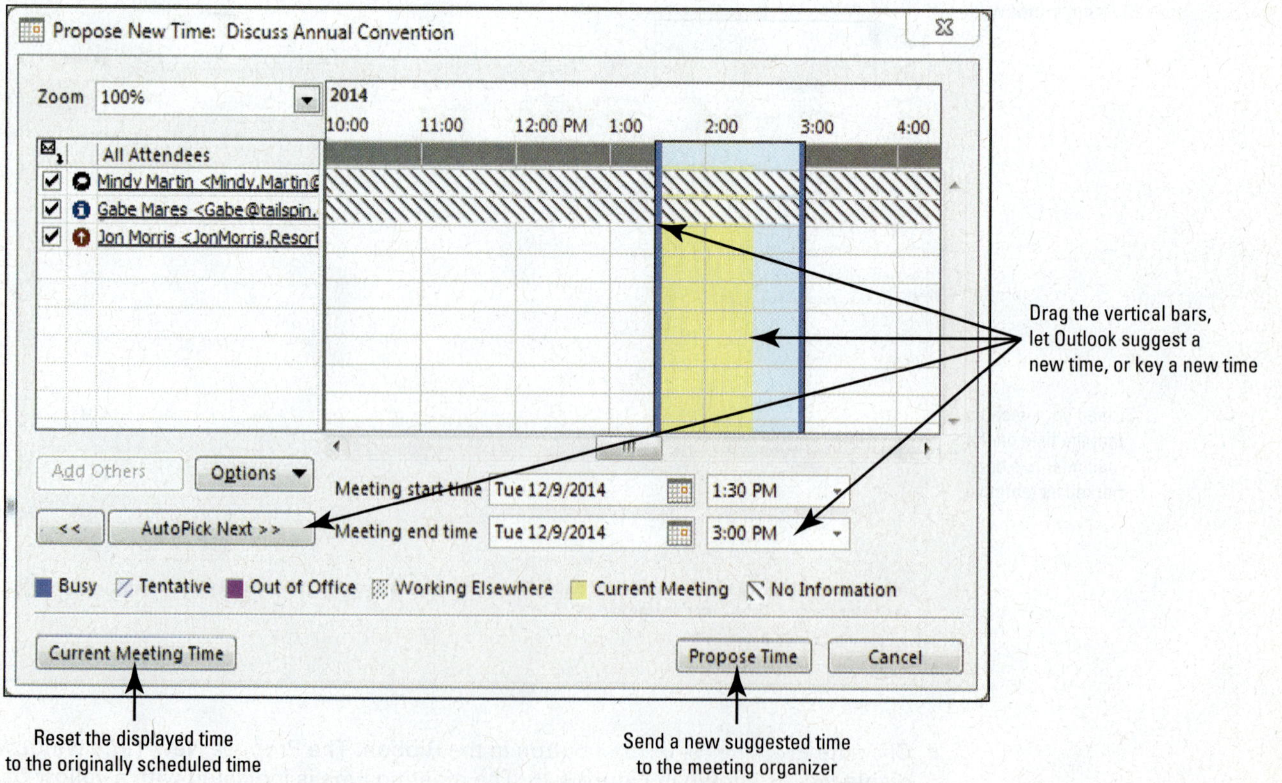

Drag the vertical bars,
let Outlook suggest a
new time, or key a new time

Reset the displayed time
to the originally scheduled time

Send a new suggested time
to the meeting organizer

6. Click the **Propose Time** button. A Message window is displayed. Both the current and proposed meeting times are listed above the message area.

7. In the message area, key the following message: **Let's add 30 minutes and conclude the meeting by offering a sampling of foods available for the convention luncheon.** [Press **Enter** twice] and sign [**your name**], as shown in Figure 9-17.

Figure 9-17

Updated meeting request

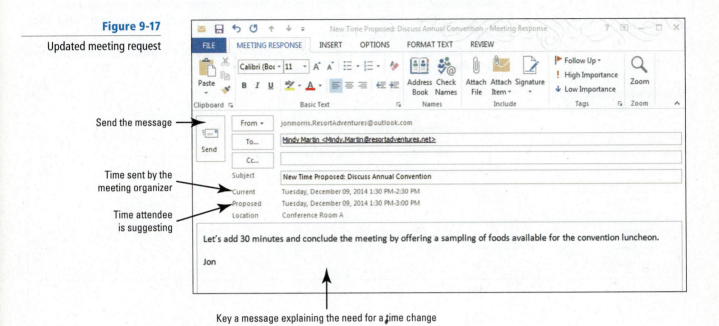

Send the message →

Time sent by the meeting organizer →

Time attendee is suggesting →

Key a message explaining the need for a time change

8. Click the **Send** button.

PAUSE. Switch to your e-mail account, if necessary. If someone else is responding to the invitation, **LEAVE** Outlook 2013 open to use in the next exercise.

Cross Ref

If you share your calendar, you can prevent some message exchanges regarding meeting times by keeping your free and busy times up-to-date in your calendar. For more information about sharing calendars, see Lesson 10.

MANAGING A MEETING

The Bottom Line

Your job as a meeting organizer is not done once you have sent your meeting invitation. As you learned earlier in this lesson, contacts you invited can respond to that invitation in one of five ways. You would be wasting valuable time if you attended a meeting all by yourself because you neglected to notice that everyone else declined your meeting request. Outlook 2013 tracks meeting responses for every meeting.

Tracking Responses to a Meeting Request

When an attendee responds to your meeting invitation, you receive a message. If the attendee included comments in the response, the comments are contained in the message. The responses are stored in the meeting information in your calendar. So, you can just open the Meeting window to view a summary of the responses. In this exercise, you will learn how to track responses.

Track Responses to a Meeting Request

GET READY. Before you begin these steps, complete the previous exercises. The mandatory attendee used in this exercise must have a different active e-mail account from yours and be able to respond to your meeting invitation.

1. In your account, click the **Mail** button in the Navigation bar to display the mailbox, if necessary. If the *Tentative: Discuss Annual Convention* message has not arrived, click the **Send/Receive All Folders** button.

2. Click the **Tentative: Discuss Annual Convention** message in the message list to preview it in the Reading Pane, as shown in Figure 9-18.

Figure 9-18

Message tentatively accepting the meeting invitation

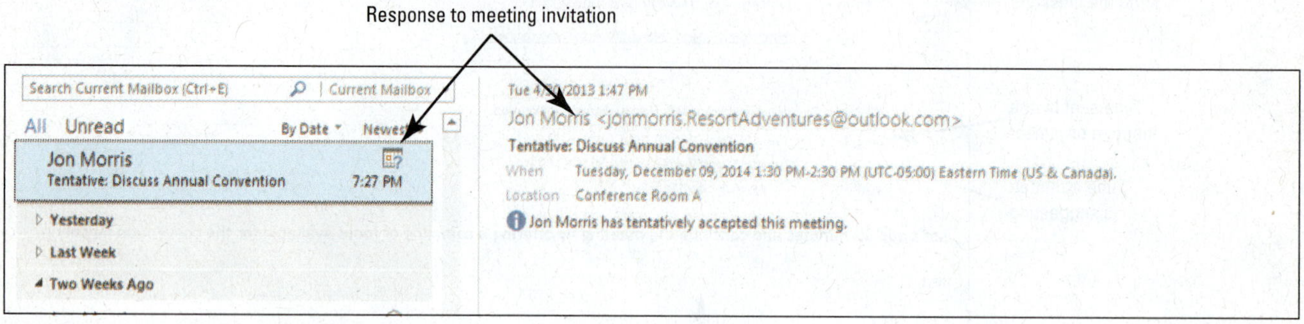

3. Click the **Calendar** button in the Navigation bar to display the Calendar folder. Click the **Month** button to display the Month view, if necessary, and navigate to next December.

4. Double-click the **Discuss Annual Convention** meeting item on the calendar. The Discuss Annual Convention – Meeting window is displayed, as shown in Figure 9-19. The InfoBar contains a summary of the responses received.

Figure 9-19

Summary of responses received

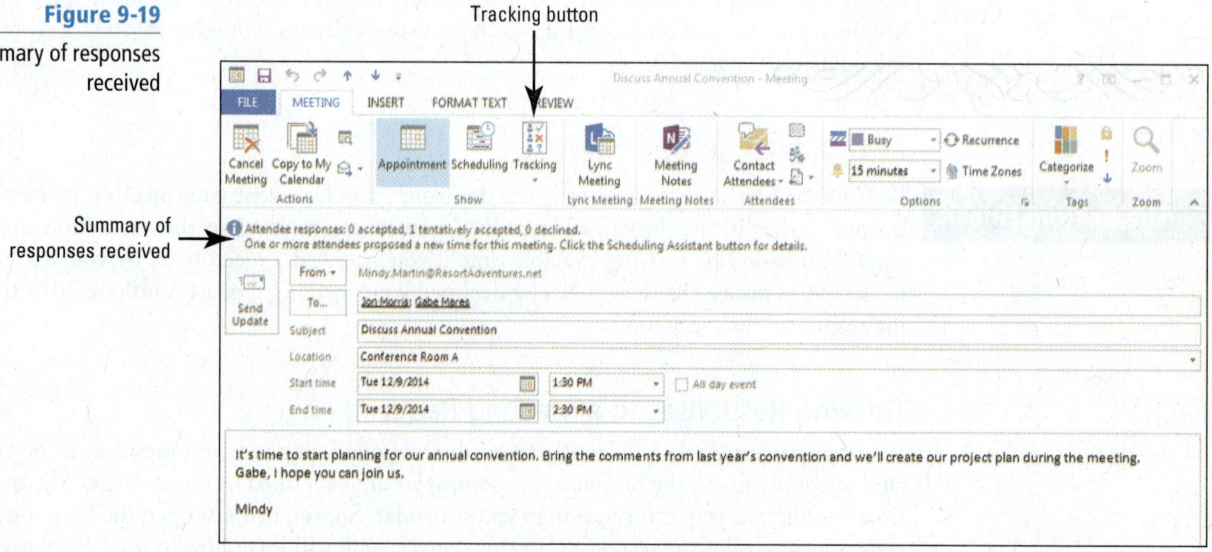

5. Click the **Tracking** button on the MEETING tab. Detailed tracking information is displayed, as shown in Figure 9-20. You can see at a glance which attendees have responded.

Figure 9-20
Detailed tracking information

Mandatory or optional   Responses received

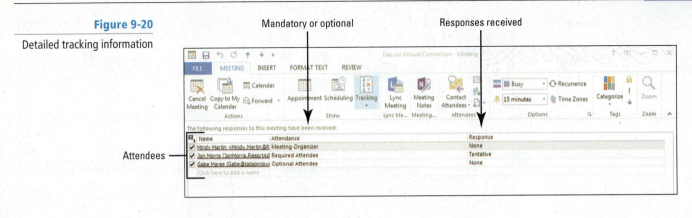

Attendees

PAUSE. LEAVE Outlook 2013 open for the next exercise.

Accepting a Proposed New Meeting Time

By default, anyone invited to the meeting can suggest a new date and time for the meeting. However, the meeting organizer has the final word on setting the meeting time. When an attendee proposes a new meeting time, the meeting organizer must evaluate the proposed time and accept or decline the proposal.

When the meeting time is changed, you need to click the Send Update or Send button to send an update message to your attendees notifying them of the new time. They must accept or decline the meeting again, as they did for the initial invitation. In this exercise, you will accept a new meeting time proposed by an attendee.

STEP BY STEP   **Accept a Proposed New Meeting Time**

GET READY. Before you begin these steps, complete the previous exercises. The mandatory attendee used in this exercise must have a different active e-mail account from yours and be able to respond to your meeting invitation.

Troubleshooting   More than one of your invitees could propose a new time for the meeting. You may choose any of the New Time Proposed e-mails to complete this exercise.

1. If necessary, open the Discuss Annual Convention Meeting request that you had open in the previous exercise.
2. Click the **Scheduling** (or **Scheduling Assistant**) button in the Show group on the Ribbon. All proposed times appear in the scheduling grid so that you can see how each time affects the mandatory attendees.

Troubleshooting   If you are using Microsoft Exchange, the Scheduling button is called Scheduling Assistant.

3. Click [**the new time proposed by your required attendee**] in the *Proposed Date and Time* box. The schedule changes to show how the new time will affect the attendees, as shown in Figure 9-21.

Another Way   You can also view the various proposed time changes by clicking View All Proposals in one of the individual meeting responses (when the meeting request is open).

Figure 9-21

Proposed time shown in Scheduling view

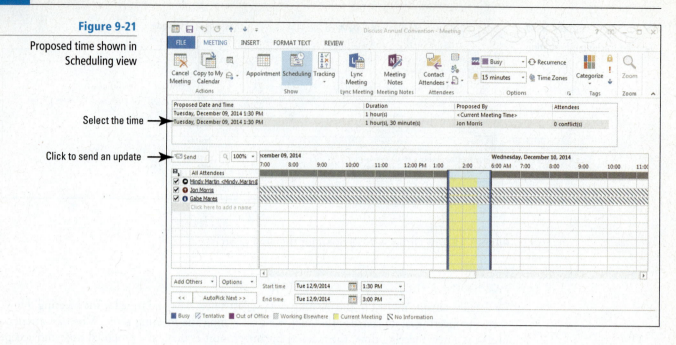

Select the time ⟶

Click to send an update ⟶

4. On the MEETING tab, click **Contact Attendees** in the Attendees group and select **Reply to All with E-mail** from the dropdown menu.

5. A message window opens. In the message body, key: **Jon had a great suggestion that we take advantage of the scheduled meeting to sample some of the food we will provide at the luncheon. I'm adding time at the end of this meeting for that purpose.** [Press **Enter** twice] and sign [**your name**].

6. On the MEETING tab, click the **Send** button above the scheduling grid.

7. Close the meeting window, if needed. Save changes if requested.

PAUSE. LEAVE Outlook 2013 open to use in the next exercise.

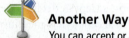

Another Way
You can accept or reject proposals in the individual meeting responses by selecting each one from the Inbox.

The Bottom Line

UPDATING A MEETING REQUEST

Whenever you are trying to get a group of people to sit at the same table at the same time, problems can emerge. One person will go out of town on an emergency business trip. Another person has to attend a meeting with a higher priority. Necessary audio-visual equipment has been shipped to a trade show. The list of potential problems is endless. Modifying a meeting and updating the attendees is a simple task in Outlook 2013.

Changing a Meeting Time

The most common modifications to a meeting are changing the time and the location of a meeting. In the previous exercise, you modified the meeting time because of a proposed change by one of the attendees. In this exercise, you will make the change yourself and send an update to the attendees. Because this is a change to the meeting time, attendees will need to respond to the meeting invitation again.

STEP BY STEP | **Change a Meeting Time**

GET READY. Before you begin these steps, complete the previous exercises. The mandatory attendee used in this exercise must have a different active e-mail account from yours and be able to respond to your meeting invitation.

1. In your account, click the **Calendar** button in the Navigation bar to display the Calendar folder. Click the **Month** button to display the Month view, if necessary.

2. Use the Date Navigator to select the month of **December**.

3. Double-click the **Discuss Annual Convention** meeting item on the calendar. The Discuss Annual Convention – Meeting window is displayed.

4. Click the *Start time* field. Key **Thursday**. [Press **Enter**]. The *End time* field automatically changes to match.

5. In the message area, select the text and [press **Delete**]. Then key **Sorry guys, we've been bumped out of Conference Room A. The next availability isn't until Thursday.** [Press **Enter** twice] and key [**your name**]. Compare your Meeting window to Figure 9-22.

Figure 9-22

Updated Meeting window

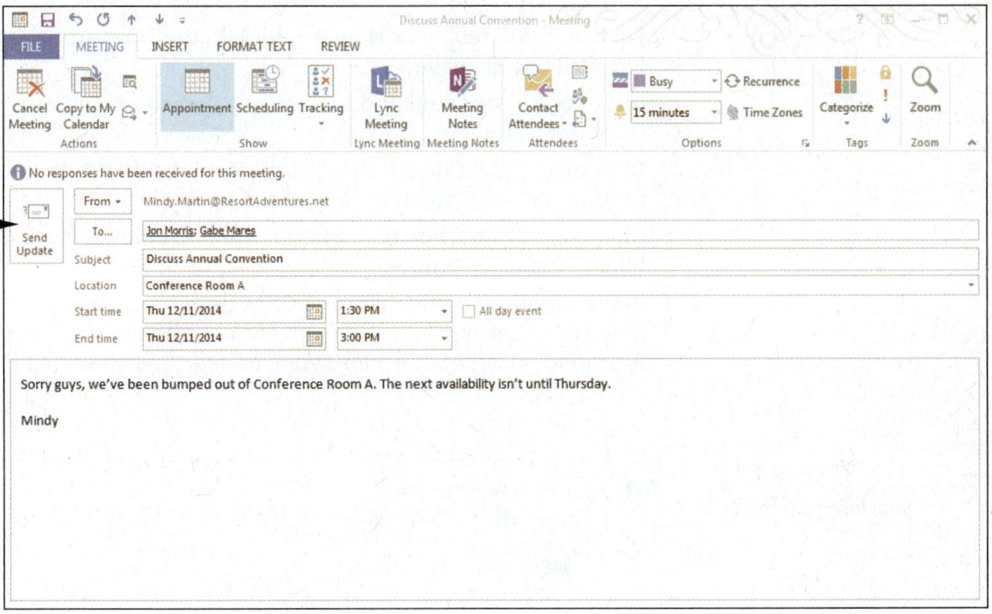

Send update to attendees →

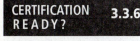

6. Click the **Send Update** button below the InfoBar to send the modified time information to the attendees.

PAUSE. Switch to the mandatory attendee's account, if necessary. If someone else is responding to the invitation, **LEAVE** Outlook 2013 open to use in the next exercise.

Scheduling a Meeting Resource

In Outlook 2013, a **resource** is an item or a location that can be invited to a meeting. Scheduling meeting resources is a great way to keep track of who needs to use each piece of equipment. Resources can include cars, presentation equipment, and conference rooms. You can invite a resource to a meeting just as you invite attendees. A resource has its own mailbox and maintains its own schedule. It accepts invitations for free times and updates its calendar. It declines invitations if the requested time is already scheduled.

Scheduling resources ensures that meetings aren't scheduled at the same time in different locations that both require the same equipment. For example, let's say the Human Resources Department is planning to show a DVD during a new-hire meeting in Conference Room A at 2:00 PM. Meanwhile, the Sales Department has a training DVD that they are planning to use in the Sales Pit during their meeting at 1:30 PM. At first glance, they looked at room availability and the schedule of the attendees and saw no conflicts. If they schedule the DVD equipment as a resource, they would realize that the DVD equipment will be in the Sales training meeting from 1:30 to 3:00 PM. It won't be available for the new-hire meeting. In this exercise, you will create a new meeting and add a computer projector resource that is essential to the meeting.

Schedule a Meeting Resource

GET READY. LAUNCH Outlook 2013 if it is not already running.

⚠️ **Troubleshooting** Scheduling a resource requires Microsoft Exchange and a resource with a separate mailbox.

1. In your account, click the **Calendar** button in the Navigation bar to display the Calendar folder.

2. On the HOME tab, click **New Meeting** in the New group. The Meeting window shown in Figure 9-1 is displayed.

3. Click the *Subject* field and key **Project Presentation Review**. In the *Location* field, key **Dept Room 62**.

4. Click the **Scheduling** (or **Scheduling Assistant**) button in the Show group on the Ribbon. Scheduling information is displayed.

5. Change the *Start time* field to **9:00 AM** and change the *End time* field to **10:00 AM**. The blue vertical lines move.

6. In the scheduling grid, click the **Click here to add a name** text in the Meeting window. Key **AV01@tailspintoys.com** and click the box just to the left of the e-mail address. A dropdown list of attendee types appears, as shown in Figure 9-23.

Figure 9-23

Scheduling a resource

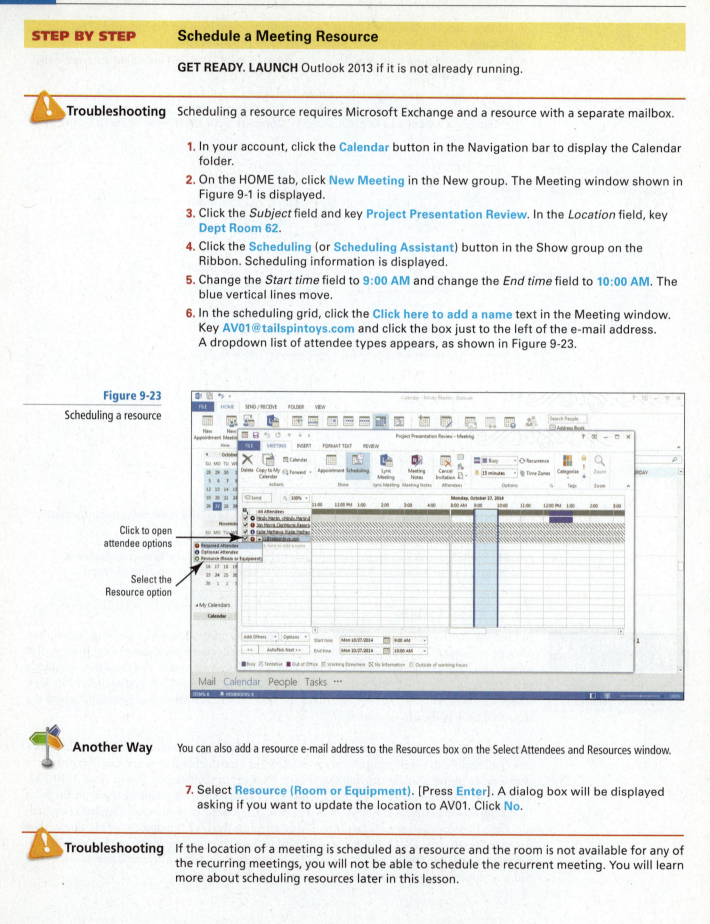

Click to open attendee options

Select the Resource option

🪧 **Another Way** You can also add a resource e-mail address to the Resources box on the Select Attendees and Resources window.

7. Select **Resource (Room or Equipment)**. [Press **Enter**]. A dialog box will be displayed asking if you want to update the location to AV01. Click **No**.

⚠️ **Troubleshooting** If the location of a meeting is scheduled as a resource and the room is not available for any of the recurring meetings, you will not be able to schedule the recurrent meeting. You will learn more about scheduling resources later in this lesson.

Another Way Even without Microsoft Exchange, you can create your own contact records for the resources you use. This enables you to select the resource from a secondary address book instead of keying the name each time you create a meeting.

8. Click the **Appointment** button in the Show group on the Ribbon.

9. Compare your Meeting window to Figure 9-24.

Figure 9-24

Meeting window with resource added

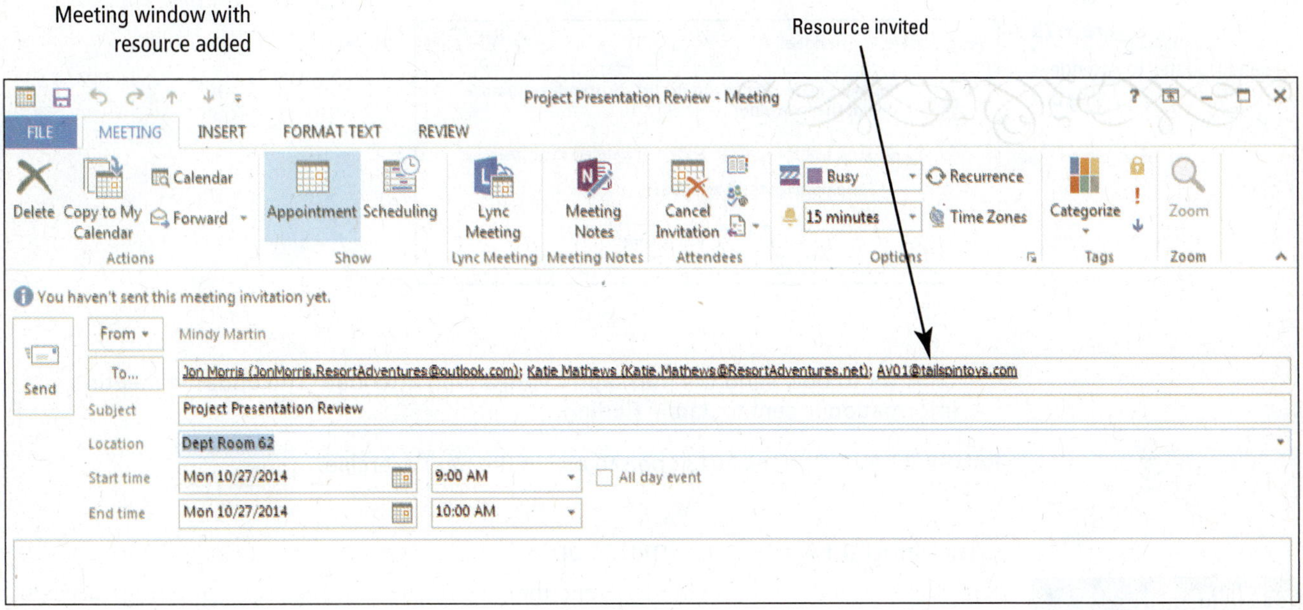

Resource invited

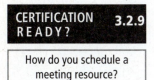

10. Click the **Send** button. Your calendar is updated to display the meeting.

PAUSE. LEAVE Outlook 2013 open to use in the next exercise.

Adding and Updating a New Attendee

<table>
<tr>
<td>

CERTIFICATION READY? 3.2.9

How do you schedule a meeting resource?

</td>
<td>

When you create a meeting, you select the attendees needed to meet the meeting's objective. When the selected attendees learn about the meeting, they can suggest other individuals who should be invited to the meeting. For example, say that you created a meeting about the continuing problems with the Project Snow software bugs. You invited the project manager, the lead software developer on the team, and the service representative working with the client. The project manager suggests that you invite the concept artist who has been working on the project as well. In this exercise, you will add an attendee to a scheduled meeting and send an updated meeting request only to the new attendee.

</td>
</tr>
</table>

STEP BY STEP **Add and Update a New Attendee**

GET READY. USE the meeting request you sent in the preceding exercise.

1. In your account, click the **Calendar** button in the Navigation bar to display the Calendar folder. Click the **Month** button to display the Month view, if necessary.

2. Double-click the **Project Presentation Review** meeting item on the calendar. The Project Presentation Review – Meeting window is displayed, as shown in Figure 9-24.

3. Click the **Scheduling** (or **Scheduling Assistant**) button in the Show group on the Ribbon.

4. Click the **Add Others** button below the scheduling grid.

5. Click **Add from Address Book**. The Select Attendees and Resources window is displayed. The mandatory attendee and the projector are already displayed in the fields.

6. Click the **Jamie Reding** contact record to add that person as an attendee and click the **Optional** button. Click **OK** to return to the Meeting window.

7. Click the **Send** button. Outlook 2013 recognizes that the list of attendees has changed and displays the Send Update to Attendees dialog box shown in Figure 9-25.

Figure 9-25

Send Updates to Attendees dialog box

8. Click **OK** to only send the message to the added attendee. The updated meeting information is sent to Jamie Reding.

PAUSE. LEAVE Outlook 2013 open to use in the next exercise.

Cancelling a Meeting or Invitation

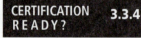

CERTIFICATION READY? 3.3.4

How do you add a new attendee to a scheduled meeting?

Regardless of how much planning went into creating a meeting, some meetings need to be **cancelled**. Reasons for cancelling a meeting are varied, such as mandatory attendees becoming unavailable or issues getting resolved before the scheduled meeting occurs. When you cancel a meeting, it is deleted from your calendar and the attendees are notified. Cancellation notices are saved in your Sent Items folder in case you need to track cancelled meetings or keep a record of the reason a meeting was cancelled. In this exercise, you will cancel a meeting and send a cancellation notice to the attendees.

STEP BY STEP **Cancel a Meeting or Invitation**

GET READY. LAUNCH Outlook 2013 if it is not already running.

Before you begin these steps, complete the previous exercises.

1. Click the **Calendar** button in the Navigation bar to display the Calendar folder. Click the **Month** button to display the Month view, if necessary.

2. Double-click the **Project Presentation Review** meeting item on the calendar. The Project Presentation Review – Meeting window is displayed.

3. On the MEETING tab, click **Cancel Meeting** in the Actions group. The InfoBar changes to let you know that the cancellation has not been sent yet.

4. Click the message body. Delete [**any existing text**] and key the following message: **This meeting was cancelled because Jon had an emergency appendectomy earlier today. He is recovering at Mountain View Hospital and we expect him to return to the office in a couple of weeks. We'll reschedule the meeting after he returns.** [Press **Enter** twice] and sign [**your name**]. Compare your Meeting window to Figure 9-26.

Figure 9-26

Cancelling a meeting

Figure 9-26

Cancelling a meeting

Click to move the cancellation to the Calendar

Click to send the cancellation to attendees

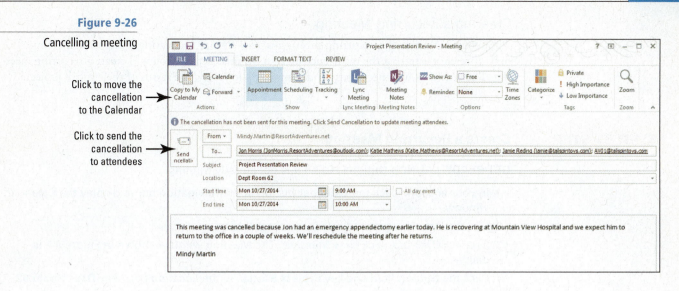

5. Click the **Send Cancellation** button. The message is sent and the meeting is removed from your calendar.

PAUSE. LEAVE Outlook 2013 open to use in the next exercise.

In the attendee's mailbox, the cancellation notice is automatically assigned a High Importance. The attendee opens the message and clicks the Remove from Calendar button in the Respond group. The attendee's calendar is updated, as shown in Figure 9-27.

Figure 9-27

Cancelled meeting in the message list

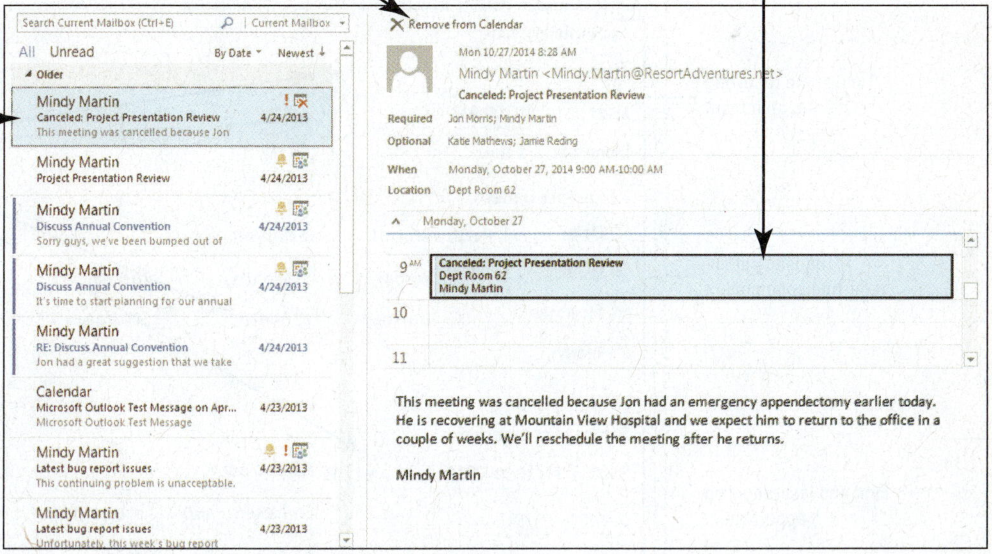

Click to delete meeting from your schedule   Cancelled meeting highlighted to catch your attention

Cancelled meeting

MANAGING A RECURRING MEETING

The Bottom Line

A **recurring meeting** is a meeting that occurs at regular intervals. The meeting always has the same attendees, location, and purpose. The interval could be a number of days, weeks, or months. For example, status meetings commonly occur at weekly or monthly intervals.

Creating a Recurring Meeting

The process of creating a recurring meeting is very similar to creating a one-time meeting. The only difference is setting the recurrence pattern. In this exercise, you will create a recurring meeting. The attendees will meet every Friday morning to review the status of their active projects.

STEP BY STEP   **Create a Recurring Meeting**

GET READY. LAUNCH Outlook 2013 if it is not already running.

1. In your account, click the **Calendar** button in the Navigation bar to display the Calendar window.
2. Use the Date Navigator to select [**the next Friday**].
3. On the HOME tab, click **New Meeting**. The Meeting window shown in Figure 9-1 is displayed.
4. Click the *Subject* field and key **Project Status**. In the *Location* field, key **Dept Room 62**.
5. Click the **Scheduling** (or **Scheduling Assistant**) button in the Show group on the Ribbon.
6. Click the **Add Others** button and click **Add from Address Book**. The Select Attendees and Resources window is displayed.
7. [Press **Ctrl**] while clicking the **four Tailspin Toys employees**. Click **Required**. Click **OK** to return to the Meeting window.
8. Change the *Start time* field to **9:00 AM** and change the *End time* field to **10:00 AM**, if necessary. The vertical lines move.
9. Click the **Recurrence** button in the Options group on the Ribbon. The Appointment Recurrence dialog box is displayed, as shown in Figure 9-28.

Figure 9-28

Appointment Recurrence dialog box

Time of the recurring appointment

Frequency of the recurring appointment

First and last recurring appointment

Default information based on data in the Meeting window

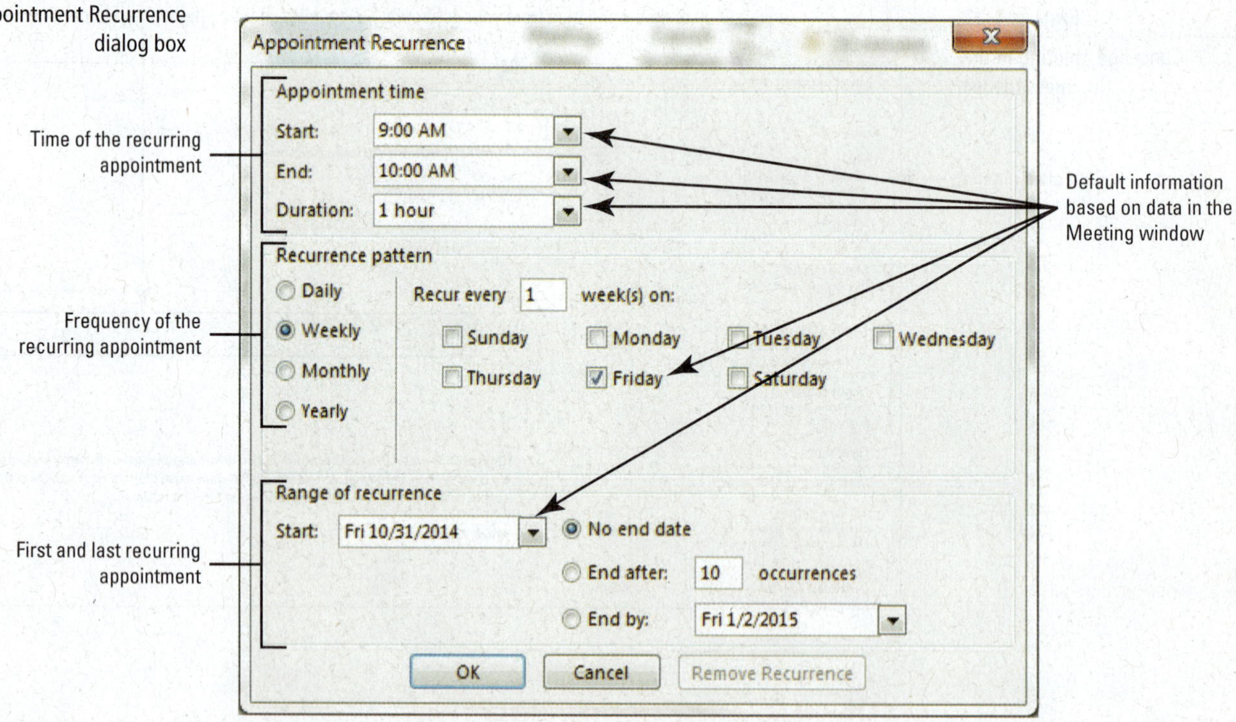

10. By default, Outlook 2013 assumes a weekly recurrence pattern on the same day you originally suggested, *Friday*. In this case, the pattern is correct. The Project Status meeting will be held every Friday. Click **OK** to accept the recurrence pattern and return to the Meeting window.

11. Click the **Appointment** button in the Show group on the Ribbon. The *To* field is automatically filled with the attendees' e-mail addresses, as shown in Figure 9-29. The recurrence pattern is listed in the information bar under the *Location* field. In this case, the meeting recurrence pattern is *Occurs every Friday effective 10/31/14*.

Figure 9-29

Meeting request for a recurring meeting

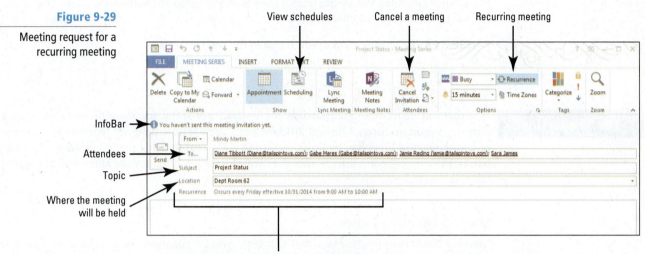

12. Click the **Send** button. Your calendar is updated, and the 9:00 AM to 10:00 AM time slot is displayed as busy for every Friday.

PAUSE. LEAVE Outlook 2013 open to use in the next exercise.

Changing One Occurrence of a Recurring Meeting

<table>
<tr><td>CERTIFICATION READY?</td><td>3.2.2</td></tr>
<tr><td colspan="2">How do you create a recurring meeting?</td></tr>
</table>

A single meeting in a series of recurring meetings is an **occurrence**. When a recurring meeting is held regularly for a long period of time, an occurrence will eventually conflict with some other event. At any time, you can change the date, time, and location of a single occurrence without affecting the other occurrences. When you change one occurrence, your calendar is updated and updates are sent to the attendees. In this exercise, you will change the time of one meeting in a series of recurring meetings.

STEP BY STEP **Change One Occurrence of a Recurring Meeting**

GET READY. Before you begin these steps, complete the previous exercise to create the recurring meeting.

1. In your account, click the **Calendar** button in the Navigation bar to display the Calendar window. Click the **Month** button to display the Month view, if necessary.

2. Double-click [the second occurrence of the Project Status] meeting item on the calendar. The Open Recurring Item dialog box is displayed, as shown in Figure 9-30, with the *Just this one* option already selected.

Figure 9-30

Open Recurring Item dialog box

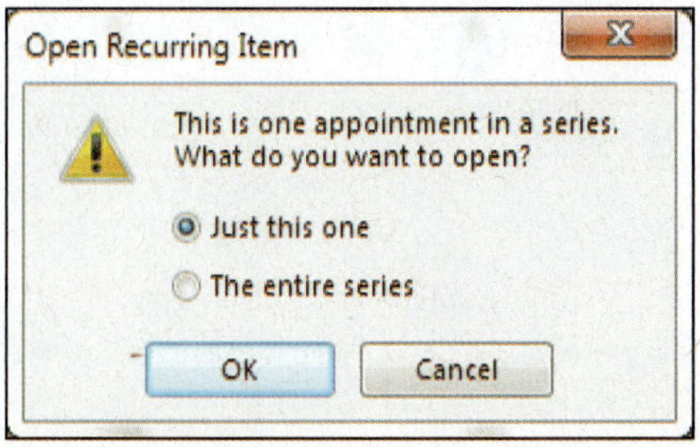

3. Click **OK** to open the single occurrence. The Project Status – Meeting Occurrence window is displayed. The meeting information applies to the single Occurrence only.

4. Click the *Start time* field. Key or select **10:00 AM** and [press **Enter**]. The *End time* field automatically changes to 11:00 AM. Click the **Send Update** button.

5. In your calendar, the single occurrence is modified to show the new time. The other occurrences are not changed.

PAUSE. LEAVE Outlook 2013 open to use in the next exercise.

SHARING MEETING NOTES

The Bottom Line

Whether you are recording the participants or details about the new sales initiative, notes are a key element in most meetings. Outlook 2013 includes a new feature designed to streamline the process of taking notes in OneNote by linking them to the actual meeting request window. As an added bonus, the meeting notes feature also gives you the ability to share your notes with the rest of the meeting's attendees.

Sharing Meeting Notes

Meeting Notes is a powerful new tool that helps you get the most out of your meetings by leveraging Outlook 2013's ability to coordinate your meetings with OneNote, Microsoft's note-taking tool. When you use Meeting Notes, Outlook 2013 will automatically add details about your meeting (date, time, location, and attendees) to the OneNote page you select. Outlook 2013 then places a link to the OneNote page within the meeting request window. After the meeting, the attendees can simply follow the link to review your notes. In this exercise, you will set up a meeting and share your meeting notes with the other attendees.

STEP BY STEP   **Share Meeting Notes**

GET READY. LAUNCH Outlook 2013 if it is not already running.

⚠️ **Troubleshooting** To complete this exercise, you need to have OneNote installed on your computer and the ability to store the notes in a shared location, such a SharePoint site or SkyDrive.

1. In your account, click the **Calendar** button in the Navigation bar to display the Calendar window.

2. On the HOME tab, click **New Meeting**. The Meeting window shown in Figure 9-1 is displayed.

3. In the *To* field, key [**your e-mail address and that of a friend**]. In the *Subject* field, key **Meeting Notes** and set the *Location* as **Executive Conference Room**.

4. Click the **Meeting Notes** button on the MEETING tab. The Meeting Notes dialog box appears, asking whether you are going to take your own notes or share them with the attendees, as shown in Figure 9-31.

Figure 9-31

The Meeting Notes dialog box

Click to create meeting notes in OneNote

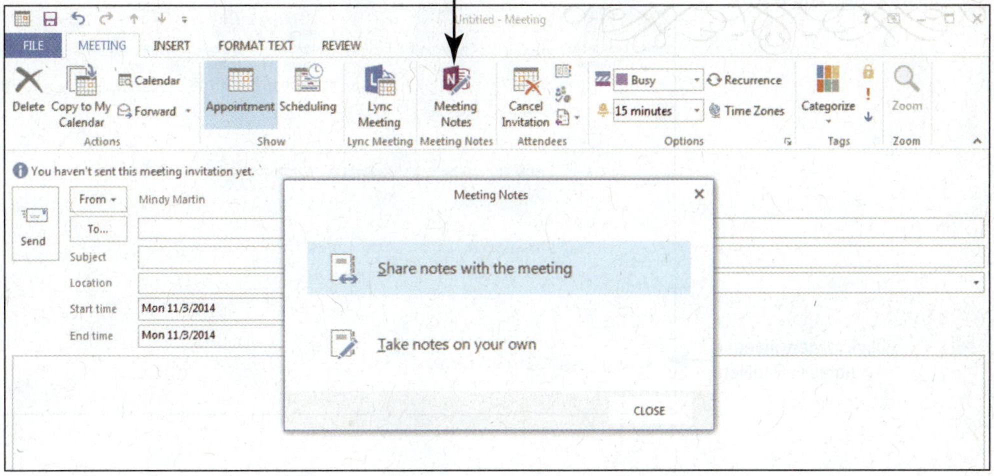

Figure 9-31

The Meeting Notes dialog box

5. Click the **Share notes with the meeting** option in the Meeting Notes dialog box. The Choose Notes to Share with Meeting dialog box opens, as shown in Figure 9-32.

Figure 9-32

The Choose Notes to Share with Meeting dialog box

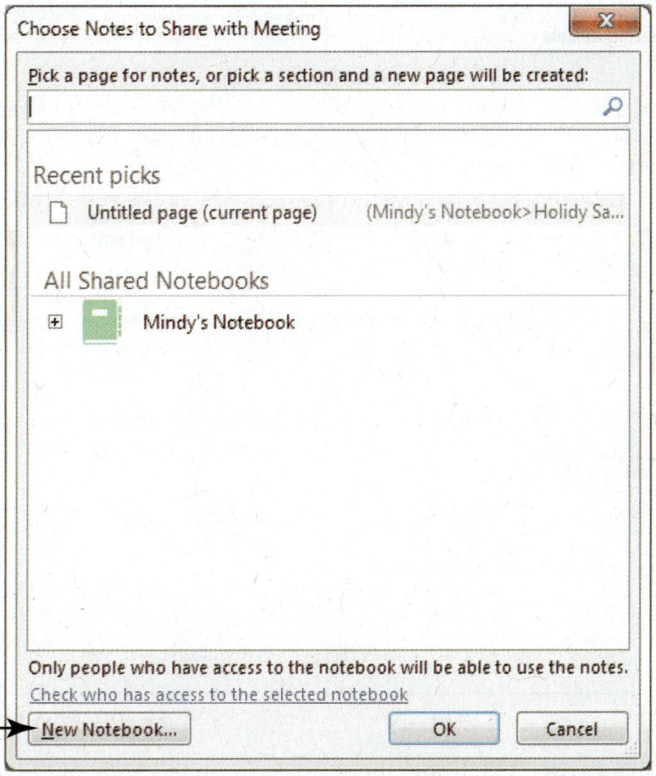

Click to create a OneNote notebook

6. Click the **New Notebook** button. A OneNote window opens asking you to name the new Notebook.

7. Select your SkyDrive or shared location and key **XX_Meeting Notes** (where the *XX* indicates your initials). Click the **Create Notebook** button.

8. Click the **Not Now** button; the Meeting Notes Notebook opens.

9. Double click the **New Section 1** tab and key **Lesson 9**. [Press **Enter**]. Close the OneNote window.

10. In the Choose Notes to Share with Meeting dialog box, navigate to the **Lesson 9** tab in the XX_Meeting Notes notebook. Click **OK**. A link to the meeting notes appears in the Meeting window, as shown in Figure 9-33.

Figure 9-33

Sharing Meeting Notes

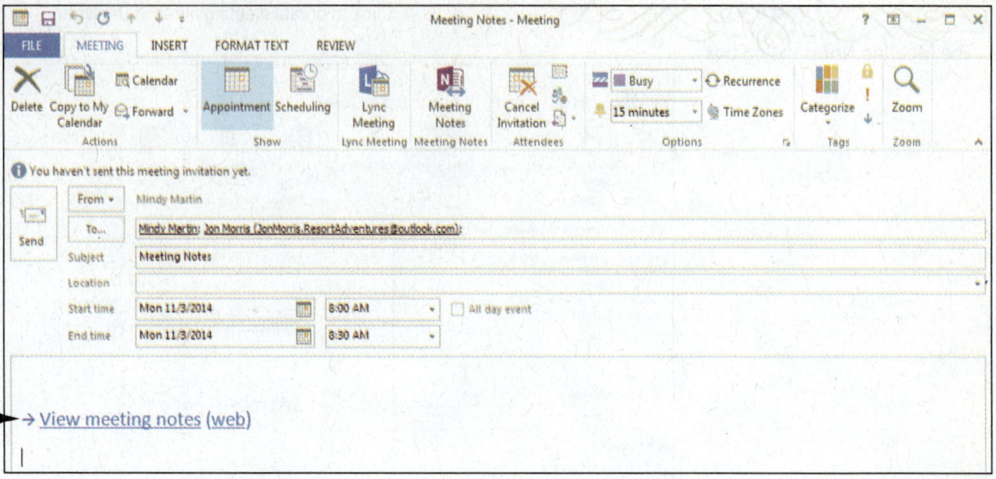

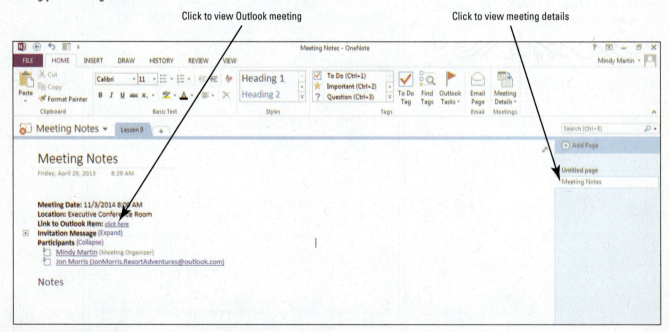

Click to view meeting
notes in OneNote → → View meeting notes (web)

11. Click **Send** to send the meeting request.
12. During the meeting, you'll want to open the Meeting Notes notebook in OneNote and click the **Meeting Notes** item in the page navigator on the right of the window. The details of the meetings appear, as shown in Figure 9-34.

Figure 9-34

Selecting your meeting details

Click to view Outlook meeting   Click to view meeting details

13. Under the word **Notes** in the body of the page, key **This is a sample of meeting notes.**
14. Click the **Link to Outlook Item:** *click here* link. The meeting window opens.
15. Close OneNote.

PAUSE. CLOSE Outlook 2013.

**CERTIFICATION
READY?   3.3.7**

How do you share meeting
notes with attendees?

SKILL SUMMARY

In This Lesson You Learned How To:	Exam Objective	Objective Number
Create a Meeting Request	Create calendar items	3.2.1
	Use the scheduling assistant	3.2.7
	Utilize Room Finder	3.2.10
	Create calendar items from messages	3.2.4
	Set calendar item importance	3.3.1
	Configure reminders	3.3.3
Respond to a Meeting Request	Respond to invitations	3.3.5
Manage a Meeting		
Update a Meeting Request	Update calendar items	3.3.6
	Schedule resources	3.2.9
	Add participants	3.3.4
	Cancel calendar items	3.2.3
Manage a Recurring Meeting	Create recurring calendar items	3.2.2
Share Meeting Notes	Share meeting notes	3.3.7

Knowledge Assessment

Matching

Match the term with its definition.

Column 1	Column 2
a. tentative	**1.** A person who should attend the meeting, but whose presence is not required.
b. scheduling grid	**2.** A single meeting in a series of recurring meetings.
c. mandatory attendee	**3.** An item or a location that can be invited to a meeting.
d. meeting	**4.** Displays scheduling information for all attendees.
e. meeting organizer	**5.** A meeting that occurs at regular intervals.
f. meeting request	**6.** A person who must attend the meeting.
g. occurrence	**7.** Indicates that a person might attend a meeting.
h. optional attendee	**8.** A scheduled activity that requires sending invitations to other people or resources.
i. recurring meeting	**9.** The person who creates the meeting and sends meeting invitations.
j. resource	**10.** The Outlook 2013 item that creates the meeting and invites attendees.

True/False

Circle T if the statement is true or F if the statement is false.

T F 1. The Meeting window is exactly like the Appointment window.

T F 2. When an attendee accepts a meeting request, the attendee's schedule displays the meeting time as tentative.

T F 3. Only people or resources in your address book can be invited to a meeting.

T F 4. Any attendee can propose a new meeting time.

T F 5. When you add an attendee, you can send updated information to only the new attendee.

T F 6. A recurring meeting can occur only 10 times.

T F 7. In order to share meeting notes, all attendees must also have OneNote.

T F 8. To be scheduled, a resource must have its own mailbox.

T F 9. Your calendar is updated when you send a meeting request.

T F 10. Any attendee can cancel a meeting.

Competency Assessment

Project 9-1: Create a One-Time Meeting

It's time to launch a new project at Tailspin Toys. Gather the team leaders in a meeting to divide the duties.

GET READY. LAUNCH Outlook 2013 if it is not already running.

1. Click the **Calendar** button in the Navigation bar to display the Calendar folder.

2. Use the *Date Navigator* to select [**next Thursday's date**].

3. On the HOME tab, click **New Meeting** in the New group. The Meeting window opens.

4. Click the *Subject* field and key **Decoder: Project Launch**. In the *Location* field, key **Dept Room 62**.

5. Click the **Scheduling** (or **Scheduling Assistant**) button in the Show group on the Ribbon.

6. Click the **Add Others** button and click **Add from Address Book**. The Select Attendees and Resources window is displayed.

7. Click **Jamie Reding's** contact information and click the **Required** button. Click **Mandar Samant's** contact information and click the **Optional** button. Click **OK** to return to the Meeting window.

8. Change the *End time* value so the meeting is one hour long. Use the Meeting Suggestions or the **AutoPick Next** button to select an open time for the meeting.

9. Click the **Appointment** button in the Show group on the Ribbon. The *To* field is automatically filled with the attendees' e-mail addresses and the *Start time* and *End time* fields are filled.

10. Click the **Send** button. Your calendar is updated, and the time slot is displayed as busy.

LEAVE Outlook 2013 open for the next project.

Project 9-2: Create a Recurring Meeting

After the Decoder project is launched, set up a recurring meeting to monitor the project's status.

GET READY. Before you begin these steps, complete the previous exercise.

1. Click the **Calendar** button in the Navigation bar to display the Calendar folder.

2. Use the Date Navigator to select [**the Thursday following the *Decoder: Project Launch* item**].

3. On the HOME tab, click New Meeting. The Meeting window is displayed.

4. Click the Subject field and key Decoder: Project Status. In the *Location* field, key Dept Room 62.

5. Click the Scheduling (or Scheduling Assistant) button in the Show group on the Ribbon.

6. Click the Add Others button and click Add from Address Book. The Select Attendees and Resources window is displayed.

7. Click Jamie Reding's contact information and click the Required button. Click Mandar Samant's contact information and click the Optional button. Click OK to return to the Meeting window.

8. Change the *Start time* field to 10:00 AM and change the End time field to 11:00 AM, if necessary. The blue vertical lines move to enclose the specified time slot.

9. Click the Recurrence button in the Options group on the Ribbon. The Appointment Recurrence dialog box is displayed.

10. Click OK to accept the weekly recurrence pattern and return to the meeting window.

11. Click the Appointment button in the Show group on the Ribbon. The *To* field is automatically filled with the attendees' e-mail addresses, and the recurrence pattern is displayed.

12. Click the Send button. Your calendar is updated and the 10:00 AM to 11:00 AM time slot is displayed as busy for every Thursday.

LEAVE Outlook 2013 open for the next project.

Proficiency Assessment

Project 9-3: Add an Attendee to a Recurring Meeting

Diane Tibbott has been assigned to the Decoder project. Add her as an attendee to the recurring Decoder project status meeting.

GET READY. Before you begin these steps, complete the previous exercises. The mandatory attendee used in this exercise must have a different active e-mail account from yours and be able to respond to your meeting invitation.

1. Click the Calendar button in the Navigation bar to display the Calendar folder.

2. Double-click the first Decoder: Project Status meeting. The Open Recurring Item dialog box is displayed.

3. Click The entire series option and click OK.

4. Click the Scheduling (or Scheduling Assistant) button in the Show group on the Ribbon. Scheduling information for the attendees is displayed.

5. Click the Add Others button and click Add from Address Book. The Select Attendees and Resources window is displayed.

6. In the *Required* field, key [the e-mail address of the person or account that is acting as your mandatory attendee] for this lesson.

7. Click OK to return to the Meeting window.

8. Click the Send button. The Send Update to Attendees dialog box is displayed.

9. Click OK. The updated meeting information is sent to Diane Tibbott and no one else.

LEAVE Outlook 2013 open for the next project.

Project 9-4: Propose a New Meeting Time

Diane is currently assigned to the TopHat project; it is coming to a close and it takes priority over the Decoder project. To be able to participate in both meetings, Diane asked you to hold the Decoder: Project Status meeting later in the day.

GET READY. Before you begin these steps, complete the previous exercises. The mandatory attendee used in this exercise must have a different active e-mail account from yours and be able to respond to your meeting invitation.

1. In the mandatory attendee's account, click the Decoder: Project Status meeting request in the message list.

2. In the Reading Pane, click Propose New Time. In the Propose New Time dialog box that appears, propose a new start time of 1:00 PM.

3. Verify that 2:00 PM is the time in the *End time* field and click Propose Time. The dialog box closes and a New Time Proposed – Message window is displayed.

4. In the message area, key [a note asking for the change in schedule].

5. Click the Send button.

LEAVE Outlook 2013 open for the next project.

Mastery Assessment

Project 9-5: Change an Occurrence of a Recurring Meeting

The TopHat project plans to camp in your meeting room for a week of intensive testing. Change the location of the first Decoder: Project Status meeting.

GET READY. LAUNCH Outlook 2013 if it is not already running.

1. Open the first Decoder: Project Status meeting in the Calendar. The Open Recurring Item dialog box is displayed.

2. Open Just this one (occurrence) of the meeting.

3. Change the location to Dept Room 50.

4. Send an update to all attendees.

LEAVE Outlook 2013 open for the next project.

Project 9-6: Cancel a Meeting

The upper management at Tailspin Toys has changed. New leadership brings new priorities. The Decoder project has been cancelled. Cancel the recurring Decoder project status meeting.

GET READY. LAUNCH Outlook 2013 if it is not already running.

1. Open the first Decoder: Project Status meeting in the Calendar. The Open Recurring Item dialog box is displayed.

2. Open The entire series of meetings and cancel the meeting.

3. Send a meeting cancellation notice to the attendees explaining the reason for the cancellation.

CLOSE Outlook 2013.

LESSON SKILL MATRIX

Skills	Exam Objective	Objective Number
Setting Calendar Options	Demonstrate how to set calendar work times	3.1.4
	Modify calendar time zones	3.1.2
	Adjust viewing details for calendars	3.1.1
Sharing Your Calendar	Share calendars	3.1.8
Working with Multiple Calendars	Create multiple calendars	3.1.5
	Overlay calendars	3.1.7
	Manage calendar groups	3.1.6
Managing Calendars	Adjust viewing details for calendars	3.1.1
	Search calendars	1.4.5
	Print calendars	1.3.2
	Delete calendars	3.1.3

© Tongshan/iStockphoto

KEY TERMS

- calendar group
- Internet Calendar Subscription
- overlay mode
- overlay stack
- side-by-side
- time zone
- UTC (Coordinated Universal Time)
- view
- WebDAV (Web-based Distributed Authoring and Versioning)
- work week

349

Mindy is a co-owner of Resort Adventures. Mindy and her partner, Jon, work different hours so that an owner is on the premises as much as possible. Their work schedules overlap for several hours a day, and they come into the office for meetings or extra hours on busy days when necessary. It's a good thing Outlook 2013 lets Mindy modify the Calendar to reflect her unusual work schedule. In this lesson, you'll customize your main Outlook 2013 calendar, create and work with a secondary calendar, share calendars, and print them.

© Tongshan/iStockphoto

SOFTWARE ORIENTATION

Outlook Calendar Options

You can customize the Outlook 2013 calendar to make it fit your needs or work patterns using the Calendar settings in the Outlook Options dialog box shown in Figure 10-1. Access these calendar options from the Backstage view, then select or modify specific settings.

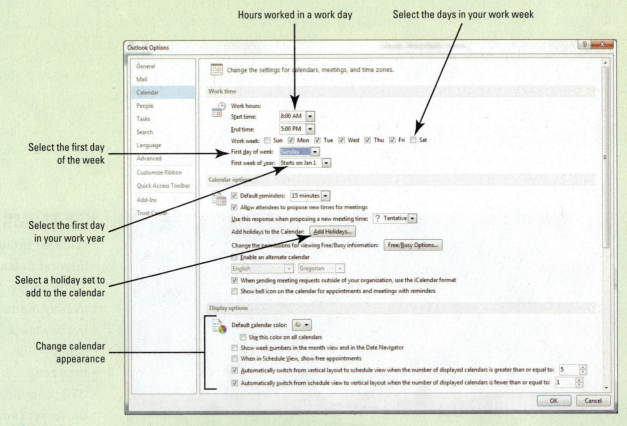

Figure 10-1
Calendar settings in the Outlook Options dialog box

SETTING CALENDAR OPTIONS

The Bottom Line

To make your calendar more useful, you can customize it in several ways. You can define your work week, display the time zones you use regularly, set your own time zone, and add holidays to the calendar.

Defining Your Work Week

Your **work week** is the hours or days you work in a calendar week. The most common work week is 8:00 AM to 5:00 PM Monday through Friday, but your work week may differ. In this exercise, you will define your work week as Tuesday through Saturday from 6:00 AM to 3:00 PM, since you don't work on Sunday and Monday.

STEP BY STEP **Define Your Work Week**

GET READY. LAUNCH Outlook 2013 if it is not already running.

1. On the FILE tab, click **Options**. The Outlook Options dialog box is displayed.
2. Click **Calendar** in the Navigation Pane. The calendar options are displayed as in Figure 10-1.
3. In the Work Time section of the window, click the **Mon** check box to deselect it and remove Monday from your work week.
4. Click the **Sat** check box to add Saturday to your work week.
5. Click the *Start time* field. Key or select **6:00 AM**. Click the *End time* field. Key or select **3:00 PM**.
6. In the *First day of the week* field, select **Tuesday** as the start of your work week. Compare your work time calendar options to Figure 10-2.

Figure 10-2

Work week defined

Work week options

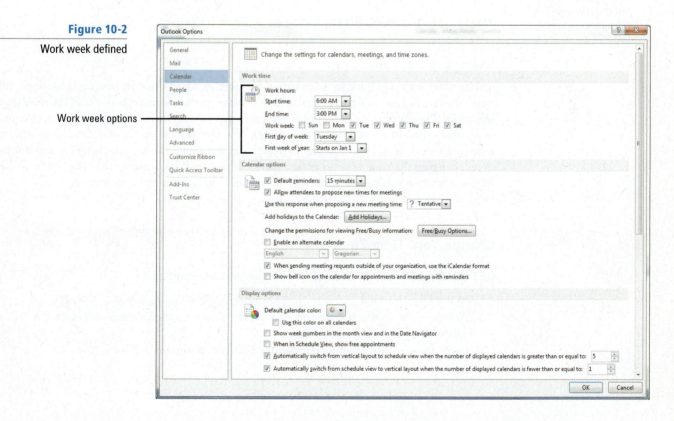

7. Click **OK** to save the modified work week.
8. Click the **Calendar** button on the Navigation bar to display the Calendar window.

9. On the HOME tab, click **Work Week** from the Arrange group to see how the modified work week affects your calendar. Note that Saturday is now a workday and Monday and Sunday have been removed to indicate that they are not workdays, as shown in Figure 10-3.

Figure 10-3

Modified Work Week view

New start time →

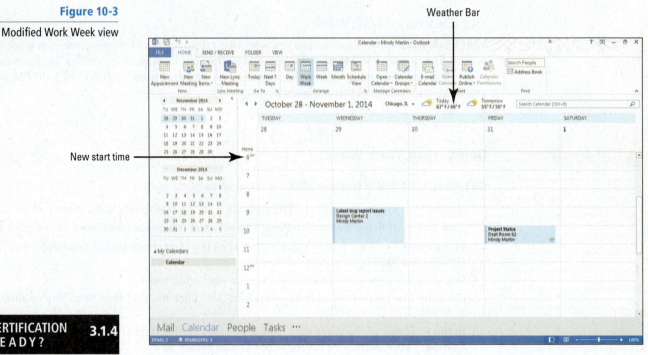

Weather Bar

PAUSE. LEAVE Outlook 2013 open to use in the next exercise.

Changing Your Time Zone

A **time zone** is a geographic location using the same standard time. In Microsoft Outlook 2013, time zones are defined in terms of the difference between their local time and **UTC (Coordinated Universal Time),** the time standard based on International Atomic Time. If you move, transfer to another office, or remain onsite at a client's office for several weeks, you can change the time zone in your calendar. If you frequently travel and stay in a different time zone for any length of time, changing the time zone to match the local time will help ensure that you don't miss any appointments. In this exercise, you will temporarily change your local time zone.

STEP BY STEP **Change Your Time Zone**

GET READY. LAUNCH Outlook 2013 if it is not already running.

1. On the FILE tab, click **Options**. The Outlook Options dialog box is displayed.
2. Click **Calendar** in the Navigation Pane. The calendar options are displayed as in Figure 10-1.
3. Scroll down to see additional calendar options, as shown in Figure 10-4.

Figure 10-4

Time Zone options

Your current time zone   Show a second time zone

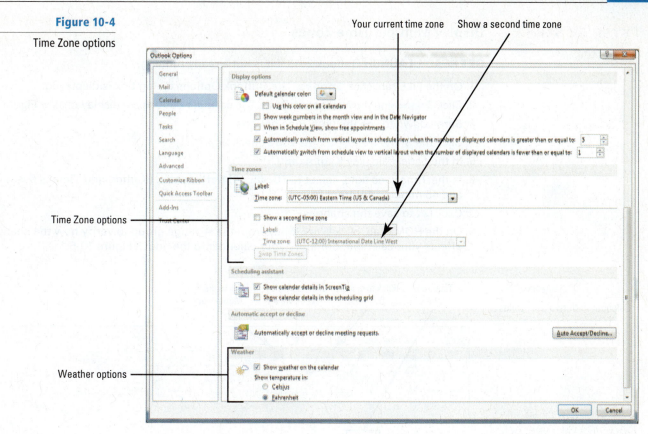

Time Zone options

Weather options

4. In the *Time Zone* field, select [a time zone that differs from your current time zone by several hours].

Take Note   Throughout this chapter you will see information that appears in black text within brackets, such as [Press Enter], or [next Friday's date]. The information contained in the brackets is intended to be directions for you rather than something you actually type word for word. It will instruct you to perform an action or substitute text. Do **not** type the actual text that appears within brackets.

5. In the *Label* field, key Training Site.
6. Click OK to save the changes.
7. On the HOME tab, click Week from the Arrange group to see how the modified time zone affects your calendar. The times of any set appointments and meetings will have been adjusted.
8. On the FILE tab, click Options.
9. Click Calendar to see the calendar options.
10. Scroll down to see the *Time Zone* field, select [your own time zone] from the list.
11. In the *Label* field, key Home.
12. Click OK to save the changes.
13. On the HOME tab, click Week from the Arrange group, if necessary, to verify that your changes have taken effect.

PAUSE. LEAVE Outlook 2013 open to use in the next exercise.

CERTIFICATION READY?   3.1.2

How do you change your time zone?

Displaying Multiple Time Zones

Depending on your business, family, and friends, you may communicate frequently with one or more businesses or individuals in a different time zone. You don't want to miss talking to an important client by calling after business hours. To easily agree on times for meetings and phone calls, it can be useful to display other time zones in your calendar. In this exercise, you will add a second time zone to your calendar.

STEP BY STEP   **Display Multiple Time Zones**

GET READY. LAUNCH Outlook 2013 if it is not already running.

1. On the FILE tab, click **Options**. The Outlook Options dialog box is displayed.
2. Click **Calendar** in the Navigation Pane. The calendar options are displayed as in Figure 10-1.
3. Scroll down to see the time zone options.
4. Click the **Show a second time zone** check box.
5. In the *Label* field, key **Kathmandu**.
6. In the *Time zone* field, select **(UTC+05:45) Kathmandu**. (Kathmandu Time is five hours and 45 minutes different from UTC.)
7. Click **OK** to save the changes.
8. On the HOME tab, click **Work Week** from the Arrange group to verify how the change affects your calendar. Compare your calendar to the one in Figure 10-5.

Figure 10-5

Calendar with two time zones

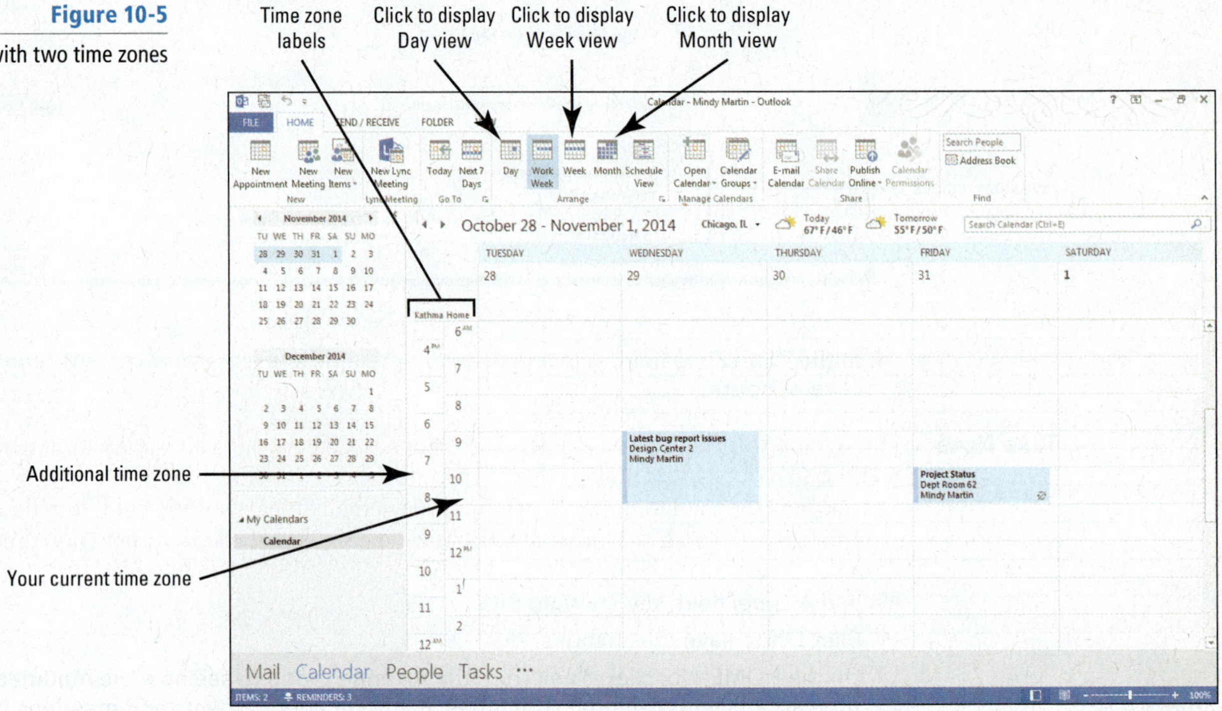

9. On the FILE tab, click **Options**. Click **Calendar** to see the calendar options.
10. Scroll down to see the time zone options and click the **Show a second time zone** check box to deselect it.
11. Click **OK** to save the changes.

PAUSE. LEAVE Outlook 2013 open to use in the next exercise.

Customizing the Weather Bar

Outlook 2013 has added a new feature, the Weather Bar, to help you be better prepared for your upcoming meetings. The Outlook 2013 Weather Bar displays the weather forecast for one to three days, depending on the view. You can customize the Weather Bar to display the forecast for up to five different cities and to display the temperature in either Fahrenheit or Celsius. In this exercise, you will customize the Weather Bar by adding a new location.

Customize the Weather Bar

GET READY. LAUNCH Outlook 2013 if it is not already running.

1. Click **Calendar** in the Navigation bar. On the HOME tab, click **Week** in the Arrange group.
2. Hover your mouse over the forecast for Today. A flyout appears with additional information, as shown in Figure 10-6.

Figure 10-6

Working with the Weather Bar

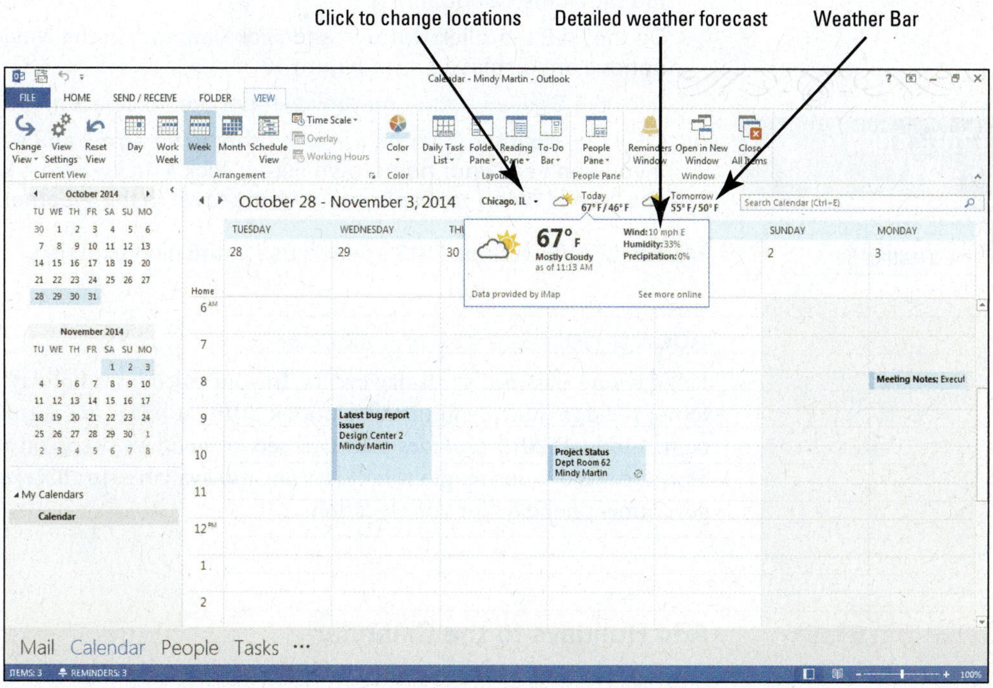

Click to change locations   Detailed weather forecast   Weather Bar

Take Note   If you click the See more online link, you'll be taken to the MSN Weather page for the selected city.

3. Click the **Weather location options** drop arrow to view your list of locations, as shown in Figure 10-7.

Figure 10-7

Weather location options

Click to add a new location   Click to change locations   Weather Bar

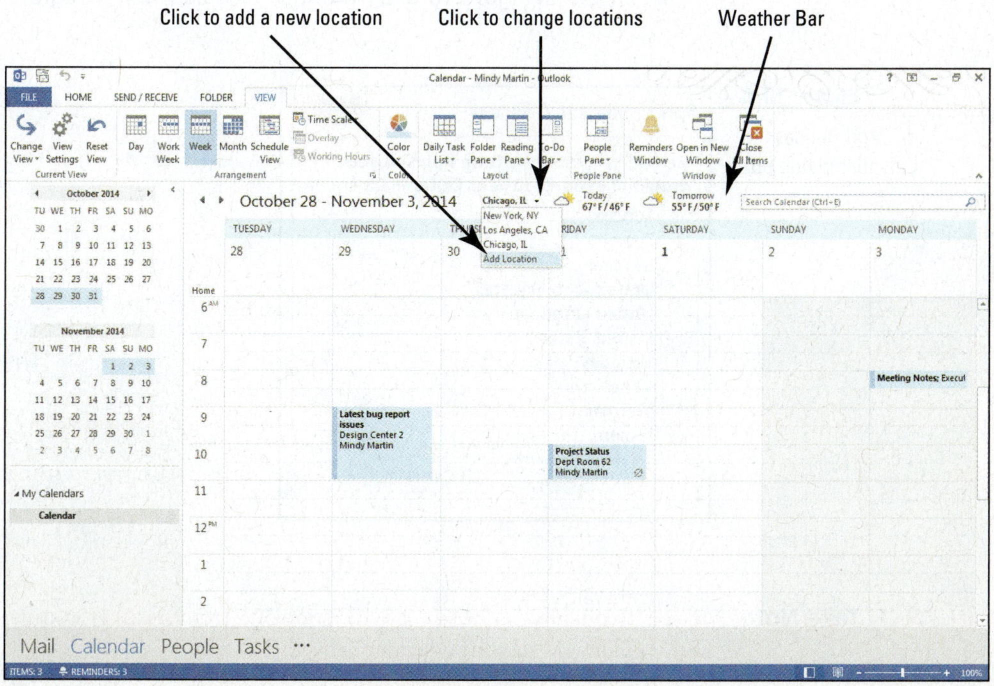

4. Click **Add Location** from drop list. In the *Enter city or Zip code* box, key **Seattle, WA** and [press **Enter**]. If prompted to select Seattle from the list, do so. The Weather Bar changes to show you Seattle's forecast.

5. On the FILE tab, click **Options**. Click **Calendar** in the Navigation Pane. The calendar options are displayed as in Figure 10-1.

6. Scroll down to see the **Weather** section, as shown in Figure 10-4.

7. Click the **Show weather on the calendar** box to deselect it. Click **OK**. The Outlook Options dialog box closes. Notice that the weather information no longer appears at the top of the calendar.

8. On the FILE tab, click **Options** and click **Calendar** in the Navigation Pane. The calendar options are displayed as in Figure 10-1.

9. Click the **Show weather on the calendar** box to select it and click **OK**.

10. Click the **Weather location options** drop down arrow and select your city from the list. If you don't see your hometown listed, click **Add Location**, key your [**home Zip code**] and [press **Enter**] to display your home town in the Weather forecast.

PAUSE. LEAVE Outlook 2013 open to use in the next exercise.

CERTIFICATION READY?   3.1.1

How do you customize the Weather Bar?

Adding Holidays to the Calendar

Holidays are classified as all-day events. In your calendar, a holiday is displayed as a banner at the top of the day. When you install Outlook 2013, holidays are not placed on your calendar by default. Outlook 2013 provides standard sets of holidays based on individual country traditions. Separate sets of some religious holidays are also available. In this exercise, you will add the official government holidays for your location.

STEP BY STEP   **Add Holidays to the Calendar**

GET READY. LAUNCH Outlook 2013 if it is not already running.

1. On the FILE tab, click **Options**. The Outlook Options dialog box is displayed.

2. Click **Calendar** in the Navigation Pane. The calendar options are displayed as in Figure 10-1.

3. Under the *Calendar options* section, click **Add Holidays**.

4. Click [**the check box next to the country or region's holiday set that you want to add**], as shown in Figure 10-8. By default, your country or region is already selected.

Figure 10-8

Add Holidays to Calendar dialog box

Add Holidays to Calendar

Select the locations whose holidays you would like copied to your Outlook Calendar:

- ☐ Tunisia
- ☐ Turkey
- ☐ Ukraine
- ☐ United Arab Emirates
- ☐ United Kingdom
- ☑ United States
- ☐ Uruguay
- ☐ Venezuela
- ☐ Vietnam
- ☐ Yemen

[OK]   [Cancel]

Take Note   If you frequently do business with someone from another country, you might consider adding their holiday set to your calendar as well.

5. Click **OK**. A small window is displayed while the holidays are added to your calendar. When the holidays are added, a message is displayed telling you that the holidays were added. Click **OK**.

Troubleshooting   If you try to add the same holiday set again, you will see duplicate holiday and event entries in your calendar. Outlook 2013 will display a warning message before adding these holidays a second time.

6. Click **OK** to close the Outlook Options dialog box.

7. On the HOME tab, click **Month** in the Arrange group to display the Month view. If necessary, click the **Forward** or **Back** button to view a month containing a holiday, as shown in Figure 10-9.

Figure 10-9

Holidays added
to the Calendar

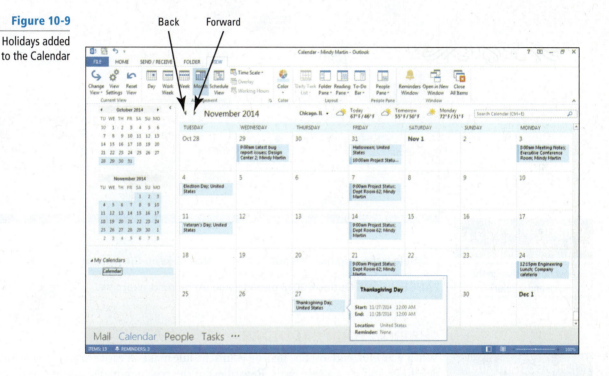

PAUSE. LEAVE Outlook 2013 open to use in the next exercise.

Changing the Calendar Color

Another way of customizing your Outlook 2013 calendar is to change the background color for the calendar grid itself. In this exercise, you will change the background color for your main Outlook 2013 calendar.

STEP BY STEP   **Change the Calendar Color**

GET READY. LAUNCH Outlook 2013 if it is not already running.

1. On the FILE tab, click **Options**. The Outlook Options dialog box is displayed. Click **Calendar**.

2. In the *Display options* section, click the **Default calendar color:** drop-down arrow and select a color you like.

Take Note   The *Use this color on all calendars* check box will apply this same background color to your custom and shared calendars as well.

3. Click **OK** to save the changes.

4. On the HOME tab, click **Month** in the Arrange group to display the Month view.

5. Click the **VIEW tab**.

6. Click the **Color** button in the Color group. Notice that the new Automatic Color matches the color you selected in the Outlook Options dialog box, as shown in Figure 10-10.

Figure 10-10

Changing the Calendar color

Click to choose a color

7. Select the original Calendar color swatch or keep the new one.

PAUSE. LEAVE Outlook 2013 open to use in the next exercise.

SHARING YOUR CALENDAR

The Bottom Line

When you work with others, sharing your schedule makes it easier to arrange meetings, determine deadlines, and set realistic goals. Regardless of the type of e-mail account you use, you can share your calendar with others. You can share calendar information through a company server using Microsoft Exchange or share your calendar using the Internet.

Sending Calendar Information via E-mail

If you don't have a Microsoft Exchange Server, you might find it useful to share your calendar information to help with trying to schedule meetings or events. In Outlook 2013, you can send a copy of your calendar to anyone using an e-mail message. In this exercise, you will send a calendar to a friend or coworker via e-mail.

STEP BY STEP **Send Calendar Information via E-mail**

GET READY. LAUNCH Outlook 2013 if it is not already running.

1. If necessary, click the **Calendar** button in the Navigation bar to display your Calendar.

2. On the HOME tab, click the **E-mail Calendar** button in the Share group. An untitled Message window is displayed along with the *Send a Calendar via E-mail* dialog box.

3. In the *Calendar* field, select **Calendar**, if necessary.

4. In the *Date Range* field, select **Next 30 days**.

Another Way

If you have more than one calendar, you can specify your alternate calendar's name here.

5. In the *Detail* field, select **Limited details**.

6. Click the **Show** button in the Advanced: section to display more options, as shown in Figure 10-11.

Figure 10-11

Send a Calendar via
E-mail dialog box

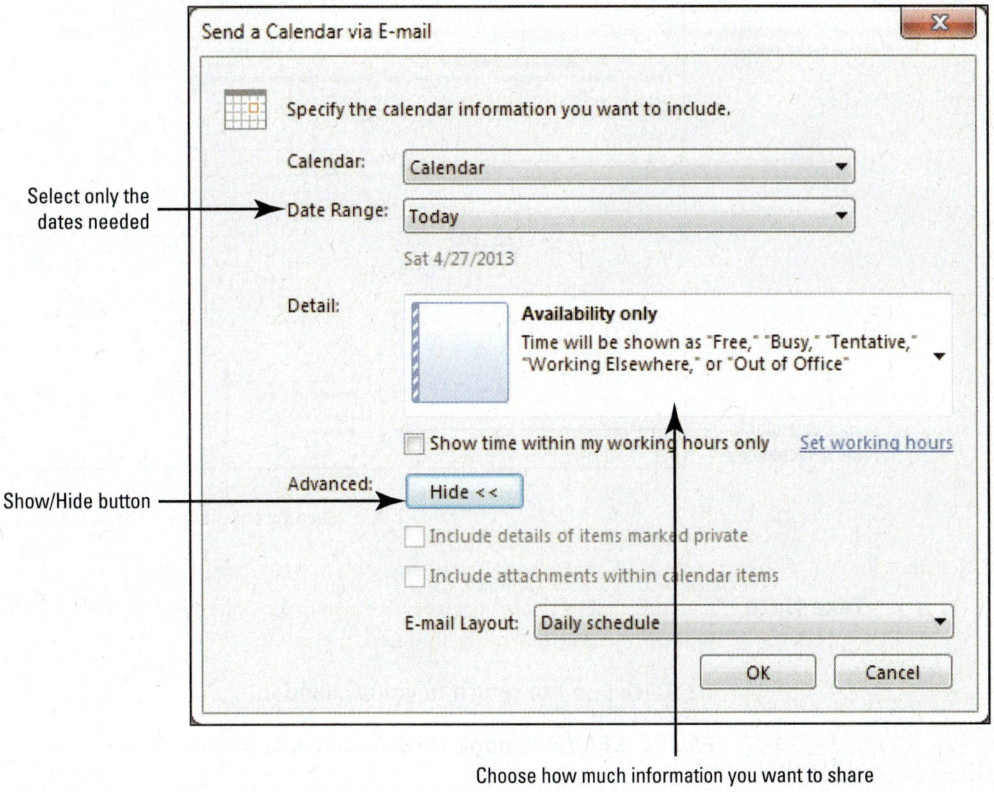

Select only the
dates needed

Show/Hide button

Choose how much information you want to share

7. In the *E-mail Layout:* field, select **List of events**.

⚠️ **Troubleshooting** Be sure to select the smallest date range necessary for the recipient's needs. Every added day increases the size of the message. Many e-mail servers restrict the size of messages that can be received. If the date range is too large or if you included unnecessary details, the message might be too large for the recipient to receive.

8. Click **OK**. The Outlook Message window displays the calendar information included in the body of the message.

9. In the *To* field, key [**the e-mail address of a friend or coworker**]. In the *Cc* field, key [**your e-mail address**].

10. In the message body above the calendar details, key **As you can see from the details below, my week is pretty open. Find a time that works for you and I'll add it to my calendar as well.** [Press **Enter**.] **Mindy**.

11. Compare your message to Figure 10-12. Scroll down the message body if necessary to view the data in the message.

Figure 10-12

Sharing a calendar via e-mail

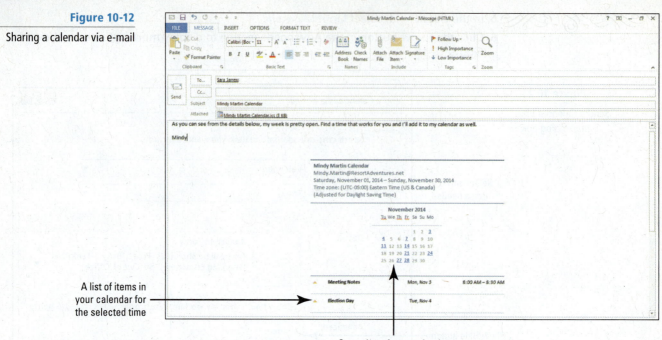

A list of items in
your calendar for
the selected time

Snap shot of your calendar

Take Note   Calendars sent in this manner are a snapshot of your calendar details, so the calendar information will not be automatically updated.

12. Click **Send** to return to your Calendar.

PAUSE. LEAVE Outlook 2013 open to use in the next exercise.

When you share a calendar with someone, they will be able to see when you are available. You select the date range you want to include and the level of detail to share, as shown in Table 10-1.

Table 10-1

Calendar Details Options

Detail Level	Description
Availability only	Time is displayed as free, busy, tentative, working elsewhere, or out of office. This is enough information for scheduling purposes.
Limited details	The attached calendar includes availability information and the subjects of all calendar items.
Full details	The attached calendar includes availability information and the complete details of all calendar items.

Publishing Calendar Information Online

Although e-mailing a snapshot of your Calendar is a useful way of making your schedule available to other people, it only sends a static view of your meetings and appointments. As schedules change, the recipient won't get updated. If you need to share your calendar with someone who is going to need your schedule information on an ongoing basis, you would be better off publishing your Calendar online to a WebDAV server. **WebDAV (Web-based Distributed Authoring and Versioning)** is a common file and calendar hosting server protocol. You can still control the amount of calendar information published and limit the number of people who can view your calendar. By default, the published calendar information is updated every 30 minutes. This means that the people you have shared the published calendar with will always have the most up-to-date information. In this exercise, you will publish a calendar to Office.com.

Publish Calendar Information Online

GET READY. LAUNCH Outlook 2013 if it is not already running.

Before you begin these steps, you must be connected to the Internet and have access to a server that supports the World Wide Web Distributed Authoring and Versioning (WebDAV) protocol. Check with your instructor if you aren't sure if your account supports this.

Troubleshooting   If you are logged into a secure Microsoft Exchange network, your Administrator may block this feature. Ask about any alternate methods for sharing calendar information outside your network.

1. If necessary, click the **Calendar** button in the Navigation bar to display the Calendar. If necessary, select your calendar and click the **Publish Online** button in the Share group.

2. Select **Publish to WebDAV Server** to open the Publish Calendar to Custom Server dialog box, which is similar to the dialog box shown in Figure 10-11.

3. In the *Location* field, key [**the address of the WebDAV server**].

4. In the *Time Span* field, select the **1 Day** previous through next **90 Days** option.

5. In the *Detail* field, select **Availability only**.

6. Click the **Advanced** button. The *Published Calendar Settings* dialog box is displayed, as shown in Figure 10-13.

Figure 10-13

The Published Calendar Settings dialog box

```
Publish Calendar to Custom Server                                    ⊠

    ┌──────────────────────────────────────────────────────┐
    │ Published Calendar Settings                      ⊠     │
    │                                                        │
    │   Upload Method:                                       │
    │   ⦿ Automatic Uploads: Upload updates periodically     │
    │   ○ Single Upload: Updates will not be uploaded        │
    │                                                        │
    │   Update Frequency:                                     │
    │   ☑ Update this calendar with the server's recommended frequency │
    │                                                        │
    │      If checked, calendar updates will be published according to the server │
    │      guidelines, regardless of Send/Receive group settings. │
    │                                                        │
    │                              [  OK  ]   [ Cancel ]     │
    └──────────────────────────────────────────────────────┘

          ☐ Show time within my working hours only   Set working hours

    [ Advanced... ]                          [   OK   ]   [ Cancel ]
```

7. Deselect the **Update Frequency** check box and click **OK**.

8. Click **OK** to publish your calendar. Key the [**username and password**] needed to access the WebDAV server, if necessary, and click **OK**. When the upload is complete, the *Send a Sharing Invitation* dialog box is displayed, as shown in Figure 10-14.

Figure 10-14

Send a Sharing Invitation dialog box

```
Send a Sharing Invitation

   ⚠    Your calendar was published
        successfully.

        Do you want to send a sharing
        invitation to let people know about
        the calendar you just published?

        [ Yes ]          [ No ]
```

9. Click **Yes**. A Share window resembling an Outlook Message window is displayed, as shown in Figure 10-15.

Figure 10-15

A Share window

Calendar to be published

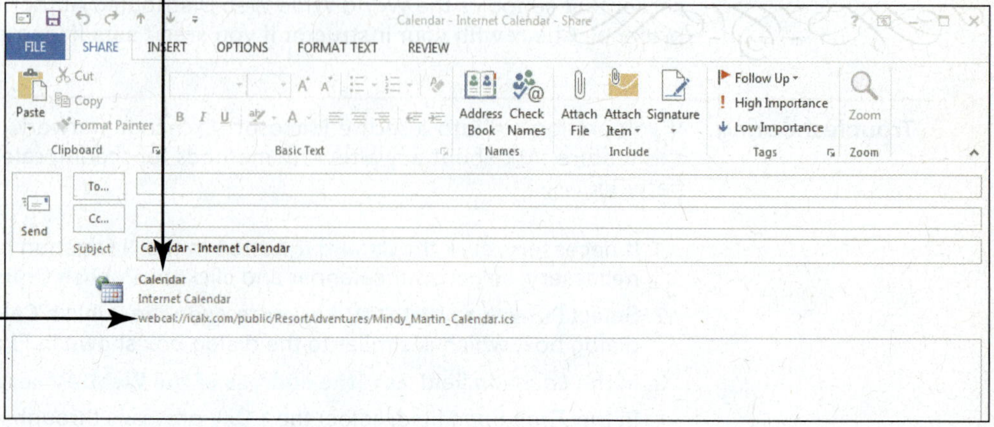

Calendar location

10. In the *To* field, key [**your e-mail address**] or that of a friend if you are working together. Click the **Send** button. The invitation is sent.

Take Note To view your calendar, the invited individual must also have access to the WebDAV server.

PAUSE. LEAVE Outlook 2013 open to use in the next exercise.

Sharing Your Calendar with Other Network Users

By default, the free/busy details of your Calendar are already shared with everyone on your Exchange network. But, you can also allow members of your Exchange Server network to see additional details and make edits to your calendar. You decide who can see your calendar and exactly what level of detail you want to share.

STEP BY STEP **Share Your Calendar with Other Network Users**

GET READY. Before you begin these steps, be sure to launch Microsoft Outlook 2013. This exercise requires a Microsoft Exchange account.

Troubleshooting If the Share Calendar button is grey on the Share group of the HOME tab, you do not have a Microsoft Exchange account configured. If this is the case, you cannot complete this exercise.

Another Way
You can also share your calendar by giving someone on your network Delegate Access to your calendar.

Cross Ref

1. If necessary, click the **Calendar** button in the Navigation bar to display the Calendar window.
2. On the HOME tab, click **Share Calendar** in the Share group. A *Sharing Invitation* message window opens.

You can find information about giving others delegate access to your calendar in Lesson 5.

3. In the *To* field, key the [**name of the individual you want to view your calendar**].
4. In the *Details* field, select **Limited Details**.
5. Click the **Send** button. A dialog box is displayed.
6. Click **OK** to confirm the information. A message is sent to the person you are sharing your calendar with notifying them that they can now open and view your calendar.

CERTIFICATION READY?   3.1.8

How do you share your calendar details with others?

PAUSE. LEAVE Outlook 2013 open to use in the next exercise.

WORKING WITH MULTIPLE CALENDARS

The Bottom Line

Keeping multiple calendars is a great way to stay organized and keep your personal information private. Outlook 2013 makes it easy to create custom calendars. You can also share calendars with others and subscribe to calendars via the Internet. Use the Outlook 2013 tools to hide and display multiple calendars and to view them in different combinations and arrangements.

Creating a Custom Calendar

Many times your work involves participation in a number of project teams. Project teams have their own set of meetings, deadlines, and tasks. In this exercise, you will create a new calendar for managing the details of a project dedicated to Resort Adventures' anniversary celebration party.

STEP BY STEP   **Create a Custom Calendar**

GET READY. LAUNCH Outlook 2013 if it is not already running.

1. On the FOLDER tab, click **New Calendar** in the New group. The *Create New Folder* dialog box is displayed, as shown in Figure 10-16.

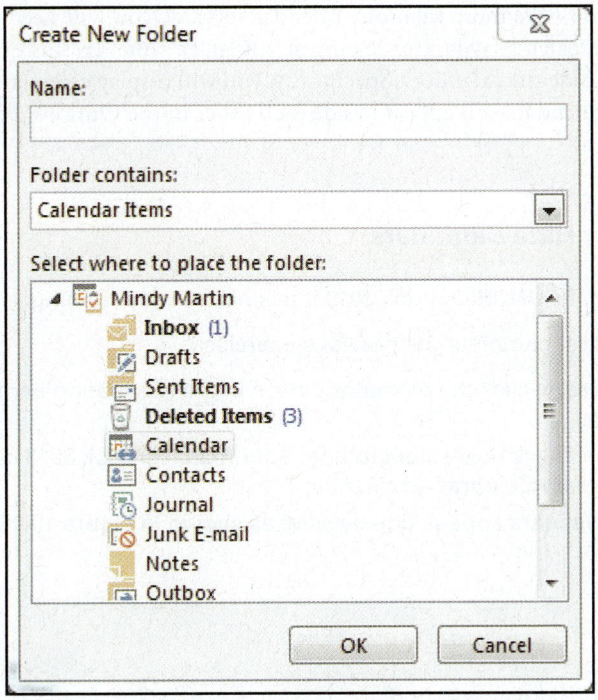

Figure 10-16

The Create New Folder dialog box

> **Create New Folder**
>
> Name:
>
> [ ]
>
> Folder contains:
>
> Calendar Items   [▼]
>
> Select where to place the folder:
>
> ▲ ▣ Mindy Martin
>   Inbox (1)
>   Drafts
>   Sent Items
>   Deleted Items (3)
>   Calendar
>   Contacts
>   Journal
>   Junk E-mail
>   Notes
>   Outbox
>
> [OK]   [Cancel]

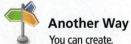

Another Way

You can create, delete, or rename a custom calendar by selecting those options in the right-click shortcut menu in the Folders Pane.

2. In the *Name* field, key **Anniversary Celebration**.
3. In the *Select where to place the folder:* field, select your main Outlook Data File.
4. Click **OK** to close the dialog box.
5. The new *Anniversary Celebration* calendar appears in the Folders Pane under the My Calendars heading, as shown in Figure 10-17.

Figure 10-17

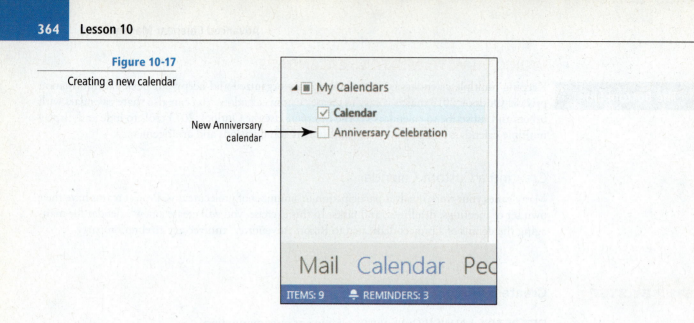

Figure 10-17

Creating a new calendar

New Anniversary calendar

PAUSE. LEAVE Outlook 2013 open to use in the next exercise.

<table>
<tr><td>CERTIFICATION READY? 3.1.5</td></tr>
<tr><td>How do you create multiple calendars?</td></tr>
</table>

Displaying or Hiding Calendars

Now that you have more than one calendar to view, you will need a way to make sure that you know which calendar you are viewing at any given time. In this exercise, you will learn how to display and hide the calendars. Specifically, you will display calendars in **side-by-side** view, which means the calendars will appear beside each other in the Outlook 2013 window.

STEP BY STEP   **Display or Hide Calendars**

GET READY. LAUNCH Outlook 2013 if it is not already running.

You must first complete the previous exercises.

1. If necessary, click the **Calendar** button in the Navigation bar to display the Calendar window.
2. Click the check boxes next to both your main Outlook 2013 calendar and the Anniversary Celebration calendar.
3. Both calendars appear side by side, as shown in Figure 10-18.

Both calendars are visible

Figure 10-18

Side-by-side calendars

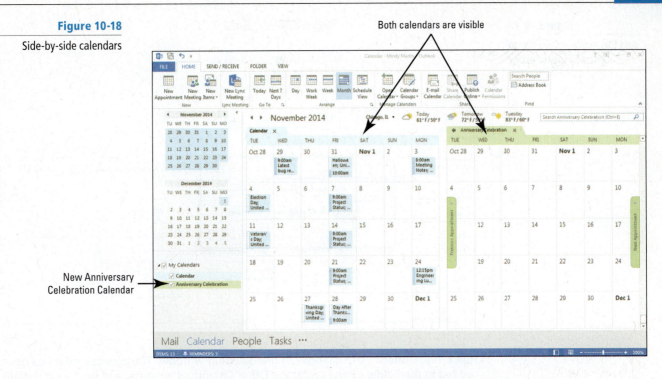

New Anniversary
Celebration Calendar

4. Click the check box next to the Anniversary Celebration calendar in the Folders Pane to clear the check box. The second calendar is now hidden from view.

PAUSE. LEAVE Outlook 2013 open to use in the next exercise.

Viewing a Calendar Shared via E-mail

In the previous section, you learned several ways to share your calendar with others. Now, you will learn how to view shared calendars. In a previous exercise, you shared a calendar via e-mail. As you saw during the exercise, a snapshot of the shared calendar appeared at the bottom of the e-mail message. In addition to the image of the calendar, the message also included a calendar attachment. You can open this calendar file and use it to view the sender's free/busy information when scheduling meetings. In this exercise, you will view a calendar shared by e-mail.

STEP BY STEP	**View a Calendar Shared via E-mail**

GET READY. LAUNCH Outlook 2013 if it is not already running. For this exercise you need to have completed the Send Calendar Information via E-mail exercise earlier in this lesson.

1. If necessary, click the **Mail** button in the Navigation bar to display the mailbox.

2. In the message list, select the Calendar sharing message sent to you by a friend or coworker. If you do not have one, locate the sharing invitation that you copied yourself on in the *Send Calendar Information via E-mail* exercise. The message is previewed in the Reading Pane.

3. Click the **Open this Calendar** button at the top of the Reading Pane. The *Add this Internet Calendar to Outlook?* message box is displayed, as shown in Figure 10-19.

Figure 10-19

Add this Internet Calendar to
Outlook? message box

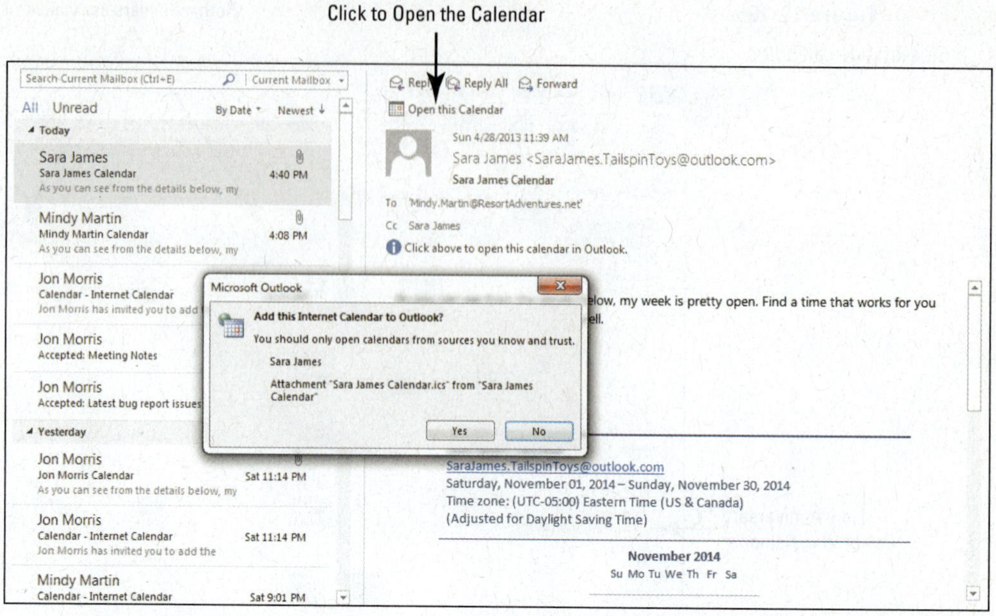

Click to Open the Calendar

4. Click **Yes**. Outlook 2013 changes to the Calendar window. The new calendar has been added to the Folders Pane under the Other Calendars heading, and both your default calendar and the one that you received via e-mail are displayed.

5. Click the check box next to the new calendar to clear the check box and view the default calendar on its own.

PAUSE. LEAVE Outlook 2013 open to use in the next exercise.

Viewing Another Network User's Calendar

In the previous section, you learned to share calendars with other users via e-mail. Now, you will learn how to view the calendars that members of your Exchange network share with you. To view someone's calendar, you must have permission. After permission is granted, you can create a link to the shared calendar that will be stored in your Folders Pane. In this exercise, you will view a network user's calendar.

STEP BY STEP   **View Another Network User's Calendar**

GET READY. LAUNCH Outlook 2013 if it is not already running.

This exercise requires a Microsoft Exchange account.

Troubleshooting   If you do not have a Microsoft Exchange account configured, you cannot complete this exercise.

Another Way
You can also open a shared calendar by clicking the Open Calendar button on the Calendar's HOME tab and selecting the Open Shared Calendar option. You will then need to click the Name button and select the name of the person who has granted you access and click OK.

1. If necessary, click the **Mail** button in the Navigation bar to display the mailbox.

2. Scroll through the Message list to locate the **Sharing Invitation message** that was sent to you in a previous exercise. Select the message so that the contents are displayed in the Reading Pane.

3. Click the **Open this Calendar** button at the top of the Reading Pane.

4. Click **Yes**. Outlook 2013 changes to the Calendar window. The new calendar has been added to the Folders Pane under the Shared Calendars heading, and both your default calendar and the one that you received via e-mail are displayed.

5. Click the check box next to the new calendar to clear the check box and view the default calendar on its own.

PAUSE. LEAVE Outlook 2013 open to use in the next exercise.

Subscribing to an Internet Calendar

An **Internet Calendar Subscription** is a downloaded calendar that is automatically updated. You can use an invitation, like the one that you created earlier in this lesson, to subscribe to an Internet calendar. You can search one of several websites that host Internet calendars, such as Office.com or iCalx.com. In this exercise, you will subscribe to the published calendar you received earlier in the lesson and a public calendar.

Subscribe to an Internet Calendar

GET READY. LAUNCH Outlook 2013 if it is not already running.

This exercise requires Internet access.

1. If necessary, click the Mail button in the Navigation bar to display the mailbox.
2. In the message list, click the Internet Calendar sharing invitation sent to you by a friend or coworker. The message is previewed in the Reading Pane.
3. Click the Subscribe to this Calendar button on the top of the Reading Pane. The *Add this Internet Calendar to Outlook and Subscribe to Updates?* dialog box is displayed, as shown in Figure 10-20.

Figure 10-20

The *Add this Internet Calendar to Outlook and Subscribe to Updates?* dialog box

Click to create a permanent link to this calendar

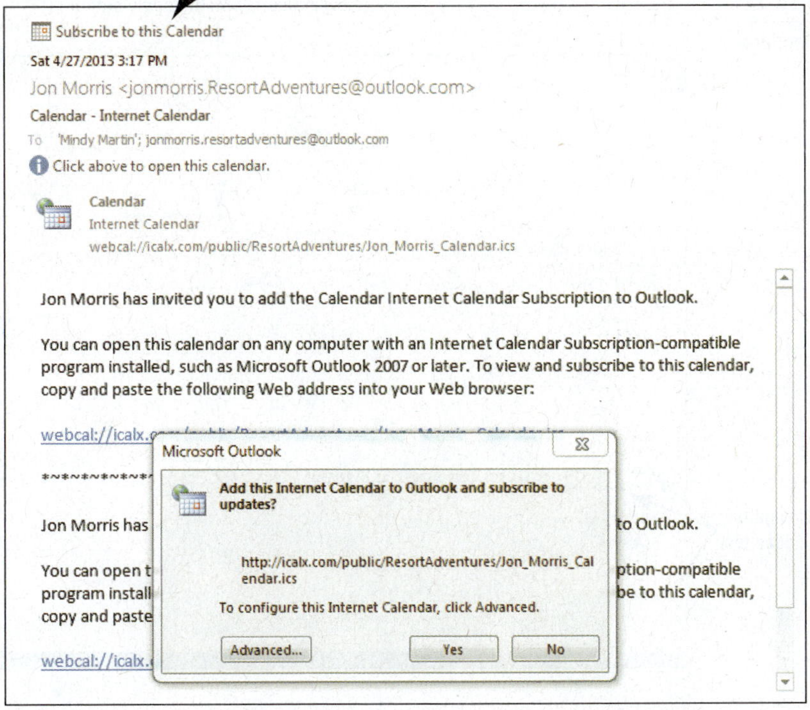

4. Click Yes. The new calendar has been added to the Folders Pane under the Shared Calendars heading.
5. Click the check box next to your default calendar to clear the check box and view the new shared calendar on its own.
6. In the Folders Pane, select [the default calendar's check box] and deselect [any other calendars].

PAUSE. LEAVE Outlook 2013 open to use in the next exercise.

Using Overlay Mode to View Multiple Calendars

You have seen how multiple calendars in Outlook 2013 can be viewed side by side, but you can also use the **overlay mode** to view a merged version of the calendars on top of each other. Color coding helps you determine which calendar holds scheduled items that appear in the merged view. Several calendars displayed in overlay mode are called an **overlay stack**. In this exercise, you will use the overlay mode to find free time that is common to all the displayed calendars.

STEP BY STEP   **Use Overlay Mode to View Multiple Calendars**

GET READY. LAUNCH Outlook 2013 if it is not already running and complete the previous exercises first.

1. If necessary, click the **Calendar** button in the Navigation bar to display the Calendar window.

2. Click the check box next to the Anniversary Celebration calendar to select it. The Anniversary Celebration calendar appears next to the default calendar.

3. Double click [**the date a week from Friday**] in the Anniversary Celebration calendar. When the *Click To Add Event* box appears, click it and key **Planning session**.

4. Click the check box next to one of the calendars under the Shared Calendars heading. All three calendars are now visible in the Side-by-Side mode, as shown in Figure 10-21.

Figure 10-21

Viewing multiple calendars

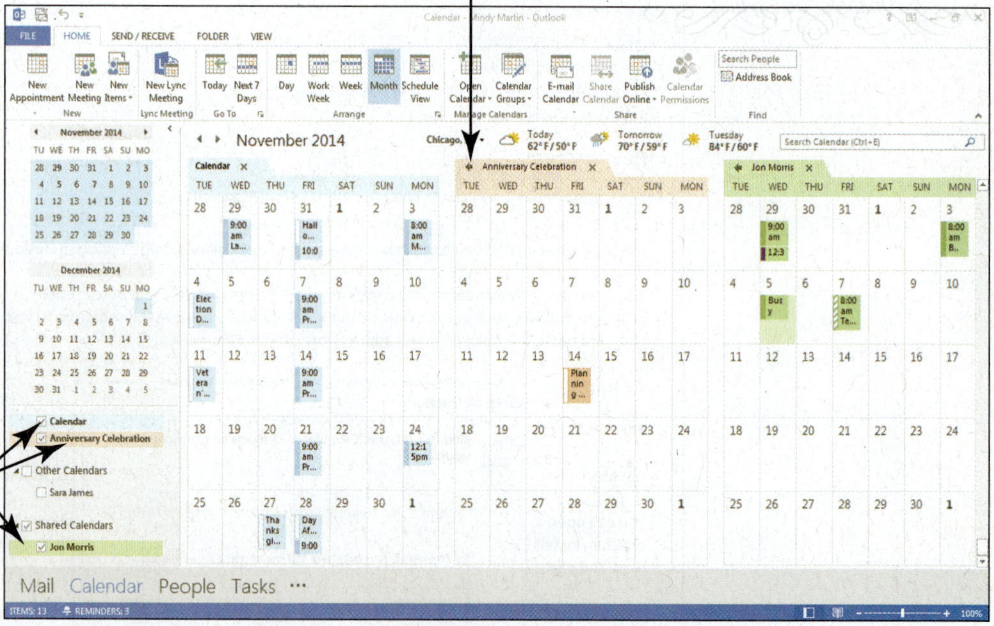

Calendars in Navigation Pane are color coded too

View in Overlay Mode toggle button

5. On the Anniversary Celebration calendar, click the **View in Overlay Mode** toggle button, which is the small left arrow next to the calendar's name. The Anniversary Celebration calendar slides over on top of the default calendar.

6. Click the **View in Overlay Mode** toggle button on the shared calendar. The calendars will be displayed in an overlay stack, as shown in Figure 10-22.

Figure 10-22

Calendars in an overlay stack

View in Side-by-Side
Mode toggle button

Events color coded to tell you
which calendar they came from

CERTIFICATION
READY?   3.1.7

How do you display
calendars in an overlay?

7. Click the check box next to the shared calendar's name to clear the check box.

8. Click the **Overlay** button on the VIEW tab to return to the Side-by-Side mode.

9. Click the check box next to the Anniversary Celebration calendar to clear the check box.

PAUSE. LEAVE Outlook 2013 open to use in the next exercise.

Creating a Calendar Group

If you have several calendars that you frequently view together, for instance, your main calendar and those of your project's team members, you may find it helpful to create a calendar group. A **calendar group** adds a heading to the Folders Pane in the Calendar and allows you to view all calendars within the group at one time. In this exercise, you will create a calendar group.

STEP BY STEP   **Create a Calendar Group**

GET READY. LAUNCH Outlook 2013 if it is not already running and complete the previous exercises first.

1. If necessary, click the **Calendar** button in the Navigation bar to display the Calendar window.

2. Click the check box next to the Anniversary Celebration calendar.

3. Click the check box next to one of the calendars under the Shared Calendars heading.

4. On the HOME tab, click **Calendar Groups** from the Manage Calendars group.

5. Select **Save as New Calendar Group** from the dropdown menu. The Create New Calendar Group dialog box is displayed, as shown in Figure 10-23.

Figure 10-23

Create New Calendar Group
dialog box

Figure 10-23

Create New Calendar Group
dialog box

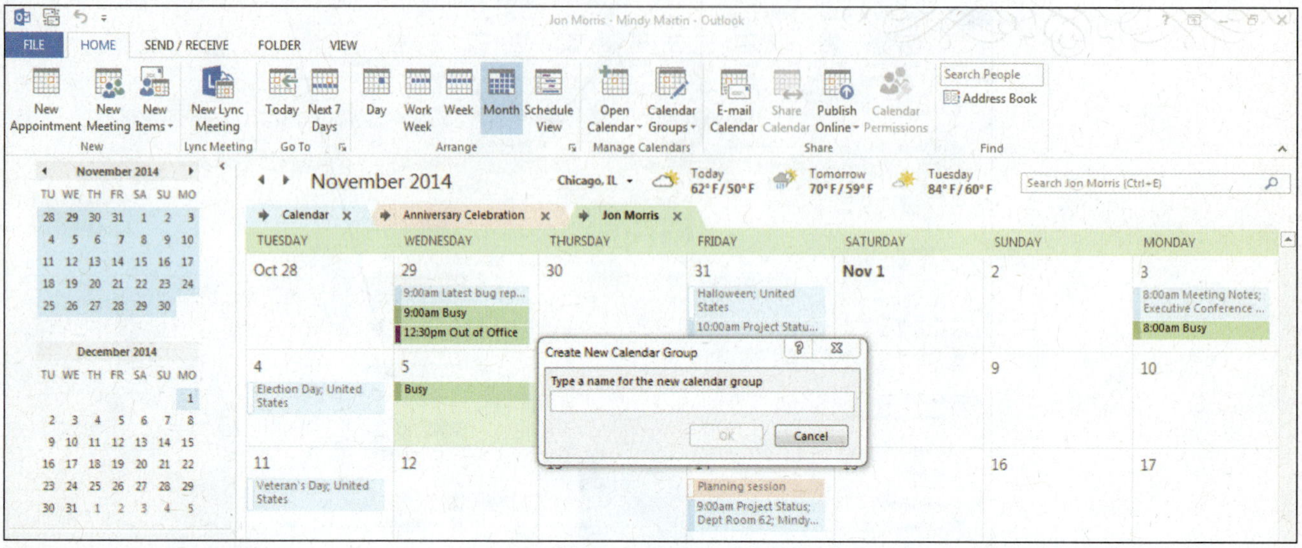

Another Way

You can use the Address Book to create a new Calendar Group. Select Create a New Calendar Group from the Calendar Groups dropdown menu and give the group a name, then use the Address Book button to add group members.

6. In the *Type a name* field, key **My Team Members** and then click **OK**. A new heading called My Team Members appears in the Folders Pane. Under this new heading are the calendars you selected to be part of the calendar group.

7. Drag another calendar from the Navigation Pane to the **My Team Members** group to add a copy of that calendar to this new group, as shown in Figure 10-24.

Figure 10-24

Calendar group in the Folders Pane

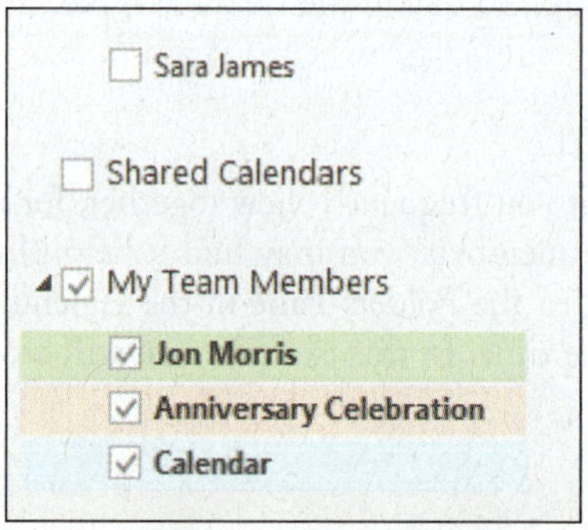

8. Deselect the check boxes for all the calendars except for the default Calendar.

PAUSE. LEAVE Outlook 2013 open to use in the next exercise.

CERTIFICATION READY?   3.1.6

How do you create a calendar group?

The Bottom Line

MANAGING CALENDARS

Outlook 2013 makes it easy to manage multiple calendars, including arranging the view, moving, and deleting calendars.

Outlook 2013 uses the same powerful search engine to help you locate items in your calendar that you use in the mailbox. Printing the calendar to produce a hard copy is one way to create a portable version of your Outlook 2013 calendar.

Arranging the Calendar View

In the Outlook 2013 Calendar, a **view** is a specific layout for the calendar details. By default, the Calendar displays appointments, meetings, and events for the current day with the Daily Task List visible below. In addition, Outlook 2013 provides a number of ways to quickly change the calendar display using the buttons on the Arrange group of the HOME tab. In this exercise, you will explore the other views available in the Calendar.

STEP BY STEP   **Arrange the Calendar View**

GET READY. LAUNCH Outlook 2013 if it is not already running.

1. If necessary, click the **Calendar** button in the Navigation bar to display the Calendar folder. If necessary, click the **Normal** view button on the status bar. This is the default Calendar view.

2. On the HOME tab, select **Work Week** in the Arrange group. Notice that the view now reflects the Tuesday through Saturday schedule you established earlier in this lesson. Your calendar view should be similar to that in Figure 10-25.

Figure 10-25

Calendar in Work Week view

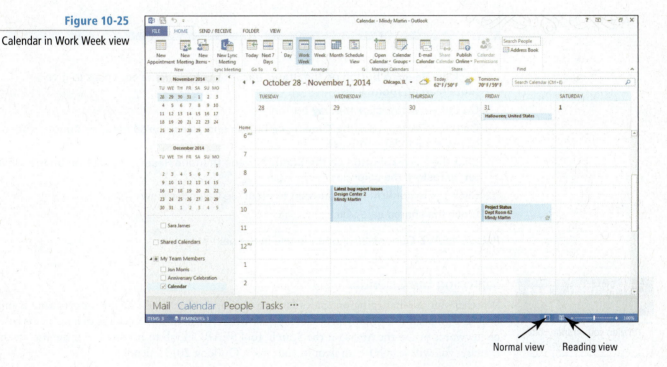

3. On the HOME tab, select **Week** in the Arrange group. Notice that the full week is displayed.

4. On the HOME tab, select **Next 7 Days** in the Go To group. Notice that you can see seven calendar days beginning with the current date.

5. On the VIEW tab, select **Month** in the Arrange group. Notice that you can see the entire month in this view.

6. In the Folders Pane, click the check box next to a shared calendar.

7. On the VIEW tab, select **Schedule View** in the Arrange group. Notice that both calendars are now stacked vertically with the time appearing along the top, as shown in Figure 10-26. Notice that appointments and time marked as busy on the calendar appear as solid blocks of time.

Figure 10-26

Calendar in Schedule View

Scheduled appointments

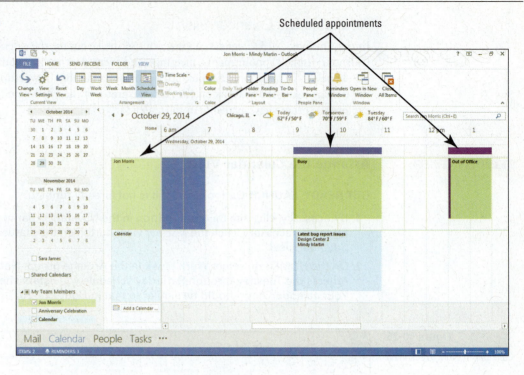

8. Click the **Reading** button on the Status bar. The Folders Pane collapses to give you more reading room.

9. On the VIEW tab, click the **Day** button.

10. On the VIEW tab, click the **Time Scale** button and select the **60 minutes** option. Notice how the calendar condenses.

11. Click the **Normal** button on the Status bar and then the **Reset View** button on the VIEW tab to restore the calendar.

12. Click **Yes** to confirm that you want to reset the Calendar view.

13. Close the shared calendar.

PAUSE. LEAVE Outlook 2013 open to use in the next exercise.

CERTIFICATION READY?   3.1.1

How do you arrange your calendar view?

Searching the Calendar

Whether you are managing one calendar or a dozen, storing your schedule information is only helpful if you can find what you are looking for when you need it. You can search for items based on keywords or use the filters on the Search Tool SEARCH tab to narrow down the list. In this exercise, you will search for an item in your main Outlook 2013 calendar.

STEP BY STEP   **Search the Calendar**

GET READY. LAUNCH Outlook 2013 if it is not already running.

1. If necessary, click the **Calendar** button in the Navigation bar to display the Calendar folder.

2. Click in the **Search Calendar (Ctrl + E)** box. The Search Tools SEARCH tab appears, as shown in Figure 10-27.

Figure 10-27

Outlook 2013 Calendar search tools

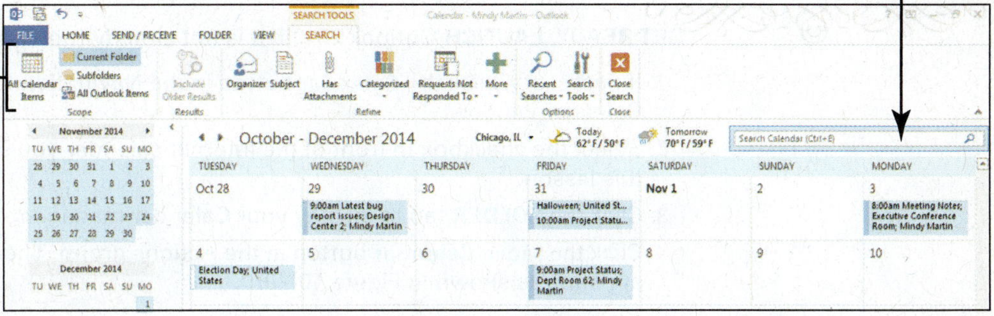

Search Tools ———

Click to start a search

3. Click the **More button** (in the Refine group) and select the **Recurring option**. A Recurring search filter appears below the Search box.

4. Click the **Recurring** down arrow and select **Yes**. Outlook 2013 displays a list of the recurring Calendar items, as shown in Figure 10-28.

Figure 10-28

Recurring Calendar items in a search results list

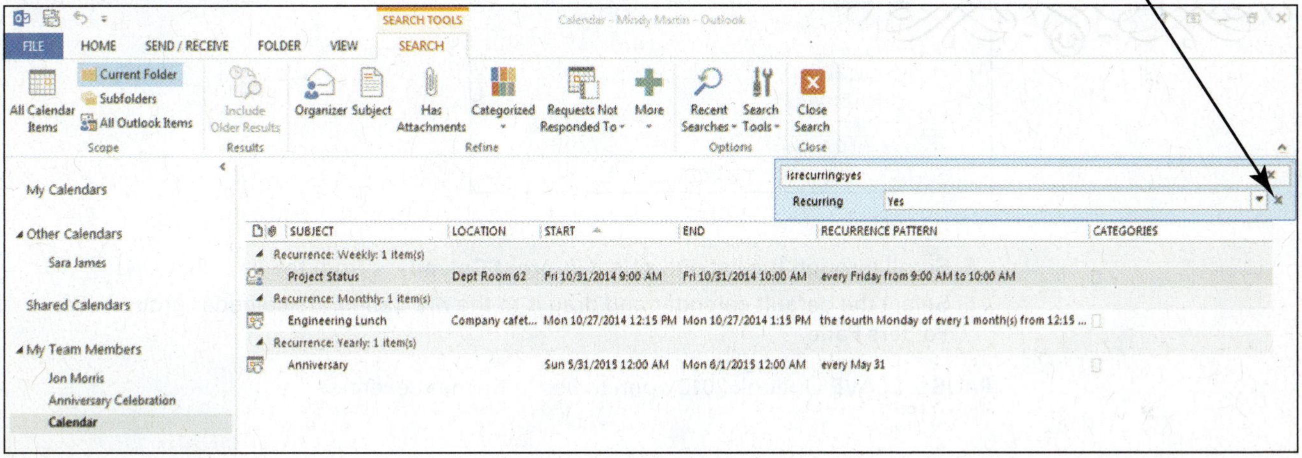

Click to clear a search parameter

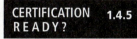

5. Click the **X** at the right of the **Recurring** search filter to clear the search box.

6. In the *Search Calendar (Ctrl + E)* box, key **Room A** to locate all of the Calendar items that take place in Conference Room A.

7. Click the **Close Search** button to return to your regular Calendar view.

PAUSE. LEAVE Outlook 2013 open to use in the next exercise.

CERTIFICATION READY? 1.4.5

How do you search for a Calendar item?

Moving a Calendar

Although Calendar groups are a great organization tool, they are not the only one available in Outlook 2013. You can use the tools on the FOLDER tab to move, copy, or rename calendars as well as open them and delete them from Outlook 2013. In this exercise, you will move calendars.

Move a Calendar

GET READY. LAUNCH Outlook 2013 if it is not already running.

1. If necessary, click the Calendar button in the Navigation bar to display the Calendar window.
2. Select the checkbox in front of the Internet calendar you subscribed to earlier in this lesson.
3. Click the FOLDER tab to display your Calendar management tools.
4. Click the Move Calendar button in the Actions group. The Move Folder dialog box appears, as shown in Figure 10-29.

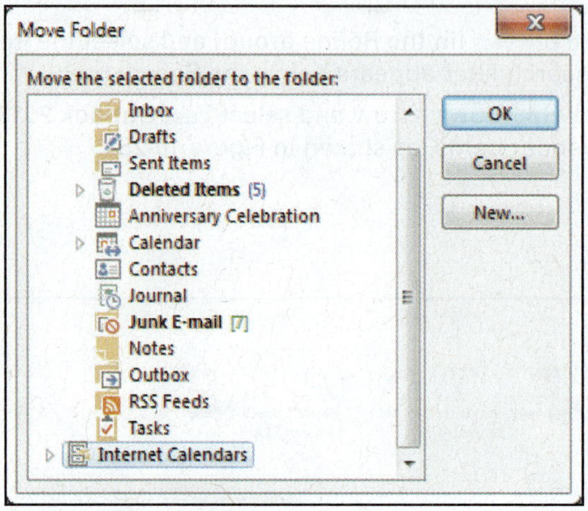

Figure 10-29

Moving a calendar in Outlook 2013

5. Scroll through the list and select Internet Calendars from the list. Click OK.
6. Select the default calendar and drag it to the My Calendars calendar group in the Folders Pane.

PAUSE. LEAVE Outlook 2013 open to use in the next exercise.

Printing a Calendar

You may find it handy to take a copy of your Outlook 2013 calendar with you to meetings or any time you need to be away from your computer. Outlook 2013 provides several different printing options for the calendar. In this exercise, you will print a weekly agenda.

Print a Calendar

GET READY. LAUNCH Outlook 2013 if it is not already running.

1. If necessary, click the Calendar button in the Navigation bar to display the Calendar window.
2. Use the Date Navigator to select [the third week of February].
3. On the FILE tab, click Print.
4. In the Printer field, select [your printer] from the drop-down menu.
5. In the Settings field, click Weekly Agenda Style. A preview of your printed page appears in the Preview pane as shown in Figure 10-30.

6. Click **Print** to send your calendar to the printer.

PAUSE. LEAVE Outlook 2013 open to use in the next exercise.

Table 10-2 describes Outlook 2013's different calendar printing options.

Table 10-2

Calendar Printing Options

Print Style	Description
Daily Style	This option prints the calendar details for a single day, including a Daily Task List. This style will print only the work hours you have defined.
Weekly Agenda Style	This option prints the calendar items on a page that looks similar to a day planner.
Weekly Calendar Style	This option prints the calendar items on a page that look similar to the Weekly Calendar view.
Monthly Style	This option prints your calendar items on a single sheet that resembles a monthly calendar.
Tri-Fold Style	This option prints your calendar items in three columns: your hourly appointments on the left, your Daily Task List in the center, and a weekly summary on the right.
Calendar Details Style	This option prints the full details of your calendar items vertically on the page, grouped by day.

Deleting a Calendar

When you're finished with a secondary calendar, you'll want to delete it to eliminate clutter. Fortunately, Outlook 2013 makes this process quick and easy. In this exercise, you will delete a calendar.

Delete a Calendar

GET READY. LAUNCH Outlook 2013 if it is not already running.

1. If necessary, click the **Calendar** button in the Navigation bar to display the Calendar window.
2. Click the check box next to the calendar that was shared with you via e-mail to select it. Deselect all the other calendars.
3. Click the **FOLDER** tab to display your Calendar management tools.
4. Click the **Delete Calendar** button in the Actions group. A confirmation message window is displayed, as shown in Figure 10-31.

Figure 10-31

Deleting a calendar in Outlook 2013

Click to Delete a calendar

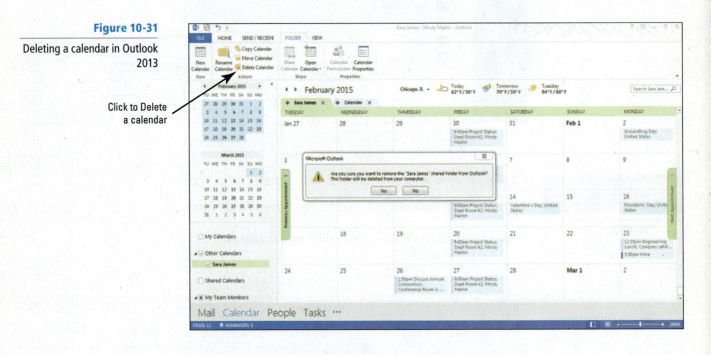

5. Click **Yes** to confirm the decision.
6. Right click the now-empty **Shared Calendars** group in the Folders Pane. A shortcut menu appears as shown in Figure 10-32.
7. Select the **Delete Group** option. A message window appears.

Figure 10-32

Deleting a calendar group

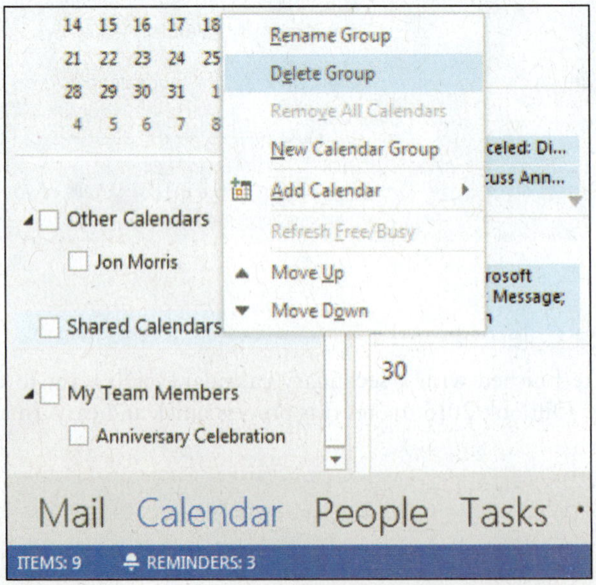

CERTIFICATION
READY?   3.1.3

How do you delete a
calendar?

8. Click **Yes** to confirm your decision.

PAUSE. CLOSE Outlook 2013 open to use in the next exercise.

SKILL SUMMARY

In This Lesson You Learned How To:	Exam Objective	Objective Number
Set Calendar Options	Demonstrate how to set calendar work times	3.1.4
	Modify calendar time zones	3.1.2
	Adjust viewing details for calendars	3.1.1
Share Your Calendar	Share calendars	3.1.8
Work with Multiple Calendars	Create multiple calendars	3.1.5
	Overlay calendars	3.1.7
	Manage calendar groups	3.1.6
Manage Calendars	Adjust viewing details for calendars	3.1.1
	Search calendars	1.4.5
	Print calendars	1.3.2
	Delete calendars	3.1.3

Knowledge Assessment

Fill in the Blank

Complete the following sentences by writing the correct word or words in the blanks provided.

1. Many people do not work on _____.
2. A common _____ is Monday through Friday.
3. Your _____ is based on your location.
4. _____ mode displays calendars on top of one another.
5. A(n) _____ calendar tracks details for specific projects separate from your default calendar.
6. Share a snapshot of your calendar information with someone not on your Microsoft Exchange network, using a(n) _____.
7. In _____ mode, calendars are displayed next to each other.
8. Time zones are defined by the difference between local time and _____.
9. Several calendars displayed in overlay mode are known as a(n) _____.

Multiple Choice

Select the best response for the following statements.

1. What is the most common work week?
   a. Sunday through Saturday
   b. Saturday and Sunday
   c. Monday through Saturday
   d. Monday through Friday

2. Which of the following is not customizable in the Outlook Options dialog box?
   a. Calendar color
   b. Custom Calendars
   c. Time zones
   d. Holidays

3. Your time zone is determined by your distance from
   a. the North Pole.
   b. UTC.
   c. Boston.
   d. the Pacific Ocean.

4. In Outlook 2013, holidays are classified as
   a. weekends.
   b. appointments.
   c. all-day events.
   d. vacations.

5. What is automatically shared with other users on a Microsoft Exchange server?
   a. Free/busy times
   b. E-mail
   c. Internet Calendar Subscriptions
   d. Holiday sets

6. What does a Sharing invitation e-mail invite the recipient to share?
   a. Your calendar details
   b. Your Outlook options
   c. Your Inbox
   d. Your free/busy information

7. What does another user on your network need in order to view your calendar?
   a. Your e-mail address
   b. A POP3 account
   c. Your IP address
   d. Your permission

8. When you share your calendar, how much detail is needed for scheduling purposes?
   a. Availability only
   b. Limited details
   c. Full details
   d. Complete calendar

9. What site does Microsoft offer for publishing Internet calendars?
   a. Microsoft Internet Calendars (MIC)
   b. Shared Calendars
   c. Microsoft My Calendar
   d. Office.com

10. What is an advantage of subscribing to an Internet calendar?
    a. Internet calendars are fun.
    b. Internet calendars are automatically updated.
    c. Internet calendars always contain useful information.
    d. All of the above.

Competency Assessment

Project 10-1: Define a Work Week

Sharon Salavaria works at a trendy restaurant in downtown Boston. The restaurant opens at 3:00 PM, stays open for late diners, and closes at 11:00 PM. This fashionable restaurant earned a culinary award for its fine cuisine—on the four days a week that it is open. Not surprisingly, it is difficult to get a table during its limited hours. Modify your calendar to match Sharon's work week.

GET READY. LAUNCH Outlook 2013 if it is not already running.

1. On the FILE tab, click **Options**.
2. Click **Calendar** to display the Calendar options.
3. Select the **Sun** and **Mon** check boxes to add them to the work week.
4. Click the **Thu** and **Fri** check boxes to clear the check boxes, removing them from the work week. The restaurant is open Saturday through Wednesday only.
5. Click the *Start time* field. Key or select **3:00 PM**.
6. Click the *End time* field. Key or select **11:00 PM**.
7. Click **OK** to save the modified work week.

PAUSE. LEAVE Outlook 2013 open to use in the next exercise.

Project 10-2: Change Your Time Zone

Arthur Yasinki has been the top salesperson at his company for the last six years. His record is amazing because he lives in Florida, but his two biggest clients are located in London and San Francisco. He displays San Francisco as his current time zone and London as his additional time zone. You will set up the additional time zone in the next project. In this project, change your current time zone to match San Francisco's time zone. If you live in the Pacific time zone, change your current time zone to the Central time zone and change the label name to South Dakota.

GET READY. LAUNCH Outlook 2013 if it is not already running.

1. On the FILE tab, click **Options**.
2. Click **Calendar** to display the calendar options.
3. In the *Time Zone* field, select **(GMT-08:00) Pacific Time (US & Canada);**. (If you live in the Pacific time zone, change your current time zone to the Central time zone.)
4. In the *Label* field, key **San Francisco**. (If you live in the Pacific time zone, change the label name to South Dakota.)
5. Click **OK** to save the changes.

PAUSE. LEAVE Outlook 2013 open to use in the next exercise.

Proficiency Assessment

Project 10-3: Display Multiple Time Zones

If you ask Arthur Yasinki for the key to his success in sales, he will laugh and respond, "It's location, location, location." Because this phrase usually refers to brick-and-mortar stores or real estate, it might be difficult to understand his answer. When you look at his calendar, it becomes clear. Arthur spends about 200 days of every year away from home at client sites. It is no wonder that he does not display the time zone where he lives. In this project, add the time zone for London to your calendar display.

GET READY. LAUNCH Outlook 2013 if it is not already running.

1. Open **Backstage** view and display the Calendar options.
2. Scroll down to see the time zone options. Click the **Show a second time zone** check box.
3. In the *Label* field, key **London**.
4. In the *Time zone* field, select **(UTC) Dublin, Edinburgh, Lisbon, London**.
5. Click **OK** to save the changes.

LEAVE Outlook 2013 open for the next project.

Project 10-4: Send Calendar Information via E-mail

Once a week, Arthur Yasinki sends a copy of his schedule to the department's administrative assistant. Without access to his calendar information, the department would have a hard time finding Arthur on a map.

GET READY. LAUNCH Outlook 2013 if it is not already running.

1. If necessary, display your Calendar.
2. On the HOME tab, click the **E-mail Calendar** button in the Share group to display the Send a Calendar via E-mail dialog box.
3. In the *Calendar:* field, select **Calendar**, if necessary.
4. In the *Date Range:* field, select **Next 7 days**.
5. In the *Detail:* field, select **Full details**.
6. Click the **Show** button in the Advanced: section to display more options.
7. In the *E-mail Layout:* field, select **List of events**.
8. Click **OK**. A new Outlook Message window is displayed with the calendar information included in the body of the message.
9. In the *To* field, key [**your e-mail address**].
10. Scroll down the message body, if necessary, to view the data in the message. Click **Send**.

LEAVE Outlook 2013 open for the next project.

Mastery Assessment

Project 10-5: Publish Calendar to Office.com

Arthur Yasinki and the department's administrative assistant are trying Outlook 2013 Internet sharing features. Arthur is publishing his calendar to Office.com. The administrative assistant will subscribe to Arthur's calendar. In this project, publish your calendar to Office.com.

Troubleshooting If you are logged in to a secure Microsoft Exchange network, your Administrator may block this feature. Ask about any alternate methods for sharing calendar information outside your network.

GET READY. LAUNCH Outlook 2013 if it is not already running.

You must also have a Microsoft account to publish your calendar to Office.com.

1. If necessary, open your **Calendar** window.
2. Click the **Publish Online** button in the Share group and then click **Publish to WebDAV Server**.
3. Click **OK**, if necessary, to view pages over a secure connection.
4. Set the options to publish *Limited details* about the next week of your calendar.
5. Click the **Only invited users can subscribe to this calendar** option and click **OK**.
6. If necessary, log in to Office.com and indicate that you want to send a sharing invitation.
7. **Send** the invitation to yourself and a friend or coworker.

LEAVE Outlook 2013 open for the next project.

Project 10-6: Subscribe to an Internet Calendar

The department's administrative assistant is looking forward to subscribing to Arthur Yasinki's published calendar. Arthur's calendar information will be up to date and easy to access.

GET READY. LAUNCH Outlook 2013 if it is not already running.

This exercise requires Internet access.

1. If necessary, open your Inbox and click the **Send/Receive All Folders** button.
2. Open the new **Share message** you received from a friend or coworker (if you did not work with a friend or coworker, open the one you sent to yourself).
3. Choose to **subscribe** to the new calendar.
4. If necessary, **sign in** to Office.com to download and display the calendar.
5. Close the **Share message** and deselect the **new calendar**.
6. To clean up after completing these projects, configure the work week to match your own schedule, set the time zone to match your location, and delete any calendar subscriptions displayed in the Folders Pane for the Calendar folder.

CLOSE Outlook 2013.

Circling Back

The Baldwin Museum of Science is planning a major event this coming August 31. Ajai Manchepalli, the Director of Special Exhibits, has worked tirelessly to arrange an exhibit of Egyptian antiquities. In a small town like Sun Ridge, Wisconsin, this is a major coup. As the plan for the event develops, Ajai must schedule a whirlwind of appointments and meetings leading up to the big event.

Project CB3-1: Modify Your Calendar

Ajai immediately adds the event to his calendar and adds his first task: update the museum's insurance plan to cover the event. Ajai will be making several calls to antiquities experts and officials in Egypt every day. Since Egypt is seven hours ahead of Wisconsin, he has decided to modify his work schedule so that he is available during the day in both Egypt and Wisconsin. Ajai also wants to share Outlook calendars with Fadi Mohammed, the Egyptian museum director.

Modify your calendar events to match Ajai's and change your work week to match his schedule, and then display Egypt's time zone so that Ajai is always aware of the time when he calls Egypt. Share your calendar with a friend or classmate to match Ajai's actions.

GET READY. LAUNCH Outlook if it is not already running.

1. Click the **Calendar** button in the Navigation bar to display the Calendar. Click the **Month** button to display the Month view, if necessary.
2. On the HOME tab, click **New Appointment**.
3. In the *Subject* field, key **Egypt: Sands of Mystery Exhibit**.
4. Select a *Start time* of **August 1** and an *End time* of **August 31**.
5. Click the **All day event** checkbox to select the option. The time fields are dimmed.
6. Click the **Save & Close** button in the Actions group on the Ribbon. The event has been added to your calendar.
7. Hover over the **Tasks** button on the Navigation bar to open the Tasks Peek.
8. Click the **Type a new task** field, and key **Update insurance for Sands of Mystery exhibit**. [Press **Enter**.] The task is created.
9. On the FILE tab, click **Options**.
10. Click **Calendar**.
11. In the Work time group, click the **Start time** field. Key or select **5:00 AM**. Click the **End time** field. Key or select **3:00 PM**.
12. Scroll down to see the time zone options.
13. In the *Time Zone* field, select **(UTC-06:00) Central Time (US & Canada)**.
14. In the *Label* field, key **Wisconsin**.
15. Click the **Show a second time zone** check box.
16. In the *Label* field, key **Egypt**.
17. In the *Time Zone* field, select **(UTC+02:00) Cairo**.
18. Click **OK** to save the changes and return to the Calendar folder.
19. Click the **Day** button to display the Day view. Note that both time zones are displayed and the calendar displays the new working hours.
20. Click the **E-mail Calendar** button in the Share group. An untitled message window is displayed along with the Send a Calendar via E-mail dialog box.
21. In the *Date Range* field, select the **Specify dates** option. Select a **Start** date of **8/1/14** and an **End** date of **8/31/14**.
22. In the *Detail* field, select **Limited details**.
23. Click **OK**.

24. In the *To* field, key [the e-mail address for a friend or classmate].
25. Click the **Send** button. The invitation is sent.

LEAVE Outlook open for the next project.

Project CB3-2: Schedule and Print Appointments

The Egypt: Sands of Mystery exhibit is scheduled for the month of August. Ajai has several appointments scheduled for next week, but his first is a meeting with the insurance agent on Monday. Your insurance agent, Susan Dryer, has requested that you and Ajai schedule a couple of hours after lunch to tour the facilities with her. Add the appointment to your calendar and print the details to take with you on a tour of the facilities with the agent.

GET READY. LAUNCH Outlook if it is not already running. Complete the previous project.

1. Point to the Tasks button on the Navigation bar to display the Tasks Peek.
2. Click the **Update insurance for Sands of Mystery exhibit** task. Drag it to the **Calendar** button on the Navigation bar. The Update insurance for Sands of Mystery exhibit – Appointment window opens.
3. Key **Susan Dryer- Insurance for Sands of Mystery** in the *Subject* field, to change the subject line for the appointment.
4. In the *Location* field, key **My office**.
5. Key a *Start time* of **12:30 PM** on next Monday and an *End time* of **2:30 PM**.
6. In the message body, key: **Remember to talk to Susan about obtaining security guards for all of the entrances and exits, our plan to upgrade the current alarm system, and transportation insurance while the exhibit is in transit** above the Task information.
7. Click the **Save & Close** button in the Actions group on the Ribbon.
8. Click the **Calendar** button in the Navigation bar to display the Calendar folder. Click the **Month** button to display the Month view, if necessary.
9. Click on the appointment with Susan Dryer and click the **Reminder** drop arrow in the Options group and select **1 hour** from the list of available times that appears.
10. Click the **Show As** down arrow in the Options group and select **Busy** to update your availability.
11. Click the **FILE** tab to open Backstage view and click **Print** in the Navigation Pane to open the Print settings page.
12. Click the **Print Options** button.
13. In the Print Style area, click **Calendar Details Style**.
14. In the *Start* box of the Print range area, select [Monday's date].
15. In the *End* box, select [Monday's date].
16. Click **Print** if you want to print the contact record using the default printer.

LEAVE Outlook open for the next project.

Project CB3-3: Schedule a Recurring Meeting

Every Friday, Ajai holds a brief status meeting to update the museum director and any interested staff members. Ajai will need to use the video conferencing resource so that the Egyptian team can participate. Ajai's family has had trouble adjusting to his new schedule and has asked that he print his calendar each week so they know when to expect him at home.

Schedule a recurring meeting with a friend or coworker to match Ajai's schedule and print your calendar.

 Troubleshooting The e-mail addresses provided in these exercises belong to unused domains owned by Microsoft. When you send a message to these addresses, you will receive an error message stating that the message could not be delivered. Delete the error messages when they arrive.

GET READY. LAUNCH Outlook if it is not already running. Complete the previous project.

1. In your account, click the **Calendar** button in the Navigation bar to display the Calendar folder.

2. Use the Date Navigator to select the [next Friday].

3. On the HOME tab, click **New Meeting**. The Meeting window is displayed.

4. Click the *Subject* field and key **Sands of Mystery Status**. In the *Location* field, key **videoconf@baldwinmuseumofscience.com** to invite the resource to your meeting.

5. Change the *Start time* field to **9:00 PM** and change the *End time* field to **9:30 PM**, if necessary.

6. Click the **Scheduling Assistant** or **Scheduling** button in the Show group on the Ribbon.

7. Click the **Click here to add a name** text below your name. Key **Steve@baldwinmuseumofscience.com**. [Press **Enter**]. Steve is the director, so click the icon next to his name and select **Required Attendee**.

8. Click the **Click here to add a name** text on the next line. Key **Fadimohammed@egyptianantiquities.eg**. [Press **Enter**]. Click the icon next to Fadi's name and select **Required Attendee**.

9. Click the **Click here to add a name** text on the next line. Key [your own e-mail address] and select **Optional Attendee**.

10. Click the **Recurrence** button in the Options group on the Ribbon. The Appointment Recurrence window is displayed.

11. Click **OK** to accept the recurrence pattern and return to the meeting window.

12. Click the **Appointment** button in the Show group on the Ribbon. The *To* field is automatically filled with the attendees' e-mail addresses, and the recurrence pattern is displayed.

13. Click the **Send** button. Your calendar is updated, and the 9:00 PM to 9:30 PM time slot is displayed as busy for every Friday.

14. Use the Date Navigator to select the month of **January**.

15. Double-click any **Sands of Mystery Status** meeting item on the calendar. The Sands of Mystery Status – Meeting window is displayed.

16. Select **The entire series** and click **OK**.

17. In the *Start time* field, **select** **9:00 AM**. In the *End time* field, select **9:30 AM**, if necessary and click **OK**.

18. Click **Scheduling Assistant** or **Scheduling** and click the **Click here to add a name** text below your name. Key **AhmedTakis@egyptianantiquities.eg**. [Press **Enter**.] Ahmed is the Mr. Mohammed's assistant, so we should add him to the meeting. Click the icon next to his name and select **Required Attendee**.

⚠ **Troubleshooting** To complete this exercise, you need to have OneNote installed on your computer and the ability to store the notes in a shared location, such a SharePoint site or SkyDrive.

19. Click the Appointment button. Click the **Meeting Notes** button on the Meeting Series tab. The Meeting Notes dialog box appears asking whether you are going to take your own notes or share them with the attendees.

20. Click the **Share notes with the meeting series** option in the Meeting Notes dialog box. The Choose Notes to Share with Meeting dialog box opens.

21. Click the **New Notebook** button. A OneNote window opens asking you to name the new Notebook.

22. Select your shared location and key **XX_Meeting Notes-CB3** (where the *XX* indicates your name). Click the **Create Notebook** button.

23. Click the **Not Now** button and the Meeting Notes Notebook opens.

24. Double click the **New Section 1** tab, if necessary to make it active, and key **Sands of Mystery Weekly Notes**. [Press **Enter**.] Close the OneNote window.

25. In the Choose Notes to Share with Meeting dialog box, navigate to the **Sands of Mystery Weekly Notes** tab in the *XX_Meeting Notes-CB3* notebook. Click **OK**. A link to the meeting notes appears in the Meeting window.

26. At the top of the message body, key: **Looks like the change in my sleep patterns has affected me this week. I'm updating the meeting so that it is scheduled during work hours.** [Press **Enter**]. **I'll be keeping track of our ongoing status notes and action items. I'm adding a link that you can use to access my notes.** [Press **Enter**] and type [your name].

27. Click **Send Update** to send the meeting request.

28. Click the **Mail** button in the Navigation bar to display the Mail folder.

29. If the **Sands of Mystery Status** message has not arrived, click the **Send/Receive All Folders** button.

30. Click the *Sands of Mystery Status* message in the message list. The message is displayed in the Preview pane.

31. To clean up Outlook after completing these projects, configure the work week to match [your schedule], set the time zone to match [your time zone], and remove the second time zone.

CLOSE Outlook.

LESSON SKILL MATRIX

Skills	Exam Objective	Objective Number
Creating New Tasks	Create and manage tasks	3.4.1
Working with Task Options	Set Outlook options	1.1.7
	Configure views	1.1.5
Managing and Completing a Task	Create and manage tasks	3.4.1
	Search for tasks	1.4.3
	Print tasks	1.3.6
Working with Assigned Tasks	Create and manage tasks	3.4.1
	Update task status	3.4.5

KEY TERMS

- **assign**
- **Completed**
- **Deferred**
- **In Progress**
- **owner**
- **recurring task**
- **task**
- **task request**
- **to-do item**

© michaeljung/iStockphoto

Developing and releasing a new product is a complicated process that can take months or years to complete. Ruth Ann Ellington knows this from first-hand experience. She has managed the product development team at Tailspin Toys, releasing three new products in five years. Ruth Ann and her team use the Tasks folder to track the multitude of tasks required to accomplish the goal of releasing solid, marketable new products. In this lesson, you will create, modify, move, and print tasks and to-do items. You will also assign a task to someone else, respond to a task request, and update the status of a task.

© michaeljung/iStockphoto

SOFTWARE ORIENTATION

The Outlook Task Window

Create and modify your tasks in the Task window shown in Figure 11-1. Use the Task window to create and track tasks that you are managing or performing. Keep your task information readily available in one location.

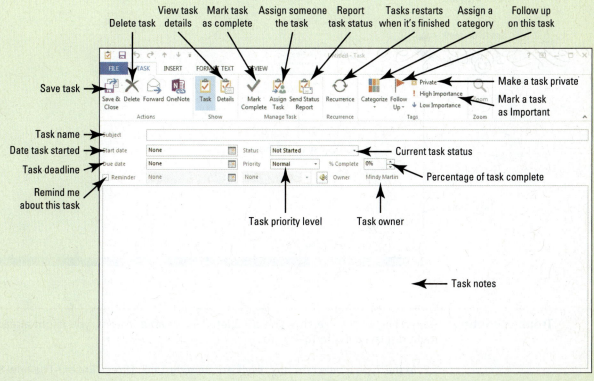

Figure 11-1
The Outlook Task window

CREATING NEW TASKS

The Bottom Line

A **task** is an Outlook 2013 item that you create. It usually has a due date and can be tracked from creation to completion. When any task is created, it is automatically flagged for follow-up. Any Outlook 2013 item that can be flagged for follow-up, including messages and contacts, is called a **to-do item**. Thus, creating a task also creates a to-do item.

Creating a One-Time Task

You create a one-time task to track your progress on a task that only needs to be completed once. For example, you would create a one-time task to register for a specific trade show. Once you have registered for the trade show, the task is complete—you don't need to return to the task every week or every month. In this exercise, you will create a one-time task.

STEP BY STEP   **Create a One-Time Task**

GET READY. Before you begin these steps, be sure to launch Microsoft Outlook 2013.

1. If necessary, click the **Tasks** button in the Navigation bar to display the Tasks folder, as shown in Figure 11-2.

Figure 11-2

The Tasks folder

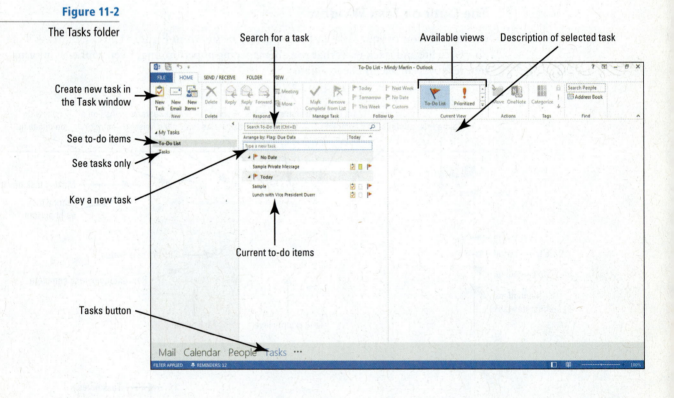

Create new task in the Task window

See to-do items

See tasks only

Key a new task

Search for a task

Available views   Description of selected task

Current to-do items

Tasks button

⚠️ **Troubleshooting**   Depending on the exercises you completed in previous lessons, you might already have some items displayed in the To-Do List.

2. In the *Type a new task* box, key **New Sample Task**. [Press **Enter**.] The new Sample task appears in the To-Do list.

Take Note Throughout this chapter you will see information that appears in black text within brackets, such as [Press **Enter**], or [**next Friday's date**]. The information contained in the brackets is intended to be directions for you rather than something you actually type word for word. It will instruct you to perform an action or substitute text. Do **not** type the actual text that appears within brackets.

Another Way
In every Outlook 2013 folder, you can create a new task by selecting Task in the New Items dropdown menu or by pressing Ctrl+Shift+K.

3. Click **New Task** on the HOME tab. A Task window is displayed, as shown in Figure 11-1.

4. In the *Subject* field, key **Create marketing brochure**.

5. In the *Due date* field, key or select the [**date four weeks from today**].

6. In the *Priority* field, select **Low**.

7. In the task note area, key **Photographer's name is Ann Beebe**. Compare your Task window to Figure 11-3.

Figure 11-3

Creating a new task

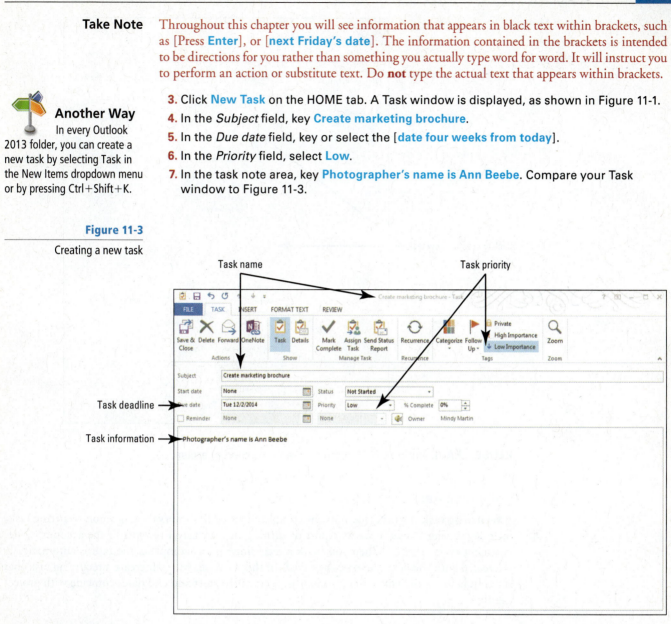

8. Click **Save & Close** in the Actions group on the Ribbon. The new task is displayed at the bottom of the To-Do list.

9. Hover the mouse over the **Tasks** button on the Navigation bar to open the **Tasks peek**.

10. In the *Type a new task* field on the peek, key **Task Peek**. [Press **Enter**.] The new Docked task appears in the To-Do list on the peek, as shown in Figure 11-4.

CERTIFICATION READY? 3.4.1

How do you create a one-time task?

Figure 11-4

Creating tasks in the
Tasks peek

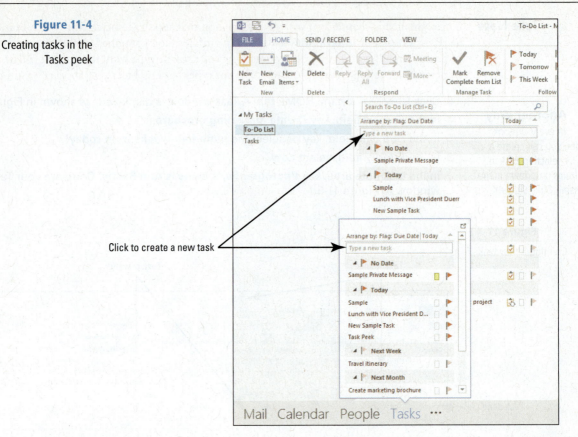

Click to create a new task

PAUSE. LEAVE Outlook 2013 open to use in the next exercise.

Creating a Recurring Task

A **recurring task** is a task that must be completed at regular intervals. Common recurring tasks include creating a weekly status report or turning in your travel receipts to the accounting department every month. When you mark a recurring task as complete, the task is automatically re-created with the next due date displayed. In this exercise, you will create a recurring task that starts in January and ends after six months. Frequently, start and end dates coincide with project deadlines.

STEP BY STEP   **Create a Recurring Task**

 Cross Ref   You can find more information on completing a task later in this lesson.

GET READY. Before you begin these steps, be sure to launch Microsoft Outlook 2013.

1. If necessary, click the **Tasks** button in the Navigation bar to display the Tasks folder.
2. Click **New Task** on the HOME tab. A Task window is displayed as shown in Figure 11-1.
3. In the *Subject* field, key **Summarize team's progress on Vault project**.
4. In the *Start date* field, select the **[second Monday in January of next year]**.
5. Click the **Recurrence** button in the Recurrence group on the Ribbon. The Task Recurrence dialog box is displayed, as shown in Figure 11-5.

Figure 11-5

Task Recurrence dialog box

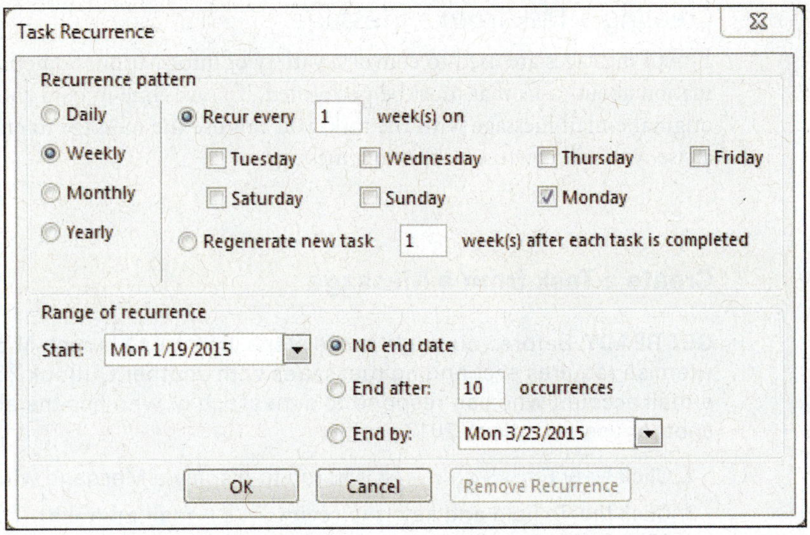

Task Recurrence ⊠

Recurrence pattern

○ Daily   ⦿ Recur every [1] week(s) on

⦿ Weekly   ☐ Tuesday   ☐ Wednesday   ☐ Thursday   ☐ Friday

○ Monthly   ☐ Saturday   ☐ Sunday   ☑ Monday

○ Yearly   ○ Regenerate new task [1] week(s) after each task is completed

Range of recurrence

Start: [Mon 1/19/2015 ▾]   ⦿ No end date

○ End after: [10] occurrences

○ End by: [Mon 3/23/2015 ▾]

[OK]   [Cancel]   [Remove Recurrence]

6. Select the **Monthly** option in the *Recurrence pattern* area.

7. Click the **End by** radio button and key or select [**the second Monday in July**]. This ends the recurring task in six months.

8. Click **OK** to return to the Task window. Compare your Task window to Figure 11-6. Depending on the current date, the number of days before the first deadline will differ.

Figure 11-6

Creating a new recurring task

Recurrence pattern

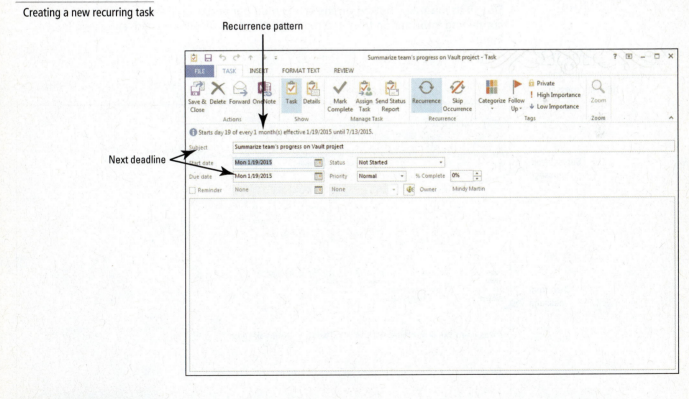

Next deadline

9. Click **Save & Close** in the Actions group on the Ribbon.

10. Examine your **To-Do List**. The new task is displayed below a heading. The heading title depends on the amount of time between today's date and the first deadline.

PAUSE. LEAVE Outlook 2013 open to use in the next exercise.

CERTIFICATION READY?   3.4.1

How do you create recurring tasks?

Creating a Task from a Message

E-mail messages are used to convey a variety of information. Sometimes, a message contains information about tasks that must be performed. To save time in data entry and to keep a record of the original e-mail message with the task, you can use the message to create a tracked task. In this exercise, you will create a task from a message.

Create a Task from a Message

GET READY. Before you begin these steps, be sure to launch Microsoft Outlook 2013. This exercise requires exchanging messages with another Outlook 2013 user with an active e-mail account who can respond to a message or who has the ability to access and use another user's Outlook 2013 profile.

1. Click **New E-mail** on the HOME tab to display a Message window.

2. Click the *To* field and key [**the recipient's e-mail address**]. The recipient is the Outlook 2013 user who will create a task from this message.

3. Click the *Subject* field and key **Travel Itinerary**.

4. In the message area, key the following message: **Hi**, [Press **Enter**] **Please give a copy of your itinerary to Arlene Huff before you leave next Friday.** [Press **Enter** twice.] **Thanks.** [Press **Enter** twice.] **Mindy**.

5. Click the **Send** button to send the message.

6. In the recipient's account, in the Mail folder, click **Send/Receive All Folders** if the Travel Itinerary message has not arrived.

7. Click the **Travel Itinerary** message in the message list.

8. Drag it to the **Tasks** button on the Navigation bar and drop it there. A Task window containing information from the message is automatically opened, as shown in Figure 11-7.

Figure 11-7

Task window showing Travel Itinerary message

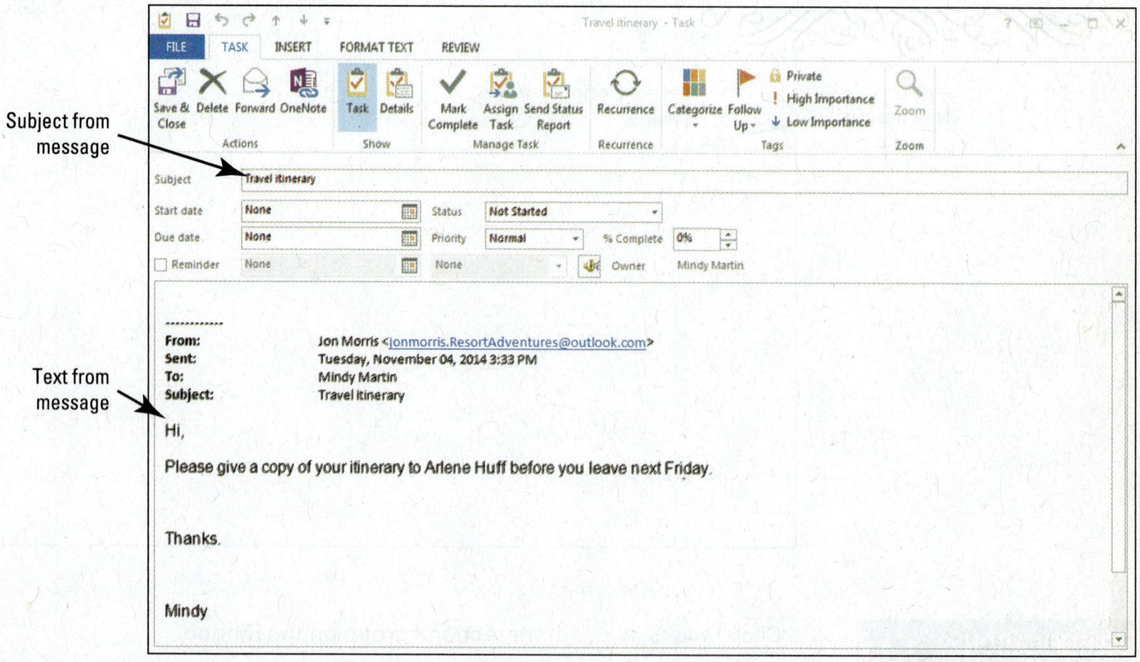

9. In the Task window, click the **Due date** field. Key or select [**next Friday's date**].

10. Click **Save & Close** in the Actions group on the Ribbon.

11. Hover over the Tasks button in the Navigation bar to display the Tasks peek. Examine your Tasks peek. The new task is displayed below the Next Week heading.

PAUSE. CLOSE the recipient's Outlook 2013 account and return to your own if necessary. If you exchanged tasks with another user so that you received the task in your mailbox, leave Outlook 2013 open to use in the next exercise.

WORKING WITH TASK OPTIONS

The Bottom Line

In this section, you will learn how to set the default task options and use the views to find the one that best meets your working style.

Setting Task Options

To make creating tasks more efficient, you can customize the default options in several ways. You can set the color for the overdue and completed flags, specify the amount of time before the due date that you want a reminder sent, and decide whether to keep copies of items you assign to someone else. In this exercise, you will set your working hours and change the Task Quick Click option.

Cross Ref   You can find more information on assigning tasks to others later in this lesson.

STEP BY STEP   **Set Task Options**

GET READY. Before you begin these steps, be sure to launch Microsoft Outlook 2013.

1. On the FILE tab, click Options. The Outlook Options dialog box opens.

2. Click Tasks in the Navigation Pane. The Outlook Options dialog box displays Task options, as shown in Figure 11-8.

Figure 11-8

The Task Options dialog box

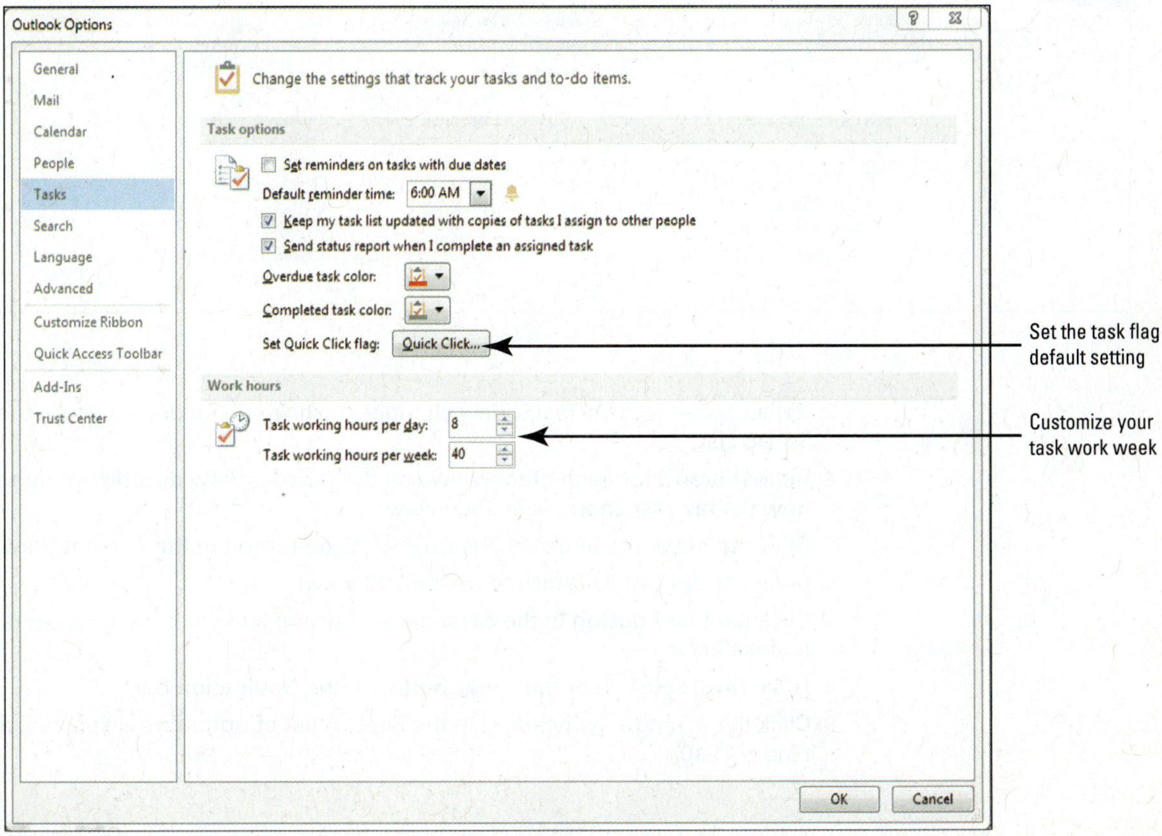

Outlook Options

General	☑ Change the settings that track your tasks and to-do items.
Mail	
Calendar	**Task options**
People	☐ Set reminders on tasks with due dates
Tasks	Default reminder time: 6:00 AM ▼
Search	☑ Keep my task list updated with copies of tasks I assign to other people
Language	☑ Send status report when I complete an assigned task
Advanced	Overdue task color: 🟥 ▼
Customize Ribbon	Completed task color: 🟥 ▼
Quick Access Toolbar	Set Quick Click flag: [Quick Click...] ←──── Set the task flag default setting
Add-Ins	**Work hours**
Trust Center	Task working hours per day: 8 ←──── Customize your task work week
	Task working hours per week: 40

OK   Cancel

3. Under the *Task options* area, click the **Quick Click** button. The Set Quick Click dialog box opens.

4. From the drop-down menu, select **Tomorrow**.

5. Click **OK**. The next time you want to flag a Mail message or a contact, click the flag column to have Outlook 2013 set the due date to *Tomorrow*.

6. In the *Work hours* area, key or select **4** in the *Task working hours per day:* box to indicate that you work only four hours a day on tasks.

7. In the *Task working hours per week:* field, key or select **20**.

8. Click **OK**.

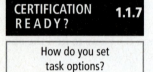

How do you set task options?

PAUSE. LEAVE Outlook 2013 open to use in the next exercise.

Working with Task Views

Each Task view displays your tasks in different ways to show more or less information and to change the way your task information is arranged. The default Tasks view is the To-Do list, which shows both mail items that you need follow up on and tasks that you need to do. In this exercise, you'll explore different Task views.

STEP BY STEP | **Work with Task Views**

GET READY. Before you begin these steps, be sure to launch Microsoft Outlook 2013.

1. If necessary, click the **Tasks** button in the Navigation bar to display the To-Do List.

2. Click the **More** button in the Current View group. The Current View gallery is displayed, as shown in Figure 11-9.

Figure 11-9

The Current View gallery

![screenshot of Outlook Current View gallery]

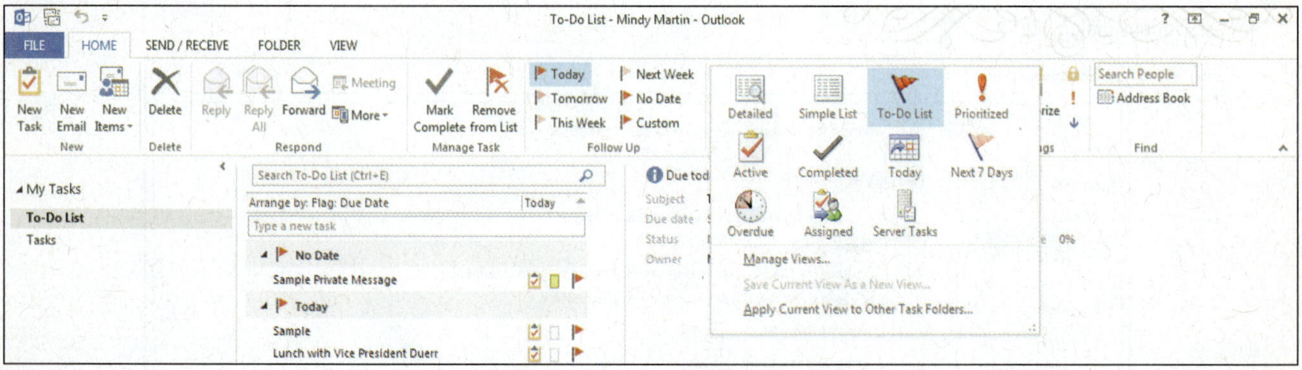

3. Select **Detailed**. The Tasks view changes to show all the details about the tasks in your To-Do List.

4. Repeat *Step 2* for each of the views on the Current View dropdown menu. Take note of how the task list changes in each view.

5. Click the **VIEW tab** and click the **Change View** button in the Current View group.

6. Select **To-Do List** to return to the default view.

7. Click the **More** button in the Arrangement group and click the **Show in Groups** option to deselect it.

8. Hover the mouse over the **Tasks** button in the Navigation bar.

9. Click the **Arrange By:** heading in the Peek. A list of options is displayed, as shown in Figure 11-10.

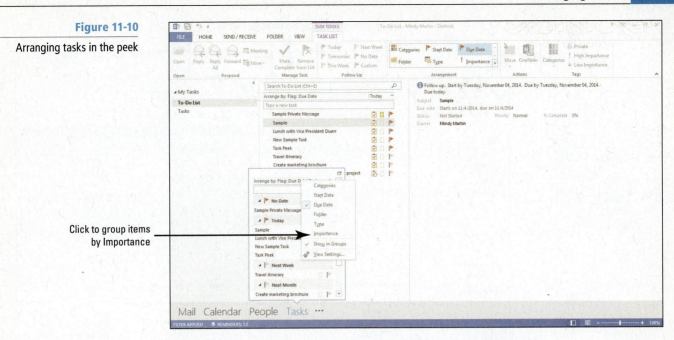

Figure 11-10

Arranging tasks in the peek

Click to group items by Importance

10. If necessary, click the **Importance** option to select it. The items in the Task peek are grouped by importance, as shown in Figure 11-11.

Figure 11-11

Task list grouped by importance

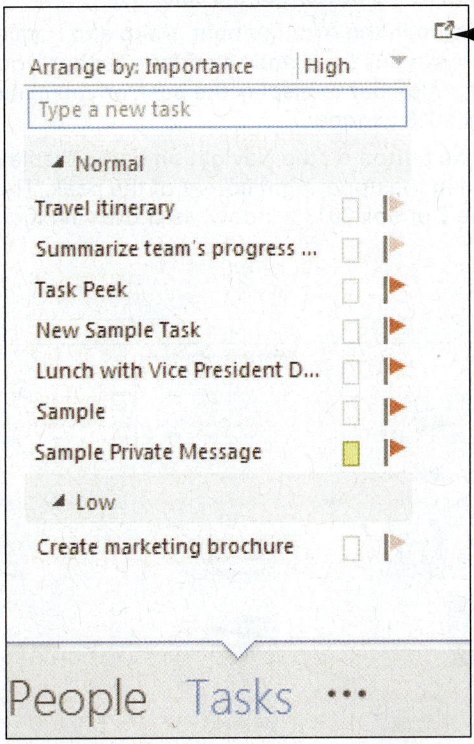

Click to dock the peek

Arrange by: Importance | High

Type a new task

▲ Normal

Travel itinerary

Summarize team's progress ...

Task Peek

New Sample Task

Lunch with Vice President D...

Sample

Sample Private Message

▲ Low

Create marketing brochure

People   Tasks   •••

11. On the VIEW tab, click **Reset View** in the Current View group.

12. When prompted, click **Yes** to confirm that you want to reset the view.

13. Because tasks have due dates, you also can view your daily tasks in the Calendar. Click the **Calendar** button in the Navigation bar.

14. Click the **Day** button in the Arrangement group on the VIEW tab.

15. In the Layout group, click the **Daily Task List** button and select the **Normal** option. The Daily Task List appears at the bottom of the window, as shown in Figure 11-12.

Figure 11-12

Viewing the Task list in Calendar

Click to display the tasks for the day

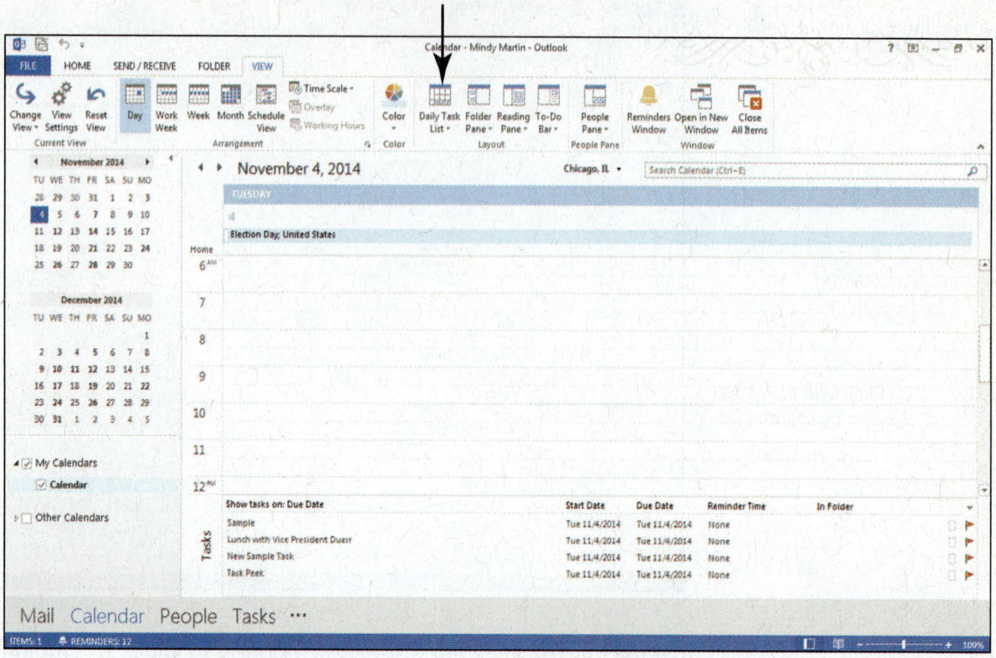

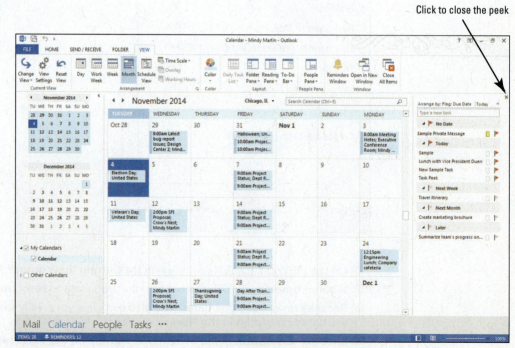

16. Click the **Week** button in the Arrangement group on the VIEW tab. Notice that each day's tasks are listed at the bottom of the calendar.

17. Click the **Month** button in the Arrangement group and notice that the tasks are no longer visible. To view your tasks and calendar together, you can hover over the Tasks button on the Navigation bar to display the peek or you can dock the peek to the right side of the Outlook 2013 window.

18. Hover over the **Tasks** button on the Navigation bar to display the Tasks peek. Click the **Dock the Peek** icon in the upper right corner of the peek. The Tasks peek appears on the right side of the Outlook 2013 window, as shown in Figure 11-13.

Figure 11-13

Viewing the Task list in a docked peek

Click to close the peek

CERTIFICATION
R E A D Y ?   1.1.5

How do you use Current
view when looking at tasks?

19. Click the **Close** button in the upper right corner of the docked peek.

PAUSE. LEAVE Outlook 2013 open to use in the next exercise.

Table 11-1 lists and describes the Outlook 2013 Task views, which you will learn to use in this exercise.

Table 11-1

Task views

Views	Description
Detailed	Similar in appearance to the Simple List, this view also includes the status, percent complete, and category of your tasks, complete or active.
Simple List	This view shows the subject and due date for all tasks, completed or not.
To-Do List	This view includes not only your active tasks, but all other To-Do items, such as messages and contacts that you have flagged for follow-up.
Prioritized	This view shows your active tasks sorted by the Priority field. Tasks at the top have a High priority.
Active	This view shows only the tasks that you have not yet marked as completed.
Completed	This view shows only the tasks that you have marked as completed.
Today	This view shows all tasks due today.
Next 7 Days	This view shows all tasks due within the next seven days.
Overdue	This view shows all tasks that are currently overdue.
Assigned	This view shows all tasks that were assigned to you or that you have assigned to someone else.
Server Tasks	If you are operating on a Microsoft Exchange network and using SharePoint 2013, this Outlook 2013 view shows all tasks created and tracked through SharePoint.

MANAGING AND COMPLETING A TASK

The Bottom Line

After a task is created, you may have to modify the task by setting its priority as High, Low, or Normal. You can change a task's status and update the amount of the task that has been completed. You can also mark a task as private, keeping the details hidden from other users.

Updating a Task

Over the lifespan of a task, many things will change, from the status to the percentage of completion to the due date. Keeping track of the status of your tasks is a key element to keeping your project on course. Tracking the status of a task includes modifying the task's status and percentage complete each time you work on it. The Status and % Complete fields work together to define your progress, as shown in Table 11-2. In this exercise, you will update an existing task.

Table 11-2

Task Status

Status	% Complete	Description
Not Started	0	The Not Started status indicates that work on the task has not yet begun.
In Progress	1–99	The **In Progress** status indicates that work on the task has started.
Completed	100	The Completed status indicates that all work on this task is finished. When you finish a task, mark it as **Completed**.
Waiting on Someone Else	0–99	The Waiting on Someone Else status indicates that your progress on the task has been postponed until you receive something (e.g., confirmation on a detail, a hard copy in the mail) from someone else.
Deferred	0–99	The **Deferred** status indicates that the task has been postponed without changing the due date or the percentage complete.

STEP BY STEP   **Update a Task**

GET READY. Before you begin these steps, you must have launched Microsoft Outlook 2013 and completed the first exercise in this lesson.

1. If necessary, click the **Tasks** button in the Navigation bar to display the Tasks folder.
2. On the HOME tab, click **Detailed** in the Current View gallery.
3. Click the **Create marketing brochure** task in the list. You know that your company cannot launch the Big Blue product line without your marketing brochure, so you will need to start work on it right away.
4. Click the **High Importance** icon in the Tags group to reflect its importance relative to other tasks.
5. Click the **Status** field for this same task. A drop list of status options is displayed. Compare your Task window to Figure 11-14.

Figure 11-14

The updated task window

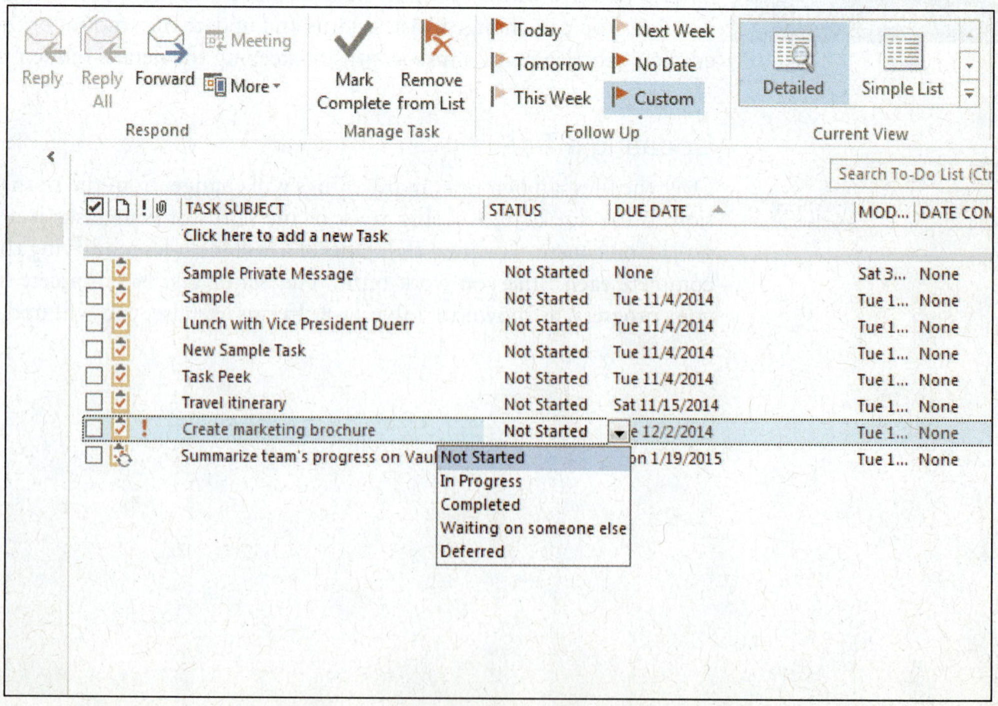

6. Select **In Progress** to indicate that you have started work.

7. Halfway through your work on the brochure, your manager stops by your desk to let you know that the release date for Big Blue has been delayed. You decide to change the status of your task to Deferred and move on to something else. Double-click the **Create marketing brochure** task. The task is opened in a Task window.

8. Click the **Status** field and select **Deferred**.

9. Click the **% Complete** field and key or select **50%**.

10. In the task note area, key the additional text: **Filename is My Documents/BigBluebrochure.docx**.

11. Click the **High Importance** icon in the Tags group to deselect it. Compare your Task window to Figure 11-15.

Figure 11-15

Deferring a task

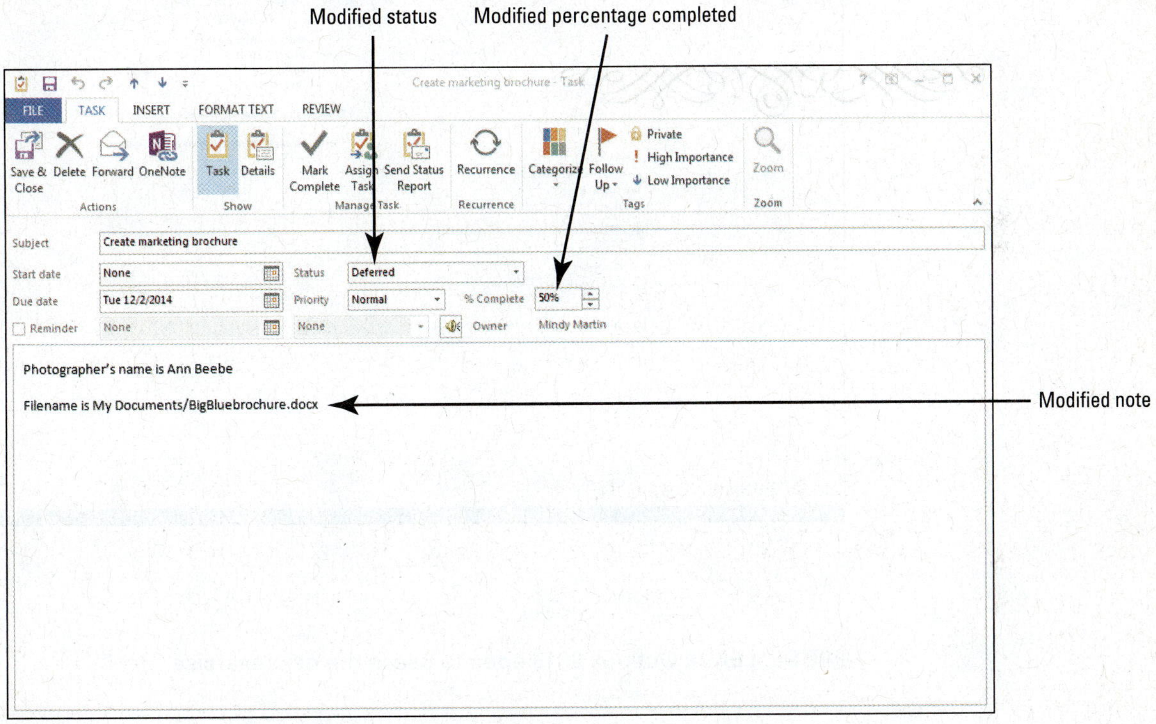

12. Click **Save & Close** in the Actions group on the Ribbon.

13. Click the **Travel Itinerary** task in the Task list. Notice that the Next Week icon is highlighted in the Follow Up group on the HOME tab.

14. Click the **Tomorrow** icon in the Follow Up group on the HOME tab.

PAUSE. LEAVE Outlook 2013 open to use in the next exercise.

CERTIFICATION READY?   3.4.1

How do you update an assigned task?

Making a Task Private

Tagging a task as private protects the details of the task from casual observers on your network. Without permission to access your account, the details of any private task will not be visible to them. In your account, your private tasks do not look different from any other task until you open the task. Once opened, the Private button in the Options group on the Ribbon will be highlighted. In this exercise, you will mark the marketing brochure as a private task.

Make a Task Private

GET READY. Before you begin these steps, you must have launched Microsoft Outlook 2013 and completed the previous exercise.

1. If necessary, click the **Tasks** button in the Navigation bar to display the Tasks folder.
2. Click the **Create marketing brochure** task and, if necessary, click the HOME tab.
3. Click the **Private** button in the Tags group. The task is classified as private, as shown in Figure 11-16.

Figure 11-16

Tagging a task as private

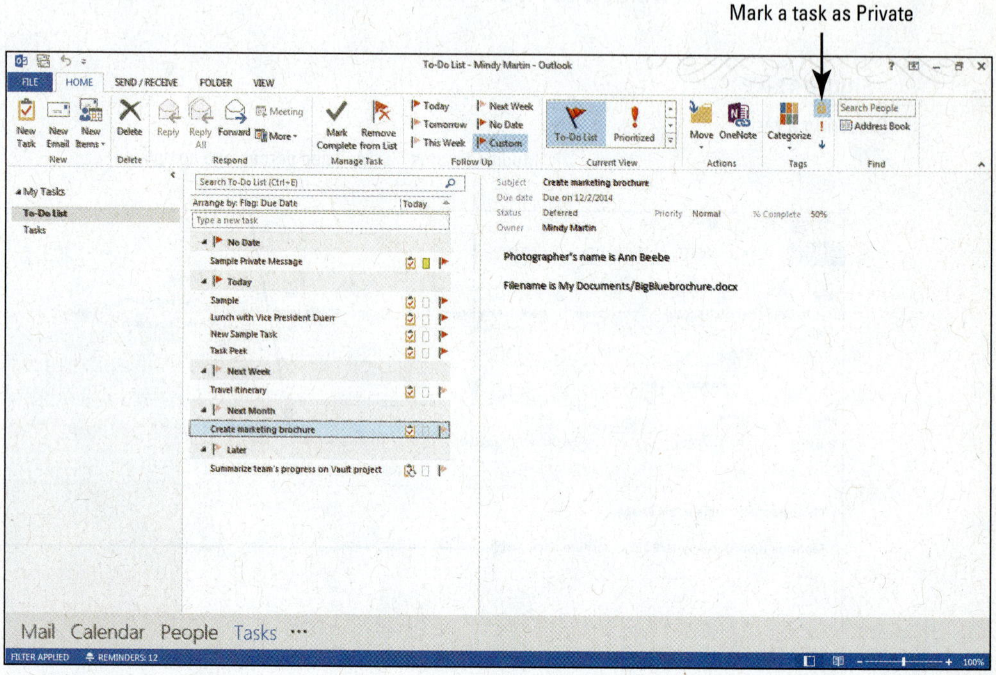

Mark a task as Private

PAUSE. LEAVE Outlook 2013 open to use in the next exercise.

Managing Task Details

Some tasks seem simple on the surface, but in the end, you find that you've expended a lot of energy driving to your client's site to complete them. If you are one of the millions of people who use Outlook 2013 to track project tasks, you might find that keeping track of details like time, billing, and mileage information for your tasks is an essential part of your business. When it comes time to submit a time sheet or issue a bill to a client, you can retrieve the information from your Tasks folder instead of trying to keep it all in your head. In this exercise, you will add details to your existing tasks, as shown in Table 11-3.

Table 11-3	Field Name	Description
Task Details Fields	Total work	Use this field to track the total amount of work spent for the task or client. You may want to track the number of days or weeks, as opposed to hours.
	Actual work	This field tracks the actual number of hours and minutes spent on a given task.
	Company	Key the client's name in this field. If you don't work with outside clients, you could enter the project manager's name or the project name used on your timecard.
	Mileage	Key information about mileage, gas prices, and the purpose of the trip.
	Billing information	Use this field to track your billing rate or any discounts you might have offered.

STEP BY STEP   Manage Task Details

GET READY. LAUNCH Microsoft Outlook 2013 if it is not already running.

1. If necessary, click the **Tasks** button in the Navigation bar to display the Tasks folder.
2. Double-click the **Create marketing brochure** task. The task is opened in a Task window.
3. Click **Details** in the Show group. The details fields are displayed in the Task window, as shown in Figure 11-17.

Figure 11-17

Viewing Task details

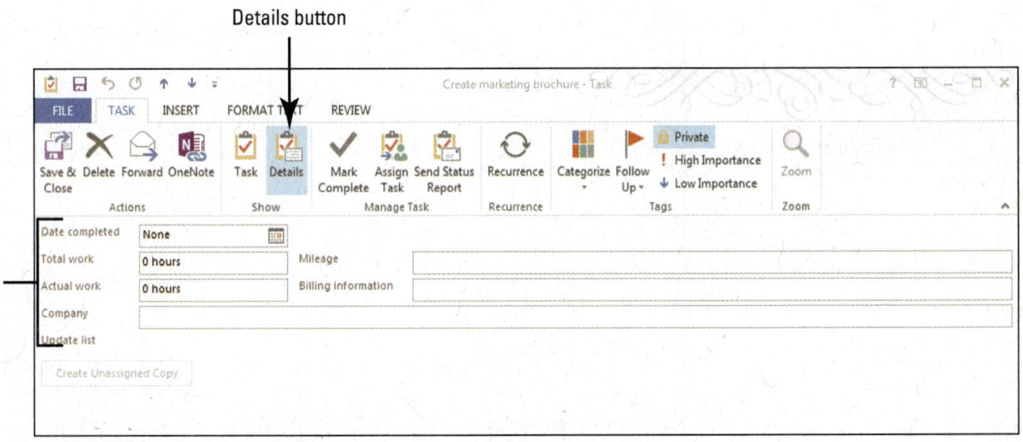

Details button

Characteristics of the selected task

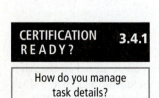

4. In the *Company* field, key **Big Blue merger**, the company's code name for its new product line.
5. In the *Actual work* field, key **23 hours** to indicate the amount of time that you have worked on the project.
6. Click **Save & Close**.

PAUSE. LEAVE Outlook 2013 open to use in the next exercise.

CERTIFICATION READY?   3.4.1

How do you manage task details?

Marking a Task as Complete

When you finish a task, you will need to mark the task as complete. Completed tasks are not displayed on your To-Do List but are visible on the Completed Tasks view. As your list of completed tasks grows over time, the Completed Tasks view becomes a record of the tasks you've accomplished. To see information about the tasks that you've marked as complete, select the Completed Tasks view. In this exercise, you will mark a task as complete.

STEP BY STEP	Mark a Task as Complete

GET READY. LAUNCH Microsoft Outlook 2013 if it is not already running. Before you begin these steps, be sure to complete the first exercise in this lesson.

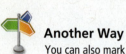

Another Way

You can also mark a task as complete by clicking Mark Complete in the Ribbon in the main Tasks feature or Task window.

1. If necessary, click the **Tasks** button in the Navigation bar to display the Tasks folder.

2. Click the follow up flag next to the **Create marketing brochure** task on the Task list. The task is moved to the Completed Tasks list so it is no longer displayed on your To-Do List.

3. Click the **HOME** tab. In the Current View gallery, click the **Completed** button to view all of your completed tasks, as shown in Figure 11-18.

Figure 11-18

Viewing Completed Tasks details

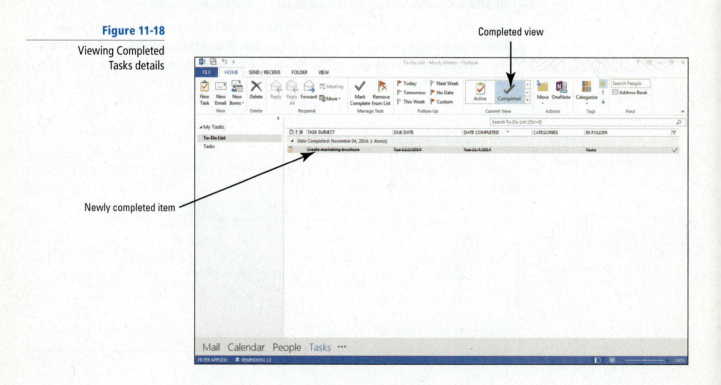

PAUSE. LEAVE Outlook 2013 open to use in the next exercise.

Searching for Tasks

The Instant Search feature makes it simple to find a task quickly, even those stored in the Mail folders. Instant Search can match your search terms with any text, including text in the Task window fields, the notes area, and the Task Details. You can also use the SEARCH TOOLS tab to filter your search results to find the task you need. In this exercise, you will use Instant Search to locate specific tasks in any folder.

Search for Tasks

GET READY. Before you begin these steps, launch Microsoft Outlook 2013 and make sure that Instant Search is enabled. You must have completed the previous exercises in this lesson.

1. In your account, click the **Tasks** button in the Navigation bar to display the Tasks folder if necessary.
2. Click the **More** button in the Current View group to open the Current View gallery of the Ribbon and select **Simple List** from the drop-down menu.
3. Click the **Search To-Do List (Ctrl + E)** box. The SEARCH TOOLS tab is displayed.
4. Verify that **All Task Items** is selected in the Scope group.
5. Key **brochure**. As you key the search text, Outlook 2013 displays the matching task items in any folder, as shown in Figure 11-19.

Figure 11-19

Task items that meet search criteria

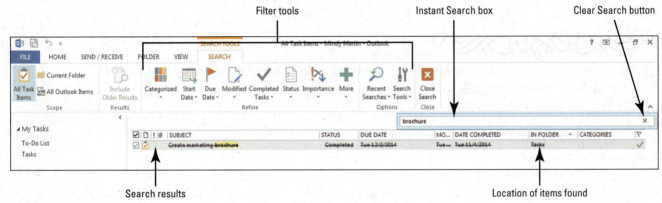

Search results   Location of items found

CERTIFICATION READY?	1.4.3

How do you search for a task?

Moving or Copying a Task to Another Folder

Even with the variety of views available in the Task module and the efficiency of the Instant Search feature, as with other Outlook 2013 modules, you can create custom folders in which to store related tasks. You may choose to create a folder for each project, for a specific time frame, or for each customer. The key is to choose an organization system that works for you. Once you have decided on a system, you can easily move items into their new location. In this exercise, you will create a folder for the Big Blue product line and move the related tasks into it.

Move or Copy a Task to Another Folder

GET READY. LAUNCH Microsoft Outlook 2013 and ensure that Instant Search is enabled. Complete the previous exercises in this lesson.

1. Right-click on the **Tasks** folder in the Folders Pane.
2. Select **New Folder** from the shortcut menu. A Create New Folder dialog box opens, as shown in Figure 11-20.

Figure 11-20

Create New Folder dialog box

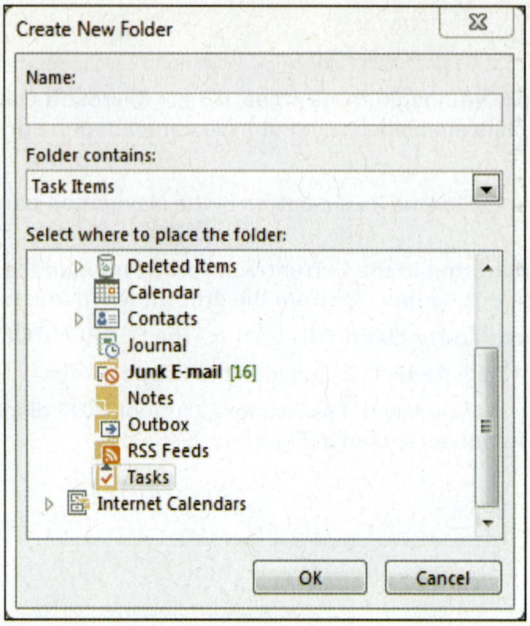

Create New Folder   ⤬

Name:

[   ]

Folder contains:

[Task Items   ▼]

Select where to place the folder:

  ▷ 🗑 Deleted Items
     📅 Calendar
  ▷ 📇 Contacts
     🕐 Journal
     📪 **Junk E-mail** [16]
     📝 Notes
     📤 Outbox
     📡 RSS Feeds
     ✅ Tasks
  ▷ 📑 Internet Calendars

        [OK]   [Cancel]

3. In the *Name:* field, key **Big Blue**.

4. Click the **Tasks** folder in the *Select where to place the folder:* area.

5. Click **OK** to create a new folder, as shown in Figure 11-21.

Figure 11-21

Big Blue folder added under
Tasks folder

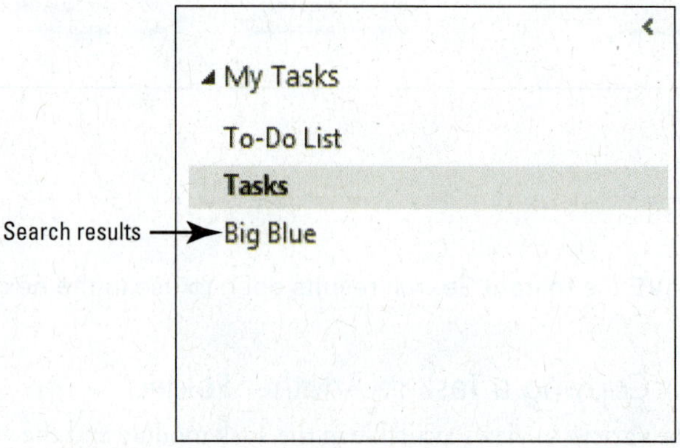

                                      ‹

    ▲ My Tasks

       To-Do List

       Tasks

Search results ⟶ Big Blue

Another Way

To copy a task, drag the item while holding the right-click button on your mouse. Select Copy Here from the shortcut menu.

6. In the Instant Search results, select the **Create marketing brochure** task.

7. Drag the item over the new Big Blue folder to move it.

PAUSE. LEAVE Outlook 2013 open to use in the next exercise.

Printing Tasks

As in other Outlook 2013 modules, tasks can be printed quickly from the Backstage view. In this exercise, you will print two tasks, one active and one completed. Table 11-4 describes the available task print styles.

Table 11-4

Task Printing Options

Print Styles	Description
Table Style	This style prints your tasks in a list, one after the other.
Memo Style	This style prints the contents of each task, including attachments.

STEP BY STEP | **Print Tasks**

GET READY. LAUNCH Microsoft Outlook 2013 if it is not already running.

1. In your account, click the Tasks button in the Navigation bar to display the To-Do List. Click the Tasks folder, if necessary.

2. Click the FILE tab and select Print.

3. Select Table Style from the Settings pane to see a preview of your printout, as shown in Figure 11-22. Click Print.

Figure 11-22

Printing tasks in List view (Table Style)

D	☑ SUBJECT	DUE DATE	✓	CATEGORIES	⚑
	☐ Sample Private Message	None		🟨 Yellow Category	⚑
	☐ Task Peek	Tue 11/4/2014			⚑
	☐ New Sample Task	Tue 11/4/2014			⚑
	☐ Lunch with Vice President Duerr	Tue 11/4/2014			⚑
	☐ Sample	Tue 11/4/2014			⚑
	☐ Travel Itinerary	Wed 11/5/2014			⚑
	☐ Summarize team's progress on Vault project	Mon 1/19/2015			⚑

Mindy Martin   1   11/4/2014 10:38 AM

4. In the Folders Pane, click the Big Blue folder to display the completed Create Marketing Brochure task.

5. Double-click the Create marketing brochure task to open it. Click the FILE tab and select Print.

6. Select Memo Style from the Settings pane to see a preview of your printout, as shown in Figure 11-23.

Figure 11-23

Printing Task details
(Memo Style)

Figure 11-23

Printing Task details
(Memo Style)

CERTIFICATION READY?   **1.3.6**

How do you print tasks?

---

7. Click **Print**.

PAUSE. LEAVE Outlook 2013 open to use in the next exercise.

WORKING WITH ASSIGNED TASKS

The Bottom Line

In the previous sections, you created, modified, and completed tasks. In this section, you will assign tasks to other Outlook 2013 users and respond to tasks assigned to you.

Assigning a Task to Another Outlook User

The task **owner** is the only Outlook 2013 user who can modify a task. The creator of a task is automatically the task owner. To transfer ownership of a task, you can **assign** the task to another Outlook 2013 user with a **task request**. By default, Outlook 2013 will keep a copy of any task you assign to someone else in your task list. If you are using a Microsoft Exchange network, your task list will be updated when the new owner updates the task on their task list.

In this exercise, you will send two task requests to your partner. When you send a task request, the recipient becomes the task owner when you click the Send button. You can recover ownership of the task only if the recipient declines the task and you return the task to your task list.

STEP BY STEP   **Assign a Task to Another Outlook User**

GET READY. LAUNCH Microsoft Outlook 2013 if it is not already running.

⚠ **Troubleshooting**   You cannot assign a task to yourself; therefore, this series of exercises requires exchanging messages with a partner using Outlook 2013. If you do not have a partner, you can use a different Outlook 2013 profile tied to a separate e-mail account. If you need to create a profile, see the Help topics for more information.

1. If necessary, click the **Tasks** button in the Navigation bar to display the Tasks folder. Click the **To-Do List** button in the Current View group on the HOME tab.
2. Click the **New Items** drop-down arrow. The drop-down menu appears.
3. Click **Task Request**. The Task Request window containing elements of a Task window and a Message window is displayed, as shown in Figure 11-24.

Figure 11-24

Task Request window

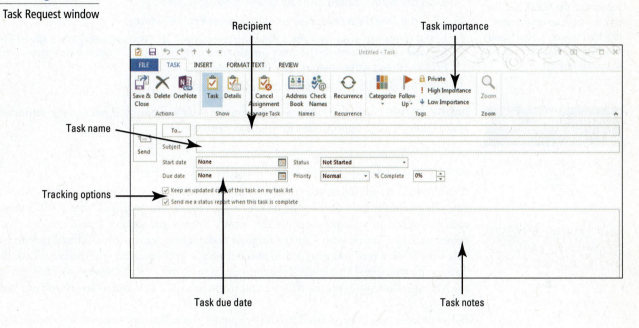

Recipient
Task importance
Task name
Tracking options
Task due date
Task notes

4. Click the **To** field and key [your partner's e-mail address]. Your partner is the Outlook 2013 user who will own this task.
5. Click the **Subject** field and key **Prepare training materials for new employees**.
6. Click the **Due date** field. Key or select [**next Friday's date**].
7. In the message area, key the following message: **Hi,** [Press **Enter**.] **Please prepare training materials and a schedule for the one-day training seminar next week.** [Press **Enter** twice.] **Thanks,** [Press **Enter** twice.] Key [**your name**].
8. Click the **Send** button to send the task request. If you kept a copy of the task, it is displayed on your To-Do List.
9. Click the **Prepare training materials for new employees** task on your To-Do List to verify that your partner is identified as the task owner, as shown in Figure 11-25.

Another Way

If you want to assign a task that already exists in your task list, open it and click the Assign Task button in the Manage Task group on the TASK tab.

Figure 11-25

Assigned task displayed after task request sent

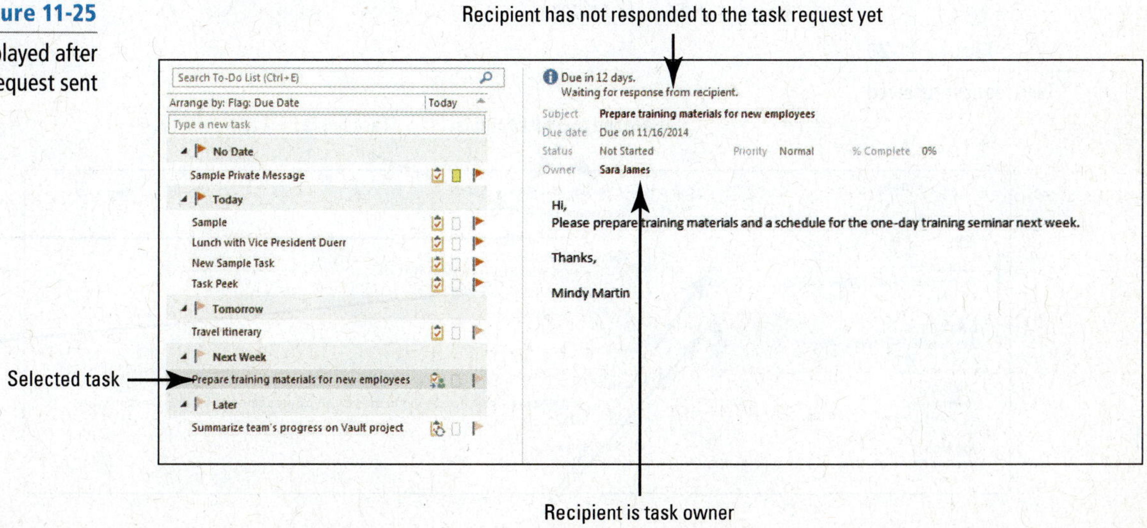

Recipient has not responded to the task request yet

Selected task

Recipient is task owner

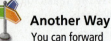

Another Way

You can forward one of your tasks to a friend or colleague. Select the task you want to forward and click Forward on the HOME tab. The task is sent as an attachment to a Mail message. Your friend can drag the attachment to their own Task list.

CERTIFICATION READY?   **3.4.1**

How do you assign tasks to others?

---

10. If necessary, click the Tasks button in the Navigation bar to display the Tasks folder.

11. Click the New Items drop-down list arrow. The drop-down menu appears.

12. Click Task Request.

13. Click the To field and key [your partner's e-mail address]. Your partner is the Outlook 2013 user who will own this task.

14. Click the Subject field and key Greet new employees.

15. Click the Due date field. Key or select [next Friday's date].

16. In the message area, key the following message: Hi, [Press Enter] It's a good idea to introduce ourselves to the new employees before the training session that starts next Friday. [Press Enter twice] Key [your name].

17. Click the Send button to send the task request.

PAUSE. CLOSE Outlook 2013 to access your partner's account, if necessary. Otherwise, leave Outlook 2013 open to use in the next exercise.

Accepting or Declining a Task Assignment

A task request is received in your mailbox like any other message. When you receive a task request, you can accept the task, decline the task, or assign the task to another Outlook 2013 user. Once a task is assigned to you, you become the owner. Even if you decline a task request, you are the owner until the person who sent the original task request returns the declined task to his or her task list. When a task you assigned to another user is declined, you will receive a Task Declined: Task Name message. Double-click the message to open it. Click the Return to Task List button in the Manage Task group on the Ribbon and then click Save & Close to return to your task list.

In this exercise, you have received two task requests. You will accept one task and decline the second.

STEP BY STEP   **Accept or Decline a Task Assignment**

GET READY. LAUNCH Outlook 2013 if it is not already running. Complete the previous exercise.

Take Note   This exercise has to be performed using tasks sent to you by a partner or in the alternate e-mail account to which you sent the tasks requests in the previous exercise.

1. Click the Mail button in the Navigation Bar to display the Mail folder, if necessary. If the task requests sent in the previous exercise have not arrived, click the Send/Receive All Folders button.

2. In the Inbox, click the Task Request: Greet new employees message to preview it, as shown in Figure 11-26.

Figure 11-26

Task request received

Respond to a task request   Task name

Search Current Mailbox (Ctrl+E)   Current Mailbox

All Unread   By Date ▾ Newest ↓

▲ Older

Sara James
Task Request: Prepare training material...   5/3/2013
‹This item contains active content. Open

Sara James
Task Request: Greet new employees   5/3/2013
‹This item contains active content. Open

Jon Morris
Travel itinerary   5/2/2013
Hi, Please give a copy of your itinerary to

Jon Morris
New Time Proposed: SFI Proposal   5/1/2013
I'm afraid I'll be tied up with the Outdoor

✓ Accept   ✕ Decline

Greet new employees

Mindy Martin

ⓘ Due in 10 days.
Assigned by Sara James on 11/4/2014 11:11 AM.

Due date   Due on 11/14/2014
Status   Not Started
Priority   Normal
Complete   0%

Hi,
It's a good idea to introduce ourselves to the new employees before the training session starts next Friday.

Sara James

Person who assigned task to you

Task deadline

Meeting request icon

3. In the Reading Pane, click the **Decline** button at the top of the message. As shown in Figure 11-27, a small dialog box is displayed asking if you want to edit the message sent with the response.

Figure 11-27

Declining Task dialog box

Declining Task ☒

⚠ This task will be declined and moved into the Deleted Items folder. Do you want to edit the response before sending it?

○ Edit the response before sending
◉ Send the response now

OK   Cancel

4. In the Declining Task dialog box, click the **Edit the response before sending** option and click **OK**.

5. At the top of the message area in the Task window, key **Sorry, I will be out of town next Friday**. [Press **Enter** twice.]

6. Compare your Task Request response to that shown in Figure 11-28.

Figure 11-28

Task Request response form

Task name

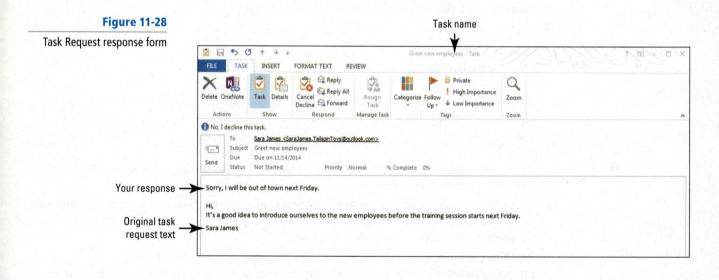

Your response →

Original task request text →

7. Click the **Send** button. Your partner has declined this task, so it is not added to his task list. However, until you—the person who originally assigned it to your partner—reclaims ownership of the task, he is still the owner.

8. In the Inbox, click the **Task Request: Prepare training materials for new employees** message. The task request is previewed in the Reading Pane.

9. In the Task window, click the **Accept** button in the Respond group on the Ribbon. The small *Accepting Task* dialog box is displayed.

10. Click **OK** to send the response now. The task acceptance is sent and the task is added to your task list.

11. Double-click the **Task Request: Greet new employees** message that your partner declined. The declined task request window opens, as shown in Figure 11-29.

Figure 11-29

Reclaiming ownership of a task

Click to add the task back to your Task List   Task name

Figure 11-29

Reclaiming ownership of a task

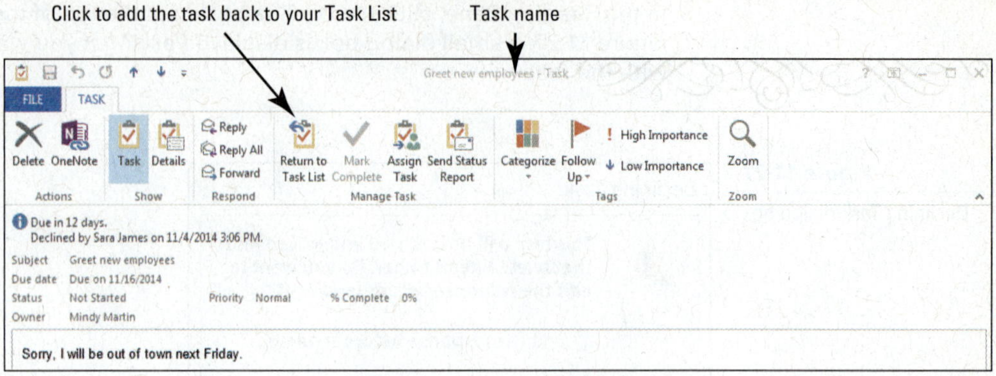

12. Click the **Return to Task List** button in the Manage Task group. The task acceptance is sent and the task is added to your task list.

PAUSE. LEAVE Outlook 2013 open to use in the next exercise.

Sending a Status Report

When you update a task assigned to you, the task copy kept on any previous owner's task list is automatically updated if the previous owner chose the tracking options when assigning the task. You can also choose to send a status report to previous task owners or other interested individuals. In this exercise, you will update the *Prepare training materials for new employees* task and send a status report to the person who assigned the task to you.

STEP BY STEP **Send a Status Report**

GET READY. LAUNCH Outlook 2013 if it is not already running. Make sure you've completed the previous exercises.

Take Note This exercise begins in your partner's account.

1. In your partner's account, click the **Tasks** button in the Navigation bar to display the Tasks folder if necessary.

2. Double-click the **Prepare training materials for new employees** task. The Task window is displayed.

3. Click the **% Complete** field. Key or select **50%**.

4. Click the **Save & Close** button to update the task.

5. Double-click the **Prepare training materials for new employees** task. The Task window is displayed.

6. Click the **Send Status Report** button in the Manage Task group on the Ribbon. A Message window is displayed. The person who assigned the task to you is displayed in the *To* field.

Take Note The *To* field is filled in automatically by Outlook 2013. To see any individuals who will be automatically updated, open the task to display the Task window and click the Details button in the Show group on the Ribbon. The *Update list* field identifies individuals who are automatically updated in the status report.

7. The message content details the task's current status.

8. Click the **Send** button.

Take Note Switch to your e-mail account.

9. In your e-mail account, click the **Task Status Report: Prepare training materials for new employees** message in your message list. The status report is previewed in the Reading Pane, as shown in Figure 11-30.

⚠️ **Troubleshooting**   If you haven't received the status report, press F9 to send and receive all messages.

Figure 11-30

Task Status Report received

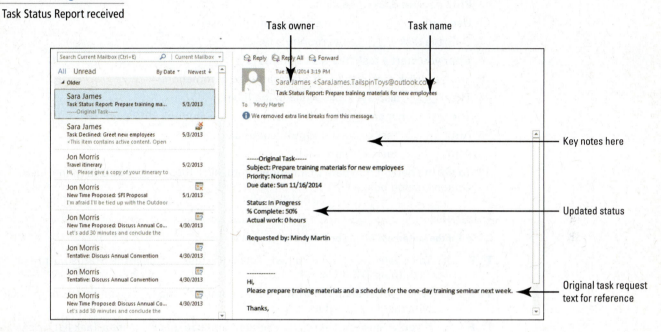

PAUSE. CLOSE Outlook 2013.

CERTIFICATION READY?   3.4.5

How do you send a status report on an assigned task?

When the status report is received, the task status report includes the original task text, the updated progress information, and any notes the task owner might want to include, as shown in Figure 11-30.

SKILL SUMMARY

In This Lesson, You Learned How To:	Exam Objective	Objective Number
Create New Tasks	Create and manage tasks	3.4.1
Work with Task Options	Set Outlook options Configure views	1.1.7 1.1.5
Manage and Complete a Task	Create and manage tasks Search for tasks Print tasks	3.4.1 1.4.3 1.3.6
Work with Assigned Tasks	Create and manage tasks Update task status	3.4.1 3.4.5

Knowledge Assessment

Fill in the Blank

Complete the following sentences by writing the correct word or words in the blanks provided.

1. To print all the details about a given task, select the task and choose the _____ on the Print page in Backstage view.
2. Use a(n) _____ to assign a task to another user.
3. Only the task _____ can modify a task.
4. After you start a task, the task's status is _____.
5. You can track a(n) _____ from creation to completion.
6. The _____ displays tasks while in the Inbox.
7. The task owner can _____ the task to another Outlook 2013 user.
8. A(n) _____ task occurs at regular intervals.
9. A(n) _____ task is postponed.
10. To set the default due date of a flagged item, click the _____ button in the Tasks Options dialog box.

True/False

Circle T if the statement is true or F if the statement is false.

T F 1. To update the status of a task, select the task and click the Status button on the Task Tools TASK List tab.

T F 2. When you mark a recurring task as complete, the task is automatically recreated with the next due date displayed.

T F 3. If you've already set up your printer, you can quickly print a Task list by clicking the Quick Print button on the Task Tools TASK List tab.

T F 4. In the Outlook Tasks Options dialog box, you can decide whether you want to keep a copy of tasks that you assigned to other people.

T F 5. To copy a task to another folder, just select the task and drag it to the new location.

T F 6. The Detailed view includes the subject, status, percent complete, and category of your tasks and To-Do items, complete or active.

T F 7. The task owner is the only Outlook 2013 user who can modify a task.

T F 8. Completed tasks are displayed on your To-Do List with a check mark indicating that the task is completed.

T F 9. Outlook 2013 will keep a copy of any task you assign to someone else in your task list.

T F 10. When you mark a task as Private, none of the details will be visible in your Reading Pane.

Competency Assessment

Project 11-1: Create a One-Time Task

Eugene Kogan is setting up a small business to bake and sell cupcakes. He believes that "personal cakes" will be popular at children's parties, open houses, and office events. Before he can get started, Eugene needs to create a list of tasks. He is a procrastinator, so he knows that deadlines are needed to keep him focused on the business. Since he already has a full-time job, he will only be able to work a few hours a week on this new venture, and he wants to update his task settings accordingly.

GET READY. LAUNCH Outlook 2013 if it is not already running.

1. On the FILE tab, click **Options**.

2. Click **Tasks**. The Outlook Options dialog box is displayed.

3. In the Work hours group, key or select **4** in the *Task working hours per day* field to indicate that you work only 4 hours a day on tasks.

4. In the *Task working hours per week* field, key or select **24** because Eugene plans to work on Saturdays as well.

5. Click **OK**.

6. If necessary, click the **Tasks** button in the Navigation bar to display the Tasks folder.

7. Click **New Task** on the HOME tab.

8. In the *Subject* field, key **Cupcakes — Identify potential clients**. In the *Due date* field, key or select [**the date two weeks from today**]. Click the **Save & Close** button in the Actions group on the Ribbon.

9. Click **New Task** on the HOME tab.

10. In the *Subject* field, key **Cupcakes — Identify competitors**. In the *Due date* field, key or select [**the date two weeks from today**]. Click the **Save & Close** button in the Actions group on the Ribbon.

11. Click **New Task** on the HOME tab.

12. In the *Subject* field, key **Cupcakes — Research prices and recurring expenses**. In the *Due date* field, key or select [**the date one week from today**]. Click the **Save & Close** button in the Actions group on the Ribbon.

13. Click **New Task** on the HOME tab.

14. In the *Subject* field, key **Cupcakes — Identify initial equipment and financial investment needed**. In the *Due date* field, key or select [**the date four weeks from today**]. Click the **Save & Close** button in the Actions group on the Ribbon.

15. Click **New Task** on the HOME tab.

16. In the *Subject* field, key **Cupcakes — Identify time investment required**. In the *Due date* field, key or select [**the date four weeks from today**]. Click the **Save & Close** button in the Actions group on the Ribbon.

17. Click **New Task** on the HOME tab.

18. In the *Subject* field, key **Cupcakes — Research and select marketing methods**. In the *Due date* field, key or select [**the date four weeks from today**]. Click the **Save & Close** button in the Actions group on the Ribbon.

19. Click **New Task** on the HOME tab.

20. In the *Subject* field, key **Cupcakes — Write a business plan**. In the Due date field, key or select [**the date six weeks from today**]. Click the **Save & Close** button in the Actions group on the Ribbon.

PAUSE. LEAVE Outlook 2013 open for the next project.

Project 11-2: Modify Tasks

Eugene has made progress on making his cupcake dream come true. Update his progress on each of the tasks.

GET READY. LAUNCH Outlook 2013 if it is not already running.

1. If necessary, click the **Tasks** button in the Navigation bar to display the Tasks folder.

2. Double-click the **Cupcakes — Identify potential clients** task. The task is opened in a Task window.

3. Click the **Status** field. Select **In Progress**.

4. Click the **% Complete** field and key or select **50%**.

5. Click the **Save & Close** button in the Actions group on the Ribbon.

6. Double-click the **Cupcakes — Identify competitors** task. The task is opened in a Task window.

7. Click the **Status** field. Select **In Progress**.

8. Click the **% Complete** field and key or select **25%**.

9. Click the **Save & Close** button in the Actions group on the Ribbon.

10. Double-click the **Cupcakes — Research prices and recurring expenses** task. The task is opened in a Task window.

11. Click the **Status** field. Select **In Progress**.

12. Click the **% Complete** field and key or select **75%**.

13. Click the **Save & Close** button in the Actions group on the Ribbon.

PAUSE. LEAVE Outlook 2013 open for the next project.

Proficiency Assessment

Project 11-3: Assign a Task to Another Outlook User

Eugene has been researching his business prospects for several weeks now. He is ready to pull the information together in a business plan. However, Eugene knows that a business plan is a critical document. For example, the business plan is necessary for obtaining funds from a bank. Although Eugene has many important business skills, he decided to ask his cousin, a technical writer at Litware, Inc., to write the business plan.

Troubleshooting   You cannot assign a task to yourself; therefore, Projects 11-3 and 11-4 require exchanging messages with a partner using Outlook 2013. If you do not have a partner, you can use a different Outlook 2013 profile tied to a separate e-mail account. If you need to create a profile, see the Help topics for more information.

GET READY. LAUNCH Outlook 2013 if it is not already running.

Take Note   This exercise is performed in your account.

1. If necessary, click the **Tasks** button in the Navigation bar.

2. Double-click the **Cupcakes — Write a business plan** task.

3. Click **Assign Task** in the Manage Task group on the Ribbon. In the *To* field, key [**the recipient's e-mail address**].

4. In the *Priority* field, select **High**.

5. In the *Due date* field, key or select [**the date four weeks from today**].

6. In the message area, key the following message: **Hi,** [Press **Enter**]. **Please let me know if you need any additional information**. [Press **Enter**.] **Thanks!**

7. Click the **Send** button to send the task request.

PAUSE. CLOSE to access your partner's account if necessary. Otherwise, leave Outlook 2013 open to use in the next exercise.

Project 11-4: Accept an Assigned Task

Eugene's cousin is helping him by sorting through all of the information necessary to create a business plan. His cousin understands the importance of creating a professional document that will give Eugene the best chance of obtaining financing from the bank. Eugene's cousin is just as excited about the new business as he is and completes the business plan in record time and marks the task as complete, which automatically updates Eugene's task list too.

GET READY. LAUNCH Outlook 2013 if it is not already running.

Take Note   This exercise is performed in your partner's account.

1. In your partner's account, view the mailbox. If the task request sent in the previous project has not arrived, click the **Send/Receive All Folders** button.
2. Click the **Task Request: Cupcakes — Write a business plan** message to preview it.
3. In the Reading Pane, click the **Accept** button at the top of the message.
4. Click **OK** to send the acceptance without editing it.
5. In the Inbox, double-click the **Task Request: Cupcakes — Write a business plan** message to open it. Mark the task as complete.
6. Click the **Send Status Report** button in the Manage Tasks group.

PAUSE. CLOSE Outlook 2013 to access your account if necessary. Otherwise, leave Outlook 2013 open to use in the next project.

Mastery Assessment

Project 11-5: Complete Tasks

At the end of two weeks, Eugene has completed several tasks on time. He marks these tasks as complete. He checks the Completed view to see his progress on this new venture.

GET READY. LAUNCH Outlook 2013 if it is not already running.

1. If necessary, display the Tasks folder.
2. Open the **Cupcakes — Identify potential clients** task.
3. Mark the task as completed using the tools on the Ribbon.
4. Select the **Cupcakes — Identify competitors** task.
5. Mark the task as completed using the tools in the Task List.
6. Mark the **Cupcakes — Research prices and recurring expenses** task as complete.
7. Change the Task view to **Completed**. These tasks, as well as the Cupcakes — Write a business plan task completed by Eugene's cousin, appear on this view.

PAUSE. LEAVE Outlook 2013 open for the next project.

Project 11-6: Search for Tasks

Eugene has been operating his cupcake business on the side for the last six months and wants to better organize his Tasks folder by creating a Cupcakes subfolder. He moves his cupcake tasks into the new folder. Seeing his progress so far helps make up Eugene's mind. It's time to take the cupcakes business full time. Afterwards, you will clean up your folders after completing all of these projects.

GET READY. LAUNCH Outlook 2013 if it is not already running.

1. In your account, right-click the **Tasks** button in the Folders Pane and create a new folder named Cupcakes.
2. Click the **Tasks** folder in the *Select where to place the folder* Bar.

3. If necessary, display the Tasks folder.

4. Use the search tools to locate all tasks containing the key word **Cupcakes**. Make sure that all task items are searched.

5. Move the found tasks to the new *Cupcakes* subfolder to move them.

6. Click the **Clear Search** button to clear the search criteria.

7. To clean up Outlook 2013 after completing these projects, restore your working hours per week **40**, working hours per day to 8, and delete the new **Cupcakes** folder.

CLOSE Outlook 2013.

LESSON SKILL MATRIX

Skills	Exam Objective	Objective Number
Working with Categories	Apply categories	2.3.4
	Categorize calendar items	3.2.6
	Sort messages	2.3.1
	Use Advanced Find	1.4.6
Working with Data Files	Create data files	1.3.8

© GlobalStock/iStockphoto

© GlobalStock/iStockphoto

Bart Duncan is a sales representative for Contoso, Ltd. He sells insurance policies to businesses. He works with large corporations, small businesses, and new businesses that are struggling to grow. Because the size of the company dictates the level of service that his company offers its clients, he chooses to categorize clients based on their employee headcount. To make the client's status easily visible, Bart uses five color categories based on size. His two most important clients have separate color categories to indicate their importance in his sales activities. In this lesson, you will use categories to color code your Outlook 2013 items. You will also learn to create, open, and close Outlook 2013 data files to help you manage your Outlook 2013 items.

SOFTWARE ORIENTATION

The Microsoft Outlook Color Categories Dialog Box

The Color Categories dialog box displayed in Figure 12-1 enables you to create, modify, and delete color categories.

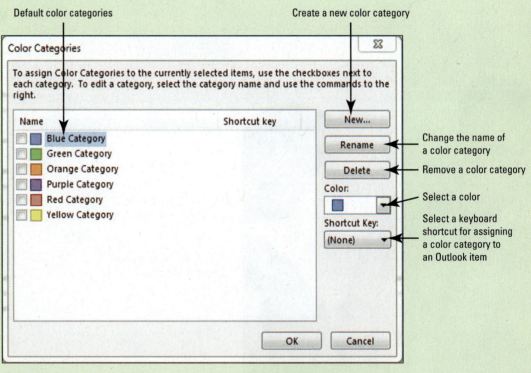

Figure 12-1

Outlook Color Categories dialog box

Use the Color Categories dialog box to customize the new color categories for your use. Refer to Figure 12-1 as you complete the following exercises.

WORKING WITH CATEGORIES

The Bottom Line

A **color category** assigns a color to an Outlook 2013 item, providing a new way to visually indicate relationships among Outlook 2013 items. For example, you might assign the red category to all Outlook 2013 items related to your supervisor. Consequently, you would mark all items related to your supervisor, including her contact record, messages you exchange with her, and meetings scheduled with her with the red color category. You can use color categories to sort or quickly find your Outlook 2013 items.

Categorizing Outlook Items

In this exercise, you will find all the Outlook 2013 items related to a specific contact and assign them to a category. Every Outlook 2013 item can be assigned to one or more color categories without opening the item. You can also create rules to assign a color category automatically to messages you send and receive.

Cross Ref You can find more information on creating rules in Lesson 5.

Take Note Throughout this chapter you will see information that appears in black text within brackets, such as [Press **Enter**], or [next Friday's date]. The information contained in the brackets is intended to be directions for you rather than something you actually type word for word. It will instruct you to perform an action or substitute text. Do **not** type the actual text that appears within brackets.

STEP BY STEP **Categorize Outlook Items**

GET READY. LAUNCH Microsoft Outlook 2013 if it is not already running.

1. Click the icon in the Navigation bar to open the additional features and select **Folders** to expand the Folders Pane to show all of your folders. Click the **Inbox** in the Folders Pane.
2. Click the **Instant Search** box. The SEARCH TOOLS tab appears in the Ribbon.
3. In the Instant Search box, key [**the name of a friend or coworker that you sent mail items to in Lessons 9 or 10**]. Outlook 2013 displays a list of items related to your friend or coworker.

Troubleshooting If you have not been completing these exercises by entering the name of a friend or coworker, key **Tibbott**. Outlook 2013 displays any items related to Diane Tibbott.

4. Click **All Outlook Items** in the Scope group on the SEARCH TOOLS tab, if necessary. All Outlook 2013 items related to the friend or coworker whose name you keyed in the Instant Search box are displayed, as shown in Figure 12-2.

Figure 12-2

Search results

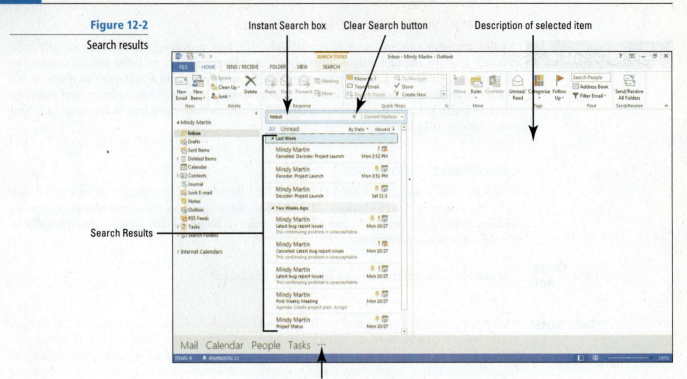

Instant Search box   Clear Search button   Description of selected item

Search Results

Click to access the Folders option

⚠️ **Troubleshooting**   The Outlook 2013 items in the search results depend on the exercises and projects you completed in previous lessons. They may differ from the results shown here.

5. Click the first item on the list. Scroll to the end of the list. If necessary, click the **More** link at the bottom of the list.

6. [Press **Shift**] and simultaneously click the **last item** on the list. All the search results are selected.

7. Right-click over the highlighted list of items. On the shortcut menu, point to Categorize and click the **Red Category** option. If you have not used the Red Category before, a dialog box allowing you to rename the category is displayed, as shown in Figure 12-3.

Figure 12-3

Rename Category dialog box

> **Rename Category**   ✕
>
> This is the first time you have used "Red Category." Do you want to rename it?
>
> Name: Red Category
>
> Color: [🟥 ▼]   Shortcut Key: (None) ▼
>
>   [Yes]   [No]

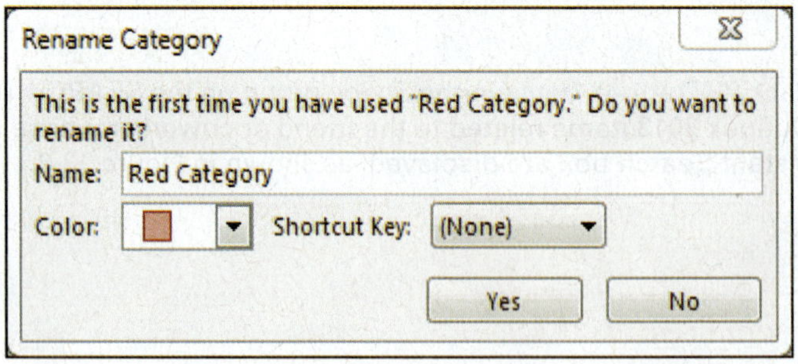

Another Way
You can add a color category before you send a new e-mail. In the Message window, click the OPTIONS tab, click the dialog box launcher in the More Options group, and select Categories.

8. Click **No** in the Rename Category dialog box. You will rename the category in the next exercise. All the items are assigned to the Red Category, as shown in Figure 12-4.

Figure 12-4

Categorizing Outlook items

Items related to Tibbott categorize as Red

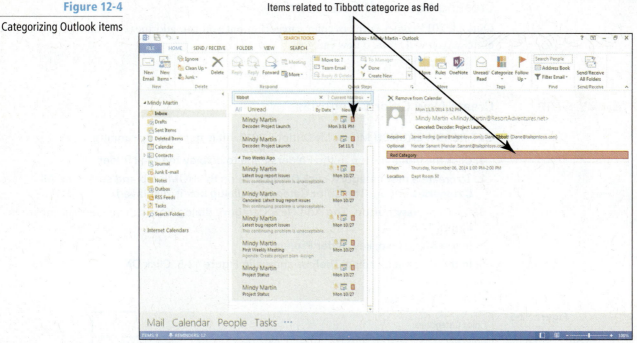

9. Click the **Close Search** button to clear the search criteria, which in this case is the name of your friend or coworker.

PAUSE. LEAVE Outlook 2013 open to use in the next exercise.

Modifying Color Categories

CERTIFICATION READY? **2.3.4**

How do you apply a category to a mail item?

If you, like most people, find that a category named Red Category is a little vague, you will be glad to know that color categories can be renamed to meet your needs. Use names that identify the Outlook 2013 items assigned to the color category. Using an individual's or a project's name more clearly identifies a color category. In this exercise, you will rename an existing color category.

STEP BY STEP   **Modify Color Categories**

Another Way
You can also access the Color Categories dialog box by right-clicking a message, pointing to Categorize, and then clicking All Categories from the list.

GET READY. LAUNCH Microsoft Outlook 2013 if it is not already running.

1. Click the **Inbox** button in the Folders Pane to display the Mail folder. A preview of the first message appears in the Reading Pane. Though you do not have to open it, an Outlook 2013 item must be selected to activate the Categorize button.

2. On the HOME tab, click the **Categorize** button in the Tags group and click the **All Categories** option from the drop-down list. The Color Categories dialog box in Figure 12-1 is displayed.

3. Click **Red Category** in the list of categories and click the **Rename** button on the right side of the dialog box. The Red Category text becomes active.

4. Key **Partner Exercises** in the activated space and [press **Enter**].

5. Click **OK** to rename the category and close the Color Categories dialog box.

Take Note   If you want to rename multiple color categories at the same time, do not click OK until after all of your changes have been made.

PAUSE. LEAVE Outlook 2013 open to use in the next exercise.

Creating New Color Categories

Outlook 2013 comes with six color categories, but you can add more as you need them. In this exercise, you will create a new category.

Create New Color Categories

GET READY. LAUNCH Microsoft Outlook 2013 if it is not already running.

1. Click the **Inbox** button in the Folders Pane to display the Mail folder.
2. To create a new category, click **Categorize** on the HOME tab and select the **All Categories** option. The Color Categories dialog box is displayed.
3. Click the **New** button. The Add New Category dialog box is displayed, as shown in Figure 12-5.
4. In the *Name* field, key **Slider Project**.
5. In the *Color* field, select **Teal**, as shown in Figure 12-5. Click **OK**.

Figure 12-5

Add New Category dialog box

Select a color   Key a name for a new category

Select a shortcut key

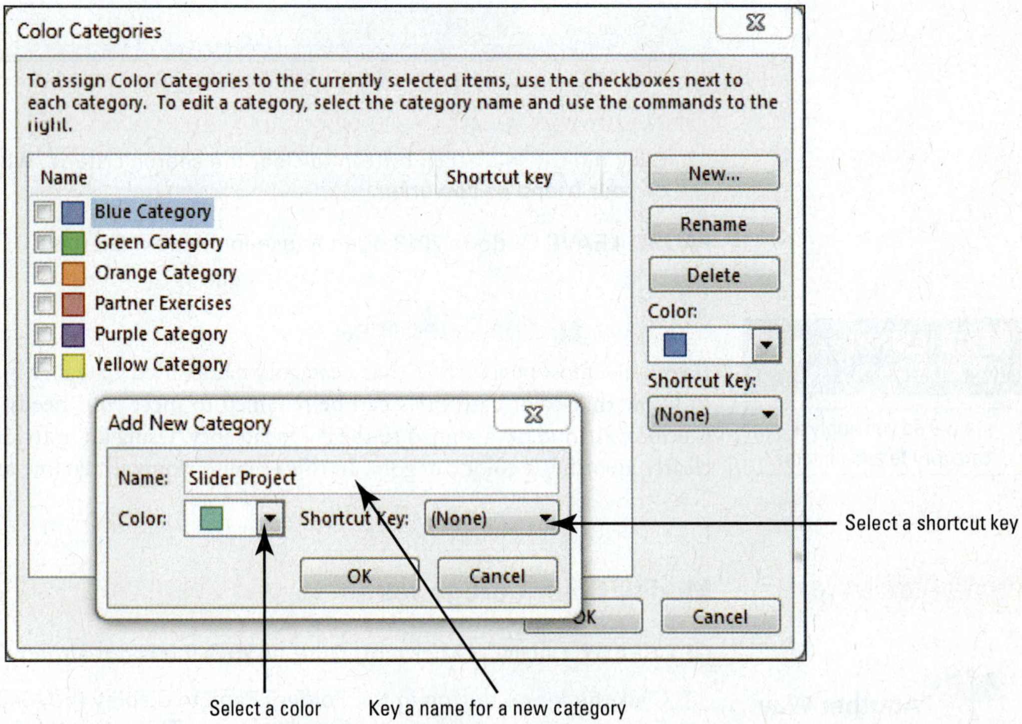

Another Way
You can also create categories that don't use a color. To create a colorless category, select None in the Color field in the Add New Category dialog box.

6. Click **OK**. The new category is displayed in the Color Categories dialog box. Because a message was selected when you created the new color category, the new category is applied to the selected message.
7. Click the **Categorize** button on the HOME tab to view the modified list of categories, as shown in Figure 12-6.

Figure 12-6

Modified list of available categories

Renamed category   New category

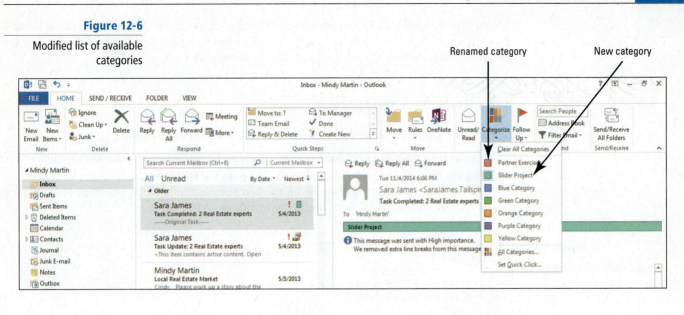

8. Select the message again, then click **Categorize** and select **Clear All Categories** to remove the category from this message.

9. Click the **Calendar** button in the Navigation bar to display the calendar.

10. Scroll ahead as needed and click on the next **Engineering Lunch appointment** that you created in Lesson 9.

11. Click the **Categorize** button on the Calendar Tools Appointment Series tab to display the available color categories.

12. Select the **Slider Project** category from the list. You should notice many categorized meetings and appointments, as shown in Figure 12-7.

Figure 12-7

Categorized calendar items

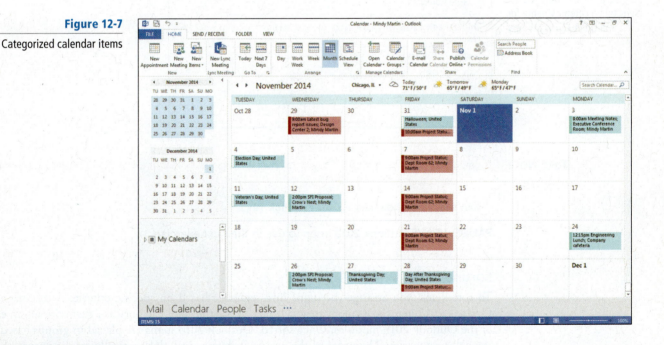

PAUSE. LEAVE Outlook 2013 open to use in the next exercise.

CERTIFICATION
READY?   2.3.4

How do you apply a category to a calendar item?

Setting a Quick Click Category

Many people find that there is one project or activity that is monopolizing their e-mail or calendar schedule. If you find that you are using the same category over and over again, you can set that category to be the default by setting it as the Quick click category. Once you have established a Quick Click, all you have to do is click the Category box to assign the Outlook 2013 item to the category. In this exercise, you will set a Quick Click category.

Set a Quick Click Category

GET READY. LAUNCH Microsoft Outlook 2013 if it is not already running.

1. If necessary, click the **Mail** button in the Navigation bar to display the Mail folder.

2. Click the **Categorize** button in the Tags group on the HOME tab and select **Set Quick Click** to select a category that will be applied automatically when you click the category box on an Outlook 2013 item, as shown in Figure 12-8.

Figure 12-8

Set Quick Click dialog box

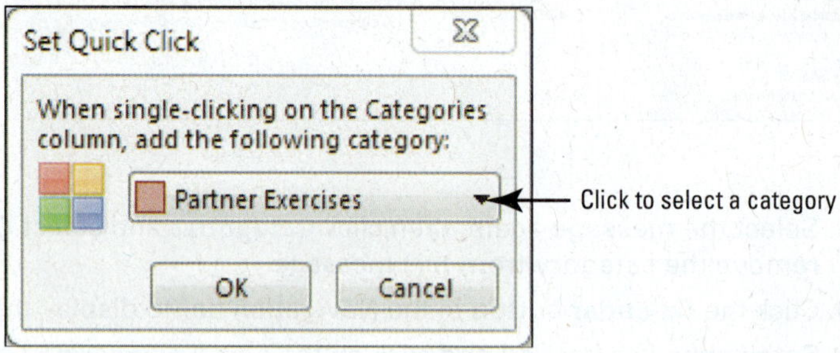

Set Quick Click

When single-clicking on the Categories column, add the following category:

Partner Exercises — Click to select a category

OK   Cancel

3. Click the drop arrow, select the **Green Category** option, and click **OK**. If you have not used the Green Category before, a message dialog box appears asking if you'd like to name it, as shown in Figure 12-9.

Figure 12-9

Selecting a category name for the Quick Click category

Rename Category

This is the first time you have used "Green Category." Do you want to rename it?

Name: Holidays

Color: [green] ▼   Shortcut Key: (None) ▼

Yes   No

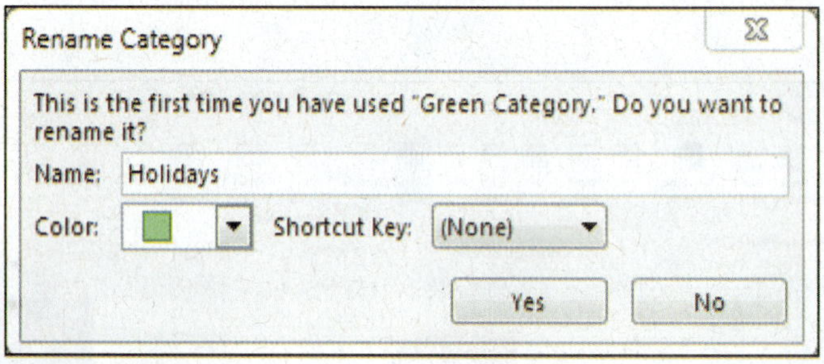

Take Note If you don't see this Rename Category dialog box, use steps 2-4 of the previous exercise to rename the Green category.

4. In the Name box, key **Holidays**. Click **Yes**.

PAUSE. LEAVE Outlook 2013 open to use in the next exercise.

Sorting Items by Color Category

To sort items, you arrange the items in a sequence based on specific criteria. After assigning Outlook 2013 items to a color category, you can use the color category as a sort criterion in each of the Outlook 2013 modules. Once sorted, Outlook 2013 items are placed in groups based on the color categories. The order of the groups is determined alphabetically by the names of the categories. For example, the category "Apple" will be placed before the category "Banana," regardless of the color assigned to the categories.

To sort by Categories, click the VIEW tab, and click Categories in the Arrangement group. The items without a category are displayed after those assigned to a color category. In this exercise, you will sort your Calendar items by color category.

STEP BY STEP   **Sort Items by Color Category**

> **GET READY. LAUNCH** Microsoft Outlook 2013 if it is not already running and be sure to complete the previous exercises.
>
> 1. If necessary, click the **Calendar** button in the Navigation bar to display the calendar.
> 2. On the VIEW tab, click **Change View** in the Current View group and select the **List** option. The calendar items are displayed in a list.
> 3. Click the **Categories** option in the Arrangement group. The items are rearranged by category. Items without an assigned category appear at the bottom of the list, as shown in Figure 12-10.

Figure 12-10

Sorting items by category

Sort by category   Click the arrow to close the category grouping

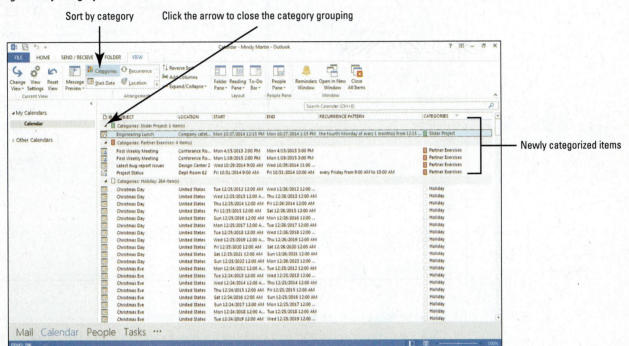

Newly categorized items

> 4. Double-click the **Category** box for the Holiday grouping. The grouping closes to hide the appointments.
> 5. On the VIEW tab, click **Change View** in the Current View group and select the **Calendar** option to restore the default view.

PAUSE. LEAVE Outlook 2013 open to use in the next exercise.

Searching for Items with Categories

The Instant Search feature allows you to search for Outlook 2013 items that meet a variety of search criteria. In previous lessons, you keyed text to use as the search criterion. You can use the Advanced Find feature to search by category or other characteristics, such as the Importance flag and sensitivity assignment. In addition, you can use Search Folders to quickly search for text within categorized messages without having to specify advanced search criteria. In this exercise, you will add a selection criterion using Advanced Find.

Search for Items with Categories

GET READY. Before you begin these steps, complete the previous exercises in this lesson.

1. Click the **Mail** button in the Navigation bar to display the Mailbox.
2. Click in the **Instant Search box** to open the SEARCH TOOLS tab.
3. Click the **Search Tools** button in the Options group and click **Advanced Find** from the drop-down list that appears. The Advanced Find window is displayed, as shown in Figure 12-11.

Figure 12-11

Advanced Find window

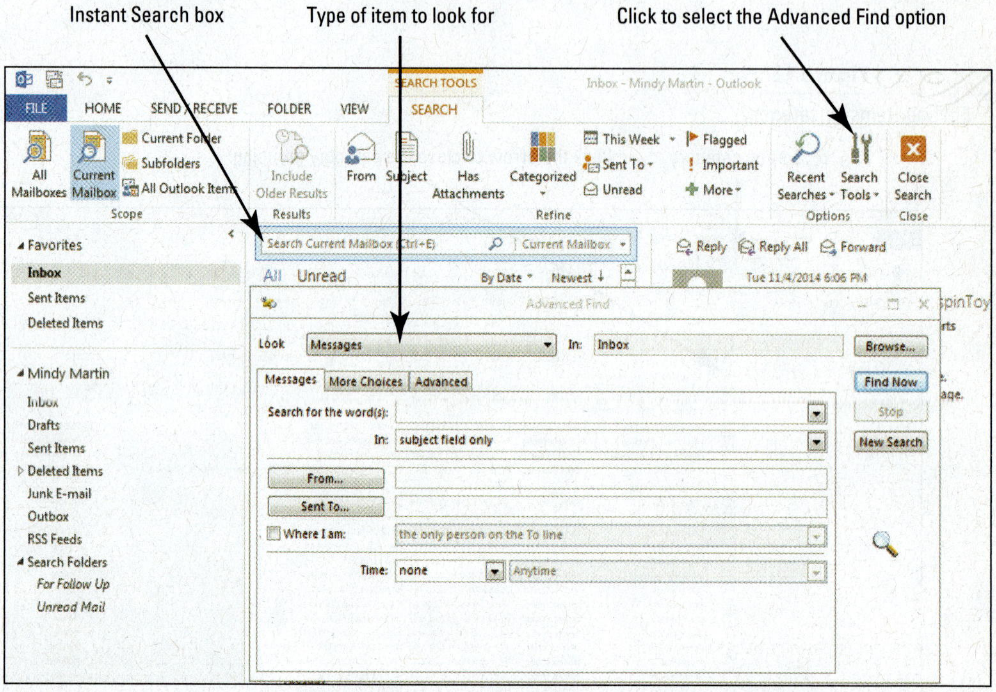

4. Click the **More Choices** tab in the Advanced Find window.
5. Click the **Categories** button and click the **Partner Exercises** check box. Click **OK** to close the Color Categories dialog box.
6. Click **Find Now**. Search results are displayed at the bottom of the Advanced Find window as they are located, as shown in Figure 12-12.

Figure 12-12

Results of searching by category

Search category

Search results

Another Way
You can also add the category option to your search criteria without using the Advanced Find window. Click Categorized in the Refine group on the SEARCH TOOLS tab and select Partner Exercises.

CERTIFICATION READY?   1.4.6

How do you use the Advanced Find feature?

The Bottom Line

7. Click the **Close** button in the upper-right corner of the Advanced Find window.

PAUSE. LEAVE Outlook 2013 open to use in the next exercise.

WORKING WITH DATA FILES

When you create an Outlook 2013 account, Outlook 2013 creates a **data file** to store all of your Outlook 2013 data. That data file is visible inside Outlook 2013 at the top-level folder in your Folders Pane. Depending on your settings, this data file might be called Outlook Data Files or Personal Folders, or it could have the same name as your e-mail address. In addition, when you use the AutoArchive feature, Outlook 2013 stores the archived data on your computer as an Outlook Data File with a .pst extension.

Cross Ref   For more information about the AutoArchive feature, see Lesson 4.

Creating a Data File

You can create your own data files by manually archiving items related to a specific project, client, or time frame and storing the information in a separate .pst file. An Outlook Data File is a convenient way to transfer Outlook data from one computer to another computer. You can even protect the data files with a password. In this exercise, you will create a new top-level Outlook Data File.

STEP BY STEP   **Create a Data File**

Another Way
You can access the New Items button on the HOME tab in every feature in Outlook 2013.

GET READY. LAUNCH Microsoft Outlook 2013 if it is not already running.

1. Click the **Mail** button in the Navigation bar to display the mailbox.
2. On the HOME tab, click **New Items** in the New group. A drop-down list of items that you can create is displayed.
3. Click the **More Items** option to display the drop-down list of new items you can create, as shown in Figure 12-13.

Figure 12-13

Creating a new Outlook Data File

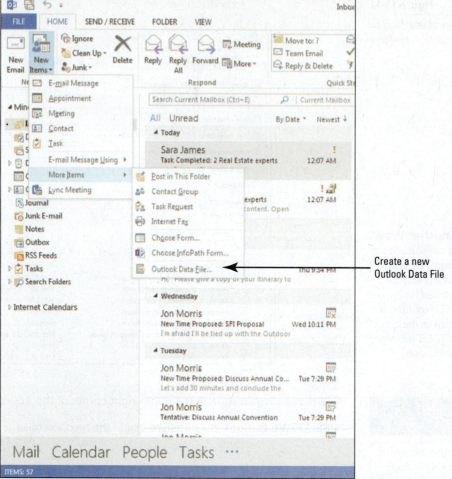

Create a new Outlook Data File

4. Click **Outlook Data File** in the drop list. The New Outlook Data File dialog box is displayed, as shown in Figure 12-14.

Figure 12-14

New Outlook Data File dialog box

Troubleshooting Depending on the settings on your PC, you might skip the dialog box in Figure 12-14. If so, just continue to Step 6.

5. Select **Outlook data file (.pst)** and click **OK**. The Create or Open Outlook Data File dialog box opens, as shown in Figure 12-15.

Figure 12-15

The Create or Open Outlook
Data File dialog box

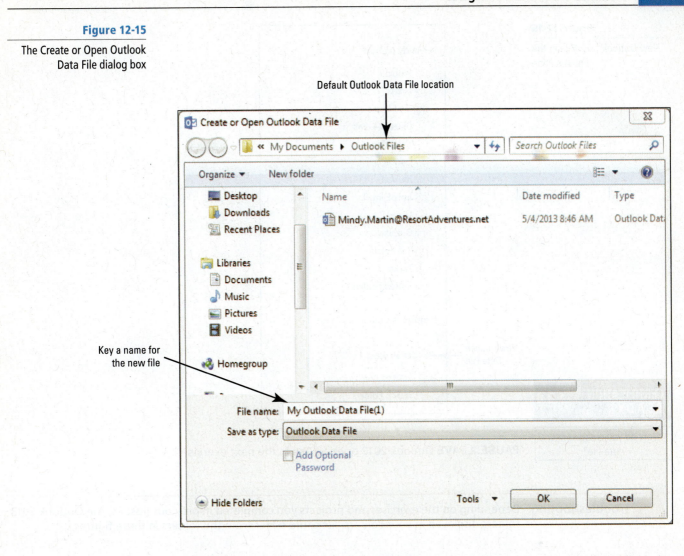

Default Outlook Data File location

Key a name for
the new file

6. In the *File name* field, key **Slider Project** and click **OK**. A new ***Slider Project.pst*** file is created on your computer, and the new Slider data file appears in the Folders Pane.

Take Note   You can see where Outlook 2013 created this file in the Account Settings. Click the FILE tab; then click Account Settings. On the Data FILES tab of the Account Settings dialog box, click Slider project.pst to see the path and file name.

7. Click the **expand arrow** next to the Slider Project folder to display its contents, as shown in Figure 12-16.

Figure 12-16

New Outlook Data File in the
Folders Pane

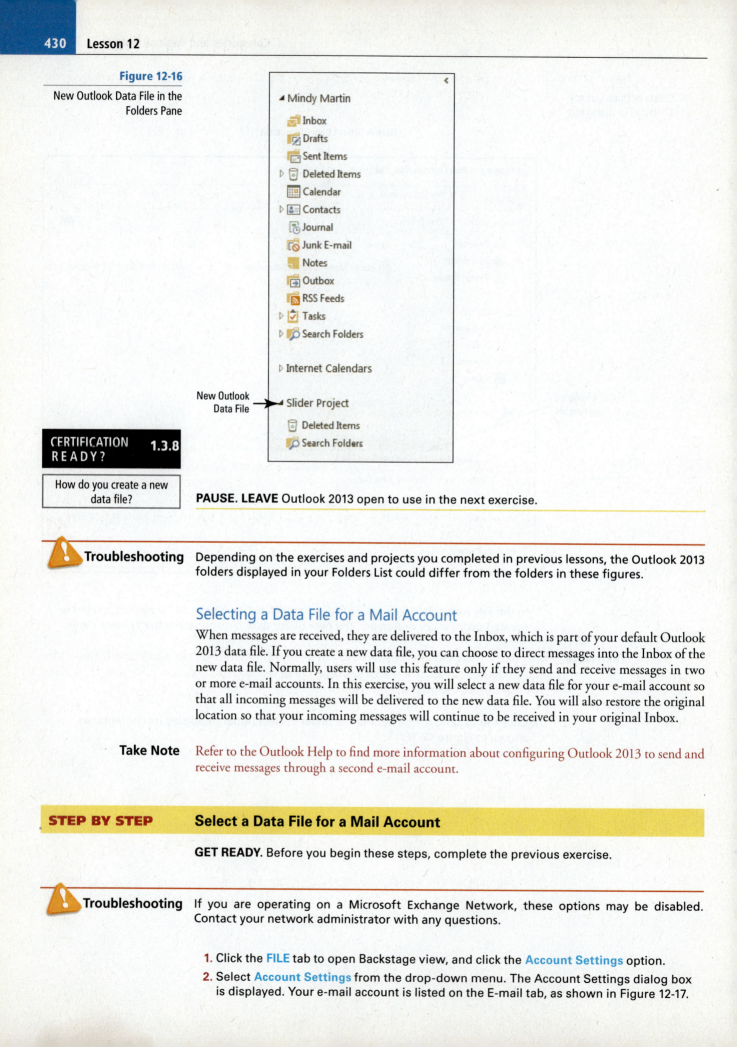

Figure 12-16

New Outlook Data File in the
Folders Pane

New Outlook
Data File →

**CERTIFICATION
READY?**   **1.3.8**

How do you create a new
data file?

PAUSE. LEAVE Outlook 2013 open to use in the next exercise.

⚠ **Troubleshooting** Depending on the exercises and projects you completed in previous lessons, the Outlook 2013 folders displayed in your Folders List could differ from the folders in these figures.

Selecting a Data File for a Mail Account

When messages are received, they are delivered to the Inbox, which is part of your default Outlook 2013 data file. If you create a new data file, you can choose to direct messages into the Inbox of the new data file. Normally, users will use this feature only if they send and receive messages in two or more e-mail accounts. In this exercise, you will select a new data file for your e-mail account so that all incoming messages will be delivered to the new data file. You will also restore the original location so that your incoming messages will continue to be received in your original Inbox.

Take Note Refer to the Outlook Help to find more information about configuring Outlook 2013 to send and receive messages through a second e-mail account.

STEP BY STEP   **Select a Data File for a Mail Account**

GET READY. Before you begin these steps, complete the previous exercise.

⚠ **Troubleshooting** If you are operating on a Microsoft Exchange Network, these options may be disabled. Contact your network administrator with any questions.

1. Click the **FILE** tab to open Backstage view, and click the **Account Settings** option.
2. Select **Account Settings** from the drop-down menu. The Account Settings dialog box is displayed. Your e-mail account is listed on the E-mail tab, as shown in Figure 12-17.

If you already receive messages from more than one e-mail account, the additional accounts will also be displayed.

Figure 12-17

Account Settings dialog box

Figure 12-17

Account Settings dialog box

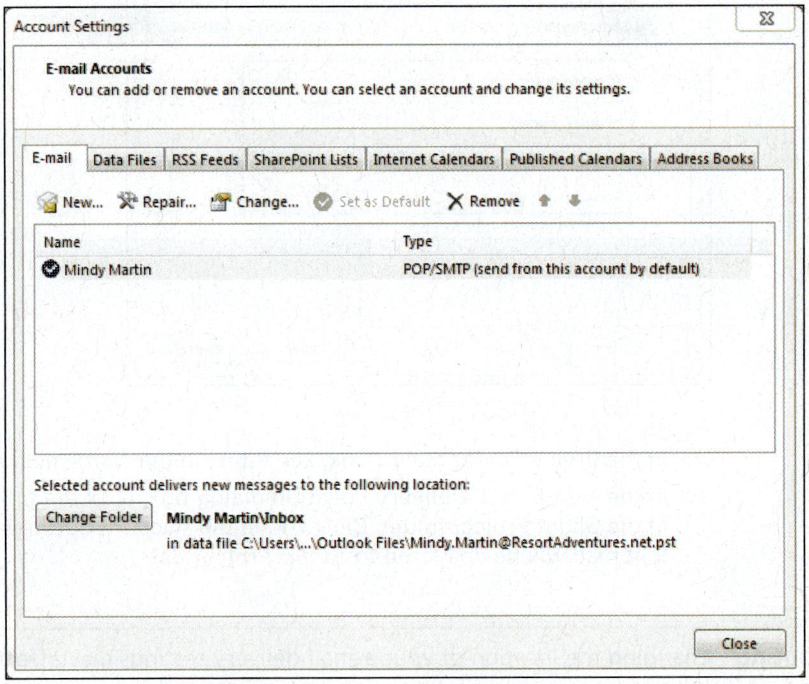

3. Click your main e-mail account to select it and click the **Change Folder** button near the bottom of the dialog box. The New E-mail Delivery Location dialog box is displayed, as shown in Figure 12-18.

Figure 12-18

New E-mail Delivery Location dialog box

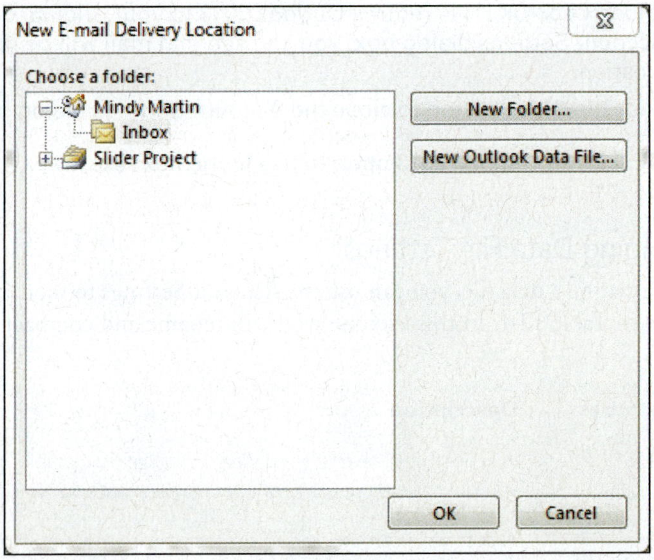

4. In the New E-mail Delivery Location dialog box, click the **Slider Project** folder. Click the **New Folder** button. The Create Folder dialog box is displayed, as shown in Figure 12-19.

Figure 12-19

Create Folder dialog box

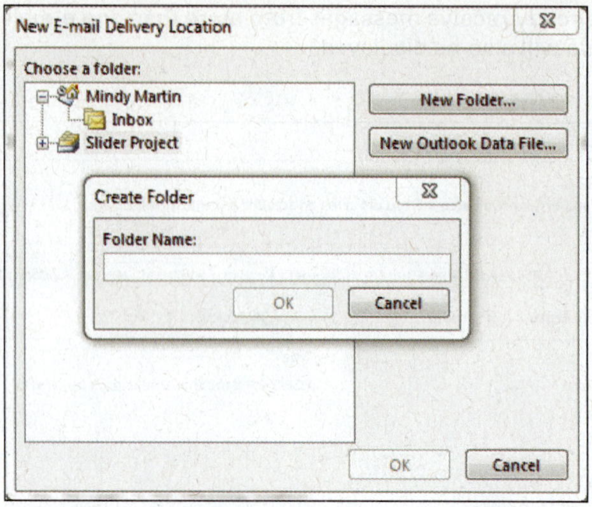

5. In the Create Folder dialog box, key **Inbox** in the *Name* field and click **OK**.

6. In the New E-mail Delivery Location dialog box, click the **Inbox** folder you just created in the Slider Project folder. Click **OK**. In the Account Settings dialog box, you can see that mail will be delivered to ***Slider Project.pst***.

Troubleshooting Changing the location of your e-mail delivery settings may affect any rules you have created or Internet calendars to which you have subscribed.

7. Click the **Change Folder** button near the bottom of the dialog box. The New E-mail Delivery Location dialog box is displayed.

8. In the New E-mail Delivery Location dialog box, click the **plus sign (+)** next to your default Outlook Data File folder and then click the **Inbox** folder in the Outlook Data File folder. Click **OK**. This returns Outlook 2013 to your original data file settings. In the Account Settings dialog box, you can see that mail will be delivered to the original location.

9. Click the **Close** button to close the Account Settings dialog box.

PAUSE. LEAVE Outlook 2013 open to use in the next exercise.

Changing Data File Settings

After creating a data file, you can use the Account Settings to modify some of its characteristics as shown in Table 12-1. In this exercise, you will rename and compact the Slider Project data file.

Table 12-1

Data file properties

Properties	Description
Name	In general, it is never a good idea to change the name of your original data file; however, you can change the name of any data files that you have created.
Change Password	A password can be used to protect the information stored in the data file. However, you are solely responsible for remembering your password. Neither Microsoft nor your network administrator will be able to help you access the data file if your password is lost or forgotten.
Compact Now	Outlook data files get very large very quickly. **Compacting** a file is a process that reduces the size of the data file.

Change Data File Settings

GET READY. Before you begin these steps, complete the previous exercise.

⚠️ **Troubleshooting**   If you are operating on a Microsoft Exchange Network, these options may be disabled. Contact your network administrator with any questions.

Another Way
You can also access a data file's properties from the Folders Pane.

1. If necessary, click the **Mail** button in the Navigation bar to display the Mail folder.
2. Right-click on the **Slider Project** folder and click **Data File Properties** in the shortcut menu.
3. Click the **Advanced** button. The Outlook Data File dialog box is displayed, as shown in Figure 12-20.

Figure 12-20

Outlook Data File dialog box

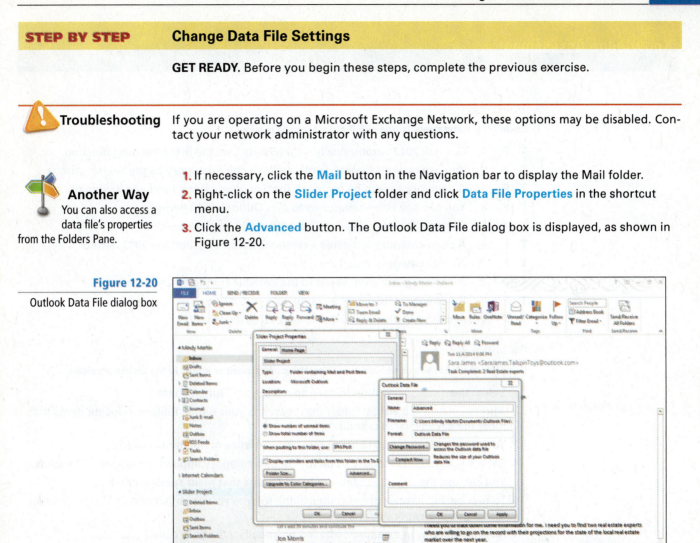

4. Click the **Compact Now** button. A small dialog box shows you the progress.
5. Click the **Name** field and key **New Slider Project**. Click **OK**.
6. Click the **OK** button to close the New Slider Project Properties dialog box.

CLOSE Outlook 2013.

SKILL SUMMARY

In This Lesson, You Learned How To:	Exam Objective	Objective Number
Work with Categories	Apply categories	2.3.4
	Categorize calendar items	3.2.6
	Sort messages	2.3.1
	Use Advanced Find	1.4.6
Work with Data Files	Create data files	1.3.8

Knowledge Assessment

True/False

Circle T if the statement is true or F if the statement is false.

T   F   1. Outlook 2013 automatically creates data files the first time it is launched.

T   F   2. You can create a Search Folder using a color category as the search criteria.

T   F   3. A category cannot be removed from an item after it has been assigned.

T   F   4. You can use color categories to sort Outlook 2013 items.

T   F   5. Outlook 2013 data files can be protected by a password.

T   F   6. A color category indicates a relationship among Outlook 2013 items.

T   F   7. A color category must use a color.

T   F   8. All messages are delivered to the data file for the e-mail account.

T   F   9. Rules cannot be used to assign color categories.

T   F   10. Archived Outlook 2013 items are stored as data files.

Fill in the Blanks

Complete the following sentences by writing the correct word or words in the blanks provided.

1. Select the _____ option to save space in your Outlook data file.

2. A(n) _____ is a virtual folder that searches your e-mail folders to locate items that meet the saved search criteria.

3. You can sort Outlook 2013 items by characteristics of the items called _____.

4. Set a(n) _____ category to be the default category applied to Outlook 2013 items.

5. You can use the _____ feature to find items that meet specific criteria.

6. To reduce the number of messages in the folders you use most often, _____ older messages in a separate folder.

7. Arranging items in a sequence based on specific criteria is called _____.

8. A(n)_____ is a color assigned to an Outlook 2013 item, providing a way to visually indicate relationships among Outlook 2013 items.

9. Actions that happen automatically when messages are received or sent are called _____.

10. All of your Outlook 2013 items are stored in a(n) _____.

Competency Assessment

Project 12-1: Assign an Outlook Item to a Color Category

Terry Crayton at Trey Research is starting a new project. After sending an e-mail to welcome Charles Fitzgerald, she realizes that it would be convenient to assign a color category to all of their correspondence.

GET READY. LAUNCH Outlook 2013 if it is not already running.

1. Click the **Mail** button in the Navigation bar to display the Mail folder, if necessary.

2. Click **New E-mail**. The Message window is displayed.

3. In the *To...* field, key **Charles@treyresearch.net**.

⚠️ **Troubleshooting** The e-mail addresses provided in these exercises belong to unused domains owned by Microsoft. When you send a message to these addresses, you will receive an error message stating that the message could not be delivered. Delete the error messages when they arrive.

4. In the *Subject* field, key **Project Team**.

5. In the message area, key the following message: **Charles,** [Press **Enter** twice.] **I look forward to working with you on the new project. The product sounds like an interesting challenge.** [Press **Enter** twice.] **Terry**.

6. Click the **Send** button.

7. Click the **Sent Items** folder in the Folders Pane.

8. Click the **Project Team** message in the message list.

9. Click **Categorize** in the Tags group. Click **Blue Category** in the dropdown list. If you have not used Blue Category before, a dialog box allowing you to rename the category is displayed.

10. Click **No** in the Rename Category dialog box, if necessary.

LEAVE Outlook 2013 open for the next project.

Project 12-2: Modify a Color Category

The new project that Terry Crayton and Charles Fitzgerald are leading has been named. Change the name of Blue Category to POD Project.

GET READY. Before you begin these steps, complete the previous exercise.

1. Click the **Mail** button in the Navigation bar to display the Mail folder, if necessary.

2. Click the **Sent Items** folder in the Folders Pane.

3. Click the **Project Team** message in the message list.

4. On the HOME tab, click **Categorize**, and click the **All Categories** option. The Color Categories dialog box is displayed.

5. Click **Blue Category** in the list of categories. Click the **Rename** button. The Blue Category text becomes active.

6. Key **POD Project**, and [press **Enter**].

7. Click **OK** to rename the category and close the Color Categories dialog box.

LEAVE Outlook 2013 open for the next project.

Proficiency Assessment

Project 12-3: Sort Items by Color Category

A week later, Terry Crayton needs to find the message she sent to Charles. Because only one message has been sent, sorting the sent messages is the simplest way to find the message.

GET READY. Before you begin these steps, complete the previous exercise.

1. Click the **Mail** button in the Navigation bar to display the Mail folder, if necessary.

2. Click the **Sent Items** folder in the Folders Pane.

3. On the VIEW tab, click **Categories** in the Arrangement group. The messages in the message list are rearranged. Messages without an assigned category appear at the top of the list.

4. Scroll down to the bottom of the message list to view the message in the POD Project category.

5. On the VIEW tab, click **Date** in the Arrangement group. The messages are resorted to the default date sort.

LEAVE Outlook 2013 open for the next project.

Project 12-4: Search Items by Category

Several weeks later, the POD Project is in full swing. Terry has added new contacts, and dozens of messages have been exchanged with POD Project team members. Searching is the easiest way to view all Outlook 2013 items associated with the project.

GET READY. Before you begin these steps, complete the previous exercise.

1. Click the **Mail** button in the Navigation bar.
2. Click in the **Instant Search** box to activate the SEARCH TOOLS contextual tab.
3. Click **Search Tools** in the Options groups, and click **Advanced Find** in the Search Tools drop-down. The Advanced Find window is displayed.
4. Click the **More Choices** tab.
5. Click the **Categories** button and select the **POD Project** checkbox. Click **OK**.
6. Click the **Browse** button to open the Select Folders dialog box.
7. Select your **Outlook Data File**, and select the **Search subfolders** box.
8. Click **OK**; then click **Find Now**. The search results are displayed at the bottom of the Advanced Find window as they are located.
9. Click the **Close** button in the upper-right corner of the Advanced Find window.

LEAVE Outlook 2013 open for the next project.

Mastery Assessment

Project 12-5: Create a Data File

Terry has been assigned to the POD Project exclusively. She creates a new data file that she will use until the project is complete.

GET READY. Before you begin these steps, complete the previous exercise.

1. Click **New Items** on the HOME tab and select **More Items**. Click **Outlook Data File** in the drop-down list.
2. Create a new Outlook data file in the Solutions folder for this Lesson named *POD Project.pst*.
3. Click **OK**.

LEAVE Outlook 2013 open for the next project.

Project 12-6: Select a Data File for a Mail Account

After creating the new data file, Terry wants to add the data file to her mail account. After making the change, you will restore your original settings.

⚠ **Troubleshooting** If you are operating on a Microsoft Exchange Network, these options may be disabled. Contact your network administrator with any questions.

GET READY. Before you begin these steps, complete the previous exercise.

1. Click the [•••] button in the Navigation bar.

2. Click the **Folders** option in the list to display the Folders List.

3. Click the **FILE** tab to open Backstage view.

4. Click **Account Settings** and select the **Account Settings** option. The Account Settings dialog box is displayed. Your e-mail account is listed on the E-mail tab.

5. Click [**your main e-mail account**] to select it, and click the **Change Folder** button near the bottom of the dialog box. The New E-mail Delivery Location dialog box is displayed.

6. In the New E-mail Delivery Location dialog box, click the **POD Project** folder.

7. Click the **New Folder** button. The Create Folder dialog box is displayed.

8. In the Create Folder dialog box, key **Inbox** in the *Folder Name* field and click **OK**.

9. In the New E-mail Delivery Location dialog box, click the **Inbox** folder you just created in the POD Project folder; then click **OK**. In the Account Settings dialog box, you can see that mail will be delivered to *POD Project.pst*.

10. Before finishing these projects, change the data file back to your default data file. Click the **Change Folder** button near the bottom of the dialog box. The New E-mail Delivery Location dialog box is displayed.

11. In the New E-mail Delivery Location dialog box, expand the top-level data file folder and click the **Inbox** folder. Click **OK**. This returns your original data file settings. In the Account Settings dialog box, you can see that mail will be delivered to the original location.

12. Click the **Close** button to close the Account Settings dialog box.

CLOSE Outlook 2013.

LESSON SKILL MATRIX

Skills	Exam Objective	Objective Number
Working with Notes	Create and manage notes	3.4.2
Working with the Journal	Create journal entries	3.4.4

KEY TERMS

- Journal
- Notes

© rcaucino/iStockphoto

Mindy Martin and Jon Morris own and operate Resort Adventures, a luxury resort. As part of their business, they run custom tours for private parties. In order to provide the best experience for their guests, they make several phone calls before the guest's visit to find out the guest's preferences and expectations. They record details of those conversations in the Outlook Journal module. In addition, as part of Mindy's job, she researches local sites even before a guest has requested a tour. She records that research in the Notes module so that she can access them at a later date. In this lesson, you will learn how to record journal entries. You will also learn how to create and categorize notes.

SOFTWARE ORIENTATION

The Microsoft Outlook Notes Window

Before you begin working with the Outlook Notes module, you need to be familiar with the primary user interface. The Notes feature, displayed in Figure 13-1, enables you to create, modify, and delete notes.

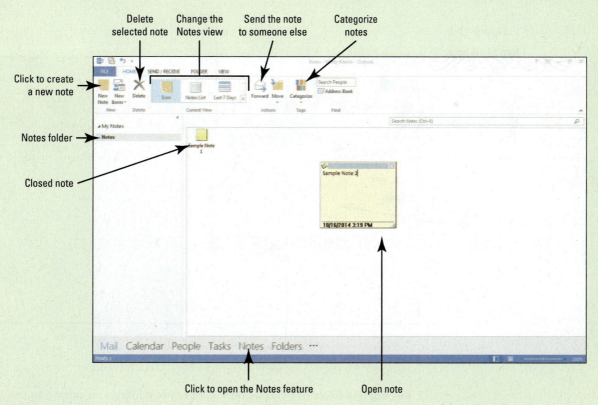

Figure 13-1

The Notes feature

Think of Outlook Notes as sticky notes that you can use to jot down quick notes and stick them on your desktop or on your Notes window. You can also use the Notes feature to record detailed notes on a specific meeting or event.

WORKING WITH NOTES

The Bottom Line

Just like the repositionable sticky notes you might have on your desk, the **Notes** module enables you to keep important information that may not be related to a particular contact or project. The Notes feature is one of the features that has been played down in Outlook 2013, but there are still a lot of things you can do with the Notes feature.

Creating a New Note

Unlike tasks, Notes do not have a due date. They simply contain a small piece of information. In this exercise, you will create a new note.

STEP BY STEP   **Create a New Note**

GET READY. LAUNCH Outlook 2013 if it is not already running.

1. Click the ⋯ icon in the Navigation bar to open the list of additional features.
2. Select **Navigation Options**. The Navigation Options dialog box is displayed.
3. In the *Maximum number of visible items box*, select the number **6**.
4. Click **OK**.
5. Click **Notes** in the Navigation bar to open the Notes feature.
6. Click the **New Note** button on the HOME tab of the Ribbon. A blank sticky note appears in the default yellow color. Below the sticky note is the current date and time, as shown in Figure 13-2.

Figure 13-2

New blank note

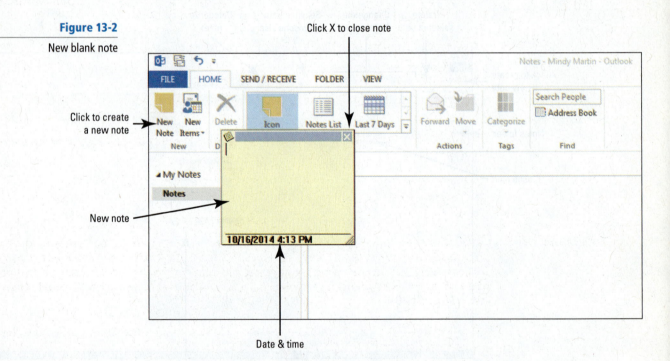

Click X to close note

Click to create a new note

New note

Date & time

7. Key **Big Red River has class 4 rapids. Possible whitewater rafting tours**.
8. Click the **Close** button (the X at the top-right corner of the note) to close the note. Your note appears as a sticky note with the note's text below it.
9. Click the **New Note** button on the Ribbon.
10. Key **Should we offer pizza if our fishing tours don't catch their dinner?**
11. Click the **Close** button (the X at the top-right corner of the note) to close the note. Notice that only the first two lines of text are displayed for the non-selected note. Your Notes folder should appear as shown in Figure 13-3.

Figure 13-3

Notes in the Notes window

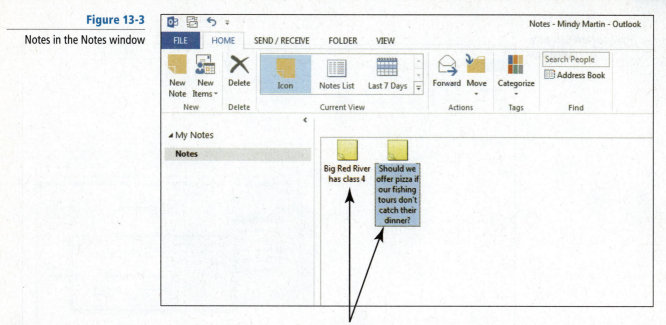

Note text

PAUSE. LEAVE Outlook 2013 open to use in the next exercise.

CERTIFICATION READY? **3.4.2**

How do you create a new note?

Categorizing Notes

Once a note has been created, you can quickly make necessary changes to it. In this exercise, you will open an existing note and categorize it.

🔍 **Cross Ref**   For more information about categories, see Lesson 12.

STEP BY STEP   **Categorize Notes**

GET READY. LAUNCH Outlook 2013 if it is not already running and be sure to complete the previous exercise.

1. If necessary, click **Notes** in the Navigation bar to open the Notes feature.
2. Click the **Big Red River** note to select it.
3. On the HOME tab, click **Categorize**.

⚠️ **Troubleshooting**   If your note disappeared when you clicked the Categorize button, then you probably opened the note. Because notes are created in a separate window, clicking a button on the Outlook 2013 application window makes it the active window and places it on top of an open note. If this happens, just minimize Outlook 2013 and close your open note. Then restore Outlook 2013.

4. Select the **All Categories** option to create a new category. The Color Categories dialog box is displayed.
5. Click the **New** button. The Add New Category dialog box is displayed.
6. In the *Name* field, key **Resort Tours,** as shown in Figure 13-4.

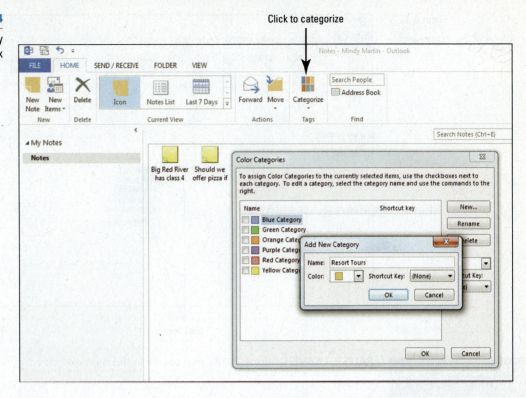

Figure 13-4

The Add New Category dialog box

Troubleshooting   Depending on the exercises you have completed, your icon color may be different from the one shown here.

7. Click the **Color** drop arrow to open the standard color palette.
8. Select **Dark Purple**.
9. Click **OK** twice to apply the color to the new Resort Tours category, as shown in Figure 13-5.

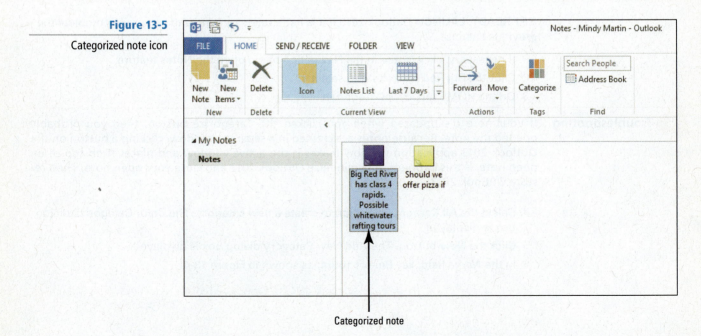

Figure 13-5

Categorized note icon

Categorized note

PAUSE. LEAVE Outlook 2013 open to use in the next exercise.

Exploring Notes Views

By default, the Notes module organizes your Notes as sticky note icons in neat rows across the Reading Pane of Outlook 2013. You can change that view in several ways, as shown in Table 13-1. All notes can be arranged by category and date from the VIEW tab. In this exercise, you will explore the Notes views to see how the content is presented in each.

Table 13-1

Notes Views

View name	Description
Icon	The default notes view shows each Note as a colored icon arranged in the order they were created.
Notes List	The notes are presented in a vertical list as a tiny colored sticky note icon followed by the note's text.
Last 7 Days	This view is presented vertically, like the Notes List, but shows only the items added in the last week.

STEP BY STEP   **Explore Notes Views**

GET READY. LAUNCH Outlook 2013 if it is not already running.

1. If necessary, click **Notes** in the Navigation bar to open the Notes feature.

2. In the Current View group on the HOME tab, click **Notes List**. The notes are now presented as a vertical list with the uncategorized notes at the top, as shown in Figure 13-6.

Figure 13-6

Exploring the Outlook Notes List view

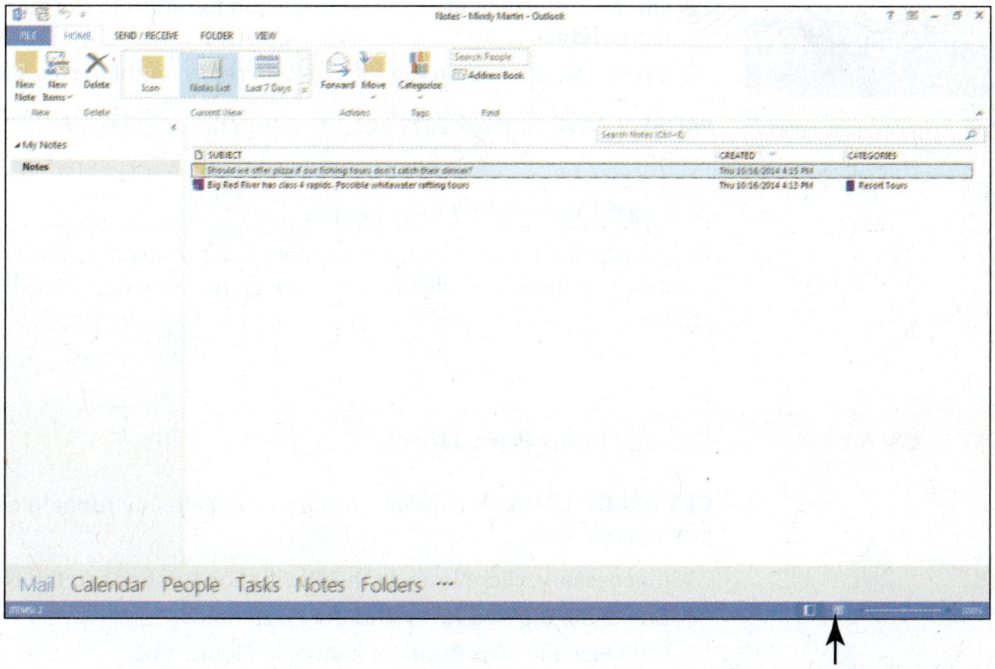

↑
Click to change to Reading View

3. In the Current View group, click **Last 7 Days**. Notice that the view is still in a vertical list. Had there been notes more than 7 days old, they would have dropped off the list.

4. In the Current View group, click **Icon**.

5. Click the **VIEW** tab.

6. Select the **Big Red River** note and drag it to the middle of the screen. Outlook 2013 allows you to stick the notes where you need them.

7. On the Status bar, click the **Reading** icon. The Folders Pane collapses.
8. In the Arrangement group, click the **Small Icons** button. The notes spread out across the screen in a balanced pattern. Notice that the Note text is also displayed, as shown in Figure 13-7.

Figure 13-7

Viewing notes as small icons in Reading view

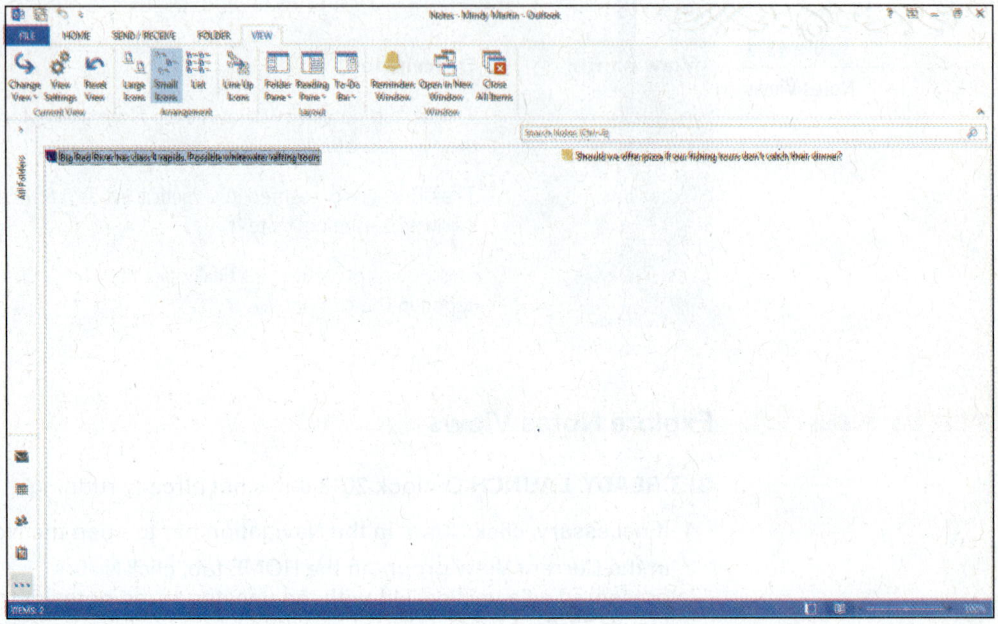

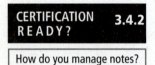

9. On the Status bar, click the **Normal** icon to return to the standard view of the Notes folder.
10. Select **Large Icons** on the VIEW tab to return to the Notes View with large icons.

CERTIFICATION READY? 3.4.2

How do you manage notes?

PAUSE. LEAVE Outlook 2013 open to use in the next exercise.

Forwarding and Printing Notes

Once a note has been created, you can forward it to someone else as an e-mail attachment. Notes can also be printed individually or as a set. In this exercise, you will forward an existing note and print it.

STEP BY STEP **Forward and Print Notes**

GET READY. LAUNCH Outlook 2013 if it is not already running and be sure to complete the previous exercise.

1. If necessary, click **Notes** in the Navigation bar to open the Notes feature.
2. Select the **Big Red River** and the **Pizza** notes.
3. Click **File** and click **Print**, as shown in Figure 13-8.

Figure 13-8

Printing multiple notes

Figure 13-8

Printing multiple notes

Click to view multiple notes

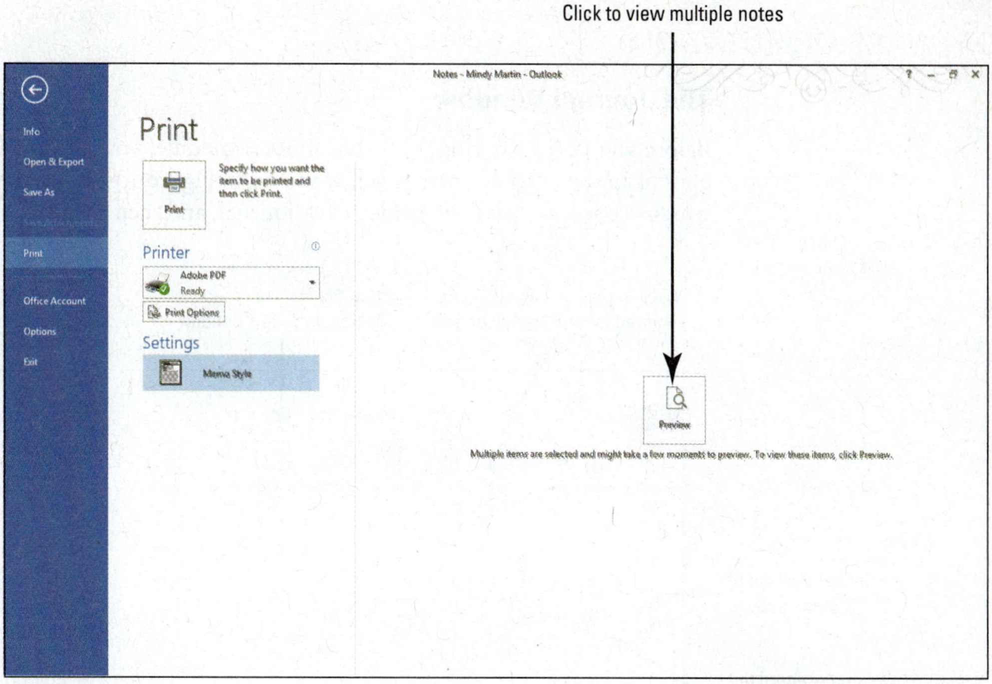

Another Way
To print a single note, right-click the note in the Reading Pane and choose Quick Print on the shortcut menu.

4. In the Preview pane, click the **Preview** button.

5. Click the **Next Page** button to view both notes when the Preview becomes available.

6. If your instructor requests, click **Print**. Turn in both Notes to your instructor.

7. Click the **Back arrow** to return to the Notes feature, if necessary.

8. Click the **Big Red River** note to select it.

9. On the HOME tab, click **Forward** in the Actions group. A new Message window appears with the note text in the Subject field and the note attached.

10. In the message area, key **Here are some notes to consider at next week's Tour Updates meeting.**

11. Address the message to yourself and click **Send**.

PAUSE. LEAVE Outlook 2013 open to use in the next exercise.

WORKING WITH THE JOURNAL

The Bottom Line

The Journal is one of the Outlook 2013 tools that has been pared down for Office 2013. The Journal can still be used to track e-mails, meetings, and task status reports that you have received from a contact. Although you can no longer use the Journal to automatically track time spent on non-Outlook documents, you can use the Duration. You also can add categories to your journal entries as with any other Outlook 2013 item.

SOFTWARE ORIENTATION

The Journal Window

Before you begin working with the Journal module, you need to be familiar with the options in the Journal Entry window shown in Figure 13-9. To access the Journal Entry window, open the full Folders List, click Journal, and then click the Journal Entry button.

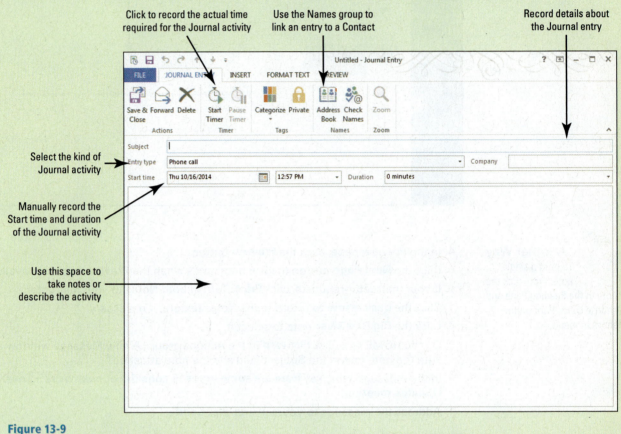

Click to record the actual time required for the Journal activity

Use the Names group to link an entry to a Contact

Record details about the Journal entry

Select the kind of Journal activity

Manually record the Start time and duration of the Journal activity

Use this space to take notes or describe the activity

Figure 13-9

The Journal Entry window

Use this figure as a reference throughout this lesson as well as the rest of this book.

Creating a Journal Entry from an Existing Outlook Item

Certain professionals, attorneys for instance, are required to keep track of the amount of time they have spent working on a particular client's case. They have to record the time spent on phone calls, e-mails, preparing documents, and holding meetings on behalf of the client. This can be done in an appointment book or by using the Journal features. Think of the **Journal** as an online diary of all activities associated with one of your contacts. In this exercise, you will create a Journal Entry to record the time you spent creating an e-mail for a client, set the Journal options for Outlook 2013, and see how that option appears within the Journal.

STEP BY STEP   **Create a Journal Entry from an Existing Outlook Item**

1. If necessary, click **Mail** in the Navigation bar to open the Inbox.
2. Select a message that you sent to yourself.
3. Click **Move** in the Move group and select **Other Folder**.
4. Select **Journal** from the available options and click **OK**. A Journal Entry window opens with the e-mail item included as an attachment.
5. In the Duration box, key **5 minutes** in the Journal Entry window.

Take Note   The Subject of the Journal entry is prepopulated with the subject of the e-mail message.

6. Click **Save & Close** in the Journal Entry window.
7. If necessary, click **Folders** in the Navigation bar to expand the Folders List.
8. Click **Journal** in the Folders List to open the Journal with the default Timeline view, as shown in Figure 13-10.

Figure 13-10

The Journal Timeline (with the To-Do Bar calendar showing)

Tracked Journal Entries

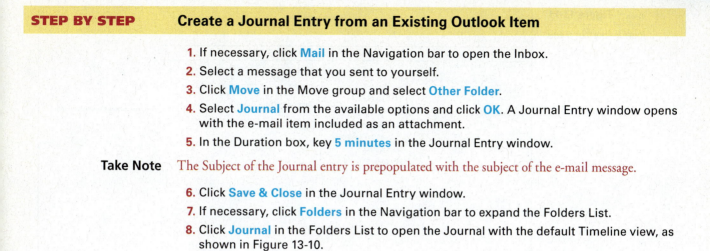

Take Note   We have added some content to the screens in this section so that you can see how your content will appear. Your screen will look different if default settings have been changed or other content has been added to your PC. Use these figures as a reference.

9. Right-click the new **Journal Entry** item in the timeline (you may need to scroll left or right if the task isn't showing). A shortcut menu is displayed, as shown in Figure 13-11.

Figure 13-11

Figure 13-11

Journal shortcut menu

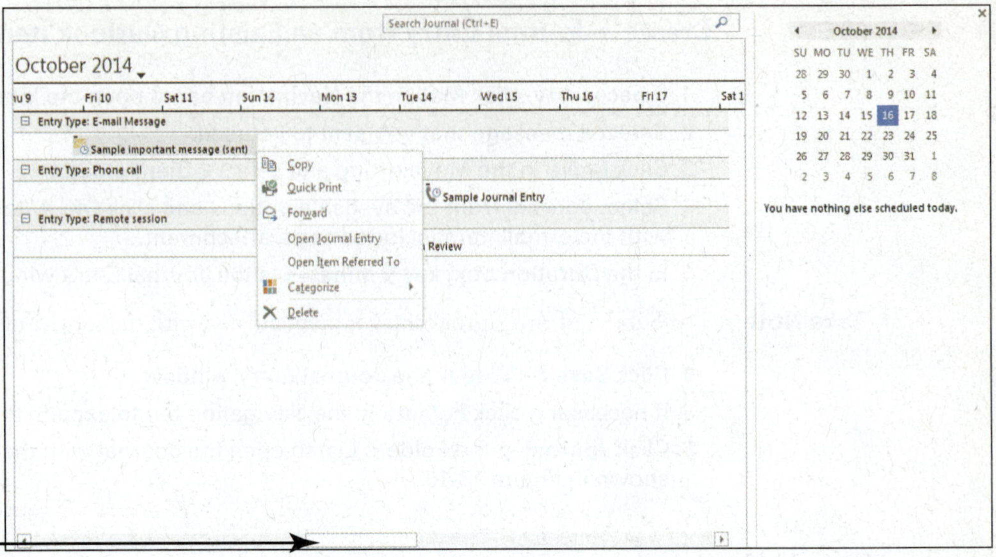

| | | | | | | | | | October 2014 | ▶ |
|Search Journal (Ctrl+E)| | | | | | | SU MO TU WE TH FR SA |

October 2014

| u 9 | Fri 10 | Sat 11 | Sun 12 | Mon 13 | Tue 14 | Wed 15 | Thu 16 | Fri 17 | Sat 1 |

☐ Entry Type: E-mail Message

  📧 Sample important message (sent)

☐ Entry Type: Phone call   📋 Copy

  📇 Quick Print

  ✉ Forward

☐ Entry Type: Remote session   Open Journal Entry

  Open Item Referred To

  ▦ Categorize ▶

  ✕ Delete

📞 Sample Journal Entry

Review

October 2014 / SU MO TU WE TH FR SA / 28 29 30 1 2 3 4 / 5 6 7 8 9 10 11 / 12 13 14 15 16 17 18 / 19 20 21 22 23 24 25 / 26 27 28 29 30 31 1 / 2 3 4 5 6 7 8

You have nothing else scheduled today.

Scroll to make task visible, if needed ⟶

⚠ **Troubleshooting**   If your document is not visible on the Journal Timeline, wait. Your Journal Entry will arrive in the journal within a couple of minutes of your saving it.

10. Click **Open Item Referred To** on the shortcut menu. The e-mail message that you selected at the beginning of this exercise opens.

11. CLOSE the Message window and return to the Journal.

PAUSE. LEAVE Outlook 2013 open to use in the next exercise.

Creating a Manual Journal Entry

If you are attending a meeting with a client, you will want to record decisions that are made and any actions that you are responsible for completing. These records are typically made on paper, but you can record these notes in a journal entry during the conversation. In addition, journal entries include a timer that can record the amount of time spent on the phone call. In this exercise, you will create a manual journal entry for a timed phone call and create a second entry to attach a document file.

STEP BY STEP   **Create a Manual Journal Entry**

GET READY. LAUNCH Outlook 2013 if it is not already running.

1. If necessary, click **Folders** in the Navigation bar and select **Journal** in the Folders List to open the Journal with the default Timeline view.

2. Click **Journal Entry** on the Ribbon. A blank Journal Entry window is displayed.

3. Click **Start Timer** in the Timer group on the Ribbon. Outlook 2013 starts a timer that will continue recording time until you stop the timer later in this exercise.

Take Note   The Journal timer records time in minutes. If you complete the call in less than 1 minute, the timer will record 0 minutes spent on the phone call.

4. If necessary, in the *Entry type* field, select **Phone call** from the list. The Phone call option is the default entry type.

5. In the *Subject* field, key **Custom Tour Expectations**.

6. In the message area, key:

Wants to take a whitewater rafting trip. [Press **Enter**.]

Wants at least one night camping by the river. [Press **Enter**.]

There will be 13 people on the trip. [Press **Enter**.]

Only 2 skilled rafters; the rest have never rafted before. [Press **Enter**.]

They don't like fish. We'll need to bring in other food for dinner. [Press **Enter**.]

They want us to include their logo which we have on file on T-shirts for the whole group to wear on the trip. [Press **Enter**.]

He will e-mail T-shirt sizes following the call.

Take Note   Throughout this chapter you will see information that appears in black text within brackets, such as [Press **Enter**] or [next Friday's date]. The information contained in the brackets is intended to be directions for you rather than something you actually type word for word. It will instruct you to perform an action or substitute text. Do **not** type the actual text that appears within brackets.

7. Click **Pause Timer** in the Timer group on the Ribbon. Outlook 2013 records the amount of time you spent on the phone creating this entry. Compare your Journal Entry window to the one shown in Figure 13-12.

Figure 13-12

Manual Journal Entry for a phone call

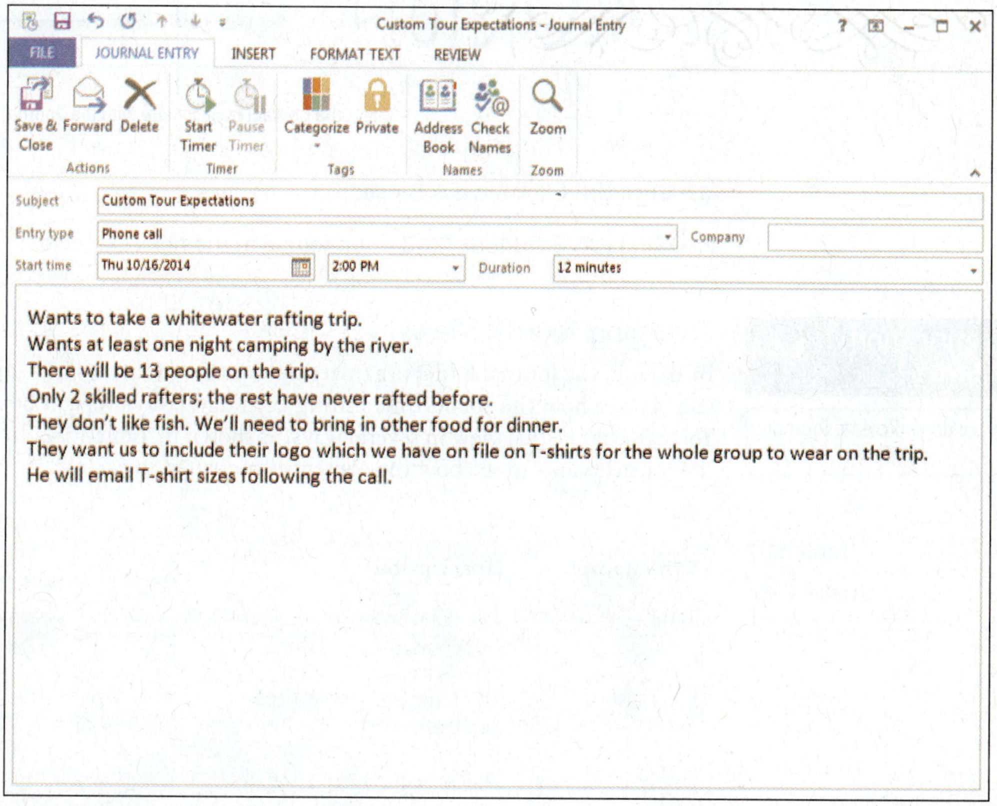

8. Click **Save & Close**.
9. Click **Journal Entry** on the Ribbon.
10. Click **Start Timer** in the Timer group on the Ribbon.
11. In the Subject field, key **T-shirt logo for Whitewater Tour**.
12. In the message area, key **Suggest this logo for Whitaker reunion**. [Press **Enter**].
13. Click the **INSERT** tab and select the **Pictures** button.
14. Navigate to your data files for this lesson and click the *Logo* file and click **Insert**.
15. In the *Entry type* field, select **Task** from the list.
16. In the Names group, click **Address Book** and select the contact record for the friend or coworker, as shown in Figure 13-13.

Figure 13-13

Associating a journal entry with a contact

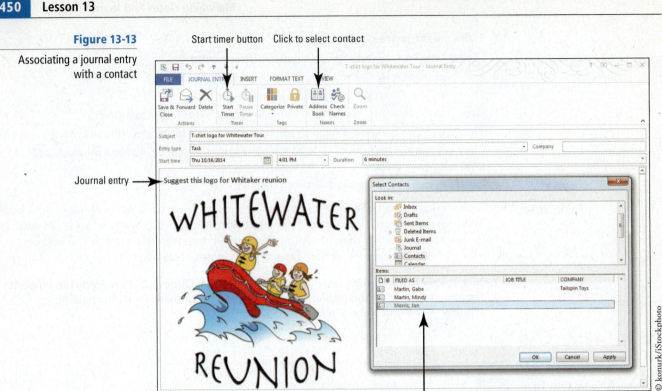

Start timer button   Click to select contact

Journal entry →

Select the Contact to associate with the Journal entry

17. Click **OK**. Click **Save & Close**.

PAUSE. LEAVE Outlook 2013 open to use in the next exercise.

Changing Journal Views

CERTIFICATION READY?   3.4.4

How do you create journal entries?

By default, the Journal folder organizes the contact's activities horizontally in a timeline fashion so you can see how you spend time during each day. All views can be arranged by date or contacts. You can change that view in several ways, as shown in Table 13-2. In this exercise, you will explore the Journal views to see how the content is presented in each.

Table 13-2

Journal Views

View name	Description
Timeline	The default view of the Journal, this view shows each entry by the date and time it was created.
Entry List	The same entries are presented in a vertical list, grouped by entry time and sorted by time.
Phone Calls	This view shows only the phone call journal entries.
Last 7 Days	Presented vertically, like the Entry List, this view only shows items added in the last week.

STEP BY STEP   **Change Journal Views**

GET READY. LAUNCH Outlook 2013 if it is not already running.

1. If necessary, click **Journal** in the Folders List. Click **Timeline** in the View group to return to the Timeline view.

2. In the Arrangement group, click **Month**. The Journal timeline condenses to show more of the month.

3. In the Current View group, click **Entry List**. The journal entries are now presented as a vertical list.

4. In the Current View group, click **Phone Calls**. Only the *Custom Tour Expectations* journal entry is visible.

5. On the **VIEW** tab, click the **Change View** button.

6. Select **Last 7 Days**. This view looks very much like the Entry List view, but includes only the entries that were recorded over the last week.

7. Click **Contact** in the Arrangement gallery. The journal entries are now grouped by contact name, as shown in Figure 13-14.

Figure 13-14

Changing the Journal view

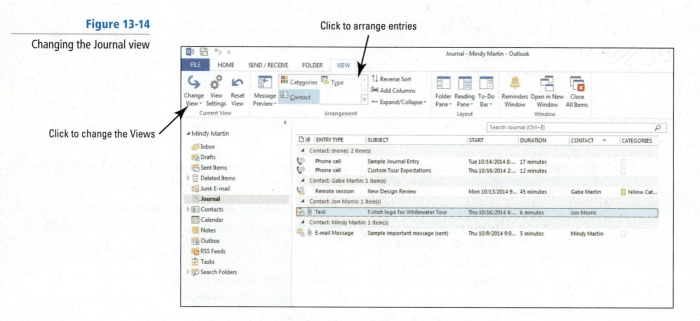

PAUSE. LEAVE Outlook 2013 open to use in the next exercise.

Modifying Journal Entries

Often you'll find that a journal entry needs to be modified; for example, you might want to add more time to a task record. In a previous exercise, you added a Custom Tour entry to your Journal. The phone call is now recorded in your Journal, but it isn't associated with any contact. To take full advantage of the Journal, your documents and Outlook 2013 items need to be tied to your contacts. In this exercise, you'll locate an entry and tie it to an existing contact.

 Cross Ref   For more information about contacts, see Lesson 6.

STEP BY STEP   **Modify Journal Entries**

GET READY. LAUNCH Outlook 2013 if it is not already running and complete the previous exercise.

1. If necessary, click **Journal** in the Folders List to open the Journal with the Timeline view. Switch to this view on the VIEW tab, if necessary.

2. Key **Custom Tour** in the **Search Journal** box and [Press **Enter**]. The SEARCH TOOLS SEARCH tab is displayed, along with a results list containing your Custom Tour Expectations entry, as shown in Figure 13-15.

Figure 13-15

Searching for a journal entry

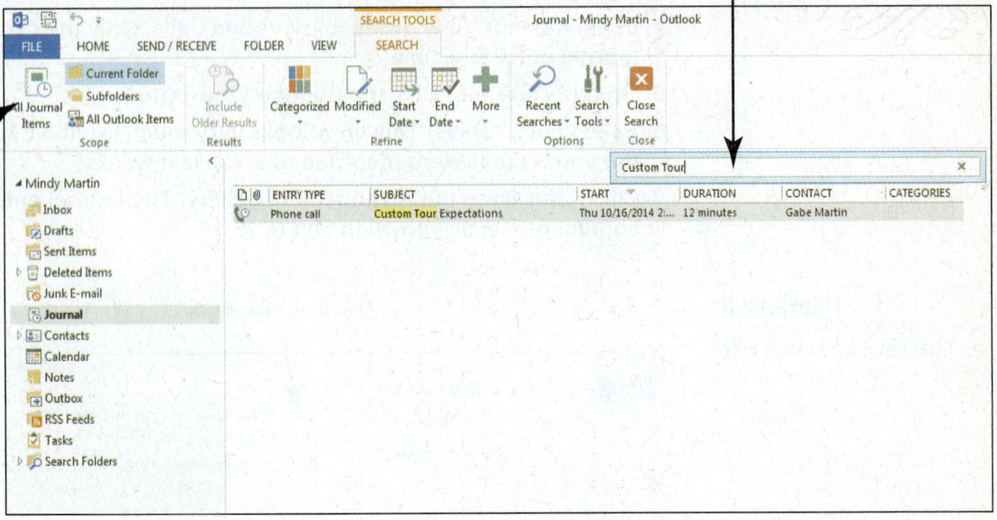

Search Journal box

Search all Journal entries

Take Note Notice that the All Journal Items button appears in the Scope group. This is particularly useful if you have a subfolder within the Journal.

3. Double-click on the **Custom Tour Expectations** entry in the results list.

4. In the Names group, click **Address Book**, and select [**the contact record for the friend or coworker**]. Click **OK**.

5. Click **Save & Close**.

6. Click the **x (Close)** icon in the Search Journal box to clear the search.

7. Double-click the **T-shirt logo for Whitewater Tour** entry in the Journal Entries list.

8. Click the **Duration** drop arrow and select **15 minutes**.

9. Click **Save & Close** to close the journal entry.

10. On the **HOME** tab, click **Timeline** in the Current View group.

11. Click **Week** in the Arrangement group.

PAUSE. LEAVE Outlook 2013 open to use in the next exercise.

CERTIFICATION READY?   **3.4.4**

How do you manage your journal entries?

Printing the Journal

Like Notes, journal entries can also be printed individually or as a set. In this exercise, you will print an existing journal entry.

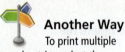

STEP BY STEP   **Print the Journal**

Another Way
To print multiple journal entries, select the journal entries you want to print before moving to the Backstage view.

GET READY. LAUNCH Outlook 2013 if it is not already running and be sure to complete the previous exercise.

1. If necessary, click **Journal** in the Folders List.

2. Select the **Custom Tour Expectations** journal entry.

3. Click **File** and click **Print**.

4. Select **Memo Style**. The journal entry appears, as shown in Figure 13-16.

Figure 13-16

Printing a journal entry

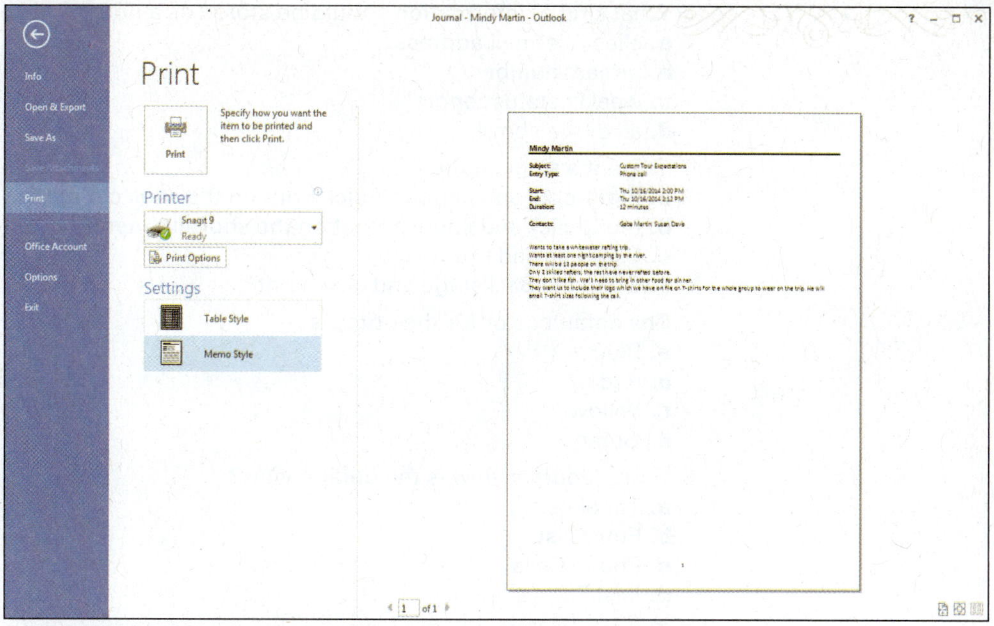

5. Click **Print**. Turn in the journal entry to your instructor.
6. Click the **Back** arrow to return to the Journal feature, if necessary.
7. Click **Timeline** in the View group to return to the Timeline view.
8. Click ••• in the Navigation bar to open the list of additional features.
9. Select **Navigation Options**. The Navigation Options dialog box is displayed.
10. Click the **Reset** button and click **OK**.

CLOSE Outlook 2013.

SKILL SUMMARY

In This Lesson You Learned How To:	Exam Objective	Objective Number
Work with Notes	Create and manage notes	3.4.2
Work with the Journal	Create journal entries	3.4.4

Knowledge Assessment

Multiple Choice

Select the best response for the following statements.

1. Double-clicking a journal entry _____.
   a. opens the related file
   b. opens the related Contact record
   c. opens the journal entry
   d. starts the timer

2. To take full advantage of the Journal, _____.
   a. the Journal must be visible at all times
   b. automatic journaling must be turned on
   c. the Subject field must be modified
   d. Journal entries must be tied to your contacts

3. What kind of information should be stored as a note?
   a. client's e-mail address
   b. project number
   c. weekly status report
   d. all of the above

4. To print a single note, _____.
   a. Right-click and choose Quick Print on the shortcut menu.
   b. Right-click and choose Print on the shortcut menu.
   c. Click File and Print.
   d. Open the Backstage and click Print.

5. The default color for the notes is _____.
   a. Blue
   b. Red
   c. Yellow
   d. Green

6. Which Journal view is the default view?
   a. Timeline
   b. Entry List
   c. Phone Calls
   d. Last 7 Days

7. The Journal records time spent on e-mail messages in the _____.
   a. Sent Mail
   b. Journal folder
   c. Inbox
   d. All of the above

8. Which of the following cannot be recorded with the journaling options?
   a. E-mail
   b. Task requests
   c. Microsoft Excel files
   d. Both A and C

9. All Journal views can be arranged _____.
   a. By Contact
   b. By Date
   c. Both A and B
   d. None of the above

10. The Subject field of a journal entry created from an existing message is populated with the _____.
    a. Message's subject line
    b. document's title
    c. file path
    d. project number

True/False

Circle T if the statement is true or F if the statement is false.

T F   1.   The default Journal view is called Entry List.

T F   2.   Notes must include a due date.

T F   3.   The Timer function can be used in all journal entries.

T F   4.   The Journal is like an online diary.

T F   5.   Journal entries must be created from the Journal folder.

T F   6.   Outlook 2013 includes an automatic journaling feature that allows you to automatically record the time spent on Outlook records for all your contacts.

T F   7.   You cannot add categories to a Journal entry.

T F   8.   By default, notes appear in the Notes module as yellow sticky notes.

T F   9.   Notes cannot be forwarded.

T F   10.   Notes are created in a separate window.

Competency Assessment

Project 13-1: Creating a Journal Entry from an Outlook Item

Susan Gilford just started a new job as a producer for a TV talk show about pets. Her job involves thinking up show ideas, making sure experts are available to talk about the topics, and making sure the set and crew are ready for show time. Susan uses the journal to track the amount of time she spends on each show concept.

GET READY. LAUNCH Outlook 2013 if it is not already running.

1. On the HOME tab, click the **New Items** button. Click **Task** to open an Untitled – Task window.
2. In the Subject field, key **Research Pet anxiety treatment options**.
3. Click **Save & Close**.
4. If necessary, click the **Tasks** button on the Navigation bar to open the Tasks feature.
5. Select the newly created task, and click **Move** in the Actions group.
6. Select **Journal** from the available options.
7. Click the **Duration** drop box and select **10 minutes**.
8. Click **Save & Close** to close the window.

PAUSE. LEAVE Outlook 2013 open for the next project.

Project 13-2: Create a New Note

Susan likes the Outlook 2013 Notes feature since she loses those little sticky notes all the time. Since she is always thinking of ideas for future shows, Susan uses Notes to record her ideas.

GET READY. LAUNCH Outlook 2013 if it is not already running and be sure to complete the previous exercise.

1. Click ••• in the Navigation bar to open the additional features list. Select **Notes**.
2. Click the **New Note** button on the Ribbon. A new blank sticky note appears in the Reading Pane. Below the sticky note is the current date and time.
3. Key **Hair loss**. [Press **Enter**.] **Do pets experience hair loss?**
4. Click the **Close** button (the small X in the top-right corner of the note).
5. Click **New Note**.
6. Key **Training**. [Press **Enter**.] **Is clicker training better than time-outs?**
7. Click the **Close** button.
8. Click **New Note**.
9. Key **Celebrities**. [Press **Enter**.] **Celebrity pets.**
10. Click the **Close** button.
11. Click **New Note**.
12. Key **Anxiety**. [Press **Enter**.] Key **Do pets have anxiety?**
13. Click the **Close** button.

PAUSE. LEAVE Outlook 2013 open for the next project.

Proficiency Assessment

Project 13-3: Categorize a Note

Susan decides to categorize the Notes for programs that will require an expert to appear. That will make it easier to find when an expert is booked.

GET READY. LAUNCH Outlook 2013 if it is not already running and be sure to complete the previous exercises.

1. Open the **Notes** folder.
2. Click the **Hair loss**, **Training**, and **Anxiety** notes to select them.
3. On the HOME tab, click **Categorize**.
4. Select the **All Categories** option to create a new category. The Color Categories dialog box is displayed.
5. Click the **New** button. The Add New Category dialog box is displayed.
6. In the *Name* field, key **Need experts**.
7. In the **Color** drop list, select **Steel**.
8. Click **OK** twice to close the open dialog boxes.
9. Apply the new color category to the three notes. The notes' icon changes color to match the category.

PAUSE. LEAVE Outlook 2013 open for the next project.

Project 13-4: Print a Note

The show's executive producer has asked a famous veterinarian to come on the show next month. He has asked Susan to bring a list of show ideas that will need a veterinarian to appear on camera. Susan prints those Notes in Memo Style.

GET READY. LAUNCH Outlook 2013 if it is not already running and be sure to complete the previous exercises.

1. Click the **Hair loss**, **Training**, and **Anxiety** Notes to select them.
2. Click **FILE** and click **Print**. Click the **Preview** button.
3. In the *Settings* field, select **Memo Style** to print each note on a separate page.
4. Click **Print**.
5. Click the **Back** arrow to return to the Notes folder, if necessary.

PAUSE. LEAVE Outlook 2013 open for the next project.

Mastery Assessment

Project 13-5: Create a Manual Journal Entry

It looks like the show on hair loss will be moving forward. Susan will place a phone call to the veterinarian, Dr. Keeler, to find out more about this tragic condition.

GET READY. LAUNCH Outlook 2013 if it is not already running and complete the previous exercises.

1. Open the **Folders List** and click **Journal**.
2. Create a new journal entry.
3. Use the Timer in the Timer group on the Ribbon to record the time spent on this project.
4. Set the Entry type as **Phone call**.
5. Set the Subject as **Hair loss research**.
6. In the message area, key:

   Dr. Keeler is very emotional.

   Has 2 patients (1 dog and 1 cat) currently losing their fur.

   Condition affects unknown numbers of animals in the wild.

   Only 1 patient's family will agree to be on camera. The other will write a letter, but they are too embarrassed to be on TV.

7. Pause the **Timer** and save the journal entry.

PAUSE. LEAVE Outlook 2013 open for the next project.

Project 13-6: Connect a Journal Entry to a Contact

After hanging up the phone, Susan realized that she forgot to associate the journal entry with Dr. Keeler's Contact record. She needs to fix that right away.

GET READY. LAUNCH Outlook 2013 if it is not already running and complete the previous exercises.

1. If necessary, open the **Journal** feature.
2. Open the **Hair loss research** journal entry.
3. Associate the journal entry with two friends or coworkers. If you have not been working with a partner, select your own Contact record and one that you created in this course.
4. Click **Save & Close** to close the journal entry.
5. If your instructor requests, print the journal entry.

CLOSE Outlook 2013.

Circling Back

Benjamin Martin is a corporate travel agent with Margie's Travel. Next month, the executives at Fourth Coffee are meeting in Orlando for a workshop. Ben must arrange travel for 15 executives from three different locations, make hotel reservations, and reserve vehicles for the 15 workshop participants.

Project 1: Organizing a Project with Data Files, Notes, and Tasks

Benjamin has just received the Fourth Coffee data file for this project. To make the project more manageable, Ben creates tasks. He plans to pass on part of the work to his assistant Tonya. To track their progress, he is going to use Outlook.

GET READY. LAUNCH Outlook if it is not already running.

1. Click the **FILE** tab to open the Backstage view, click **Account Settings** and select the **Account Settings** option. The Account Settings dialog box is displayed.
2. Click the **DATA FILES** tab, and click **Add**. The Create or Open Outlook Data File dialog box is displayed. Navigate to the data files for this lesson and select *Fourth Coffee.pst*.
3. Click **OK** to return to the Account Settings dialog box and click the **Close** button to close the Account Settings dialog box as well.
4. If necessary, click the **Folders** button to show your folders in the Folders Pane. Click the **expand arrow** next to the Fourth Coffee data file. Click **Project Inbox**.
5. Click the **Fourth Coffee Meeting** message in the message list. You need to create task items to ensure that you don't forget anything.
6. Click **New Items** in the New group on the HOME tab. Select **Task** from the list.
7. In the *Subject* field, key **Fourth Coffee – Hotel Arrangements for 15**.
8. In the *Due date* field, key or select the date for **next Thursday**.
9. In the *Priority* field, select **High**.
10. Click the **Save & Close** button in the Actions group on the Ribbon.
11. Repeat the same process to create the following two tasks.

Subject	Due Date	Priority
Fourth Coffee – Car Rentals for 15	next Thursday	Normal
Fourth Coffee – Flight Arrangements for 15	next Wednesday	High

12. Maggie, the office manager at Margie's Travel, wants you to follow up with her when the arrangements are made, so you decide to create a task from the message. Click **Move** in the Move group and select **Other Folder** from the dropdown list. Select the **Tasks folder** in the Fourth Coffee data file. Click **OK**.
13. In the *Subject* field, key **Follow up with Maggie on the Fourth Coffee arrangements**. In the *Due Date* field, select next **Friday's date**. Click **Save & Close**.
14. Check to see if Maggie included any notes from her Fourth Coffee meeting. Click the **Orlando Meeting Notes** folder to take a look.
15. Click the **Julie is free to work on the Fourth Coffee arrangements** note and drag it to the **Tasks folder**. The task window opens.
16. In the *Subject* field, change the text to read **Assign Julie some of the Fourth Coffee Arrangements**. Click **Save & Close**.

LEAVE Outlook open for the next project.

Project 2: Manage a Project with Data Files, Notes, and Tasks

Julie Valdez has offered to help make the arrangements. Assign Julie the task of making flight reservations from Seattle to Orlando. You will need to make car reservations on the phone for the entire Fourth Coffee team. Record your time spent on the phone call with the car rental agency in a manual Journal entry and mark that task as complete.

GET READY. LAUNCH Outlook if it is not already running.

⚠ **Troubleshooting**   The e-mail addresses provided in these exercises belong to unused domains owned by Microsoft. When you send a message to these addresses, you will receive an error message stating that the message could not be delivered. Delete the messages when they arrive.

1. If necessary, click the **Tasks** button in the Navigation bar to display the Tasks folder.

2. Click the **New Items** arrow and click the **Task Request** option.

3. Click the *To* field and key **Julie@margiestravel.com**.

4. In the *Subject* field, key **Fourth Coffee - Make five reservations to Orlando from Seattle**.

5. In the *Due date* field, key or select [the date for next Friday].

6. In the *Priority* field, select **High**.

7. In the task note area, key the following list of names. These executives are traveling from Seattle to Orlando.

   Terry Adams

   Kari Hension

   Tamara Johnston

   Paula Nartker

   Benjamin C. Willett

8. Click the **Send** button to send the task request. Click **Yes** to add the task to your Tasks folder.

9. Click the **Fourth Coffee** Journal folder in the Folder list.

10. Click **Journal Entry** on the Ribbon.

11. Click **Start Timer** in the Timer group on the Ribbon.

12. If necessary, in the *Entry type* field, select **Phone call** from the list.

13. In the *Subject* field, key **Fourth Coffee Car Rental**.

14. In the message area, key: **Rental agent's name is Enrique.** [Press **Enter**.] **He only has 12 cars available for the date of the meeting.** [Press **Enter**.] **He is calling another agency while I'm on hold.** [Press **Enter**.] **The other agency has agreed to provide the remaining 3 cars for the days required. Enrique will handle the rental agreement with the other agency so that Fourth Coffee personnel will all pick up their cars at the same location.** [Press **Enter**.] **The confirmation number for all 15 cars is XUT2975K-34.**

15. Click **Pause Timer** in the Timer group on the Ribbon.

16. Click **Save & Close**.

17. If necessary, click the **Tasks** button in the Navigation bar to display the Tasks folder.

18. Double-click the **Fourth Coffee – Car Rentals for 15** task and mark it as complete.

LEAVE Outlook open for the next project.

Project 3: Assign Fourth Coffee Items to a Color Category

Ben frequently handles large travel projects for Fourth Coffee. He decided to create a color category that matches the color category used for Fourth Coffee in his physical file cabinets. Ben searches for all Fourth Coffee tasks and prints his status in a Table Style.

GET READY. LAUNCH Outlook if it is not already running.

1. If necessary, click the **Tasks** button in the Navigation bar to display the Tasks folder.

2. Click the **Change View** in the Current View group of the Ribbon and select **To-Do List** from the dropdown menu.

3. Click one of the **Fourth Coffee** tasks.

4. Click the **Categorize** button and click the **All Categories** option. The Color Categories dialog box is displayed.

5. Click **Orange Category** in the list of categories. Click the **Rename** button. The Orange Category text becomes active.

6. Key **Fourth Coffee** and [press **Enter**].

7. Click **OK** to rename the category and close the Color Categories dialog box.

8. Select the remaining **Fourth Coffee** tasks. Click the **Categorize** button on the HOME tab. Click the **Fourth Coffee** category in the dropdown list.

9. Click the **Orlando Meeting Notes** folder and select all of the notes.

10. Click the **Categorize** button and click the **Fourth Coffee** category.

11. Display the **Tasks** folder.

12. In the Instant Search box, verify that **Search All Task Items** is selected.

13. In the Instant Search box, key **Fourth Coffee**.

14. Click the **FILE** tab and select **Print**.

15. Select **Memo Style** and click **Print**.

16. Make sure that all the Fourth Coffee items are in the **Fourth Coffee.pst** and close the data file.

CLOSE Outlook.

Matrix Skill	Objective Number	Lesson Number
Manage the Outlook Environment	**1**	
Customize Outlook Settings	1.1	
Include original messages with all reply messages	1.1.1	3
Change text formats for all outgoing messages	1.1.2	2, 3
Customize the Navigation Pane	1.1.3	1
Block specific addresses	1.1.4	4
Configure views	1.1.5	1, 6, 11
Manage multiple accounts	1.1.6	3
Set Outlook options	1.1.7	1, 3, 11
Automate Outlook	1.2	
Change quoted text colors	1.2.1	3
Create and assign signatures	1.2.2	2, 7
Apply Quick Steps	1.2.3	5
Create and manage rules	1.2.4	5
Create auto-replies	1.2.5	5
Print and Save Information in Outlook	1.3	
Print messages	1.3.1	2, 3
Print calendars	1.3.2	8, 10
Save message attachments	1.3.3	2
Preview attachments	1.3.4	2
Print contacts	1.3.5	7
Print tasks	1.3.6	11
Save messages in alternate formats	1.3.7	2
Create data files	1.3.8	12
Search in Outlook	1.4	
Create new search folders	1.4.1	7
Search for messages	1.4.2	3

Matrix Skill	Objective Number	Lesson Number
Search for tasks	1.4.3	11
Search for contacts	1.4.4	7
Search calendars	1.4.5	10
Use advanced find	1.4.6	12
Use Search by Location	1.4.7	3
Manage Messages	**2**	
Create a Message	2.1	
Create messages	2.1.1	2
Forward messages	2.1.2	2
Delete messages	2.1.3	4
Add/Remove message attachments	2.1.4	2
Add cc and bcc to messages	2.1.5	2
Add voting options to messages	2.1.6	3
Reply to all	2.1.7	2
Reply to sender only	2.1.8	2
Prioritize messages	2.1.9	3
Mark as private	2.1.10	3, 8
Request delivery/read receipt	2.1.11	3
Redirect replies	2.1.12	3
Delegate access	2.1.13	5
Format a Message	2.2	
Format text	2.2.1	2
Insert hyperlinks	2.2.2	2
Apply themes and styles	2.2.3	2
Insert images	2.2.4	2
Add a signature to specific messages	2.2.5	2
Format signatures	2.2.6	2
Create and use Quick Parts	2.2.7	2
Organize and Manage Messages	2.3	
Sort messages	2.3.1	3, 12
Move messages between folders	2.3.2	4
Add new local folders	2.3.3	4
Apply categories	2.3.4	12

Matrix Skill	Objective Number	Lesson Number
Configure junk e-mail settings	2.3.5	4
Cleanup messages	2.3.6	4
Mark as read/unread	2.3.7	4
Flag messages	2.3.8	4
Ignore messages	2.3.9	4
Sort by conversation	2.3.10	4
Set attachment reminder options	2.3.11	2
Manage Schedules	**3**	
Create and Manage Calendars	3.1	
Adjust viewing details for calendars	3.1.1	10
Modify calendar time zones	3.1.2	10
Delete calendars	3.1.3	10
Demonstrate how to set calendar work times	3.1.4	10
Create multiple calendars	3.1.5	10
Manage calendar groups	3.1.6	10
Overlay calendars	3.1.7	10
Share calendars	3.1.8	10
Create Appointments, Meetings, and Events	3.2	
Create calendar items	3.2.1	8, 9
Create recurring calendar items	3.2.2	8, 9
Cancel calendar items	3.2.3	9
Create calendar items from messages	3.2.4	8, 9
Set calendar item times	3.2.5	8
Categorize calendar items	3.2.6	12
Use the scheduling assistant	3.2.7	9
Change availability status	3.2.8	8
Schedule resources	3.2.9	9
Utilize Room Finder	3.2.10	9
Organize and Manage Appointments, Meetings, and Events	3.3	
Set calendar item importance	3.3.1	9
Forward calendar items	3.3.2	8
Configure reminders	3.3.3	3, 4, 8, 9
Add participants	3.3.4	9

Matrix Skill	Objective Number	Lesson Number
Respond to invitations	3.3.5	9
Update calendar items	3.3.6	9
Share meeting notes	3.3.7	9
Create and Manage Notes, Tasks and Journals	3.4	
Create and manage tasks	3.4.1	11
Create and manage notes	3.4.2	13
Attach notes to contacts	3.4.3	6
Create journal entries	3.4.4	13
Update task status	3.4.5	11
Manage Contacts and Groups	**4**	
Create and Manage Contacts	4.1	
Create new contacts	4.1.1	6, 7
Delete contacts	4.1.2	6
Import contacts from external sources	4.1.3	7
Edit contact information	4.1.4	6, 7
Attach an image to contacts	4.1.5	6
Add tags to contacts	4.1.6	6
Share contacts	4.1.7	6, 7
Manage multiple address books	4.1.8	7
Create and Manage Groups	4.2	
Create new contact groups	4.2.1	6
Add contacts to existing groups	4.2.2	6
Add notes to a group	4.2.3	6
Update contacts within groups	4.2.4	6
Delete groups	4.2.5	6
Delete group members	4.2.6	6

A

action   Determines what happens when a message meets the conditions defined in an Outlook message handling rule.

address book   Stores names and email addresses.

appointment   A scheduled activity that does not require sending invitations to other people or resources.

archive   Store messages in a separate PST file to reduce the number of messages in the folders you use most often.

assign   Transfer ownership of a task to another Outlook user.

attachment   File sent as part of an email message.

Attachment Reminder   A tool will scan each message you create to see whether it mentions something that should be attached.

attribute   File characteristic such as size, subject, or sender.

AutoArchive   Automatic function that archives messages.

AutoComplete   Automatically completes the names of the months and days of the week.

AutoPreview   Displays the first three lines of every message in the message list.

Auto-reply   An email message that goes out automatically when you receive a message notifying the sender that you are not in the office during this time period.

availability indicator   The availability indicator uses a color or pattern to let others know if you are available and how definite your schedule is for a specific period.

B

Backstage view   The view that opens when you click the FILE tab, containing commands for managing files, setting program options, and printing.

banner   Text displayed at the top of a day to indicate an event.

Bcc   A field that enables you to send a copy of the message to individuals who you think should be informed about the message content without notifying the other recipients.

Blocked Senders list   is a collection of email address that you have designated as junk mail. All future messages from these sender's email address will go straight to the Junk Email folder.

busy   An activity is scheduled for this time period. You are not available for other activities.

C

Calendar group   A group of related calendars that are grouped together for easy viewing.

Calendar Snapshot   A picture of your calendar at a specific moment.

cancel   Delete a meeting.

Categorized Mail Standard Search Folder   that displays messages with an assigned color category.

Cc   A field that enables you to send a copy of the message to individuals who you think should be informed about the message content but from whom you don't expect

character   A letter, number, punctuation mark, or symbol.

clip art   A single piece of readymade art, often appearing as a bitmap or a combination of drawn shapes.

color category   Color assigned to an Outlook item, providing a way to visually indicate relationships among Outlook items.

compact   Process that reduces the size of a data file.

complete   Designates that a task is 100 percent finished.

condition   Identifies the characteristics used to determine the messages affected by a rule.

contact   Collection of information about a person or company.

Contacts folder   Electronic organizer that enables you to create, view, and edit contact information.

Contact Group   Group of individual contacts saved together as a single contact

Contact Index   In the Contacts folder, all contacts are stored alphabetically in the Contact Index.

Conversation   A view that enables you to organize every email message you send or receive about the same subject together into one conversation group.

Coordinated Universal Time (UTC)   The time standard used by Outlook which is based on International Atomic Time.

crop   To remove a portion of a picture or shape that is not needed. The cropped portion is hidden until you compress the picture.

Custom Search Folder   A virtual folder that searches your email folders to locate items that meet the custom search criteria

D

Data file   File containing stored Outlook data. It is identified by the .pst extension.

Deferred   Status indicating that a task has been postponed without changing the deadline or the percentage complete.

Deleted Items folder   Deleted items are held in this folder until the folder is emptied. Emptying this folder removes the items from your computer.

delivery receipt   Tells you that the message has arrived in the recipient's mailbox.

desktop shortcut   An icon placed on the Windows desktop that launches an application, opens a folder, or opens a file.

digital ID   Contains a private key that remains on your computer and a public key you give to your correspondents to verify that you are the message sender.

distribution list   *see Contact Group.*

Drafts folder   Outlook messages you write but haven't sent are stored in this folder.

Draft indicator   An icon that appears on the message item in the message list, and will stay there until you either send the message or delete the reply that you added

duplicate contact   Contact records containing the same information.

E

electronic business card   Digital version of paper business cards. They can be sent as attachments, used as signatures, and used to create a contact record.

encryption   Scrambles the text so that only the recipient with a key can decipher the message.

event   An activity that lasts one or more days.

exception   Identifies the characteristics used to exclude messages from being affected by the rule.

F

feature   The different components that make up Outlook: Calendar, Contacts, Journal, Mail, Notes, Tasks.

fields   Specific bits of information that Outlook stores about an item.

fly-out   A menu or pane that opens floating above the main window instead of docked to a fixed place on the screen and which changes the way every other pane appears.

folder   Common name for Outlook components.

fonts   Typefaces that are used to display characters, numbers, and symbols in your PowerPoint presentations.

Format Painter   A tool to copy character and paragraph formatting.

Formatting attributes   Special formatting, such as bold or italic, that you can apply to characters within your text to give them special emphasis.

Free   No activities are scheduled for this time period. Indicates an attendee is available for a meeting.

G

gallery   A dropdown window containing multiple options within a group.

group   Ribbon segment containing related commands.

group schedule   Displays scheduling information for several people. Requires Microsoft Exchange 2000 or a more recent version of Microsoft Exchange.

H

hyperlink   An address that refers to another location, such as a Web site, a different slide, or an external file.

Hypertext Markup Language (HTML)   Formatting language that enables you to format text and insert items such as horizontal lines, pictures, and animated graphics for viewing on the World Wide Web (web).

I

iCalendar (.ics)   An updatable calendar format that is interchangeable between most calendar and email applications.

Internet Calendar Subscription   A downloaded calendar in .ics format that is automatically updated.

import   Bring information into a file from an external source.

In Progress   Status indicating that work on the task has started.

Inbox folder   By default, new messages are placed in this folder when they arrive.

InfoBar   Banner containing information added automatically at the top of a message.

Information Rights Management (IRM)   An Outlook feature that allows you to control how the recipient can use a message.

Instant Search   Outlook's enhanced search tool that includes two features that you can use to filter through the results: Search Suggestions List and the SEARCH Contextual tab.

item   A record stored in Outlook.

J

Journal   An online diary of all activities associated with one of your Contacts.

Junk E-Mail folder   Messages identified as spam are placed in this folder when they arrive.

L

Large Mail   A standard Search Folder that displays messages larger than 100 kilobytes.

M

MailTips   Messages that Outlook provides you in the InfoBar to alert you when you might be in danger of making an email mistake.

mandatory attendee   A person who must attend a meeting.

meeting   A scheduled activity that requires sending invitations to other people or resources.

meeting organizer   The person who creates the meeting and sends meeting invitations.

meeting request   Outlook item that creates a meeting and invites attendees.

message header   Text automatically added at the top of a message. The message header contains the sender's email address, the names of the servers used to send and transfer the message, the subject, the date, and other basic information about the message.

N

Navigation Bar   Provides access to Outlook components such as Contacts and the Calendar folder.

Notes   An Outlook feature that enables you to keep important information that may not be related to a particular contact or project.

O

occurrence   A single meeting in a series of recurring meetings.

optional attendee   A person who should attend the meeting but whose presence is not required.

Out of Office (availability)   Indicates that you are unavailable because an activity is scheduled for this time period and you will be out of the office.

Outbox folder   Outgoing messages are held in this folder until you are connected to the Internet. When an Internet connection is detected, the message is sent.

overlay mode   Displays calendars on top of each other.

overlay stack   Several calendars are displayed on top of each other.

owner   The only Outlook user who can modify a task.

P

Peek   A fly-out panel that shows what is happening in another Outlook feature.

People Hub   The People Hub is the main view of the contacts in your Contacts folder, consisting of the Contact Index and a contact card.

plain text   Text without any formatting.

private   Feature that protects the details of an activity from a casual observer, but it does not ensure privacy.

Private key   The portion of the digital ID that remains on your computer.

Publick key   The portion of the digital ID that you give to your correspondence.

Q

Quick Access Toolbar (QAT)   Toolbar that can be customized to contain commands from any tab.

Quick Parts   A gallery that contains blocks of text and/or images that you can reuse again and again to complete messages with content that needs to be sent out repeatedly.

Quick Response   Customizable shortcuts that you can use to perform several functions at the same time.

Quick Steps   Customizable shortcuts that you can use to perform several functions at the same time.

Quick Style   Built-in formatting for text, graphics, SmartArt diagrams, charts, WordArt, pictures, tables, and shapes.

R

read receipt   Tells you that the message has been opened in the recipient's mailbox.

Reading Pane   Displays the text of a selected email message.

recurring appointment   An appointment that occurs at regular intervals.

recurring meeting   A meeting that occurs at regular intervals.

recurring task   A task that must be completed at regular intervals.

resource   An item or a location that can be invited to a meeting.

restore   Make an item available for use. For example, moving an item out of the Deleted Items folder restores it for use.

retention rules   Guidelines that determine the length of time correspondence must be kept.

Really Simple Syndication (RSS)   A method that allows you to subscribe to content from a variety of Web sites offering the service.

ribbon   Contains commands organized into groups that are located on tabs.

Rich Text Format (RTF)   Formatting system that uses tags to format text.

rule   Defines an action that happens automatically when messages are received or sent.

S

Safe Senders List   A list of people whom you know and can trust that the messages they send should be regarded as safe.

ScreenTip   Brief description of an item's purpose displayed when the mouse hovers on the item.

Search Folder   A virtual folder that searches your email folders to locate items that meet the saved search criteria.

secondary address book   The address book for an additional Contacts folder.

sensitivity   Suggests how the recipient should treat the message and the type of information in the message. Sensitivity settings include normal, personal, private, and confidential.

Sent Items folder   Items are automatically moved to this folder after they have been sent.

side-by-side mode   Displays two or more calendars next to each other in the Calendar folder.

signature   Text or images that may be automatically placed at the end of outgoing messages.

SmartArt graphic   A visual representation of information and ideas that can be used with other images and decorative text.

Social Connector   The Social Connector is a tool that allows you to synchronize Outlook with social network accounts, such as Facebook or LinkedIn.

sort   Arrange items in a sequence based on specific criteria.

spam   Unsolicited email sent to many email accounts.

spoofing   Providing false information in a message header.

Status bar   Identifies the number of items in the active feature. For example, when the Contacts tool is active, the number of contacts stored is displayed in the status bar.

style   A set of formatting attributes that users can apply to a cell or range of cells more easily than setting each attribute individually.

subject   Topic of a message.

T

task   An Outlook item that can be tracked from creation to completion.

task request   A task assigned to another user.

Tasks folder   Store tasks in this folder.

template   An existing rule provided by Outlook that contains specific pieces that can be customized to create new rules.

tentative   An activity is scheduled for this time period, but the activity might not occur. You might be available for other activities.

theme   A set of formatting choices that include colors, a fonts (including heading and body text fonts), and theme effects (including lines and fill effects).

tile   An icon placed on the Windows Start screen that launches an application, opens a folder, or opens a file

Title bar   A banner across the top of a window that identifies the application and the active feature

time zone   A geographic area using the same standard time.

To Do Bar   Feature that summarizes information about appointments and tasks.

to-do item   Any Outlook item flagged for follow-up.

U

Unread Mail   Standard Search Folder that displays unread messages.

V

view   A specific layout for viewing details about the items in an Outlook feature.

virtual folder   A folder that does not contain the actual items it displays.

W

WebDAV (Web-based Distributed Authoring and Versioning)   A common file and calendar hosting server protocol.

wizard   A feature that guides you through steps for completing a process in Microsoft Office applications.

work week   The hours or days you work in a calendar week.

Index